The Prentice-Hall Encyclopedia of Mathematics

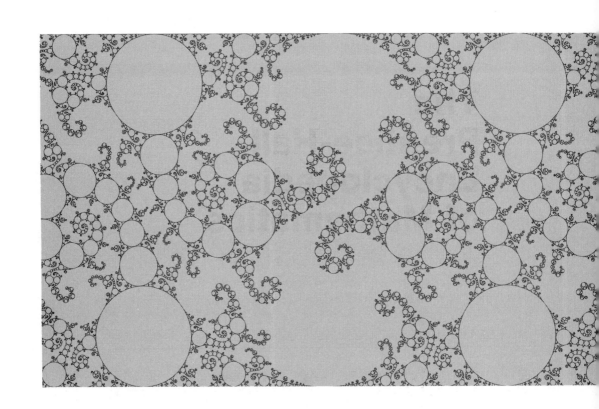

The Prentice-Hall Encyclopedia of Mathematics

by Beverly Henderson West,
Ellen Norma Griesbach, Jerry Duncan Taylor,
and Louise Todd Taylor

PRENTICE-HALL, INC. *Englewood Cliffs, New Jersey*

Library of Congress Cataloging in Publication Data

Main entry under title:

The Prentice-Hall encyclopedia of mathematics.

Includes index.
1. Mathematics—Dictionaries. I. West,
Beverly Henderson, 1939-
QA5.P7   510'.3'21   82-5352
ISBN 0-13-696013-8   AACR2

10 9 8 7 6 5 4 3 2 1

Printed in the United States of America

Frontispiece produced by C. McMullen, D. Mumford, and
D. Wright at I.B.M. Thomas J. Watson Research Center as
part of a research project on Kleinian fractals with
B. Mandelbrot.

A *fractal* is a shape with very irregular boundary. The study
of fractals is a recent topic of high-level mathematical
research. New applications are continually being discovered. The rich variety of fractals is shown by the illustrations on pp. 80, 276, 317, and 566. These are excerpted
from Benoit B. Mandelbrot, *The Fractal Geometry of
Nature* (W. H. Freeman and Co., 1982). Copyright © 1982
by Benoit B. Mandelbrot.

PRENTICE-HALL INTERNATIONAL, INC., *London*
PRENTICE-HALL OF AUSTRALIA, PTY. LTD., *North Sydney*
PRENTICE-HALL OF CANADA, LTD., *Toronto*
PRENTICE-HALL OF INDIA PRIVATE LTD., *New Delhi*
PRENTICE-HALL OF JAPAN, INC., *Tokyo*
PRENTICE-HALL OF SOUTHEAST ASIA PTE. LTD., *Singapore*
WHITEHALL BOOKS LIMITED, *Wellington, New Zealand*

Contents

v

Preface

The Prentice-Hall Encyclopedia of Mathematics is a comprehensive resource in mathematics for students, teachers, and nonprofessionals. In a single volume, it gives definitions, formulas, explanations, historical information, and guides to further study, as well as glimpses of the curiosities and applications that make mathematics exciting.

This book gives precise definitions of mathematical terms, explains the formal terminology, and emphasizes the unifying concepts of mathematics.

But mathematics is far more than definitions, formulas, and equations—and so is the Encyclopedia. This book includes puzzles, games, projects, and interesting applications.

In addition, the Encyclopedia presents some of the history of mathematics. Although makers of mathematics can be just as interesting as the makers of machines or music or war, most people can name ten inventors, composers, or generals more easily than they can name even five mathematicians. To help make mathematicians better known, many articles in the Encyclopedia tell not only about the development of mathematical ideas but also about the people who developed them and the uses that have been made of their theories.

Finally, this book emphasizes the fact that mathematics is not a collection of separate disciplines. Most topics in mathematics are related to other topics. For instance, a logician may sometimes use more topology than logic; one topologist may use algebraic methods, another may use geometry. These relationships can be seen both in the text of the articles and in the many cross-references.

How the Book is Organized

The Prentice-Hall Encyclopedia of Mathematics consists of eighty articles on broad mathematical topics, arranged alphabetically. Numerous additional topics are covered under subheadings in a more general article.

Some sections begin on a very elementary level, because these are topics on which many junior high students have foundered. Others are written to interest the general reader at any level. And still others contain provocative sidelights for more advanced students. Difficult topics are covered in language that is as simple as possible.

Nearly every article begins with a working definition of its topic. This definition is followed by examples, explanations, and definitions of related terms. Most articles end with a brief historical treatment of the topic being discussed, activities or practical applications, and annotated references for further reading.

To enhance the historical material, the Encyclopedia begins with a time line that shows the development of mathematics and how it is related to other areas of history. A separate biographical list at the back of the book gives the nationality and dates for persons mentioned in the articles.

At the end of the Encyclopedia are also a list of symbols, a number of tables (of measure, square and cube roots, logarithms, trigonometry), a bibliographical index of authors and titles, and a detailed general subject index.

How the Book Can Be Used

The Prentice-Hall Encyclopedia of Mathematics can be used effectively:

- for *research* on a particular topic, term, symbol, or person.
- as a *reference guide* to other sources.
- as a *classroom supplement* because it contains examples, charts, and graphs illustrating most elementary mathematical topics and many advanced ones.
- for *browsing,* as each article is virtually independent of other articles. In many cases sections within articles can be understood without reading the entire article. In order to help the reader scan an article, key words have been *italicized* or printed in **bold-face** type.

How to Find What You're Looking For

- To find information on a mathematical *topic* or on a particular *mathematician,* use the index at the end of the book.
- To find *articles related to a given article,* see the cross-references at the end of the article and note any term in the article printed in small CAPITAL LETTERS. A capitalized term indicates that there is a separate article on that topic.
- To find *other sources,* locate the article on that topic by using the

general index and then see the references listed in that article. Particular authors or titles can be located in the bibliographical index.

- To find a *symbol*, see the table of mathematical symbols in APPENDIX I.
- To find various *mathematical tables*, see also APPENDIX I.
- To find *historical information*, consult the time line at the beginning of the book, the biographical list in APPENDIX II, or the general index.

You may find some sections of the Encyclopedia hard to understand. Many discuss very difficult material. Don't let these worry you—you can skip over them. At some other time you may return to a difficult section and find it easier. If it is a topic you wish to pursue, try the references for help.

It is our hope that you will find *The Prentice-Hall Encyclopedia of Mathematics* a useful reference tool and an intriguing introduction to more advanced topics in mathematics.

BEVERLY HENDERSON WEST
ELLEN NORMA GRIESBACH
JERRY DUNCAN TAYLOR
LOUISE TODD TAYLOR

Acknowledgments

We give grateful recognition to Keith Henderson, Ken Olum, and Becky Henderson, our most dogged critics. They have each, from their junior high to college years, been continually involved in this project, reviewing and criticizing, contributing ideas and materials for text and illustrations, and programming for the index.

We are also indebted to former teacher Carolyn Gray, who has thoughtfully contributed much time and expertise over many years. We are grateful to historian Morris Kline, who made valuable suggestions in the historical sections, and to logician and teacher Catherine Wagner, who provided careful consultation, especially for the sections on logic and mathematical foundations. It is, however, we authors who must bear responsibility for any errors that may occur in the final product.

We appreciate the help from reviewers Ron Ward, Barbara Elder Weller, Jerry Kaplan, Carolyn Lucas, Mark Broadie, and Constanta Manu, who dealt in depth with the entire awkward manuscript. We gratefully acknowledge the special support provided by James E. West, and by Judy Adams, Terry Anderson, Guram Berishvili, Richard E. Burt, Barry De Libero, Cay Gibian, Pauline Halpern, Faith Hanson, David W. Henderson, Carolyn Jackson, Helga Metzler, Smoke Torres, Marguerite Wheeler, Lois Williams, Inez Wolins, and Nancy Zobel. And we thank all the many other people, too numerous to list individually, who have assisted us in various aspects of the project.

This encyclopedia has been an unusually long-term undertaking. We owe special thanks to editor Ellen Roberts, who started it all and should share the success of its completion; to editorial assistant Dwight Richardson, who pulled it together in the intermediate stages; and to editor Carol Barkin, who cheerfully encouraged us and took over the substantial task of finishing it.

Finally, we express special gratitude to designer George Whipple, whose splendid ideas, quiet competence, and immense patience made sense of a difficult task of presentation.

Time Line

On the following two pages is a rough chronology of the history of mathematics. The names of the most important mathematicians are printed in boldface type. The overall development of mathematical ideas is traced through the time line by italic labels. These point out only the highlights; in several instances there were later, or earlier, contributions to the same subject. The mathematical chronology is accompanied by a sampling of non-mathematical events, in lightface type, to give some historical perspective.

The lifespans of various mathematicians overlap, and many of them worked on different topics at different times. We have dealt with this difficulty by placing each name at a time corresponding to some major work. The numbers such as (1) (25) that follow each mathematician's name refer to the italic mathematical ideas to which that person contributed. For all mathematicians on the time line, more information is given in the biographical list, pp. 653–658.

More specialized and detailed chronologies appear in the articles on COMPUTERS, p. 103; EQUATIONS, p. 158; and PI (π), pp. 394–395.

Time Line

3000 B.C. Egyptian hieroglyphic numerals (3000 B.C.) (1)
Babylonian culture (3000 B.C.);
 cuneiform notation (2400 B.C.) (1)
Great Pyramid (2800 B.C.) *Development of*
  numeral systems;
2000 B.C. Stonehenge, England (1700 B.C.) *bookkeeping;*
Abraham (1700 B.C.) *practical problems*
Rhind or Ahmes Papyrus (1650 B.C.) (1) *of arithmetic*
Tutankhamen (reign: 1360–1350 B.C.) *and geometry* (1)
Moses (1250 B.C.)
1000 B.C. David (1000 B.C.)
Queen Dido's Problem (800 B.C.) (1)
800 B.C. First Olympics (776 B.C.)
Founding of Rome (753 B.C.)
600 B.C. Pythagoras (2) (21)
500 B.C. Confucius (551–479 B.C.) *Ancient Greek*
Buddha (563–483 B.C.) *mathematics:*
Zeno (2) *beginnings of*
Socrates (469–399 B.C.) *number theory,*
  formal geometry,
400 B.C. Peloponnesian Wars (431–404 B.C.) *logic* (2)
Plato (2)
Aristotle (2)
300 B.C. Euclid (2)
Alexander the Great (356–323 B.C.)
Archimedes (2)
Punic Wars (264–241, 218–201, 149–146 B.C.)
Sieve of Eratosthenes (230 B.C.) (2)
Conics of Apollonius (225 B.C.) (2)
200 B.C. Hannibal's crossing the Alps, with elephants (218 B.C.)
Hipparchus (2) (3)
Julius Caesar (100–44 B.C.)
B.C.
 Jesus of Nazareth (4 B.C.–30 A.D.)
A.D.
 Book of *Chou Pei Suan Ching* (40 A.D.)
Hero (or Heron) (2)
100 Papermaking in China (100 A.D.) *Beginnings of*
Menelaus of Alexandria (2) (3) *trigonometry,*
Claudius Ptolemy (2) (3) *by astronomers*
  (3)
Claudius Galen, definitive medical works on anatomy and
 physiology (130–200)
200 Diophantus (2) (4) (21) *Beginnings of*
400 Hypatia (2) *algebra* (4)
Fall of Rome (476)
500 Aryabhata (5) *Hindu and Arabian*
Mohammed (570–632) *influence on geometry,*
  algebra, and numeral
600 Brahmagupta (5) *systems; introduction*
Use of zero by Hindus (628) (5) *of zero* (5)
700 Charlemagne (reign: 771–814)
Translation of Hindu mathematics to Arabic (775) (5)
al-Khowârizmî, *Hisab aljabr w'al muqabalah* (4) (5)
800 Peak of Mayan civilization (800)
Alfred the Great (reign: 871–899)
1000 Lief Ericson's landing in America
 (1002)
William the Conqueror, Battle of *Hindu and Arabic*
 Hastings (1066) *mathematics,*
  brought to
1100 Omar Khayyám (4) (5) (22) *Western Europe* (6)
Bhaskara (4) (5)
1200 Fibonacci (Leonardo of Pisa), translation of Arabic
 mathematics to Latin (1200) (4) (6)
Universities founded at Oxford and Paris (1200)
Mongols rose under Genghis Khan (1206–1227)
Magna Carta (1215)
Gothic cathedrals with flying buttresses
Roger Bacon, pioneer for experimentation and mathematics
 in physical science (1214–1292)

Marco Polo set off for China (1271)
1300 Building of the Alhambra by Moors (1238–1354)
Black Death, struck Europe, costing England a third of its
 population (1348–1350)
Nicole Oresme (14)
1400 Joan of Arc, saved Orléans (1429), burned at stake (1431)
Fall of Constantinople (1453)
Gutenberg Bible (1454)
First printed mathematics books (1478),
 introduction of + and − signs (1489) (7)
Columbus discovered America (1492)
1500 Michael Stifel (7) *Negative numbers* (7)
Leonardo da Vinci (8) *Perspective* (8)
Albrecht Dürer (8)
Michelangelo, Sistine Chapel (1508–1512)
Protestant Reformation (1517)
Magellan, circumnavigation of globe (1519)
1520 Scipione del Ferro (9) *Solving*
Antonio Maria Fior (9) *equations* (9)
Nicolas Copernicus, astronomer
1540 Tartaglia (Niccolò Fontana) (9)
Girolamo Cardano (9) (10) *Imaginary*
Lodovico Ferrari (9) *numbers* (10)
Mercator map projection (1568) (20)
Discovery of circulation of blood in lungs, Michael Servetus,
 (1537)
1560 Elizabeth I (reign: 1558–1603)
Tycho Brahe, astronomer (1546–1601)
First permanent settlement in North America, St. Augustine,
 Florida (1565)
1580 Francois Viète (9) (11) *Introduction*
Simon Stevin (11) *of decimals* (11)
William Shakespeare (1564–1616)
Defeat of the Spanish Armada (1588)
1600 Settling of Jamestown, Virginia (1607)
John Napier (11) (12) *Logarithms* (12)
Jobst Bürgi (12)
Landing of Pilgrims, Plymouth,
 Massachusetts (1620)
1620 Slide rule (12) *Astronomy by*
Henry Briggs (12) *telescope,*
Adriaen Vlacq (12) *laws of*
Galileo (13) *planetary*
Johann Kepler (2) (13) *motion* (13)
Building of the Taj Mahal (1632–1654)
Harvard College established (1636)
Gerard Desargues (20) *Coordinate*
Rene Descartes (9) (14) (26) *system* (14)
1640 Pierre de Fermat (14) (15) (21) *Probability*
Blaise Pascal (15) (16) (20) *theory* (15)
Mersenne's Laws for musical pitch
1660 Royal Society founded in London (1662); French Academy
 founded in Paris (1666)
Robert Hooke, physics and microscopy, discovery of cells in
 plants (1635–1703) *Calculating*
Isaac Newton (9) (13) (17) *machines* (16)
Gottfried Wilhelm von Leibniz (16) (17) (18) (25)
Girolamo Saccheri (22) *Infinitesimal*
1680 Johann Sebastian Bach (1685–1750) *calculus* (17)
Peter the Great (reign: 1689–1725)
1700 Gabriel Cramer (18) *Determinants* (18)
Emilie de Breteuil Châtelet (17)
Leonhard Euler (17) (19) (28)
Thermometers (Fahrenheit 1718, Centigrade 1742)
Maria Theresa, Empress of Austria (reign: 1740–1780)

1750   Benjamin Franklin's kite experiment (1752)
       George Washington (1732–1799)
       Jean le Rond d'Alembert (19)
       Johann Heinrich Lambert, irrationality of π (1767) (19)
       Wolfgang Amadeus Mozart (1756–1791)
       Catherine the Great (reign: 1762–1796)
       James Watt's steam engine (1767)
       Discovery of oxygen, Joseph Priestly (1774)
       Thomas Jefferson (1743–1826)
       American Declaration of Independence (1776)
1780   Ludwig van Beethoven (1770–1827)
       French Revolution (1789–1814)
       Metric System (1790–1795)   *Complex*
       Gaspard Monge (20)   *numbers* (19)
1800   **Jean-Robert Argand** (19)   *Projection* (20)
       Joseph Fourier, summing sine functions
       Jane Austen, novelist (1775–1817)
       Carl Friedrich Gauss (2) (4) (19) (21) (22) (28)
       Sophie Germain (21)   *Number theory* (21)
       Smallpox vaccination, Edward Jenner (1796)
       Electric battery; first submarine; steamboats; steam locomo-
          tives (early 1800s)
       Napoleonic Empire (1804–1815)
       Jean Victor Poncelet (20)
1820   Augustin-Louis Cauchy, limits
       Nicolai Ivanovich Lobachevsky (22)
       Janos Bolyai (22)   *Non-Euclidean*
       Evariste Galois (9)   *geometry* (22)
       Braille reading method for the blind (1834)
       Charles Babbage (16) (32)
       Lady Ada Byron Lovelace (32)
       Beginnings of modern photographic processes (1835–1840)
       **Impossibility proved for trisection of angle or duplication of
          cube (1837)** (2)
       Queen Victoria (reign: 1837–1901)
       Charles Dickens, novelist (1812–1870)
       Augustus DeMorgan (26)
1840   **Arthur Cayley** (23)   *Matrices* (23)
       Anesthetics introduced into surgery (1840s)
       William Rowan Hamilton (24)
       Hermann Grassman (24)   *Vectors* (24)
       Joseph Liouville, transcendental numbers (1844)
       Sewing machine (1846)
1850   **George Boole** (25) (26)   *Symbolic logic* (25)
       Karl Marx, *Communist Manifesto* (1848)
       Harriet Beecher Stowe, *Uncle Tom's Cabin* (1852)
       George Friedrich Bernhard Riemann (19) (22)
       Richard Dedekind (27)
       John Venn (26)   *Sets* (26)
       First transatlantic cable (1858)
1860   Charles Darwin, *The Origin of Species* (1859)
       Internal combustion engine (1860)
       Abraham Lincoln (1809–1865)
       U.S. Civil War (1861–1865)
       Pasteurization (1864)
       Lewis Carroll (Charles Dodgson), logic
       Mark Twain (Samuel Langhorne Clemens) (1835–1910)
       Principles of heredity, Gregor Mendel (1866)
       Typewriter (1868)
       Transcontinental railroad (1869)
1870   Sonya Kovalevsky, differential equations
       Georg Cantor (26) (27)   *Infinite sets* (27)
       Telephone, Alexander Graham Bell (1876)
       Thomas Edison, inventor (phonograph 1877,
          incandescent light bulb 1879)

1880   Ferdinand Lindemann, **π is transcendental (1882)**
       Electromagnetic waves, Heinrich Hertz (1887)
1890   Booker T. Washington, Black educator (1856–1915)
       Giuseppe Peano (25)
       X-rays; First public motion picture (1895)
       Henri Poincare (28)   *Topology* (28)
       Discovery of electron (1897)
       Rocket propulsion (1898)
       David Hilbert (30)
1900   Sigmund Freud, founder of psychoanalysis (1856–1939)
       Mahatma Gandhi (1869—1948)
       Wireless telegraphy, Guglielmo Marconi (1901)
       Helen Keller, blind and deaf author and
          lecturer (1880–1968)
       Pablo Picasso, painter (1881–1973)
       First powered flight, Wright brothers (1903)
       Marcel Grossman (24) (29)
       Albert Einstein (29)   *Relativity* (29)
       Conquest of earth's poles (North by Robert Peary
          1906–1909, South by Roald Amundsen 1911)
       Early plastics; first mass production
          of automobiles (1909)
1910   **Alfred North Whitehead** (30)   *Logical*
       Bertrand Russell (30)   *foundations of*
       Luitzen E. J. Brouwer (30)   *mathematics* (30)
       Jim Thorpe, American Indian athlete (1888–1953)
       World War I (1914–1918)
       Russian Revolution (1917)
       Prohibition (1917, repealed 1933)
       Babe Ruth, baseball (1895–1948)
1920   **Women's Suffrage (19th amendment) (1920)**
       Emmy Noether (31)   *Abstract algebra* (31)
       Trial of John T. Scopes, found guilty of teaching
          evolution in the public schools (1925)
       William Faulkner, novelist (1897–1962)
       First nonstop flight over Atlantic, Charles Lindbergh (1927)
       First television broadcasting (England 1927, U.S. 1930)
       Penicillin, Alexander Fleming (1928)
1930   First analog computer, Vannevar Bush (1930) (32)
       Kurt Gödel (30)
       Adolf Hitler comes to power (1933)
       Jesse Owens, American athlete, first to win three Olympic
          events (1914–1980)
       Enrico Fermi, atomic physicist (1901–1954)
       J. Robert Oppenheimer, atomic physicist (1904–1967)
       Hans Bethe, energy physicist (1906–   )
1940   World War II (1939–1945)   *Computers* (32)
       Atomic bombs dropped on Hiroshima
          and Nagasaki (1945)
       United Nations established (1946)
       First digital computers (Aiken 1944, ENIAC 1946)
       John von Neumann (32)
       State of Israel established (1948)
1950   First hydrogen bomb (1952)
       Sputnik I (1957)
1960   First men in space (U.S.S.R., U.S. 1961)
       Computer graphics (early 1960s) (32)
       First successful human heart transplant (1967)
       U.S. lands men on moon (1969)
1970   Solution of Four Color Problem, Kenneth Appel and Wolf-
          gang Haken (1976) (32)
       Fractal geometry, Benoit Mandelbrot (1970s) (32)
       Rigidity counterexample, Robert Connelly (1977) (2)
1980   **Breakthrough computer algorithm to test for large prime
          numbers (1980–1981)** (32) (21)

The
Prentice-Hall
Encyclopedia
of Mathematics

ALGEBRA

ALGEBRA: the branch of mathematics characterized by the use of *variables* and operations relating these variables; ARITHMETIC generalized to include variables as well as REAL NUMBERS.

A *variable* is a symbol for which one or more quantities may be substituted. For example, in the ALGEBRAIC EXPRESSION $4x$, where

$$4x = x + x + x + x,$$

x is a variable, and it can be replaced by any real number, for example, $1, 2, 3, \frac{1}{2}, -5$, or 0. On the other hand, to make the algebraic expression

$$4y = 8$$

a true statement, the variable y can be replaced only by 2.

When variables represent real numbers, they can act like numbers in any ARITHMETIC OPERATION. Variables can be added, subtracted, multiplied, or divided (excluding division by zero). And it is possible to raise a variable to a power or to extract a root of a variable.

Algebra enables you to express what is known about some variable (or variables) in terms of a *mathematical sentence*—an EQUATION or an INEQUALITY—and to perform operations on the two sides of a mathematical sentence in order to find the value (or values) of the variable. Usually an equation is solved by performing one or more operations on both sides of the equation in order to isolate the variable on one side. Then the other side of the equation will give the solution.

Example.
$$3x + 4 = 19$$ subtracting 4 from both sides
$$3x = 15$$ dividing both sides by 3
$$x = 5$$

Using algebra, you can solve problems that cannot easily be solved with arithmetic alone.

Example.   On the route home from a game twenty football players quenched their thirst with either a Coke @ 65¢ or milk @ 40¢. The coach paid $10.75 for their drinks. How many drank Coke?

Solution: Let x represent the number of players who drank Coke. Then $20 - x$ represents the number who drank milk. The cost may be represented by

$$0.65x + 0.40(20 - x) = 10.75$$
$$0.65x + 8.00 - 0.40x = 10.75$$
$$(0.65 - 0.40)\, x = 10.75 - 8.00$$
$$0.25x = 2.75$$
$$x = 11.$$

APPLICATIONS

Algebra has numerous practical applications. In fact, every time you work with an equation or formula that includes unknown quantities, you are using algebra.

A bank uses algebra for computations on savings accounts that receive INTEREST. If money is invested at *simple* interest, the formula is

$$A = P + (P \times R \times T) \quad \text{where} \quad \begin{aligned} A &= \text{amount} \\ P &= \text{principal} \\ R &= \text{rate, as a DECIMAL} \\ T &= \text{time, in years.} \end{aligned}$$

There are four variables in this formula. But for a customer who invests $3,000 at 10% for twelve years, values of the variables P, R, and T may be substituted in the equation. Then A would be the only remaining variable, and its value could be calculated by the formula.

$$A = 3000 + (3000 \times 0.10 \times 12) = \$6600, \quad \text{the amount in}$$
the customer's account after twelve years.

On the other hand, someone who invests $3,000 at 10% may ask how long it will take for the account to grow to $7,000. In this case, values may be substituted for P, R, and A. Then T is the remaining variable, and the equation can be solved for T:

$$7000 = 3000 + (3000 \times 0.10 \times T)$$
$$4000 = 300\ T$$

$$T = \frac{4000}{300} = 13\tfrac{1}{3} \text{ years.}$$

The computations necessary to solve such equations can be done by COMPUTERS that can be programmed to operate with variables as well as with real numbers. In the example of investment at simple interest—an equation in four variables—the computer can be programmed to compute any one variable given the other three.

Another application of algebra is to various types of work–time problems. For example, suppose that one computer can do all of a bank's bookkeeping for a day in three hours, and that a slower computer can do the same job in five hours. If the first computer works on the job for one hour and then breaks down, how long will it take the slower computer to finish the job? The problem can be solved algebraically by letting

w = total amount of work to be done
$\tfrac{1}{3}w$ = amount of work done by C_1 (before breakdown)
$\tfrac{2}{3}w$ = amount of work left to be done by C_2 (from $w - \tfrac{1}{3}w$)
5 = number of hours for C_2 to complete entire job
t = number of hours for C_2 to finish job.

Then a PROPORTION can be set up as follows:

$$\frac{\text{time for } C_2 \text{ to do entire job}}{\text{time for } C_2 \text{ to finish job}} = \frac{\text{total amount of work}}{\text{amount of work left to be done by } C_2}$$

$$\frac{5}{t} = \frac{w}{\tfrac{2}{3}w}$$

$$t \times w = 5 \times \tfrac{2}{3} \times w$$

$$t = 5 \times \tfrac{2}{3}$$

$$t = \tfrac{10}{3} = 3\tfrac{1}{3}.$$

Algebra can be applied to problems involving distance, rate, and time. It can be applied to problems of keeping proportions constant when quantities are changed—for example, when a cook cuts a recipe by a third or when a pharmacist wants to make a certain quantity of a 3% solution.

Finally, algebra has a host of applications in the physical sciences. In the very readable book *The Realm of Algebra*, Isaac Asimov devotes the last chapter to ''Putting Algebra to Work.'' Asimov tells a tale suggesting how Galileo applied algebra to the results of his experiments with rolling balls to calculate the rate at which a falling body accelerates, how Isaac Newton used algebra to arrive at his formula for the gravitational pull between two bodies, and how Henry Cavendish—working with Newton's formula for gravitation and the results of some experiments with large and small balls—used algebra to approximate the weight of the earth.

HISTORY OF ALGEBRA

The solution of equations dates back to the ancient Egyptians and Babylonians, and it can be traced through the early Greeks. Some ancient Greek mathematicians solved problems strictly by GEOMETRY rather than algebra, but others took an algebraic approach using equations. The highest point of Alexandrian Greek algebra was reached in the third century A.D. by Diophantus, who is sometimes called the "father of algebra."

But Diophantus did not find all the solutions that can be found today. He was interested only in positive rational solutions, and he was satisfied when he had found a single answer.

Diophantus was the first to substitute abbreviations or symbols for frequently used words. Yet other mathematicians in his day and for centuries thereafter continued to write mathematical sentences completely in words.

The title "father of algebra" might more appropriately be awarded to the Arabian mathematician Al-Khowarizmi, who really launched algebra in the Western world. In the ninth century, Al-Khowarizmi published a treatise, *Hisab al-jabr w' al muqabalah,* in which he gave a clear and complete exposition of how to solve linear equations by performing the same operation on both sides of an equation. The title of his work has been translated as "The Science of Restoring and Cancelling." This probably refers to the process of restoring a missing term, as in the solution of $x - 5 = 10$ (where 5 must be restored to each side of the equation), and to cancelling, or division, as in the solution of $3x = 9$ (where each side must be divided by 3).

Al-Khowarizmi also showed how to solve quadratic (or second-degree) equations. Although he was not the first to do this, his work became so influential when it was translated into Latin in the thirteenth century that it came to stand for the whole science of solving equations. It is from the title of his treatise that we get our word "algebra."

The history of algebra from the thirteenth through the seventeenth centuries is the story of how more solutions to equations were found and how equations of higher degree came to be solved. This is told in detail in the article on EQUATIONS. By the end of the seventeenth century, mathematicians accepted both negative and irrational solutions to equations, solved equations of the third and fourth degree, and used the same symbolic notation, or shorthand, used in algebra today.

The important developments in algebra after the seventeenth century were extending the idea of variable and discovering the possibility of developing an algebra that did not follow the ground rules, or FIELD PROPERTIES, of conventional arithmetic.

In the nineteenth century, several mathematicians developed systems of algebra in which a *variable* was used to represent something other than a REAL NUMBER. George Boole, an English logician, developed an algebra in which variables represented classes, or SETS. (*Boolean algebra* later had enormously important applications in the development of computers). An Irish mathematician, William Rowan Hamilton, was one of several mathematicians to develop algebras in which variables represented VECTORS. And an English mathematician, Arthur Cayley, showed how a variable could represent a whole array of numbers, or MATRIX. (*Vector algebra* and *matrix algebra* are used extensively in physical sciences, natural sciences, and social sciences—wherever many quantities may be changing at the same time.)

Extending the concept that a variable could stand for things other than real numbers had unexpected consequences, however. When Hamilton developed his algebra with variables that are vectors, he discovered that it was necessary to change an important FIELD PROPERTY of conventional algebra. In conventional algebra, multiplication is *commutative:* that is, $a \times b = b \times a$. But in Hamilton's algebra, multiplication is *not* commutative: $a \times b \neq b \times a$.

The discovery that it was possible to develop an algebra in which one or more of the field properties of conventional algebra did not apply led to the development of many new algebras, each with its own set of ground rules, or *structure*. And the development of these new algebras led in turn to *abstract algebra*, the study of different algebraic systems.

An outstanding contributor in the field of abstract algebra was Emmy Noether. In the 1920's, she made important discoveries about the structure of noncommutative algebras. Although there have been few women in the history of mathematics, Emmy Noether was a notable exception. In the words of the historian E. T. Bell, "She was the most creative abstract algebraist in the world." (See references, Bell, p. 261.)

REFERENCES

Irving Adler, *Thinking Machines: A Layman's Introduction to Logic, Boolean Algebra, and Computers* (The John Day Co., 1961); the extension of abstract algebra to the design of COMPUTERS. By explaining how to treat variables as something other than real numbers, Adler uses an algebra of classes, an algebra of propositions, an

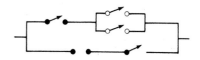

algebra of switching circuits, and finally Boolean algebra to design circuits that calculate and perform deductive reasoning.

Isaac Asimov, *The Realm of Algebra* (Houghton Mifflin, 1961; Fawcett paperback).

Deborah Hughes-Hallett, *The Math Workshop: Algebra* (W. W. Norton & Co., 1980); an exceptionally readable textbook for students who have not had algebra or who need a complete review.

W. W. Sawyer, ''Algebra,'' *Scientific American,* September 1964; reprinted in *Mathematics in the Modern World: Readings from Scientific American* (W. H. Freeman & Co., 1968), pp. 102–110; good description of the more abstract algebras.

References on the history of algebra

Howard Eves, *An Introduction to the History of Mathematics* (Holt, Rinehart and Winston, 1964, 1969).

Historical Topics for the Mathematics Classroom, 31st Yearbook of the National Council of Teachers of Mathematics (1969), pp. 233–260; an overview of the history of algebra. Diophantus, Al-Khowarizmi, Boole, Hamilton, and Cayley are discussed further in this book.

Biographical references

E. T. Bell, *Men of Mathematics* (Simon and Schuster, 1937; Fireside paperback); another historical source, covering primarily the years 1600 to 1900; a chapter each on Hamilton, Cayley, and Boole.

Teri Perl, *Math Equals: Biographies of Women Mathematicians + Related Activities* (Addison Wesley, 1978), Ch. 10, ''Emmy Noether,'' pp. 173–194.

Herbert Westren Turnbull, *The Great Mathematicians* (New York University Press, 1961), pp. 55–60; more on Diophantus.

For more on algebra, see ALGEBRAIC EXPRESSIONS, EQUATIONS, and INEQUALITIES.

ALGEBRAIC EXPRESSIONS

ALGEBRAIC EXPRESSION: any *variable* or *constant* or any combination of variables and constants related by ARITHMETIC OPERATIONS.

Examples. $5y + z$ $\dfrac{x + 2}{3x - 1}$ $5x^4 - 3x^3 + 2x + 9$

$|2y - 3|$ $\sqrt{7x}$ $\frac{1}{2}x + yz$

Constant: a symbol, usually a numeral, that represents exactly one quantity.

Variable: a symbol, usually a letter, for which one or more quantities may be substituted.

Algebraic expression	Constant(s)	Variable(s)
$5x$	5	x
$3y^2 - 4$	3 and 4	y
$\frac{1}{2}y + z$	$\frac{1}{2}$	y and z

Sometimes a variable is used to represent a whole SET of quantities. Then the individual members of the set are distinguished by the use of a *subscript*—a numeral written to the lower right of the variable. For example, the set of scores made by a group on a test could be represented by the variable t, and the individual scores could be represented by t_1, t_2, t_3 ... (read "t sub 1, t sub 2, t sub 3").

TERMINOLOGY

Term: when plus or minus signs separate an algebraic expression into parts, each part is a *term*. If an expression is not separated by plus or minus signs, the entire expression is a single term.

Examples.   *Algebraic Expressions*   *Terms*

$$3x^2 - 7x + 6 \qquad 3x^2, -7x, \text{ and } 6$$
$$4(x - y) + 5 \qquad 4(x - y) \text{ and } 5$$

Coefficient: within a term, any FACTOR is a coefficient of the other factors. Usually, though, ''coefficient'' refers to a *numerical* or constant factor.

Examples.   *Term*   *Coefficient*

$3x^2$ 3 is the coefficient of x^2

$-7y$ -7 is the coefficient of y

cx c is the coefficient of x,
        where c may be a constant factor.

When a term includes no numerical factor, the coefficient is understood to be 1.

Examples. $x^2 = 1x^2 \qquad -x^2 = -1x^2$

It is common practice not to write the numeral for the coefficient when it is 1 or -1.

Like (or Similar) Terms: terms that are exactly alike or that differ only in their numerical coefficients.

Examples.   Of $3x^2y$, $7x^2y$, and $7x^2y^2$, only $3x^2y$ and $7x^2y$ are like terms. Like terms may be combined:

$$3x^2y + 7x^2y + 7x^2y^2 = (3 + 7)x^2y + 7x^2y^2 = 10x^2y + 7x^2y^2$$

An algebraic expression is not considered *simplified* until all like terms are combined.

TYPES OF ALGEBRAIC EXPRESSIONS

Monomial: an algebraic expression of exactly one term.

Examples. $xyz \qquad -7y^3 \qquad \dfrac{5x}{2} \qquad 3(2a + b)$

Binomial: an algebraic expression of exactly two terms.

Examples. $5x - y \qquad 6(x - z) - 2(c + d) \qquad \frac{1}{2}c + \frac{1}{4}d$

Trinomial: an algebraic expression of exactly three terms.

Examples. $9x^2 - xy - 8y^2$ $a + b + c$ $x^3 - 5x + 1$

Multinomial: an algebraic expression of two or more terms.

Examples. $\dfrac{4}{x} + 2x - 7$ $3 - \sqrt{2x}$

Polynomial: an algebraic expression of one or more terms in which there are *no* variables in a denominator and *no* variables under a radical sign; where n is a positive integer, an expression of the form

$$ax^n + bx^{n-1} + cx^{n-2} \ldots + kx^0$$

In a polynomial *in one variable,* the terms are usually arranged so that the exponents of the variable are in descending order.

Examples. $x - 7$ $6y^4 - 5y^3 - 2y^2 + 3y + 1$

In a polynomial *in two variables,* the terms are arranged so that the exponents of one of the variables are in descending order.

Examples. $5x^4 - 2x^3y + x^2y^2 + 7xy^3 - y^4$, or

$$-y^4 + 7y^3x + y^2x^2 - 2yx^3 + 5x^4$$

A polynomial is said to be of a certain *degree,* which is always equal to the degree of its highest degree term. The degree of any term is equal to the exponent of the variable if there is only one variable or to the sum of the exponents if there are two or more variables in the term.

Examples.

Polynomial	*Degree*
$x^3 - 1$	3rd
$x^2 + 2xy + y^2$	2nd
$xy + 3y$	2nd

ARITHMETIC OPERATIONS

It is possible to perform ARITHMETIC OPERATIONS on algebraic expressions.

Addition: to add two algebraic expressions, you write the sum and combine like terms.

Example. $(10x^2 + 3x - 8) + (7x^2 - 10) = 17x^2 + 3x - 18$

or,

$$
\begin{array}{r}
10x^2 + 3x - 8 \\
+ 7x^2 - 10 \\
\hline
17x^2 + 3x - 18
\end{array}
$$

Subtraction: to subtract one expression from another, you reverse the sign of each term in the expression to be subtracted and then proceed as in addition.

Example. $(10x^2 + 3x - 8) - (7x^2 - 10)$

$$= 10x^2 + 3x - 8 - 7x^2 + 10$$

$$= 3x^2 + 3x + 2$$

or,

$$
\begin{array}{r}
10x^2 + 3x - 8 \\
- 7x^2 - 10 \\
\hline
\end{array}
\quad = \quad
\begin{array}{r}
10x^2 + 3x - 8 \\
+ -7x^2 + 10 \\
\hline
3x^2 + 3x + 2
\end{array}
$$

Multiplication: to multiply two expressions, you multiply each term of the first expression by each term of the second and then combine like terms.

Examples. $(2x + 4)(3x - 7)$

$$= 2x(3x) + 2x(-7) + 4(3x) + 4(-7)$$

$$= 6x^2 - 14x + 12x - 28$$

$$= 6x^2 - 2x - 28$$

$$
\begin{array}{r}
3x^2 + x + 2 \\
\times x - 4 \\
\hline
3x^3 + x^2 + 2x \\
- 12x^2 - 4x - 8 \\
\hline
3x^3 - 11x^2 - 2x - 8
\end{array}
$$

Division: to divide a polynomial by a monomial, you divide each term of the polynomial by the monomial and simplify the results.

Example. $(3x^3y + 7xy^2 - xy^3) \div xy$

$$= \frac{3x^3y}{xy} + \frac{7xy^2}{xy} - \frac{xy^3}{xy}$$

$$= 3x^2 + 7y - y^2$$

To divide a polynomial by a polynomial, you arrange both expressions in descending order of powers of the desired variable and proceed by long division in the same manner as in arithmetic.

Examples. $(2x^2 + x - 15) \div (x + 3) = 2x - 5$

$$
\require{enclose}
\begin{array}{r}
2x - 5 \\
x + 3 \enclose{longdiv}{2x^2 + x - 15} \\
\underline{2x^2 + 6x } \\
- 5x - 15 \\
\underline{- 5x - 15} \\
0 \quad \text{Remainder}
\end{array}
$$

$$(x^2 - 5) \div (x + 3) = x - 3 + \frac{4}{x + 3}$$

$$
\begin{array}{r}
x - 3 \\
x + 3 \enclose{longdiv}{x^2 + 0x - 5} \\
\underline{x^2 + 3x } \\
- 3x - 5 \\
\underline{- 3x - 9} \\
+ 4 \quad \text{Remainder}
\end{array}
$$

The second example illustrates the insertion of zero terms for missing powers of the variable in the dividend (the number to be divided) to aid in long division.

The remainder of the second example is not zero, but the division process reaches an end when the degree of the variable in the remainder is less than the degree of the variable in the divisor.

BINOMIAL THEOREM

You can raise an algebraic expression to a power by repeated multiplication.

Examples.

$(x - 4)^2 = (x - 4)(x - 4) = x^2 - 8x + 16$

$(x - 4)^3 = (x - 4)(x - 4)(x - 4) = (x^2 - 8x + 16)(x - 4)$

$$= x^3 - 12x^2 + 48x - 64$$

For an algebraic expression with exactly two terms—a binomial such as $(x + y)$—the results of such repeated multiplication look like this:

$$(x + y)^0 = 1$$
$$(x + y)^1 = x + y$$
$$(x + y)^2 = x^2 + 2xy + y^2$$
$$(x + y)^3 = x^3 + 3x^2y + 3xy^2 + y^3$$
$$(x + y)^4 = x^4 + 4x^3y + 6x^2y^2 + 4xy^3 + y^4$$
$$(x + y)^5 = x^5 + 5x^4y + 10x^3y^2 + 10x^2y^3 + 5xy^4 + y^5$$
$$(x + y)^6 = x^6 + 6x^5y + 15x^4y^2 + 20x^3y^3 + 15x^2y^4 + 6xy^5 + y^6.$$

There is a pattern to this display:

- $(x + y)^n$ always has $n + 1$ terms.
- in every term, the exponents of x and y sum to n.
- the terms are arranged in descending powers of x:

$$x^n, \ x^{n-1}y^1, \ x^{n-2}y^2, \ldots, \ x^2y^{n-2}, \ x^1y^{n-1}, \ y^n.$$

- the coefficients form a pattern called *Pascal's triangle* (after Blaise Pascal, the French mathematician who discovered this pattern in the seventeenth century):

$$
\begin{array}{llccccccccccc}
(x + y)^0: & & & & & & 1 & & & & & \\
(x + y)^1: & & & & & 1 & & 1 & & & & \\
(x + y)^2: & & & & 1 & & 2 & & 1 & & & \\
(x + y)^3: & & & 1 & & 3 & & 3 & & 1 & & \\
(x + y)^4: & & 1 & & 4 & & 6 & & 4 & & 1 & \\
(x + y)^5: & 1 & & 5 & & 10 & & 10 & & 5 & & 1 \\
(x + y)^6: & 1 & 6 & & 15 & & 20 & & 15 & & 6 & 1 \\
\end{array}
$$

Do you see how this pattern is formed?

Each row begins and ends with one, and each intermediate number is the sum of the numbers above it. The display can be continued as follows:

$$
\begin{array}{lccccccccc}
(x + y)^6: & 1 & 6 & 15 & 20 & 15 & 6 & 1 & & \\
(x + y)^7: & 1 & 7 & 21 & 35 & 35 & 21 & 7 & 1 & \\
(x + y)^8: & 1 & 8 & 28 & 56 & 70 & 56 & 28 & 8 & 1 \\
\end{array}
$$

Raising a binomial to a power is called *expanding the binomial,* and the result is called a *binomial expansion.* The need to do this occurs often in mathematics. The shortcut method following the above general rules is called the *binomial theorem.* The binomial theorem allows you to write down the expansion of $(x + y)^7$ without multiplying out each step.

Example.

$$(x + y)^7 = \bigcirc x^7 + \bigcirc x^6y + \bigcirc x^5y^2 + \bigcirc x^4y^3 + \bigcirc x^3y^4 + \bigcirc x^2y^5 + \bigcirc xy^6 + \bigcirc y^7$$

$$= \textcircled{1}x^7 + \textcircled{7}x^6y + \textcircled{21}x^5y^2 + \textcircled{35}x^4y^3 + \textcircled{35}x^3y^4 + \textcircled{21}x^2y^5 + \textcircled{7}xy^6 + \textcircled{1}y^7$$

(The coefficients were filled in from Pascal's triangle.)

In expanding a binomial, the most difficult part usually is finding the coefficients. There are a number of different ways to do this. Pascal's triangle is an easy method to remember, and it is handy for small n.

Another method to find the coefficient for each term is to look at the *preceding term*, multiply its coefficient by its power of x, and divide by the ordinal (nth) number of that preceding term.

$$\left(\begin{array}{c} \text{coefficient} \\ \text{of any term} \end{array}\right) = \frac{\left(\begin{array}{c} \text{coefficient of} \\ \text{preceding term} \end{array}\right)\left(\begin{array}{c} \text{power of } x \text{ of} \\ \text{preceding term} \end{array}\right)}{\left(\begin{array}{c} \text{ordinal number of} \\ \text{preceding term} \end{array}\right)}$$

Example.

$$
\begin{array}{cccccccccc}
& \text{1st term} & & \text{2nd term} & & \text{3rd term} & & \text{4th term} & & \text{5th term} \\
(x + y)^4 = & \bigcirc x^4 & + & \bigcirc x^3y & + & \bigcirc x^2y^2 & + & \bigcirc xy^3 & + & \bigcirc y^4 \\
= & \textcircled{1}x^4 & + & \textcircled{4}x^3y & + & \textcircled{6}x^2y^2 & + & \textcircled{4}xy^3 & + & \textcircled{1}y^4
\end{array}
$$

$$\frac{1 \times 4}{1} \qquad \frac{4 \times 3}{2} \qquad \frac{6 \times 2}{3} \qquad \frac{4 \times 1}{4}$$

If a binomial such as $(2a - b)$ already includes a numerical coefficient in one or both of its terms, when the binomial is expanded the coefficients must be carried throughout the expansion and eventually must be multiplied by the coefficients from the binomial theorem.

Example.

$$(2a - b)^3 = \bigcirc(2a)^3 + \bigcirc(2a)^2(-b) + \bigcirc(2a)(-b)^2 + \bigcirc(-b)^3$$

$$= \textcircled{1}(2a)^3 + \textcircled{3}(2a)^2(-b) + \textcircled{3}(2a)(-b)^2 + \textcircled{1}(-b)^3$$

$$= \quad 8a^3 \quad - \quad 12a^2b \quad + \quad 6ab^2 \quad - \quad b^3$$

(Binomial coefficients 1,3,3,1 are from Pascal's triangle.)

There is a third way to calculate the coefficients of a binomial expansion, because of this fact: the coefficient of $x^{n-k}y^k$ in $(x + y)^n$ is the number of *combinations* of n things taken k at a time, $_nC_k$. See PERMUTATIONS AND COMBINATIONS.

For more on the uses of algebraic expressions, see EQUATIONS and INEQUALITIES.

ANGLES

ANGLE: (in geometry) the figure formed by two distinct rays starting from the same endpoint. A ray is a portion of a LINE starting at one point and going on forever in one direction. *Distinct* rays cannot be part of the same line.

Symbol: ∠

Sides of an Angle: the two rays.

Vertex of an Angle: the common endpoint.

Interior of an Angle: the part of the plane between the sides of the angle.

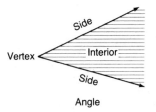

Angle

ANGLE: (in trigonometry) the angle formed by the rotation of a ray around its endpoint to a new position.

Sides of the Angle: the two different positions of the ray, with the starting position called the *initial side* and the final position called the *terminal side*.

Vertex of the Angle: the point about which the ray is rotated.

Positive Angle: the angle formed when the ray is rotated in a counterclockwise direction.

Negative Angle: the angle formed when the ray is rotated in a clockwise direction.

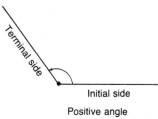

Positive angle
(counter-clockwise)

MEASURE OF AN ANGLE

The measure of an angle is a measure of the *opening* between the two ~~'es~~ and does not depend on the length of the sides. One way to ~~measure~~ the opening between the sides of an angle would be to construct ~~some~~ convenient circle with the vertex of the angle at its center. You ~~could~~ then consider what fractional part of the total circumference of the ~~circle~~ is included between the two sides of the angle.

The size of the circle does not matter. Though the length of the arc cut

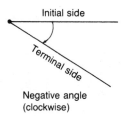

Negative angle
(clockwise)

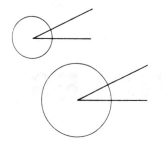

The measure of an angle tells what fractional part of the entire circumference is subtended by the angle

off, or *subtended,* would vary with the size of the circle, the angle would subtend the same *fractional part* of any circle.

Measuring an angle in terms of a circle dates back to the early Greek geometers (about 500 B.C.). Even more ancient is the set of *units* most often used to express the measure of an angle. The Babylonians (2000–1600 B.C.) first divided a circle into 360 equal parts called *degrees,* for astronomical purposes, thereby providing one convenient unit for expressing the measure of any angle.

Degree: the measure of a central angle that subtends or cuts off $\frac{1}{360}$ of a circle; $\frac{1}{360}$ of a complete rotation about a point. A degree is divided into 60 *minutes.* A minute is divided into 60 *seconds.*

An angle of 36 degrees, 22 minutes, and 35 seconds would be written 36° 22′ 35″. An angle of this size is shown in the illustration.

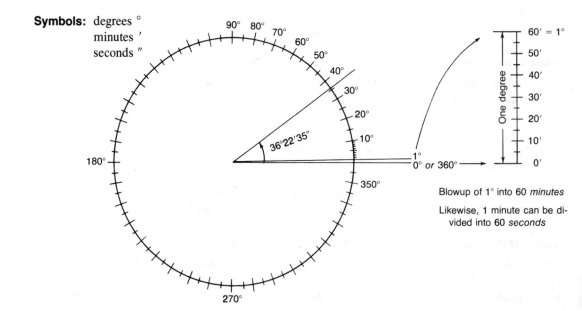

Symbols: degrees °
minutes ′
seconds ″

Blowup of 1° into 60 *minutes*

Likewise, 1 minute can be divided into 60 *seconds*

Degrees are the unit of angle measure most commonly used, and you may never need to know any other. However, another unit of angle measure does become necessary in higher mathematics, particularly in CALCULUS. That is the measure of an angle by *radians,* the ratio of arc length to radius in a circle.

$$\text{radian measure of an angle} = \frac{\text{arc length}}{\text{radius}}$$

Again, the size of the circle does not matter, because for a given angle the ratio of arc length to radius will always be the same.

Radian: the measure of a central angle of a circle that subtends or cuts off an arc equal in length to the radius of the circle.

$$\text{one radian} = \frac{5 \text{ cm arc length}}{5 \text{ cm radius}} = 1$$

$$2\pi \text{ radians} = \frac{\text{circumference}}{\text{radius}} = \frac{2\pi r}{r}$$

$$\pi \text{ radians} = \frac{\text{half-circumference}}{\text{radius}} = \frac{\pi r}{r}$$

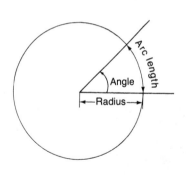

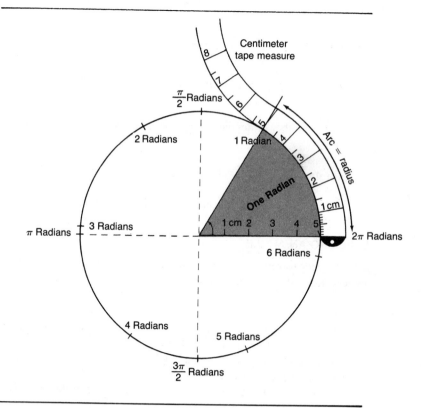

Relationship between Degrees and Radians

Because degrees and radians are two units for measuring the same thing, it is possible to convert an angle measure from one to the other by knowing the relationship between them.

One full circle (or one complete revolution) contains 360°, or 2π radians. Therefore

$$360° = 2\pi \text{ radians}$$

$$1° = \frac{2\pi}{360} \text{ radians (approximately 0.01745 radians)}$$

$$1 \text{ radian} = \frac{360°}{2\pi} \text{ (approximately 57° 17' 45'')}$$

To convert from radians to degrees:

$$\text{number of radians} \times \frac{360}{2\pi} = \text{number of degrees}$$

Example. $\frac{\pi}{3}$ radians $\times \dfrac{360}{2\pi} = 60°$

To convert from degrees to radians:

$$\text{number of degrees} \times \frac{2\pi}{360} = \text{number of radians}$$

Example. $90° \times \dfrac{2\pi}{360} = \dfrac{\pi}{2}$ radians

(approximately 1.57 radians)

LABELING AN ANGLE

It is easier to refer to a particular angle in a geometric figure if the angle is labeled. An angle is usually labeled in one of three ways:

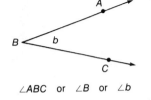

$\angle ABC$ or $\angle B$ or $\angle b$

- An angle may be labeled by three letters with the first letter standing for a point on one ray, the middle letter for the vertex, and the last letter for a point on the other ray;
- An angle may be labeled by a single letter at its vertex *if* there is only one angle at that vertex;
- An angle may be labeled by a single small letter in the interior of the angle.

WAYS OF CLASSIFYING ANGLES

There are numerous ways of classifying angles. One way is according to their *measure*:

Right Angle: an angle with a measure of 90°. A right angle is usually marked in a diagram in this way: ⌐⌐

Acute Angle: an angle with a measure of less than 90°.

Obtuse Angle: an angle with a measure of more than 90° but less than 180°.

Straight Angle: an angle with a measure of 180°; an angle formed by two rays extending in opposite directions from a common point.

Reflex Angle: an angle with a measure of more than 180° but less than 360°.

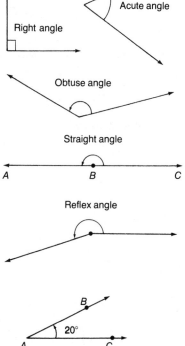

Another way of classifying angles is by their *relationship to other angles:*

Congruent Angles: angles with the same measure.

Complementary Angles: two angles with a combined measure equal to 90°. One angle is said to be the *complement* of the other. Complementary angles may or may not be next to each other. The two acute angles of a right triangle are complementary.

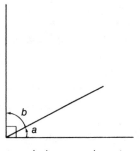

∠a and ∠b are complementary

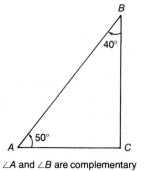

∠A and ∠B are complementary

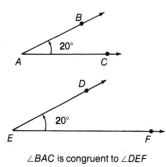

∠BAC is congruent to ∠DEF
∠BAC ≅ ∠DEF

Supplementary Angles: two angles with a combined measure equal to 180°. One angle is said to be the *supplement* of the other. Supplementary angles may or may not be next to each other.

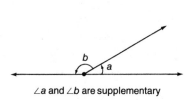

∠a and ∠b are supplementary

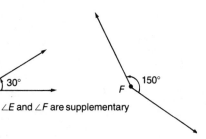

∠E and ∠F are supplementary

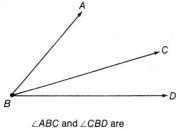

∠*ABC* and ∠*CBD* are
adjacent angles

∠*ABC* and ∠*ABD* are *not*
adjacent angles

Adjacent Angles: two angles in the same plane with a common vertex and a common side but with no interior points in common.

Vertical Angles: the pair of opposite angles formed by two intersecting lines. Vertical angles have equal measure.

Alternate Interior Angles: when two lines are cut by a transversal (a third line), any two nonadjacent angles that are inside the two lines and on opposite sides of the transversal. Notice that the alternate interior angles form a **Z**. If the alternate interior angles are equal, the lines cut by the transversal are parallel.

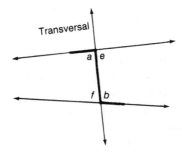

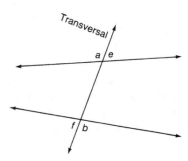

∠*a* and ∠*b* are alternate interior angles

∠*e* and ∠*f* are alternate interior angles

∠*a* and ∠*b* are alternate exterior angles

∠*e* and ∠*f* are alternate exterior angles

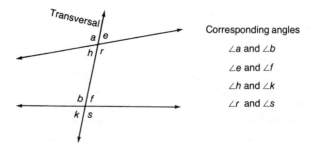

∠*a* and ∠*b* are vertical angles

∠*e* and ∠*f* are vertical angles

∠*a* and ∠*e* are *not* vertical angles

Alternate Exterior Angles: when two lines are cut by a transversal (a third line), any two nonadjacent angles that are on the outside of the two lines and on opposite sides of the transversal. If the alternate exterior angles are equal, the lines cut by the transversal are parallel.

Corresponding Angles: when two lines are cut by a transversal (a third line), any two angles that are on the same side of the lines and on the same side of the transversal. If the corresponding angles are equal, the lines cut by a transversal are parallel.

Corresponding angles

∠*a* and ∠*b*

∠*e* and ∠*f*

∠*h* and ∠*k*

∠*r* and ∠*s*

A third way of classifying angles is by the *context* in which they occur or in which they are being discussed:

Central Angle: an angle formed by two radii of a circle.

Angle of Elevation: the angle formed by the horizontal ray and the line of sight when you look up at an object.

Angle of Depression: the angle formed by the horizontal ray and the line of sight when you look down at an object.

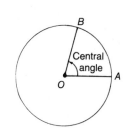

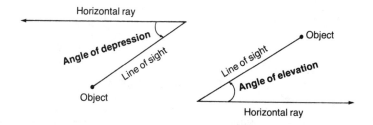

ANGLE OF INCIDENCE AND ANGLE OF REFLECTION

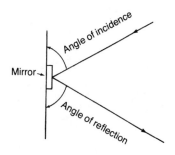

Two additional examples of angles classified according to context are the angle of incidence and the angle of reflection. The *angle of incidence* is the angle at which light or sound or an object strikes a surface. And the *angle of reflection* is the angle at which light, sound, or an object bounces back from the surface.

An interesting property of the angle of reflection is that it is *always equal* to the angle of incidence. For example, if a billiard ball strikes the table's edge at an angle of 30°, it will be reflected at an angle of 30°.

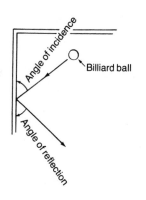

The fact that the angle of incidence and the angle of reflection are always equal can be used to make *indirect measurements*. For instance, you could approximate the height of a flagpole in this way. To estimate the height, you first place a mirror on the ground. Next you move back until you can see the top of the flagpole in the mirror. Then you must measure the distance you are from the mirror, the distance the mirror is from the flagpole, and your height at eye level. (See figure, p. 22.)

Your height at eye level and the distance you are from the mirror form two legs of a right triangle. Similarly, the height of the flagpole and the distance the pole is from the mirror form two legs of another right triangle. Since the angle of incidence and the angle of reflection are equal and since both triangles contain corresponding right angles, triangles *ABC* and *CDE* are *similar*. Therefore, corresponding sides have the same RATIO, and you can find the height of the flagpole by solving the following PROPORTION:

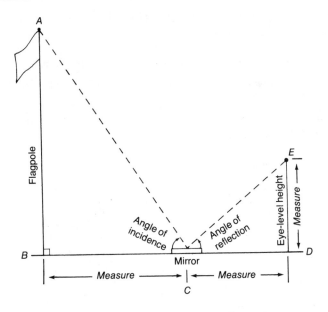

$$\frac{\text{Height of flagpole}}{\text{Your height at eye level}} = \frac{\text{Distance from pole to mirror}}{\text{Distance from you to mirror}}$$

$$\frac{AB}{ED} = \frac{BC}{CD}$$

For more about similar triangles, see SIMILARITY. For more on solving proportions, see PROPORTIONS.

TRISECTION OF THE ANGLE

Using only an unmarked straightedge and compass, it is possible to divide a *line* segment into *any* number of equal parts. And using these same tools, it is also possible to *bisect* any *angle* (divide it into two equal parts). For demonstrations of these constructions, see GEOMETRIC CONSTRUCTION. Because these two constructions are relatively simple, it is natural to suppose that there would be a way to *trisect* an *angle* (divide it into three equal parts), using only a straightedge and compass. But trisecting the angle is one of the three famous construction problems of antiquity—none of which can be solved using only a straightedge and compass. (The other two are squaring the circle, which is discussed under CIRCLE, and duplication of the cube, which is discussed under GEOMETRIC CONSTRUCTION.)

Of the three, trisecting the angle is the one that appeals most to amateur mathematicians. And mathematics journals still receive letters from people who believe they have solved it. One *false solution* tempts many beginning geometry students: they set their compasses for some distance and mark off points equidistant from the vertex on each side of the angle (indicated in the illustration by a dotted arc). Then they connect those two points with a line segment, trisect the line segment, and connect the two points of trisection with the original vertex. The method appears to work for a small angle. But if the same construction is applied to an obtuse angle, it becomes clear that the angle has not been divided into three equal parts. The center angle ($\angle COD$) subtends a much larger arc than the angles on either side ($\angle AOC$ and $\angle DOB$), so the central angle is of much larger measure.

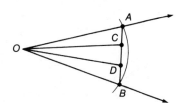

$AC = CD = DB$

$\angle AOC \overset{?}{=} \angle COD \overset{?}{=} \angle DOB$

Although mathematicians were unable to solve the problem of trisecting the angle with straightedge and compass alone, they were able to trisect it by other means. Many of their solutions used curves other than circles. For example, Hippias (425 B.C.), a Greek scholar, trisected the angle using a curve called the quadratrix. Archimedes (250 B.C.) achieved a trisection of the angle using a spiral. Other mathematicians used other curves, including the CONIC SECTIONS. Archimedes also demonstrated a way to trisect the angle using only a compass and a straightedge with two marks on it.

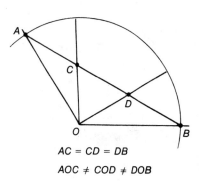

$AC = CD = DB$

$AOC \neq COD \neq DOB$

Many mathematical discoveries were made as a result of attempts to trisect the angle. Yet despite the best efforts of the best mathematicians, the problem remained unsolved. Finally, in the nineteenth century, it was realized that it would always remain so, for by means of ALGEBRA it was proved that it is impossible to trisect an angle with straightedge and compass alone.

Reference on methods of angle trisection

Martin Gardner, ''Mathematical Games: The persistence (and futility) of efforts to trisect the angle,'' *Scientific American,* June 1966.

ANGLES IN THREE DIMENSIONS

Spherical Angle: an angle formed on the surface of a sphere, rather than in a plane, by intersecting great circles. (A great circle is the intersection of the sphere with a plane passing through the center of the sphere.) Spherical angles are discussed under spherical GEOMETRY and spherical TRIGONOMETRY.

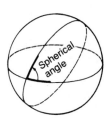

Dihedral Angle: an angle formed by the intersection of planes rather than by the intersection of lines.

Face of a dihedral angle: a half-plane forming one side of the angle.

Edge of a dihedral angle: the line of intersection of the planes forming the angle.

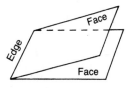

Dihedral angle

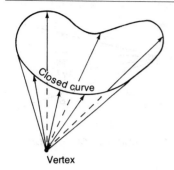

Closed curve

Vertex

Solid Angle: the geometric figure formed in space by the rays from a point (the vertex) that pass through a closed curve.

Measure of a solid angle

A solid angle is measured by the *amount of surface area of a unit sphere,* centered at the vertex, which the angle cuts off (*subtends*). The unit of measure of a solid angle is the *steradian.* There are a total of 4π steradians about a point in space, because the surface AREA of the unit sphere is $4\pi(1)^2$.

Polyhedral Angle: a solid angle for which the closed curve is a POLYGON, a geometric figure formed by the intersection of the lateral faces of a POLYHEDRON at a vertex.

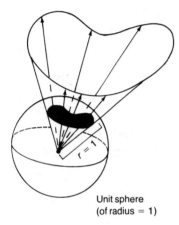

Unit sphere
(of radius = 1)

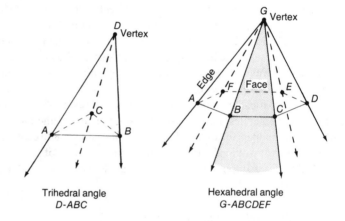

Trihedral angle
D-ABC

Hexahedral angle
G-ABCDEF

Face of a polyhedral angle: the portion of a plane forming a side of the angle.

Edge of a polyhedral angle: an intersection of two faces.
Vertex of a polyhedral angle: the point of intersection of the edges.

Polyhedral angles are named by the number of faces.

REFERENCE

Elizabeth A. Wood, *Science from Your Airplane Window* (Houghton Mifflin, 1968; Dover, 1975), pp. 72–79 and 108–129; a wonderful reference on angles and what you can do with them, this includes a goniometer for measuring angles on the spot; a superb air-travel companion, yet full of interesting and useful information even if you are earthbound.

For other applications of angles, see geographical COORDINATES.

Practical ways to measure angles "in the field" are explained under TRIGONOMETRY, the science of triangles, angles, and their relationships.

AREA

AREA: an amount of flat surface; the number of square unit regions contained in a two-dimensional or PLANE surface. The word "area" is from Latin, meaning level piece of ground.

Examples. Numbers are used to describe area in the following ways:

Dave says that he lives on a 300-acre farm.

A piece of notebook paper covers approximately 605 square centimeters.

A box of floor tiles holds enough to cover 30 square feet.

The surface of the earth contains approximately 196,938,800 square miles, or 510,051,790 square kilometers.

CALCULATION OF AREA

Area is calculated by counting or approximating the number of square unit regions covered by the surface in question. In many cases this counting process can be shortcut by a formula.

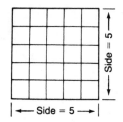

Area = 5 × 5
     = 25 square units

Areas of Quadrilaterals

Square: area = side × side

$$A = s^2$$

Rectangle: area = length × width

$$A = lw$$

area = base × height

$$A = bh$$

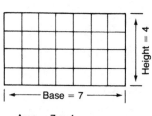

Area = 7 × 4
     = 28 square units

Parallelogram: area = base × height

$$A = bh$$

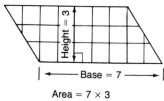

Area = 7 × 3
   = 21 square units

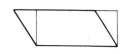

Any side can serve as a base. Height is measured *perpendicular* to the side chosen as base. Notice that the area of a parallelogram is equal to the area of the rectangle of the same base and height.

Trapezoid: area = average base × height

$$A = \frac{b_1 + b_2}{2} h = \tfrac{1}{2}h(b_1 + b_2)$$

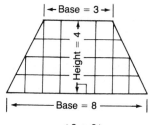

Area = $\left(\dfrac{3 + 8}{2}\right)$ × 4
   = 22 square units

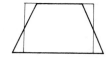

Height is the *perpendicular* distance between the parallel bases. Notice that the area of a trapezoid is equal to the area of the rectangle with the average base and the same height.

Areas of Triangles

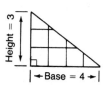

Area = $\tfrac{1}{2}(4 × 3)$
   = 6 square units

Triangle: area = $\tfrac{1}{2}$ base × height

$$A = \tfrac{1}{2}bh$$

Any side can serve as base. Height is the *perpendicular* distance to the base from the opposite vertex. Notice that the area of a triangle is equal to half the area of the rectangle of the same base and height.

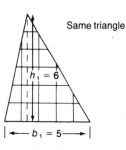

Same triangle

$h_1 = 6$

$|\leftarrow b_1 = 5 \rightarrow|$

Area = $\frac{1}{2}(5 \times 6)$
= 15 square units

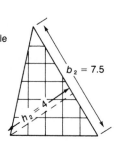

$b_2 = 7.5$

$h_2 = 4$

Area = $\frac{1}{2}(7.5 \times 4)$
= 15 square units

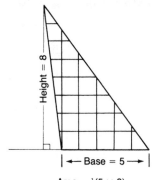

Height = 8

$|\leftarrow$ Base = 5 $\rightarrow|$

Area = $\frac{1}{2}(5 \times 8)$
= 20 square units

Sometimes the perpendicular distance from vertex to opposite base lies entirely outside the triangle.

Hero's Theorem

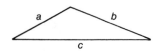

Hero (also known as Heron) was a first century Greek mathematician who expressed the area of a triangle in terms of its three sides. This is especially useful if a height is difficult to measure as, for example, on a triangular plot of land mostly covered by a large lake.

The area of any triangle with sides a, b, c is given by the following process: First calculate

$$s = \tfrac{1}{2}(a + b + c)$$

which is the *semiperimeter* (half the PERIMETER). Then

area = the *square root* of the product $s(s - a)(s - b)(s - c)$

$$A = \sqrt{s(s - a)(s - b)(s - c)}$$

The proof of Hero's theorem involves a great deal of algebra. For an explanation of square root, see ARITHMETIC OPERATIONS.

Reference for proof of Hero's Theorem

Harold R. Jacobs, *Geometry* (W. H. Freeman & Co., 1974), pp. 356–358.

Examples.

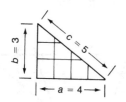

$s = \frac{1}{2}(4 + 3 + 5) = \frac{1}{2}(12) = 6$

area $= \sqrt{6\,(6 - 4)(6 - 3)(6 - 5)}$

$= \sqrt{6 \times 2 \times 3 \times 1}$

$= \sqrt{36}$

$= 6$ square units, which you can see is the same area calculated by the formula $A = \frac{1}{2}bh$.

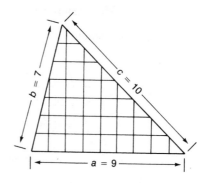

$s = \frac{1}{2}(9 + 7 + 10) = \frac{1}{2}(26) = 13$

area $= \sqrt{13\,(13 - 9)(13 - 7)(13 - 10)}$

$= \sqrt{13 \times 4 \times 6 \times 3}$

$= \sqrt{936}$

$=$ approximately 30.59 square units

Area of a Circle

Circle: area $=$ pi $\times$ square of the radius

$$A = \pi r^2$$

where $\pi =$ approximately 3.14

See PI and CIRCLE for more about this number and for the history of finding the area of a circle.

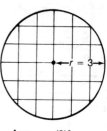

Area $= \pi\,(3)^2$
$=$ approximately
28.26 square units

Areas of Other Figures

Many areas can be calculated by *counting* squares or by *subdividing* the figure into sections for which the area can easily be calculated.

Examples.

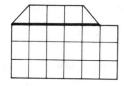

Trapezoid plus rectangle *or*

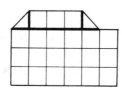

Two rectangles plus two triangles

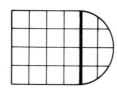

Square plus semicircle

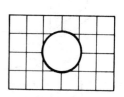

Rectangle minus circle

More examples.

Counting   Subdivision into triangles

 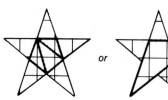

or

Area = about 9½ square units

Areas of Even More Irregular Figures

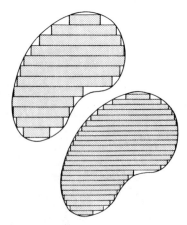

These figures too can be subdivided, by a series of equally spaced parallel lines. Between each pair of parallel lines, draw the biggest rectangle that will fit inside the figure. The area of each rectangle can easily be calculated, and the sum of these areas approximates the area of the irregular figure.

A more accurate approximation can be made if the spacing between the parallel lines is made smaller. The actual area of the whole irregular figure is the *limit* of a sequence of approximations to the area, with each approximation having a shorter distance between the parallel lines. The branch of mathematics known as integral CALCULUS is concerned with finding this limit.

SURFACE AREA OF A SOLID

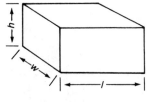

Area may refer to the amount of surface enclosing a three-dimensional, or solid, object.

Cube: surface area = area of 6 square sides

$$S = 6s^2$$

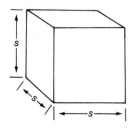

Rectangular Solid: surface area = area of top and bottom, plus area of front and back, plus area of two ends

$$S = 2lw + 2lh + 2wh$$

Cylinder: surface area = area of 2 ends, plus area of sides

$$S = 2\pi r^2 + 2\pi rh$$

where π = approximately 3.14

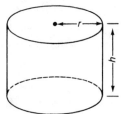

Sphere: surface area = 4π × square of radius

$$S = 4\pi r^2$$

where π = approximately 3.14

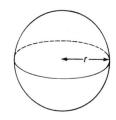

See PI for more about this number π.

PRACTICAL APPLICATIONS OF AREA

Area is one topic of mathematics in which the practical applications are direct and obvious. For instance, you need to know how to calculate area to buy many items:

- The amount and the cost of floor tile or carpeting are determined by the area of the floor to be covered. How many 9-inch or 12-inch tiles would you need to cover the floor of your room? Or how many square yards of carpeting?
- The amount of paint needed for a job depends on the area to be covered; the label on the can tells how many square feet that amount of paint will cover. For instance, if you were to paint the four walls and ceiling of a room with a brand of paint that will cover 400 square feet per gallon, you would need to make a calculation like the following:

$$\text{number of cans to buy} = \frac{\text{total area to be painted, in ft}^2}{400 \text{ ft}^2 \text{ per can}}$$

where

area to be painted = area of ceiling, plus
area of each wall, minus
area of doors and windows

- Fertilizer is sold with instructions to apply 10 pounds per 100 square feet. If you are fertilizing a lawn or garden, you would need to calculate its area. Then

$$\text{number of pounds to buy} = \left(\text{area, in ft}^2 \right) \times \left(\frac{10 \text{ lb}}{100 \text{ ft}^2} \right).$$

- Other situations that commonly involve the calculation of area are comparing the sizes of houses or estimating the size or value of a house. Property taxes on a house are usually based on the number of square feet contained in the dwelling. Contractors often estimate the cost of building a house in terms of the number of square feet called for in the plan. The amount of insulation needed for a home must be calculated according to the area, in square feet or square meters, to be insulated.

- The surface area of a solid must be calculated to determine the amount of material necessary to make a box or a can, or the amount of paper or fabric necessary to wrap or cover an object.

For related articles see: MEASURE, METRIC SYSTEM; TRIANGLES, QUADRILATERALS; PI, CIRCLE.

For the question of the largest area that can be enclosed by a fixed length of boundary (such as fencing), see Queen Dido's Problem in PERIMETER.

Tables of units of measure for area are included in APPENDIX I.

ARITHMETIC

ARITHMETIC: the art of calculating by performing operations on a set of elements.

In the conventional arithmetic taught in elementary school, calculating is done by performing any of the four basic arithmetic operations—addition, subtraction, multiplication, or division—on the set of positive REAL NUMBERS. (For more on conventional arithmetic, see ARITHMETIC OPERATIONS.)

However, the definition of arithmetic does not restrict the set of elements that can be used or the kinds of operations that can be performed. And by changing either the operations or the set of elements, it is possible to create different arithmetics. The following examples illustrate three different kinds of arithmetic:

MODULAR ARITHMETIC: an arithmetic constructed to use a *finite* rather than infinite set of numbers.

Example. The digits on a clock form a finite set of 12 numbers. When you add time on a clock, you are using modular arithmetic. Specifically, you are calculating in arithmetic *modulo* 12, or mod 12.

$12 + 1 \equiv 1 \pmod{12}$ because when 1 hour is added to 12 o'clock, it is 1 o'clock.

$8 + 7 \equiv 3 \pmod{12}$ because 3 o'clock is 7 hours later than 8 o'clock.

Symbol: $\equiv$
> is equivalent to, or
> is congruent to

Modular arithmetic is sometimes called *clock arithmetic,* because the clock face gives a perfect model. But the clock face need not be an ordinary clock with 12 integers.

Example.   Arithmetic modulo 5 has only 5 elements. The model is a clock face with only 5 integers. The top of the clock could read either 5 or 0.

$3 + 4 \equiv 2 \pmod 5$ because if you start at 3 and move 4 numbers in a clockwise direction, you end up at 2.

You can see that some sums in modular arithmetic give the same answer as in ordinary arithmetic. For example, $3 + 1 \equiv 4 \pmod 5$. For other sums, ordinary arithmetic would give an answer outside that finite set of numbers. Therefore some technique, such as a clock face, is needed to keep the answers for all sums within the finite set. Again, $3 + 4 = 7 \equiv 2 \pmod 5$.

There is another, equivalent, approach to modular arithmetic. In arithmetic modulo m, the m elements $\{0, 1, 2, \ldots, m - 1\}$ form the possible *remainders* that can occur when any integer is divided by m. Thus you can calculate in arithmetic modulo m by making an ordinary arithmetic calculation, then dividing the result by m to find the remainder, which is the answer (mod m). For instance, $3 + 4 = 7 \equiv 2 \pmod 5$ because $7 \div 5$ gives a remainder of 2. Notice that there are many other numbers which are equivalent to 2 (mod 5), for example, 12 and 17.

The standard notation

$$a \equiv b \pmod m \quad \text{read ``}a\text{ is congruent to } b \text{, modulo } m\text{''}$$

means that a and b have the same remainder when divided by m.

Example. $7 \equiv 12 \pmod 5$ This says, in effect, that if you start at the top of a mod 5 clock face and count either 7 or 12, you will end up at the same point, 2.

Arithmetic modulo 5 has some interesting properties, which are discussed under FIELD PROPERTIES.

Casting Out Nines

Arithmetic modulo 9 is the basis of the arithmetic checking procedure called *"casting out nines."* The idea is that an arithmetic sum should be congruent modulo 9 to the sum of the remainders modulo 9 of the addends, an idea that is most easily shown by an example.

Example. $1261 \equiv 1 \pmod 9$
            $356 \equiv 5 \pmod 9$
          $+\ 7910 \equiv +\ 8 \pmod 9$
            $\overline{9527}$ $\overline{14}$
          $\equiv 5 \pmod 9$ $\equiv 5 \pmod 9$

These two numbers should be the same. If they are *not* the same, you have made an error. (If they *are* the same, it is still possible, though less likely, that you have made an error. An error that differs from the correct answer by a multiple of 9 will not show up.)

Actually, this procedure would work for any modulus *m*, but 9 is particularly convenient. This is because one quick way to calculate the remainder mod 9 for any number at all is to sum the digits (repeating, if necessary) until you have a single digit mod 9. For example,

$9527 \equiv (9 + 5 + 2 + 7) \pmod 9 \equiv 23 \pmod 9 \equiv 5 \pmod 9$.

Furthermore, any digit of 9 may be *cast out,* because it will not affect the remainder mod 9: $\cancel{9}527 \equiv 527 \pmod 9$. And any combination of digits that add to 9 may also be cast out of a number for the same reason: $\cancel{952}7 \equiv 5 \pmod 9$.

Thus, a much quicker check of the addition may be obtained in this manner.

Example. $12\cancel{6}1 \equiv 1 \pmod 9$
            $35\cancel{6} \equiv 5 \pmod 9$
          $+\ 7\cancel{9}10 \equiv +\ 8 \pmod 9$
            $\overline{\cancel{9}52\cancel{7}} \qquad \overline{14}$
          $\equiv 5 \pmod 9 \qquad \equiv 5 \pmod 9$
                  Check

Casting out nines may also be used to check a multiplication problem.

Example. $73\cancel{4}6 \equiv 2 \pmod 9$
          $\times\ \cancel{1}0\cancel{8}3 \equiv \times\ 3 \pmod 9$
            $\overline{22038} \qquad \equiv 6 \pmod 9$
            58768
            $\underline{73460}$
            $7\cancel{9}5571\cancel{8}$
          $\equiv 24 \pmod 9$
          $\equiv 6 \pmod 9 \qquad$ Check

For more on modular arithmetic, see the example of finite field under FIELD PROPERTIES.

Reference on modular arithmetic

Constance Reid, *From Zero to Infinity: What Makes Numbers Interesting* (Thomas Y. Crowell Co., 1955), pp. 122–136. The chapter on the number 9 begins with casting out nines and expands to algebraic problems in modular arithmetic, leading to interesting and surprising results in number theory. Reid's chapter does a lovely job of explaining modular arithmetic and introducing its applications.

ARITHMETIC WITHOUT NUMBERS: an arithmetic in which operations are performed on elements other than numbers.

Example.   Rotation of a square.

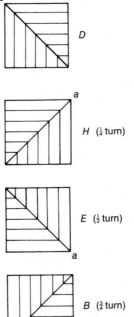

Consider the square shown. The letter *a* marks one corner so you can more easily tell the position of the square.

Consider the square under the following clockwise rotations: Let *D* represent the original position of the square. Then *D* also represents a 360° rotation (one complete rotation) of the square.

Let *H* represent a 90° rotation ($\frac{1}{4}$ of a full turn). Let *E* represent a 180° rotation ($\frac{1}{2}$ of a full turn). And let *B* represent a 270° rotation ($\frac{3}{4}$ of a full turn).

Let the operation * be defined so that *E* * *B* means performing *E* and then *B* on the square.

Example. *E * B*

The original square is in this position.

E is performed first.

Then *B* is performed. The result is the same as the result of performing *H* on the original square.

Therefore *E * B = H*.

Other calculations which may be made in this arithmetic are the following:

$$H * D = H \qquad B * H = D \qquad E * H = B \qquad H * H = E$$

Applications of the rotation of a square include designing wallpaper patterns and planning color schemes. For example, consider a design of four parts to be colored with four colors. Possible color schemes can be listed by making a square and labeling the four corners with the colors. Place the square on a blank piece of paper and position each part of the design outside one corner of the square. This gives one possible color scheme; others can be found by rotating the color square, leaving the design parts in their original corner positions. Rotations of the square give some, but not all, of the possible color schemes. Others appear if

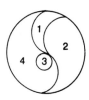

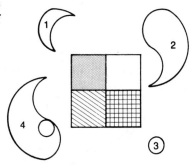

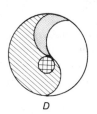
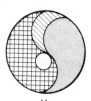
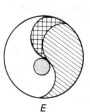
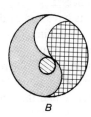

D	H	E	B
No or full rotation of color square	$\frac{1}{4}$ rotation of color square	$\frac{1}{2}$ rotation of color square	$\frac{3}{4}$ rotation of color square

Color schemes given by rotation of square

you flip the square—and an arithmetic can be developed that includes flips as well as rotations.

References on arithmetic with rotation

Albert B. Bennett, Jr. and Leonard T. Nelson, *Mathematics: An Informal Approach* (Allyn & Bacon, 1979), pp. 432–434, "Mapping Figures onto Themselves."

M. Holt and Z. Dienes, *Let's Play Math* (Walker & Co., 1973), pp. 88–94.

J. Troccolo, "A Strip of Wallpaper," *Mathematics Teacher,* January 1977, pp. 55–58.

TRANSFINITE ARITHMETIC: an arithmetic in which operations are performed on cardinal NUMBERS assigned to INFINITE SETS.

A *cardinal number* tells *how many* members are in a set. For instance, $\{a, b, c, d\}$ has cardinal number 4. In an infinite set there are infinitely many members. However, not all infinite sets are the same "size." *Transfinite numbers* are cardinal numbers indicating the size or magnitude of infinite sets.

The natural, or counting, numbers $\{1, 2, 3, 4, 5, 6, \ldots\}$ form the smallest infinite set. The cardinal number that tells how many natural numbers are in this infinite set is called *aleph null* and is written $\aleph_0$, the Hebrew letter *aleph* with a zero subscript. The transfinite number $\aleph_0$ is also the cardinal number for any other *countable* infinite set. A countable set is any set that can be listed in one-to-one correspondence with the natural numbers, such as the set of unit FRACTIONS:

$$
\begin{array}{cccccccccc}
1 & 2 & 3 & 4 & 5 & 6 & 7 & 8 & 9 & 10 \ldots \\
\updownarrow & \updownarrow & \updownarrow & \updownarrow & \updownarrow & \updownarrow & \updownarrow & \updownarrow & \updownarrow & \updownarrow \\
\frac{1}{1} & \frac{1}{2} & \frac{1}{3} & \frac{1}{4} & \frac{1}{5} & \frac{1}{6} & \frac{1}{7} & \frac{1}{8} & \frac{1}{9} & \frac{1}{10} \ldots
\end{array}
$$

Since these two sets can be put in one-to-one correspondence, both sets have the cardinal number $\aleph_0$.

Transfinite arithmetic can be performed on transfinite numbers such as $\aleph_0$. But, because transfinite arithmetic uses numbers assigned to infinite sets, the rules for performing operations are different from those of conventional arithmetic. For instance, in transfinite arithmetic, a part may equal the whole.

Example. $\aleph_0 + 4 = \aleph_0$

Consider two sets—one an infinite set that can be put in one-to-one correspondence with the natural numbers and the other a finite set of four elements:

{natural numbers} has the cardinal number $\aleph_0$, by definition of $\aleph_0$;
{a, b, c, d} has the cardinal number 4, because it has 4 elements.

But the sum of these two sets can be put in one-to-one correspondence with the natural numbers by first listing the finite set and then the infinite set, as follows:

1	2	3	4	5	6	7	8	9	10 ...
$\updownarrow$	$\updownarrow$	$\updownarrow$	$\updownarrow$	$\updownarrow$	$\updownarrow$	$\updownarrow$	$\updownarrow$	$\updownarrow$	$\updownarrow$
a	b	c	d	1	2	3	4	5	6 ...

Consequently, the cardinal number of the combined set remains $\aleph_0$.

This phenomenon of transfinite arithmetic extends to the combination of two *infinite* sets—the result might *not* be a "bigger" infinite set.

Example. $\aleph_0 + \aleph_0 = \aleph_0$

Consider two infinite sets, each having the cardinal number $\aleph_0$ and having no elements in common:

$$\text{Set } 1 = \{5, 10, 15, 20, 25, 30, \ldots\}$$
$$\text{Set } 2 = \{3, 8, 13, 18, 23, 28, \ldots\}$$

The sum of these two sets can be put in one-to-one correspondence with the set of natural numbers by alternating elements, as follows:

1	2	3	4	5	6	7	8	9	10	11	12 ...
$\updownarrow$	$\updownarrow$	$\updownarrow$	$\updownarrow$	$\updownarrow$	$\updownarrow$	$\updownarrow$	$\updownarrow$	$\updownarrow$	$\updownarrow$	$\updownarrow$	$\updownarrow$
3	5	8	10	13	15	18	20	23	25	28	30 ...

Therefore, the cardinal number of the combined set is also $\aleph_0$, the cardinal number of each of the component sets.

In transfinite arithmetic there are other transfinite numbers besides $\aleph_0$. There are $\aleph_1, \aleph_2, \aleph_3, \ldots$. The cardinal number $\aleph_1$ is used to denote an infinite set so numerous that it cannot be put in one-to-one correspondence with the natural numbers, that is, a set that cannot be counted.

The set of REAL NUMBERS, for example, is too numerous to be counted. The real numbers cannot be put in one-to-one correspondence with the natural numbers. However, the size of the set of real numbers has not been proved equivalent to $\aleph_1$. (It was the discovery of the uncountability of the real numbers that launched Georg Cantor on his studies of INFINITY and his development of transfinite arithmetic.)

The transfinite number $\aleph_1$ represents the number of elements in some smallest uncountable set. Then $\aleph_2$ denotes the next size, or magnitude. That is, $\aleph_2$ represents the smallest number so numerous that it cannot be put in one-to-one correspondence with a set having cardinal number $\aleph_1$. The transfinite numbers go on in this manner and are used to denote different orders, or magnitudes, of infinity.

For references on the arithmetic of infinite sets, see INFINITY.

GROUPS

Common properties of all these arithmetics, including conventional arithmetic, are a *set of elements* and a *binary operation* that has been defined on that set. A binary operation is an operation performed on exactly two elements at a time. For instance, in the examples above, 8 + 7, $E * H$, $\aleph_0 + \aleph_0$ are all illustrations of binary operations.

Furthermore, in each of the above arithmetics, the following are true:

- There is an *identity element*.
- Each element has an *inverse*.
- The operation satisfies the axiom of *closure*.
- The operation satisfies the axiom of *associativity*.

For definitions and discussion of these properties, see FIELD PROPERTIES.

Any set of elements with a binary operation that exhibits all four of the above field properties constitutes what is known in mathematics as a *group*. The importance of the group concept is that it allows mathematicians to study simultaneously not only the three systems illustrated in this article but others as well. See the references.

REFERENCES

Teri Perl, *Math Equals: Biographies of Women Mathematicians + Related Activities* (Addison-Wesley, 1978), pp. 68–72 and 179–194; some mathematical activities that further explain and illustrate arithmetic. Groups, presented in a number of interesting ways, provide an introduction to the abstract ALGEBRA of Emmy Noether. Modular arithmetic is discussed as a first step to understanding the work of Sophie Germain, a self-educated and creative French mathematician in the period just after the French Revolution. She was denied university admission and position because she was a woman, but she was admired and supported by leading mathematicians. Biographies of both women are also provided.

Reference on groups

LeRoy C. Dalton and Henry D. Snyder, eds., *Topics for Mathematics Clubs* (National Council of Teachers of Mathematics, 1973), Ch. 3, "Groups," by Roy Dubisch; an excellent presentation of different kinds of groups—groups of PERMUTATIONS, SYMMETRY groups, modular arithmetics—and what can be done with them.

ARITHMETIC OPERATIONS

ARITHMETIC OPERATIONS: the four basic arithmetic operations are *addition, subtraction, multiplication,* and *division;* two other operations used sometimes in arithmetic and often in algebra are *raising to a power* and *extracting a root.*

Addition, subtraction, multiplication, and division are called *binary* operations because the operations are performed on exactly *two* numbers at a time. The operations of raising to a power and extracting a root are called *unary* operations because the operations are done on *one* number.

Symbol: + plus

ADDITION: the process of finding the total number of elements in two disjoint sets (sets which have no elements in common).

Example.

	Set A		Set B		
	O O O	added to	O O O O O	gives	O O O O O O O O
	3	+	5	=	8

To *add* the two sets above, you must find the total number of balls in both sets combined. The most primitive approach to adding is to count the total number of members in the two groups. However, on the basis of experience and repeated drill, you come to know certain addition facts, such as $3 + 5 = 8$, without counting. And once you have learned the addition facts for all the possible pairs of integers from 0 to 9, you use these facts to add larger numbers without counting.

The two most common ways of writing addition problems are the following:

$$3 + 5 = 8$$

$$\begin{array}{rl} 3 & addend \\ +5 & addend \\ \hline 8 & sum \end{array}$$

42

The process of addition can be extended to other numbers besides whole numbers:

Examples.   Addition of FRACTIONS: Addition of DECIMALS:

$$\frac{1}{3} + \frac{1}{3} = \frac{2}{3}$$

$$\begin{array}{r} 2.5 \\ + \ 3.4 \\ \hline 5.9 \end{array}$$

Addition is *commutative*. That is, the order of the addends makes no difference.

Examples. $4 + 3 = 3 + 4$

$a + b = b + a$, for any real numbers a and b.

Addition is *associative*. That is, the grouping of the addends makes no difference.

Examples. $3 + (4 + 5) = (3 + 4) + 5$

$a + (b + c) = (a + b) + c$

For more on the properties of addition, see FIELD PROPERTIES.

SUBTRACTION: the process of finding the difference between the number of elements in one set and the number in another; the process of taking one set away from another set.

Symbol: $-$ minus

Example.   *Set A*   *Set B*

□ □ □		□ □ □		
□ □ □	minus	□ □	gives	□ □
□				

7	$-$	5	$=$	2

The two most common ways of writing subtraction problems are the following:

$$7 - 5 = 2$$

$$\begin{array}{rl} 7 & \textit{minuend} \\ -5 & \textit{subtrahend} \\ \hline 2 & \textit{difference} \end{array}$$

The process of subtraction can be extended to other numbers besides whole numbers.

Examples.   Subtraction of FRACTIONS: Subtraction of DECIMALS:

$$\frac{7}{9} - \frac{5}{9} = \frac{2}{9}$$

$$\begin{array}{r} 8.6 \\ - \ 5.2 \\ \hline 3.4 \end{array}$$

Subtraction is the inverse of addition: subtraction "undoes" addition. The problem $7 - 5$ can be thought of as finding the number which when added to 5 will give 7.

Subtraction is not commutative.

Example. $7 - 5 \neq 5 - 7$

Subtraction is not associative.

Example. $(9 - 4) - 2 \neq 9 - (4 - 2)$
$$5 - 2 \neq 9 - 2$$
$$3 \neq 7$$

Symbol: $\times$ times

MULTIPLICATION: the process of finding the total number of elements in a given number of sets where each set has the same number of members.

Example.   ▽ ▽ ▽
             ▽ ▽ ▽   4 sets, each having 3 members
             ▽ ▽ ▽ $4 \times 3 = 12$
             ▽ ▽ ▽

There are several ways to write a multiplication problem:

$$4 \times 3 = 12 \qquad \begin{array}{r} 4 \\ \times 3 \\ \hline 12 \end{array} \begin{array}{l} \textit{multiplicand (factor)} \\ \textit{multiplier (factor)} \\ \textit{product} \end{array}$$

$4 \cdot 3 = 12$ (Raised dot indicates multiplication.)

$4(3) = 12$
$(4)(3) = 12$ (Parentheses indicate multiplication.)

ab means $a \times b$ (With variables, no special symbol for mul-
$3y$ means $3 \times y$ tiplication is needed. The symbols for the quantities to be multiplied are simply written side by side.)

The multiplicand and the multiplier are also called FACTORS.

The process of multiplication can be extended to other numbers besides whole numbers.

Examples.   Multiplication of   Multiplication of
              FRACTIONS: DECIMALS:

$$\frac{2}{3} \times \frac{4}{5} = \frac{8}{15} \qquad \begin{array}{r} 2.3 \\ \times\, 0.4 \\ \hline 0.92 \end{array}$$

Multiplication is commutative.

Examples. $2 \times 3 = 3 \times 2$ and $ab = ba$

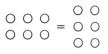

Multiplication is associative.

Examples. $2 \times (3 \times 4) = (2 \times 3) \times 4$ and $a(bc) = (ab)c$

For more on the properties of multiplication, see FIELD PROPERTIES.

DIVISION: the process of finding how many times one number (the *divisor*) is contained in another number (the *dividend*); the process of determining how many subsets of a given size are contained within a set.

Symbol: ÷ divided by

Examples.   There are 5 sets of 3 in 15.

$$15 \div 3 = 5$$

There are 6 lengths of $\frac{1}{2}$ in 3 cm.

$$3 \div \frac{1}{2} = 6$$

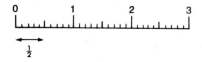

There are three ways to write a division problem:

$$15 \div 3 = 5 \qquad 3\overline{)15}^{\,5} \qquad \frac{15}{3} = 5$$

$$\text{divisor}\overline{)\,\text{dividend}}^{\,\text{quotient}}$$

Sometimes the division does not come out even. The number left over is called the *remainder*.

Example.
$$3\overline{)14}^{\,4}$$
$$\underline{12}$$
$$2 \quad \text{Remainder}$$

This remainder may be written as a fraction with the divisor as the denominator.

Example. $14 \div 3 = 4\frac{2}{3}$

The process of division can be extended to other numbers besides whole numbers.

Examples.   Division of FRACTIONS: Division of DECIMALS:

$$\frac{2}{3} \div \frac{4}{9} = \frac{3}{2}$$

$$\begin{array}{r} 3\ 4. \\ .2\overline{)6.8} \end{array}$$

Division is the inverse of multiplication. The problem $8 \div 4$ can be thought of as finding the number which when multiplied by 4 will give 8. For this reason, dividing by a number is also defined as multiplying by the *reciprocal* (multiplicative inverse) of the number.

Examples. $8 \div 4 = 8 \times \frac{1}{4} = \frac{8}{4} = 2$

$$\frac{2}{3} \div \frac{4}{9} = \frac{2}{3} \times \frac{9}{4} = \frac{18}{12} = \frac{3}{2}$$

Division is not commutative.

$$8 \div 4 \neq 4 \div 8$$
$$2 \neq \tfrac{1}{2}$$

Division is not associative.

$$16 \div (4 \div 2) \neq (16 \div 4) \div 2$$
$$16 \div 2 \neq 4 \div 2$$
$$8 \neq 2$$

For more on the properties of division, see FIELD PROPERTIES.

RAISING TO A POWER (Involution): the process of finding the product when some number is used as a factor a given number of times.

Example.   The *third* power of 2 is 8, because $2 \times 2 \times 2 = 8$.

Notation: $2^3 = 8$ $base^{exponent} = power$

The expression "2^3" indicates that 2 is to be used as a factor 3 times. The number that is to be used as a factor is called the *base;* the number that indicates how many times the base is to be used as a factor is called the *exponent;* the result is called a *power.*

More Examples. $3^2 = 3 \times 3 = 9$

$$2^4 = 2 \times 2 \times 2 \times 2 = 16$$
$$(\tfrac{1}{4})^3 = \tfrac{1}{4} \times \tfrac{1}{4} \times \tfrac{1}{4} = \tfrac{1}{64}$$

When the exponent is 2 or 3, there are special names for the powers:

3^2 is read "three *squared*" because using a number as a factor twice gives the area of a square with sides equal to the given number. 5^3 is read as "five *cubed*" because using a number as a factor three times gives the volume of a cube with edges equal to the number.

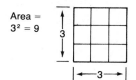

Area = $3^2 = 9$

The other powers are named as follows:

2^4—the fourth power of two, or two to the fourth.
2^5—the fifth power of two, or two to the fifth, and so on.

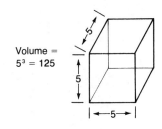

Volume = $5^3 = 125$

For more on raising to a power, see EXPONENTS.

EXTRACTING A ROOT (Evolution): the process of finding a number that can be used as a factor a given number of times to produce the original number.

Symbol: $\sqrt{}$

$$\sqrt[index]{radicand} = root$$

Example. The *fifth* root of $32 = 2$ because $2 \times 2 \times 2 \times 2 \times 2 = 32$.

$$\sqrt[5]{32} = 2$$

Radical sign: this symbol $\sqrt{}$ means that a root is to be extracted. (The word "radical" comes from the Latin word "radix," meaning "root.") Credit for inventing the radical sign is given to Christoff Rudolff, a German mathematician of the sixteenth century.

By convention, to avoid confusion, a radical of *even* index refers to the *positive* root; that is, $\sqrt{4} = 2$, although -2 is another square root of 4.

Index: the number in the upper left-hand corner of the radical sign, indicating which root is to be extracted. If no index is written, the index is assumed to be 2.

Examples. $\sqrt{9} = \sqrt[2]{9}$ (read "square root of 9")
$\sqrt[3]{8}$ (read "cube root of 8")
$\sqrt[4]{16}$ (read "fourth root of 16")

Radicand: the number or algebraic expression under the radical sign.

Example. $\sqrt[3]{8}$ 8 is the radicand.

Another way to indicate that a root is to be extracted is by using *fractional exponent notation*. For details, see EXPONENT.

Examples. $\sqrt{9} = 9^{\frac{1}{2}}$ $\sqrt[4]{16} = 16^{\frac{1}{4}}$

Extracting a root is the inverse operation of raising to a power. For example, $\sqrt{9}$ could be thought of as finding the number which when squared equals 9.

$$\sqrt{9} = \square \quad \text{means} \quad \square^2 = 9.$$
$$3^2 = 9.$$

Therefore, $\sqrt{9} = \boxed{3}$.

These examples have all been carefully chosen so that the radicands are integral powers of some whole number. However, it is possible to extract a root of a rational number that is *not* an integral power of a whole number.

Example. $\sqrt{6.25} = 2.5$

It is also possible to extract a root of a number that is *not* an integral power of any *rational number*. But if the radicand is not an integral power of a rational number, the root will not be rational. For example, the number 3 is not the square of any rational number. Therefore $\sqrt{3}$ is *irrational*. And any finite decimal expressing such a root is only an approximation.

Examples. $\sqrt{3} \doteq 1.732$

where $\doteq$ means "approximately equal"

$\sqrt{2} \doteq 1.414$

For more on such irrational roots, see RATIONAL AND IRRATIONAL NUMBERS.

Square Root Algorithm

There is an algorithm (method) for extracting the square root of any *positive real number* to as many decimal places as you like:

(1) Place the number under the radical sign and, starting from the decimal point, mark off the digits in *groups of two* to the right and to the left. Each group is called a *period*. For example,

$$\sqrt{123456.7890} = \sqrt{12\ \ 34\ \ 56.78\ \ 90}$$
$$\sqrt{12345} = \sqrt{01\ \ 23\ \ 45}.$$

(2) Consider the first period. Find the integer that when squared comes closest to the value of the first period without exceeding it, and write that number above the first period. Then square the number you have written and subtract the square from the first period.

(3) Bring down the second period and write it beside the remainder. Then double the entire number written above the radical sign and write it to the left of the remainder and the second period as a kind of trial divisor.

(4) Estimate how many times this trial divisor, when multiplied by 10, would go into the number to the right of it. Place your estimate over the radical sign above the second period, *and* at the end of the trial divisor.

(5) Multiply the last digit above the radical sign by the newly created divisor and subtract the product from the dividend. (If the product is greater than the dividend, go back to the preceding step and make a smaller estimate.)

(6) Bring down the third period beside the new remainder. Double the entire number that appears above the radical and write this double to the left of the remainder as the new divisor.

(7) Repeat the procedure described in steps 4 and 5.

The process of bringing down periods may be continued until the answer reaches a desired level of precision. (In the example, the last remainder is so small that the next digit of the answer would have to be zero. Therefore the answer can be safely rounded to 7.19, accurate to two decimal places.)

The decimal place in the answer is placed directly above the decimal point in the radicand.

This method of extracting a square root is time-consuming. Fortunately, the advent of inexpensive CALCULATORS that take square roots has meant that few people need to extract square roots by hand.

(1) $\sqrt{51.7} = \sqrt{51.70\ 00}$

(2)
$$\begin{array}{r} 7 \\ \sqrt{51.70\ 00} \\ 49 \\ \hline 2 \end{array}$$

(3)
$$\begin{array}{r} 7 \\ \sqrt{51.70\ 00} \\ 49 \\ \hline 14)\ 2\ 70 \end{array}$$

(4)
$$\begin{array}{r} 7.\ 1 \\ \sqrt{51.70\ 00} \\ 49 \\ \hline 141)\ 2\ 70 \end{array}$$

(5)
$$\begin{array}{r} 7.\ 1 \\ \sqrt{51.70\ 00} \\ 49 \\ \hline 141)\ 2\ 70 \\ 1\ 41 \\ \hline 1\ 29 \end{array}$$

(6)
$$\begin{array}{r} 7.\ 1 \\ \sqrt{51.70\ 00} \\ 49 \\ \hline 141)\ 2\ 70 \\ 1\ 41 \\ \hline 142)\ 1\ 29\ 00 \end{array}$$

(7)
$$\begin{array}{r} 7.\ 19 \\ \sqrt{51.70\ 00} \\ 49 \\ \hline 141)\ 2\ 70 \\ 1\ 41 \\ \hline 1429)\ 1\ 29\ 00 \\ 1\ 28\ 61 \\ \hline 39 \end{array}$$

More on Roots

The roots that can be extracted depend upon the index and the radicand.

$$\sqrt{0} = 0 \quad \sqrt[8]{0} = 0$$
zero radicand

- If the radicand is zero, there is only one root, regardless of the index.

$$\sqrt[3]{27} = 3 \quad \sqrt[3]{-27} = -3$$
odd index

- If the index is an odd number, there will be one real root. The sign of the root matches the sign of the radicand.

$$\sqrt{64} = 8 \quad \sqrt[4]{16} = 2$$

even index,
positive radicand

- If a square or even root is to be extracted and the radicand is *positive*, there are *two* real roots—one positive and one negative. For example,

$$\sqrt{64} \text{ could be 8 or } -8,$$

$$\sqrt[4]{16} \text{ could be 2 or } -2.$$

But to avoid confusion, the convention is established that the $\sqrt{}$ symbol itself always refers to the *positive* real root.

$$\sqrt{-4} \neq 2 \quad (2 \times 2 = 4,$$
$$\text{not } -4)$$
$$\sqrt{-4} \neq -2 \quad (-2 \times -2 = 4,$$
$$\text{not } -4)$$

even index,
negative radicand:
no real root

- If the index is even and the radicand is *negative*, there will be *no* real root. *In the real number system you cannot take an even root of a negative number*. Even roots of negative numbers are called *imaginary numbers* (as opposed to real numbers). For an explanation of imaginary numbers, see COMPLEX NUMBERS.

ORDER OF OPERATIONS

If more than two numbers are to be added or multiplied, the operations must be repeated, but the order in which the work is carried out makes no difference.

Examples. To add $6 + 2 + 7$
you add $6 + 2 = 8$, and then add $8 + 7 = 15$;
or you add $2 + 7 = 9$, and then add $9 + 6 = 15$.

To multiply $3 \times 5 \times 4$
you multiply $3 \times 5 = 15$, and then multiply $15 \times 4 = 60$;
or you multiply $5 \times 4 = 20$, and then multiply $20 \times 3 = 60$.

However, if other operations are involved in an expression or if more than one type of operation is to be done, the order is important.

Parentheses can be used to indicate the order of operations. The rule is to do the operation inside the parentheses first.

Examples. $(5 + 2) \times 3 = 7 \times 3 = 21$
$5 + (2 \times 3) = 5 + 6 = 11$

If more than one pair of parentheses is used, the rule is to start with the innermost ones first. In this case brackets, [ ], and braces, { }, may be used like larger parentheses.

Examples. $[\, 4 + (2 \times 3)\,] \div 2 = (4 + 6) \div 2 = 10 \div 2 = 5$

If there are no parentheses or if there is more than one operation inside the parentheses, the following rules have been agreed upon:
(1) First, do the operations inside the parentheses, starting with the innermost one.
(2) Then do powers and roots in order from left to right.
(3) Then do multiplications and divisions in order from left to right.
(4) Last, do additions and subtractions in order from left to right.

Examples. $6 + 4 \times 3 = 6 + 12 = 18$

$$3 + 2^2 \times 5 - 4 \times 2 + 15 \div 3 + \sqrt[3]{8} =$$
$$3 + 4 \times 5 - 4 \times 2 + 15 \div 3 + 2 =$$
$$3 + 20 - 8 + 5 + 2 =$$
$$23 - 8 + 7 =$$
$$15 + 7 =$$
$$22$$

The order outlined above is the same order a computer follows in performing arithmetic operations. One popular way to remember the order of the basic operations is by the following phrase:

My	Dear	Aunt	Sally
u	i	d	u
l	v	d	b
t	i	i	t
i	s	t	r
p	i	i	a
l	o	o	c
i	n	n	t
c			i
a			o
t			n
i			
o			
n			

OTHER WAYS OF PERFORMING OPERATIONS

A method of performing an arithmetic operation is called an *algorithm*. And for some of the operations such as multiplication, long division, and extracting a root, there are several different algorithms. For example, instead of using the conventional algorithm for division, you could divide one number into another by repeated subtraction.

Examples.

$15 \div 3$

$$
\begin{array}{r}
15 \\
-③ \\
\hline
12 \\
-③ \\
\hline
9 \\
-③ \\
\hline
6 \\
-③ \\
\hline
3 \\
-③ \\
\hline
0
\end{array}
$$

There are
five 3's:
$15 \div 3 = 5$

$27 \div 4$

$$
\begin{array}{r}
27 \\
-④ \\
\hline
23 \\
-④ \\
\hline
19 \\
-④ \\
\hline
15 \\
-④ \\
\hline
11 \\
-④ \\
\hline
7 \\
-④ \\
\hline
3
\end{array}
$$

Six 4's with a
remainder of 3:
$27 \div 4 = 6\frac{3}{4}$

An interesting example of a different algorithm for multiplication is the method used by the ancient Egyptians. Their method—called *duplation and mediation* (or doubling and halving)—allowed them to multiply without memorizing the multiplication table beyond the multiples of two.

To multiply two numbers using duplation and mediation, you arrange the two numbers as shown below and repeatedly double the numbers in one column and halve the numbers in the other until the column of halves is reduced to one. (If a number cannot be halved exactly, disregard the remainder.) You then add the numbers from the doubles column that correspond to an odd number in the halves column. The total will be the product of the two original numbers.

Example.

	17	×	42	
half of 17 =	8		84	= double 42
half of 8 =	4		168	= double 84
half of 4 =	2		336	= double 168
half of 2 =	1		672	= double 336

Now add the numbers from the doubles column that correspond with an odd number from the halves column.

$$
\begin{array}{c|c|c}
17 & & 42 \\
1 & + & 672 \\
& & \overline{714}
\end{array}
\qquad
\begin{array}{l}
\text{pairs with odd numbers} \\
\text{from halves column}
\end{array}
$$

$$
\begin{array}{|c|c|c|}
17 & \times & 42
\end{array} = 714
$$

For further information on this method, consult the references below.

Professor Jakow Trachtenberg, who fled first the Russian Revolution and then the Germany of World War II, devised during years spent in concentration camps a system of high-speed multiplication, division, addition, subtraction, and extraction of square roots. Most steps in this system are performed mentally, shortening computation time by as much as 80 percent compared to conventional methods. One need only be able to count to 11 to master the entire system. For details, see references.

REFERENCES

References on historical algorithms

Helen A. Merrill, *Mathematical Excursions* (1933; Dover, 1957), Ch. 1–3, pp. 1–31; further explanation of the why's of mediation and duplation.

David Eugene Smith, *History of Mathematics* (Ginn, 1925; Dover, 1958), Vol. 2, pp. 88–155; a comprehensive treatment of other historical methods for arithmetic operations.

References on the Trachtenberg System

Ann Cutler, *Instant Math (Based on the Trachtenberg System of Basic Mathematics)* (Doubleday & Co., 1962); "for children from 8 to 80," stressing ease, speed, and accuracy.

The Trachtenberg Speed System of Basic Mathematics, translated and adapted by Ann Cutler and Rudolph McShane (Doubleday & Co., 1960).

CALCULATORS

CALCULATOR: a device that can perform arithmetic computations.

The modern desk calculator or hand calculator consists of at least three components: an input unit, an output unit, and an arithmetic unit.

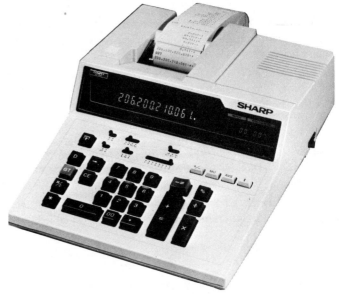

Courtesy of Sharp Electronics Corporation.

Input

Numbers and operations to be performed are entered into a calculator by pressing marked buttons on the keyboard. The sequence in which the buttons are pressed depends on whether the calculator uses algebraic or reverse Polish notation.

With *algebraic entry*, the numbers and operations are entered just as they would be written in an algebraic expression. For example, to add 5 and 7, you would press ⑤ , ⊞ , and ⑦ in that order.

In calculators using *reverse Polish notation,* both numbers are entered before the operation. Thus to add 5 and 7, you would press ⑤ , ⑦ , and ⊞ . Once you are used to it, reverse Polish notation can be more efficient.

Output

A record of the numbers entered and the results of computation may be displayed electronically or printed on paper.

Arithmetic Unit

Any calculator can perform the four basic ARITHMETIC OPERATIONS, and most can find the reciprocal of a number $\boxed{1/x}$, the square root of a number $\boxed{\sqrt{x}}$, and any percent of a number $\boxed{\%}$. Some raise a number to a power $\boxed{n^x}$ and automatically compute factorials $\boxed{n!}$. Some have been programmed for STATISTICS or for financial calculations. Others handle TRIGONOMETRIC FUNCTIONS, LOGARITHMS, and exponentials. Still others are preprogrammed to work with MATRICES, determinants, and COMPLEX NUMBERS. And some calculators can be programmed to perform a whole sequence of operations without having their buttons pushed each time.

CALCULATORS VERSUS COMPUTERS

Calculators and COMPUTERS are very similar, although in general a calculator is a small device that is carried around to do simple calculations while a computer sits in a room and runs complicated programs. Both can calculate or compute.

Making calculations on a computer is not as direct as making them on a calculator, because the computer must be programmed—instructions must be input and stored before a program can begin. However, the computer is then much faster and can perform a complicated or repetitive calculation automatically, whereas a simple calculator requires the appropriate keys to be pressed every time each part of the calculation is done.

Example. You could add the numbers from 1 to 100 on a computer with a very short program (see COMPUTER PROGRAMMING), but on a basic calculator you would have to type

Some calculators can do the things a computer can do, such as remembering short programs. A calculator becomes a computer if all of the following conditions are satisfied:

- It has a *memory* capable of storing a quantity of both data and instructions.
- There is a way to give the machine *instructions*.
- It can make *logical decisions* about whether one number is greater than or less than another number and alter the sequence of computation according to the result.

These *programmable calculators* are really computers, although they are less flexible and slower than most computers.

Scientific calculator, not programmable
Courtesy of Sharp Electronics Corporation.

IMPLICATIONS OF USING THE CALCULATOR

Just as the automobile, by making transportation easier and faster, has radically changed a whole society, so has the calculator, by making calculations easier and faster. The electronic calculator has already made slide rules and other mechanical calculators obsolete. Printed tables of powers and roots are hardly needed. Nor, if a person has the right calculator, are logarithmic, trigonometric, or interest tables. In addition, many calculators automatically convert units of measure and money from one system to another.

Because of its speed and portability, a hand calculator enables people to total bills, balance checkbooks, figure stock dividends, and compare prices almost instantaneously. What was once tedium has become fun. Many calculators come equipped with games for both entertainment and education.

Advances in technology continually make calculators smaller and cheaper. A calculator can now be incorporated in a wristwatch. And steady price reductions in calculators and computers now give individuals and classrooms access to simple calculators.

Some people worry about calculators in the classroom, fearing that students will become too dependent on them and will not learn basic arithmetic skills. Others view them simply as time-saving devices that take the drudgery out of mathematics. And still others see the calculator as a teaching device that students enjoy.

In education and in society, calculators have changed the form of computations. For example, a calculator uses only DECIMAL fractions. Two decimal fractions accurate to ten digits can now be multiplied before your finger is removed from the equals key. This means that decimal fractions will be more widely used than the common FRACTIONS that have long been more familiar.

It is impossible to make predictions about a field changing as rapidly as that of calculator technology. And it is harder yet to predict the changes in our life style, but the fact that changes are coming cannot be denied.

The calculator on the left was manufactured just a few years after the one on the right, but improvements in miniaturization enable far more intricate circuitry to fit in a smaller space. The newer calculator is less than half the thickness of the older model, yet it will calculate dozens of functions that were totally absent from the earlier machine.

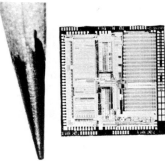

Courtesy of Hewlett-Packard Company.

CALCULATOR TECHNOLOGY

The basic design of a calculator is the same as the design of a digital COMPUTER. Both store information on *chips,* integrated electronic circuits mounted on tiny squares about 0.2 inch or 0.5 centimeter on a side. Each chip contains thousands of transistors. A programmable calculator may be built on a single chip, a minicomputer on several chips, and a large computer on many of them. For details, see references.

REFERENCES

The Calculator Information Center, 1200 Chambers Rd., Columbus, Ohio 43212; write for further information and collected references for classroom uses of calculators.

References on calculator technology

Eugene W. McWhorter, "The Small Electronic Calculator," *Scientific American,* March 1976, pp. 88–98; a detailed explanation of how calculators work, their electronics, and chip technology.

Scientific American, September 1977; an issue devoted to the microelectronics that make calculators.

References on calculator games

Edwin Schlossberg and John Brockman, *The Pocket Calculator Game Book* (William Morrow & Co., 1975), and *The Pocket Calculator Game Book No. 2* (William Morrow & Co., 1977).

There are innumerable books, many in paperback, on calculator games. Look in the mathematical recreation section of your library or bookstore.

For a history of calculators and computers, see COMPUTERS.

CALCULUS

CALCULUS (or Infinitesimal Calculus): a branch of higher mathematics that deals with *variable,* or changing, quantities. Calculus is based on the concept of *infinitesimals* (exceedingly small quantities) and on the concept of *limits* (quantities that can be approached more and more closely but never reached). There are two related branches of calculus: *differential calculus* and *integral calculus.*

The word "calculus" is the Latin word for "pebble," and since pebbles were used by the ancients in reckoning, the word soon gained the added meaning of "reckoning" or "computation"—a meaning that is reflected in our word "*calcul*ation." The word has been applied to various systems of calculation, but "calculus" alone, or "the calculus," usually refers to the calculus of infinitesimals described in this article.

Calculus is one of the most important branches of mathematics. If you are given a FUNCTION relating two variables, calculus enables you to find more information much more quickly than is possible with ARITHMETIC and ALGEBRA alone. Calculus has long had applications in the physical sciences—physics, chemistry, and engineering—and more recently in the biological and social sciences as well.

The study of calculus requires a good working knowledge of algebra. Nevertheless, some of the most basic ideas can be understood without getting into the details of computation.

DIFFERENTIAL CALCULUS: a method of calculating the changes in one variable produced by changes in a related variable.

A RELATION between two variables x and y in which every value of x is paired with exactly one value of y is called a FUNCTION. In such a relation, y is said to be a function of x, and the relation is abbreviated in calculus as $y = f(x)$.

Differential calculus provides methods of examining the *change* in y

due to a *change* in *x,* where *y* is a function of *x.* One method is to examine the GRAPH of the function. On the graph, notice the changes in *y* resulting from a one-unit change in *x* at different points along the curve.

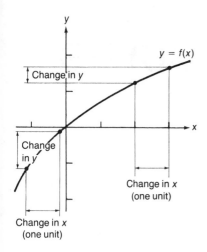

The change in *y* due to a change in *x* of one unit depends on the *shape* of the curve. At the left, where the graph rises steeply, the change in *y* is much greater than at the right, where the graph rises more slowly. Differential calculus is concerned with the graph of a function and how steeply the graph rises (or falls) from left to right. The measure of steepness is called *slope.*

Finding Slope on a Graph

The SLOPE of a *line* can be determined by any two points on the line.

The slope is the RATIO of $\dfrac{\text{vertical change between the 2 points}}{\text{horizontal change between the 2 points}}$.

Example.

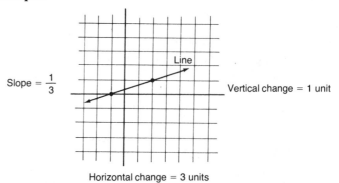

A line that rises more steeply will have a greater slope.

The slope of a *curve* at any given point is equal to the slope of a line *tangent* to the curve at that point. (A tangent line is a line that touches a curve at one and only one point.)

But a *curve* has a *different slope* at each point. And all these slopes taken together determine precisely the shape of the curve. How can the slope of a curve be calculated? How do you find the slope of the tangent line at each point? If your curve were drawn on graph paper, you could probably make a good approximation to the tangent line at any given point and then read its slope by counting squares in the vertical and horizontal directions between two points on the tangent line. However, this is a tricky business because the tangent line is supposed to touch the curve in only *one* point. The fact that only one point is certain makes it hard to know exactly where to draw the tangent line because two points are needed to determine a straight line.

Example.

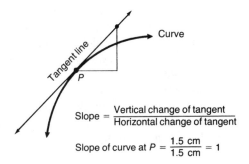

Slope = $\dfrac{\text{Vertical change of tangent}}{\text{Horizontal change of tangent}}$

Slope of curve at $P = \dfrac{1.5 \text{ cm}}{1.5 \text{ cm}} = 1$

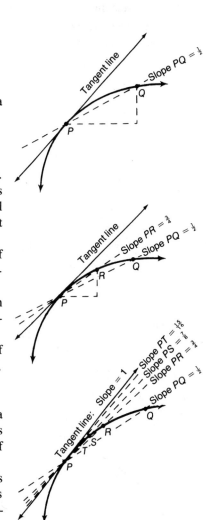

Calculus solves this problem by using the concept of *limit*. Finding a slope by a limit is illustrated by the following sequence of steps:

Suppose you want to find the slope of this curve at P.

(1) First consider point Q, which is near P and also on the curve. You can calculate the slope of $\overline{PQ}$ because you have two points between which you can measure vertical change and horizontal change. The slope of $\overline{PQ}$ may be close to the slope of the tangent at P, but it is certainly not the same.

(2) Consider another point R, closer to P but still on the curve. If you calculate the slope of $\overline{PR}$, you will then have a closer approximation to the slope of the tangent at P.

(3) If you choose another point even closer to P than R, you can calculate the slope of this line and get an even closer approximation.

(4) The slope of the tangent at P is in fact the *limit* of the slopes of the lines $\overline{PQ}, \overline{PR}, \overline{PS}, \overline{PT}$, and so on, where each point $Q, R, S, T, \ldots$ is chosen closer and closer to P on the curve.

When you understand the idea that the slope of the line tangent to a curve is the *limit* of slopes which *can* be calculated (because *two* points are known on $\overline{PQ}, \overline{PR}, \overline{PS} \ldots$), you have grasped a basic concept of calculus.

To calculate the *exact* slope of a curve, more than careful drawing is required: the techniques of ALGEBRA are needed. Using algebra, it is possible to calculate the slope at *any* point on the graph of a function.

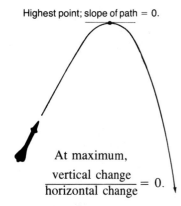

Highest point; slope of path = 0.

At maximum,

$$\frac{\text{vertical change}}{\text{horizontal change}} = 0.$$

Uses of Differential Calculus

Calculus can be applied wherever related quantities are *changing*.

One important application of differential calculus is in solving *problems of optimization*—problems of finding the maximum or minimum values for a given function. An example is finding out how high a certain rocket will fly. The path, or curve, the rocket will follow can be graphed if you know the velocity with which the rocket will be fired and the angle of its firing. From the graph, you can see that when the rocket reaches its maximum height, the slope of its path will be zero. (At that point, there will be no vertical change.)

The path is the graph of some function $y = f(x)$. The slope of this function at any point can be found with calculus, and the point where the slope is zero is the maximum for the function.

Other applications of calculus involve *problems of motion*. Simple algebra is enough to deal with problems of uniform motion—motion at a constant speed or velocity. But if the velocity *changes*, as when a car accelerates from rest to highway speed, the situation becomes more complicated.

As one steps on the accelerator of a car, the *acceleration* changes as a function of time. Acceleration affects the *velocity* of the car, and velocity is also a function of time. The *distance* the car moves along the highway is yet another function of time, which is affected by a changing velocity and a changing acceleration. In a given amount of time, the changes in distance, velocity, and acceleration are all matters for calculus.

INTEGRAL CALCULUS: the calculation of *sums* of *infinitesimals*.

Infinitesimals are exceedingly small quantities. Finding a *sum* of infinitesimals involves finding a *limit*, as follows:

Consider the problem of trying to measure *distance along a curved path* using only a straight yardstick or meterstick.

(1) An *approximation* of the distance along the curved path can be made by marking a number of points on the path, measuring straight-line segments between them, and summing the lengths of these segments.

(2) A better approximation can be made in the same way using more points on the line.

(3) If the path is subdivided again and again, the individual pieces eventually become infinitesimally small.

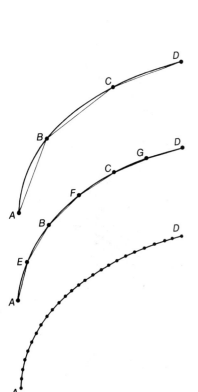

(4) The actual distance along the curve is the *limit* of the sums of straight-line distances between points, as the curve is subdivided at more and more points.

Uses of Integral Calculus

Integral calculus can be used to calculate quantities like distance, AREA, and VOLUME. These calculations are simple if the lines are straight and the boundaries are rectangular or triangular. But if a path is not straight, or if a boundary is curved or irregular, then these calculations require a *limiting* process, as illustrated in the distance problem.

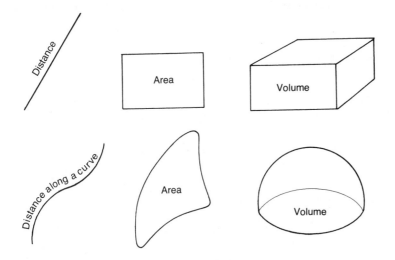

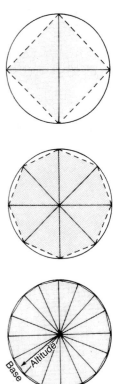

The general idea is to slice up an irregular figure into little pieces which can be approximated. Then, as the number of slices is increased (making more but smaller pieces), the limit of the sum of the pieces will give the exact quantity desired.

Even before the integral calculus was formally developed, slicing and summing was used by the seventeenth-century German astronomer Johannes Kepler to calculate the area enclosed by a planet in its orbit around the sun. First, Kepler calculated the area of a CIRCLE by dividing it into an exceedingly large number of tiny TRIANGLES, each having a vertex at the center and its base on the circumference. Kepler reasoned that when the base of the triangle became exceedingly small, the altitude would equal the radius of the circle. Since the area of a triangle is $\frac{1}{2} \times$ the base $\times$ the altitude, Kepler concluded that the area of a circle should equal the *sum* of the areas of all those tiny triangles or

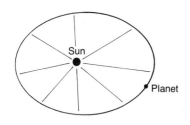

$\frac{1}{2} \times$ the sum of all bases $\times$ the altitude of each triangle

$= \frac{1}{2} \times$ circumference of the circle $\times$ radius of the circle

$= \frac{1}{2} \times 2\pi r \times r$

$= \pi r^2$.

. Then, using a similar method, he calculated the area enclosed by an *ellipse,* which is the shape of the planetary orbits.

As with differential calculus, the finding of the limits involved in integral calculus usually requires the techniques of algebra. But the geometric idea of slicing and summing is the heart of the matter. If you understand this basic idea, you can probably approximate a distance, an area, or a volume as closely as you desire.

For further illustration of calculating by slicing and summing, see AREA and VOLUME.

THE RELATION BETWEEN DIFFERENTIAL AND INTEGRAL CALCULUS

Although there is no obvious connection between the problems of finding slopes and calculating sums, such a connection does exist. Slope-finding and sum-finding turn out to be inverse or opposite processes (the *Fundamental Theorem of Calculus*). Their relationship is very important to actual calculation.

THE HISTORY OF CALCULUS

The method of slicing and summing dates back to the third century B.C., when it was used by Archimedes of Syracuse. Archimedes described how he used this method to calculate the area of curved figures and the volume of a sphere. His treatise, *The Method,* was lost to the world until 1906, when it was found on an ancient palimpsest (a parchment scroll that has been erased and reused) underneath some religious writings. Upon reading *The Method,* twentieth-century mathematicians were astonished at how close Archimedes had come to discovering the methods of infinitesimal calculus.

Yet, despite Archimedes' excellent beginning, the calculus as we know it today was not discovered until nearly 2000 years later—after other mathematicians seeking solutions to various practical problems made important contributions. Kepler worked on the problem of finding the VOLUME of wine barrels of various dimensions. Others worked on calculating the areas of irregular figures. Still others tried to find the tangents to a curve, an important practical problem in the grinding of lenses.

Credit for discovering a general, rather than a particular, approach to all these problems goes to Isaac Newton of England and Gottfried Wilhelm von Leibniz of Germany. Working independently of one another, both brought algebra into the solution of knotty problems in physics and geometry, and both discovered the fundamental fact that differential calculus (slope finding) is *directly related* to integral calculus (sum finding). By the end of the seventeenth century, Newton and Leibniz had each developed the calculus.

REFERENCES

Lancelot Hogben, *Mathematics for the Million* (published in Great Britain and by W. W. Norton & Co. in the U.S., in many editions, from 1936 to 1967), Ch. XI in the first edition, "The Arithmetic of Growth and Shape."

W. W. Sawyer, *What Is Calculus About?*, New Mathematical Library (Random House, 1961).

References on the history of calculus

Historical Topics for the Mathematics Classroom, 31st Yearbook of the National Council of Teachers of Mathematics (1969), Ch. VII, "The History of Calculus," including several capsules on individual contributions.

Teri Perl, *Math Equals: Biographies of Women Mathematicians + Related Activities* (Addison-Wesley, 1978), pp. 37–51. The calculus is presented to explain the work of Emilie du Châtelet, a French expository mathematician. Her best known work was an excellent translation and analysis of Newton's *Principia* that helped to spread his ideas from England to continental Europe in the eighteenth century.

Biographical references on Newton and Leibniz

Eric T. Bell, *Men of Mathematics* (Simon & Schuster, 1937; Fireside paperback) pp. 90–130; both Newton and Leibniz.

I. Bernard Cohen, "Isaac Newton," *Scientific American,* December 1955; reprinted in *Mathematics in the Modern World: Readings from Scientific American* (W. H. Freeman & Co., 1968), pp. 40–44.

Frederick C. Kreiling, "Leibniz," *Scientific American,* May 1968; reprinted in *Mathematics: An Introduction to Its Spirit and Use: Readings from Scientific American* (W. H. Freeman & Co., 1978), pp. 33–38.

See also HISTORY.

CIRCLE

Symbol: ⊙

The symbol ⊙*A* represents a circle in which the center is at *A*.

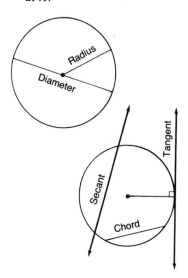

CIRCLE: the SET of all POINTS in a PLANE that are the same distance (equidistant) from a fixed point, called the *center*.

LINES IN A CIRCLE

Radius (plural, *radii*): a line segment from the center to any point on the circle. For a given radius and a given center there is only one possible circle.

Chord: a line segment from any point on the circle to any other point on the circle.

Diameter: a line segment from any point on the circle, through the center, to another point on the circle. The diameter is a chord (the *diametral chord*) passing through the center of the circle; it is the longest chord possible in a circle.

Secant: a straight line intersecting the circle at two points.

Tangent: a straight line intersecting the circle at exactly one point. The point at which the tangent intersects the circle is called the *point of tangency,* or *point of contact*. The radius is perpendicular to the tangent at the point of contact.

ARCS OF A CIRCLE

Arc: part of the circle between any two points on the circle. The symbol $\overarc{AB}$ represents an arc between the points *A* and *B*.

Semicircle: an arc equal to half a circle. Any diameter divides a circle into two semicircles.

Major Arc: an arc larger than a semicircle.

Minor Arc: an arc smaller than a semicircle.

ANGLES IN A CIRCLE

Central Angle: an ANGLE with the vertex at the center of the circle and with sides along two radii.

Measure of Arc: the measure of its central angle (for example, a 30° arc is one whose central angle is 30°). An entire circle contains 360°.

Inscribed Angle: an angle with the vertex on the circle and with sides along two chords.

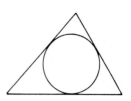

SPECIAL CIRCLES

Concentric Circles: two or more circles in the same plane with the same center, but with radii of different length.

Inscribed Circle: a circle constructed within a POLYGON and tangent to every side of the polygon.

Circumscribed Circle: a circle constructed about a polygon with every vertex of the polygon lying on the circle.

Every triangle has an inscribed circle (whose center is the intersection of the angle bisectors) and a circumscribed circle (whose center is the intersection of the perpendicular bisectors of the sides). See GEOMETRIC CONSTRUCTION.

Polygons of four or more sides may or may not have an inscribed circle and a circumscribed circle.

Tangent Circles: circles that intersect at exactly one point.

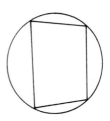

Concentric circles

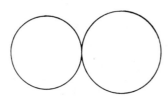

Inscribed circle

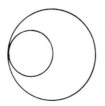
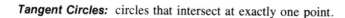

Internally tangent circles   Externally tangent circles

REGIONS DEFINED BY CIRCLES

Interior: the set of all points inside a circle.

Exterior: the set of all points outside a circle.

Segment: a region bounded by an arc of a circle and its chord.

Sector: a region bounded by an arc of a circle and two radii.

Annulus: a region between two concentric circles.

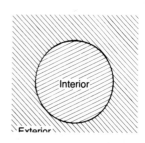

Circumscribed circle

Interior

Exterior

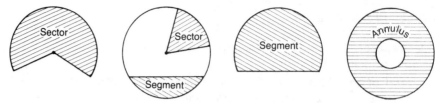

FORMULAS FOR THE CIRCLE

Circumference: the distance around the circle.

$$C = \pi d$$
or
$$C = 2\pi r$$

The circumference is equal to PI times the length of the diameter (or twice pi times the length of the radius).

Area: the number of square units contained in the interior of the circle.

$$A = \pi r^2$$

The area of a circle is equal to pi times the square of the length of the radius.

THAT NUMBER π OR PI

$\pi =$ approximately 3.14 or $\frac{22}{7}$

From the most ancient times, mathematicians recognized that the RATIO of the circumference of a circle to the length of the diameter was always a little more than three. And, in fact, the exact ratio for *all* circles is denoted by the Greek letter π, called "pi."

$$\pi = \frac{\text{circumference of a circle}}{\text{diameter of a circle}}$$

$$= \text{approximately } 3.14 \text{ or } \tfrac{22}{7}$$

Pi is an *irrational number,* which means that it has a never ending, never repeating DECIMAL expansion. (See RATIONAL AND IRRATIONAL NUMBERS.) The infinite decimal may be approximated to whatever accuracy is desired.

Quadrature of the Circle

The same number π that is the ratio of circumference to diameter of a circle occurs in the formula for the *area* of a circle, as was proved by the ancient Greeks. (Kepler's explanation is shown in the article on integral CALCULUS.) Greek mathematicians tried to calculate the value of π from the area of the circle: they reduced this problem to *quadrature* or *squaring* of the circle—the attempt to construct a square of area exactly equal to the area of a circle.

Quadrature of the circle, using only a straightedge and compass, became one of the three famous unsolved GEOMETRIC CONSTRUCTION problems of antiquity. The difficulty in squaring the circle lies in the fact that since the area of a circle is πr^2, the side of a square of the same area would have to be ($\sqrt{\pi}$) r. It turns out that it is impossible with straightedge and compass alone to *construct* $\sqrt{\pi}$. In fact, it is not possible to find π or $\sqrt{\pi}$ by any construction method. Furthermore, it is impossible to calculate an exact value for π by any method at all. Nevertheless, throughout recorded history better and better approximations have been made for this elusive number.

The Early History of Finding the Area of a Circle, or of Finding π

For hundreds of years before the birth of Christ, mathematicians knew how to calculate the AREA of a POLYGON (a closed plane figure for which every side is a straight line segment). The area of any polygon could be divided into some number of TRIANGLES. The area of each triangle could be found by the formula $A = \frac{1}{2}bh$, where b = base and h = height. And the total area of a polygon could be calculated by adding together the areas of the triangles within it. However, the ancients were never able to compute exactly the area of a *circle*.

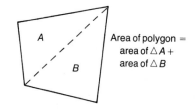

Area of polygon = area of △A + area of △B

Finding area of polygon by triangulation

One of the early approximations to the area of a circle is found in the Rhind Papyrus, an Egyptian document believed to have been recorded by the scribe Ahmes in about the year 1650 B.C. The solution was to construct a square with a side $\frac{8}{9}$ of the diameter of the given circle. Thus the Egyptian mathematicians were saying that

$$\text{area of square} = \text{area of circle}$$

$$s^2 = \pi r^2$$

$$8^2 = \pi \left(\tfrac{9}{2}\right)^2$$

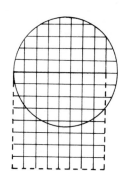

which implies $\pi = (\tfrac{16}{9})^2 = 3.1605$—not a bad approximation for the correct rounded value of 3.1416.

The most significant contribution in calculating both the area and the circumference of a circle was made by a man generally considered one of the greatest mathematicians of all time—Archimedes of Syracuse, who lived and worked in the third century B.C. Archimedes' genius was not limited to any one branch of science. In addition to numerous contributions to mathematics, he also wrote on astronomy, mechanics, and hydrostatics. Archimedes' ingenuity in inventing war machines became legendary when Rome attacked Syracuse in 212 B.C. According to various reports, Archimedes designed catapults that hurled great

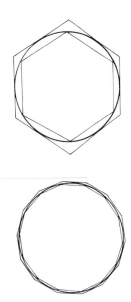

boulders onto the invading fleet, hooks and pulleys that hoisted enemy ships out of the water, and ''burning glass'' reflectors that set fire to the ships by focusing the sun's rays. Yet despite all these inventions, the might of Rome ultimately prevailed and Syracuse fell.

Though the Roman commander gave specific orders to spare the life of the great scientist, Archimedes was killed in the sacking of the city. According to legend, he was concentrating on a diagram in a sand tray when approached by a pillaging Roman soldier. The soldier is said to have run his spear through Archimedes when the old geometer commanded, ''Disturb not my circle.''

Archimedes' method of calculating the area of a circle was to relate it to the area of regular polygons, which could be computed by known methods. He observed that the area of a circle was somewhat greater than the area of a polygon inscribed in it, and somewhat less than the area of a polygon circumscribed around it. He also observed that increasing the number of sides of the inscribed and circumscribed polygons made the area of the polygons closer to that of the circle.

Thus Archimedes started with inscribed and circumscribed hexagons and successively doubled the number of sides until the inscribed and circumscribed polygons each had 96 sides. He computed the areas of these 96-sided polygons and approximated the area of the circle lying between them. Such a process was known as the *method of exhaustion*, for it was an effort to exhaust, or eliminate, the differences in area between the polygons and the circle.

Using the fact that the area of the circle is πr^2, Archimedes calculated π to be greater than $3\frac{10}{71}$ and less than $3\frac{10}{70}$, or somewhere between 3.1408 and 3.1428, an accuracy which was not improved upon for hundreds of years.

See PI for subsequent events and more details on the history of this number.

APPLICATIONS OF THE CIRCLE

Ever since the invention of the wheel, people have found innumerable uses for the circle.

Attempts at perpetual motion machines; this one was proposed by the Marquis of Worcester in 1663.

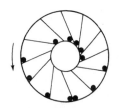

Wheel

Clock

Compass

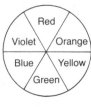

Color wheel

Circular Form in Art and Architecture

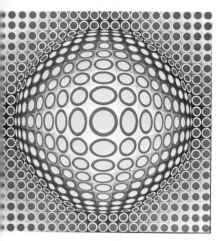

"Vega 222," by Victor Vaserely, 1969–70
Courtesy of Sidney Janis Gallery, New York.

"The Family at Work," engraving by Crispin de Passe de Oude (Dutch, 1565–1637)
Courtesy of Theodore B. Donson, Inc.; photo by Jon Reis, Herbert F. Johnson Museum of Art, Cornell University.

"The Adoration of the Magi" by Fra Angelico and Fra Filippo Lippi
Courtesy of the National Gallery of Art, Washington.

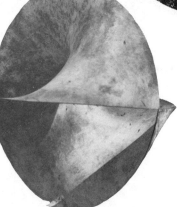

Bronze sculpture, untitled, by Robert Engman
Courtesy of Hirshhorn Museum and Sculpture Garden, Smithsonian Institution.

Plan for *Tempietto of San Pietro* in Montorio, Rome, by Donato Bramante, 1502
Courtesy of Electa Editrice, Milano.

You can find circles almost anywhere, in nature as well as in manufactured objects.

Ripples on a water surface
where a pebble has dropped

Growth rings of a tree

Eternity

Wedding band

Halo

Symbolically the circle represents eternity (being without end) and perfection (of shape). These ideas are represented in many signs and ceremonies.

Ancient Chinese symbol for the union
of two opposing forces, Yang and Yin,
which are found in everything in nature.

Ceremonial dance

The circular form is powerful in artistic works—in painting, sculpture, photography, and architecture.

REFERENCES

Martin Gardner, ''Mathematical Games: The diverse pleasures of circles that are tangent to one another,'' *Scientific American*, January 1979; a number of varied and interesting problems.

Bruno Munari, *Discovery of the Circle* (George Wittenborn, 1966, 1970); dozens of interesting facts about circles, their uses, and their symbolism are discussed and beautifully illustrated.

The idea of endlessness represented by the circle is used in LOGIC. A *circular argument* is one that comes back to its starting point. This argument is discussed under DEFINITIONS and MATHEMATICAL SYSTEMS.

A circle may be considered as a special form of *ellipse*. See CONIC SECTIONS.

A circle is the shape that will enclose the largest area with a fixed length of boundary (such as fencing). See Queen Dido's Problem in the article on PERIMETER.

COMPLEX NUMBERS

COMPLEX NUMBER: a member of the most general or inclusive set of numbers used in ALGEBRA; a number that can be expressed in the form $a + bi$, where a and b are REAL NUMBERS and $i = \sqrt{-1}$.

IMAGINARY NUMBER: the square root of a negative number.

In the eighteenth century the letter "i" was introduced to stand for $\sqrt{-1}$. And since any negative number can be expressed as some positive number times -1, any imaginary number can be expressed as some real number times i. For example, $\sqrt{-9}$ can be expressed as $\sqrt{9 \times -1}$ or $3 \times \sqrt{-1}$ or $3i$. And $\sqrt{-7}$ can be expressed as $\sqrt{7 \times -1}$ or $\sqrt{7}\,i$.

The complex numbers include all the *real numbers,* all the *imaginary numbers,* and all the numbers consisting of both a real number part and an imaginary number part.

The real numbers include all the *rational numbers* (numbers that can be expressed as a ratio of two integers) and all the *irrational numbers* (such as $\sqrt{2}$, $\sqrt{3}$, π). (See RATIONAL AND IRRATIONAL NUMBERS.) The rational numbers include all the integers, both positive and negative; all the fractions, both positive and negative; and the integer zero. The irrational numbers also include both positives and negatives and, surprisingly, are even more numerous than the rationals. The set of real numbers can be represented by a real NUMBER LINE. Every real number corresponds to exactly one point on the line, and every point on the line corresponds to exactly one real number:

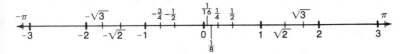

At first glance, it might appear that the set of real numbers is so immense that it would contain a solution for any possible equation. But this is not the case. Consider, for example, the equation $x^2 = -1$. What number multiplied times itself equals -1? There is no real number that will satisfy this equation because every real number multiplied by itself gives a positive product.

Since the sixteenth century, mathematicians have been using such "non-real" numbers as $\sqrt{-1}$ to solve other problems. For example, in 1545, Girolamo Cardano, an Italian mathematician, solved the following problem by using the square root of negative 15.

Problem: How can you divide the number 10 into 2 parts so that the product of the 2 parts is 40?

Solution: $5 + \sqrt{-15}$ and $5 - \sqrt{-15}$,

$$
\begin{array}{ll}
\text{because} \quad
\begin{array}{r}
5 + \sqrt{-15} \\
+5 - \sqrt{-15} \\
\hline
10
\end{array}
\quad \text{and} \quad
&
\begin{array}{r}
5 + \sqrt{-15} \\
\times \; 5 - \sqrt{-15} \\
\hline
25 + 5\sqrt{-15} \\
- 5\sqrt{-15} \; - \quad -15 \\
\hline
25 + \quad 0 \quad + \quad 15 = 40
\end{array}
\end{array}
$$

In the seventeenth century, numbers such as $\sqrt{-15}$ and $\sqrt{-1}$ were given the name "imaginary numbers."

Any complex number can be expressed in the form $a + bi$, where a and b stand for any real numbers and i stands for $\sqrt{-1}$. A complex number with no imaginary part—a real number—can be expressed by $a + bi$ where b equals zero.

Example.   If $a = 7.2$ and $b = 0$,
then $a + bi = 7.2$ (a real number).

A complex number with no real part—an imaginary number—can be expressed by $a + bi$ where a is equal to zero and b is not equal to zero.

Example.   If $a = 0$ and $b = 5$,
then $a + bi = 5i$ (an imaginary number).

And finally, a complex number with *both* a real part and an imaginary part can be expressed as $a + bi$ where neither a nor b is equal to zero.

Example.   If $a = 4$ and $b = 10$,
then $a + bi = 4 + 10i$.

The inclusiveness of the complex number system is shown in the following diagram:

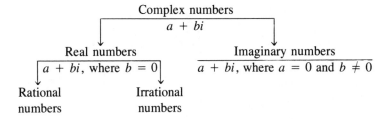

OPERATIONS WITH COMPLEX NUMBERS

Any two complex numbers can be added, subtracted, multiplied, or divided (excluding division by zero).

Addition: to find the sum of two complex numbers, you add the two real components together and then add the two imaginary components together.

Example.
$$
\begin{array}{r}
(3 + 2i) \\
+\ (-7 + 5i) \\
\hline
(-4 + 7i)
\end{array}
$$

Subtraction: to find the difference between two complex numbers, you subtract the real component of one from the real component of the other, and then subtract the imaginary component of the one from the imaginary component of the other.

Example.
$$
\begin{array}{r}
(11 + 5i) \\
-\ \ (7 + 2i) \\
\hline
(4 + 3i)
\end{array}
$$

Multiplication: to find the product of two complex numbers, you multiply the real components together, you multiply the imaginary components together, and you multiply the real components by the imaginary components.

Example.
$$
\begin{array}{r}
(2\ + 3i) \\
\times\ (5\ -\ i) \\
\hline
+10\ +\ \ 15i \\
-2i\ -\ 3i^2 \\
\hline
10\ +\ 13i\ -\ 3i^2
\end{array}
$$

The product of two complex numbers can be further simplified by evaluating the powers of i. The following table gives values of the powers of i through i^4.

$$i^1 = \sqrt{-1}$$
$$i^2 = -1$$
$$i^3 = -\sqrt{-1} = -i$$
$$i^4 = 1$$

This cycle of 4 repeats itself. For example,
$$i^5 = i^4 \text{ (or 1)} \times i = i^1$$

In the example above, when i^2 is replaced with -1, the value of the whole expression is simplified:

$$10 + 13i - 3i^2 = 10 + 13i - (3 \times -1)$$
$$= 10 + 13i + 3$$
$$= 13 + 13i.$$

Thus $(2 + 3i) \times (5 - i) = 13 + 13i$.

Division: to find the quotient of one complex number divided by another, you multiply both numerator and denominator by the *conjugate* of the denominator. The conjugate of a complex number is the same as the complex number except that the sign of the *bi* term is reversed.

Number	Conjugate
$a + bi$	$a - bi$
$3 - 2i$	$3 + 2i$
$-4 + i$	$-4 - i$

Example.

$$\frac{7}{3 + i} = \frac{7 \times (3 - i)}{(3 + i) \times (3 - i)} = \frac{21 - 7i}{9 - i^2} = \frac{21 - 7i}{10} = \frac{21}{10} - \frac{7}{10}i$$

FIELD PROPERTIES

The set of complex numbers constitutes a mathematical *field*. Therefore the complex numbers possess all the properties described in the article on FIELD PROPERTIES.

GRAPHING A COMPLEX NUMBER

Since every complex number contains two terms—a real term and an imaginary one—it is possible to express a complex number as an *ordered pair*. The first element in the pair represents the real number part and the second element represents the imaginary part. For example, the number $3 + 2i$ would be written $(3, 2)$ in ordered-pair notation.

Because complex numbers are really ordered pairs, they can be shown by a GRAPH on a COORDINATE SYSTEM consisting of two intersecting NUMBER LINES—a number line of real numbers and a number line of imaginary numbers. The set of points that can be represented on such a coordinate system is said to form a *complex plane*.

Examples. *In a + bi form*   *In ordered-pair form*

$-3 + 2i$	$(-3, 2)$
$5 - 3i$	$(5, -3)$
7	$(7, 0)$
$-8i$	$(0, -8)$

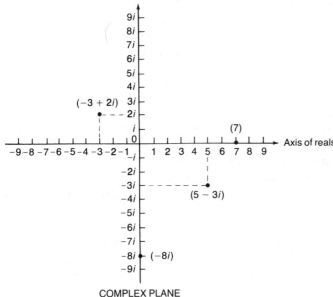

COMPLEX PLANE

Absolute Value of a Complex Number

The *absolute value* of a complex number is its *distance from the origin* in the complex plane.

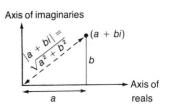

Notation: $|a + bi|$, read "the absolute value of *a* plus *bi*."

The absolute value, or distance from the origin, of a point $a + bi$ can be calculated by the PYTHAGOREAN THEOREM as follows:

$$|a + bi| = \sqrt{a^2 + b^2}$$

Examples. $|7| = 7$

$|-8i| = 8$

$|-3 + 2i| = \sqrt{9 + 4} = \sqrt{13} \doteq 3.6$, approximately

$|5 - 3i| = \sqrt{25 + 9} = \sqrt{34} \doteq 5.8$, approximately

These four complex numbers are illustrated on the graph, so you can confirm these absolute values, or distances from the origin.

HISTORY AND APPLICATIONS

One of the first Europeans to use imaginary numbers was Girolamo Cardano of Italy in the sixteenth century. Yet even after Cardano had shown how such numbers could be used to solve problems, he still dismissed the idea of working with them as being "as subtle as it would be useless." The attitude that numbers representing the square roots of negative numbers were mysterious quantities without practical significance led the seventeenth-century Frenchman René Descartes to give them the name "imaginary."

However, in spite of general skepticism, mathematicians continued to work with imaginary numbers. In the eighteenth century, Leonhard Euler, a Swiss, introduced the shorthand symbol "i" to stand for $\sqrt{-1}$. In the same century, a Norwegian surveyor, Caspar Wessel, and another Swiss mathematician, Jean Robert Argand, showed how both real and imaginary numbers could be graphed. And in the nineteenth century, Carl Friedrich Gauss of Germany introduced the name "complex number" to refer to any number that could be expressed in the form $a + bi$.

Gauss proved that when the sets of all the real numbers, all the imaginary numbers, and all the numbers having both real and imaginary parts are added together, the resulting set of numbers—the *complex numbers*—is sufficient to provide a solution to any polynomial EQUATION. For example,

$$x^2 = -1 \text{ has two complex solutions, } x = \pm i.$$
$$x^2 - 10x + 40 = 0 \text{ has two complex solutions, } x = 5 \pm \sqrt{15}\, i.$$
$$x^7 + 3x + 1 = 0 \text{ has seven complex solutions.}$$

In general an nth degree polynomial equation will have n complex solutions. Gauss's statement is known as the *Fundamental Theorem of Algebra*.

Gradually, applications for complex numbers were found in the physical sciences. In the eighteenth century, the German mathematician Johann Lambert used complex numbers to project a map of the three-dimensional earth onto a two-dimensional surface (see PROJECTION). In the same century, the French mathematician Jean d'Alembert used complex numbers in his theory of hydrodynamics.

However, the person who probably deserves the most credit for taking the mystery out of complex numbers was the Irish mathematician William Rowan Hamilton. Working in the nineteenth century, Hamilton emphasized that complex numbers were ordered pairs of real numbers—that $a + bi$ can be completely represented by the ordered pair (a, b). He pointed out the need for ordered pairs to represent a quantity with *two dimensions,* such as a force having a certain magnitude and a certain direction.

Hamilton also demonstrated how complex numbers could be used to represent the *rotation* of a directed quantity (called a VECTOR) about a point. The use of complex numbers to represent the rotation of a directed quantity turned out to have an extremely important application in electrical engineering, because alternating electric current and voltage can be expressed as rotating vectors.

In the twentieth century, the American mathematician and engineer Charles P. Steinmetz used complex numbers to develop the theory of electrical circuits.

REFERENCES

Martin Gardner, "Mathematical Games: The imaginableness of imaginary numbers," *Scientific American,* August 1979, pp. 18–24.

Ian Stewart, "Gauss," *Scientific American,* July 1977, pp. 122–131.

Sir Edmund Whittaker, "William Rowan Hamilton," *Scientific American,* May 1954; reprinted in *Mathematics and the Modern World: Readings from Scientific American* (W. H. Freeman & Co., 1968), pp. 49–52.

See also REAL NUMBERS and HISTORY.

COMPUTER PROGRAMMING

COMPUTER PROGRAM: a list of instructions to be executed, or carried out, by a COMPUTER.

Mandelbrot Fractal Landscape

Suitably programmed, the computer can be made to perform many unexpected tasks. In this instance, R. F. Voss used the computer to illustrate a *fractal* theory of the Earth's relief. (See page iv.)

In computer terminology, the computer itself is referred to as the *hardware*. Hardware is capable of performing certain operations on data at lightning speed. However, in every operation that a computer performs, it follows a detailed sequence of instructions called a *program*. A computer program, sometimes referred to as the *software,* tells the hardware exactly what data to use, gives step-by-step instructions for carrying out each operation on the data, and then instructs the hardware what to do with the results.

The person who writes this detailed set of instructions is a *computer programmer*. It is the job of a computer programmer to analyze the task that the computer is to perform and divide it into its component operations. A detailed method of performing some task is called an *algorithm*. Often the hardest part of programming is finding the best algorithm to use; that is, to discover the best sequence of operations for a computer solution of the problem. The programmer must then write instructions for performing the operations in the correct order. And the instructions must be written in a language that the computer can understand.

The hardware provides incredible speed and accuracy in performing laborious calculations. However, the intelligent decisions concerning what calculations are necessary to solve a problem must be made by a computer programmer and specifically written into the software. When you hear about a computer that is able to play chess, you may be tempted to think that computers can do almost anything. However, the fact is that an ingenious programmer can program a computer to do almost anything.

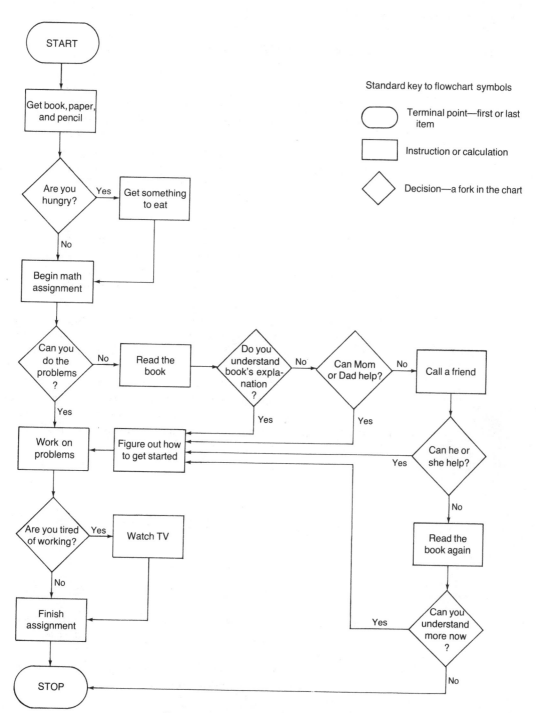

START

Get book, paper, and pencil

Are you hungry? — Yes → Get something to eat

No

Begin math assignment

Can you do the problems? — No → Read the book → Do you understand book's explanation? — No → Can Mom or Dad help? — No → Call a friend

Yes

Work on problems ← Figure out how to get started

Do you understand book's explanation? — Yes

Can Mom or Dad help? — Yes

Can he or she help? — Yes

No

Read the book again

Are you tired of working? — Yes → Watch TV

No

Finish assignment ← Yes

Can you understand more now? — No

STOP

Standard key to flowchart symbols

Terminal point—first or last item

Instruction or calculation

Decision—a fork in the chart

Flow chart for doing math assignment

81

STEPS IN COMPUTER PROGRAMMING

Organizing

A *flow chart* is a plan, or visual outline, that pictures the steps in a program. It can help the programmer organize these steps. A flow chart is especially important when the program to be written is complicated and has many sub-parts. In a flow chart, variously shaped boxes, each with a special meaning, are used to picture the steps. The order in which the steps are to be carried out is shown by arrows. See page 81.

Coding

Once all the steps of a program have been planned or organized into a flow chart, the program must be translated into a language that the computer can understand, or decode. Many *programming languages* have been devised to simplify the task of giving instructions to a computer. Some of the most popular are listed in the table on the next page, and a sample program is given in four of these languages to sum the integers from 1 to 100. This problem is discussed also under CALCULATORS; these samples show that a short computer program can do the job much more quickly.

In contrast to the flexibility of language used in a flow chart, statements written in a programming language must follow exactly the rules of that language. For example, in a flow chart for finding the average of five test scores, the instruction to divide the sum of the scores by 5 could be written in a number of ways:

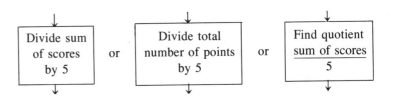

If the same instruction were to be programmed in Fortran, a name is assigned to the sum of the scores and another name to the average. Once the names have been assigned, there is only one way to write the division statement. If the sum were named S and the average A, the statement would be written (in Fortran),

$$A = S/5.0 \quad \text{where / means ``divided by.''}$$

Programming Languages

Date introduced	Language		Principal uses
1954	Fortran	(FORmula TRANslator)	scientific and engineering calculation
1956	Lisp	(LISt Processor)	artificial intelligence
1969	Cobol	(COmmon Business-Oriented Language)	business
1960	Algol	(ALGOrithmic Language)	scientific and general programming
1962	APL	(A Programming Language)	general programming; model building
1964	PL/1	(Programming Language 1)	business; scientific calculation
1965	Basic	(Beginner's All-purpose Symbolic Instruction Code)	teaching; very small computers
1971	Pascal	(named after Blaise PASCAL, who made one of the first adding machines)	teaching; general programming
1980	Ada	(named after Lady ADA Byron Lovelace, who wrote early instructions for Charles Babbage's Difference and Analytic Engines)	real-time control processes, such as the ongoing operation of an airplane; official military language

Sample programs, in four languages, to sum the integers from 1 to 100.

Fortran:

```
       PROGRAM SUMUP
       SUM = 0
       DO 10 I = 1,100
10     SUM = SUM + I
       WRITE (5,100) SUM
100    FORMAT (F10.4)
       END
```

Basic:

```
20   X=0
30   FOR I=1 to 100
40   X=X+I
50   NEXT I
60   PRINT X
70   END
```

Lisp:

```
(defun sumup (n)
    (cond ((zerop n) 0)
        (t (plus n (sumup (sub1 n))))))
(sumup 100)
```

Pascal:

```
Program Sumup;
var x,i:integer;
begin
    x:=0;
    for i:=1 to 100 do x:=x+i;
    write(x);
end.
```

When a program is coded to be run through the computer, it usually contains each of these types of statements:

- *Input statements* specify the form of the data to be read into the computer. For example, an input statement will indicate whether the data are to be alphabetic or numeric (whether they are words or numbers). If the data are numeric, an input statement will specify whether the numbers are integers or decimal fractions.
- *Arithmetic statements* indicate what operations are to be performed on the data. For example, in a program for posting checks and deposits in bank accounts, an arithmetic statement might instruct the machine to subtract the amount of a particular check from the balance of that account.
- *Control statements* tell the computer what to do next, possibly depending on some condition or the values of some data. Control statements differ from arithmetic statements in that they affect the operation of the computer rather than the values of the data.
- *Output statements* specify the form in which the output is to be produced. For example, if the output is a list of names in alphabetical order, an output statement will specify whether the list is to be printed in a vertical column or printed in horizontal rows with several names to a line. An output statement will indicate whether the names are to be separated by punctuation, or whether blank spaces are to be left between the names, and so on.

Input

A coded program must be read into the computer in some way. This can be done by punched cards or tapes, or a program may be entered directly by a terminal keyboard.

Here is a sample punched card for performing the operation

$$X = Q + \left(\frac{Z}{23.5} - 62 \times Y \right).$$

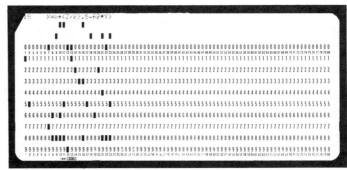

Common Codes for Computer Input

In the Hollerith code for punched cards, the numerals 0 through 9 are each represented by a single punch in a vertical column. For example, 9 is one punch at the bottom of a vertical column. Alphabetic characters are each represented by a combination of two punches in the same vertical column. Special characters may be represented by as many as three punches.

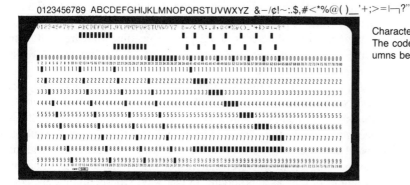

Characters are listed across the top. The code is punched in vertical columns below each character.

Hollerith code for punched cards

The paper tape code is different, but it is also made by combinations of punches in vertical columns.

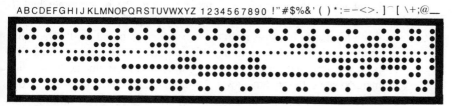

One paper tape code

Debugging

Next, the program must be given a trial run to check for errors. Errors in a computer program are called *bugs,* and the process of correcting any errors in the plan of the program or in the coding is called *debugging.* Errors must be corrected before the program will run correctly.

Output

When all errors have been corrected, the computer will run the program and produce the results, or output. The information usually comes out of the computer on a printed page. However, the output may also be on cards, tape, or TV screen (cathode-ray tube).

HISTORY

The history of computer programming is the story of how computers became able to handle more and more instructions, or programs, and how they became more flexible. On the earliest electronic computer, the ENIAC, constructed at the University of Pennsylvania in the 1940s and completed in 1946, a programmer programming the machine to perform a certain job set up a particular pattern of electrical circuits. To program the machine to do a different job, wires had to be unplugged and a new pattern set up. Thus, in the infancy of the computer, programming and debugging were time-consuming jobs. Sometimes hundreds of wires had to be reconnected, and just one wire hooked up to the wrong terminal was a bug that would foul up the whole program.

An enormous contribution was made to computer science by John von Neumann, an American mathematician who saw that the job of changing the computer circuitry to perform different tasks could be accomplished by the computer itself. He saw that programs could be coded and stored in memory in the same way that data could, and that the machine could interpret patterns of binary numbers as either instructions or data as appropriate. In that way, reprogramming the computer became simply putting a new batch of numbers into it, to be interpreted by the control unit.

Now stored in the computer are other programs, including *compilers* to translate instructions written in programming language into machine language. In the early days of programming, the programmer had to write his instructions in a language very close to the one used by the machine itself. Because a digital COMPUTER is based on the fact that electrical circuits must be in one of two states—on or off—the machine language is based on the *binary* NUMERAL SYSTEM. In the binary numeral system, the statement $3 + 2 = 5$ would appear as $11 + 10 = 101$. For people unfamiliar with the binary numeral system, working with machine language was difficult. The invention of programming languages, which are much closer to English than machine language, and the storing within the computer of compilers to translate programming languages, opened the field of computer programming to many more people and simplified the process.

REFERENCES

David H. Ahl, ed., *Basic Computer Games* (Workman Publishing Co., 1978); more than a hundred challenging games for solo or group play, from lunar landing to the stock market, with complete programs. See also *More Basic Computer Games* (Creative Computing Press, 1979).

David H. Ahl, ed., *Computers in Mathematics: A Sourcebook of Ideas* (Creative Computing Press, 1980); a huge softbound book, full of useful material from *Creative Computing:* problems, puzzles, art and graphing, programming ideas for the classroom, from elementary to advanced. Many activities are included that do not require a computer.

Bob Albrecht, *My Computer Likes Me When I Speak in Basic* (dilithium Press, 1978); an informal paperback workbook that teaches BASIC, the general purpose programming language.

Jerome A. Feldman, "Programming Languages," *Scientific American,* December 1979, pp. 94–116; what the languages do, how they work, and how they differ.

Nicholas Findler, "Computer Poker," *Scientific American,* July 1978, pp. 144–151; models of decision-making in the real world.

Roger Kaufman, *A Fortran Coloring Book* (M.I.T. Press, 1978); guaranteed to teach FORTRAN and plenty about computers in hilarious fashion.

Stephen J. Rogowski, *Problems for Computer Solution* (Creative Computing Press, 1979); ninety problems from eleven different areas of mathematics, with a thorough discussion of and references for each. A teacher's edition is available with solutions and in-depth analysis.

Eric Weiss, ed., *Computer Usage Fundamentals* (McGraw-Hill, 1975).

Biographical references

Teri Perl, *Math Equals: Biographies of Women Mathematicians + Related Activities* (Addison-Wesley, 1978), pp. 101–125; something of the life and work of Ada Byron Lovelace, one of the first people to be involved with computer programming. She worked with Charles Babbage on his analytical and difference engines, forerunners of the modern computer.

Frances Benson Stonaker, *Famous Mathematicians* (J. B. Lippincott, 1966); chapters on von Neumann and Norbert Wiener.

John von Neumann, *The Computer and the Brain* (Yale University Press, 1958); a slim volume of public lectures with a short biographical preface by Klara von Neumann, his wife.

See COMPUTERS for more references.

The question of *computability* is discussed at the end of MATHEMATICAL SYSTEMS.

COMPUTERS

COMPUTER: a device for automatically performing operations on data. *Data* is the collective term for all information, numerical and otherwise, that may be acted on by a computer.

There are two basic types of computer—the *analog computer* and the more common *digital computer*.

An *analog computer* is one in which changes in physical quantities are represented in the computer by changes in some model, or analog. A simple example of this principle is a mercury thermometer, which measures changes in temperature by analogous changes in the height of a column of mercury. Usually, though, the analog in an analog computer is varying electrical voltage. For example, an analog computer might be used in an oil refinery to keep track of the amount of oil flowing through the pipes. An increase in the oil flow could be represented by an increased voltage in the computer. With this information, the computer might be programmed to open and close valves automatically to keep the oil flow constant. One important use of analog computers is to simulate many possible conditions. By varying the voltages in an analog computer, scientists attempt to predict the effects of variations in gravity, air pressure, temperature, and the like.

A *digital computer* processes information in the form of numbers, or digits. Unlike an analog computer, which works with quantities that may assume any value along a continuum, a digital computer works with quantities that may assume only certain values. Some values, in the case of the digital computer, are not possible. The difference between the kinds of quantities these two computers process is analogous to the difference between rising temperatures and rising prices. As the temperature rises from 30° to 35°, it will pass every possible point between those two temperatures. But as the price of a single candy bar rises from 30¢ to 35¢, the price must be in some whole number of cents; it will not be 31.337786¢ per bar.

In an analog computer many things happen at once, but a digital computer must proceed step by step. A digital computer can do only one operation at a time; operations and data must be divided into certain discrete units. The key, however, to the usefulness of a digital computer is its accuracy and extremely high speed—it can perform millions of these discrete operations per second without error.

Digital computers (henceforth called simply "computers") work not only with numbers, but also with anything that can be coded in numbers such as symbols, letters, words, and positions of pieces in a chess game. Thus, a computer can perform complex calculations, correct papers, put a list of names in alphabetical order, or play chess. If information about diseases is encoded as symbols, a computer can help to diagnose illness and prescribe medication.

Control console of an electronic digital computer

HOW A COMPUTER WORKS

A digital computer works on the *binary* NUMERAL SYSTEM. The binary system contains only two digits, 0 and 1, and any number is represented by a sequence of the two. In computer science, a binary digit is called a *bit*. A group of bits used to represent a single character is called a *byte*. In the computer, the bits 0 and 1 are represented by an electric switch being "off" or "on."

A computer contains a multitude of tiny electronic switches, operated by electric currents. These switches can open or close (turning another current on or off) nearly a billion times a second. They are connected in various ways to form LOGIC circuits which can count, add, remember numbers, and so on (see SET and its references). While it takes hundreds of thousands of such circuits to form a computer, they are so fast that the computer can still do millions of separate operations each second.

Binary counting

0 =	0
1 =	1
2 =	10
3 =	11
4 =	100
5 =	101
6 =	110
7 =	111
8 =	1000
9 =	1001
10 =	1010
11 =	1011
12 =	1100
13 =	1101
14 =	1110
15 =	1111
16 =	10000
.	.
.	.
.	.

Computers are really rather simple-minded. No computer ever does anything more complicated than simple arithmetic or comparing numbers and deciding what to do next based on this comparison. Computers do fantastic things not because they are smart, but because they are fast. There is nothing a computer can do that a ten-year-old could not do with enough time (say several million years) and a perfect memory.

COMPONENTS OF A COMPUTER

The physical machinery of a computer, including the wires and electronic circuits, is referred to as *hardware*. The COMPUTER PROGRAM, or instructions for this machinery, is called *software*.

Hardware

The central part of a digital computer, its "brain," is a *processor,* or *central processing unit* (CPU). Attached to the processor and controlled by it are *storage* (or *memory*), which stores information and programs, and various *input* and *output* devices, which connect the computer to the world outside and the people using it.

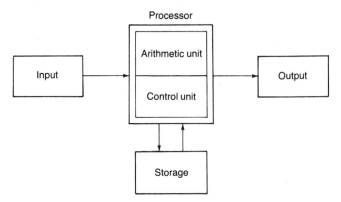

Hardware components of a computer

Processor

The processor is the only part of a computer that does anything on its own. It is the device that looks at the instructions in a program and carries them out; it tells the machine what to print. All the other parts of a computer exist only to allow the processor to be instructed and to do its work. The processor has two components: an *arithmetic unit* and a *control unit*.

The *arithmetic unit,* or *logic unit,* performs the basic ARITHMETIC OPERATIONS—addition, subtraction, multiplication, and division. (Because of the computer's fantastic speed, these basic operations are enough to carry out much more complex operations. For example, values for TRIGONOMETRIC FUNCTIONS are calculated by SERIES; that is, by the addition of many terms, each involving multiplication and division.) Furthermore, the arithmetic unit can make numerical comparisons—greater than, equal to, and less than. The comparison operation, which enables the computer to arrange data in numerical or alphabetical order or to do different things in different situations, is particularly important in the business of *data processing.*

The *control unit* directs all phases of the execution of a program: it decides what should be done; it controls retrieval of information; it tells the arithmetic unit which operations to perform; it relays the results to the output unit or memory.

Input and Output

Input to a computer is generally done on a *terminal,* which works like a typewriter. A computer *user* sits at a terminal and types commands to the computer; the computer types its responses on the terminal. This "typing" can either be printed on paper or displayed on a television screen (called a CRT, for cathode ray tube).

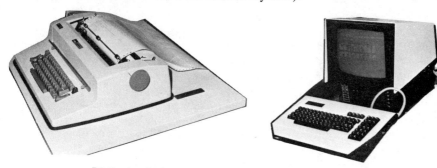

Printing terminal   CRT terminal, or screen

An alternative is to prepare instructions for a computer on *punchcards,* using a *keypunch.* The deck of cards is then read into the computer by a *card reader.* Another input device is *punched paper tape,* like ticker tape. The computer may also be given previously prepared instructions from *storage* on *magnetic disks* or *magnetic tapes.*

Output from the computer can be generated at the terminal, or by a *line printer* (which is like a typewriter but hundreds of times faster because it types a whole line at once), or by a *plotter* (which can draw graphs and intricate designs).

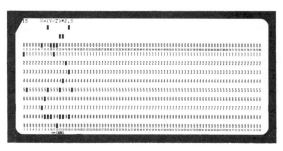

Computer punch-card

Keypunch

Line printer

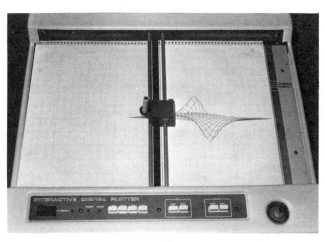

Plotter

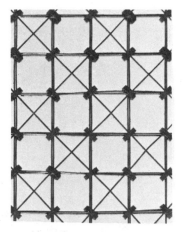

Magnetic core memory
Courtesy of Digital Computer Museum.

Storage

In order for a computer to work, it must remember the program it is running, the data it is working with, and other information. Since it is inconvenient to type in a program every time you want to run it, or data that is to be used repeatedly, the computer must be able to store it from day to day.

Most common is some sort of *magnetic* storage. All kinds of magnetic storage use the same idea: pieces of material are magnetized in one of two directions, each direction representing a binary digit. In magnetic *core* memory there are fine iron "doughnuts," threaded onto wires, that can be magnetized circularly clockwise or counterclockwise. Other memory systems use magnetic *disks*, magnetic *tapes*, and even magnetic *bubbles*.

By the mid 1950's, the first magnetic disks gave data processing an enormous boost. Now stored information could be retrieved much faster than from punched cards or tapes. Here the fifty spinning aluminum disks of IBM's RAMAC (for RAndoM ACcess) contained five million characters of information. In a fraction of a second, a read/write mechanism could find the right magnetic spot and retrieve data from any point on the disk.

Courtesy of International Business Machines Corporation.

Magnetic disks

A magnetic disk is a circular piece of magnetic material, like a phonograph record, that can be magnetized by a recording head that almost touches the disk as it turns. *Magnetic tape* is a long strip of magnetic material, similar to ordinary recording tape, $\frac{1}{2}$ inch wide and as much as 3200 feet long, that is wound onto reels. A disk is faster to use than tape, because a reading device does not have to go through all of it to get at the correct program; you might compare this to finding a particular song on an LP record or on a tape cassette.

There are two types of storage: short-term and long-term. Short-term storage, or *primary memory,* is used to hold within the computer whatever information the computer needs for the program it is executing. Access to this memory is fast, but storage here is more expensive per bit. Therefore data and programs not in immediate use are stored outside the computer in slower but less expensive *long-term storage* devices such as magnetic disks or tapes. When this information is to be used, it must be transferred to short-term memory.

Magnetic tape drives

Software

Software for a computer consists of all the COMPUTER PROGRAMS it uses: those that people write for their own use and those that the computer uses to run itself and talk to its users. The basic program that any computer runs is called a *monitor,* and it runs continuously whenever the computer is on. On a small system, the monitor might run like this:

1. See if the user has typed a key. If so, go on to step 2. If not, keep looking until a key is typed.
2. See what the key is. If it is a carriage return, signifying the end of a line, go on to step 3. If it is not a carriage return, remember it and go back to step 1.
3. Look at the whole line just typed. It should be a command, so search through the list of available commands, matching them against what the user has typed. If the command is in the list, go on to step 4. If the command is not in the list, go on to step 5.
4. Follow the instructions of what to do next (for example, run a particular program, tell the time of day). Then return to step 1.
5. The computer cannot do whatever the user asked for if the command is not in the list (perhaps there was a typing error), so tell the user by printing "unrecognized command." Then return to step 1 so he or she can try again.

Of course in a large system the monitor is more complicated, but the basic idea is the same.

Another program basic to a computer is a *compiler.* A compiler is a program that automatically translates "high-level" *programming languages* (like Basic, Fortran, or Pascal) that resemble English and that people can easily understand, into binary *machine language* that the processor can understand.

Another common type of software is a *text editor,* a program that allows the user to create and modify other programs or written materials, to look over what has been done so far, and to correct errors.

Large monitors, or *operating systems,* communicate with terminals and printers, decide when to run each program, respond to users' requests, and so on. This is especially important on a timesharing system. *Timesharing* is a scheme by which many people use the same computer at the same time. Since most of the time a person uses at a computer is spent deciding what to do next, timesharing is a great advantage: while one person decides what to do, the computer can run a program for another. If several people all want programs run at once, the computer alternates among them.

Computers also may have special-purpose programs for such tasks as preparing manuscripts or solving equations.

DO COMPUTERS MAKE MISTAKES?

All a computer does is follow the instructions it is given, right or wrong. If the computer goes wrong, it is usually the fault of the *programmer*, not the computer. To be sure, sometimes there is some failure of the hardware, but then the computer almost always stops entirely (called *crashing*). If the computer makes an error in your bank balance, it is because the program has a *bug*—a mistake or omission. Programs must tell a computer what to do at every step, and programmers usually do not think of every possible situation that must be covered when they first write a program. Finding and correcting bugs is called *debugging*. Very complicated programs are hard to debug—sometimes a program retains a hidden flaw for years after it has been pronounced "bug free." Such bugs appear only in some rare circumstance that the programmer has overlooked.

CAN A COMPUTER THINK?

Computers exceed some mechanical sorts of human thinking because of *speed* and *capacity*. A chess-playing computer can test the consequences of hundreds or thousands of moves in the time a human player can think out only a few. Of course, the human player is very clever at disregarding foolish possibilities, whereas the computer must consider many more—but the computer's speed still puts it ahead of all but the best human players. A computer can carry out tasks that for sheer size are too complex for humans to manage. (See TOPOLOGY: the four-color problem.)

But can a computer *think?* No, said Ada Byron Lovelace, who lived in the nineteenth century and worked with Charles Babbage on his analytical and difference engines, forerunners of the modern computer. She was one of the first people to write instructions for computing machines, and she well understood their capabilities. She wrote:

> The Analytical Engine has no pretensions whatever to *originate* anything. It can do whatever we *know how to order it* to perform. It can *follow* analysis, but it has no power of *anticipating* any analytical revelations or truths. Its province is to assist us in making *available* what we are already acquainted with.*

This has become famous as "Lady Lovelace's Objection" to the idea that a computer might think.

By itself a computer cannot think. But perhaps a computer could be

*Teri Perl, *Math Equals: Biographies of Women Mathematicians + Related Activities* (Addison-Wesley, 1978), p. 108.

programmed to think. It would need to be told how to do the thinking, with numbers and symbols. If we understood exactly how people think or what thinking means, a computer could be programmed to do it. Attempts to reproduce human thought are called *artificial intelligence* research.

Suppose a computer were to follow some program similar to human thought. Would it be thinking or just simulating thought? After all, say some people, all the computer can do is to follow complex instructions, and this mechanical process is not like human thought. Others say that perhaps our brains follow similar sets of instructions of which we are unaware. To avoid this controversy, British logician A. M. Turing devised the *Turing Test:* A person, perhaps a psychologist, sits at a terminal that is connected either to a computer or to another terminal operated by a human—the psychologist does not know which. If the psychologist cannot distinguish the computer's responses from human responses, the computer will be considered to be thinking.

Artificial intelligence is a tantalizing idea, but can it be realized? We do not yet know.

HISTORY OF COMPUTING MACHINES

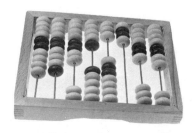

Modern Russian abacus

Japanese soroban

For thousands of years, people have sought means to calculate more rapidly and accurately. To this end, they have invented devices to perform at least a part of the computation process automatically, thereby increasing the speed of computation and reducing the chance of human error. The oldest such device is the *abacus,* the origin of which is so ancient that it cannot be accurately dated. The abacus may have been used by the Babylonians and was certainly used by the Greeks and Romans. It was important to European clerks and businessmen up through the Renaissance, and it is still used today, particularly in the Soviet Union and the Orient.

The abacus consists of counters, usually strung on rows of wires, with each row representing a separate power of ten. Addition is performed by moving the counters in one direction, and subtraction by moving them in the opposite direction. When ten counters have been added on a row, they are pushed back, and one counter is added on the row above. The abacus indicates when to carry in addition and when to borrow in subtraction.

Some versions of the abacus have fewer beads in each row. For the Roman, Japanese, and Chinese abaci, the beads in the top rows represent five units each.

In the seventeenth century, several devices were invented to simplify the task of computation. In 1614, a Scottish mathematician, John

Napier, invented a gadget called *Napier's rods,* or *Napier's bones.* Napier's rods were long sticks with a multiplication table on each face. Each side would be a strip as shown. Each strip was thus divided into rectangles, and each rectangle was split by a diagonal, separating the tens digit from the units digit.

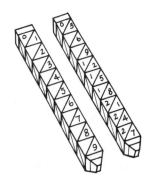

Napier's Bones

$$1 \times 3 = 3$$
$$2 \times 3 = 6$$
$$3 \times 3 = 9$$
$$4 \times 3 = 12$$
$$5 \times 3 = 15$$
$$6 \times 3 = 18$$
$$7 \times 3 = 21$$
$$8 \times 3 = 24$$
$$9 \times 3 = 27$$

To multiply two numbers together, such as 3176×2, one chose Napier's rods corresponding to the first number and lined them up beside each other, as illustrated above. Then the product of that number times an integer from 1 to 9 could be obtained by adding the digits in each resulting parallelogram in the row corresponding to the integer. Thus, each parallelogram corresponded to one digit of the answer, and the answer to a *multiplication* problem could be obtained using only *addition.*

In the 1620's, two Englishmen, Edmund Gunter and William Oughtred, invented the *slide rule,* a small analog computer for multiplication and division. (See LOGARITHMS).

Slide rule, set to multiply 2×3 along bottom of slide. See LOGARITHMS for explanation.

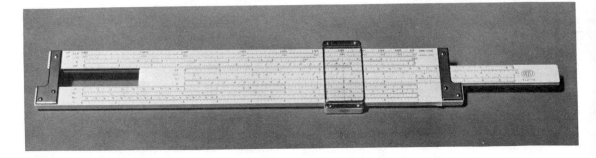

Nineteenth or Early Twentieth
Century Reckoning Machines

Thacher Rule, by Edwin Thacher, Pittsburgh, 1892

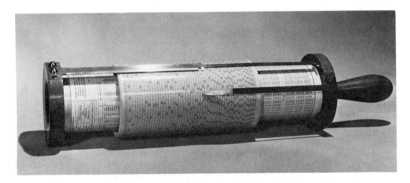

Fuller Rule, by George Fuller, England, 1897
"A calculating slide rule equivalent to a straight slide rule 83 feet 4 inches long."

The Adix Machine
(Mannheim, Germany)

The Lightning Adding Machine
(Standard Trading Co., N.Y.)

Photographs courtesy of the History of Science Collections, Cornell University Libraries.

From a simple slide rule were developed fancier versions which gave greater accuracy. For example, the Thacher rule is essentially a 30-foot slide rule. Although it is only about 18 inches long, its scales are arranged to give a great deal of space between digits, which means that it can be read accurately to five significant digits.

The twelve-inch slide rule was widely used as an indispensable portable calculating device for over three hundred years. Slide rules were carried by every engineer and by many other people until the advent, in the 1970s, of the pocket electronic CALCULATOR.

Still in the seventeenth century, in 1642, a nineteen-year-old French mathematician, Blaise Pascal, invented a little machine about the size of a shoe box that could *add* and *subtract*. Pascal's device contained interlocking wheels with ten positions, from 0 to 9. When one wheel moved from position 9 up to 0, the next higher wheel moved forward a notch; Pascal's machine could carry and borrow automatically.

Thirty years later, Gottfried Wilhelm von Leibniz, a German mathematician, invented a mechanical device that was supposed to *multiply* automatically; but, because of the imperfect tooling of the day, it was never very accurate. Until the twentieth century, mechanical calculating machines were still pretty primitive by today's standards.

Even today, adding machines and nonelectronic desk calculators are based on mechanical principles of toothed wheels, although electricity is often used to turn the wheels.

Early in the nineteenth century, an English mathematician, Charles Babbage, designed a machine called a "difference engine" that was intended to perform the laborious and repetitive work necessary to compute mathematical tables. Babbage persuaded the British government to invest 17,000 pounds in his invention, and he invested almost a third as much of his own money. However, because of limitations in tooling and engineering, the complicated machine could not be constructed and was eventually abandoned.

Instead of giving up, Babbage dreamed of an even more complicated machine, "the analytical engine," which was to have the essential features of a modern digital computer: an input-output system, a memory, a control unit, and an arithmetic unit. Babbage began work on his analytical engine in 1834, and he continued to invest time and money in it until his death in 1871. But again, the available technology was inadequate for the construction of such a precise instrument.

In the twentieth century, though, Babbage's dream was realized. Howard Aiken and others completed construction of the first digital computer, the Mark I, in 1944 at Harvard University. The Mark I was an electromechanical machine that measured 50 feet by 8 feet. It could carry out instructions on data fed into it on punched paper tape, and it could print out the results. Two years later, construction of the first

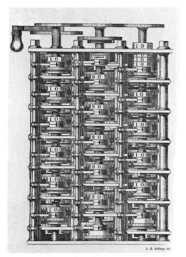

"It was commenced 1823.
This portion put together 1833.
This construction abandoned 1842.
This plate was printed 1889."

From Henry Prevost Babbage, *Babbage's Calculating Engines*, Collection of Papers (E. & F. Spon, London, 1889). Printed courtesy of the History of Science Collections, Cornell University Libraries.

electronic computer, the ENIAC, was finished by John Mauchly and J. Presper Eckert of the University of Pennsylvania.

The next significant advance in the design of computers was the internal storage of software. After working with the early computers—the Mark I and the ENIAC—John von Neumann, an American mathematician, saw that much work and many chances for error could be eliminated by coding instructions and storing them in memory in the same way that data is stored (see history of COMPUTER PROGRAMMING). Working at the Institute for Advanced Study at Princeton, New Jersey, von Neumann designed a computer with internally stored programs to translate programming languages into machine language, to direct details of input and output, and to perform a variety of other operations. Von Neumann's design was so successful that it provided the basis of most computers developed thereafter. The extent to which von Neumann advanced computer technology has been compared to a person's looking at the Wright brothers' plane and designing a jumbo jet.

The history of computer hardware since the ENIAC has been a steady progress toward smaller, faster, more powerful machines. The first computers were built with *vacuum tubes*—the ENIAC contained over 18,000. Then in the 1950's, vacuum tubes were replaced, as *transistor technology* was applied to the construction of computers. Computers built with transistors were smaller and faster. They used less electricity and were subject to fewer breakdowns.

In the late 1960's, *integrated circuit technology* was developed, and

Computer chip

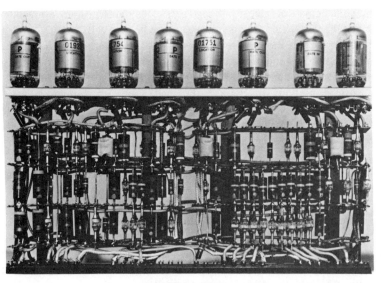

Vacuum tubes

hundreds of transistors and other circuit components could be etched on a silicon chip about the size of a fingernail. Since then the number of components that can be combined on one chip has increased dramatically, doubling nearly every year (that is, from 10 to approximately 400,000 in fifteen years).

The photograph below shows a 1980 IBM logic module containing up to 118 silicon logic chips, each containing up to 704 circuits, on three levels of wiring. Each module measures approximately 5 in. × 5 in. × 2 in.; these modules can be arranged to contain more than three quarters of a million logic circuits in four cubic feet of space. Most of this space, however, is consumed not by the logic circuits, but by cooling apparatus. The silicon chips are in the squares on the bottom. The rest of the apparatus contains spring-loaded pistons in contact with each chip; these carry heat away through a metal plate to a chilled water system. This cooling design is necessary for such dense packing of these modules, but it consumes an enormous amount of space. Computer technology developments in superconductivity can eliminate this bulk.

A device even smaller and faster than an integrated circuit is the *Josephson Junction*, based on the phenomenon of superconductivity, which works only at very low temperatures (4.2° Kelvin; see MEASURE) and must therefore be immersed in liquid helium. Superconductor technology overcomes speed constraints and heat production problems that limit computer expansion. Furthermore, like each of the previous technological advances, it drastically reduces the size and cost of computers, and reduces the amount of power needed to run them.

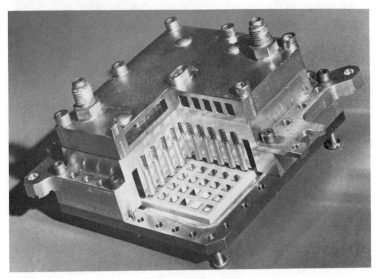

Photographs courtesy of International Business Machines Corporation.

Logic pack

As a result of these advances, *minicomputers* not much larger than an ordinary filing cabinet have been rented or sold by the thousands. In 1950, there were fifteen computers in the United States. In 1973, there were over 100,000, more than half of which were minicomputers. Now even smaller *microcomputers* are available at a price one person can afford. And devices like the Josephson Junction will enable a large room-sized computer of 1980 to be replaced by something the size of a football. The miniaturization of computer components has been accompanied by dramatically lower manufacturing costs, and the revolution is still in progress.

The search for automatic computing devices has brought us to levels of automation unforeseeable to pioneers in the field. And the consequences of transferring an enormous load of computation and clerical work from human beings to machines are only beginning to be understood and evaluated.

The history of computing machines is summarized in a chronology on the next page.

The first transistorized computer, the TX-O, restored to its original state, as it looked at MIT in the late fifties.

Courtesy of Digital Computer Museum.

A personal computer system of the early eighties, with color and graphics capabilities and high speed microprocessor.

Courtesy of International Business Machines Corporation.

Chronology of Computing Machines

? B.C.	Abacus
1614	John Napier (Scotland) invented a device called Napier's Bones, to make multiplication easier.
1620s	Edmund Gunter and William Oughtred (England) developed the slide rule. (See LOGARITHM.)
1642	Blaise Pascal (France) invented a machine for adding and subtracting.
1671	Gottfried Wilhelm von Leibniz (Germany) developed a machine for multiplying automatically.
1812	Charles Babbage (England) designed the "difference engine" intended to figure out and print mathematical tables.
1834	Charles Babbage developed the design of his "analytical engine," a powerful computing machine with many of the features of a modern computer.
1876	E. D. Barbour (United States) invented the first adding machine to use tape.
1889	Herman Hollerith (United States) developed punch cards to process data from the 1890 census.
1930	The first modern analog computer was constructed by Vannevar Bush and others (United States).
1944	The first modern digital computer, Mark I, was constructed by Howard Aiken and others (United States).
1946	The first electronic digital computer, ENIAC, was constructed by John Mauchly, J. Presper Eckert and others (United States).
1940s	John von Neumann (United States) greatly improved computer design by designing the memory unit to store programs as well as data.
1950s	The first commercial computers were mass produced.
1960s	Transistors were incorporated into computers, making them faster and more efficient.
late 1960s	Integrated circuits were incorporated into computers; minicomputers became available.
1974	First computer designed for hobbyists was announced, at a cost under $1000.

REFERENCES

Irving Adler, *Thinking Machines: A Layman's Introduction to Logic, Boolean Algebra, and Computers* (The John Day Co., 1961); from ALGEBRA to the design of circuits that calculate and perform deductive reasoning.

Karen Billings and David Moursund, *Are You Computer Literate?* (dilithium, 1979); a self-instruction paperback.

Paul M. Chirlian, *Understanding Computers* (dilithium, 1978); aims to provide an understanding of what computer languages are and how they operate in a computer.

Charles and Ray Eames, *A Computer Perspective* (Harvard University Press, 1973); a stunning collection of photographs and commentary from an extensive IBM exhibit.

David N. Groves and James L. Poirot, *Computers and Data Processing* (Sterling Swift Publishing Co., 1978); a good introduction.

Henry Jacobowitz, *Electronic Computers,* A Made Simple Book (Doubleday, 1963); an excellent paperback compendium of all the building blocks of both analog and digital computers. Details are clearly explained and illustrated.

Raymond G. Kenyon, *I Can Learn About Calculators and Computers* (Harper & Bros., 1961). Written for young people, it includes directions for making one's own calculating machines, from the abacus and Napier's Bones to digital and analog computers. Just reading the plans for these projects explains essential features of and differences between digital and analog computers.

Ronald D. Levine, "Supercomputers," *Scientific American,* January 1982, pp. 118–135; detailed explanation of how computer scientists approach complex problems needing immense amounts of "number crunching." The secret is to program a computer to do several operations simultaneously, an approach called vector processing.

Herman Lukoff, *From Dits to Bits: A Personal History of the Electronic Computer* (Robotics Press, 1979); recounts the intense atmosphere of discovery and frustration involved in the development of the ENIAC, with many photographs.

Merl K. Miller and Charles J. Sippl, *Home Computers: A Beginner's Glossary and Guide* (dilithium, 1978); a background reference book for beginners that will also help you evaluate microcomputer systems.

James L. Poirot and David N. Groves, *Computers and Mathematics* (Sterling Swift Publishing Co., 1979); designed for use by students with different backgrounds in mathematics. More advanced topics are presented as chapters progress.

James Poirot and David Groves, *Computer Science for the Teacher* (Sterling Swift Publishing Co., 1976); enjoyed by computer students as well.

Scientific American, September 1966; a whole issue devoted to computers. This magazine often has interesting articles on computers, for example:

> Philip Morrison and Emily Morrison, ''The Strange Life of Charles Babbage,'' April 1952; reprinted in *Mathematics in the Modern World: Readings from Scientific American* (W. H. Freeman & Co., 1968). pp. 52–56.

References on the abacus

Jesse Dilson, *The Abacus: A Pocket Computer* (St. Martin's Press, 1968); details of the operation of the abacus; includes the good story of how the oriental abacus has held its own in competition with computers.

There are many other good books on the abacus, both for young people and adults.

See COMPUTER PROGRAMMING for details on how instructions are written and given to a computer and for further references, including a source on Ada Byron Lovelace.

See CALCULATORS for comparison of calculator and computer. See MATRICES for reference to *computer graphics*. See SET for a discussion of the logic used in computer design.

CONGRUENCE

Symbols:

$\cong$ is congruent to
$\not\cong$ is *not* congruent to

CONGRUENCE: in geometry, the relationship between figures having the same shape and the same size; if two figures are *congruent,* they can be made to coincide exactly.

The top part of the symbol, $\sim$, is the sign for SIMILARITY and indicates identical shape. The bottom part of the symbol, $=$, is the equality sign, indicating identical size.

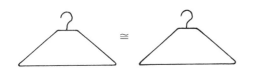  

If two figures have exactly the same shape and size, it is possible to imagine picking up one of the figures and placing it on the other in such a way that the fit is perfect, in other words, so the two figures *exactly coincide.* To make the figures coincide, it will be necessary to *translate* (move without changing direction or orientation) at least one of them. In addition, it may be necessary to *rotate* one of the figures or even to *reflect* it (flip it over). In any case, if the figures can be turned in such a way that they coincide when one is *superimposed* on (placed on top of) the other, they are congruent.

 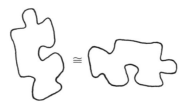 

Only translation is necessary   Translation *and rotation* are necessary   Translation *and reflection* are necessary

In the illustrations, the members of each pair are congruent. However, one of the figures may need to be rotated or reflected to appear congruent.

It is possible for two plane figures to have the same shape but not the same size. Such figures share similarity but not congruence. It is also possible for two figures to have the same size in terms of AREA, but not the same shape. A rectangle 4 meters by 3 meters has an area of 12 square meters, as does a rectangle 6 meters by 2 meters. However, as the illustration shows, they do not have the same shape and are not congruent.

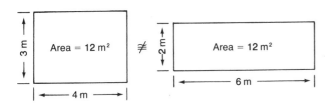

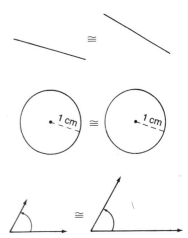

Same shape, different size—
not congruent

CONGRUENT PLANE FIGURES

For any two congruent plane figures, it must be possible to superimpose one on the other in such a way that the two figures coincide. However, for certain types of plane figures it is possible to determine whether or not two figures are congruent without superimposing one on the other. That is, for certain plane figures the conditions sufficient to insure that two figures are congruent have already been established. Below are some common plane figures together with the conditions sufficient to guarantee congruence.

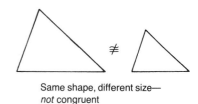

- Line segments: Any two LINE segments are congruent if they have the same length.
- Circles: Any two CIRCLES are congruent if their radii are congruent.
- Angles: Any two ANGLES are congruent if they have the same measure. The same measure means the same number of degrees or the same number of radians. (Angles are measured in terms of the size of the opening between the two sides, not in terms of the lengths of the sides.)
- Polygons: Any two POLYGONS are congruent if their corresponding sides are congruent *and* their corresponding angles are congruent.

Corresponding angles are angles that occur in the same relative position on two figures when the figures are oriented in the same way. For example, angle A corresponds to angle A' and to angle A''.

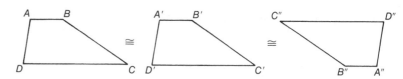

Corresponding sides are the sides between corresponding pairs of angles. Side *AB* corresponds to side *A'B'* and to side *A"B"*.

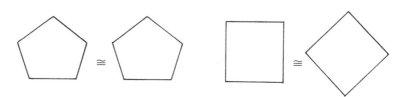

- Triangles: AS TRIANGLES are a special case of polygons, any two triangles are congruent if corresponding sides are congruent *and* corresponding angles are congruent.

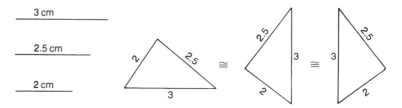

However, a triangle is a polygon with unique properties. One is that when the sides of a triangle are fixed, the angles are fixed as well. That is, with three sides of given lengths, it is possible to construct only one triangle. By taking this property into account, it is possible to determine whether or not two triangles are congruent without measuring the size of every side and every angle. It is possible to show that:

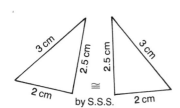

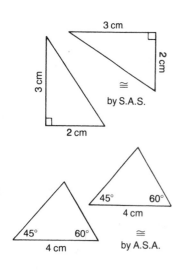

Two triangles are congruent if their corresponding sides are congruent. This condition is usually abbreviated S.S.S., for Side-Side-Side.

Two triangles are congruent if two corresponding sides and the angle between them are congruent. This condition is usually abbreviated S.A.S., for Side-Angle-Side.

Two triangles are congruent if two corresponding angles and the side between them are congruent. This condition is usually abbreviated A.S.A., for Angle-Side-Angle.

CONGRUENT SPACE FIGURES
(Congruent Solids)

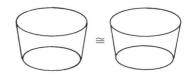

Any two space figures are congruent if they have exactly the same shape *and* size. If it were possible for two congruent solids to occupy the same space, they would exactly coincide.

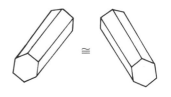

The mass-produced goods of our modern society provide many examples of congruent solids. Links of a jewelry chain, or of a tractor chain, are congruent. Any two teacups from the same set of china dishes are congruent. Any two coins of equal value are practically congruent, and vending machines are designed to identify congruent coins and funnel them into the appropriate slots. And duplicate keys are made by machines that cut the shaft of the duplicate so that it is congruent to that of the original.

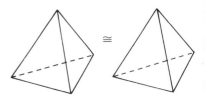

MORE ON GEOMETRIC CONGRUENCE

In solving a problem of congruence between geometric figures, it is necessary to remember which parts are congruent and which are not. In order to clarify which parts are congruent with one another, mathematicians often mark congruent parts with an equal number of slashes or hatch marks. For example, in the two triangles, side AB is congruent to side DE, so both are marked with a single slash. Similarly, angle A is congruent to D, and both are marked with double slashes. And side AC is congruent to side DF and marked with triple slashes.

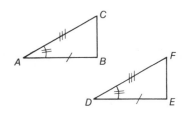

Pairs of congruent solids

Reference on geometric congruence

H. A. Elliott, James MacLean, and Janet Jorden, *Geometry in the Classroom* (Holt, Rinehart & Winston of Canada, 1968), pp. 89–94.

Marking congruent parts

APPLICATION OF CONGRUENCE TO MASS PRODUCTION

Congruent solids are so common to us today that it is hard to realize that just 200 years ago they were not common at all. As late as the eighteenth century, most goods were still manufactured by hand. (The word "manufacture" comes from two Latin words meaning "made by hand.") And as the goods were handmade by different craftsmen, no two manufactured items were exactly alike.

The man who changed all this and revolutionized the manufacturing industry was Eli Whitney (1765–1825). Whitney was the American who invented the cotton gin. By cleaning cotton more rapidly and with less labor, the cotton gin made millions of dollars for Southern planters. But it didn't make a dime for Whitney. After he had borrowed substantial sums of money to set up a plant to produce the gins, someone stole his patent, leaving Whitney with little besides his heavy debts.

In order to repay these debts Whitney signed a contract in 1798 with the U.S. government to manufacture and deliver 10,000 muskets within two years. In those days, all guns were handcrafted by skilled gunsmiths. Every gun was slightly different, and it took many hours of work to produce a single gun. When by 1800 Eli Whitney had delivered only 500 of the 10,000 guns he had promised, the government asked him to appear before some officials to explain the delay. As the story goes, he came into the room with a sackful of musket parts: ten barrels, ten stocks, ten hammers, and so on. Whitney separated the parts into piles on the floor and asked one of the officials to select at random a part from each pile. To everyone's amazement, Whitney then assembled a musket from these random choices.

For two years, instead of handcrafting muskets, Eli Whitney had been developing machine tools that could turn out uniform or *congruent* parts. With uniform parts already produced, fewer skilled craftsmen were needed to rapidly assemble the guns. Moreover, congruent parts made repairing the muskets vastly simpler.

Although Whitney was late in his delivery of the 10,000 muskets, his ideas and example gave the young American manufacturing industry the boost it needed. Whitney's concept of producing congruent items by machine and his capacity to carry it out marked the beginning of mass production in the United States.

AN EXCURSION TO THE FOURTH DIMENSION

The question of congruence between two figures asks whether the figures can be made to coincide, either in actuality or in imagination, by rigid motions (translation, rotation, reflection). Further examination of these motions leads to an intriguing consideration of dimensions.

Consider a right footprint and a left footprint; because they can be made to coincide by flipping one over onto the other, they are congruent. Notice that the footprints are *two*-dimensional figures, yet one must be flipped in *three*-dimensional space in order to make them coincide.

When one figure is a *reflection* of the other, an additional dimension is needed for the rigid motion bringing one to coincide with the other.

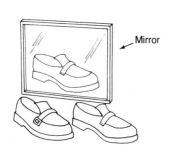

Mirror

What happens with a three-dimensional figure? Consider a pair of shoes. They have the same size and the same shape, except that the left shoe is a reflection of the right shoe. These shoes cannot be made to coincide in three-dimensional space; a *fourth* dimension is necessary to "flip" one to coincide with the other!

In three-dimensional space, the closest we can come to superimposing one shoe on the other is to turn one inside out (like a rubber glove), but this certainly would not make the left shoe look like the right. The notion of a fourth dimension allows a mathematician to consider the shoes as superimposable in imagination; they are labeled *oppositely congruent*.

Mathematicians often consider spaces of four (or more) dimensions. People cannot ordinarily *visualize* more than three dimensions, but the concept of higher dimensional spaces is very helpful in extending mathematical systems.

Another glimpse of higher dimensions is provided in the article on POLYHEDRA.

CONGRUENCE IN ARITHMETIC

The general idea of congruence is an exact equivalence. In geometry, congruence is the exact coincidence of geometric figures. In arithmetic, the word ''congruence'' has a numerical meaning and a different symbol:

$$12 \equiv 5 \;(\text{mod } 7),$$ read as ''twelve is congruent to five modulo seven,'' which means that 12 divided by 7 has a remainder of 5.

See *modular arithmetic* under ARITHMETIC for an introduction to this idea and its usefulness.

CONIC SECTIONS

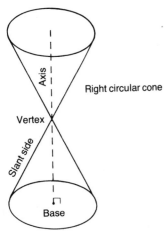

Right circular cone

Vertex

Axis

Slant side

Base

CONIC SECTIONS: the PLANE curves that can be formed by the intersection of a plane with a right circular cone. They include the *circle, ellipse, parabola,* and *hyperbola.*

Circular Cone: a three-dimensional figure formed by a straight LINE moving around the circumference of a CIRCLE *and* always passing through a fixed POINT that is not in the plane of the circle.

The circle becomes the *base* of the cone; the fixed point is the *vertex.* The moving line forms the *slant side.* The *axis* is a line from the vertex to the center of the circular base. As shown in the diagram, a cone has two sections.

The figure is a *right circular cone* if the axis is perpendicular to the base.

Conic sections may be defined in one of two ways:

- by the way in which a PLANE intersects a right circular cone
- by a LOCUS of points

Both ways are illustrated in the chart on pages 114–115.

O

DRAWINGS OF CONIC SECTIONS

Circle

The easiest way to draw a circle is with a drawing compass, setting the metal point at the center of the circle and the pencil at the distance of the radius from the point, and then twirling the compass through 360°.

If you do not have a compass or if you wish to make a very big circle, you can use a pencil, a piece of string, and a thumbtack. Tie one end of the string around the pencil and tack the other end to the center at the desired distance from the pencil. Keeping the string taut and the pencil perpendicular to the surface, move the pencil all the way around.

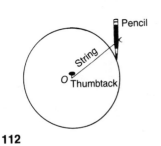

Pencil

String

O Thumbtack

Ellipse

An ellipse can be drawn using a pencil, a piece of string, and *two* thumbtacks. Put the two thumbtacks a distance apart on a board (for instance, 8 centimeters apart). Tie the string to form a loop (for instance, 20 centimeters of string) that will go around the tacks and be held taut by the pencil. With the pencil always holding the loop of string taut and always held perpendicular to the board, move the pencil around to draw the ellipse. The two thumbtacks are the foci of the ellipse.

If you change either the distance between the tacks or the length of the string, you will get different ellipses.

Parabola

A parabola can be obtained by folding a piece of thin paper. First, draw a straight dark line on the paper—this is the directrix. Also make a dark dot on the paper, anywhere except on the line—this dot is the focus. Fold the dot onto the line and crease the paper. Do this over and over again, each time folding the dot to a different point on the line, until you can see the parabolic shape formed along the side of all the creases. You can now draw the parabola along this curve.

Hyperbola

A hyperbola can also be made by folding paper. Draw a dark circle on a piece of thin paper. Mark a dark dot outside the circle. Fold the dot onto the circle and make a crease in the paper. Repeat this step again and again, each time folding the dot to a different point on the circle, until you can see the hyperbolic shape formed along the edges of all the creases. You can draw in both branches of the hyperbola. The dot and the center of the circle are the two foci of the hyperbola.

APPLICATIONS OF CONIC SECTIONS

The conic sections have been studied at least since the fourth century B.C. About 225 B.C., the Greek geometer Apollonius wrote *Conic Sections,* a series of eight books in which he thoroughly investigated these curves and introduced the names ellipse, parabola, and hyperbola. His work was a study in pure rather than applied mathematics. Yet today each of the conic sections appears in many ways in everyday life.

Circle

Applications of the circle are illustrated in the CIRCLE article.

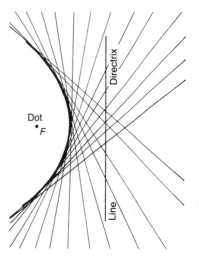

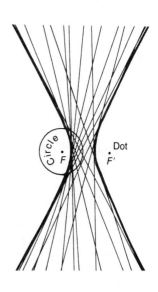

Name of conic section	Definition by *intersection of plane with right circular cone*	

Circle

Circle: the curve produced by the intersection of the cone with a plane passing through the cone parallel to the base

Ellipse

Ellipse: the curve produced by the intersection of the cone with a plane passing through only one part of the cone, and not parallel to a slant side.

Parabola

Parabola: the curve produced by the intersection of the cone with a plane passing through the cone parallel to a slant side.

Hyperbola

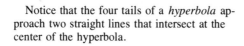

Hyperbola: the two-branched curve produced by the intersection of the cone with a plane passing through the cone at a greater angle to the base than that of a slant side (so the plane intersects both parts of the cone).

Notice that the four tails of a *hyperbola* approach two straight lines that intersect at the center of the hyperbola.

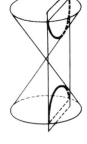

Projections of Conic Sections

You can easily produce all of the conic sections with the aid of a flashlight. Since the light comes out of the flashlight in the form of a cone, you can project the different shapes by shining the flashlight on the wall at different angles.

For a *circle,* you should hold the flashlight parallel to the floor.

If you tip the flashlight slightly, the circle will become an *ellipse.*

To get a *parabola,* you must hold the flashlight so that one side of the beam of light is parallel to the wall.

As you tilt the flashlight farther down toward a perpendicular position with the floor, the curve becomes a *hyperbola.* You get only half the hyperbola because the light forms a single cone, not a double one.

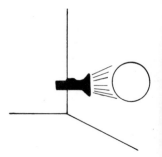

Definition by
locus of points

Circle: the locus of all points in a plane that are a given distance from a given point.

   The given point (*O*) is the *center*. The given distance is the *radius* (*r*).

A circle can be considered an ellipse with both foci at the center.

$$AO = BO = CO = r$$

Ellipse: the locus of all points in a plane such that for each point on the curve, the *sum* of the distances from two given points is a constant.

   These two given points (*F* and *F'*) are *foci* (plural of *focus*). The distance from a point on the ellipse to a focus is a *focal radius*.

$$PF + PF' = QF + QF' = RF + RF'$$

Parabola: the locus of all points in a plane such that each point on the curve is the same distance from a given point as it is from a given line.

   The given point (*F*) is the *focus*. The given line is the *directrix*. The distance from the point on the parabola to the directrix must be measured perpendicular to the directrix.

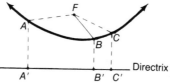

$$AF = AA' \quad BF = BB' \quad CF = CC'$$

Hyperbola: the locus of all points in a plane such that for each point on the curve the absolute value of the *difference* of its distances from two given points is a constant. (To find the *absolute value* of the difference, subtract the smaller distance from the larger.)

   The given points (*F* and *F'*) are *foci*. The distance from a focus to a point on the hyperbola is a *focal radius*.

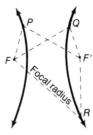

$$|PF - PF'| = |QF - QF'| = |RF - RF'|$$

See GRAPHS of second degree equations for examples of *equations* of conic sections.

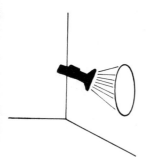
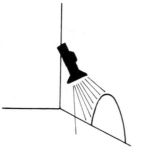
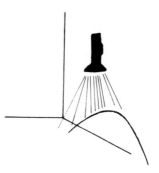

Ellipse

The planets move about the sun in paths that are elliptical. This fact was discovered by Johannes Kepler, a German astronomer, in 1609, some 1800 years after the Greeks' thorough study of conics. The discovery that the paths of heavenly bodies could be described by an abstract geometric curve was an amazing scientific feat, accomplished by extraordinary INDUCTION and by laborious computation on vast amounts of astronomical data. The assertion that the planets move in elliptical orbits is Kepler's first law of planetary motion.

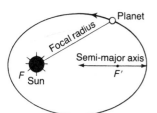

In the same year, Kepler stated a second law of planetary motion—that the focal radius vector between a planet and the sun moves at a rate which sweeps out equal areas in equal time intervals. Ten years later, he added a third law—that the time needed for a planet to make a complete revolution around the sun depended on the size of its elliptical orbit. (Specifically, he stated that the square of the time period for one revolution is proportional to the cube of the orbit's semi-major axis, half the distance across the ellipse at its maximum.)

Kepler's three laws of planetary motion apply to all heavenly bodies that revolve around another one. For instance, moons and man-made satellites follow elliptical orbits about their planets.

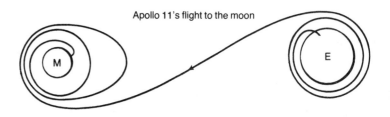

Apollo 11's flight to the moon

An interesting property of the ellipse is that a straight line or ray from one focus will be reflected from the side of the ellipse exactly through the other focus. (The original ray from one focus and the reflected ray through the other focus make equal angles with the ellipse.) There are rooms with elliptical dome-shaped ceilings, such as the Mormon Tabernacle in Salt Lake City, Utah, and the Whispering Gallery in the United States Capitol in Washington, D.C., that demonstrate this property. A pin dropped at one focus can be heard at the other very clearly, even though the foci are some distance apart. All sound waves emanating from one focus toward the ceiling are reflected through the other and arrive at the second focus at the same time, enabling a person at the second focus to hear all the reflected sounds together.

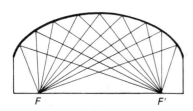

Parabola

Parabolic curves are seen in the steel cables of a suspension bridge or in the supporting arch of a highway or railroad bridge, for it is this shape which naturally holds up a uniformly weighted road surface.

A baseball in flight, a stream of water projected upward, and a bullet shot from a gun all follow parabolic paths (neglecting air resistance).

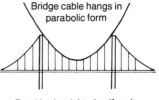

Bridge cable hangs in parabolic form

Road bed weighted uniformly

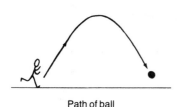

Path of ball

Path of water

Parabolic arch supporting bridge

Parabolas also form the central cross-sections of automobile headlight reflectors and the mirrors of large telescopes, because all rays from the focus are reflected parallel to the axis of a parabola, and vice versa.

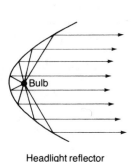

Headlight reflector

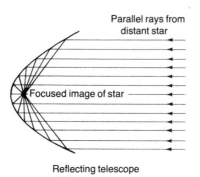

Parallel rays from distant star

Focused image of star

Reflecting telescope

Hyperbola

A cylindrical lampshade casts hyperbolic shadows on a wall.

A jet plane flying faster than the speed of sound (about 770 miles per hour) is followed by a conic shock wave. When this shock wave intersects the ground, it creates a sonic boom, which is heard only within a hyperbola formed by the intersection of the shock wave and the ground. Along the hyperbola of intersection, people at different places hear the sonic boom at the same time. See diagram on next page.

A system of long-range navigation (LORAN) for ships is based on hyperbolas. There are transmitting stations several hundred miles apart which act as foci of hyperbolas. A ship's pilot notes the time difference

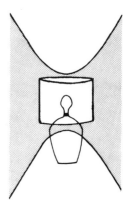

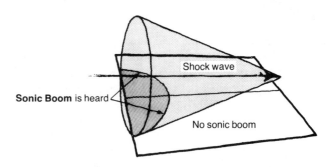

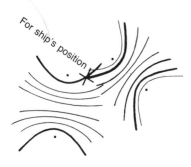

between the signals sent by different stations as they are received aboard ship. For a pair of transmitted signals, the time difference corresponds to a distance difference from the transmitting stations, so the ship's pilot knows he is located somewhere on a two-branched hyperbola between the stations. LORAN charts are published with whole families of hyperbolas for a pair of transmitting stations, with each hyperbola labeled in microseconds of time difference. (Such a chart will actually have families of hyperbolas for several pairs of transmitting stations, each family being printed in a different color to avoid confusion.) The pilot can pinpoint his ship's location by also timing the signal difference from a second pair of transmitting stations. He now knows he is located on a certain hyperbola for each pair of stations, so his precise position is where these hyperbolas intersect.

REFERENCES

Martin Gardner, "Mathematical Games: On conic sections, ruled surfaces, and other manifestations of the hyperbola," *Scientific American,* September 1977, pp. 24–39.

Henrietta O. Midonick, *The Treasury of Mathematics* (Philosophical Library, 1965), pp. 1–12 on Apollonius, including portions of his original writings.

Teri Perl, *Math Equals: Biographies of Women Mathematicians + Related Activities* (Addison-Wesley, 1978), Ch. 1, "Hypatia," pp. 9–26. Hypatia of Alexandria (A.D. 370–415) was a mathematical scholar and teacher of high repute; one of her writings was a book, *On the Conics of Apollonius.*

For the serious reader

Julian Lowell Coolidge, *A History of the Conic Sections and Quadric Surfaces* (Oxford University Press, 1945; Dover, 1968).

See also GRAPHS of second-degree equations.

COORDINATES

COORDINATES: any set of numbers used to locate a POINT on a NUMBER LINE, in a PLANE, or in space.

A *coordinate system* consists of one or more number lines, used as reference lines, to identify points by sets of numbers. A coordinate system gives every point an identification.

CARTESIAN, OR RECTANGULAR, COORDINATE SYSTEMS

Early in the seventeenth century two French mathematicians, Pierre de Fermat and René Descartes, each working independently, came up with the idea of using two *perpendicular number lines* to identify points in a *plane*. Every point could be represented by a *pair* of numbers, each of which represents the distance in the direction of one of the number lines. This rectangular coordinate system is called Cartesian, in honor of Descartes. The following words are used to describe a Cartesian coordinate system:

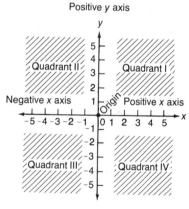

Axis (plural, *axes*): one of the two intersecting perpendicular number lines.

Horizontal Axis (usually called the *x-axis*): the horizontal number line.

Vertical Axis (usually called the *y-axis*): the vertical number line.

Origin: the point where the two axes intersect, which is at zero on both number lines.

Quadrant: one of the four regions into which the axes divide the plane. Quadrants are numbered counterclockwise, starting in the upper right-hand region where both number lines are positive.

Cartesian Coordinates: an *ordered pair* of numbers (*x, y*), which locates a point in the plane.

Abscissa: the first number of the ordered pair, giving the location of the point in the direction of the x-axis.

Ordinate: the second number of the ordered pair, giving the location of the point in the direction of the y-axis.

Examples.

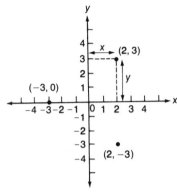

For this point, $x = 2$ and $y = 3$. Thus (2,3) can be located by: starting at the origin, moving along the x-axis 2 units, then moving up, parallel to the y-axis, 3 units.

Cartesian Coordinates in Three-Dimensional Space: an *ordered triple* of numbers (x, y, z), representing distances in the directions of *three* mutually perpendicular axes.

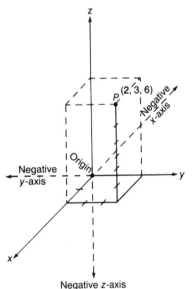

The Cartesian coordinate axes in three-dimensional space are three number lines, called the x-axis, y-axis, and z-axis. The axes intersect at the origin, which is zero on all three number lines.

The accompanying diagram portrays in two dimensions the three-dimensional axis system. You need to look at it with a three-dimensional perspective. Consider the y-axis and z-axis as lying in the plane of this page, perpendicular to each other, and the x-axis as coming out of the page, perpendicular to both.

The diagram shows the point P $(2, 3, 6)$, for which $x = 2$, $y = 3$, and $z = 6$. This point, P, can be located by moving from the origin as follows:

2 units along the x-axis,

3 units along a line parallel to the y-axis, then

6 units along a line parallel to the z-axis.

The diagram also shows the usual way in which the axes are labeled x, y, and z. However, there are other possible orientations of the axes. Shown here are the two possibilities for orienting the axes with the z-axis being the one sticking out perpendicular to the page. A "right-handed" system means that when the fingers of the *right* hand are curled from the positive x-axis to the positive y-axis, the thumb always points along the positive z-axis. The important thing is always to *label* axes so there can be no confusion.

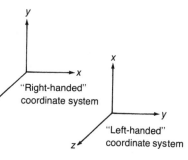

"Right-handed" coordinate system

"Left-handed" coordinate system

POLAR COORDINATE SYSTEM

You have seen that a point in a plane can be represented in Cartesian coordinates by a pair of numbers telling the location of the point with respect to two perpendicular axes.

In the *polar coordinate system* an entirely different pair of numbers will do the same job of locating a point in a plane, using only the *origin* and a *horizontal axis* for reference. The point P can be represented by the *distance* of P from the origin O, and the *angle* between the horizontal axis and the line OP.

The terminology of the polar coordinate system:

Pole: the origin O.

Polar Axis: the horizontal line through the origin.

Polar Coordinates: an *ordered pair* of numbers (r, θ) which identify a point P in the plane.

r: the first number of the ordered pair, giving the *distance* of P from the origin O.

θ: the second number of the ordered pair, giving the measure of the *angle* between the positive polar axis and the line OP. This angle is measured in a *counterclockwise* direction and is usually represented by the Greek letter θ (theta).

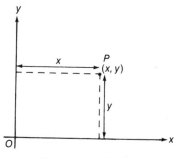

Cartesian coordinates

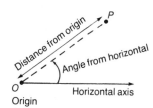

Polar coordinates

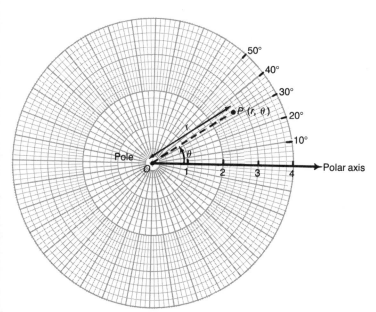

Examples.

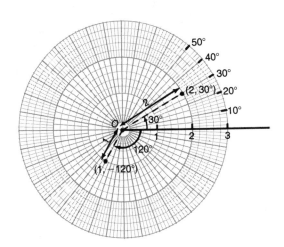

For this point,
$r = 2$ units and $\theta = 30°$

Thus $(2, 30°)$ can be located in polar coordinates by:

rotating a ray about the origin, counterclockwise, from the polar axis through the angle $30°$,

then measuring the distance 2 units from the origin along the ray

For convenience in locating points according to this system, there is a special *polar coordinate graph paper,* illustrated here and under GRAPHS.

Polar coordinates are useful because they make some equations much simpler. For instance, compare the equations that locate all the points on a circle with radius of one, centered at the origin.

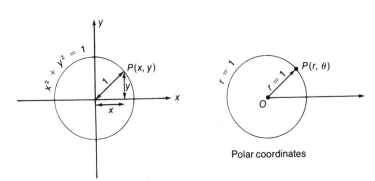

Cartesian coordinates

Polar coordinates

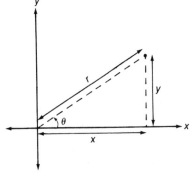

You can see the relationships between polar coordinates and Cartesian coordinates if you draw both coordinate systems on the same graph. Formulas for changing from one coordinate system to the other were derived from this diagram, using TRIGONOMETRY.

• To change from polar coordinates to Cartesian coordinates:

$$x = r \cos \theta$$
$$y = r \sin \theta$$

Example.

Polar coordinates (3, 30°), so $r = 3$, $\theta = 30°$.
$x = 3 \cos 30° = 3 \times 0.866 = 2.598 \doteq 2.6$
$y = 3 \sin 30° = 3 \times 0.5 = 1.5$
Cartesian coordinates (2.6, 1.5)

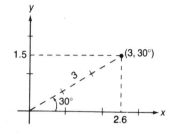

• To change from Cartesian coordinates to polar coordinates:

$$r = \sqrt{x^2 + y^2}$$

$$\tan \theta = \frac{y}{x}$$

Example.

Cartesian coordinates (2, 2), so $x = 2$, $y = 2$.
$r = \sqrt{2^2 + 2^2} = \sqrt{8} = 2\sqrt{2} = 2 \times 1.414 \doteq 2.8$
$\tan \theta = \frac{2}{2} = 1$, so $\theta = 45°$
Polar coordinates (2.8, 45°)

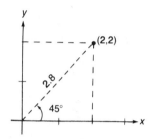

GEOGRAPHICAL COORDINATES

The lines of latitude and longitude form a coordinate system on the earth.

The *parallels of latitude* are circles parallel to the Equator, the great circle on the earth's surface which is equally distant from the North and South Poles. The latitude is an *angular* distance, measured in degrees, from the Equator. Thus the latitude at the Equator is zero degrees, and at either pole, ninety degrees. Parallels north of the Equator give north latitude, while those south give south latitude.

Meridians, the lines of *longitude*, run from the North Pole to the South Pole, perpendicular to the parallels of latitude. The Equator is divided into 360 circular degrees, and the meridians are labeled by degrees to show where they cross the Equator. One meridian is chosen as the Prime Meridian, which has zero degrees longitude. The other meridians are measured with respect to the Prime Meridian.

Although any meridian may be chosen as the Prime Meridian, the one

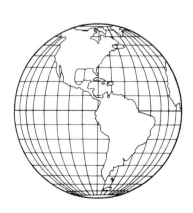

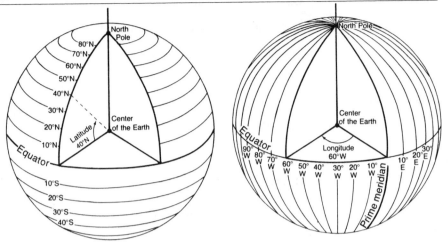

most generally accepted runs through Greenwich, England, where there is a famous observatory. From the Greenwich meridian, longitude is measured both east and west to 180 degrees. The 180° meridian is directly opposite the Prime Meridian on the globe, in the Pacific Ocean, and serves as the International Date Line. The kinks in the actual date line simply allow the countries that cross the 180° meridian to keep the same day within their boundaries.

Thus a coordinate system of latitude and longitude covers the entire surface of the earth. Small-scale globes and maps have space to draw these lines only every ten degrees or so, but larger scale maps can show latitude and longitude for each degree. Since a degree may cover as much as 69 miles on the earth's surface, the degree may be further subdivided into minutes (sixty to a degree) and seconds (sixty to a minute) to pinpoint a location. For example, the *World Almanac* locates New York City at 40° 45′ 06″ latitude north, 73° 59′ 39″ longitude west.

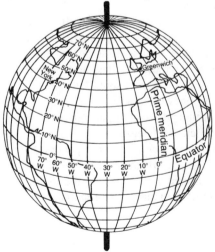

If you did not have a map at hand or did not know where you were on a map, could you determine the latitude and longitude of your position on the earth's surface? Yes, you could.

First, consider the matter of longitude. You know that the earth rotates once every twenty-four hours. Different locations around the earth experience high noon at different times. The time at Greenwich, England, is set so that at noon the sun appears at its zenith all along the Prime Meridian. For each hour of lag between high noon at Greenwich and high noon at another location there is a 15 degree difference in longitude. This difference is computed by dividing the number of degrees in the earth's circumference by the number of hours in a day: $\frac{360}{24} = 15°$.

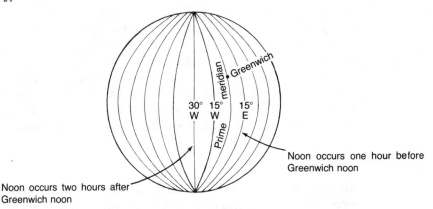

Noon occurs one hour before Greenwich noon

Noon occurs two hours after Greenwich noon

After about 1735, sailors were able to carry very good chronometers, or clocks, which kept the time as it was on the Prime Meridian. Then the longitude could be calculated:

longitude = 15° × (number of hours before or after 12:00 Greenwich time that high noon occurs)

Since the invention of the radio, time calculations can be made with high precision without relying on a chronometer.

Now, what about latitude? Latitude can be calculated by the ANGLE of elevation at which stars appear in the heavens. In the Northern Hemisphere this is particularly easy, because the North Star always appears directly over the North Pole. If you can measure from the horizon the angle made by your line of sight when observing the North Star, that angle will equal your latitude.

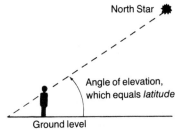

Sailors measured this angle of elevation of the North Star with a sextant. You can try it with the angle-measuring device described under TRIGONOMETRY.

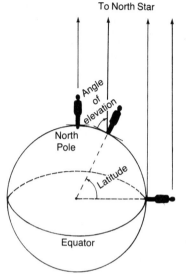

To North Star

Angle of elevation

North Pole

Latitude

Equator

Why is the angle of elevation of the North Star equal to the latitude? The North Star is so far away from the earth that all lines to it appear to be perpendicular to the Equator. Consider the diagram:

If you were to stand at the North Pole, you would see the North Star directly overhead. The angle of elevation would be 90°, and the latitude at the North Pole is 90°.

On the other hand, if you were to stand at the Equator, the North Star would appear to be on the horizon. The angle of elevation would then be 0°, and the latitude at the Equator is also 0°.

If you were to move from the Equator to the North Pole, the angle of elevation of the North Star and the latitude would both increase at the same rate, from 0° to 90°.

Naturally, it is extremely useful to have a coordinate system for the surface of the earth. For instance, a ship in distress in the middle of the ocean can give its location in terms of latitude and longitude and a plane can be dispatched directly toward it. When a balloonist attempted a newsworthy transatlantic crossing, the journalists reported daily on his latitude and longitude, thus telling us just what progress he had made. These geographical coordinates identify every point on the earth's surface. And conversely, with the coordinates, every point can be located.

REFERENCES

David Greenhood, *Mapping* (University of Chicago Press, 1964); a great deal more on geographical coordinates, written very clearly and interestingly.

Lancelot Hogben, *Mathematics for the Million* (published in Great Britain and by W. W. Norton and Co. in the U.S., in many editions, from 1936 to 1968); coordinate systems, both Cartesian and geographical, are discussed in considerable detail.

For more on the use of coordinate systems, see GRAPHS and SLOPE.

DECIMALS

DECIMAL FRACTION: a FRACTION in which the denominator is some power of ten.

The word "decimal" comes from the Latin word "decem," meaning "ten." A decimal fraction is usually written in a single line, with a dot or *decimal point* separating the whole number from the proper fraction.

Examples. $0.7 = \dfrac{7}{10}$ $\qquad 0.06 = \dfrac{6}{100} = \dfrac{6}{10^2}$

$\qquad\qquad 2.5 = \dfrac{25}{10}$ $\qquad 0.317 = \dfrac{317}{1000} = \dfrac{317}{10^3}$

In a decimal fraction, the denominator is not written but rather is understood to be some power of ten. Exactly what power of ten is in the denominator is indicated by the number of digits to the right of the decimal point.

In the decimal number 217.04, the numerals to the left of the decimal point represent the whole number two hundred seventeen (2 hundreds + 1 ten + 7 ones), and the numerals to the right of the decimal point represent the fraction four-hundredths (0 tenths + 4 hundredths). This number is shown in a chart on the next page, illustrating how decimal fractions follow the regular place value pattern of our decimal NUMERAL SYSTEM.

CONVERTING FRACTIONS TO DECIMALS

Any common fraction (any fraction that can be expressed as the RATIO of two integers) can be converted to a decimal fraction by *dividing the denominator into the numerator.*

	Hundred thousands	Ten thousands	Thousands	Hundreds	Tens	Ones	Tenths	Hundredths	Thousandths	Ten thousandths	Hundred thousandths	Millionths
Powers of 10 represented by each place	10^5 or 100,000	10^4 or 10,000	10^3 or 1000	10^2 or 100	10^1 or 10	10^0 or 1	$\frac{1}{10^1}$ or $\frac{1}{10}$	$\frac{1}{10^2}$ or $\frac{1}{100}$	$\frac{1}{10^3}$ or $\frac{1}{1000}$	$\frac{1}{10^4}$ or $\frac{1}{10,000}$	$\frac{1}{10^5}$ or $\frac{1}{100,000}$	$\frac{1}{10^6}$ or $\frac{1}{1,000,000}$
Places illustrated by example				2	1	7 .	0	4				
Names of Places	hundred thousands	ten thousands	thousands	hundreds	tens	ones	tenths	hundredths	thousandths	ten thousandths	hundred thousandths	millionths

Example.   Terminating decimal:

$$\frac{3}{8} = 8\overline{)3.000}\ \ \overset{0.375}{}\ \ \begin{array}{c} 2\,4 \\ \hline 60 \\ 56 \\ \hline 40 \\ 40 \\ \hline\hline \end{array} = \frac{375}{1000}$$

These are *equivalent* fractions—three numerical representations of the same number

- If, as in the example, in the process of division you reach a point where there is no remainder, the decimal fraction is called a *terminating decimal* (or *finite decimal*).
- On the other hand, for some fractions the division process never ends. No matter how far the division is carried, there will always be a remainder greater than zero. For these fractions there is a pattern of a repeated digit or a repeated sequence of digits; hence they are called *repeating decimals* (or *periodic decimals*).

Examples.   Repeating decimals:

$$\frac{2}{3} = 3\overline{)2.0000}\ \overset{.6666\ldots}{}\ \begin{array}{c}1\,8\\ \hline 20\\18\\ \hline 20\\18\\ \hline 20\\18\\ \hline 2\end{array}$$

$$\frac{5}{11} = 11\overline{)5.000000}\ \overset{.454545\ldots}{}\ \begin{array}{c}4\,4\\ \hline 60\\55\\ \hline 50\\44\\ \hline 60\\55\\ \hline 50\\44\\ \hline 60\\55\\ \hline 5\end{array}$$

A shorthand notation for a repeating or periodic decimal is to write a bar or a dot over the repeating set of digits. This repeating set is called the *period* or the *repetend*. For example,

$$\frac{2}{3} = 0.6666\ldots = 0.\overline{6} \text{ or } 0.\dot{6}$$

$$\frac{5}{11} = 0.454545\ldots = 0.\overline{45} \text{ or } 0.\dot{4}\dot{5}$$

$$\frac{12222}{99000} = 0.123454545\ldots = 0.123\overline{45} \text{ or } 0.123\dot{4}\dot{5}$$

Terminating decimal

$$\frac{1}{25} = 25\overline{)\begin{array}{l} 0.04 \\ 1.00 \end{array}}$$

$$\begin{array}{r} 0 \\ \hline \textcircled{1}00 \\ 00 \\ \hline \textcircled{10}0 \\ 100 \\ \hline \textcircled{0} \end{array}$$

$$\frac{1}{25} = 0.04$$

Repeating decimal

$$\frac{2}{7} = 7\overline{)\begin{array}{l} 0.2857142\ldots \\ 2.0000000\ldots \end{array}}$$

$$\begin{array}{r} 0 \\ \hline \textcircled{2}0 \\ 14 \\ \hline \textcircled{6}0 \\ 56 \\ \hline \textcircled{4}0 \\ 35 \\ \hline \textcircled{5}0 \\ 49 \\ \hline \textcircled{1}0 \\ 7 \\ \hline \textcircled{3}0 \\ 28 \\ \hline \textcircled{2}0 \\ 14 \\ \hline \textcircled{6} \end{array}$$

Remainders →
start to
repeat,
forming
cycle

.
.
.

$$\frac{2}{7} = 0.285714285714\ldots$$

$$= 0.\overline{285714}$$

Any common fraction will convert to either a terminating or a repeating decimal. To see why this is true, consider the fraction

$$\frac{k}{n}, \quad \text{where} \left\{ \begin{array}{l} k \text{ stands for any integer and} \\ n \text{ stands for any integer except } 0. \end{array} \right.$$

When the denominator n is divided into the numerator k, a remainder will appear at each step of the division process, as circled in the examples in the margin. The remainder can be any integer, $0, 1, 2, 3, \ldots$, up to one less than n.

When the division process arrives at the point where there are only zeros left in the dividend, continue dividing, bringing down zeros from the dividend. Then,

- if a zero remainder occurs, the fraction converts to a terminating decimal.
- if no zero remainder occurs, the fraction converts to a repeating decimal.

This is because by the time the division process reaches the nth step, if not before, one of the remainders will have to be repeated. For example, if $n = 7$, the possible remainders are $0, 1, 2, 3, 4, 5,$ or 6. By the time the division process reaches the seventh step, either there has been a step with zero remainder, or one of the other possible remainders will have to be repeated. When a remainder is repeated, a cycle is formed, resulting in the same set of digits in the quotient that was obtained when that remainder first appeared.

CONVERTING DECIMALS TO FRACTIONS

- Any *terminating decimal* can be converted to a common fraction. The numerator of the common fraction will be the decimal fraction without the decimal point; the denominator will be ten raised to a power equal to the number of digits to the right of the decimal point in the decimal fraction.

Examples. $0.375 = \dfrac{375}{10^3} = \dfrac{375}{1000}$

$4.06 = \dfrac{406}{10^2} = \dfrac{406}{100}$

- Any *repeating decimal* can be converted to a common fraction by the algebraic process outlined here step by step.

(1) Write an equation setting the decimal equal to n.

(2) Multiply both sides of the equation by a power of ten equal to the number of digits repeating. (For example, if one digit repeats, multiply by 10^1 or 10. If two digits repeat, multiply by 10^2 or 100, and so on.)

(3) Subtract the first equation from the second.

(4) Solve the resulting equation for n, and reduce the result if possible.

Note: Under this procedure, the decimal 0.999 ... converts to 1.

NONTERMINATING, NONREPEATING DECIMALS

Although all terminating and repeating decimals can be converted to common fractions, there are other decimal numbers that cannot, for example, a number like .101100111000 .... Furthermore, there also are decimals resulting from certain ARITHMETIC OPERATIONS that neither terminate nor repeat. The result of taking the square root of 3 is such a decimal. The square root of 3 carried out to three places is 1.732 ... , carried out to four places it is 1.7321 ... , and carried out to six places it is 1.732051 .... But no matter how many times the square root operation is carried out, the answer will never come out even and there will never be a pattern of repeating digits. Thus, the decimal number representing $\sqrt{3}$ is an infinite decimal sequence that cannot be converted to a common fraction.

Numbers like the square root of three that cannot be expressed as common fractions are called *irrational numbers* (see RATIONAL AND IRRATIONAL NUMBERS). The term "irrational" means that these numbers cannot be expressed as the RATIO of two integers. Another irrational number is PI (π), the ratio of the circumference of a CIRCLE to its diameter. The approximate value of π is 3.141592 .... But it has been proved that these digits never terminate or repeat, and so π cannot be expressed *exactly* as a common fraction or as a finite decimal fraction.

However, irrational numbers can be *approximated* by decimal fractions, and the approximation can be done as accurately as you wish by computing more and more decimal places.

ROUNDING OFF

In computations with decimals it is often desirable to use only a certain number of decimal places. For example, if you want to check the distance from one city to another on the odometer of a car, you may not be interested in measuring the distance to the nearest tenth of a mile

Example. To convert $5.\overline{3}$ = 5.333 ... to a fraction:

(1) $n = 5.\overline{3} = 5.333 \ldots$

(2) One digit, 3, repeats.
$10n = 53.\overline{3} = 53.333 \ldots$

(3)
$$\begin{array}{r} 10n = 53.333\ldots \\ -\quad n = 5.333\ldots \\ \hline 9n = 48 \end{array}$$

(4) $n = \dfrac{48}{9} = \dfrac{16}{3}$

so $n = 5.\overline{3} = \dfrac{16}{3} = 5\dfrac{1}{3}$

even though the odometer records distance that accurately. Instead, you may prefer to round off the odometer readings to the nearest mile.

Eliminating the decimal places beyond some desired level of accuracy is called *rounding off*. Rounding off takes into account the value of the digits beyond the desired point:

- If the first digit to be dropped is *less than 5*, it is dropped, along with all subsequent digits.
- If the first digit to be dropped is *greater than 5*, the last digit retained is increased by 1.

Examples.	*Odometer reading*	*Rounded off to the nearest mile*	*Rounded off to the nearest 10 miles*
	83,438.2	83,438	83,440
	56,721.9	56,722	56,720
	5,104.6	5,105	5,100

- If the first digit to be dropped is *equal to 5*, there is a convention to deal with the fact that the digit 5 is exactly in the middle:

   if the preceding digit is even, round down, keeping the last digit even;

   if the preceding digit is odd, round up, making the last digit even.

This way, in the long run, half the numbers get rounded up and half down.

Examples.   1.45 = 1.4 to the nearest tenth
1.55 = 1.6 to the nearest tenth

To find an answer to a desired level of accuracy, you usually carry the calculation to one more than the desired number of places and then round off to the desired place.

Example. $\frac{2}{11}$ = 0.18181818 . . .   = 0.182 to the nearest thousandth
= 0.18   to the nearest hundredth
= 0.2   to the nearest tenth

ARITHMETIC OPERATIONS WITH DECIMALS

Arithmetic operations are often simpler with decimal fractions than with common fractions. In fact, decimals may be treated in arithmetic operations exactly as if they were whole numbers. However, care must be taken to place the decimal point properly in the results.

Addition

To add decimal fractions, arrange the numbers to be added in a column so that all the decimal points are exactly lined up with one another. (Keeping the decimal points lined up means that tenths are in a column with tenths, hundredths are in a column with hundredths, and so on.) Then add the numbers exactly as if they were whole numbers. Place the decimal point in the sum directly below the decimal points in the numbers to be added.

Examples.

```
  0.50           1.25
  0.33           0.075
  0.25        + 13.1
  0.20          14.425
+ 0.17
  1.45
```

Numbers named by common fractions are often easier to add if they are expressed in decimal form.

Example. $\frac{1}{2} + \frac{1}{3} + \frac{1}{4} + \frac{1}{5} + \frac{1}{6}$

Adding as common fractions with a common denominator of 60:

$$\frac{1}{2} + \frac{1}{3} + \frac{1}{4} + \frac{1}{5} + \frac{1}{6}$$

$$= \frac{1 \times 30}{2 \times 30} + \frac{1 \times 20}{3 \times 20} + \frac{1 \times 15}{4 \times 15} + \frac{1 \times 12}{5 \times 12} + \frac{1 \times 10}{6 \times 10}$$

$$= \frac{30}{60} + \frac{20}{60} + \frac{15}{60} + \frac{12}{60} + \frac{10}{60}$$

$$= \frac{87}{60} = \frac{29}{20} = \left(20\overline{)29.00}^{\,1.45} \right)$$

```
 20
 ──
 90
 80
 ──
100
100
```

On the other hand, by converting to decimals (rounded off to two places where necessary):

$$\frac{1}{2} = 0.50$$
$$\frac{1}{3} = 0.33$$
$$\frac{1}{4} = 0.25$$
$$\frac{1}{5} = 0.20$$
$$+ \ \frac{1}{6} = 0.17$$
$$\overline{ 1.45}$$

Subtraction

To subtract decimal fractions, place the number to be subtracted under the other number, keeping the decimal points exactly in line. (Lining up the decimal points means that tenths are under tenths, hundredths are under hundredths, and so on.) If one of the numbers has fewer decimal places than the other, zeros may be added to the right of the last decimal place till that number has as many decimal places as the other. Then subtract as if the numbers were whole numbers. Place the decimal point in the difference directly below the decimal points in the given numbers.

Examples.
$$\begin{array}{r} 1.3 \\ -\ 0.5 \\ \hline 0.8 \end{array}
\qquad
\begin{array}{r} 1.3 \\ -\ 0.51 \\ \hline \end{array}
=
\begin{array}{r} 1.30 \\ -\ 0.51 \\ \hline 0.79 \end{array}$$

Multiplication

To multiply decimal fractions, arrange the numbers for multiplication and multiply them as if they were whole numbers. Count the total number of decimal places in both the numbers being multiplied. Place the decimal point in the product so that the number of digits to the right of the decimal point is equal to the total number of decimal places in the two numbers being multiplied.

Example. $2.7 \times 0.08 =$

$$\begin{array}{r} 2.7 \ \leftarrow 1 \text{ decimal place} \\ \times \ \ 0.08 \ \leftarrow 2 \text{ decimal places} \\ \hline 0.216 \ \leftarrow 3 \text{ decimal places} \end{array}$$

The same result could be obtained by writing the decimals as common fractions:

$$2.7 \times 0.08 = \frac{27}{10} \times \frac{8}{100} = \frac{216}{1000} = 0.216$$

$$\qquad\quad\ \uparrow \qquad \uparrow \qquad \uparrow$$
$$\qquad\quad 10^1 \quad\ 10^2 \quad\ 10^3$$

Division

Decimal fractions are most easily divided if the divisor is a whole number. If the divisor is not a whole number, multiply both the dividend (the number to be divided) *and* the divisor by a power of ten large enough to make the divisor a whole number. Arrange the divisor and dividend as usual for long division, and divide as if the numbers were whole numbers. Place the decimal point in the quotient (the result) directly above the decimal point in the dividend.

Example. $23.484 \div 5.7 = \dfrac{23.484}{5.7} = \dfrac{23.484 \times 10}{5.7 \times 10} = \dfrac{234.84}{57}$

$$
= 5.7)\overline{23.484} \quad\quad \begin{array}{r} 4.12 \\ \hline \end{array}
$$

```
        4.12
 = 5.7)23.484
        228
        ───
         6 8
         5 7
         ───
         1 14
         1 14
         ────
```

The same result could be obtained by writing the decimals as common fractions:

$$
\frac{23.484}{5.7} = \frac{\dfrac{23484}{1000}}{\dfrac{57}{10}} = \frac{23484}{1000} \times \frac{\cancel{10}^{\;1}}{57} = \frac{23484}{5700}
$$

```
           4.12
 5.700)23.48400
        22800
        ─────
          684 0
          570 0
          ─────
          114 00
          114 00
          ──────
```

HISTORY OF DECIMAL FRACTIONS

Babylonian clay tablets dating back to the twentieth century B.C. reveal that the Babylonians wrote fractions much the way we write decimal fractions. But the Babylonian NUMERAL SYSTEM was *sexagesimal* (based on powers of sixty) rather than decimal (based on powers of ten). So Babylonian numerals reading

$$
2\ 27\ 18 \quad \text{could mean} \quad 2 + \frac{27}{60} + \frac{18}{60^2}.
$$

The sexagesimal system was also later used by the ancient Greeks.

By the fifteenth century A.D., mathematicians in China, India, and Persia were using *decimal* fractions. Some European mathematicians may have studied the Oriental works. Medieval mathematicians used something like decimal fractions in computing square root tables. Nevertheless, the credit for introducing and popularizing the use of decimal fractions in Europe should probably go to three sixteenth-century mathematicians—François Viète of France, Simon Stevin of Belgium, and John Napier of Scotland.

In a mathematical treatise published in 1579, Viète strongly urged the use of decimal fractions instead of sexagesimal fractions. And he illustrated how this could be done by using decimal fractions throughout his book. Even more influential than Viète's work was a little book entitled *The Tenth,* published in 1585 by Simon Stevin. Stevin urged the use of decimal fractions on the grounds that they greatly simplified computation. He pointed out that decimal fractions could be added, subtracted, multiplied, and divided as easily as whole numbers.

However, neither Stevin nor Viète used the decimal point to separate the whole number from the fraction. At different places in Viète's work, he used various separators—a vertical bar between the whole number and fraction, a comma between the two, and smaller type for printing the fractions:

$$27|847 \qquad 27,847 \qquad 27^{847}.$$

Stevin employed a cumbersome notation that indicated the power of ten of the denominator for each digit of the fraction. For example, Stevin wrote the number 27.847 as

$$\overset{\textcircled{0}\textcircled{1}\textcircled{2}\textcircled{3}}{2\ 7\ 8\ 4\ 7} \qquad \text{or as} \qquad 27\ \textcircled{0}\ 8\ \textcircled{1}\ 4\ \textcircled{2}\ 7\ \textcircled{3}.$$

The mathematician who won acceptance for the decimal point was John Napier. Although Napier did not invent the decimal point, he used it throughout the English translation of his book on logarithms, *Descriptio,* published in 1616. Then in a book published the next year, he used a comma in place of a decimal point and instructed his readers that either a dot or a comma could be used to separate the decimal fraction from the whole number. Books on logarithms were eagerly read by both mathematicians and astronomers in the seventeenth century, and Napier's use of decimal fractions was important in introducing this form of writing fractions to a large number of readers.

However, the form for writing decimals has never been internationally standardized. In the United States, decimal fractions are written with a dot on the baseline—3.18. In Britain, decimals are written with a raised dot—3·18. In other European countries, such as France and Germany, a comma is used in place of a dot—3,18. And in the Scandinavian countries, the fractional part of a decimal number is written in smaller raised digits—3,^{18}.

Today, in addition to our decimal monetary system, the increasing use of the METRIC SYSTEM and the growing number of CALCULATORS and COMPUTERS make decimal fractions the most common form of fraction.

REFERENCES

Historical Topics for the Mathematics Classroom, 31st Yearbook of the National Council of Teachers of Mathematics (1969); historical material on Viète, Stevin, and Napier.

David Eugene Smith, *History of Mathematics, Volume II: Special Topics of Elementary Mathematics* (Ginn, 1925; Dover, 1958), pp. 228–247; more on the history of decimal fractions.

See also NUMERAL SYSTEMS, PERCENT, RATIONAL AND IRRATIONAL NUMBERS, REAL NUMBERS, SCIENTIFIC NOTATION, and SIGNIFICANT DIGITS.

DEDUCTION

DEDUCTION: the process of reasoning from statements accepted as true to reach a conclusion.

The statements accepted as true are called *premises*. A premise may be either a statement assumed to be true or a statement previously proved true. Deduction is the process of using LOGIC to show that if the premises are true, the conclusion must necessarily be true.

(premise)	**Example.** (1) Lisa is the oldest child in her family.
(premise)	(2) Mary is Lisa's sister.
(conclusion)	(3) Therefore, Lisa is older than Mary.

Deductive reasoning is sometimes called *a priori* reasoning, meaning "knowable without reference to experience." That is, a priori reasoning relies only on the logical structure of an argument, rather than on experience beyond the facts listed in the premises.

DEDUCTIVE REASONING

Sherlock Holmes, the fictional detective, is famous for making simple but remarkable deductions. To decode a message written entirely in stick figures, Holmes made deductions like the following:

(premise)	(1) The letter occurring most frequently in written English is "e."
(premise)	(2) The figure occurring most frequently in the stick-figure message is 入 .
(premise)	(3) The stick-figure message can be decoded into English.
(conclusion)	(4) Therefore, the figure 入 probably stands for "e."

The argument proceeds from a general statement about the English language to a particular statement about a particular code.

Not every attempt at deductive reasoning is correct. For instance, the following argument is *not* a proper deduction:

(1) All squares are rectangles.   (premise)
(2) Figure *ABCD* is a rectangle.   (premise)
(3) Therefore, *ABCD* is a square.   (conclusion)

This conclusion is false. Consider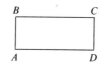

Where is the error in reasoning? Statements (1) and (2) are true, but conclusion (3) cannot logically be drawn from them. Conclusion (3) rests on a premise that is not given and is not true—that all rectangles are squares. Although all squares are rectangles, not all rectangles are squares.

A deductive argument in which the conclusion follows inescapably from the premises is said to be *valid*. In a valid deduction, if each of the premises is true, the conclusion is true. But if one of the premises is false, the conclusion may be true or false. This cannot be determined from the given premises.

Example.   (1) Anyone who is in the kitchen can hear the telephone   (premise)
                       when it rings.
                 (2) John is in the kitchen.   (premise)
                 (3) John can hear the telephone when it rings.   (conclusion)

If premise (2) is false, we cannot draw a conclusion. John may be in another room where he can still hear the phone, or he may be a hundred miles away.

How can you know whether a deduction is valid? You must examine the basic structure of an argument. You can turn to LOGIC for assistance. With logic you can strip away distracting detail and see more easily which types of argument are valid deductions.

DEDUCTIVE REASONING IN A MATHEMATICAL SYSTEM

Mathematics is sometimes referred to as a deductive science, because the reasoning of mathematics shows clearly that certain results follow logically from certain premises.

In a MATHEMATICAL SYSTEM, however, it is necessary to start with a few basic or general premises that are not proved true but rather are assumed true. These basic assumptions are called *axioms,* and a logical system based on a set of axioms is called an *axiomatic system.* Furthermore, deductive reasoning in mathematics is sometimes called *axiomatic reasoning* because every mathematical system must be built on a set of axioms.

The conclusions that are proved by deduction in a mathematical system are called *theorems.* Theorems are proved from the axioms, and then the proved theorems, together with the axioms, are used to prove new theorems.

Example of a Deductive Proof

The following theorem arises in plane GEOMETRY:

It is possible to construct, using only compass and straight-edge, an equilateral TRIANGLE on a given straight-line segment.

Given: a straight-line segment *AB*.   A●————●B

Proof:

(1) Construct circle *A* having *A* as center and *AB* as radius.
(by axiom: a circle may be constructed from any center with any radius)

(2) Construct circle *B* having *B* as center and *AB* as radius.
(by same axiom)

(3) From point *E* where these two circles intersect, draw straight lines *AE* and *BE*.
(by axiom: a straight line may be drawn from any point to any other point)

(4) $AB = AE$
(by definition of circle: all radii are equal)

(5) $AB = BE$
(by same definition)

(6) $AE = BE$
(by axiom: things equal to the same thing are equal to each other)

(7) Therefore, $\triangle ABE$ is equilateral, and it is constructed on given line segment *AB*.
(conclusion, because $AB = AE = BE$)

INDIRECT DEDUCTION

Deductive reasoning may also be done *indirectly.* Mathematical logic assumes that a statement is either *true* or, if not true, *false;* no "maybe" is allowed. Therefore, it is sometimes possible to prove a statement true by proving its opposite, or negative, false. This is done by proving that *the negative statement leads to a contradiction,* that is, by proving that the negative of the desired conclusion leads to a contradiction of a premise. Hence, this indirect reasoning process is often called *reductio ad absurdum*, the Latin phrase for "reduction to the absurd."

Example.

(1) Jessie and David are the same age.	(premise)
(2) David and Sarah are *not* the same age.	(premise)
Prove that Sarah and Jessie are not the same age.	(desired conclusion)
(3) Assume that Sarah and Jessie *are* the same age.	(assumption of negative of conclusion)
(4) Then, by (1), David and Sarah must be the same age, which contradicts (2).	(contradiction of premise)
(5) Therefore, (3) is false, which means that Sarah and Jessie are *not* the same age.	(conclusion)

PARADOXES

A paradox occurs when apparently valid deductive reasoning leads to a contradiction of a fact or premise.

Zeno, a Greek philosopher of the fifth century B.C., proposed a famous paradox concerning a race between Achilles, the legendary Greek hero, and a tortoise. When the race begins, the tortoise is given a head start. Zeno asked whether Achilles would ever overtake the tortoise. He pointed out that by the time Achilles reaches the tortoise's starting point, the tortoise will have moved ahead to a new point. When Achilles gets to this second point, the tortoise will again have moved ahead, although by a shorter distance. The tortoise, though slow, moves steadily forward. Therefore, although the distance between Achilles and the tortoise will be getting smaller and smaller, according to Zeno, the tortoise will nevertheless always be ahead.

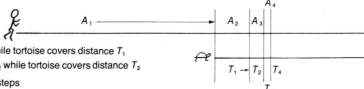

First step: Achilles runs distance A_1 while tortoise covers distance T_1
Second step: Achilles runs distance A_2 while tortoise covers distance T_2
... and so on, for an *infinite number* of steps
During each step, while Achilles is catching up, the tortoise is moving ahead

It is evident that in reality the speedy Achilles can overtake the creeping tortoise, but where is the error in reasoning? Why does Zeno's conclusion contradict this obvious fact? The error is in the hidden assumption that an infinite amount of time is required to cover a distance divided into an infinite number of segments. That assumption is false. The time intervals t_1, t_2, t_3, ... , that are required for Achilles to run the distances A_1, A_2, A_3, ... form an infinite SEQUENCE, which may nevertheless have a finite sum. The details of this resolution of Zeno's paradox can be shown by CALCULUS.

In the twentieth century, the English philosopher Bertrand Russell proposed the following "barber paradox":

> The only barber of a village posts a notice that while, of course, he does not shave those who shave themselves, he does shave all those people who do not shave themselves. Then one day as the barber stands in front of the mirror shaving himself, he realizes that his advertisement places him in an impossible dilemma: if he shaves himself, then he should not be shaved by the barber; yet if he does not shave himself, he, the barber, must shave himself!

This is a variation on a more general paradox:

> If all sets are separated into two types: those that contain themselves, and those that do not, then what about the set of all sets that are not members of themselves? The set of all sets that are not members of themselves *is* a member of the set of all sets that do *not* include themselves, but this membership makes it at the same time a member of a set that includes itself.

Contradictions like these two paradoxes have not been resolved by mathematicians except by avoiding such classifications. For further discussion of paradoxes and the trouble they bring to the foundations of mathematics, see MATHEMATICAL SYSTEMS.

REFERENCES

Harold R. Jacobs, *Geometry* (W. H. Freeman & Co., 1974), especially pp. 1–67 on the nature of deductive reasoning.

References on logical paradoxes

Morris Kline, *Mathematics in Western Culture* (Oxford University Press, 1953; Galaxy paperback), Ch. XXV, "Paradoxes of the Infinite."

W. V. Quine, "Paradox," *Scientific American,* April 1962; reprinted in *Mathematics in the Modern World: Readings from Scientific American* (W. H. Freeman & Co., 1968), pp. 200–208; a most thorough discussion.

References on Zeno's four paradoxes

Eric T. Bell, *Men of Mathematics* (Simon & Schuster, 1937; Fireside paperback), pp. 24–25.

Carl B. Boyer, *A History of Mathematics* (John Wiley & Sons, 1968), pp. 82–84.

Morris Kline, *Mathematical Thought from Ancient to Modern Times* (Oxford University Press, 1972), pp. 34–37.

References on decoding

Sir Arthur Conan Doyle, *The Return of Sherlock Holmes* (McClure & Co., 1905; numerous later editions), ''The Adventure of the Dancing Men.''

Martin Gardner, *Codes, Ciphers and Secret Writing* (Simon & Schuster, 1972); how to crack codes, how to construct hard-to-break ciphers, lots of ways to send secret messages.

Harold R. Jacobs, *Mathematics as a Human Endeavor* (W. H. Freeman & Co., 1970), pp. 399–405; includes wartime codes.

David Kahn, *The Codebreakers* (Macmillan, 1967); over 1000 pages of fascinating history—the classic and comprehensive reference on decoding.

Collections of deductive puzzles

Oswald Jacoby, *Mathematics for Pleasure* (McGraw-Hill; Fawcett paperback, 1962); 150 entertaining brainteasers.

Raymond M. Smullyan, *What Is the Name of This Book? The Riddle of Dracula and Other Logical Puzzles* (Prentice-Hall, 1978); a most entertaining course in logic and paradoxes, ending up in the heart of twentieth-century breakthroughs in the foundations of mathematics.

Dozens of other excellent deductive puzzle books are published by Dover Publications, 180 Varick St., New York, NY 10014. You can write for a current list of Mathematical Recreations.

See LOGIC for more on formal deductive reasoning, including references.

See INDUCTION for another kind of reasoning.

See also MATHEMATICAL SYSTEMS and PROOFS.

For other examples of deductive proofs, see PYTHAGOREAN THEOREM, the explanation of the VOLUME of a pyramid, the uncountability of the REAL NUMBERS.

DEFINITIONS

DEFINITION: a statement that gives the meaning of a word or symbol in terms that have been previously defined or accepted as undefined.

Example. A triangle = a figure formed by the three straight line segments joining three points not in a straight line.

A good definition of "triangle" should enable the person who reads and understands it to know whether something is a triangle or not. In this respect, a mathematical definition is not too different from the definitions you find in an ordinary dictionary. In more formal terms, a mathematician would say that a good definition of any concept x should enable a reader to separate the world into two mutually exclusive categories—things that are x and things that are not x.

However, in other respects, formal mathematical definitions often differ from the definitions found in a dictionary. A conventional dictionary definition may give several meanings of a single word. But a mathematical definition usually gives exactly *one* meaning of the word, symbol, or operation being defined. Even when different mathematical definitions of the same term are used, they are generally mathematically equivalent.

Example.

Ordinary definition

A relation =
(1) a narration; a recital or telling; an account
(2) a relative; a kinsman or kinswoman
(3) a connection; a relationship

Mathematical definition

A relation = a set of ordered pairs

144

A mathematical definition is *precise*. Mathematical precision requires that there be no possible ambiguity. The following illustrates an ambiguity that allows an unintended meaning.

Example.   This definition is *not* precise:

A triangle = a figure formed by the intersection of three straight line segments in three distinct points.

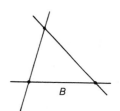

This definition allows figures *A* and *B* each to be called a triangle, whereas only figure *A* represents a conventional mathematical triangle.

Ideally, a mathematical definition is worded so carefully that there is exactly one meaning. Precise definitions are essential to any MATHEMATICAL SYSTEM.

Another difference between mathematical definitions and those found in an ordinary dictionary is that dictionary definitions tend to be circular, whereas mathematical definitions must be *noncircular*. If you look up the word "weary" in a dictionary, you may find that it means "tired." If you look up "tired," you may find that it means "fatigued." And if you look up "fatigued," you may find that it means "weary." These three definitions go round in a circle. And any dictionary that defines every word in terms of other words in the dictionary is bound to be circular. Indeed, the main reason our dictionaries are helpful is that we already know a great number of words before we ever consult one. Can you imagine trying to learn the meaning of, say, a Finnish word using only a Finnish dictionary?

In order to avoid circularity in mathematical definitions, modern mathematicians have come to the conclusion that *not every term can be defined*. Consider "point" and "line." How can you define them? If you were to say that a point is the intersection of two lines and that a line is what connects two points, you would certainly have circularity. If you were to define point as that which has no length or breadth, and line as that which has no breadth, then you would have to define "length" and "breadth," and you would no doubt come full circle very quickly by this route as well.

Thus, some basic terms, called *primitives*, must be left *undefined*, and then other terms can be defined in terms of them. Some terms in mathematics that may be used as primitives are, in geometry: POINT, LINE, and PLANE; in set theory: SET; in number theory: NUMBER.

PROPERTIES OF A MATHEMATICAL DEFINITION

- A mathematical definition must be stated *only in terms that have previously been defined or accepted as undefined*.

Example. A relation = a *set* of *ordered pairs*.

undefined term or primitive

previously defined

This requirement assures that the definition is noncircular.

- A mathematical definition must be *consistent* with previously accepted axioms and with other definitions.

Example. A *fractional exponent* is defined to be consistent with the laws of EXPONENTS. The law for multiplication says that to multiply two terms with a common base, you add the exponents.

$$a^2 \times a^3 = a^{(2 + 3)} = a^5$$

According to this law

$$a^{\frac{1}{2}} \times a^{\frac{1}{2}} = a^1 \text{ or } a$$

But any term that when multiplied by itself gives a as the product must equal $\sqrt{a}$. Therefore, $a^{\frac{1}{2}}$ must be defined to be $\sqrt{a}$.

- In a mathematical definition, the term being defined and the defining phase should be *interchangeable*.

Example. If a triangle = a figure formed by the three straight-line segments joining three points not in a straight line,

then a figure formed by the three straight-line segments joining three points not in a straight line = a triangle.

This requirement assures that the definition is precise.

- A mathematical definition must be *restrictive;* it must define exactly the term in question and not a more general term.

Example. This definition is *not* restrictive enough:

> A square = a four-sided plane figure with all four sides equal.

The definition does not distinguish a square from a rhombus.

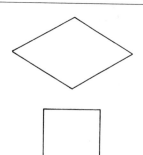

The following definition is restrictive to a square:

> A square = a four-sided plane figure with all four sides equal and meeting in right angles.

- A mathematical definition should be *concise*. In order to achieve *simplicity* (sometimes called *elegance*), mathematicians prefer to state definitions in as few terms as possible. Usually no condition that is implied by the other conditions is added to a definition.

Example. A triangle = a closed plane figure having three sides and three angles, that is formed by the three straight-line segments joining three points not in a straight line.

Since the definition requires joining three points not in a straight line, the figure can only be a closed plane figure with three sides and three angles.

The requirement that mathematical definitions be concise is not as important as the other requirements. Occasionally in the interests of clarity a condition implied by the other conditions is added to a definition.

HISTORY

One of the great achievements of Euclid, the Greek geometer of around 300 B.C., and his contemporaries was to recognize that in a MATHEMATICAL SYSTEM, not every statement can be proved. Certain basic propositions, called *axioms* (or *postulates*), have to be assumed, that is, accepted without proof. Then these axioms and a set of definitions can be used to prove other propositions. Without axioms, every proposition would have to be proved in terms of some other proposition, and the result would be circular reasoning.

Although Euclid recognized the need for axioms, he did not recognize the similar need for undefined terms. Euclid attempted to define all terms including "point," "line," and "plane." However, his definitions made use of such terms as "part," "length," and "breadth," which were not explicitly defined.

It was not until the nineteenth century that mathematicians came to realize that undefined terms are to definitions what axioms are to proofs. These *primitives* provide a starting point that keeps all the other definitions from being circular. Once it became clear that undefined terms were necessary, mathematicians agreed on the few basic terms that would remain undefined in each mathematical system; then they arrived at logically precise definitions of the remaining terms.

REFERENCE

Imre Lakatos, *Proofs and Refutations* (Cambridge University Press, 1976); an amusing discussion, in the form of a dialogue, about the difficulties of formulating a precise definition of "polyhedron."

For related articles, see MATHEMATICAL SYSTEMS and PROOFS.

EQUATIONS

EQUATION: a mathematical sentence in which two expressions are connected by a symbol of equality; a symbolic statement that two mathematical expressions represent the same quantity.

Mathematical sentences, like the sentences that you read and write every day, are used to communicate ideas. However, in a mathematical sentence, symbols are used instead of words. In writing a mathematical sentence, you use symbols to represent numbers, symbols to express relations between numbers, and symbols to represent arithmetic operations. A mathematical sentence can be either an *equation* or an IN-EQUALITY.

A mathematical sentence may be true or it may be false or it may be neither true nor false.

Examples. $4 + 3 = 7$ (Four plus three equals seven.)   (True)
$4 + 3 = 8$ (Four plus three equals eight.)   (False)

These sentences are called *closed* because they are either always true or always false.

$x + 5 = 12$ (The sum of a number, represented by x, and five is equal to twelve.)   (Neither true nor false)

This sentence is called *open* because it may be either true or false, depending on what number is substituted for the *variable x*. If $x = 7$, the sentence is true. If x is equal to any number other than 7, the sentence is false.

An *identity* is an equation that is always true. When an identity contains one or more variables, the equation must be true no matter what numbers are substituted for the variables. Although the equal sign,

=, is often used to state an identity, there is a special identity sign, ≡ (read as "identically equal").

Examples of identities.

$4 + 2 \equiv 1 + 5$

$1 + x \equiv x + 1$ True for *any* value of x.

$(a + b)^2 \equiv a^2 + 2ab + b^2$ True, for *any* values of a and b.
For example, if $a = 3$ and $b = 4$, then
$$(3 + 4)^2 = 3^2 + 2 \times 3 \times 4 + 4^2$$
$$7^2 = 9 + 24 + 16$$
$$49 = 49$$

SOLUTION OF OPEN SENTENCES

The number or numbers that make an open sentence true are called *solutions,* or *roots.* The SET of all roots of an open sentence is called the *solution set,* or *truth set.*

Examples.

$3y = 24$ The only solution is $y = 8$, because $3 \times 8 = 24$. The solution set is $\{8\}$.

$x^2 - 5x + 6 = 0$ There are two values of x that make this equation a true sentence: $x = 2$ and $x = 3$. The solution set is $\{2, 3\}$.

Solving a sentence means finding the number, or numbers, if any, that make the open sentence true—this usually requires techniques of ALGEBRA. The method of solving an equation depends upon the type of equation and the number of variables.

CLASSIFICATION OF POLYNOMIAL EQUATIONS BY DEGREE

Equations in One Variable

The *degree* of an equation in one variable is equal to the greatest EXPONENT of the variable.

Terms and examples.

Linear, or first degree: $2x - 5 = 7$

Quadratic, or second degree: $x^2 - 5x + 6 = 0$

Cubic, or third degree: $2x^3 - x^2 - 7x + 6 = 0$

Quartic (or *biquadratic*), or fourth degree: $x^4 - 17x^2 + 16 = 0$

Polynomial, or *n*th degree, for $n = $ any integer.

The linear, quadratic, cubic, and quartic equations are polynomial equations of first, second, third, and fourth degrees, respectively.

A polynomial is said to be in *standard form* when the terms are arranged in descending powers of the variable, with the constant term at the end, as in the examples.

Equations in Two Variables

The degree of a sentence in two variables is equal to the highest *sum* of exponents of the variables that appear in one term.

For example, $7xy$ is a second degree term, because the sum of the exponents of x and y is $1 + 1$, or 2. And $7xy^2$ is a third degree term because the sum of the exponents of x and y is $1 + 2$, or 3.

Terms and examples.

Linear, or first degree: $x + y = 7$

Quadratic, or second degree: $y = 3x^2 + 4$ $xy = 12$

SOLVING AN EQUATION IN ONE VARIABLE

Linear Equations

The basic principle in solving a linear equation in one variable is to add, subtract, multiply, or divide both sides of the equation by the same number until the variable is *isolated* on one side of the equation.

Example. $2x - 5 = 7$

Add 5 to both sides of the equation, in order to isolate the term with x.

$2x - 5 + 5 = 7 + 5$

$2x \qquad = 12$

Divide both sides of the equation by 2, in order to obtain x alone.

$$\frac{2x}{2} = \frac{12}{2}$$

$x = 6$ Solution, or root.

Quadratic Equations

There are several different methods of solving quadratic equations in one variable. The method illustrated here is the use of a formula that can be applied to any quadratic equation.

In order to solve a quadratic equation by the formula, you must first write the equation in the following *standard form:*

$$ax^2 + bx + c = 0 \text{ where } a \text{ is the coefficient of } x^2 \ (a \neq 0),$$
$$b \text{ is the coefficient of } x, \text{ and}$$
$$c \text{ is the constant term.}$$

Then, as any standard algebra text will show, the solutions are given by the *quadratic formula:*

$$x = \frac{-b \pm \sqrt{b^2 - 4ac}}{2a} \quad \text{where the } \pm \text{ symbol is read ''plus or minus.''}$$

Generally there will be two solutions to every quadratic equation—one using the plus sign, the other using the minus sign.

Example.   Find the roots of the equation $x^2 + 6x = 7$. In order to solve this equation, you must first put it in standard form. Then you will be able to find values for a, b, and c and use the quadratic formula.

First arrange the terms in standard order

$$x^2 + 6x - 7 = 0;$$

then match the coefficients and constants of this equation with a, b, and c as given above:

the coefficient of x^2 is 1, so $a = 1$;
the coefficient of x is 6, so $b = 6$;
the constant term is -7, so $c = -7$.

Then these values for a, b, and c may be substituted into the quadratic formula:

$$x = \frac{-b \pm \sqrt{b^2 - 4ac}}{2a}$$

$$= \frac{-(6) \pm \sqrt{6^2 - 4 \times 1 \times (-7)}}{2 \times 1}$$

$$= \frac{-6 \pm \sqrt{36 + 28}}{2}$$

$$= \frac{-6 \pm \sqrt{64}}{2}$$

$$= \frac{-6 \pm 8}{2}$$

$$= \frac{-6 + 8}{2} \quad \text{or} \quad \frac{-6 - 8}{2}$$

$$= \frac{2}{2} \qquad = \frac{-14}{2}$$

$$= 1 \qquad = -7$$

The roots of the equation are 1 and -7. You can check that either of these answers does indeed satisfy the original equation by substituting them for x in $x^2 + 6x = 7$.

Other Equations in One Variable

For a detailed discussion of methods of solving polynomial equations beyond the linear and the quadratic and for solving equations that are not polynomials at all, you should consult an algebra textbook. However, you can often attack such a problem without any formal algebra. Sometimes when you confront an equation for which you have no method, you can find at least one solution by "inspection," or guessing.

Example. Solve $x^3 - x = 0$.

Can you guess a solution? Can you guess another solution? Yet another?

There are three roots to this equation: $x = 0$, $x = 1$, and $x = -1$.

A helpful bit of information about polynomial equations is that the number of different roots to any given equation cannot be greater than the degree of equation. Hence, in this example you can rest assured that there are no more than three different solutions.

SOLVING AN EQUATION IN TWO VARIABLES

If a single equation involves two variables, x and y, there may be an infinite number of (x, y) pairs of numbers that will satisfy the equation. For example, given the equation $x + y = 7$, you could make an endless list of (x, y) pairs that would have a sum of 7. In fact, you could make a GRAPH in a rectangular COORDINATE system that would show an infinite number of possible solutions to this equation.

Example. $x + y = 7$

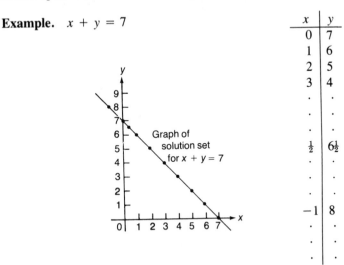

x	y
0	7
1	6
2	5
3	4
.	.
.	.
.	.
$\frac{1}{2}$	$6\frac{1}{2}$
.	.
.	.
-1	8
.	.
.	.

Graph of solution set for $x + y = 7$

SOLVING SIMULTANEOUS EQUATIONS

A *pair* of equations in two variables, even if each single equation has an infinite number of solutions, may have an infinite number of solutions *or* a finite number of solutions *or* no solution at all.

Such a pair of equations is called a *system* of *simultaneous equations,* because two different conditions are put upon the same two variables at the same time.

Example. Find two numbers whose sum is 7 and whose difference is 1. This is equivalent to the following system:

$$x + y = 7 \quad \text{and} \quad x - y = 1.$$

The solution set is the single pair $x = 4$, $y = 3$.

One way to solve such a system of equations is *algebraically.*

Example. This system can be solved by adding the equations:

$$\begin{array}{r} x + y = 7 \\ x - y = 1 \\ \hline 2x \quad\;\; = 8 \\ x = 4 \end{array}$$

Now $x = 4$ can be substituted into the first equation, giving $4 + y = 7$. The solution is $y = 3$. The solution of the system is the ordered pair $(4, 3)$.

Another approach to simultaneous equations is *geometric*. Remember that any single equation in two variables can be graphed on a rectangular coordinate system. The *solution* of two simultaneous equations will be the *intersection* of their graphs.

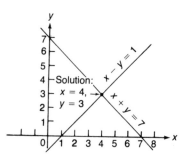

Example. $x + y = 7$

$x - y = 1$

One solution—a single point.

A system of equations that has no solution is one for which the graphs of the equations do not intersect.

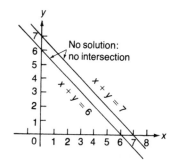

Example. $x + y = 7$

$x + y = 6$

No solution—graphs do not intersect.

A system of equations that has an infinite number of solutions is one for which the two equations have the same graph.

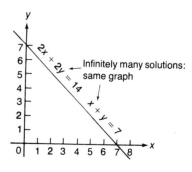

Example. $x + y = 7$

$2x + 2y = 14$

Infinite number of solutions—all points on the line.

A system of equations need not be linear. You can still use graphs to analyze the number of solutions.

Example. $x + y = 2$

$x^2 + y^2 = 4$

Two solutions—two points of intersection.
The graph of the second equation is a circle—see GRAPHS.

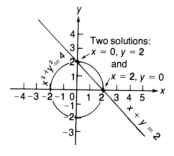

HISTORY OF SOLVING EQUATIONS

When you use the standard techniques for solving equations, they seem so clear and logical that you might think they were fairly easy to discover. The truth is, though, that the methods and symbols used to solve equations were gradually developed over a period of centuries.

The earliest attempts at solving problems that today would be solved as algebraic equations were written out in words instead of in symbols. The method of stating and solving the problem in words has been called the *rhetorical* approach. It was used by Babylonian mathematicians nearly four thousand years ago to solve many problems, including some quadratic equations. The Babylonians did not have a general method of solving such problems. Instead, they had various specific examples worked out, and they used these examples rather like recipes for solving other problems.

Most early Greek mathematicians approached problems using geometry rather than algebra. They were able to solve a number of problems, but the geometric approach was cumbersome and time-consuming. Other Greeks solved problems rhetorically, using ALGEBRA but writing out the problem and the solution in words.

However, in the third century A.D., a Greek mathematician named Diophantus introduced the idea of abbreviating the statement of an equation by replacing some of the words and phrases with symbols. Nevertheless, Diophantus' algebra was still largely rhetorical. And his idea of using symbols to state and solve equations was ignored until the sixteenth century.

Meanwhile, one of the earliest descriptions of how to solve an equation by performing the same operation on both sides of the equation appeared in A.D. 825 in a famous book by the Arabian mathematician Al-Khowarizmi. The title was *Hisab al-jabr w' al muqabalah,* and it is from this title that our word ''algebra'' (*al-jabr*) is derived. Unlike Diophantus, Al-Khowarizmi used no symbols. His algebra was completely rhetorical, yet he gave a clear and thorough exposition of how to solve both linear and quadratic equations. He solved quadratic, or second degree, equations by completing the square, the method by which the quadratic formula is derived.

In the twelfth century, the *Hisab-al-jabr* was translated into Latin by Leonardo of Pisa, an Italian mathematician also known as Fibonacci. The translation of Al-Khowarizmi's work gave European mathematicians a general method of solving quadratic equations, but it was not until the sixteenth century that general methods were discovered for solving cubic (third-degree) and quartic (fourth-degree) equations.

There was much competition among Italian mathematicians to solve the general cubic equation. At the heart of the story are Antonio Fior and Niccolo Fontana, who was nicknamed Tartaglia, the stutterer. Fior had been taught by his teacher, Scipione del Ferro, how to solve a cubic equation of the form $x^3 + mx = n$. Tartaglia claimed that he too could solve such an equation, and Fior challenged him to a contest. Shortly before the contest Tartaglia discovered how to solve a cubic equation of the form $x^3 + px^2 = n$, and since Fior could not solve both types, Tartaglia was the winner.

After the contest, Girolamo Cardano, another Italian, wheedled Tartaglia's secret method from him by promising never to reveal it. Eventually, though, Cardano published the method, leading to another dispute. Today it is generally believed that the solving of the general cubic equation was the result of the work of several mathematicians.

A method of solving the general quartic equation was discovered by one of Cardano's pupils, Lodovico Ferrari. The general solutions to both the cubic and quartic equations were published by Cardano in 1545 in his *Ars Magna*. Cardano considered not only the positive rational solutions to equations but the negative and irrational roots as well.

François Viète, a French mathematician of the sixteenth century, provided the last giant step toward the use of modern symbolic notation. Previous notations had used entirely different letters for x^3 and x^2. For example, Diophantus had used κ^γ and Δ^γ. Viète, though, used the *same* letter to represent the variable and added another symbol to stand for the power of the variable: AC for A cubum, or A^3, and AQ for A quadratum, or A^2. Viète was also the first to use letters as coefficients before variables, as in $ax^2 + bx + c$, and he introduced $+$ and $-$ signs, although he never used a sign for equality.

Solutions to third and fourth degree equations were discovered in the sixteenth century, but the problem of the general quintic (fifth degree) equation continued to plague mathematicians. Finally, early in the nineteenth century, an Italian physician, Paolo Ruffini, and a Norwegian mathematician, Niels Abel, each independently proved the impossibility of a general solution to polynomial equations of degree higher than four.

But though not all higher degree equations can be solved algebraically, some can. In 1831, a young French mathematician, Evariste Galois, was able to classify those that can be solved by means of the concept of *group* (see ARITHMETIC). Unfortunately, Galois was unable to develop his theory further; he was killed in a duel the following year at the age of twenty-one. Nevertheless, group theory has been studied by other prominent mathematicians and is today an important topic of higher mathematics.

The slow development of modern concise algebraic notation is illustrated by the following table. Each entry represents the equation $x^2 - 6x = 20$.

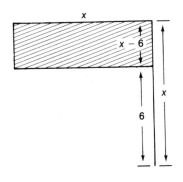

Babylonians (about 1700 B.C.)

"I have multiplied equal length and width, thus obtaining area. Then I subtracted from the area six times the length: twenty. Required: length."

$$(x \text{ times } x - 6 \text{ times } x = 20)$$

Euclid (300 B.C.)

"If a certain straight line be diminished by six, the rectangle contained by the whole and the diminished segment is equal to twenty."

$$(x \,(x - 6) = 20)$$

Diophantus (about A.D. 250)

$Δ^γ \bigwedge ςⓢ \quad \text{ἐστι} \quad κ$

$$(x^2 - x6 \quad = \quad 20)$$

Al-Khowarizmi (A.D. 850)

"What must be the amount of a square, which, when six roots of that square are subtracted from it, becomes equivalent to twenty?"

$$(x^2 - 6x = 20)$$

Cardano (1545)

"quadratum m 6 rebus aequalis 20"

$$(x^2 \quad - 6 \quad x \quad = \quad 20)$$

Viète (1591)

"1AQ − 6A aequatur 20"

$$(x^2 \quad - 6x \quad = \quad 20)$$

REFERENCES

Historical Topics for the Mathematics Classroom, 31st Yearbook of the National Council of Teachers of Mathematics (1969), pp. 233–256 and 260–263; much more detail on notation and methods of solving equations.

Biographical references

Eric T. Bell, *Men of Mathematics* (Simon & Schuster, 1937; Fireside paperback), Ch. 20, "Genius and Stupidity: Galois," pp. 362–377.

Richard W. Feldmann, "The Cardano–Tartaglia Dispute," *Mathematics Teacher,* March 1961, pp. 160–163.

Oystein Ore, *Cardano: The Gambling Scholar* (Princeton University Press, 1953; Dover, 1965).

The history of solving equations is discussed from a different perspective under ALGEBRA and HISTORY.

For other mathematical sentences and how to solve them, see INEQUALITIES. For equations of a line, see SLOPE. For examples of equations of curves, see GRAPHS.

See also FUNCTIONS, RELATIONS, and PROPERTIES OF EQUALITY.

EXPONENTS

EXPONENT: a number or symbol that is placed to the upper right of another number or symbol called the *base,* and that denotes in mathematical shorthand certain ARITHMETIC OPERATIONS to be performed on the base.

Example. 2^5 represents a *product.* The *exponent* 5 indicates that the *base* 2 is to be used as a FACTOR 5 times.

$$2^5 = 2 \times 2 \times 2 \times 2 \times 2 = 32$$

The product of this repeated multiplication is called a *power;* for example, 32 is the fifth power of 2. The word "power" is also used to refer to the exponent; 2 to the fifth power equals 32.

POSITIVE EXPONENT

An exponent that is a *positive whole number n* indicates a *product* in which the base is used as a factor n times.

$$b^n = \underbrace{b \cdot b \cdot b \ldots}_{n \text{ factors}}$$

Examples. $8^3 = 8 \times 8 \times 8 = 512$

$x^4 = x \cdot x \cdot x \cdot x$

$(a + b)^2 = (a + b) \cdot (a + b) = a^2 + 2ab + b^2$

$5^1 = 5$ (Note that an expression without an exponent could be rewritten with an exponent of 1; for example, $7 = 7^1$.)

NEGATIVE EXPONENT

An exponent that is a *negative number* indicates that a *reciprocal* is to be taken:

b^{-n} is the reciprocal of b^n; that is, $b^{-n} = \dfrac{1}{b^n}$

159

$$b^{-n} = \frac{1}{b^n}$$

Examples.

$$8^{-3} = \frac{1}{8^3} = \frac{1}{8 \cdot 8 \cdot 8} = \frac{1}{512}$$

$$x^{-4} = \frac{1}{x^4} = \frac{1}{x \cdot x \cdot x \cdot x}$$

$$(a + b)^{-2} = \frac{1}{(a + b)^2} = \frac{1}{(a + b) \cdot (a + b)} = \frac{1}{a^2 + 2ab + b^2}$$

$$5^{-1} = \frac{1}{5}$$

FRACTIONAL EXPONENT

$$b^{\frac{1}{n}} = \sqrt[n]{b}$$

An exponent that is a *positive unit fraction* (fraction with a numerator of 1) indicates that a *root* of the base is to be extracted. The *n*th *root* of the base is a number that when used as factor *n* times gives a product equal to the base. For example, the fourth root of 81 is 3 because $3 \times 3 \times 3 \times 3 = 81$. This can be expressed symbolically either as $\sqrt[4]{81} = 3$ or as $81^{\frac{1}{4}} = 3$.

Examples. $8^{\frac{1}{3}} = \sqrt[3]{8} = 2$

$$x^{\frac{1}{4}} = \sqrt[4]{x}$$

$$(a + b)^{\frac{1}{2}} = \sqrt[2]{a + b}$$

A *positive fractional exponent* in which *the numerator is not equal to 1* indicates that *two operations* are to be performed—extracting a root and raising to a power.

$$b^{\frac{m}{n}} = b^{(\frac{1}{n})m} = (\sqrt[n]{b})^m$$

The denominator of the fractional exponent indicates what root is to be extracted from the base. The numerator of the fraction indicates how many times this root is to be used as a factor.

Examples. $8^{\frac{2}{3}} = (\sqrt[3]{8})^2 = 2^2 = 4$

$$x^{\frac{3}{4}} = (\sqrt[4]{x})^3$$

In these examples, the root is first extracted and then the result is raised to a power. However, reversing the operations would not change the results, because it is also true that

$$b^{\frac{m}{n}} = b^{m(\frac{1}{n})} = \sqrt[n]{b^m}$$

Examples. $8^{\frac{2}{3}} = \sqrt[3]{8^2} = \sqrt[3]{64} = 4$

$$x^{\frac{3}{4}} = \sqrt[4]{x^3}$$

An exponent that is a *negative unit fraction* also indicates that two operations are to be performed—taking a root and taking a reciprocal.

Examples. $8^{-\frac{1}{3}} = \dfrac{1}{8^{\frac{1}{3}}} = \dfrac{1}{\sqrt[3]{8}} = \dfrac{1}{2}$

$$x^{-\frac{1}{4}} = \dfrac{1}{x^{\frac{1}{4}}} = \dfrac{1}{\sqrt[4]{x}}$$

Finally, a *negative fractional exponent* in which *the numerator is not 1* indicates that *three operations* are to be performed—raising to a power, extracting a root, and taking a reciprocal.

Example. $8^{-\frac{2}{3}} = \dfrac{1}{8^{\frac{2}{3}}} = \dfrac{1}{\sqrt[3]{8^2}} = \dfrac{1}{4}$

Decimal Exponents

At first glance, the expression $32^{0.6}$ may look quite forbidding. However, the exponent 0.6 is simply a DECIMAL fraction, that can be rewritten as a common fraction: $0.6 = \frac{6}{10} = \frac{3}{5}$. And the definitions for fractional exponents have been given.

Example. $32^{0.6} = 32^{\frac{3}{5}}$
$$= (32^{\frac{1}{5}})^3$$
$$= (\sqrt[5]{32})^3$$
$$= 2^3$$
$$= 8$$

ZERO EXPONENT

$$\boxed{b^0 = 1}$$

A zero exponent for any nonzero base denotes a result equal to 1.

Examples. $8^0 = 1$
$$x^0 = 1$$
$$(a + b)^0 = 1$$

LAWS OF EXPONENTS

Multiplication

$$\boxed{b^m b^n = b^{m+n}}$$

To multiply two expressions with the same base, retain the common base and add the exponents together.

Examples.

$$5^6 \cdot 5^2 = 5^{6+2} = 5^8 \quad [\text{Note: } (5 \cdot 5 \cdot 5 \cdot 5 \cdot 5 \cdot 5) \cdot (5 \cdot 5) = 5^8]$$

$$x^{\frac{1}{4}} \cdot x^{\frac{1}{2}} = x^{\frac{1}{4}+\frac{1}{2}} = x^{\frac{3}{4}}$$

$$(a + b)^3 \cdot (a + b)^1 = (a + b)^4$$

Division

$$\boxed{\frac{b^m}{b^n} = b^{m-n}}$$

To divide one expression by another with the same base, retain the common base and subtract the exponent of the divisor from the exponent of the dividend.

Examples.

$$\frac{5^6}{5^2} = 5^{6-2} = 5^4 \quad [\text{Note: } \frac{5 \cdot 5 \cdot 5 \cdot 5 \cdot 5 \cdot 5}{5 \cdot 5} = 5 \cdot 5 \cdot 5 \cdot 5 = 5^4]$$

$$\frac{x^{\frac{1}{2}}}{x^{\frac{1}{4}}} = x^{\frac{1}{2}-\frac{1}{4}} = x^{\frac{1}{4}}$$

$$\frac{(a + b)^3}{(a + b)^1} = (a + b)^{3-1} = (a + b)^2$$

Raising to a Power

$$\boxed{(b^m)^n = b^{mn}}$$

To raise an exponential expression to a power, multiply the exponents.

Examples.

$$(5^6)^2 = 5^{6 \cdot 2} = 5^{12} \quad [\text{Note: } (5 \cdot 5 \cdot 5 \cdot 5 \cdot 5 \cdot 5)(5 \cdot 5 \cdot 5 \cdot 5 \cdot 5 \cdot 5) = 5^{12}]$$

$$(x^{\frac{1}{2}})^{\frac{1}{4}} = x^{\frac{1}{2} \cdot \frac{1}{4}} = x^{\frac{1}{8}}$$

$$[(a + b)^1]^3 = (a + b)^{1 \cdot 3} = (a + b)^3$$

Extracting a Root

$$\boxed{\sqrt[n]{b^m} = b^{\frac{m}{n}}}$$

To extract a root of an expression, divide the exponent of the expression by the *index* of the radical (the number that indicates what root is to be taken).

Examples.

$$\sqrt[2]{5^6} = 5^{\frac{6}{2}} = 5^3 \quad [\text{Note: } \sqrt{5 \cdot 5 \cdot 5 \cdot 5 \cdot 5 \cdot 5} = 5 \cdot 5 \cdot 5 = 5^3]$$

$$\sqrt[6]{x^{\frac{1}{2}}} = x^{\frac{1}{2} \div 6} = x^{\frac{1}{12}}$$

$$\sqrt[3]{(a + b)^{12}} = (a + b)^{\frac{12}{3}} = (a + b)^4$$

Using the Laws of Exponents

The laws of exponents are useful in two ways. First, they simplify the work involved in performing certain arithmetic operations. To divide 2^{10} by 2^6 without using the laws of exponents, you could perform the repeated multiplications indicated by the exponents and then divide:

$$\frac{2^{10}}{2^6} = \frac{2 \cdot 2 \cdot 2 \cdot 2 \cdot 2 \cdot 2 \cdot 2 \cdot 2 \cdot 2 \cdot 2}{2 \cdot 2 \cdot 2 \cdot 2 \cdot 2 \cdot 2} = \frac{1024}{64} = 16$$

However, with the law of exponents for division, the problem is reduced to the following:

$$\frac{2^{10}}{2^6} = 2^{10-6} = 2^4 = 2 \cdot 2 \cdot 2 \cdot 2 = 16$$

In effect, this law of exponents has divided numerator and denominator by 2 six times:

$$\frac{2^{10}}{2^6} = \frac{2 \cdot 2 \cdot 2 \cdot 2 \cdot \cancel{2} \cdot \cancel{2} \cdot \cancel{2} \cdot \cancel{2} \cdot \cancel{2} \cdot \cancel{2}}{\cancel{2} \cdot \cancel{2} \cdot \cancel{2} \cdot \cancel{2} \cdot \cancel{2} \cdot \cancel{2}} = 2 \cdot 2 \cdot 2 \cdot 2$$

$$= 2^4 = 16$$

Second, the laws of exponents help to clarify why negative exponents, zero exponents, and fractional exponents are defined as they are. The laws of exponents are written *because they describe what happens to positive integer exponents*. Then the negative, zero, and fractional exponents are designed to fit these same laws.

Consider the problem

$$\frac{2^6}{2^{10}} .$$

Since it is true that

$$\frac{2^{10}}{2^6} = 2^4 = 16 \quad \text{(or } \frac{16}{1}\text{)},$$

it must be true that

$$\frac{2^6}{2^{10}} = \frac{1}{2^4} = \frac{1}{16} .$$

However, according to the law of exponents for division,

$$\frac{2^6}{2^{10}} = 2^{6-10} = 2^{-4} .$$

Thus 2^{-4} must equal $\frac{1}{16}$, or $\frac{1}{2^4}$.

Similarly, the laws of exponents can be used to show why any non-zero number raised to the zero power is equal to 1. It is known that when any number other than zero is divided by itself, the result is 1. For example, $\frac{8}{8} = 1$. But 8 can be rewritten as a power of 2: $8 = 2^3$. And the division problem

$$\frac{8}{8} \text{ can be rewritten as } \frac{2^3}{2^3}.$$

According to the law of exponents for division,

$$\frac{2^3}{2^3} = 2^{3-3} = 2^0 .$$

However, since

$$\frac{2^3}{2^3} \text{ is simply } \frac{8}{8}$$

in different notation, the results of these two division problems must be equal. Thus, 2^0 must equal 1.

Finally, the laws of exponents can help clarify why fractional exponents are defined as roots. The fourth root of 81 is 3 because $3 \cdot 3 \cdot 3 \cdot 3 = 81$. However, according to the laws of exponents,

$$81^{\frac{1}{4}} \cdot 81^{\frac{1}{4}} \cdot 81^{\frac{1}{4}} \cdot 81^{\frac{1}{4}} = 81^{\frac{1}{4}+\frac{1}{4}+\frac{1}{4}+\frac{1}{4}} = 81^1 = 81.$$

Thus $81^{\frac{1}{4}}$ must be one way of writing the fourth root of 81; in other words, $81^{\frac{1}{4}} = 3$.

EXPONENTIAL GROWTH AND DECAY

Many types of growth and decay occur at a rate that involves a *variable exponent*.

Example.   If a certain bacteria reproduces at a rate that doubles the size of the colony every twenty-four hours, an original population of 1000 bacteria will grow as shown in the table.

$t = time$ measured in days	$N = number\ of\ bacteria$ in population	
0	1000, or	1000×2^0
1	2000, or	1000×2^1
2	4000, or	1000×2^2
3	8000, or	1000×2^3
4	16,000, or	1000×2^4
5	32,000, or	1000×2^5

For any time t, $N = 1000 \times 2^t$.

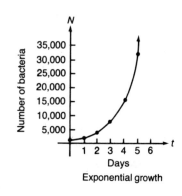

Exponential growth

A population such as this, with $N = 1000 \times 2^t$ giving its size at any given time t, is called an *exponential* FUNCTION of the time, because the variable t appears as an exponent. And since the population N increases as t increases, this is called an *exponential growth function*. The GRAPH of an exponential growth function rises from left to right at an *ever increasing rate*. In the example, in the first day the population increases by 1000, in the third day by 4000, in the fifth day by 16,000.

Many populations of living creatures grow naturally at an exponential rate. The *base* for a particular exponential growth function will depend on the growth rate of the population. And, of course, additional considerations such as death rates, food supplies, effects of crowding, and birth control make for modifications of the natural exponential growth. Nevertheless, exponential growth occurs frequently. Even money in a savings account at compound INTEREST grows exponentially.

An opposite phenomenon, called *exponential decay,* is illustrated by the disintegration of radioactive substances such as radium, uranium, and polonium. These elements decay at *ever decreasing rates*.

Example.   Polonium is a radioactive element, useful in the laboratory and in industry, discovered in 1898 by Pierre and Marie Sklodovska Curie in the process of their discovery of radium. Like other radioactive substances, polonium is always decaying by emitting radiation. Emitted particles of radiation cause flashes on a fluorescent screen, so the decay rate can be measured. After about 138 days, a sample of polonium will be decaying at only half the original rate; half the sample will have decayed. Although the sample may appear to be the same, it will now contain only half the original amount of pure polonium. After another 138 days, the decay rate will be halved again, and so on. Thus, the *half life* of polonium is 138 days.

A sample of polonium that is decaying at a rate of R when it is first observed will decay as shown on next page.

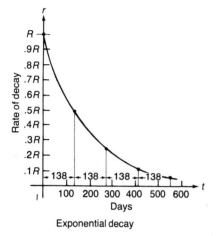

Rate of decay

Days

Exponential decay

$t = time$ measured in days	$r = rate\ of\ decay$ of polonium
0	R , or $R \times 2^0$
138	$\dfrac{R}{2}$, or $R \times 2^{-1}$
276	$\dfrac{R}{4}$, or $R \times 2^{-2}$
414	$\dfrac{R}{8}$, or $R \times 2^{-3}$
552	$\dfrac{R}{16}$, or $R \times 2^{-4}$

R = rate of decay when first observed.

For any time t, $r = R \times 2^{-\frac{t}{138}}$.

Notice that the decay rate of radioactive material will never actually reach zero, although it will get closer and closer. The decay becomes ever slower. Mathematically, this is the behavior of a function that is *negatively* exponential.

Cobalt-60, a radioactive element used in medical radiotherapy, decays much more slowly. It takes 5.26 years for the decay rate of cobalt-60 to be halved. The graph of the decay of cobalt-60 falls less steeply from left to right than that of polonium. Yet the essential characteristics of negative exponential decay will still predominate. The decay rate will be ever smaller, approaching but never reaching zero as time goes on.

HISTORY OF EXPONENT NOTATION

The Greek mathematician Archimedes (250 B.C.) recognized the need for a symbol to refer to the power of a number. Archimedes used the Greek word "myriad" to refer to ten thousand, or 10^4, and he used "myriad of myriads" to refer to $10^4 \times 10^4$, or 10^8. Throughout succeeding centuries, mathematicians used a variety of symbols for exponents, including letters, Roman numerals, numerals in circles, and even pictures. The chart illustrates a few notations for the quantities written today as $7x^2$ and $7x^3$.

	$7x^2$	$7x^3$
1559 Jean Buteo	7 ◇	7 ⬠
1585 Simon Stevin	7②	7③
1590 François Viète	7Q	7C
1610 Pietro Cataldi	7 ₂	7 ₃
1619 Jobst Bürgi	$\overset{ii}{7}$	$\overset{iii}{7}$

Finally, in 1637, the French mathematician and philosopher René Descartes published a work introducing the notation for positive integral exponents used today. Later in the same century, the great English mathematician Sir Isaac Newton extended Descartes' system of exponential notation to include negative and fractional exponents. Newton wrote in a letter, "Since algebraists write a^2, a^3, a^4, etc. for aa, aaa, $aaaa$, etc., so I write $a^{\frac{1}{2}}$, $a^{\frac{3}{2}}$, $a^{\frac{5}{3}}$ for $\sqrt{a}$, $\sqrt{a^3}$, and $\sqrt{c\ a^5}$ [meaning $\sqrt[3]{a^5}$], and I write a^{-1}, a^{-2}, a^{-3} for $\frac{1}{a}, \frac{1}{aa}, \frac{1}{aaa}$, etc." (See references below, *Historical Topics for the Mathematics Classroom*, p. 331.)

REFERENCES

Isaac Asimov, *The Realm of Numbers* (Houghton Mifflin Co., 1959; Fawcett paperback); a good elementary exposition of exponents.

Historical Topics for the Mathematics Classroom, 31st Yearbook of the National Council of Teachers of Mathematics (1969), pp. 327–331; more on Newton and the history of exponent notation.

See also LOGARITHMS.

FACTORS
AND MULTIPLES

FACTOR: if a, b, and c are integers and if a times b equals c ($a \times b = c$), then a and b are *factors* of c.

Examples.   *Factors of 48*   *because*

1
48         $\big\}$ $1 \times 48 = 48$

2
24         $\big\}$ $2 \times 24 = 48$

3
16         $\big\}$ $3 \times 16 = 48$

4
12         $\big\}$ $4 \times 12 = 48$

6
8          $\big\}$ $6 \times 8 = 48$

Any factor of a given number divides the number evenly—with a zero remainder. Thus, factors are sometimes called *divisors*. (See ARITHMETIC OPERATIONS.)

Factoring: the process of finding the factors of a given number.

The work in factoring can be presented in what is known as a *factor tree*. In a factor tree any number that can be factored is represented on the next lower line of the tree as the product of two factors. The tree is continued until no number in the bottom line can be factored further. The factor tree for a number can be arranged in different ways. Yet for any given number, the set of factors on the bottom line of the tree will always be the same.

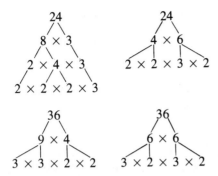

Prime Factor: a factor greater than 1 that can be factored only into itself and 1. (See NUMBERS.)

Example.   *Factors of 12*

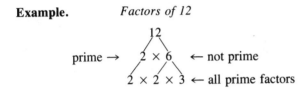

Prime Factorization: the process of finding all the prime factors of a given number.

The bottom line of every factor tree represents the prime factors of the number. And, except for the order of the factors, the bottom line of the factor tree for any number will always be the same. The *fundamental theorem of arithmetic* states that every integer greater than one can be expressed as a product of prime factors in one and only one way, except for the order of the factors.

Greatest Common Factor (G.C.F.): the largest factor common to a given set of integers.

Example.

Set of integers   *Factors*

96   1, 2, 3, 4, 6, 8, 12, 16, 24, 32, 48, 96
60   1, 2, 3, 4, 5, 6, 10, 12, 15, 20, 30, 60
48   1, 2, 3, 4, 6, 8, 12, 16, 24, 48

The factors common to 96, 60, and 48 are underscored. The greatest common factor is 12.

Example. *Set of integers* *Factors*

35	1, 5, 7, 35
54	1, 2, 3, 6, 9, 18, 27, 54

The greatest common factor (G.C.F.) of 35 and 54 is 1. When the greatest common factor of a set of numbers is 1, these numbers are said to be *relatively prime*.

The greatest common factor can be found by using the factor trees of numbers. The bottom line of a factor tree gives the set of prime factors for that number. The greatest common factor of a set of numbers will be the product of the common prime factors.

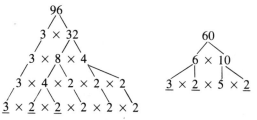

Common prime factors: one 3 and two 2's
G.C.F.: $3 \times 2 \times 2 = 3 \times 4 = 12$

MULTIPLE: if a, b, and c are whole numbers and if a times b equals c $(a \times b = c)$, then c is a multiple of a and of b.

Examples. $6 \times 8 = 48$, so 48 is a multiple of 6 and of 8.
$9 \times 4 = 36$, so 36 is a multiple of 9 and of 4.

The set of multiples for a whole number can be determined by multiplying it by each member of the set of whole numbers: $\{0,1,2,3,4,\ldots\}$. For example, the set of multiples of 3 begins as follows:

$$\{0 \times 3, 1 \times 3, 2 \times 3, 3 \times 3, 4 \times 3,\ldots\}, \text{or}$$
$$\{ \quad 0, \quad\quad 3, \quad\quad 6, \quad\quad 9, \quad\quad 12, \ldots \}$$

The set of multiples of any whole number (except zero) is an infinite set. And zero is a multiple of every whole number.

Common Multiple: a number that is a multiple of two or more given whole numbers.

Example.   *Some common multiples of 8 and 6*

$$24 \begin{cases} (\underline{8} \times 3 = 24) \\ (\underline{6} \times 4 = 24) \end{cases}$$

$$48 \quad (8 \times \underline{6} = 48)$$

$$72 \begin{cases} (\underline{8} \times 9 = 72) \\ (\underline{6} \times 12 = 72) \end{cases}$$

Least Common Multiple (L.C.M.): the smallest number that is a common multiple of two or more given numbers.

Examples.   *Numbers*   *Least common multiple*

Numbers	Least common multiple
8 and 6	24
10 and 30	30
5 and 7	35

If two numbers are relatively prime, then the least common multiple is the product of the two numbers.

Factor trees can be used in finding the least common multiple of a set of numbers:

Example.   and   6

$$3 \times ②$$ This factor has already been included.

Factors of LCM: three 2's

one 3

LCM: $= 2 \times 2 \times 2 \times 3 = 24$

FACTORING ALGEBRAIC EXPRESSIONS

Factor trees show how integers can be factored. But some ALGEBRAIC EXPRESSIONS can be factored also.

Examples.   *Expression*   *Factors*

Expression	Factors
$3x + 27$	3 and $(x + 9)$
$x^2 - 4$	$(x + 2)$ and $(x - 2)$

You can check to see if the factors of an expression are correct by multiplying them together.

Examples.

Expression	Factors	Product
$3x + 27$	3 and $(x + 9)$	$(x + 9)$

$$\begin{array}{r} (x + 9) \\ \times\ 3 \\ \hline 3x + 27 \end{array}$$

$x^2 - 4$	$(x + 2)$ and $(x - 2)$	

$$\begin{array}{r} x\ \ + 2 \\ x\ \ - 2 \\ \hline x^2 + 2x \\ -\ 2x - 4 \\ \hline x^2 + 0\ \ - 4 \\ = x^2 - 4 \end{array}$$

For more on factoring of algebraic expressions, consult any algebra text.

PERFECT, ABUNDANT, DEFICIENT, AND AMICABLE NUMBERS

Mathematicians have long enjoyed playing with factors. And some—such as the Pythagoreans, a group of scholars in ancient Greece—took this play rather seriously. The Pythagoreans were particularly fascinated with the results of adding together all the factors of a number—including 1 but excluding the number itself—and then comparing this sum to the original number. In fact, they classified numbers according to whether this sum was equal to the number itself, greater than the number, or less than the number. Their names for these classes are still used occasionally.

If a number is exactly equal to the sum of all its factors other than itself, the number is said to be *perfect*.

Example.   *Factors of 6*

$$\begin{array}{r} 1 \\ 2 \\ +\ 3 \\ \hline \end{array}$$

Sum of factors $= 6$ Sum of factors of 6 $=$ number 6; thus, 6 is perfect.

If the sum of all the factors of a number—including 1 but excluding the number itself—is greater than the number, the number is said to be *abundant*.

Example.   *Factors of 18*

$$
\begin{array}{r}
1 \\
2 \\
3 \\
6 \\
+\ 9 \\
\hline
\end{array}
$$

Sum of factors = 21   Sum of factors of 18 > number
18; thus, 18 is abundant.

And if the sum of the factors of a number—including 1 but excluding the number itself—is less than the number, the number is said to be *deficient*.

Example.   *Factors of 8*

$$
\begin{array}{r}
1 \\
2 \\
+\ 4 \\
\hline
\end{array}
$$

Sum of factors = 7   Sum of factors of 8 < number 8;
thus, 8 is deficient.

Another interesting relationship between a few numbers is that the sum of the factors of one number *a* will equal another number *b* and the sum of the factors of *b* will equal *a*. Such numbers are called *amicable* (or friendly) *numbers*.

Example.   *Factors of 284*   *Factors of 220*

Factors of 284	Factors of 220
1	1
	2
2	4
	5
4	10
	11
71	20
	22
+ 142	44
Sum of factors = 220	55
	+ 110
	Sum of factors = 284

Thus, 220 and 284 are amicable numbers.

Perfect numbers are rare: 6 is perfect, and so is 28, but the next is 496, and the fourth is 8128. The fifth does not occur until 33,550,336, and the sixth is 8,589,869,056. The number of digits soon becomes too large to list or comprehend. Nevertheless, the idea is intriguing and the search continues. Only the first four perfect numbers were known prior to the fifteenth century. The list grows more rapidly in the age of modern computers: in 1979 at the Lawrence Livermore Laboratory in California, the twenty-seventh perfect number was discovered—it has 13,395 digits!

Amicable numbers are less rare—more than 600 pairs are known, with thirty-odd digits or less: first 220 and 284, then 1184 and 1210, then 2620 and 2924, and so on.

For more information on perfect and amicable numbers, see references.

PRIME AND COMPOSITE NUMBERS

Mathematicians have also done much more serious work with factors and factoring. For example, if an integer other than 1 has only two factors—itself and 1—it is said to be a *prime number*. All other integers are called *composite numbers*. And several important mathematical theorems, such as the fundamental theorem of arithmetic, are statements about prime numbers.

REFERENCES

Martin Gardner, ''Mathematical Games: A short treatise on the useless elegance of perfect numbers and amicable pairs,'' *Scientific American,* March 1968; reprinted in *Mathematics: An Introduction to Its Spirit and Use: Readings from Scientific American* (W. H. Freeman and Co., 1978), pp. 63–66.

Ivars Peterson, ''Quickening the Pursuit of Primes,'' *Science News,* March 6, 1982, p. 158; a clear explanation of a modern mathematical breakthrough—a new computer algorithm that can test in seconds whether a 100-digit number is prime. Before 1981, this task would have taken more fast computer time than the age of the universe!

See also prime NUMBERS.

FIELD PROPERTIES

FIELD: a set of NUMBERS on which two ARITHMETIC OPERATIONS, addition and multiplication, can be performed *and* which satisfy the following six *field properties:* closure, commutativity, associativity, distributivity, identity elements, and inverses.

In a field there must be a set and two operations, called addition ($+$) and multiplication ($\times$), that can be performed on that set. Addition and multiplication are the traditional arithmetic operations unless defined otherwise (see the later section on *finite fields*).

Furthermore, when either of these operations is performed on members of the set, there must be a *unique solution;* that is, for each addition or multiplication problem there can be only one right answer. An example of such a set would be the natural, or counting, numbers $\{1, 2, 3, \ldots\}$. Any two or more members of this set can be added or multiplied, and for each addition or multiplication problem there is only one right answer. Such a set of numbers, or number system, constitutes a field if it possesses all six *field properties*.

CLOSURE: a set is *closed* under a particular operation if whenever that operation is performed on any two members of the set, the answer is a member of the set.

For example, $\{0, 1\}$ is closed under multiplication. If any two members of the set are multiplied, the answer is a member of the set:

$$0 \times 0 = 0 \qquad 0 \times 1 = 0 \qquad 1 \times 1 = 1.$$

However, this same set, $\{0, 1\}$, is not closed under addition:

$$0 + 0 = 0 \qquad 0 + 1 = 1,$$

but $1 + 1 = 2$, and 2 is not a member of the set.

> *Closure*
>
> If a and b belong to the set, then $a + b$ and $a \times b$ also belong to the set.

The set of REAL NUMBERS is closed under addition, for when two r₁
numbers are added, the result is a real number; it is also closed un₁
multiplication, for when two real numbers are multiplied, the result i₁
real number. Furthermore, the set of real numbers is closed under su₁
traction, and closed under division if division by ZERO is excluded.

In any number system, the property of closure must be examin₁
under *each* operation. The set of natural numbers (all positive intege₁
is closed only under addition and multiplication, whereas the set ₁
integers (positive, negative, and zero) is closed under addition, mul₁
plication, and subtraction.

Commutativity
$a + b = b + a$
$a \times b = b \times a$

COMMUTATIVITY: a set is commutative under a given operation
whenever that operation is performed on any two numbers, the *order*
the numbers can be changed without affecting the result.

For example, the real number system is commutative under additio₁
Thus

$$4 + 3 = 3 + 4 \qquad\qquad 2.6 + 1.9 = 1.9 + 2.6$$
$$7 \quad = \quad 7 \qquad\qquad\qquad 4.5 \quad = \quad 4.5$$

$a + b = b + a$, where a and b are any two real numbers

Furthermore, the real number system is commutative under multiplic₁
tion. That is, when two real numbers are multiplied, the product is r₁
changed by changing the order of the numbers:

$$4 \times 3 = 3 \times 4 \qquad\qquad 2.6 \times 1.9 = 1.9 \times 2.6$$
$$12 \quad = \quad 12 \qquad\qquad\qquad 4.94 \quad = \quad 4.94$$

$a \times b = b \times a$, where a and b are any two real numbers

Thus, the set of real numbers is said to be commutative under bo₁
addition and multiplication, because under these two operations any tw₁
of its members can be commuted (placed in a different order).

However, the real number system is *not* commutative under the op₁
ations of subtraction and division. In subtraction and division, changi₁
the order of the elements being operated on changes the result:

$$4 - 3 \neq 3 - 4 \qquad\qquad 8 \div 2 \neq 2 \div 8$$
$$1 \quad \neq \quad -1 \qquad\qquad\qquad 4 \quad \neq \quad \tfrac{1}{4}$$

Associativity
$a + (b + c) = (a + b) + c$
$a \times (b \times c) = (a \times b) \times c$

ASSOCIATIVITY: a set is associative under a given operation if whe₁
ever that operation is performed, the pairing, or *grouping*, of eleme₁
does not affect the result.

The real number system is associative under addition. The following examples illustrate that when three or more real numbers are added together, changing the grouping of the numbers—changing which two numbers are added together first and so on—does not change the answer:

$$4 + (3 + 2) = (4 + 3) + 2$$
$$4 + 5 \quad = \quad 7 + 2$$
$$9 \quad = \quad 9$$

$$2.7 + (1.9 + 3.8) = (2.7 + 1.9) + 3.8 = 8.4$$

The real number system is also associative under multiplication:

$$4 \times (3 \times 2) = (4 \times 3) \times 2$$
$$4 \times 6 \quad = \quad 12 \times 2$$
$$24 \quad = \quad 24$$

The real number system, however, is not associative under subtraction and division. In performing the operations of subtraction and division, changing the grouping of the elements changes the answer:

$$(12 - 4) - 2 \neq 12 - (4 - 2) \qquad (12 \div 4) \div 2 \neq 12 \div (4 \div 2)$$
$$8 - 2 \quad \neq \quad 12 - 2 \qquad\qquad 3 \div 2 \quad \neq \quad 12 \div 2$$
$$6 \quad \neq \quad 10 \qquad\qquad\qquad 1\tfrac{1}{2} \quad \neq \quad 6$$

DISTRIBUTIVITY: this property refers to the relationship between two operations. In multiplying one number by the sum of two other numbers, two operations are involved. The sum may be taken first and then the multiplication performed, or each of the numbers to be summed can first be multiplied by the common factor and then the results added together. This is called the distributive principle.

> *Distributivity*
> $a \times (b + c) =$
> $a \times b + a \times c$

The distributive property (or principle) can be illustrated by a concrete example. Suppose Mike works 3 hours on Friday evenings and 7 hours on Saturdays at a service station and he is paid $5 per hour. One way to figure his wages for a week is to figure that he works 3 + 7 hours, or 10 hours; and 10 times $5 gives him $50 in wages. Another way his wages could be figured is that 3 hours of work at $5 an hour plus 7 hours of work at $5 an hour gives him $15 plus $35, or $50. Thus

$$5 \times (3 + 7) = (5 \times 3) + (5 \times 7)$$

The multiplier 5 in this example is said to be *distributed* to both the 3 and the 7.

In the real number system, multiplication is distributive over addition; for any real numbers a, b, and c

$$a \times (b + c) = ab + ac$$

Moreover, in the real number system, multiplication is also distributive over subtraction; for any real numbers a, b, and c

$$a \times (b - c) = ab - ac$$

IDENTITY ELEMENTS: the *additive identity element* is a number that when added to any given number always results in a sum identical to the given number.

In the real number system, the additive identity element is 0.

$$4 + 0 = 4 \qquad 2.9 + 0 = 2.9$$

The *multiplicative identity element* is a number that when multiplied times any given number always results in a product identical to the given number.

In the real number system, the multiplicative identity element is 1.

$$5 \times 1 = 5 \qquad \pi \times 1 = \pi$$

Identity elements

For addition, 0 is the identity element if
$$a + 0 = a.$$
For multiplication, 1 is the identity element if
$$a \times 1 = a.$$

INVERSES: the *additive inverse* of a given number is that number that when added to the given number gives the additive identity element, namely zero.

In the following pairs of numbers, the two numbers are the additive inverses of each other because the sum of each pair is zero:

Pairs of additive inverses	Sum
6, −6	$6 + (-6) = 0$
3.14, −3.14	$3.14 + (-3.14) = 0$
$-\pi$, π	$-\pi + \pi = 0$

Inverses

Additive inverses are a and $-a$, if
$$a + (-a) = 0.$$
Multiplicative inverses, for $a \neq 0$, are a and $\frac{1}{a}$, if
$$a \times \frac{1}{a} = 1.$$

A helpful way to visualize the additive inverses is to think of the NUMBER LINE. Numbers may be paired on the line so that they are the same distance from the origin but on opposite sides of the origin. Each number in such a pair is the additive inverse of the other (sometimes called the *opposite*, or the *negative*), and the sum of each pair is always exactly zero. Zero is its own additive inverse because $0 + 0 = 0$.

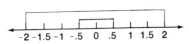

The *multiplicative inverse* of a given number is that number that when multiplied by the given number gives a product equal to the multiplicative identity element, namely 1.

In the following pairs of numbers, the two numbers are the multiplicative inverses of each other because the product of each pair is one.

Pairs of multiplicative inverses	Product
$\frac{1}{2}$, 2	$\frac{1}{2} \times 2 = 1$
$-\frac{5}{8}$, $-\frac{8}{5}$	$-\frac{5}{8} \times -\frac{8}{5} = 1$
π, $\frac{1}{\pi}$	$\pi \times \frac{1}{\pi} = 1$

A helpful way to think of the multiplicative inverse is to notice that the multiplicative inverse of a number is always the *reciprocal* of the number, that is, 1 divided by the number. For example, the reciprocal of 7 is 1 divided by 7, or $\frac{1}{7}$.

The reciprocal of $\frac{1}{4}$ is 1 divided by $\frac{1}{4}$ or $\frac{1}{\frac{1}{4}}$ or 4.

In each example the product is 1: $7 \times \frac{1}{7} = 1$ and $\frac{1}{4} \times 4 = 1$. One is its own multiplicative inverse, or reciprocal, because $1 \times 1 = 1$.

Zero has no multiplicative inverse because zero times any number gives zero, not 1. According to the definition of reciprocal, zero can have no reciprocal because $\frac{1}{0}$ is undefined. In a field, every element *except zero* must have a multiplicative inverse.

Not every number system, however, has inverses. In the set of integers there is an additive inverse for every integer, but there is no multiplicative inverse because there are no fractions in the set of integers, only whole numbers. In the set of natural numbers there is no additive inverse because there are no negative numbers, and no multiplicative inverse because there are no fractions.

WHICH SETS OF NUMBERS CONSTITUTE FIELDS?

A review of all the field properties gives a table showing their occurrence in various sets of numbers under the various possible operations. (See page 180.)

Three number systems possess all the field properties under addition and multiplication: the REAL NUMBERS, the RATIONAL NUMBERS, and the COMPLEX NUMBERS. Each of these sets of numbers constitutes a field.

		Natural numbers	Integers	Rational numbers	Real numbers	Complex numbers
Closure If a and b belong to set, then $a + b$ and $a \times b$ belong to set	+	✓	✓	✓	✓	✓
	×	✓	✓	✓	✓	✓
	−	no	✓	✓	✓	✓
	÷	no	no	✓*	✓*	✓*
Commutativity $a + b = b + a$ $a \times b = b \times a$	+	✓	✓	✓	✓	✓
	×	✓	✓	✓	✓	✓
	−	no	no	no	no	no
	÷	no	no	no	no	no
Associativity $a + (b + c) =$ $(a + b) + c$ $a \times (b \times c) =$ $(a \times b) \times c$	+	✓	✓	✓	✓	✓
	×	✓	✓	✓	✓	✓
	−	no	no	no	no	no
	÷	no	no	no	no	no
Distributivity $a \times (b + c) =$ $a \times b + a \times c$	+	✓	✓	✓	✓	✓
	−	no	✓	✓	✓	✓
Identity elements $a + 0 = a$ $a \times 1 = a$	+	none	✓	✓	✓	✓
	×	✓	✓	✓	✓	✓
Inverses $a + (-a) = 0$ $a \times (\frac{1}{a}) = 1$	+	none	✓	✓	✓	✓
	×	none	none	✓*	✓*	✓*

*except ZERO. These systems exclude division by 0, and 0 has no inverse.

The integers and the natural NUMBERS do not possess all the field properties, and these two sets of numbers do not constitute fields.

EVERYDAY APPLICATIONS OF FIELD PROPERTIES

Although the average nonmathematician may be unfamiliar with the names of the field properties, everyone who can perform the basic arithmetic operations is familiar with the properties themselves. Indeed, almost everybody takes advantage of them in performing arithmetic operations. If you are $15 overdrawn at the bank, you know that you must deposit $15 into your account. (You know that $+15$ is the additive inverse of -15.) If you are adding a long column of figures, you may add going up the first time and then check by adding down the column. (You know that addition is commutative and that changing the order in which the figures are added does not change the answer.)

Also, if you are adding a column of figures like this one, you may add some other way besides up or down. You may notice that the top pair of digits and the bottom pair both equal 10. Thus, you may sum up those two pairs first and then add 4 to the total to get 24. (You know that addition is associative and the pairing of the figures does not affect the result.)

$$
\begin{array}{r}
3 \\
7 \\
4 \\
8 \\
+\ 2 \\
\end{array}
$$

If you wish to buy three water pistols at 29¢ each, you might not figure the total price by multiplying 3 times 29. Instead, you might multiply 3 times 30 and then subtract 3. (If you make use of this kind of shortcut, you are taking advantage of the distributive property; you know that $3 \times (30 - 1) = (3 \times 30) - (3 \times 1)$.) In fact, every time you multiply numbers by the traditional method, you are using the distributive property.

$$
\begin{array}{r}
256 \\
\times \quad 124 \\
\hline
1024 \\
512 \\
256 \\
\hline
31744 \\
\end{array}
$$

$$
\begin{aligned}
256 \times 124 &= 256 \times (100 + 20 + 4) \\
&= 256 \times 100 + 256 \times 20 + 256 \times 4 \\
&= \quad 25600 \quad + \quad 5120 \quad + \quad 1024 \\
&\qquad\ \ \text{third} \qquad\quad \text{second} \qquad\ \text{first} \\
&\qquad\ \ \text{line} \qquad\qquad \text{line} \qquad\quad \text{line}
\end{aligned}
$$

Many examples could be added here, all illustrating the fact that although the names of the field properties may be unfamiliar, the properties themselves are known and used by almost everyone.

FINITE FIELDS

It is possible to have a *finite field*, that is, a field with a finite number of elements.

Example. The integers {0, 1, 2, 3, 4} form a finite field, provided that addition and multiplication are defined as shown in the tables.

+	0	1	2	3	4
0	0	1	2	3	4
1	1	2	3	4	0
2	2	3	4	0	1
3	3	4	0	1	2
4	4	0	1	2	3

Addition
(mod 5)

You can calculate the entries in the tables by adding or multiplying in the ordinary way, dividing the result by 5, and entering the *remainder* in the table. This is a *modular* ARITHMETIC, specifically, arithmetic mod 5.

With these tables you can verify the properties of closure, commutativity, associativity, and distributivity, and that 0 is the additive identity element and 1 is the multiplicative identity element.

Additive inverses can be found by the sums that yield zero:

1 and 4 are additive inverses, because $1 + 4 = 4 + 1 = 0$ (mod 5).

2 and 3 are additive inverses, because $2 + 3 = 3 + 2 = 0$ (mod 5).

×	0	1	2	3	4
0	0	0	0	0	0
1	0	1	2	3	4
2	0	2	4	1	3
3	0	3	1	4	2
4	0	4	3	2	1

Multiplication
(mod 5)

Multiplicative inverses can be found by the products that yield one:

1 and 4 are each their own multiplicative inverses, because
$1 \times 1 = 1$ (mod 5) and $4 \times 4 = 1$ (mod 5).

2 and 3 are multiplicative inverses of each other, because
$2 \times 3 = 1$ (mod 5) and $3 \times 2 = 1$ (mod 5).

Hence, all the field properties are satisfied for the integers mod 5.

Not every modular arithmetic, however, constitutes a field.

×	0	1	2	3
0	0	0	0	0
1	0	1	2	3
2	0	2	0	2
3	0	3	2	1

Multiplication
(mod 4)

Example. The integers mod 4 do *not* form a field. This can be shown by looking at the table for multiplication mod 4. You can see that 1 and 3 are each their own multiplicative inverse. But 2 has *no* multiplicative inverse mod 4, because no product with 2 yields 1. Therefore, the integers mod 4 cannot be a field.

In general, the set of integers modulo a *prime number* forms a finite field, whereas the set of integers modulo a *composite number* is *not* a field. (A prime number has no FACTORS other than itself and one; a composite number has other factors.)

REFERENCES

M. Scott Norton, *Finite Mathematical Systems,* Exploring Mathematics on Your Own Series (Webster, 1963); excellent further exploration of finite fields and field properties.

See ARITHMETIC for more explanation of modular arithmetic and for a discussion of *group,* a concept related to field.

See also history of ALGEBRA or VECTORS.

FRACTIONS

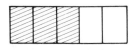

$\frac{3}{5}$ of this rectangle is shaded

FRACTION: a numeral representing some part of a whole;

a numeral of the form a/b or $\frac{a}{b}$ (meaning a divided by b)

where a may represent any number, and b may represent any number except zero.

$\frac{3}{5}$ Numerator
     Denominator

Numerator: the numeral above the bar, telling *how many* parts are being considered.

Denominator: the numeral below the bar, *naming* the parts.

The numerator and denominator are called the *terms* of the fraction.

FRACTIONAL NUMBER: the concept of NUMBER represented by a fraction:

- the concept of *parts of a whole*.
- the concept of *division*.

$$\frac{3}{5} = 3 \div 5 \qquad \frac{x^2}{7} = x^2 \div 7$$

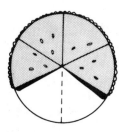

$\frac{2}{6}$, or $\frac{1}{3}$, of this pie has been removed

Parts of a Whole

If a chocolate bar were divided into three equal pieces, how much of the bar would there be in each piece? Obviously, the answer must be less than one, because each piece is less than the whole bar. It is only 1 out of 3 parts, or $\frac{1}{3}$, of the chocolate bar.

The numerals that represent parts of a whole are called *fractions*, from the Latin word "fractus," meaning "broken." Fractions are

184

named according to the number of parts into which the whole has been
divided. Thus, if something is divided into 8 equal parts, the parts are
called "eighths." If the whole is divided into 13 equal parts, the parts
are called "thirteenths," and so on. However, due to their frequent use,
some special fraction names have come into our language. The word
"half" comes from an Indo-European word meaning "to cut," and
"quarter" comes from "quattuor," the Latin word for "four."

Fractions are often necessary for making a MEASURE when part of a
unit is required.

Fractions are used to indicate values between two integers on the
NUMBER LINE. See the sections that follow on rational numbers and
density.

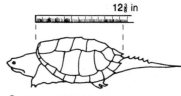

Oscar, a snapping turtle with
shell measuring 12¾ in

A Way of Indicating Division

Fractions are used to express division, as well as to represent parts of
a whole. The fraction ⅔ means two out of three equal parts, *and* it means
two divided by three. Imagine three wilderness backpackers who have
planned an afternoon snack ration of a chocolate bar each. Unfortunately a squirrel makes off with one of the bars, so the three hikers must
now evenly divide two bars—they will each get two out of three parts, or
⅔, of a bar.

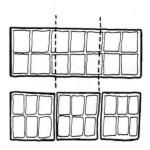

Often a fraction is best expressed in the form of a DECIMAL fraction,
especially if you are using a calculator or computer. In such a case the
division indicated by the common fraction has been carried out.

$$\frac{7}{8} = 7 \div 8 = 0.875 \qquad 8)\overline{7.000} \;\; 0.875$$

For any fraction a/b, where b is not equal to zero, "division" means
that the statement "$a/b = c$" is *exactly equivalent* to the statement
"$a = b \times c$."

$$\frac{a}{b} = c \iff a = b \times c$$

$$\frac{26}{2} = 13 \iff 26 = 2 \times 13$$

TYPES OF FRACTIONS

$$\frac{7}{23} \quad \frac{5}{4} \quad \frac{3}{1} \quad \frac{-3}{4}$$

Common fractions
(integer terms)

Common Fraction (or *simple fraction*): a fraction in which the numerator and denominator are both integers.

Proper Fraction: a fraction in which the numerator is less than the denominator. A proper fraction always expresses a quantity less than one.

Improper Fraction: a fraction in which the numerator is equal to or greater than the denominator. An improper fraction expresses a quantity equal to or greater than one.

$$\frac{1}{8} \quad \frac{2}{7} \quad \frac{6}{11} \quad \frac{-7}{8}$$

Proper fractions
(numerator less than denominator)

The name "improper" suggests that people were once uncomfortable with fractions greater than one. But, mathematically speaking, there is nothing wrong or improper about them. In fact, an improper fraction such as $\frac{4}{3}$ is often easier to use in ARITHMETIC OPERATIONS than the equivalent mixed number.

$$\frac{3}{2} \quad \frac{8}{7} \quad \frac{4}{4} \quad \frac{-6}{5}$$

Improper fractions
(numerator equal to or greater
than denominator)

Mixed Number: a number consisting of an integer and a proper fraction.

Any mixed number can be changed to an improper fraction. For example,

$$1\tfrac{1}{7} = 1 + \tfrac{1}{7} = \tfrac{7}{7} + \tfrac{1}{7} = \tfrac{8}{7}.$$

$$1\tfrac{1}{7} \quad 4\tfrac{2}{3} \quad -3\tfrac{1}{8}$$

Mixed numbers
(integer and proper fraction)

Likewise, any improper fraction in which the numerator and denominator are not equal can be written as a mixed number. For example,

$$\tfrac{3}{2} = \tfrac{2}{2} + \tfrac{1}{2} = 1 + \tfrac{1}{2} = 1\tfrac{1}{2}.$$

$$\frac{0}{16} = 0 \qquad \frac{0}{-3} = 0$$

$$\frac{0}{12765} = 0$$

Zero fractions
(numerator zero)

Zero Fraction: a fraction in which the numerator is zero.

A zero fraction equals zero, because

$$\frac{0}{a} = \square \text{ means } 0 = a \times \square.$$

As long as $a \neq 0$, the only number that can be substituted for $\square$ is zero.

Undefined Fraction: a fraction with a denominator of zero. It is not possible to have a fraction in which the denominator is zero. Such a fraction would be *undefined*. This is because if $\frac{3}{0} = \square$, then $3 = 0 \times \square$. Since zero times any number equals zero, there is no number that can be substituted for □ to make a true equation. And this would be true if the numerator were any number other than zero.

If $\frac{0}{0} = \square$, then $0 = 0 \times \square$. Since zero times any number equals zero, *any* number can be substituted for □ and the equation will still be true. Since a single answer cannot be determined when zero is divided by zero, $\frac{0}{0}$ is said to be *indeterminate*.

In general, because division by zero does not work out for any numerator a,

$$\frac{a}{0} \text{ is } \textit{undefined}.$$

Unit Fraction: a fraction in which the numerator is one.

A fraction in which the denominator is one represents an *integer*. For example,

$$\frac{6}{1} = 6, \quad \frac{35}{1} = 35, \quad \frac{-2}{1} = -2.$$

$$\frac{1}{6} \qquad \frac{1}{35}$$

Unit fractions
(numerator one)

Complex Fraction: a fraction in which the numerator or denominator, or both, is a *fraction*.

Remember that

$$\frac{\frac{2}{3}}{\frac{5}{9}} \text{ means } \frac{2}{3} \div \frac{5}{9}.$$

$$\frac{4\frac{1}{2}}{3} \qquad \frac{5}{\frac{3}{10}} \qquad \frac{\frac{2}{3}}{\frac{5}{9}}$$

Complex fractions
(terms can be fractions)

By dividing the fractions (see p. 191), a complex fraction can be rewritten as a common fraction.

Reciprocal of a number: the fractional number that results from dividing 1 by that number.

The reciprocal of a common fraction is another common fraction. The numerator and denominator have been interchanged.

The reciprocal of a number is its *multiplicative inverse* (see FIELD PROPERTIES).

The reciprocal of 6 is $\frac{1}{6}$.

The reciprocal of a is $\frac{1}{a}$.
(where $a \neq 0$)

EQUIVALENT AND LIKE FRACTIONS

The reciprocal of $\frac{3}{5}$ is $\frac{5}{3}$.

The reciprocal of $\frac{a}{b}$ is $\frac{b}{a}$.
(where $a \neq 0$, $b \neq 0$)

Equivalent fractions: fractions that represent equal value; numerals that name the same fractional number.

The reciprocal of $\frac{1}{7}$ is $\frac{7}{1} = 7$.

Example.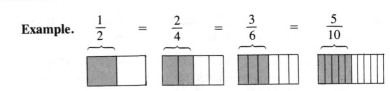

$$\frac{1}{2} = \frac{2}{4} = \frac{3}{6} = \frac{5}{10}$$

Equivalent fractions are obtained whenever the numerator and denominator of a fraction are *multiplied* by the same number.

$$\frac{a}{b} = \frac{a \times c}{b \times c} = \frac{ac}{bc}$$

Examples. $\dfrac{1}{2} = \dfrac{1 \times 3}{2 \times 3} = \dfrac{3}{6}$

Equivalent fractions are also obtained when numerator and denominator of a fraction are both *divided* by the same number.

$$\frac{a}{b} = \frac{a \div c}{b \div c}$$

Examples. $\dfrac{5}{10} = \dfrac{5 \div 5}{10 \div 5} = \dfrac{1}{2}$

(This principle is called *cancelling* when written $\dfrac{5}{10} = \dfrac{1 \times \cancel{5}}{2 \times \cancel{5}} = \dfrac{1}{2}$.)

Multiplying or dividing both numerator and denominator by the same number is the same as multiplying or dividing the whole fraction by *one*, so the value of the fraction is unchanged.

Reducing a fraction is the process of obtaining an equivalent fraction by dividing both the numerator and denominator of a fraction by the same *whole number* (other than one).

Example. $\dfrac{18}{24} = \dfrac{18 \div 2}{24 \div 2} = \dfrac{9}{12} = \dfrac{9 \div 3}{12 \div 3} = \dfrac{3}{4}$ reduced to lowest terms or simplest terms

The fraction is *simplified* or *reduced to lowest terms* when the only whole number that evenly divides both numerator and denominator is one. If two fractions are equivalent, they will be the same when reduced to lowest terms.

Another test for the equivalence of fractions is *cross-multiplication* of the terms. Cross-multiplication gives equal products if, and only if, the fractions are equivalent.

Examples.

$$\frac{3}{4} \overset{?}{\bowtie} \frac{9}{12} \qquad \frac{5}{3} \overset{?}{\bowtie} \frac{10}{7}$$

$$3 \times 12 \overset{?}{=} 4 \times 9 \qquad 5 \times 7 \overset{?}{=} 3 \times 10$$

$$36 = 36 \qquad\qquad 35 \neq 30$$

$$\text{so,}\ \frac{3}{4} = \frac{9}{12} \qquad\qquad \text{so,}\ \frac{5}{3} \neq \frac{10}{7}$$

fractions are
equivalent

fractions are
not equivalent

Like Fractions: fractions with the same denominator.

Example. $\dfrac{1}{8}$, $\dfrac{7}{8}$, and $\dfrac{13}{8}$ are like fractions.

The denominator of like fractions is called the *common denominator*. If two like fractions cannot be simplified to equivalent like fractions with a smaller common denominator, then their denominator is called the *least common denominator* (L.C.D.). In adding or subtracting fractions, it is usually necessary to convert unlike fractions to equivalent like fractions—to convert them to fractions having a common denominator.

ARITHMETIC OPERATIONS WITH FRACTIONS

Addition

To add two like fractions, place the sum of the numerators over their common denominator.

Example. $\dfrac{1}{4} + \dfrac{2}{4} = \dfrac{3}{4}$

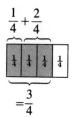

$$\frac{1}{4} + \frac{2}{4}$$

$$= \frac{3}{4}$$

> *Addition of like fractions:* $\dfrac{a}{b} + \dfrac{c}{b} = \dfrac{a + c}{b}$

To add two fractions which are *not* like fractions, first convert them to *equivalent like fractions,* and then add as described above.

Example. $\dfrac{1}{3} + \dfrac{1}{2} = \dfrac{1 \times 2}{3 \times 2} + \dfrac{1 \times 3}{2 \times 3} = \dfrac{2}{6} + \dfrac{3}{6} = \dfrac{2 + 3}{6} = \dfrac{5}{6}$

Converting to like fractions

$\dfrac{1}{2}$ + $\dfrac{1}{3}$ = $\dfrac{5}{6}$

$$\begin{array}{l} \textit{Addition of} \\ \textit{unlike} \\ \textit{fractions:} \end{array} \quad \frac{a}{b} + \frac{c}{d} = \frac{a \times d}{b \times d} + \frac{c \times b}{d \times b} = \frac{ad}{bd} + \frac{bc}{bd} = \frac{ad + bc}{bd}$$

A common denominator is bd.

Subtraction

To subtract *like* fractions, place the difference of the numerators over the common denominator.

Example. $\dfrac{4}{5} - \dfrac{2}{5} = \dfrac{2}{5}$

$$\textit{Subtraction of like fractions:} \quad \frac{a}{b} - \frac{c}{b} = \frac{a - c}{b}$$

To subtract fractions which are not like fractions, convert them to *equivalent like fractions*, and then subtract.

$$\begin{array}{l} \textit{Subtraction} \\ \textit{of unlike} \\ \textit{fractions:} \end{array} \quad \frac{a}{b} - \frac{c}{d} = \frac{a \times d}{b \times d} - \frac{c \times b}{d \times b} = \frac{ad}{bd} - \frac{bc}{bd} = \frac{ad - bc}{bd}$$

To perform arithmetic operations with mixed numbers, it is usually easier to change the mixed numbers to improper fractions. Sometimes, for addition and subtraction, they may be left as mixed numbers. But in the case of subtraction, it may then be necessary to "borrow" by re-writing the first number.

Example. $4\frac{1}{3} - 2\frac{2}{3}$

<table>
<tr><td align="center">*By mixed
numbers*</td><td align="center">*By improper
fractions*</td></tr>
<tr><td align="center">$4\frac{1}{3} = \quad 3\frac{4}{3}$</td><td align="center">$4\frac{1}{3} = \quad \frac{13}{3}$</td></tr>
<tr><td align="center">$- 2\frac{2}{3} = -2\frac{2}{3}$</td><td align="center">$- 2\frac{2}{3} = -\frac{8}{3}$</td></tr>
<tr><td align="center">$\overline{\qquad 1\frac{2}{3}}$</td><td align="center">$\overline{\qquad \frac{5}{3} = 1\frac{2}{3}}$</td></tr>
</table>

Multiplication

To multiply two fractions, place the product of the two numerators over the product of the two denominators.

Example. $\dfrac{3}{5} \times \dfrac{2}{3} = \dfrac{3 \times 2}{5 \times 3} = \dfrac{6}{15} = \dfrac{2}{5}$

$\frac{3}{5}$ of $\frac{2}{3}$ (or $\frac{2}{3}$ of $\frac{3}{5}$) is the doubly shaded portion, or $\frac{6}{15}$.

To multiply fractions there is no need to convert to like fractions.

However, to multiply mixed numbers, it is better to convert the mixed numbers to equivalent improper fractions.

Example. $2\frac{1}{3} \times 3\frac{1}{4} = \dfrac{7}{3} \times \dfrac{13}{4} = \dfrac{7 \times 13}{3 \times 4} = \dfrac{91}{12} = 7\frac{7}{12}$

> *Multiplication of fractions:* $\dfrac{a}{b} \times \dfrac{c}{d} = \dfrac{ac}{bd}$

Division

To divide one fraction by another, *multiply* the first fraction by the *reciprocal* of the second.

Examples. $\dfrac{1}{2} \div \dfrac{1}{4} = \dfrac{1}{2} \times \dfrac{4}{1} = \dfrac{4}{2} = 2$

How many times will $\frac{1}{4}$ go into $\frac{1}{2}$? Two.

$\dfrac{1}{6} \div \dfrac{1}{3} = \dfrac{1}{6} \times \dfrac{3}{1} = \dfrac{3}{6} = \dfrac{1}{2}$

How many times will $\frac{1}{3}$ go into $\frac{1}{6}$? One half.

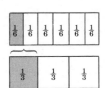

Multiplying by the reciprocal of the divisor is really a shortcut to multiplying the numerator and denominator of a complex fraction by the same number. For instance,

$$\tfrac{1}{2} \div \tfrac{2}{3} = \frac{\frac{1}{2}}{\frac{2}{3}} = \frac{\frac{1}{2} \times \frac{3}{2}}{\frac{2}{3} \times \frac{3}{2}} = \frac{\frac{3}{4}}{1} = \tfrac{3}{4}.$$

This shortcut division process is sometimes described as *inverting the divisor and then multiplying*.

$$\text{Division of fractions: } \frac{a}{b} \div \frac{c}{d} = \frac{a}{b} \times \frac{d}{c} = \frac{ad}{bc}.$$

FRACTIONS AS RATIONAL NUMBERS

A RATIONAL NUMBER is any number which can be expressed as a quotient of two integers,

$$\frac{a}{b}, \text{ with the divisor } b \text{ not equal to zero.}$$

Hence every fraction is a rational number. Furthermore, every whole number, every integer, and every mixed number is also a rational number, for each of these can be expressed as a fraction.

$$58 = \frac{58}{1} \qquad -1 = \frac{-1}{1} \qquad 4\tfrac{1}{2} = \frac{9}{2}$$

However, there is no single way to express a rational number as a fraction. Instead, there are infinitely many ways. For instance,

$$0 = \tfrac{0}{1} = \tfrac{0}{2} = \tfrac{0}{3} = \dots, \quad \text{and} \quad 1 = \tfrac{1}{1} = \tfrac{2}{2} = \tfrac{3}{3} = \dots,$$

and so on. For each rational number there is a whole SET of *equivalent fractions*. And each set of equivalent fractions represents exactly *one* rational number.

Because each set of equivalent fractions represents exactly one rational number, a set such as

$$\{\tfrac{1}{2}, \tfrac{2}{4}, \tfrac{3}{6}, \tfrac{4}{8}, \tfrac{5}{10}, \dots\}$$

corresponds to exactly one point on the NUMBER LINE.

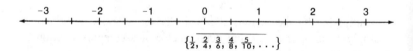

DENSITY OF FRACTIONS

How many rational numbers are there? If you think about it, you can see that there must be at least as many fractions as there are integers, because any integer such as 3, -257, or 120,000 could be the denominator of a fraction such as

$$\frac{1}{3} \quad \frac{1}{-257} \quad \frac{1}{120,000} \cdot$$

Thus, since there are infinitely many integers, there must be infinitely many fractions.

But suppose the field is narrowed a bit. How many fractions are there between $\frac{1}{4}$ and $\frac{1}{3}$? To start counting these fractions, you might try finding the fraction that is exactly halfway between $\frac{1}{4}$ and $\frac{1}{3}$. One way to find it is as follows:

(1) Subtract the smaller fraction from the larger one.

$$\tfrac{1}{3} - \tfrac{1}{4} = \tfrac{4}{12} - \tfrac{3}{12} = \tfrac{1}{12}$$

(2) Take half the difference between the two.

$$\tfrac{1}{2} \times \tfrac{1}{12} = \tfrac{1}{24}$$

(3) Add this number to the smaller fraction.

$$\tfrac{1}{4} + \tfrac{1}{24} = \tfrac{6}{24} + \tfrac{1}{24} = \tfrac{7}{24}$$

Thus $\frac{7}{24}$ is the fraction exactly halfway between $\frac{1}{4}$ and $\frac{1}{3}$.

However, if you could find the fraction halfway between $\frac{1}{4}$ and $\frac{1}{3}$, you ought to be able to find the fraction $\frac{1}{3}$ of the way between them using the same method; and you can:

(1) Subtract the smaller fraction from the larger one.

$$\tfrac{1}{3} - \tfrac{1}{4} = \tfrac{4}{12} - \tfrac{3}{12} = \tfrac{1}{12}$$

(2) Take one third the difference between the two.

$$\tfrac{1}{3} \times \tfrac{1}{12} = \tfrac{1}{36}$$

(3) Add this number to the smaller fraction.

$$\tfrac{1}{4} + \tfrac{1}{36} = \tfrac{9}{36} + \tfrac{1}{36} = \tfrac{10}{36}$$

And using the same method, you could find the fraction $\frac{1}{4}$ of the way between the two fractions or $\frac{1}{40}$ of the way between them or $\frac{1}{400}$ of the way or $\frac{1}{4,000,000}$ of the way. In fact, there is no end to the number of fractions to be found between $\frac{1}{4}$ and $\frac{1}{3}$. And there is no end to the number of fractions to be found between any two fractions. The fact that between any two fractions, no matter how close they may be, there are infinitely many other fractions is known in mathematics as the *property of density*.

HISTORY OF FRACTIONS

The history of how we came to understand and to write a fraction such as $\frac{3}{4}$ the way we do is a long one. Over the centuries, progress in learning to calculate with fractions has been slow, and it has not always been straightforward. Today's student who has trouble mastering fractions may take some comfort in knowing that in ancient times even mathematicians found fractions difficult to work with.

Surprisingly, though, the earliest mathematical records demonstrate a way of writing fractions that made them relatively easy to use. The Babylonians as early as 2000 B.C. wrote fractions very much the way we write decimal fractions. While our decimal fractions are based on powers of ten (like our numeral system), Babylonian fractions were based on powers of sixty, in keeping with their sexagesimal numeral system. Where we use a decimal point to separate the whole number from the fraction, the Babylonians left a space. Thus the number $1\frac{1}{2}$, which we write 1.5, would have been written 1 30 (meaning $1\frac{30}{60}$) by the Babylonians. In Babylonian numerals this actually appeared as ⟨ ⟩ . (See NUMERAL SYSTEMS.)

The next oldest records of the use of fractions come from Egypt. The *Rhind* or *Ahmes Papyrus,* a collection of mathematical problems and tables dating back to 1650 B.C., reveals that the Egyptian system for calculating with fractions was neither as complete nor as easy to work with as that of the Babylonians. Except for the fraction $\frac{2}{3}$, which the Egyptians used frequently and for which they had a special symbol $\mathcal{Z}$ or φ , all Egyptian fractions were expressed as *unit* fractions, with a numerator of one. Fractions were written with either an oval or a dot over the denominator, and the numerator was understood to be one. For example, the fraction $\frac{1}{4}$ would have been written $\overset{\circ}{4}$ or $\overset{\bullet}{4}$, which in Egyptian numerals appeared as |||| or $\overset{\circ}{\wedge}$. Fractions that could not be expressed as single unit fractions were written as the sum of two or more different unit fractions. For example, $\frac{2}{5}$ was written not as $\frac{1}{5} + \frac{1}{5}$, but as $\frac{1}{3} + \frac{1}{15}$. As an aid to computation, tables were prepared giving the double of various fractions in terms of different unit fractions. The *Ahmes Papyrus* contains a table giving the doubles of all fractions with odd denominators from $\frac{1}{5}$ through $\frac{1}{101}$. The doubling of $\frac{1}{101}$ shows how cumbersome this method could be:

$$2 \times \tfrac{1}{101} = \tfrac{1}{101} + \tfrac{1}{202} + \tfrac{1}{303} + \tfrac{1}{606}$$

The various Greek mathematicians (600 B.C. to A.D. 600) were not particularly adept at working with fractions. For one thing, the number "one," or unity, had a mystic significance to many Greek scholars. They believed that "one" was an indivisible building block of philosophy and mathematics that ought not to be broken into parts. When Greek mathematicians did work with fractions, they preferred to think of them as RATIOS. For example, $\frac{3}{4}$ was the ratio of 3 units to 4 units.

Greek tradespeople and merchants, however, had no such qualms about working with fractions, and they used them freely. Not only did they have a way of expressing unit fractions, but they developed various ways of writing other fractions. One way was to put one accent after the numerator and two accents after the denominator. For example, $\frac{3}{4}$ would have been written $3'4''$ ($\gamma'\delta''$ or $\Gamma'\Delta''$).

The Romans also used fractions, especially in their monetary system and in weighing and measuring. They frequently expressed fractions in terms of twelfths; their pound was divided into twelve ounces, their foot into twelve inches.

Throughout the Middle Ages, fractions were included in arithmetic books used to teach students to calculate; however, they were not written as they are today. Our form—with the numerator over the denominator—was probably first introduced into Europe by the Arabs, who may have gotten it from the Hindus. The first records in Europe appear during the twelfth century, and after that time the numerator-over-denominator form became more and more common.

In 1585 a Flemish mathematician named Simon Stevin published a little book called *The Tenth,* in which he strongly advocated the use of DECIMAL fractions. Stevin's argument was that when fractions are written in decimal form, they become as easy to work with as integers. For example, it is as easy to add 5.75 and 2.50 as it is to add 575 and 250.

Stevin did not use the decimal point. It appeared in the next century in several math books, and the dot—or an equivalent—has been used since then to separate a whole number from a decimal fraction. Nearly 3500 years after the Babylonians first wrote fractions in terms of powers of 60, Europeans found their way back to a similar way of writing fractions.

OTHER OCCURRENCES OF FRACTIONS

DECIMALS are fractions in which the denominator is a power of ten.

$$0.05 = \frac{5}{100} = \frac{5}{10^2}$$

PERCENT is a fraction in which the denominator is one hundred.

$$5\% = \frac{5}{100}$$

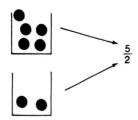

A fraction may express a RATIO, for purposes of comparison. And an equality between two ratios is expressed as a PROPORTION.

$$3:4::6:8 \qquad \text{or} \qquad \frac{3}{4} = \frac{6}{8}$$

Fractions are also used to express PROBABILITY. For example, a probability of $\frac{3}{4}$ indicates that a particular event will occur, on the average, three times in every four trials.

All definitions and operations described for fractions of real numbers apply as well to fractions in which the terms are ALGEBRAIC EXPRESSIONS or COMPLEX NUMBERS.

Examples.

$$\frac{1}{x} + \frac{1}{y} = \frac{y}{xy} + \frac{x}{xy} = \frac{y + x}{xy}$$

$$\frac{3 + i}{2 - i} = \frac{3 + i}{2 - i} \times \frac{2 + i}{2 + i} = \frac{6 + 5i + i^2}{4 - i^2} = \frac{5 + 5i}{5} = 1 + i$$

because $i^2 = -1$

Finally, a topic that fascinates many people is that of *continued fractions,* such as

$$1 + \cfrac{1}{2 + \cfrac{1}{2 + \cfrac{1}{2 + \cfrac{1}{2 + \cdots}}}}$$

(This, believe it or not, equals the square root of 2.) For further discussion of continued fractions, see references.

REFERENCES

Isaac Asimov, *The Realm of Numbers* (Houghton Mifflin Co.; Fawcett paperback, 1959), ''Broken Numbers,'' pp. 57–73; an excellent explanation of fractions in nontechnical language.

Harald M. Ness, Jr., ''Another look at fractions,'' *Arithmetic Teacher,* Vol. 20, No. 1, January 1973; considers fractions as the quotients of two numbers (rather than as parts of a whole) and develops all operations from this definition.

Historical references

Carl B. Boyer, *A History of Mathematics* (John Wiley & Sons, 1968),
   pp. 13–16; an explanation of the unit fractions of the Egyptians.

Historical Topics for the Mathematics Classroom, 31st Yearbook of the
   National Council of Teachers of Mathematics (1969), pp. 95–98,
   135–157.

Robert Swain, *Understanding Arithmetic* (Holt, Rinehart, 1963), pp.
   135–136; more on the history of writing fractions.

Reference on continued fractions

C. D. Olds, *Continued Fractions,* New Mathematical Library (Random
   House, 1963).

FUNCTIONS

FUNCTION: a SET of *ordered pairs* (x, y) in which each value of x is paired with exactly one value of y.

Example. A sales tax table that a cashier uses assigns a tax to every purchase total. This table represents a function.

For a 55 ¢ purchase, the tax is 4¢. For any purchase, the table gives an ordered pair (purchase, tax); for example, (.55, .04).

A function can be regarded as a *rule* that assigns exactly one value to some variable y for each given value of a variable x. The given variable x is called the *independent* variable; the other variable y to which values are assigned is called the *dependent* variable. The rule, or function, may be expressed by a table, an EQUATION, or a GRAPH.

Examples. The equation $y = 3x - 1$ is a function that for every value of x assigns to y the value of one less than three times x.

A graph records gas pressure as a function of time. This could be used by a utility company to monitor the system and to spot leaks.

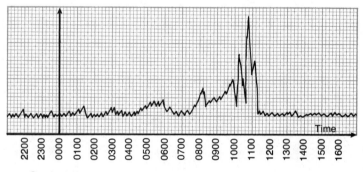

Gas pressure

Notation

A function may be represented by a single letter, such as f, g, or F. Then $f : x$ or $f (x)$ represents the y value, which is obtained by the function operating on x.

Arrow notation: $f : x \rightarrow 3x - 1$

$\underbrace{}_{\substack{\text{first} \\ \text{element}}}$ $\underbrace{}_{\substack{\text{second} \\ \text{element}}}$

Equation notation: $f(x) = 3x - 1$

$\underbrace{}_{\substack{\text{first} \\ \text{element}}}$ $\underbrace{}_{\substack{\text{second} \\ \text{element}}}$

$f(x)$ is read "f of x," meaning "function of x." This is one instance in mathematics when the parentheses do *not* indicate multiplication.

FUNCTION MACHINE

A function is sometimes explained by using the model of a *function machine*. A function machine, when it is fed a number x, will give out a certain number y to be paired with the first. For any given function, the machine is set to determine this pairing.

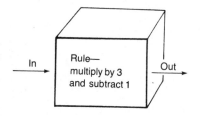

Example.   A function machine is set to multiply by three and then subtract one. Suppose that the following numbers are fed into the machine: 2, 0, and 5:

Number fed in	Rule: Multiply by 3 and subtract 1	Number that comes out
2	3 × 2 − 1	5
0	3 × 0 − 1	−1
5	3 × 5 − 1	14

The function gives a set of ordered pairs:

$$\{(2, 5), (0, -1), (5, 14)\}.$$

DOMAIN AND RANGE

The *domain* of a function is the set of x values specified for the function; the *range* is the set of y values that result.

For the function $y = 3x - 1$, the domain might be specified to include only the values $\{2, 0, 5\}$ as in the above example. On the other hand, the domain might be an infinite set. For any real number x, the equation $y = 3x - 1$ gives a real number y, so the domain of this function could be the set of all real numbers.

If a domain is not specified, it is understood to be all real numbers x for which the value of the function can be computed.

GRAPHING FUNCTIONS

A function can be represented by a GRAPH on a COORDINATE system.

Examples.

$f(x) = 3x - 1$

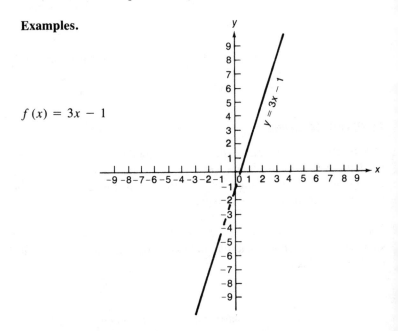

a patient's temperature chart

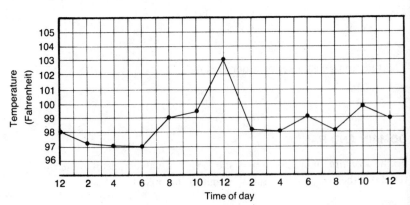

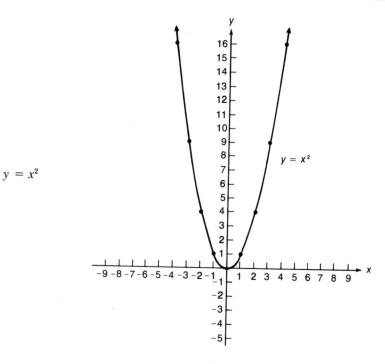

$y = x^2$

OTHER FUNCTIONS

Many functions cannot be defined by a simple formula, but can be defined by other methods.

Example. The United States Postal Service insures parcels according to a schedule. The table represents a function, because for any amount of insurance desired (x), the table gives the fee (y).

Special Services—Domestic Mail Only

INSURANCE

For Coverage Against Loss or Damage
Fees (in addition to postage)

Liability	Fee
$0.01 to $20	0.45
20.01 to 50	0.85
50.01 to 100	1.25
100.01 to 150	1.70
150.01 to 200	2.05
200.01 to 300	3.45
300.01 to 400	4.70

The function can be graphed, and because the graph looks like a set of steps, this type of function is called a *step function*.

The fee *y* is a function *F* of the amount of insurance *x*, so the function can also be written in function notation as follows:

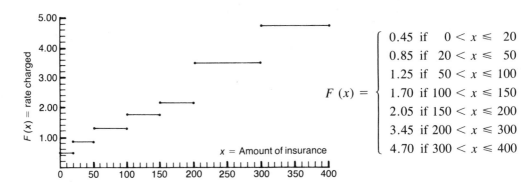

$$F(x) = \begin{cases} 0.45 & \text{if} \quad 0 < x \leq 20 \\ 0.85 & \text{if} \quad 20 < x \leq 50 \\ 1.25 & \text{if} \quad 50 < x \leq 100 \\ 1.70 & \text{if} \quad 100 < x \leq 150 \\ 2.05 & \text{if} \quad 150 < x \leq 200 \\ 3.45 & \text{if} \quad 200 < x \leq 300 \\ 4.70 & \text{if} \quad 300 < x \leq 400 \end{cases}$$

FUNCTION AS A RELATION

A function is also a RELATION. Specifically, a function is a relation in which each element in the domain is paired with *exactly one* element in the range.

Although a function is a relation, *not all relations are functions*. The key is that only those relations that assign a *unique y* to every *x* are functions.

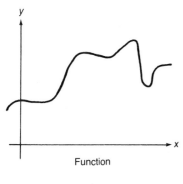

Function

Not a function

Examples. The upper graph represents a function. The lower graph represents a relation that is *not* a function, because for some values of *x* there are several values of *y*.

For more examples, see RELATIONS.

FUNCTION AS A MAPPING

A function *f* from a set *X* to a set *Y* can be called a *mapping* that pairs or sends each element *x* of set *X* to a unique element *y* of set *Y*.

Notation: $f : x \rightarrow y$ or $x \overset{f}{\rightarrow} y$

Image: an element *y* of set *Y* is the image of the element *x* of set *X* if *x* is sent to *y* by the mapping *f*. The image of *x* can be written $f(x)$, which is read "*f* of *x*."

Domain: in a function from *X* to *Y*, the set *X* is the domain. Every element in the domain must have an image.

Range: in a function from *X* to *Y*, the set of all images is the range.

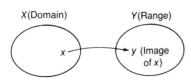

Although a mapping may be expressed in equation form or represented by a standard graph, it is often presented as a diagram that pairs the elements in the domain with their images in the range by arrows.

Types of Mappings

Set X   Set Y

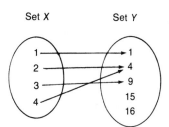

onto versus into: in a mapping f from X to Y, if every element in Y is an image of some element in X, then f is said to map X *onto* Y. Otherwise, the function f is said to map X *into* Y.

one-to-one: in a mapping f from X to Y, if no two different elements in X have the same image in Y, then the mapping is *one-to-one*.

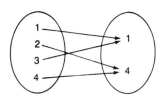

Examples. The upper mapping is an *into* mapping because 15 and 16 are elements of set Y, but they are not images of any element in set X. The mapping is not one-to-one because 4 is the image of both 2 and 4. The domain of the function is $\{1, 2, 3, 4\}$ and the range is $\{1, 4, 9\}$.

The middle mapping is *onto* because set Y contains only the elements 1 and 4, and both are images of at least one element in set X. The mapping is not one-to-one because 2 and 4 are images of more than one element in set X. The domain of the mapping is $\{1, 2, 3, 4\}$ and the range is $\{1, 4\}$.

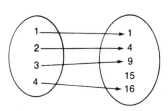

The lower mapping is *one-to-one* because each image in set Y is the image of exactly one element from set X. The mapping is *into* because 15 is in set Y and is not an image. The domain of the mapping is $\{1, 2, 3, 4\}$, and the range is $\{1, 4, 9, 16\}$.

Uses of the Mapping Concept

Some mathematicians, especially those in transformational GEOMETRY and TOPOLOGY, like the mapping concept of a function. They look not only at what happens to individual elements in the domain, but also at what happens to entire sets of elements.

In the diagram, the rectangle A is mapped into circle B. A mathematician might ask about this mapping: Does the function f always map rectangles to circles? Do circles map into rectangles? Are points on the boundary of a rectangle sent to points on the boundary of a circle? Are nearby points in X always carried to nearby points in Y? The mapping concept helps a mathematician think about such questions.

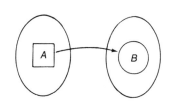

THE IMPORTANCE OF FUNCTIONS

Many relationships that you may take for granted are functions. For example, the *d*istance that you travel in two hours is a function of the *r*ate per hour at which you are traveling: $d = 2r$. The *s*ize of the motion picture projected on a screen is a function of the *d*istance that the projector is from the screen: $s = kd^2$, where k is some constant factor.

Scientists, though, do not take these relationships for granted. In fact, one of the primary goals of the physical sciences is to take a set of ordered pairs of numbers arrived at through observation of some physical phenomenon and try to discover the rule, or function, that describes the set of pairs. Functions that describe many phenomena in the physical world have already been discovered. One example is the Law of Falling Bodies, discovered by Galileo, an Italian astronomer and physicist in the sixteenth century. Galileo discovered that the *d*istance an object falls is *not* a function of its weight, but *is* a function only of the *t*ime it is falling: $d = \frac{1}{2}gt^2$, where g is the constant acceleration due to *g*ravity. When dropped from the same height or distance, a heavy object and a lighter one will hit the ground at the same time. Galileo allegedly confirmed the fact by dropping objects of different weights from the leaning tower of Pisa.

A more recent example of the discovery of a function describing a relationship in the physical world is the function that relates matter and energy. Early in the twentieth century, the German-born physicist Albert Einstein discovered that the amount of *e*nergy released when *m*atter is changed into energy can be expressed by the formula $E = mc^2$, where c is the *c*onstant velocity of light. Einstein's discovery of this function was a crucial step in the development of atomic energy.

FUNCTION: A UNIFYING CONCEPT

In reading this article, you may have noticed that the word "function" is used in slightly different ways. Sometimes it refers to a *set* of ordered pairs, sometimes to the *relationship* between the first and second elements in a set of ordered pairs, and sometimes to the *formula* stating the relationship. The different ways of using the word are not due to carelessness. They are rather the result of a change that has occurred in the way mathematicians define functions.

Originally, physical scientists described the *relationship* between a quantity x that changed and a quantity y that changed as x changed. As early as the fourteenth century, the French mathematician Nicole Oresme showed how a relationship between two varying quantities could be graphed. In the seventeenth century, such a relationship was given the name "function" by the German mathematician Gottfried Wilhelm von Leibniz. However, it was not until the eighteenth century that the idea of function was seen to be a concept unifying various branches of mathematics and physics.

The man chiefly responsible for developing the notation to express functions as *formulas,* or equations, was Leonhard Euler, a Swiss mathematician of the eighteenth century who was the first to use the notation ''$f(x)$'' for ''function of x.'' Euler was a prolific writer in both pure and applied mathematics. He wrote important calculus and analysis texts based on the concept of function. His work in other areas paved the way to viewing trigonometric ratios and logarithms as functions. For over a century, Euler's concept of a function held full sway. It still reigns in the physical sciences and in much of mathematics.

In the late nineteenth century, a German mathematician named Georg Cantor developed a theory of *sets* that was to have a profound effect on mathematics. Cantor argued that the idea of set was even more general and more basic than the idea of number. Although Cantor's ideas were at first ridiculed, mathematicians gradually came to the conclusion that Cantor was right. Consequently, they began to redefine various mathematical concepts in terms of sets. One such concept was ''function.''

Instead of defining a function as a relation between variables—a definition considered unsatisfactory because the terms ''relation'' and ''variable'' are both hard to define—most mathematicians today prefer to define a function as a set of ordered pairs in which every first element is different. This definition is also felt to be more general, applying not only to numbers but to sets of other things as well.

BIOGRAPHICAL REFERENCES

Eric T. Bell, *Men of Mathematics* (Simon & Schuster, 1937; Fireside paperback); a chapter each on Leibniz, Euler, and Cantor describes their mathematical contributions in considerable detail.

Frederick C. Kreiling, ''Leibniz,'' *Scientific American,* May 1968; reprinted in *Mathematics: An Introduction to Its Spirit and Use: Readings from Scientific American* (W. H. Freeman & Co., 1978).

GEOMETRIC CONSTRUCTION

GEOMETRIC CONSTRUCTION: a figure drafted or sketched using only two tools, a straightedge and a compass. ("Construction" is also used alone to denote this process.)

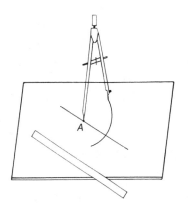

A *straightedge* is an object with at least one straight edge, along which a line segment can be drawn. The straightedge used in making geometric constructions is not marked off in units like a ruler and thus cannot be used for measuring or for drawing line segments of a certain length.

A *compass* is a device that looks like an upside-down **V**. At one end of the **V** is a sharp metal point to hold that end of the compass in a fixed position, and at the other end is a writing instrument such as a pencil. The angle of the compass can be adjusted to move the pencil point and the metal point closer together or farther apart, but when it is being used, the distance between the two points remains fixed. A compass is used to construct circles or arcs of circles.

Since the days of the Greek philosopher-mathematicians, geometers have distinguished between a construction and a drawing. A formal construction was to be done using only an unmarked straightedge and a compass. Because Euclid, in his famous *Elements* (about 300 B.C.), explicitly stated these limitations on a construction, the straightedge and compass are often referred to as Euclidean tools.

The compass used by Euclid and the early Greeks was somewhat different from a modern one. A Euclidean compass was collapsible and could not hold a distance when lifted from the paper. However, Euclid demonstrated that the length of any line segment can be reproduced on any other line—that a measurement can be transferred from one place to another. The transfer can be accomplished more easily with a modern compass that can be set to a specific distance. But because the transfer can be accomplished with either compass, the two are said to be equivalent tools.

Formal constructions in plane geometry are still done using only a straightedge and compass. These limitations make construction something like a game that has to be played by the rules. You can construct a surprising number of intricate figures, and many people enjoy the challenge of trying to construct new ones, using only the Euclidean tools.

BASIC CONSTRUCTIONS

In this section are directions for making a number of geometric constructions:

(1) a congruent line segment
(2) a perpendicular to a line at a point on the line
(3) a perpendicular to a line from a point not on the line
(4) a perpendicular bisector of a line segment
(5) a congruent angle
(6) a parallel line
(7) the division of a line segment into any number of equal parts
(8) an angle bisector
(9) an arc bisector
(10) a tangent to a circle at a point on the circle
(11) a tangent to a circle from a point outside the circle
(12) a circle circumscribed about a triangle
(13) a circle inscribed in a triangle.

Each of these constructions is justified by theorems that are proved in any plane GEOMETRY text. So if you don't see why a given construction procedure works, you can ask someone who knows plane geometry or consult a text for proofs of the relevant theorems.

The notation used in the constructions is explained as follows:

AB = the distance between A and B
$\overline{AB}$ = the LINE segment from A to B
$\overrightarrow{AB}$ = the ray starting at A, passing through B,
        and continuing indefinitely
$\overleftrightarrow{AB}$ = the line passing through both A and B and
        extending indefinitely in both directions
$\overparen{AB}$ = the arc of a circle between A and B.

Finally, one general direction applies to making *any* geometric construction: each construction should be carefully done with a very fine pencil to approach the ideal of LINES and POINTS without width as closely as possible and to determine intersection points as accurately as possible. The lines in the illustrations are thickened only for clarity of explanation.

1. A Congruent Line Segment

(a line segment equal in length to another line segment)

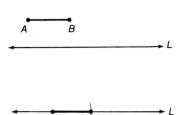

Given line segment $\overline{AB}$ and a line L, construct on L a line segment $\overline{A'B'}$ that is congruent to $\overline{AB}$.

Set one point of the compass at A and the other at B, thus setting the compass to the distance between A and B. Label a point A' on L. Place one point of the set compass at A' and construct an arc that crosses L, determining B'.

$\overline{A'B'}$ is congruent to $\overline{AB}$.

2. A Perpendicular to a Line at a Point on the Line

Given line L and point X on the line, construct a perpendicular to the line at X.

With X as center and with a convenient radius, construct arcs intersecting L at A and B.

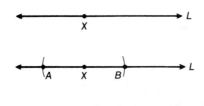

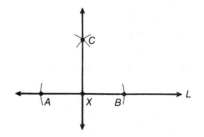

With a radius greater than $\frac{1}{2}AB$, construct arcs, with centers at A and B, that intersect at C.

Draw $\overleftrightarrow{CX}$. $\overleftrightarrow{CX}$ is perpendicular to line L.

3. A Perpendicular to a Line from a Point not on the Line

Given line L and point X not on the line, construct a perpendicular to the line from X.

With X as center and with a convenient radius, construct an arc intersecting line L at B and C.

With centers at B and C, construct arcs of the same radius, greater than $\frac{1}{2}BC$, so that they will intersect at D.

Draw $\overleftrightarrow{DX}$. $\overleftrightarrow{DX}$ is perpendicular to line L.

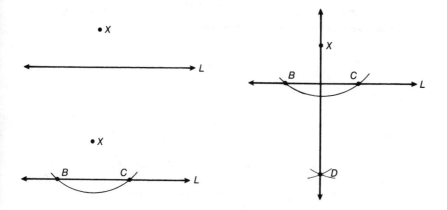

4. The Perpendicular Bisector of a Line Segment

Given line segment $\overline{AB}$, construct the perpendicular bisector.

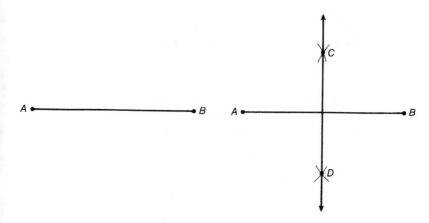

With radius greater than $\frac{1}{2}AB$, construct arcs of the same radius, with centers at A and B, that intersect at C and D.
Draw $\overleftrightarrow{CD}$. $\overleftrightarrow{CD}$ is the perpendicular bisector of $\overline{AB}$.

5. A Congruent Angle

Given an angle ∠*ABC* and a ray $\overrightarrow{DE}$, construct an angle congruent to the given angle, using the ray as one side.

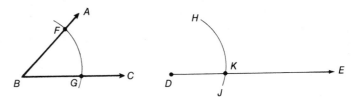

With *B* as center and with a convenient radius, construct an arc intersecting $\overrightarrow{BA}$ at *F* and $\overrightarrow{BC}$ at *G*. With the same radius, and with the center at *D*, construct an arc $\overset{\frown}{HJ}$, intersecting $\overrightarrow{DE}$ at *K*.

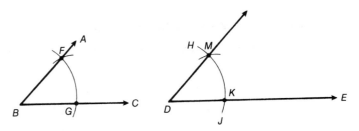

With center at *G*, set compass to length *FG*. With center at *K*, construct an arc intersecting arc $\overset{\frown}{HJ}$ at *M*.

Draw $\overrightarrow{DM}$. ∠*MDE* is congruent to ∠*ABC*.

6. A Parallel Line

Given a line *L* and a point *X* not on the line, construct a line through *X* parallel to *L*.

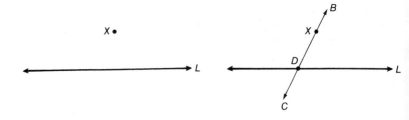

Through *X* draw any oblique line $\overleftrightarrow{BC}$ that intersects line *L* at *D*.

With *X* as a vertex and $\overrightarrow{XB}$ as one side, construct ∠*BXE* congruent to ∠*XDG*, where *G* is another point on *L*, (as in construction 5).

Extend ray $\overrightarrow{XE}$ to *F*. Line $\overleftrightarrow{FE}$ is parallel to line *L*.

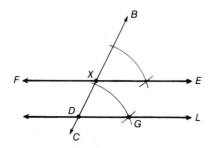

7. The Division of a Line Segment into Any Number of Equal Segments

Given a line segment $\overline{AB}$, divide it into any given number n of equal segments (this illustration uses $n = 3$; the same technique will work for any integer n).

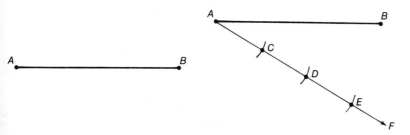

From A, draw any ray $\overrightarrow{AF}$ that is not on $\overline{AB}$.

On $\overrightarrow{AF}$ choose a convenient length, such as AC, and, starting at A, mark it off n times. (For $n = 3$, this means $AC = CD = DE$.)

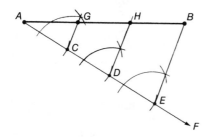

Draw $\overline{EB}$, the line from the last point marked on $\overrightarrow{AF}$.

Construct *lines parallel* to $\overline{EB}$, through all other points marked on $\overrightarrow{AF}$ (as in construction 6).

The intersections of these parallel lines with $\overline{AB}$ divide AB into n equal segments. $AG = GH = HB$.

8. An Angle Bisector

Given an angle $\angle ABC$, construct the ray that bisects the angle.

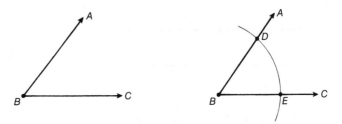

With B as a center and with a convenient radius, construct an arc intersecting $\overrightarrow{BA}$ at D and $\overrightarrow{BC}$ at E.

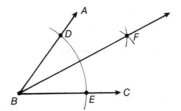

With D and E as centers and with a radius greater than $\frac{1}{2}DE$, construct arcs in the interior of $\angle ABC$ that intersect at F.

Draw $\overrightarrow{BF}$. $\overrightarrow{BF}$ is the bisector of $\angle ABC$.

9. An Arc Bisector

Given arc $\overset{\frown}{AB}$ of a circle, construct the line that bisects the arc.

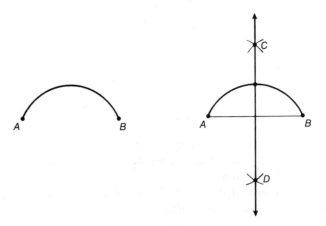

Draw chord $\overline{AB}$.

Construct the *perpendicular bisector* of chord $\overline{AB}$ (as in construction 4).

This line, $\overleftrightarrow{CD}$, is the bisector of arc $\overparen{AB}$.

10. A Tangent to a Circle at a Point on the Circle

Given a point X on a circle O, construct a tangent to the circle at X.

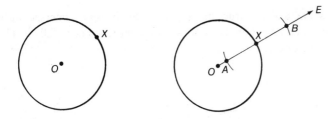

Draw radius $\overline{OX}$ and extend it through X to E.

With X as center and with a convenient radius, construct arcs intersecting $\overrightarrow{OE}$ at A and B.

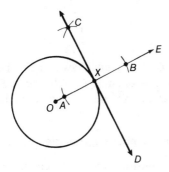

With centers at A and B and with a radius greater than $\frac{1}{2}AB$, construct arcs that intersect at C.

Draw $\overline{CX}$ and extend it through X to D. Line $\overleftrightarrow{CD}$ is tangent to circle O at X.

11. A Tangent to a Circle from a Point
Outside the Circle

Given a point X outside a circle O, construct a tangent to the circle from X.

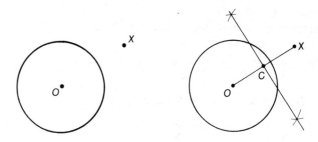

Draw $\overline{OX}$ and construct its *perpendicular bisector*, intersecting $\overline{OX}$ at C (as in construction 4). It does not matter whether C falls inside or outside the circle.

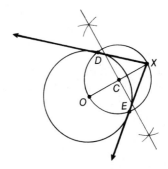

With C as center and OC as radius, draw a circle. This circle passes through O and X and intersects circle O at D and at E.
Draw $\overrightarrow{XD}$ and $\overrightarrow{XE}$. $\overrightarrow{XD}$ and $\overrightarrow{XE}$ are tangents to circle O.

12. A Circle Circumscribed about a Triangle

Given triangle ABC, construct the circle circumscribed about the triangle.

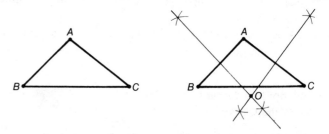

Construct the *perpendicular bisectors* (as in construction 4) of two sides of the triangle, for example, the perpendicular bisectors of $\overline{AB}$ and $\overline{AC}$. Label the intersection of the perpendicular bisectors as O.

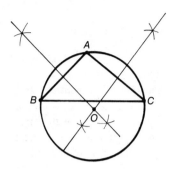

With O as center and OA as radius, construct a circle that should also pass through B and C. Circle O is circumscribed about triangle ABC.

13. A Circle Inscribed in a Triangle

Given a triangle ABC, construct the circle inscribed in the triangle.

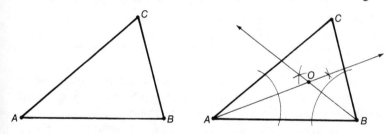

Bisect any two angles of the triangle (as in construction 8), for example, $\angle A$ and $\angle B$. Label the intersection of the angle bisectors as O.

From O construct a line *perpendicular* to one side of the triangle (as in construction 3). Label the intersection F.

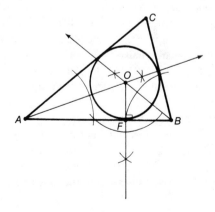

With O as center and $\overline{OF}$ as radius, construct a circle. Circle O is inscribed in triangle ABC.

LIMITATIONS OF EUCLIDEAN TOOLS

Because such a large number of geometric figures can be constructed solely by means of straightedge and compass, it was not at all obvious that these tools were inadequate to construct certain other figures. As a result, many mathematicians over the centuries worked on three construction problems that are now known as the *three famous problems of antiquity:* the squaring of the CIRCLE, the trisection of the ANGLE, and the duplication of the cube. The first two are discussed in the indicated articles; the third is presented here.

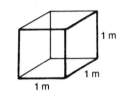

1 m

1 m

1 m

$V = 1 \times 1 \times 1 = 1$ cubic meter

DUPLICATION OF THE CUBE

The problem of duplicating the cube was to construct a cube with exactly *twice the volume of a given cube.* There are conflicting stories about the origin of this problem, but according to one story, the god Apollo was angry, and to appease his anger, he required an altar twice as large as the existing one. Because the altar to Apollo was located on the island of Delos, the duplication of the cube is sometimes referred to as the *Delian problem.*

Imagine the altar in the shape of a cube. If the cube measures one meter in each direction, the volume of the cube will be length times width times height ($1 \times 1 \times 1$), or one cubic meter. What would be the volume of a cube twice as large? Clearly, the answer is two cubic meters. But what would be the length of the side of a cube whose volume equals two cubic meters?

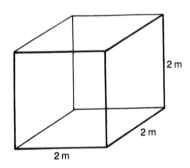

2 m

2 m

2 m

$V = 2 \times 2 \times 2 = 8$ cubic meters

The volume of a cube 2 meters on a side is $2 \times 2 \times 2$, or 8 cubic meters. So the length of the side of a cube containing two cubic meters must be between one and two meters. Finding the exact number that can be used as a factor three times to give 2 is called finding the *cube root of 2,* written $\sqrt[3]{2}$. If the volume of any cube is expressed as V, the volume of a new cube twice as large must be $2 \times V$. And the side of the new cube will be $\sqrt[3]{2 \times V}$, or $\sqrt[3]{2} \times \sqrt[3]{V}$. Although we may be able to find the cube root of V equal to the edge of the original cube, we would still need to construct $\sqrt[3]{2}$.

It is possible to construct the *square* root of two using Euclidean tools. A square with sides one unit long has a diagonal equal to the square root of two. According to the PYTHAGOREAN THEOREM, the sum of the squares of the two legs of a right triangle equals the square of the hypotenuse. Therefore, a square built on the diagonal of a square one

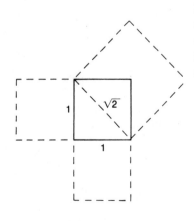

1

$\sqrt{2}$

1

unit on a side must be two square units in area. And the diagonal itself must be $\sqrt{2}$.

But the *cube* root of two is not so easily found. Some ingenious solutions to this problem were discovered by the Greeks and mathematicians who followed them; however, they all depended on something more than Euclidean tools. Archytas, a Pythagorean in about 400 B.C., gave a solution that hinges on finding the intersection of a torus (a doughnut-shaped solid), a cylinder, and a cone. That is, Archytas came up with equations that amounted to finding the geometric intersection that is pictured. (Neither the original cube nor the duplicated cube is pictured, only the resulting geometric intersection problem. See references for more detail.)

Another solution was to treat the problem as a series of PROPORTIONS. Still other solutions made use of various curves, including CONIC SECTIONS. However, *no* solution to the problem was found using only a straightedge and compass, and in the nineteenth century it was proved, by means of ALGEBRA, that such a solution is impossible.

Although mathematicians in the field of plane geometry may still do constructions using only the Euclidean tools, drawings in applied sciences like engineering and drafting are made with protractors, marked straightedges, French curves, and a host of powerful drawing tools that allow the construction of figures impossible using straightedge and compass alone.

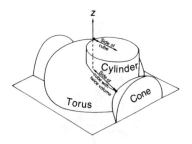

Archytas' solution to duplication of the cube

REFERENCES

H. A. Elliott, James MacLean, and Janet Jorden, *Geometry in the Classroom* (Holt, Rinehart and Winston of Canada, 1968), pp. 107–147; a presentation of intuitive, informal methods of creating a variety of geometric figures.

Martin Gardner, ''Mathematical Games: Geometric constructions with a compass and a straightedge, and also with a compass alone,'' *Scientific American*, September 1969; reprinted in *Mathematics: An Introduction to Its Spirit and Use: Readings from Scientific American* (W. H. Freeman & Co., 1978); an entertaining collection of unusual constructions.

Historical Topics for the Mathematics Classroom, 31st Yearbook of the National Council of Teachers of Mathematics (1969), pp. 192–204; discussion of the history of ancient Greek constructions and later adaptations.

Dale Seymour and Reuben Schadler, *Creative Constructions* (Creative Publications, P.O. Box 10328, Palo Alto, California 94303; 1974);

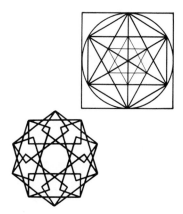

From *Creative Constructions.*

another source of intricate geometric designs composed from basic constructions, as shown in margin.

Reference on duplication of the cube

R. F. Graesser, "Archytas' duplication of the cube," *Mathematics Teacher,* May 1956, pp. 393–395; full algebraic and geometric details.

For other geometric constructions, see ANGLES (attempts to trisect an angle), CIRCLE (attempts to square the circle, or to construct π), GOLDEN SECTION (golden section, golden rectangle), NUMBER LINES (distances representing integers, rational numbers, and certain irrational numbers), POLYGONS (regular polygons).

GEOMETRY

GEOMETRY: the branch of mathematics that deals with space and figures in space and with properties of those figures, such as size and shape.

SOME TYPES OF GEOMETRY

Plane Geometry: the geometry that deals with figures in a two-dimensional PLANE.

Solid Geometry: the geometry that deals with figures in three-dimensional space.

Spherical Geometry: the geometry that deals with figures on the surface of a sphere.

Euclidean Geometry: the geometry (plane and solid) based on Euclid's postulates.

Non-Euclidean Geometry: any geometry that changes Euclid's postulates.

Analytic Geometry: the geometry that deals with the relation between ALGEGRA and geometry, using GRAPHS and EQUATIONS of lines, curves, and surfaces to develop and prove relationships.

ORIGINS

The word "geometry" comes from two Greek words: "ge" meaning "earth" and "metria" meaning "measure." As the word's origin indicates, geometry was originally concerned with practical problems such as measuring tracts of land. But there were other practical problems—such as carpentry and construction—and even before the ancient Greeks, people were concerned with them and wrote works that included geometric arguments. The *Sulvasutras,* an ancient Indian treatise on altar construction and temple building, is an example. Geometric theorems like the PYTHAGOREAN THEOREM appear in Babylonian cuneiform texts and in the Chinese *Chou Pei.*

A milestone in Western culture occurred in the third century B.C. when the Greek mathematician Euclid incorporated logical reasoning into his geometry, which became the model for classical geometry based on axioms and postulates.

CLASSICAL (FORMAL) GEOMETRY

About 300 B.C. Euclid published his *Elements,* in which geometry is presented as a formal system of reasoning.

> Euclid gathered together the
> geometric knowledge of his time,
> and arranged it
> not just in a hodge-podge manner,
> but,
> he started with what he thought were
> self-evident truths
> and then proceeded to
> PROVE all the rest by
> LOGIC.
> A splendid idea, as you will admit.
> And his system has served
> as a model
> ever since.
>
> From Lillian Lieber,
> *The Education of T. C. Mits**

Euclidean geometry was the heart of nearly all mathematics prior to the seventeenth century. In fact, until Descartes introduced the notation of ALGEBRA into geometry in the 1630's, Euclidean geometry had stood for almost two thousand years without being changed or challenged. And although today there are geometries that do not share the basic assumptions of Euclidean geometry, they do, as do other branches of mathematics, still follow the pattern of *formal reasoning* established in Euclidean geometry.

Any formal geometry is based on *assumptions*—a set of *undefined terms* and a set of statements about them that are called *postulates,* or *axioms.*

From these assumptions, you define new terms and *prove* other statements by the logical process of DEDUCTION. The statements that are proved from the postulates by deduction are called *theorems* or *propositions*.

Thus, any formal geometry is a collection of postulates and the theorems that may be deduced from them. Euclid made his set of axioms and postulates as small as possible, following the ancient Greek ideal of simplicity of form. The Greeks tried to reduce even geometric drawing to its most basic ingredients. So an additional idea important to the study of Euclidean geometry is that of GEOMETRIC CONSTRUCTION. Since the time of Euclid, formal geometric construction allows only two tools: an unmarked straightedge and a compass.

Euclid's Axioms and Postulates

Axioms

(1) Things that are equal to the same thing are also equal to one another.
(2) If equals be added to equals, the wholes are equal.
(3) If equals be subtracted from equals, the remainders are equal.
(4) Things that coincide with one another are equal to one another.
(5) The whole is greater than the part.

Postulates

(1) A line can be drawn from any point to any point. (In Euclidean geometry, a line is a *straight line*.)
(2) A finite line segment can be extended to a line of any length.
(3) A circle can be drawn with any center and at any distance from that center.
(4) All right angles are equal to one another.
(5) Through a given point not on a given line can be drawn only one line parallel to the given line (the *parallel postulate*).

(*Parallel lines* are lines in the same plane that never intersect, or meet, no matter how far they are extended.)

The *parallel postulate* is stated in the form given in 1795 by John Playfair, a Scottish mathematician and physicist. The fifth postulate is not necessary for a great deal of geometry. In fact, mathematicians long wondered if it were necessary at all. In the course of their wonderings, they stated it in several different forms—Playfair's version is the most popular. The axioms and postulates with this substitution are equivalent to Euclid's original system, and it was this form of the fifth postulate that led to the discovery of non-Euclidean geometry.

NON-EUCLIDEAN GEOMETRY

In 1829 a Russian, Nikolai Ivanovich Lobachevsky, took the revolutionary step of publishing the first formal geometry that changed one of Euclid's basic assumptions—in particular, the parallel postulate. Lobachevsky created a new geometry in which through a given point *more* than one line could be drawn parallel to a given line, yet the new system was as mathematically valid as Euclidean geometry.

This was one of the biggest breakthroughs in mathematics. It freed geometry, and even other branches of mathematics, from the notion that there is a single collection of obvious truths on which all mathematics must be based. It opened the possibility of taking different collections of carefully chosen and explicitly stated assumptions and making from them different MATHEMATICAL SYSTEMS.

Some of Lobachevsky's ideas had been anticipated, even before Euclid's time, according to the writings of Aristotle in the fourth century B.C. (See references below, Toth.) Later, about A.D. 1100, Omar Khayyam, a Persian mathematician and poet who wrote the famous *Rubaiyat,* actually proved some theorems that are now recognized as theorems in non-Euclidean geometry. Khayyam's works were translated into Latin in the early eighteenth century by an Italian priest, Girolamo Saccheri, who extended these ideas. But neither Saccheri nor other mathematicians of his time saw where Khayyam's work could lead; they were totally engrossed in trying to prove that the fifth postulate followed from the other four.

A century later, as Lobachevsky showed that a different fifth postulate created a different geometry, Janos Bolyai of Hungary and Carl Friedrich Gauss of Germany were working independently along similar lines. And in 1854, Bernhard Riemann of Germany suggested an entirely different formal non-Euclidean geometry, in which *no* line could be drawn parallel to a given line. The door was now wide open for the creation of still more geometries—different from but as mathematically valid as Euclidean geometry.

The non-Euclidean geometries that grew from Lobachevsky's and Riemann's ideas are called respectively *hyperbolic* geometry and *elliptic* geometry. You will notice in the following examples that for these geometries "line" does not mean "straight line." This is a handy result of the fact that in any geometry, line is undefined. Because it is, mathematicians are free to specify a line different from a straight line.

Hyperbolic geometry assumes that through a given point not on a line, *more than one* line can be drawn parallel to the given line.

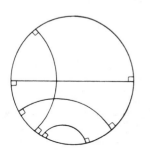

Models for hyperbolic geometry

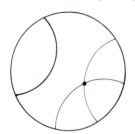

Example.   The interior of a circle forms a model for hyperbolic geometry if *lines* are defined to be all *circular arcs that meet the boundary of the circle at right angles* and all *diameters of the circle.*

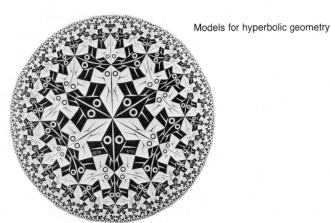

By mathematician H. S. M. Coxeter

From *Introduction to Geometry*, 2nd edition
(John Wiley & Sons, 1961, 1969), p. 285.

By graphic artist M. C. Escher,
"Circle Limit I," woodcut, 1958

Models for hyperbolic geometry

Two works of art show many of these lines. Since parallel lines are lines that never meet, then in this model through a given point not on a line there can be drawn more than one line parallel to the given line.

Elliptic geometry assumes that through a given point not on a straight line, *no* line can be drawn parallel to the given line.

Example.   A concrete example of elliptic geometry is *spherical geometry,* for which the earth's surface provides a model. As any airplane pilot knows, the shortest distance between two points on the surface of the earth is along a *great circle*. A great circle is the intersection of a sphere with a plane through its center. Examples of great circles are the meridians of longitude and the equator (but not the other parallels of latitude, because their planes do not go through the center of the sphere). Likewise, a line in spherical geometry is a *great circle*. And spherical geometry is non-Euclidean, because any two great circles intersect. That is, through a given point not on a great circle there can be drawn *no* great circle parallel to (not intersecting) a given great circle.

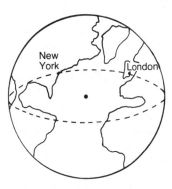

Models for elliptic geometry

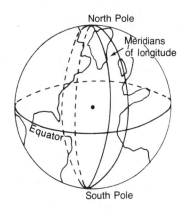

Surprising Results in Spherical Geometry

Spherical geometry, the geometry of the earth's surface, is non-Euclidean because all lines (great circles) meet. Therefore, parallel lines are impossible. But this is not the only difference from Euclidean geometry.

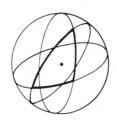

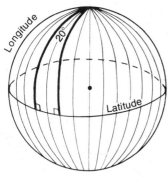

Angle sum = 90° + 90° + 20° = 200°

Angle sum = 90° + 90° + 100° = 280°

Another surprising fact concerns *spherical triangles*. A spherical triangle lies on the surface of a sphere and has for sides the arcs of great circles. The ANGLES of a spherical triangle have a greater sum than the angles of a plane TRIANGLE. *The angles of every spherical triangle sum to <u>more</u> than 180°.*

For example, consider the surface of the earth as marked into geographical COORDINATES. Every meridian of longitude follows a great circle, and the equator is also a great circle. So any triangle formed by two meridians and the equator is a spherical triangle. The angle between any meridian and the Equator is 90°, so any spherical triangle formed by two meridians and the Equator already has 180° in the two angles at the Equator. The angle sum of such a triangle will indeed be greater than 180°.

Furthermore, the sums of the angles of different spherical triangles may be different. In the example, the sum depends on the angle between the meridians; a larger angle between the meridians gives a larger sum. In fact, the *excess over 180°* of the angle sum of a spherical triangle is in direct PROPORTION to the AREA of the triangle. So, measuring the excess allows you to compute the *area:*

$$A = \frac{\pi}{180} R^2 E, \quad \text{where} \quad \begin{array}{l} A = \text{the area of a spherical triangle;} \\ R = \text{the radius of a sphere;} \\ E = \text{the excess, in degrees,} \\ \quad \text{of the angle sum over } 180°. \end{array}$$

The calculation of area by measuring only the angles is used by geographers, cartographers, and surveyors to calculate areas of large triangles on the earth's surface.

TRANSFORMATION GEOMETRY—ANOTHER APPROACH

The classical axiomatic approach is not the only way to do geometry. The ancient Egyptians and Babylonians used spherical geometry in navigation and astronomy without referring to a formal axiom system. In fact, spherical geometry has almost always been done without such a formal system, which would be cumbersome.

A nonaxiomatic approach to geometry in general is preferred by many contemporary mathematicians. This approach, sometimes called *transformation geometry,* considers geometry the study of the properties of a figure that do not change under motions of the figure.

What kinds of motion can a figure undergo? Examples are *translation*, *rotation*, and *reflection*. These are called *rigid motions* because the figures remain rigid; size, shape, and distances within the figure are unchanged. Most classical geometry deals with rigid motions that leave distances unchanged.

Other motions of figures are possible. Some nonrigid motions are the bases of other geometries.

Projective geometry: the geometry that deals with the properties of figures that are unchanged by PROJECTION. *Projection* is like casting a shadow. This science evolved from artists' studies of perspective.

Topology: the geometry that deals with the properties of figures that are unchanged by distortion. *Distortion* is stretching or deforming. TOPOLOGY is sometimes called "rubber sheet geometry."

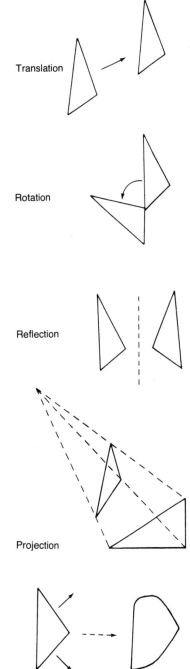

Translation

Rotation

Reflection

Projection

Distortion

REFERENCES

References on geometry and its history

Lewis Carroll (Charles Dodgson), *Euclid and His Modern Rivals* (Macmillan, 1885; Dover, 1973); a drama defending Euclid's masterpiece against "new" texts. The topic is entirely serious for mathematician Dodgson, but he uses the light touch of Carroll (the author of *Alice in Wonderland*) to keep the reader's attention.

Howard Eves, *An Introduction to the History of Mathematics,* 3rd ed., (Holt, Rinehart & Winston, 1969), Ch. 5, pp. 112–139; a concentrated yet readable discussion of Euclid and his *Elements*.

T. L. Heath, *The Thirteen Books of Euclid's Elements* (Cambridge University Press, 1926; Dover, 1956); a famous translation, with commentary, for the mathematician.

Historical Topics for the Mathematics Classroom, 31st Yearbook of the National Council of Teachers of Mathematics (1969), pp. 165–231; a great variety of interesting historical notes on geometry, both Euclidean and non-Euclidean.

Harold R. Jacobs, *Geometry* (W. H. Freeman & Co., 1974); a splendid text of Euclidean geometry, with an excellent chapter on spherical and other non-Euclidean geometries.

Morris Kline, "Geometry," *Scientific American,* September 1964; reprinted with other excellent articles on geometry in *Mathematics in the Modern World: Readings from Scientific American* (W. H. Freeman & Co., 1968) and in *Mathematics: An Introduction to Its Spirit and Use: Readings from Scientific American* (W. H. Freeman & Co., 1978).

A. Seidenberg, "The Ritual Origin of Geometry," *Archive for History of Exact Sciences,* Vol. 1, pp. 488–527; much detail, from ancient Greece and before, to India, Egypt, and Babylonia.

Imre Toth, "Non-Euclidean Geometry before Euclid," *Scientific American,* November 1969, pp. 87–98.

A. M. Welchons, W. R. Krickenberger, and Helen R. Pearson, *Essentials of Solid Geometry* (Ginn, 1964); an excellent small text that includes spherical geometry.

I. M. Yaglom, *Geometric Transformations,* translated from Russian, New Mathematical Library (L. W. Singer Co., 1962).

References for fun with geometry

Frederick J. Almgren, Jr., and Jean E. Taylor, "The Geometry of Soap Films and Soap Bubbles," *Scientific American,* July 1976.

Pierre Berloquin, *100 Geometric Games* (Charles Scribner's Sons, 1976).

C. V. Boys, *Soap-Bubbles: Their Colours and the Forces Which Made Them* (1911; Dover, 1959); a classic, written for the layman or beginning scientist.

Matila Ghyka, *The Geometry of Art and Life* (Sheed & Ward, 1946; Dover, 1977).

Eugene F. Krause, *Taxicab Geometry* (Addison-Wesley, 1975); an entirely different but simple and concrete non-Euclidean geometry, and a delightful book. See also Martin Gardner, "Taxicab geometry offers a free ride to a non-Euclidean locale," *Scientific American,* November 1980, pp. 18–30.

C. Stanley Ogilvy, *Excursions in Geometry* (Oxford University Press, 1969); easy-to-prove nontrivial theorems that are too often just around the corner from the usual geometry course; intellectual stimulus for people who liked geometry but felt the play ended just when the plot got interesting.

T. Sundara Row, *Geometric Exercises in Paper Folding* (The Open Court Publishing Co., 1905; Dover, 1966).

Evans G. Valens, *The Number of Things: Pythagoras, Geometry, and Humming Strings* (E. P. Dutton & Co., 1964); a delightful presentation of geometry, ending with a splendid long section on extension to music.

For illustrative articles on geometry, see

LINES, POINTS, PLANES, LOCUS
ANGLES, PERIMETER, AREA, VOLUME
TRIANGLES, QUADRILATERALS, POLYGONS, POLYHEDRONS
CIRCLE, CONIC SECTIONS
SIMILARITY, CONGRUENCE, SYMMETRY
GEOMETRIC CONSTRUCTION, GOLDEN SECTION
PYTHAGOREAN THEOREM
PROJECTION, TOPOLOGY

GOLDEN SECTION

GOLDEN SECTION: the division of a line segment into two unequal parts so that the RATIO of the whole segment to the longer part is the same as the ratio of the longer part to the shorter part.

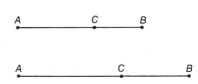

Each segment is divided so that

$$AB : AC = AC : CB, \quad \text{or} \quad \frac{AB}{AC} = \frac{AC}{CB}.$$

This is called dividing the segment into the *extreme and mean ratio*. It is also called the *Divine Proportion*. *AC* is the *Golden Mean* between *CB* and *AC+CB*.

The term "Golden Section" has been used since the nineteenth century. The verb "to section" means "to cut," so "Golden Section" refers to this special cut, or division, that is seen far more often than you might suspect.

Although there is evidence that the Golden Section was known and used by the ancient Egyptians and Babylonians, it was studied and made famous about 500 B.C. by the Greek philosopher Pythagoras and his fellow scholars, now known as the Pythagoreans. The Pythagoreans were a group of Greek aristocrats engaged in a serious study of mathematics and philosophy for theoretical and aesthetic ends, rather than practical ones. Although it is rarely noted, the Pythagoreans included a number of women. In fact, Pythagoras' wife Theano is said to have become a teacher in their school and to have discussed the Golden Mean in one of her treatises. Theano and two of her daughters are credited with having continued her husband's studies and teaching after his death. The Pythagorean Order endured for more than two hundred years. It was a secret and mystical cult that attached deep significance to various numbers and geometric shapes. The star-shaped symbol of the

227

order, the Pentagram of Pythagoras, is the fabled source of the Golden Section.

The pentagram may be constructed from a regular pentagon, the GEOMETRIC CONSTRUCTION of which is described under POLYGON. You may then either

- extend all the sides of the pentagon until they meet, *or*
- draw in all the diagonals and erase the pentagon.

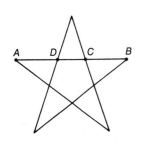

In either case you will now have a pentagram that is full of Golden Sections. Not only does *C* divide *AB,* but *D* divides *AC* into extreme and mean ratio, and this happens on all sides of the star.

Thus, the pentagram is a good place to *see* Golden Sections. However, it may be more useful to be able to divide *any* line segment into extreme and mean ratio.

GEOMETRIC CONSTRUCTION OF THE GOLDEN SECTION

Using only straightedge and compass, the construction of the Golden Section of any line segment $\overline{AB}$ proceeds like this:

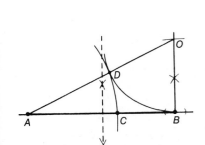

(1) Construct a perpendicular at *B*.
(2) Bisect $\overline{AB}$ and mark off $BO = \frac{1}{2}AB$.
(3) Make a circle with center at *O* and radius *BO*.
(4) Draw $\overline{OA}$.
(5) Label the point *D* where *OA* meets the circle.
(6) With *A* as center and *AD* as radius, make an arc intersecting $\overline{AB}$.
(7) The intersection is *C*.
(8) Now $\dfrac{AB}{AC} = \dfrac{AC}{CB}$.

For individual construction steps, see GEOMETRIC CONSTRUCTION.

NUMERICAL RATIO OF THE GOLDEN SECTION

The ratio of the Golden Section is usually called ϕ (Phi).

$$\frac{AB}{AC} = \frac{AC}{CB} = \phi = 1.618, \text{ approximately}$$

The exact value of ϕ is

$$\frac{1 + \sqrt{5}}{2}$$

which can be calculated as shown:

(1) Let $CB = 1$ unit. Then $AC = \phi$ units and $AB = \phi + 1$ units.

(2) $\dfrac{AB}{AC} = \dfrac{AC}{CB}$, so $\dfrac{\phi + 1}{\phi} = \dfrac{\phi}{1}$.

(3) This says $\phi + 1 = \phi^2$, or $\phi^2 - \phi - 1 = 0$.

(4) This quadratic EQUATION has two solutions: $\phi = \dfrac{1 \pm \sqrt{5}}{2}$

(5) $\dfrac{1 + \sqrt{5}}{2} \doteq 1.618$ and gives the distance we called ϕ.

$\dfrac{1 - \sqrt{5}}{2} \doteq -.618$, which is unacceptable for a distance because

it is negative.

(6) Hence ϕ, the ratio of the Golden Section, is given by the first

solution, $\dfrac{1 + \sqrt{5}}{2}$.

The number ϕ is a funny one. Notice that the solution that did not give the distance ϕ was approximately $-.618$, which is $1 - \phi$. You will find other interesting relations if you divide 1 by ϕ, or if you calculate ϕ^2, in decimal form.

The number ϕ keeps popping up in unexpected places. The ancient Greeks found this ratio occurring in many geometric figures. Ever since, people have been fascinated by it, "seeing" it in nature, art, and music.

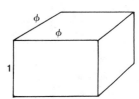

A FEW OCCURRENCES OF ϕ

In Ancient Egypt

The quantity ϕ (often approximated by $\frac{10}{6}$ or $\frac{16}{10}$) occurs often in the proportions of ancient Egyptian structures erected some 5000 years ago. The "Golden Chamber" of the tomb of Rameses IV measured 16 ells × 16 ells × 10 ells, which is approximately in the ratio of $\phi : \phi : 1$.

Many pieces of Egyptian furniture found in tomb chambers had an overall shape of $\phi : 1 : 1$.

Another volume often used in Egyptian tombs is $\phi^2 : \phi : 1$. The center of a chamber with these dimensions is a distance of ϕ from each of the eight vertices.

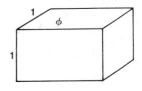

There are theories that much of the construction of the pyramids, such

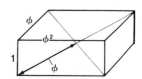

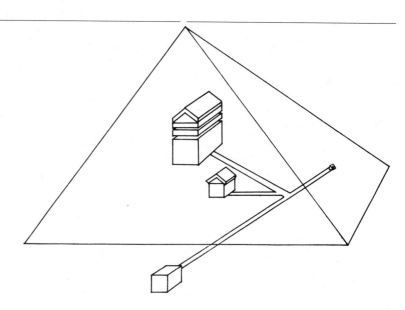

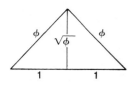

as the Great Pyramid of Cheops, was of triangular forms based on ratios involving ϕ. Measurements of this pyramid show, to accuracy on the order of 0.1%, two right triangles with sides in the ratio $1:\phi:\phi$. Although such measurements strongly indicate that the Egyptians knew about the Golden Section, little written evidence remains and authorities are undecided whether these ratios were plan or coincidence.

In Music

The harmonious major sixth interval is given by two notes that have a ratio approximately equal to ϕ.

Modern Hungarian pianist and composer Béla Bartok made extensive use of the "Sectio Aurea" (Golden Section) in his music, often using it at the climax of a piece or at the beginning of a recapitulation.

C = 256 cycles/second
E = 162 cycles/second
A = 432 cycles/second

$\dfrac{532}{256} = 1.58$

$\dfrac{256}{162} = 1.68$

In Human and Animal Proportions

Artists are vitally concerned with proportions. German engraver Albrecht Dürer early in the sixteenth century produced a four-volume *Treatise on Human Proportions*. Many others have also studied the proportions of the human body, and the ratio ϕ occurs frequently.

The search for ϕ is not limited to human forms. Some believers feel that all animals can be analyzed in a way that will show ϕ as the basic proportion. An example is the horse, which has been analyzed to give several different ratios involving ϕ.

ϕ *Analysis in Human and Animal Proportions*

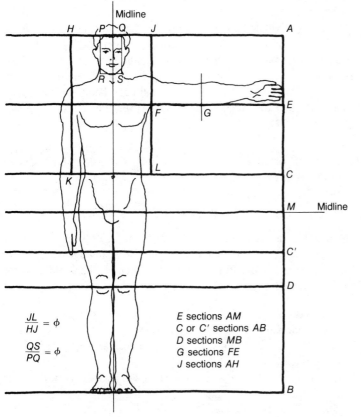

Midline

H P Q J A

R S

E

F G

L

K C

M Midline

C'

D

$$\frac{JL}{HJ} = \phi$$

$$\frac{QS}{PQ} = \phi$$

E sections *AM*
C or C' sections *AB*
D sections *MB*
G sections *FE*
J sections *AH*

B

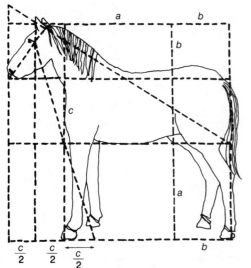

a b

b

c

a

a

$$\frac{c}{2} \quad \frac{c}{2} \quad \frac{c}{2}$$

b

$$\frac{a}{c} = \phi$$

$$\frac{c}{b} = \sqrt{\phi}$$

$$\frac{a}{b} = \phi\sqrt{\phi}$$

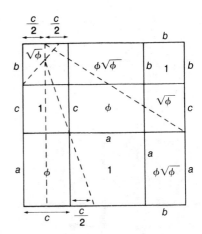

$$\frac{c}{2} \quad \frac{c}{2}$$

b

$\sqrt{\phi}$

b $\phi\sqrt{\phi}$ b 1 b

c 1 c ϕ $\sqrt{\phi}$ c

a

a ϕ 1 $\phi\sqrt{\phi}$ a

$c \quad \frac{c}{2}$ b

Adapted from Matila Ghyka, *The Geometry of Art and Life*, (Sheed and Ward, 1946; Dover, 1977).

231

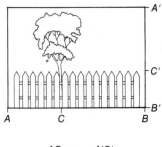

$$\frac{AC}{CB} = \phi = \frac{A'C'}{C'B'}$$

In Artistic Layout

In many paintings and design layouts, an important element will be placed where it divides the horizontal or vertical dimension of the overall work in the Golden Section. If you take a ruler and calculator and experiment with some magazine advertisements, you will probably find examples where the ratios are surprisingly close to ϕ. Artistic analysis involving the Golden Section is far more intricate than this simple fact, but that is beyond the scope of this book. (See the references, especially Ghyka and Hambidge.)

GOLDEN RECTANGLE: a rectangle constructed using the segments $\overline{AC}$ and $\overline{CB}$ from the Golden Section as sides.

Construction of the Golden Rectangle

A Golden Rectangle can of course be constructed by first dividing a line segment, $\overline{AB}$, in the Golden Section and then using those lengths for the sides of the rectangle. But that extra first step can be avoided by the following direct GEOMETRIC CONSTRUCTION:

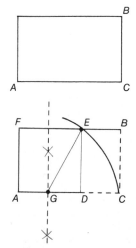

(1) Start with a square ($ADEF$).
(2) Bisect one side (point G on side $\overline{AD}$).
(3) With G as center and GE as radius, draw an arc, meeting $\overrightarrow{AD}$ extended at C.
(4) Extend $\overline{FE}$, and using a compass set to length AC, mark B so that $FB = AC$.
(5) Then $ACBF$ is a Golden Rectangle.

This can be confirmed by calculating the ratio $\dfrac{AC}{CB}$ as follows:

(1) If we let $AD = 2$ units, then $GD = 1$ unit and $ED = 2$ units.
(2) Therefore, by the PYTHAGOREAN THEOREM, $GE = \sqrt{1^2 + 2^2} = \sqrt{5}$ units.
(3) $GC = GE = \sqrt{5}$ units.
(4) $AC = AG + GC = 1 + \sqrt{5}$ units.
(5) $CB = 2$ units.
(6) Hence, $\dfrac{AC}{CB} = \dfrac{1 + \sqrt{5}}{2} = \phi$, the ratio of the Golden Section.

The Golden Rectangle in Art

The Golden Rectangle is considered the rectangular shape most pleasing to the eye. Many famous painters have used the Golden Rectangle in their paintings, and architects have used it in their design of buildings.

"Composition with Red, Yellow, and Blue, 1936–1942" by Piet Mondrian

The Tate Gallery, London. © BEELDRECHT, Amsterdam/VAGA, New York, 1982.

The most famous example is the Greek Parthenon, fifth century B.C. This building has been much analyzed in terms of Golden Rectangles and related forms (see references, Hambidge), although nobody can be certain whether the designers planned it this way.

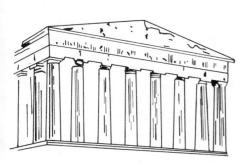

The Parthenon, Athens, 5th century B.C.

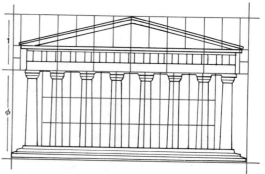

Hambidge points out these Golden Rectangles in the facade of the Parthenon as a few of the many often subtle, occurrences of φ.

In the twentieth century, Swiss-French architect Le Corbusier explicitly used the Golden Section and the Golden Rectangle both in painting and in architecture. Dutch artist Piet Mondrian, on the other hand, did not deliberately use the Golden Rectangle in his work, yet some of his paintings are full of them. This observation at least supports the claim that the Golden Rectangle's proportions are aesthetically particularly pleasing.

Although art critics may argue about who uses the Golden Rectangle and who doesn't, the mathematicians can produce a fascinating and indisputable occurrence of the Golden Rectangle, inside a regular icosahedron (see POLYHEDRA). The corners of the icosahedron coincide with the corners of three Golden Rectangles!

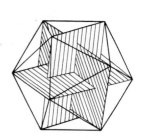

CONTINUOUS PROPAGATION OF THE DIVINE PROPORTION

The Golden Section is *self-propagating*. If a line segment, $\overline{AB}$, is divided into extreme and mean ratio at C, then the smaller segment, $\overline{CB}$, always has exactly the length that divides the larger segment, $\overline{AC}$, into extreme and mean ratio. This process continues indefinitely.

C divides $\overline{AB}$ in the Golden Section.

Locate D so $AD = CB$; then D divides $\overline{AC}$ in the Golden Section.
Locate E so $AE = DC$; then E divides $\overline{AD}$ in the Golden Section.
Locate F so $AF = ED$; then F divides $\overline{AE}$ in the Golden Section.
And so on. . . .

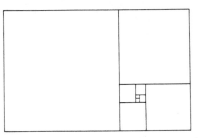

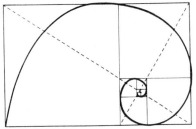

The Golden Rectangle is also self-propagating. If a square is removed from one end, the rectangle that remains is also a Golden Rectangle. This process too can be continued indefinitely.

This sequence may be used to sketch the *equiangular spiral,* so called because it makes the same angle with every radius drawn from its its center. For the spiral propagated in the Golden Rectangle, this angle is approximately 73°; the center of the equiangular spiral is located at the intersection of the diagonals of the successive rectangles. (An equiangular spiral is also a *logarithmic spiral*—see GRAPHS on polar coordinate paper.)

Equiangular spirals are often seen in nature. They have a property of balance—for instance, a horn that grows along an equiangular spiral maintains the same center of mass. The shell of the chambered nautilus, the swirling of celestial bodies in many galaxies, the cloud formation of hurricanes, and the path of a moth flying into a bright light are all equiangular spirals, although their angles may differ from that in the Golden Rectangle.

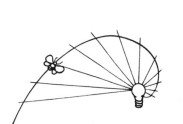

Moth flying at 65° angle to light's rays

Spiral galaxy, in Ursa Major
Palomar Observatory Photograph.

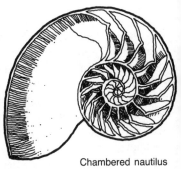

Chambered nautilus

The arrangement of seeds in a sunflower, or the pattern on the base of a pineapple or pine cone are other examples of equiangular spirals—see the Fibonacci SEQUENCE.

REFERENCES

H. E. Huntley, *The Divine Proportion: A Study in Mathematical Beauty* (Dover, 1970); an excellent reference for all aspects of the Golden Section which shows the occurrence of ϕ again and again in regular polygons and polyhedra and in conic sections, while also providing historical and aesthetic discussions.

References on art and architecture

Matila Ghyka, *The Geometry of Art and Life* (Sheed & Ward, 1946; Dover, 1977).

Jay Hambidge, *The Elements of Dynamic Symmetry* (first published in Europe, 1919–1920; Dover, 1967).

Jay Hambidge, *The Parthenon and Other Greek Temples: Their Dynamic Symmetry* (Yale University Press, 1924).

Michael Holt, *Mathematics in Art* (Van Nostrand Reinhold Co., 1971).

Peter Tompkins, *Secrets of the Great Pyramid* (Harper and Row, 1971), pp. 189–213; detailed discussion of the Golden Section and measurements of the pyramid.

References on the occurrence of φ and spirals in nature

Theodore Andrea Cook, *The Curves of Life* (Constable & Co., London, 1914; Dover, 1979).

"The Spiral Way," *Natural History,* August–September 1974, pp. 50–55; includes discussion of other spirals and intriguing facts, both natural and mathematical, about them.

D'Arcy Thompson, *On Growth and Form* (Cambridge University Press, 1917; shorter revision, 1961).

References on the Pythagoreans

Carl B. Boyer, *A History of Mathematics* (John Wiley & Sons, 1968), pp. 52–67.

Historical Topics for the Mathematics Classroom, 31st Yearbook of the National Council of Teachers of Mathematics (1969), especially pp. 31–35.

Lynn M. Osen, *Women in Mathematics* (M.I.T. Press, 1974), pp. 15–18; discusses the contributions of women to the Pythagoreans.

The Golden Section and Golden Rectangle are closely related to *Fibonacci numbers*, discussed under SEQUENCES AND SERIES.

GRAPHS

GRAPH: a drawing or visual representation that shows the relationship between two or more sets of numbers.

GRAPHING: the process of making a graph.

GRAPHING STATISTICAL DATA

A graph can be made for any sets of data or information (usually numbers) that are given in related pairs. For example, the number of cars sold each month by an agency provides a collection of data which can be graphed to show trends. A graph often gives a better idea of the relationship between the numbers (in this case, between the month and the number of cars sold that month) than one is likely to get from a table that merely lists them. The graph illustrates a situation such as growth and decline at a glance, and it is more likely to catch a reader's attention.

This is a *broken line graph*. The horizontal axis is a NUMBER LINE representing one set of numbers (in this case the months, in order); the vertical axis is a number line representing the second set of numbers (in this case the number of cars sold). The points that represent the data are located for each month, and these points can be joined from left to right in a series of line segments to show sales trends.

Such a line graph is commonly used when one of the sets of numbers to be compared represents *time*. For example, you might use a broken line graph to show the hourly change in temperature from 8 A.M. to 8 P.M. on a certain day, or to show the change in the population of the United States from 1900 to 1980.

Other types of graphs, however, may also be used to display data. Notice how each type illustrated emphasizes different features of the same car-sales data.

A *bar graph,* also called a *column graph* (or, if there are no spaces

Number of cars sold

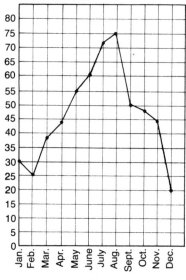
Month

Number of cars sold each month
by the Bowen Motor Company

January	30
February	26
March	38
April	44
May	55
June	61
July	72
August	75
September	50
October	48
November	44
December	20

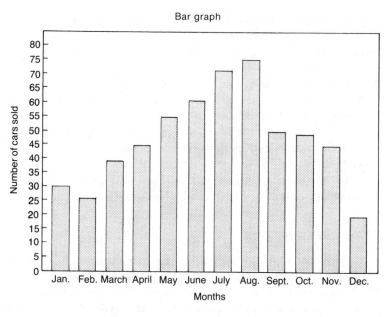

Bar graph

<!-- Y-axis: Number of cars sold; X-axis: Months -->

between bars, a *histogram*), consists of a series of parallel bars all of the same width, each of which represents one of the numbers in one set. The corresponding number in the second set is then represented by the *length* of each bar. That is, a bar representing the number 2000 would be twice as long as a bar representing 1000. The bars of a bar graph may be arranged either horizontally or vertically.

Number of cars sold

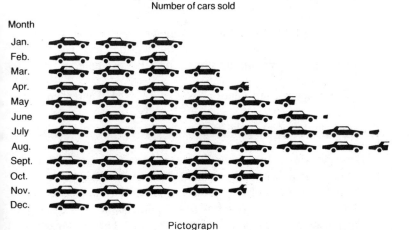

Pictograph

A *pictograph*, or *pictorial unit graph*, uses drawings—of cars, animals, people, or whatever is appropriate—to illustrate the relation be-

Circle graph

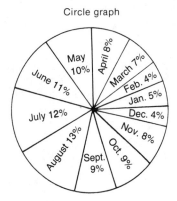

Percentage of cars sold each month

tween two sets of numbers. Pictorial unit graphs are made on the same principle as bar graphs, but they are used frequently in newspapers and magazines because they are more likely to catch a reader's attention than are other types of statistical graphs. One disadvantage of a pictograph, however, is that it is not as accurate as a line graph or a bar graph. You can see from the example that it is more difficult to tell how many cars were sold each month.

A *circle graph,* sometimes called a *pie chart,* divides a circle into sections to show the relationships between the individual sets of numbers and the whole. In the case of car sales, the whole circle represents the total number of cars sold in the year 1980. Then each section represents the PERCENT of the annual sales during a particular month.

GRAPHING EQUATIONS

Another example of data that can be graphed is a table relating Celsius and Fahrenheit temperature MEASURES. Again, you can make a broken line graph, with the horizontal axis representing one temperature scale and the vertical axis the other. Both of the scales require number lines in the negative direction as well as in the positive direction, and the lines intersect at the zero point on each scale.

But notice what happens when these Celsius-Fahrenheit points are connected—they form a straight line. In fact, this straight line is the graph of an *equation,*

$$F = \tfrac{9}{5}C + 32 \quad \text{where} \quad \begin{aligned} C &= \text{Celsius temperature,} \\ F &= \text{Fahrenheit temperature.} \end{aligned}$$

For any value of C, a Celsius temperature, you can calculate the equivalent F or Fahrenheit temperature from this equation, and you will find you have another point on the straight line. For example,

$5°$ Celsius is equivalent to $\tfrac{9}{5} \times 5 + 32 = 41°$ Fahrenheit.

If you locate this point on the graph, you will see that it also falls on the line.

Thus, every point of this straight line is part of the graph illustrating the relationship between Celsius and Fahrenheit temperature measures. The variables are C and F, representing two sets of numbers, and the relationship between the two sets is given by the equation $F = \tfrac{9}{5}C + 32$.

Any equation in two variables can be graphed, because the equation gives the relationship between two sets of numbers. The Celsius-Fahrenheit relation is but one example.

An equation is graphed on a rectangular COORDINATE SYSTEM com-

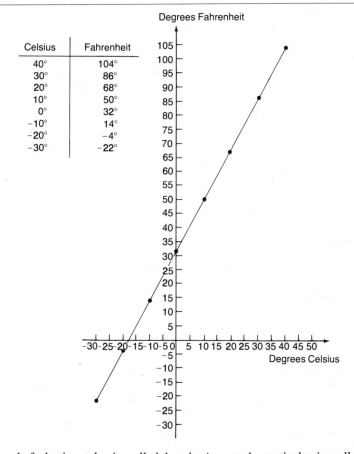

Celsius	Fahrenheit
40°	104°
30°	86°
20°	68°
10°	50°
0°	32°
-10°	14°
-20°	-4°
-30°	-22°

posed of a horizontal axis, called the *abscissa,* and a vertical axis, called the *ordinate.* Each axis is a number line, and the axes intersect at the *origin,* where each number line reads zero.

Frequently, the two variables in an equation are labeled x and y. It is traditional to represent the values of x on the horizontal axis and the values of y on the vertical axis.

Example. $y = x^2$

A general approach to graphing an equation is to make a table of x, y pairs that satisfy the equation and then to locate or plot these points on the graph. Continue until you have enough points on the graph to be sure how they should be connected from left to right.

For example, in the graph of $y = x^2$, you might be uncertain exactly how the graph would go from $(0, 0)$ to $(1, 1)$. You could investigate this section by adding to your table $x = \frac{1}{2}$, for which $y = \frac{1}{4}$. Now it is clearer what sort of curve the graph follows in this region.

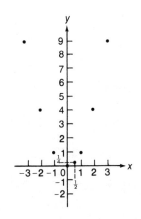

$y = x^2$

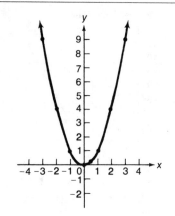

x	y
3	9
2	4
1	1
0	0
−1	1
−2	4
−3	9
$\frac{1}{2}$	$\frac{1}{4}$

Linear, or First-Degree, Equations

A *linear equation* is one that has a straight-line graph.

Example. $2x - 3y = 12$

x	y
0	−4
1	−$\frac{10}{3}$
2	−$\frac{8}{3}$
3	−2
4	−$\frac{4}{3}$
5	−$\frac{2}{3}$
6	0
.	.
.	.
.	.

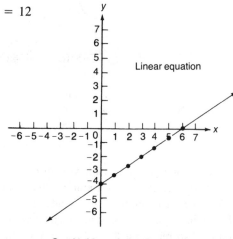

Graph of $2x - 3y = 12$

Equations that have straight-line graphs are always algebraically equivalent to the *general linear equation,*

$$ax + by + c = 0, \quad \text{where} \quad x \text{ and } y \text{ are the variables,}$$
$$a, b, \text{ and } c \text{ are real numbers,}$$
$$a \text{ and } b \text{ are not both zero.}$$

Example.

$$F = \tfrac{9}{5}C + 32$$

is algebraically equivalent to

$$5F = 9C + 5 \times 32$$
$$= 9C + 160$$

multiplying both sides of the equation by 5 in order to remove fractions

which is algebraically equivalent to

$$0 = 9C - 5F + 160$$

adding $-5F$ to both sides of the equation in order to have zero on one side

which is a general linear equation in the variables C and F.

Any equation that can be put in the form $ax + by + c = 0$ has a straight-line graph, and is called a linear (or *first-degree*) equation. Whenever you can recognize an equation as linear, you will not need a lengthy x and y table for graphing it, because two points are enough to determine a straight line.

Other forms of linear equations and their graphs are discussed more fully in the SLOPE article.

Second-Degree Equations

Nonlinear equations may be graphed by making a careful table of x, y pairs for which the equation is true.

Example. $xy = 12$

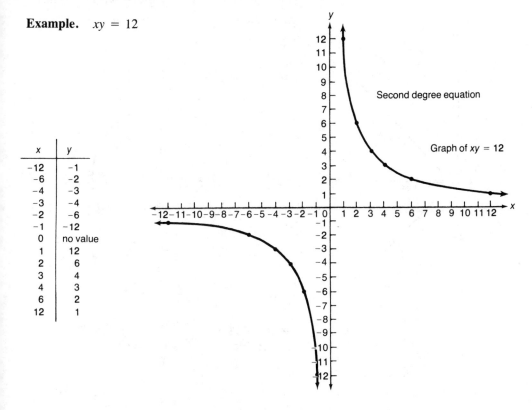

x	y
-12	-1
-6	-2
-4	-3
-3	-4
-2	-6
-1	-12
0	no value
1	12
2	6
3	4
4	3
6	2
12	1

Second degree equation

Graph of $xy = 12$

Second-degree equations are those algebraically equivalent to the form

$$Ax^2 + Bxy + Cy^2 + Dx + Ey + F = 0,$$

where   *x* and *y* are variables,

        A, B, C, D, E, and *F* are real numbers,

        A, B, and *C* are not all equal to zero.

These are called *second*-degree equations because the exponents of the variables in each term sum to at most *two*. The possible variable terms with exponent sum two are x^2, xy, and y^2.

Example. $xy = 12$ is algebraically equivalent to

          $xy - 12 = 0$ which is a general second-degree equation with $B = 1$, $F = -12$, and A, C, D, E each equal to zero.

The graphs of second-degree equations are CONIC SECTIONS.

Examples.   The graph of $xy = 12$ is a *hyperbola;*

          the graph of $x^2 - y^2 = 1$ is another *hyperbola;*

          the graph of $x^2 + y^2 = 25$ is a *circle;*

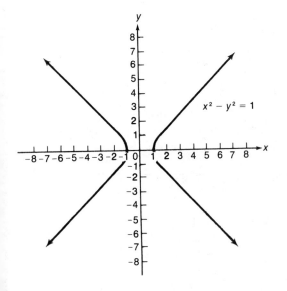

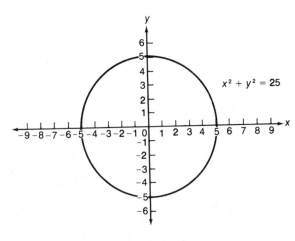

the graph of $x^2 + 4y^2 = 100$ is an *ellipse;*

the graph of $x = y^2$ is a *parabola.*

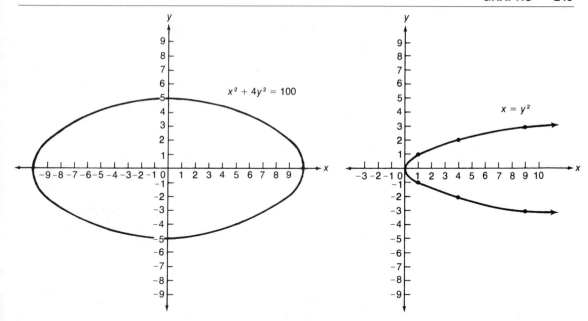

You can confirm the graph of each of these equations by making a table of x, y pairs for which the equation is true. And the x, y table technique may be used to graph any other equation in two variables.

In turn, it is true that many graphs other than straight lines and conic sections can also be described by equations, although for irregular graphs these equations can often be difficult to find and are usually approximated.

Examples.

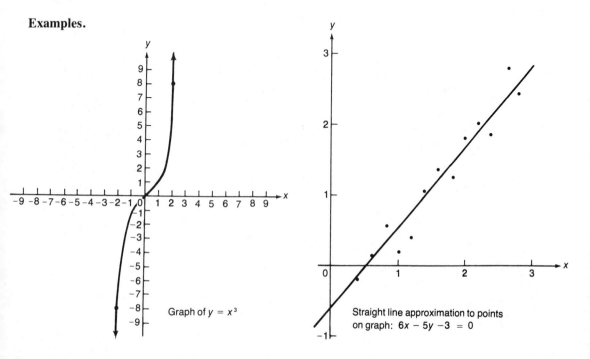

Graph of $y = x^3$

Straight line approximation to points on graph: $6x - 5y - 3 = 0$

OTHER KINDS OF GRAPHS AND GRAPH PAPERS

Any relation between two quantities can be graphed. Relations may be not only tables of statistical data and equations but others, such as INEQUALITIES for which a graph may cover an entire area, or FUNCTIONS for which the graphs may be discontinuous (not all in one piece).

Examples.

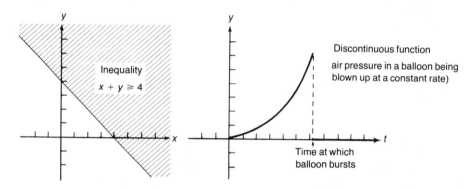

Inequality

$x + y \geq 4$

Discontinuous function

air pressure in a balloon being blown up at a constant rate)

Time at which balloon bursts

Furthermore, graphs need not be limited to two-dimensional Cartesian-coordinate systems. There are many other kinds of graphs and paper to plot them on.

Isometric graph paper uses three rather than two sets of parallel lines. You can therefore use isometric paper to sketch a three-dimensional surface.

Isometric graph paper used to show three dimensions

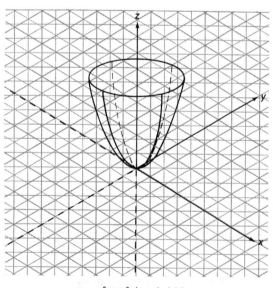

$z = x^2 + y^2$ (paraboloid)

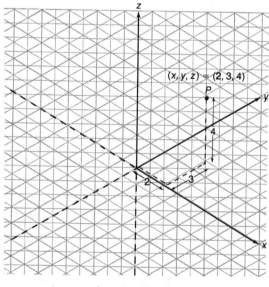

$(x, y, z) = (2, 3, 4)$

Logarithmic graph paper is based on LOGARITHMS. Semi-log graph paper has one axis marked on a logarithmic scale. Log-log graph paper has both axes marked on logarithmic scales. Graphing *x* or *y* on a logarithmic scale is actually graphing log *x* or log *y*, because of the spacing of the lines. For certain functions this has enormous advantages.

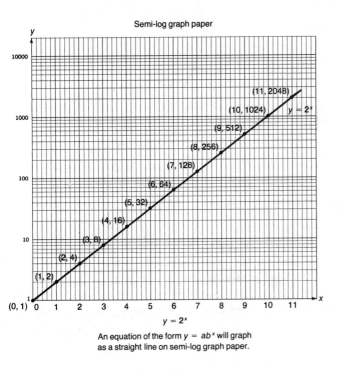

Semi-log graph paper

$y = 2^x$

An equation of the form $y = ab^x$ will graph as a straight line on semi-log graph paper.

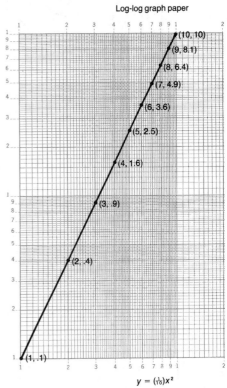

Log-log graph paper

$y = (\tfrac{1}{10})x^2$

An equation of the form $y = ax^b$ will graph as a straight line on log-log graph paper

Polar-coordinate graph paper is based on the polar COORDINATE system in which every point is located by

     r, its distance from the origin, and

     θ, its angle from the polar axis.

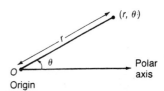

For certain curves, polar coordinates are more useful than Cartesian coordinates, as is shown on the next page.

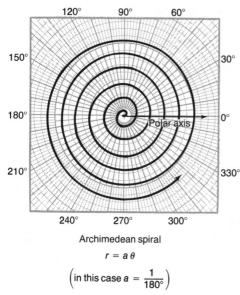

Archimedean spiral

$$r = a\theta$$

$$\left(\text{in this case } a = \frac{1}{180°}\right)$$

Polar graph paper

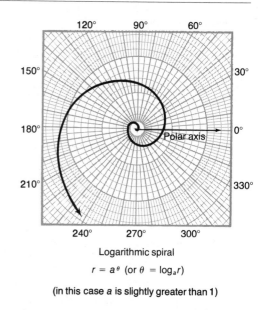

Logarithmic spiral

$$r = a^\theta \text{ (or } \theta = \log_a r)$$

(in this case a is slightly greater than 1)

ESTIMATION FROM A GRAPH

It is often necessary to read values *from* a graph. For instance, after a graph is obtained by plotting some points of statistical or experimental data, an experimenter will predict y values for other values of x.

For example, an experiment might give the points shown. And one might reasonably ask for an estimated y at $x = 2$ and at $x = 6$.

A smooth graph of this situation might follow the dotted line, so one way to estimate those y's is to read them from the sketched curve. This would give:

$$\text{when } x = 2, y \doteq 1.4$$
$$\text{when } x = 6, y \doteq 9,$$

where the symbol $\doteq$ means *approximately* equal.

Of course, you might have dotted in a slightly different curve, so your estimated y values might be different. For $x = 2$, estimated y values would probably differ only slightly, but for $x = 6$, the estimated y values might vary quite a bit. This is because it is difficult to be sure how to continue a curve beyond the last given point, and it is especially difficult if the curve is steeply rising.

This example actually illustrates two different types of estimation:

Extrapolation is the estimation of a value *beyond* the given points.

Interpolation is the estimation of a value *between* given points.

In general, interpolation is more reliable than extrapolation.

x	y
1	1
3	2
4	3
5	5

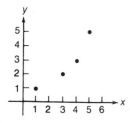

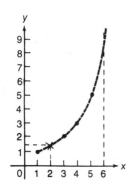

Linear interpolation is one method used to estimate y values, particularly if one does not have a good picture. This method connects the closest two points by a straight *line* and estimates the third point as if it were on that line.

In the above example, since $x = 2$ is *halfway* from $x = 1$ to $x = 3$, the estimated y by linear interpolation will be *halfway* from 1 to 2. Hence,

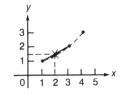

$$\text{when } x = 2, \ y \doteq 1.5$$

According to the dotted curve picture, a better estimated y is slightly *less* than 1.5, but 1.5 is reasonably close.

Linear interpolation is very useful if you are using a table (of square roots or LOGARITHMS or TRIGONOMETRIC FUNCTIONS) which does not contain exactly the point you need.

Example. $\sqrt{2} = 1.414$

$\sqrt{3} = 1.732$

What about $\sqrt{2.3}$?

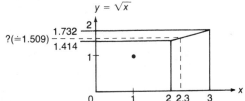

$y = \sqrt{x}$

Since 2.3 is $\frac{3}{10}$ of the way from 2 to 3, $\sqrt{2.3}$ is approximately $\frac{3}{10}$ of the way from $\sqrt{2}$ to $\sqrt{3}$.

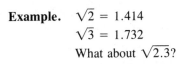

$\sqrt{2} \ \ = 1.414$

$\sqrt{2.3} \doteq 1.414 + \frac{3}{10} (1.732 - 1.414) = 1.509$

$\sqrt{3} \ \ = 1.732$

This estimated value is close to the actual value: $\sqrt{2.3}$ = 1.51657...

GRAPH THEORY

The word ''graph'' has another meaning in a branch of mathematics called *graph theory*. Graph theory is the study of networks, such as the Seven Bridges of Koenigsberg (see TOPOLOGY). Euler's paper on this problem published in 1736 was the beginning of graph theory. It is now one of the fastest growing branches of modern mathematics.

A network, or graph, in graph theory consists of a set of points with lines connecting some of the points.

A network graph reduces a circulation plan to its bare essentials. Rail and air transport routes, rush-hour traffic flow, and complex electric circuitry are just a few of the problems that can be simplified and handled by graph theory.

There are intriguing *games* associated with graph theory, such as the game of Sim. Two players start with the six points at the corners of a hexagon and take turns drawing a line between any two points, without redrawing a line. They use different-colored pencils, and the first player

A network graph

A directed graph, or digraph

to complete (or be forced to complete) a *triangle* with three of the six starting points as vertices is the loser.

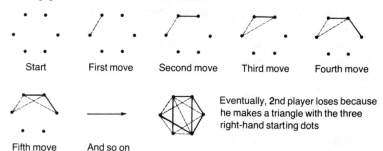

REFERENCES

References on graph theory

John N. Fujii, *Puzzles and Graphs* (National Council of Teachers of Mathematics, 1966); a number of interesting verbal problems solvable by graph theory.

Martin Gardner, "Mathematical Games: Graphs that can help cannibals, missionaries, wolves, goats and cabbages get there from here," *Scientific American,* February 1980; explores theorems on directed graphs and discusses applications—including round-robin tournaments, ordering of preferences, and scheduling for manufacturing.

Martin Gardner, "Mathematical Games: Sim, Chomp and Race Track: new games for the intellect," *Scientific American,* January 1973, pp. 108–113; further discussion of games played on graph paper.

Oystein Ore, *Graphs and Their Uses,* New Mathematical Library (L. W. Singer Co., 1963); this book is entirely on networks and graph theory, rather than on any other kinds of graphs.

References on statistical graphs and graphs of relations

Lancelot Hogben, *Mathematics for the Million* (published in Great Britain, and by W. W. Norton & Co. in the U.S., in many editions, from 1936–1968); contains an enormous and fascinating chapter on graphing and its applications.

Harold R. Jacobs, *Mathematics: A Human Endeavor* (W. H. Freeman & Co., 1970); pp. 422–430 for statistical graphs; pp. 84–121 for functions and their graphs; pp. 122–128 for interpolation and extrapolation.

See also STATISTICS, COORDINATE SYSTEMS, EQUATIONS, INEQUALITIES, FUNCTIONS, and SLOPE.

HISTORY

HISTORY

A comprehensive history of mathematics is beyond the scope of this book. However, many of the important developments are presented here in order to provide an overall picture—a framework to which you can add other information. (Also see the time line at the beginning of the book, and the biographical index in APPENDIX II.)

The historical development of the REAL NUMBER system traces a path almost exactly parallel to the overall history of mathematics. Nearly every time people have learned to manipulate NUMBERS in more sophisticated ways in order to solve more complicated problems, they have had to expand their idea of the real number system.

Unquestionably, the first real numbers used were the *natural,* or counting, *numbers.* The earliest written records of various cultures include references to counting numbers. And even tribes that have not developed a writing system invariably have some type of NUMERAL SYSTEM.

With the development of agriculture and trade in ancient civilizations, there arose a need to *divide* things. Land had to be redivided among owners after each flood. Units of grain, wool, and salt had to be divided when traded for other goods. And as a result of all this division, there arose a need for numbers to represent quantities smaller than one. Both the Babylonians and the Egyptians were using RATIONAL NUMBERS or FRACTIONS to represent such quantities at least two thousand years before the birth of Christ.

When a thriving culture began to flourish on the Greek islands and peninsula about 800 B.C., these people too used the natural numbers and the positive rational numbers in conducting their business. However, in Greek civilization there came to be a sharp distinction between the arithmetic computations of scribes and tradespeople and the pure mathematics of philosophers and scholars.

One famous band of Greek scholars was the Pythagorean Order. Although it originally consisted of the disciples of the Greek mathematician Pythagoras (about 580–500 B.C.), the Pythagorean school continued to attract scholars for nearly two hundred years after the death of the master. The Pythagoreans were a secret fellowship of aristocrats devoted to the study of mathematics and number lore. These men and women believed that the counting numbers, and particularly the number one, were of divine origin. The Pythagoreans strove to preserve the unity of integers in all of their computations. For example, they thought of *rational fractions* not as parts of a whole, but rather as RATIOS of whole numbers.

Ironically, these scholars who so revered the whole numbers were the discoverers of *irrational numbers,* numbers that *cannot* be expressed as a ratio of whole numbers. The Pythagoreans, in their work with geometry, discovered that it is possible for two line segments to be *incommensurable*. Two line segments are incommensurable when there is no unit of length, no matter how tiny, that measures both of them a whole number of times. The side and diagonal of a square are two such incommensurable segments. If the side of a square is one unit long, there is no number that can be expressed as the ratio of two integers that will give the length of the diagonal. The length of that segment, therefore, is an *irrational number,* and by the PYTHAGOREAN THEOREM, its length is $\sqrt{2}$.

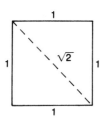

The discovery of irrational numbers appalled the Pythagoreans. They could prove to themselves that such numbers must exist, yet their existence appeared to undermine the whole Pythoragorean philosophy, which had rested firmly on the primacy of the whole numbers. Consequently, the Pythagoreans resolved to conceal the existence of such numbers from the rest of the world. According to legend, the pledge to secrecy was so sacred that at least one Pythagorean, Hippasus, was drowned for revealing the secret.

However, by the third century B.C. the Greeks had developed ways of operating with irrational numbers by introducing the idea of *rational approximation*. For practical purposes, irrational numbers can be approximated by rational numbers and the closeness of the approximation can be determined by comparing DECIMAL expansions of the rational number and the irrational number. (See RATIONAL AND IRRATIONAL NUMBERS.)

The next real number to be discovered was ZERO. Zero is such an integral part of our present numeral system that you may be surprised to discover that ancient Egyptian and Greek mathematicians computed without it. The Babylonians apparently did have a zero placeholder that functioned the way the digit zero functions in a number like 407. But credit for discovering that zero is a *number* probably goes to the Hindus. Some sources suggest that the first systematic use of zero is found in an arithmetic by a seventh century Hindu mathematician, Brahmagupta. However, of much greater importance to the mathematics of Western Europe was the use of zero by the Arabian mathematician Al-Khowarizmi in his *Hisab al-jabr wa'l muqabalah*, a treatise on ALGEBRA written around A.D. 825. In the thirteenth century this work was translated into Latin by the Italian mathematician Leonardo of Pisa, known as Fibonacci, who popularized the Hindu-Arabic numerals in the Western world.

During the Renaissance, Europeans began to use *negative numbers,* which the Hindus and Arabs had been using freely. The impetus for the use of SIGNED NUMBERS (both positive and negative) came from two sources: the increase in commerce and bookkeeping that characterized the Renaissance, and the revival of interest in pure mathematics, especially algebra. It is difficult, if not impossible, to attribute the discovery of negative numbers to any one person. One of the earliest uses of + and − signs is found in a German business arithmetic by Johann Widman, published in 1489. Widman did not use the signs to indicate operations but rather to indicate a surplus or deficiency. During the sixteenth century, various algebraists recognized negative numbers as solutions to equations. And in 1545, the Italian mathematician Girolamo Cardano included negative numbers as solutions to equations in his great *Ars Magna,* which was considered the standard work in algebra for years thereafter.

But Cardano also encountered problems to which there was no solution in the set of numbers already discovered. That is, there was no solution in the set of *real numbers*—the set that includes the positive and negative rational numbers, the positive and negative irrational numbers, and zero. Consider, for example, the problem of finding the square root of −1, the solution to the EQUATION $x^2 = -1$. Since any real number times itself equals a positive real number, there is *no* real number to represent $\sqrt{-1}$ or the *square root of any negative number.*

Cardano and other sixteenth-century algebraists refused to stop when they arrived at the square root of a negative number. Instead, they used these nonreal numbers to solve other problems. For example, Cardano solved this problem by using the square root of negative fifteen.

Problem: How can you divide the number 10 into two parts so that the product of the two parts is 40?

Solution: $(5 + \sqrt{-15})$ and $(5 - \sqrt{-15})$, because

$$
\begin{array}{c}
5 + \sqrt{-15} \\
+\ 5 - \sqrt{-15} \\
\hline
10
\end{array}
\quad \text{and} \quad \times
\begin{array}{c}
5 + \sqrt{-15} \\
5 - \sqrt{-15} \\
\hline
25 + 5\sqrt{-15} \\
-\ 5\sqrt{-15} - -15 \\
\hline
25 \qquad\quad +15 = 40
\end{array}
$$

In this one example Cardano toyed with the possibility of taking the square root of a negative number, but he dismissed the whole idea as being too fanciful. Nevertheless, other algebraists continued to be interested in such numbers, and in the seventeenth century, the French mathematician René Descartes gave the name *"imaginary"* to numbers involving the square root of a negative number. He in turn gave the name *"real"* to the large class of rational and irrational numbers (positive, negative, and zero) that could be located on a real NUMBER LINE. In the nineteenth century, the German mathematician Carl Friedrich Gauss introduced the term COMPLEX NUMBER to describe any number composed of real *or* imaginary numbers.

Since the acceptance of all the real numbers in the sixteenth century, mathematicians have come to recognize many important properties of the real numbers, and they have come to understand the importance of viewing the real numbers as a complete system. (See FIELD PROPERTIES.)

The end of the seventeenth century was a high-water mark in the mathematical development of Western Europe. Two men working independently—Sir Isaac Newton of England and Gottfried Wilhelm von Leibniz of Germany—developed the infinitesimal CALCULUS. The calculus proved to be a powerful mathematical tool that enabled mathematicians to solve difficult problems involving area, volume, and motion. During the eighteenth century, mathematicians found numerous applications for the calculus.

However, the calculus made use of ideas that mathematicians had long avoided—the concepts of *infinity* and the *infinitesimal*. (See INFINITY.) During the nineteenth century, mathematicians worked to incorporate these difficult concepts into the calculus in such a way that it would rest on a logically consistent foundation. Among those who sought to give the calculus a rigorous foundation was the French mathematician Augustin-Louis Cauchy, who used the notion of a *limit* as its basis. As an example of a limit, consider the fixed value approached by an infinite SERIES, which is the sum of an infinite SEQUENCE. The sum $\frac{1}{2} + \frac{1}{4} + \frac{1}{8} + \frac{1}{16} \ldots$ approaches closer and closer to 1 as more terms are added. Thus, 1 is the limit of that infinite series, although the sum never actually reaches 1.

The efforts of Cauchy and others to place calculus on a solid foundation made mathematicians look at the real numbers in a new light. An infinitely repeating decimal could now be viewed as an infinite series approaching a rational number as a limit. For example, the number $0.33333\ldots$ could be thought of as the series

$$\frac{3}{10} + \frac{3}{100} + \frac{3}{1000} + \frac{3}{10,000} + \ldots$$

a series that approaches the number $\frac{1}{3}$ as a limit.

The work of another nineteenth-century French mathematician, Joseph Liouville, led to another discovery about the real numbers. He found that there are some irrational numbers that are not the solution to any polynomial EQUATION of the form

$$ax^n + bx^{n-1} + \ldots + px + q = 0.$$

An example is $2^{\sqrt{3}}$. Such numbers are called *transcendental numbers*, and the rest of the real numbers, each of which *is* the solution to some polynomial equation, are called *algebraic numbers*.

Interestingly, the discovery of transcendental numbers in the nineteenth century provided the key to a riddle of GEOMETRIC CON-STRUCTION that had puzzled mathematicians since the time of the ancient Greeks. They had asked, "Is it possible, using only a straightedge and compass, to construct a square with an area exactly equal to that of a given circle?" It turns out that only algebraic numbers can be constructed with straightedge and compass—and not all of them, at that. You *can* construct any rational number and *some* irrational numbers, such as $\sqrt{2}$ (See NUMBER LINE), but *none* of the transcendental numbers. When in 1882 German mathematician C. F. Lindemann showed that π is transcendental, he proved the impossibility of ever squaring the circle. The side of such a square would be $r\sqrt{\pi}$, and the transcendental $\sqrt{\pi}$ cannot be constructed. (See CIRCLE.)

Finally, there was yet another major development in the nineteenth century: the revolutionary work of three geometers hit the mathematics community with such force that the shock waves affected nearly every branch of mathematics, including the understanding of the nature of the real number system. Previously, in Euclid's geometry there was a set of statements called *postulates,* which were not proved but were assumed to be true because the truth of these statements was intuitively obvious. One famous postulate was Euclid's fifth—that through a given point P not on line $L,$ only one straight line can be drawn parallel to $L.$ For centuries, mathematicians had worried about that postulate. They had felt that it was really a theorem and could be proved by LOGIC and DEDUCTION to be true in terms of the other postulates. (See GEOMETRY for more precise detail.)

However, in the nineteenth century, three men working independently—Gauss of Germany, Lobachevsky of Russia, and Bolyai of Hungary—demonstrated that it was possible to develop a logically consistent geometry assuming the opposite of Euclid's fifth postulate: that through a given point P not on line $L,$ any number of lines can be drawn parallel to $L,$ or, no lines can be drawn parallel to $L.$ No longer were the postulates statements of universal truth. Gauss, Lobachevsky, and Bolyai had demonstrated that postulates were merely assumptions and that it was possible to develop logically consistent systems on the basis of different assumptions.

Suddenly nothing in mathematics could be taken for granted as obviously true or obviously self-consistent—not even the real number system. In fact, establishing the postulates, or assumptions, underlying the real number system became an increasing important goal as mathematicians discovered that their work was logically consistent only if the real number system was consistent.

A significant step toward providing a postulational basis for the real numbers was taken by the Italian logician Guiseppe Peano. In the 1890s, Peano developed a set of five postulates that he felt provided a logical foundation for the real numbers. In the twentieth century, other mathematicians, including David Hilbert, Bertrand Russell, and Alfred North Whitehead, continued the search for a logical foundation for the real number system.

In 1931, a young Austrian mathematician, Kurt Gödel, proved a disturbing theorem showing that systems such as those of Peano, Hilbert, Russell, and Whitehead would always include some statements that can never be proved true or false; that is, some "undecidable" statements. (See MATHEMATICAL SYSTEM, foundations section.) Yet despite Gödel's theorem, the search for a logical foundation for the real numbers goes on; we cannot yet conclude the history of the real number system.

REFERENCES

Robert Hackworth and Joseph Howland, *History of Real Numbers,* a module from Introductory College Mathematics, The Saunders Series in Modular Mathematics (1976).

David Eugene Smith, *History of Mathematics,* 2 volumes (Ginn, 1923; reprinted by Dover, 1958)—accurate, exhaustive, well illustrated—in short, marvelous; the most comprehensive yet accessible sourcebook for details of mathematical history. Volume 1 discusses historical periods from prehistoric to late nineteenth-century, covering over 1100 mathematicians. Geographic areas include China, Japan, India, Persia, and Arabia, where mathematics existed in many ways independent of the West. Volume 2 is arranged by topics, from numerals, arithmetic operations, calculating machines, fractions, and decimals through irrational and complex numbers, geometry, pi, and others, up to trigonometry and calculus.

Other general references on the history of mathematics

Carl B. Boyer, *A History of Mathematics* (John Wiley & Sons, 1968); a popular chronological, comprehensive college text.

Florian Cajori, *A History of Mathematics,* 3rd ed. (Macmillan, 1919; revised Chelsea, 1980); a comprehensive, compact single-volume history that tells exactly what more than 1600 mathematicians from all over the world did, in a smooth narrative full of interesting asides.

Howard Eves, *An Introduction to the History of Mathematics,* 3rd ed. (Holt, Rinehart & Winston, 1969); another popular text, very clearly presented.

Historical Topics for the Mathematics Classroom, 31st Yearbook of the National Council of Teachers of Mathematics (1969); an excellent reference with capsule histories of all areas of mathematics written by numerous authors; each has several pages of interesting facts, with a bibliography.

Morris Kline, *Mathematical Thought from Ancient to Modern Times* (Oxford University Press, 1972); a massive, detailed, and authoritative work arranged first by mathematical topics and then chronologically within topics, detailing steps leading to conceptual breakthroughs. Kline has deftly sorted out the sheer bulk of mathematical thought.

Morris Kline, ed., *Mathematics: An Introduction to Its Spirit and Use: Readings from Scientific American* (W. H. Freeman & Co., 1978), pp. 6–45; a fine collection of original articles, introduced within a historical framework. Articles about the Rhind Papyrus, Cardano, Pascal, Descartes, Newton's writing, Leibniz, and the invention of analytic geometry are included.

Morris Kline, ed., *Mathematics in the Modern World: Readings from Scientific American* (W. H. Freeman & Co., 1968), pp. 30–83; original biographical articles (Descartes, Newton, Laplace, Hamilton, Babbage, Clifford, Maxwell, Ramanujan, and ''Bourbaki'') collected and introduced within an overall perspective.

Morris Kline, *Mathematics in Western Culture* (Oxford University Press, 1953; Galaxy paperback); a classic reference that explains in detail why and how mathematical developments arose; for example, how fifteenth-century artists' studies of perspective led to projective geometry.

Edna E. Kramer, *The Nature and Growth of Modern Mathematics* (Hawthorn Books, 1970; Princeton University Press, 1982); very pleasant reading; comprehensive but with many anecdotes and clear explanations of the mathematics necessary to understand the history.

Henrietta O. Midonick, *The Treasury of Mathematics* (Philosophical Library, 1965); a single collection of 54 original texts, including Apollonius on CONIC SECTIONS; the Rhind Papyrus; Babylonian cuneiform texts; portions of Boole's *Laws of Thought* and Euclid's *Elements;* writings of Cantor, Descartes, Gauss, Leibniz, and Newton; and a number of selections from India, Latin America, and the Orient. Sources are translated and presented with photographs, diagrams, and historical and biographical material.

Frank Swetz, "The Evolution of Mathematics in Ancient China," *Mathematics Magazine,* January 1979, pp. 10–19; an exposition of early Chinese mathematical accomplishments, revealing sophisticated approaches to arithmetic and algebra.

Claudia Zaslavsky, *Africa Counts* (Prindle, Weber, & Schmidt, 1973); an informative and well-illustrated pioneering work on the history of mathematics in Africa.

Biographical references

Arthur Beckhard, *Albert Einstein* (G. P. Putnam's Sons, 1959; Avon paperback).

Eric T. Bell, *Men of Mathematics* (Simon & Schuster, 1937; Fireside paperback); Zeno, Eudoxus, Archimedes, Descartes, Fermat, Pascal, Newton, Leibniz, the Bernoullis, Euler, Lagrange, Laplace, Monge, Fourier, Poncelet, Gauss, Cauchy, Lobachevsky, Abel, Jacobi, Hamilton, Galois, Sylvester, Cayley, Weierstrass, Kovalevsky, Boole, Hermite, Kronecker, Riemann, Kummer, Dedekind, Poincaré, and Cantor.

Julian Lowell Coolidge, *The Mathematics of Great Amateurs* (Oxford University Press, 1949; Dover, 1963); Plato, Omar Khayyám, Franceschi, da Vinci, Dürer, Napier, Pascal, Arnauld, DeWitt, Hudde, Brouncker, L'Hôpital, Buffon, Diderot, Horner, and Bolzano.

Joseph and Frances Gies, *Leonard of Pisa and the New Mathematics of the Middle Ages* (Thomas Y. Crowell Co., 1969).

Oystein Ore, *Cardano: The Gambling Scholar* (Princeton University Press, 1953; Dover, 1965); includes translation from Latin of Cardano's *Book on Games of Chance*.

Lynn M. Osen, *Women in Mathematics* (M.I.T. Press, 1974); Hypatia, Agnesi, du Châtelet, Germain, Herschel, Somerville, Kovalevsky, and Noether.

Teri Perl, *Math Equals: Biographies of Women Mathematicians + Related Activities* (Addison-Wesley, 1978); Hypatia, du Châtelet,

Agnesi, Germain, Somerville, Lovelace, Kovalevsky, Young, and Noether.

Constance Reid, *Hilbert* (Springer-Verlag, 1970); a complete and fascinating biography of a truly great twentieth-century mathematician.

Scientific American: The starred articles are reprinted in two books of readings collected and introduced by Morris Kline:

*Mathematics in the Modern World (W. H. Freeman & Co., 1968)

**Mathematics: An Introduction to Its Spirit and Use (W. H. Freeman & Co., 1978)

April 1952:	Philip and Emily Morrison, "The Strange Life of Charles Babbage"*
June 1953:	James R. Newman, "Review of *Cardano, The Gambling Scholar* by Ore"**
May 1954:	Sir Edmund Whittaker, "William Rowan Hamilton"*
July 1955:	I. Bernard Cohen, "An Interview with Einstein"
December 1955:	I. Bernard Cohen, "Isaac Newton"*
April 1956:	Warren Weaver, "Lewis Carroll: Mathematician"
October 1959:	A. C. Crombie, "Descartes"* **
December 1959:	James R. Newman, "Review of *Blaise Pascal: The Life and Work of a Realist* by Mortimer"**
May 1968:	Frederick C. Kreiling, "Leibniz"**
July 1977:	Ian Stewart, "Gauss"

Francis Benson Stonaker, *Famous Mathematicians* (J. B. Lippincott Co., 1966); Euclid, Archimedes, Aryabhatta, Al-Khowarizmi, Descartes, Newton, Lagrange, Gauss, Galois, von Neumann, and Wiener—interesting biographies for young readers spanning the history of mathematics.

Herbert Westren Turnbull, *The Great Mathematicians* (New York University Press, 1961); also in James R. Newman, *World of Mathematics,* Vol. 1; Thales, Pythagoras, Eudoxus, Euclid, Archimedes, Apollonius, Pappus, Diophantus, Kepler, Napier, Descartes, Pascal, Newton, the Bernoullis, Euler, Maclaurin, Lagrange, Gauss, and Hamilton.

Additional historical material is included in most other articles in this book. See particularly COMPUTERS, EQUATIONS, FRACTIONS, GEOMETRY, NUMBERS, NUMERAL SYSTEMS, PI, PROJECTION, PYTHAGOREAN THEOREM.

INDUCTION

INDUCTION: the process of arriving at a conclusion by generalizing from particular observations; reasoning from the particular to the general.

INDUCTIVE REASONING

Forming generalizations from particular observations is a common occurrence. For example, a child who is burned by a hot radiator may conclude that all radiators are hot. A person who tastes a hard green apple may come to the conclusion that all green apples are sour. A few particular observations are used as the basis for generalizations about a whole class of things, and these are examples of inductive reasoning.

Inductive reasoning is used to discover patterns and relationships. But induction involves a certain amount of intelligent *guesswork*. And not all conclusions drawn by the process of induction are correct. For instance, although you might conclude that green apples are sour, there are some tasty varieties of apples that are green when ripe and are not sour.

Erroneous induction can also occur in mathematics.

Example. Consider the quantity $n^2 - n + 41$.

If you substitute $n = 1$, or $n = 2$, or $n = 3$ into this formula, you will get 41, 43, or 47, which are three *prime numbers*.

You might be tempted to conclude that substituting any positive integer for n will yield a prime number.

Further evidence supporting this conclusion can be found by substituting many other numbers for n, such as 4, 5, 6, 7, 8, 9, 10, 19, 20, 25, 28, ...

However, if you substitute 41 for n, you will get $(41)^2 - 41 + 41 = (41)^2$, which is *not* a prime number.

Therefore the observation that this formula yields prime numbers does *not* generalize to *any* positive integer *n*.

So, inductive thinking must be undertaken with caution.

Need for Proof of Inductions

A conclusion reached by inductive reasoning may be true or false. In mathematics it is necessary to test the conclusion and to prove that it is true or that it is false. The last example illustrates this need, because it proves that the inductive conclusion (that the formula would always produce prime numbers) was false. An induction cannot be trusted without PROOF. For this reason, an inductive conclusion without proof is called an *incomplete induction*.

However, a proof of an inductive conclusion may be difficult to supply. One example of an induction in mathematics that has not yet been proved either true or false is Goldbach's conjecture. Christian Goldbach was a Russian mathematician who in 1742 posed this question in a letter to fellow mathematician Leonhard Euler. Goldbach's conjecture is so apparently simple that many professional and amateur mathematicians have since tried to prove it.

Goldbach's conjecture: "Every even integer greater than four can be expressed as the sum of two odd prime numbers."

Supporting examples.

$$12 = 7 + 5 \qquad 26 = 7 + 19 \qquad 54 = 13 + 41$$

By using a computer, the truth of this conjecture has been shown for millions of integers, and for no even integer has it been found false. But no proof has ever been given that it is true for *all* even integers greater than four.

The Vital Role of Inductive Reasoning

Although inductive reasoning may not provide a proof of a conclusion, induction is the heart of experimental science. Most scientific principles have been discovered by inductive reasoning. In many sciences, demonstrative proof may be impossible, but all scientists search for confirmation of their theories and test their inductive conclusions as fully as possible.

Mathematics is usually considered a *de*ductive science because DE-

DUCTION is the method by which mathematicians usually try to prove their inductive conclusions. However, underlying all of mathematics is the *in*ductive reasoning that produces the ideas.

A GAME OF INDUCTION

There is an intriguing game called *Eleusis* that is based on inductive thinking. Eleusis is played with two decks of ordinary playing cards by four or more players. The dealer decides on a ''secret rule'' for a proper order of playing the cards (for example, that odd and even numbers will alternate, regardless of color). The players must try to discover the rule.

On each play, a player tries a card. If the dealer says it correctly follows the rule, then it may be added to the ''main line'' of correct cards. Cards that are incorrect are placed on ''sidelines'' below the card they were meant to follow. In the example, Q♦ was meant to follow 4♣, but was incorrect.

Example.

Main Line of correct cards, played from left to right

The players keep making inductive guesses, or theories, based on the evidence they have so far, and they experiment with their theories to uncover the underlying rule.

Eleusis was invented in 1956 by Robert Abbott, a student at the University of Colorado, who was studying the psychological phenomenon of sudden insight. Mathematicians and other scientists have become fascinated with the game because it is a model of the induction central to the scientific method.

Reference on Eleusis

Martin Gardner, ''Mathematical Games: On Playing New Eleusis, the game that simulates the search for truth'' (*Scientific American*, October 1977); much more detail, including amended rules and scoring.

MATHEMATICAL INDUCTION: a formal method of *proving* that a statement about a positive integer n is true for *all* positive integers n, by:

(1) proving that the statement is true for the first integer; then
(2) proving that if the statement is true for n, it must be true for $(n + 1)$.

How Mathematical Induction Works

Proving something by mathematical induction is like knocking down a chain of dominoes. To successfully set up a chain reaction to knock down all the dominoes, you must do both of the following:

(1) You must knock down the first domino, and
(2) You must also space the dominoes so that each one, in falling, will knock down the next.

These steps correspond exactly to the steps of a mathematical induction. Knocking down the first domino, or proving a statement for the first integer, is what allows a mathematical proof to begin. Spacing the dominoes so that each pushes over the next is what allows the proof to continue until all the dominoes fall or until all the integers are included.

Step 2 provides that if a mathematical statement is true for the first integer, it is true for the second integer. And then, since the statement is true for the second integer, step 2 can again be used to prove the statement for the third integer. And if the statement is true for the third integer, it likewise must be true for the fourth, and so on. In this manner the statement is proved for all integers n. An example is shown on the next page.

Because formal mathematical induction includes a *proof*, it is sometimes called *complete induction*.

Example.   Prove that the sum of the first n positive integers is $\frac{1}{2}n(n + 1)$. That is, show the truth of the

$$statement:\ 1 + 2 + 3 + 4 + \cdots + n = \tfrac{1}{2}n\,(n + 1).$$

(1) Is the statement true for $n = 1$?
   Yes, because $1 = \frac{1}{2}\,(1)\,(1 + 1) = \frac{1}{2}\,(1)\,(2) = 1$.
(2) Assume that the statement is true for n, and then add $n + 1$ to both sides:

$$
\begin{aligned}
1 + 2 + 3 + 4 + \cdots + n + (n + 1) &= \tfrac{1}{2}n\,(n + 1) + (n + 1) \\
&= \tfrac{1}{2}n\,(n + 1) + 1\,(n + 1) \\
&= (\tfrac{1}{2}n + 1)\,(n + 1) \\
&= \tfrac{1}{2}\,(n + 2)\,(n + 1) \\
&= \tfrac{1}{2}\,(n + 1)\,[(n + 1) + 1]
\end{aligned}
$$

This equation now has the same form as the original statement, for $(n + 1)$ as well as for n. The truth of this statement for any n does indeed imply that the statement is true for $n + 1$ also.

The mathematical induction is now complete. Both steps 1 and 2 have been proved, so the statement has been proved true for *all* integers n.

REFERENCES

References on mathematical or complete induction

Martin Gardner, "Mathematical Games: The 'jump proof' and its similarity to the toppling of a row of dominoes," *Scientific American,* May 1977; a serious but entertaining discussion.

I. S. Sominskii, *The Method of Mathematical Induction,* translated from Russian (Blaisdell, 1961).

*References on inductive thinking, or
incomplete induction*

Harold R. Jacobs, *Mathematics: A Human Endeavor* (W. H. Freeman & Co., 1970), Ch. 1, "The Mathematical Way of Thinking," especially pp. 12–16.

Bruce E. Meserve and Max A. Sobel, *Introduction to Mathematics* (Prentice-Hall, 1973), Ch. 1, "Explorations with Mathematics."

For related articles, see LOGIC and DEDUCTION.

INEQUALITIES

INEQUALITY: a mathematical sentence in which two expressions are connected by a symbol of inequality; a symbolic statement that two mathematical expressions either do not or may not represent the same quantity.

An inequality is one kind of *mathematical sentence*; it uses one of these symbols to express a RELATION between numbers. A mathematical sentence also uses symbols for NUMBERS and symbols for ARITHMETIC OPERATIONS. It makes a statement in symbols to express ideas of equality or inequality. (See also EQUATIONS.) A mathematical sentence may be true, or it may be false, or it may be neither true nor false.

Symbols:

$\neq$ is not equal to
$>$ is greater than
$<$ is less than
$\geq$ is greater than or equal to
$\leq$ is less than or equal to

Examples. $9 > 5$ (Nine is greater than (True) five.)

$7 + 5 < 11 - 8$ (The sum of seven (False) and five is less than the difference of eleven and eight.)

These sentences are called *closed* because they are either always true or always false.

$3x \leq 15$ (Three times a num- (Neither true ber, represented by nor false) x, is less than or equal to fifteen.)

This sentence is called *open* because it may be either true or false depending on what number is substituted for the *variable* x. If $x \leq 5$, the sentence is true. If $x > 5$, the sentence is false.

SOLUTION OF OPEN SENTENCES

The number or numbers that make an open sentence true are called *solutions*, or *roots*. The SET of all roots of an open sentence is called the *solution set*, or *truth set*.

Example. $x + 5 \geq 8$ This inequality has many solutions.
The solution set is {all numbers ≥ 3}.

Solving a sentence means to find the number or numbers, if any, that make the open sentence true. This usually requires the techniques of ALGEBRA. The method for solving an inequality depends upon the degree of the inequality and the number of variables.

CLASSIFICATION OF INEQUALITIES BY DEGREE

Inequalities in One Variable

The *degree* of a sentence in one variable is equal to the greatest EXPONENT of the variable, if all exponents are whole numbers.

Terms and Examples.   *Linear*, or first degree: $3(x - 2) > 7x - 2$
Quadratic, or second degree: $y^2 \geq 4$
Polynomial, or *n*th degree, for $n =$ any positive integer: $x^n > x$.

The linear and quadratic inequalities are polynomial inequalities of first and second degree, respectively.

A polynomial is said to be in *standard form* when the terms are arranged in descending powers of the variable, with the constant term at the end; for instance, $3x^3 - 7x^2 + 13$.

Inequalities in Two Variables

The degree of a sentence in two variables is equal to the highest *sum* of exponents of the variables appearing in one term.

Terms and Examples.   *Linear*, or first degree: $3x - y > 8$
Quadratic, or second degree: $x^2 + y^2 \leq 25$ $xy > 12$

SOLVING AN INEQUALITY IN ONE VARIABLE

Linear Inequalities

The basic approach to solving a linear inequality in one variable is to add, subtract, multiply, or divide both sides of the inequality by the same number until the variable is *isolated* on one side of the inequality.

Any such operation is permitted if it gives an *equivalent sentence,* that is, a sentence with the same solution set. However, when you are working with an inequality rather than an equation, you must pay special attention to negative FACTORS in order to obtain equivalent inequalities:

> To *multiply* or *divide* an inequality by a *negative* number, you must *reverse* the direction of the inequality.

Consider, for example, the inequality

$$1 > -2.$$

If both sides are multiplied by -1, the resulting terms will be -1 and $+2$.

$$1\,(-1) \quad ? \quad -2\,(-1)$$
$$-1 \quad ? \quad 2$$

Thus the inequality sign must be reversed in order for the sentence to be true:

$$-1 < 2$$

You must remember this principle in order to solve an inequality with variables and negative factors.

Example. $-x > 2$

> To multiply both sides by -1, you must reverse the direction of the inequality to obtain an equivalent inequality.

$$x < -2$$

The solution set for this inequality therefore is $x < -2$, which may be *graphed* on a NUMBER LINE as shown.

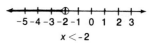

$$x < -2$$

In summary, a linear inequality in x may be solved by isolating x according to some combination of the following operations, each of which gives an equivalent inequality:

The *open circle* at $x = -2$ indicates that $x = -2$ is *not* part of the solution set.

• You may add to or subtract from both sides of an inequality the same number (positive or negative).

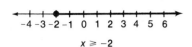

$x \geqslant -2$

The *closed circle* at $x = 2$ shows that $x = -2$ *is* part of this solution set.

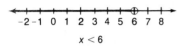

$x < 6$

When two inequalities are combined by "*and*," the solution is where their graphs *overlap*.

- You may multiply or divide both sides of an inequality by the same positive number.
- You may multiply or divide both sides of an inequality by the same negative number *if* you also reverse the direction of the inequality.

Examples.   • $7x + 3 \geqslant -11$ Add -3 to both sides

$\qquad 7x \quad\;\; \geqslant -14$

$\qquad\quad x \quad\;\; \geqslant -2$ Divide both sides by 7

• $\dfrac{x}{-3} > -2$ Multiply both sides by -3 and reverse inequality

$\quad x \; < 6$

• $7x + 3 \geqslant -11$ *and* $\dfrac{x}{-3} > -2.$

Solve each inequality separately, as above, giving

$$x \geqslant -2 \quad and \quad x < 6.$$

The solution set of these combined inequalities may be shown as follows:

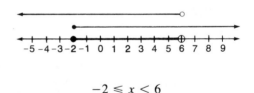

$$-2 \leqslant x < 6$$

The combined inequality of this example may be written as a single statement $-2 \leqslant x < 6$ that says x may be any number between -2 and 6, including $x = -2$, but not $x = 6$.

Quadratic or Polynomial Inequalities

Inequalities of second, or higher, degree are most easily solved when they can be arranged with *zero* on one side and then factored into linear FACTORS. Different combinations of linear inequalities will then provide possible solutions. The possible combinations will depend on whether the product of factors is >0 or <0.

Example. $x^2 + x > 2$

$x^2 + x - 2 > 0$

$(x + 2)(x - 1) > 0$

Add -2 to both sides to obtain zero on the right.

Factor the polynomial on the left.

For the product of two factors to be greater than zero, or positive, either both factors are positive *or* both factors are negative. These are the only possibilities.

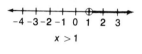

both factors positive   *or*   both factors negative

$x + 2 > 0$ *and* $x - 1 > 0$ $x + 2 < 0$ *and* $x - 1 < 0$

$x > -2$ *and* $x > 1$ $x < -2$ *and* $x < 1$

This combination is satisfied when $x > 1$.   This combination is satisfied when $x < -2$.

The solution set for the original quadratic inequality, $x^2 + x > 2$, is therefore:

$x < -2$ *or* $x > 1$

When two inequalities are combined by "*or*," the solution is the union of *both* individual graphs.

In this example, the combined inequality can*not* be written as a single statement because x cannot at the same time be less than -2 and greater than 1.

INEQUALITIES IN TWO VARIABLES

If a single inequality involves two variables, x and y, there may be an infinite number of (x, y) pairs of numbers that will satisfy the inequality. For example, if $x + y \geq 7$, then $(0, 7)$, $(1, 7)$, $(2, 7)$ all satisfy this inequality, as do $(1, 6)$, $(2, 6)$, $(3, 6)$ and $(0, 8)$, $(0, 9)$, $(0, 10)$. In fact, there are so many possible pairs that an organized list of them is impossible. The best way to show the solution set of an inequality in two variables is usually with a GRAPH.

Example. $x + y \geqslant 7$

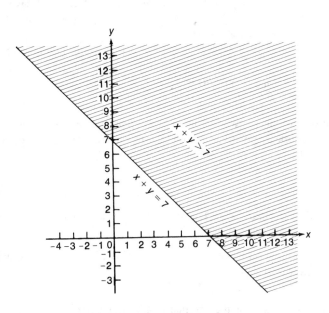

THE TRIANGLE INEQUALITY

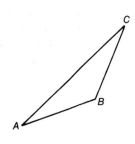

A classical inequality is the *triangle inequality:*

The sum of the lengths of two sides of a triangle is always greater than the length of the third side.

When $|AB|$ = distance between point A and point B, then the triangle inequality is written

$$|AB| + |BC| \geqslant |AC|.$$

(The only time that $|AB| + |BC| = |AC|$ is when the triangle has collapsed, with B on the line segment between A and C.)

REFERENCES

Edwin Beckenbach and Richard Bellman, *An Introduction to Inequalities,* New Mathematical Library (L. W. Singer Co., 1961); this monograph for high school students points out that mathematicians are often more interested in inequalities than in equations; gives classical inequalities and problems of maximum and minimum.

P. P. Korovkin, *Inequalities,* Popular Lectures in Mathematics series, translated from Russian (Blaisdell, 1961); sixty-two problems, with solutions, showing the uses of inequalities in higher mathematics.

The various relations of inequality are *binary* RELATIONS that possess some, but not all, of the PROPERTIES OF EQUALITY.

INFINITY

INFINITE: unlimited, endless.

FINITE: having limits; capable of being counted, measured, or determined.

There is a *finite* number of letters in the Roman alphabet—twenty-six to be exact. A first-grader who has learned her letters can sit down and print the entire alphabet from A to Z. When she gets to Z, she has reached the end of the alphabet; there are no letters beyond Z.

On the other hand, a first-grader who has learned to count cannot sit down and count to the last, or highest, number. Even if she counted all day long every day for the rest of her life, she would never reach the end of the natural numbers. No matter what number she stopped with, it would always be possible to add 1 to that number or to double that number or to multiply that number times itself. It is impossible to complete the counting process because there is no end to the natural numbers. The set of natural numbers is *infinite*.

An *infinite* quantity should not be confused with a very large number. For example, if a swimming pool were filled with sand, the pool would contain an extremely large number of grains of sand. There would be so many that it would be impossible for one person to count them one at a time. But there would be a finite number. And if enough people working together counted long enough, or if one person estimated, it would be possible to count or calculate the number of grains needed to fill the pool.

In fact, by using an estimation procedure, the Greek mathematician Archimedes (about 250 B.C.) demonstrated that the number of grains of sand needed to fill a sphere the size of the earth would not be infinite. It would be an enormously large number indeed, but it would still be a finite number. British astronomer Sir Arthur Eddington claimed that the number of electrons in the universe is finite. In *The Expanding Universe*

(Cambridge University Press, 1933) he estimated this staggeringly big finite number—1,290,000,000,000,000,000,000,000,000,000,000, 000,000,000,000,000,000,000,000,000,000,000,000,000,000, 000,000,000 (1.29×10^{87} in SCIENTIFIC NOTATION)—still not an infinite quantity. And many eminent scientists, including Albert Einstein, have held that even the universe itself is not infinite in extent.

Although it is impossible to observe something infinite in the physical world, mathematicians have long been able to conceive of, or imagine, the infinite. In plane geometry, for example, a straight LINE is conceived of as extending on forever in opposite directions. It is said to have an infinite length. A plane is conceived of as having two infinite dimensions—length and width. Thus an ideal geometric plane is an infinite flat surface. A straight line is conceived of as consisting of infinitely many points, between any two of which, no matter how close together, there are infinitely many other points.

INFINITY: an unbounded quantity.   **Symbol:** ∞

Infinity is not a number. It is a quantity beyond any number. Since the natural numbers go on forever, it is impossible for there to be a last number. Thus, infinity can be approached but never reached.

Consider what would happen if you divided a number such as 1 by a smaller and smaller divisor:

$$\frac{1}{1} = 1 \qquad \frac{1}{\frac{1}{1000}} = 1000$$

$$\frac{1}{\frac{1}{10}} = 10 \qquad \frac{1}{\frac{1}{1,000,000}} = 1,000,000$$

$$\frac{1}{\frac{1}{100}} = 100 \qquad \frac{1}{\frac{1}{1,000,000,000,000}} \quad 1,000,000,000,000$$

In this example, the divisor approaches closer and closer to zero but will never reach it no matter how many zeros are added to the denominator.

As the divisor in this example becomes smaller and smaller, the quotient becomes larger and larger. As the divisor approaches zero, the quotient approaches infinity. This can be symbolized as follows:

$$\text{In the equation } \frac{1}{b} = c, \text{ as } b \rightarrow 0, \ c \rightarrow \infty.$$

However, just as the divisor approaches but never reaches zero, so the quotient approaches but never reaches infinity.

POINT AT INFINITY (Ideal Point): a point added to the plane where two parallel lines are said to meet.

Parallel lines are sometimes said to intersect in *a point at infinity,* and parallel planes are said to intersect in *a line at infinity.* Since, in Euclidean geometry, infinity can be approached but never reached, this becomes another way of saying that parallel lines (and parallel planes) do not intersect in Euclidean geometry.

Nevertheless, mathematicians have been able to invent GEOMETRIES in which parallel lines do intersect. For example, in projective geometry, parallel lines are conceived of as intersecting at a point on some bounding, or limiting, curve. And artists, in their use of perspective, demonstrate that although parallel lines such as railroad tracks do not in fact intersect, they do appear to meet at a point in the distance. For more on projective geometry and *point at infinity* in art, see PROJECTION.

INFINITE SET: any SET for which the counting of its members would never end.

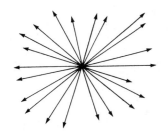

One example of an infinite set is the set of lines that can be drawn through a given point. There is no end to the number of straight lines that can be drawn through a given point. Yet it is possible to talk about that set of lines as a whole, as distinct from the infinite set of lines that do not pass through the point.

An infinite set may be *unbounded,* that is, it may have no first element, or beginning, and no last element. The set of all integers, both positive and negative, is such a set. This set has no smallest element and no largest element.

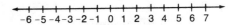

An infinite set may have *one bound,* or limit. An example of such a set would be the set of all positive integers. This set has a smallest element, the number 1, but it has no largest element.

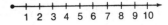

Finally, an infinite set may be *bounded* by a first element and a last element. The set of FRACTIONS, or RATIONAL NUMBERS, between and including 0 and 1 is such a set. This set has a smallest element, 0, and a largest element, 1, but the set of numbers in between is unlimited. Some examples of its members are $\frac{1}{2}, \frac{1}{3}, \frac{1}{4}, \frac{1}{5}, \frac{1}{6}, \ldots \frac{1}{69}, \ldots \frac{1}{217} \ldots$. You can see that the denominator can be increased forever. Thus there is an infinite set of fractions between 0 and 1 with a numerator of 1. And this set of fractions is a subset of the infinite set of all the fractions between 0 and 1.

HISTORY

Similar to the concept of infinity, an unbounded large quantity, is the concept of *infinitesimal,* an infinitely small nonzero quantity. These concepts are linked because

$$\frac{1}{b} = c \text{ approaches infinity when } b \text{ approaches zero.}$$

Mathematicians used these intuitive concepts long before they understood their logical foundation. Archimedes (250 B.C.) employed the concept of the infinitesimal in developing his formulas for area and volume. Nineteen hundred years later, Isaac Newton and Gottfried Wilhelm von Leibniz used these concepts in developing infinitesimal CALCULUS.

Although in many kinds of calculations the usefulness of the concepts infinite and infinitesimal was undeniable, many mathematicians worried about working with them. As early as the fourth century B.C., the philosopher Aristotle had argued that an unknowable such as infinity exists only as a potentiality, a kind of useful fiction. He stated that a "proper" or completed infinity did not exist. Even after the discovery of the calculus, which has so many applications, mathematicians continued to be skeptical about basing a branch of mathematics on a concept as formless and imprecise as infinity. As a result, they formalized the concept of *potential infinity,* a variable that becomes larger than any given real number. Another view of potential infinity is the idea of a finite set that can be increased indefinitely. In these views, infinity is never actually reached.

However, in the nineteenth century three mathematicians became interested in the properties of an *actual infinity*, that is, in the properties of an infinite set. These were Augustus De Morgan, a British algebraist, and Richard Dedekind and Georg Cantor, two German mathematicians. De Morgan and Dedekind pointed out that in an infinite set, a part can be placed in one-to-one correspondence with the whole. This characteristic had been noticed before by Galileo, among others. Galileo observed that for every integer there is exactly one perfect square.

Integer	Square of the Integer
1	1
2	4
3	9
4	16
5	25
6	36
.	.
.	.
.	.

Since it is possible to pair every integer with its perfect square, it seemed to Galileo as if in some curious way there were as many perfect squares as there were integers. Three hundred years later, De Morgan, Dedekind, and Cantor showed that this is indeed the case. If in pairing integers with perfect squares you were to stop at some point, say at the number 101, it would not be true that there are as many perfect squares as integers. Between 0 and 101, there are 100 integers and only 10 perfect squares. With a finite set, a part cannot be found equivalent to the whole. But since there is no stopping—as both sets are infinite—it will be possible to match every integer with a perfect square, on and on, forever. Thus Dedekind concluded that the defining characteristic of an infinite set is that a part can be put in one-to-one correspondence with the whole.

More than anyone else, Georg Cantor deserves the credit for initiating a serious study of infinite sets. Cantor was able to show that not only is it possible to consider an actual infinity, or an infinite set, but it is also possible to perform arithmetic operations on such sets. Cantor referred to the number of members of such sets as *transfinite numbers,* and he developed a *transfinite arithmetic* with rules for adding and multiplying transfinite numbers quite different from the rules of finite arithmetic. (For an explanation of transfinite numbers and transfinite arithmetic, see ARITHMETIC.)

Furthermore, Cantor showed that not all transfinite numbers are the same size. That is, not all infinite sets are of the same order of magnitude. Infinite sets that can be put into a one-to-one correspondence with the natural, or counting, numbers are the smallest infinite sets. These are said to be *denumerable,* or *countable,* infinite sets, and Cantor used the Hebrew letter aleph ($\aleph$) with a zero subscript $\aleph_0$ (aleph null) to symbolize such sets. For larger transfinite numbers, he used the symbols $\aleph_1, \aleph_2, \aleph_3, \ldots$

Cantor's work with infinite sets was completely new. In fact, his theories were so revolutionary that few of his contemporaries could understand or appreciate them. On the contrary, a number of nineteenth-century mathematicians attacked and ridiculed his work. And without ever receiving proper acclaim for his achievement, Cantor died in a mental hospital in 1918. Eventually, though, his work was taken seriously, and the consequences were far-reaching. Today there is hardly a branch of mathematics that has not been affected by Cantor's theory of sets. In evaluating his contribution to the field of mathematics, David Hilbert, a noted twentieth-century mathematician, is reported to have said that Cantor led mathematics into the paradise of infinity, "and no one shall drive us out." (See references—Bell, p. 577, and Boyer, p. 7.)

REFERENCES

Isaac Asimov, *Realm of Numbers* (Houghton Mifflin Co., 1959; Fawcett paperback), Ch. 10, "Endlessness."

Carl Boyer, "Mathematical Infinity," *Collier's Encyclopedia* (1972), Vol. 13, pp. 5–7; an exceptionally fine presentation for a reader with some mathematical background.

George Gamow, *One Two Three . . . Infinity* (Viking Press, 1947; Mentor paperback); a very popular exposition of numbers in science.

Martin Gardner, "Mathematical Games: The hierarchy of infinities and the problems it spawns," *Scientific American,* March 1966; reprinted in *Mathematics: An Introduction to Its Spirit and Use: Readings from Scientific American* (W. H. Freeman & Co., 1978).

Lillian R. Lieber, *Infinity: Beyond the Beyond the Beyond* (Rinehart, 1953); one of her charming books designed to make mathematics more comprehensible, written in a sort of free verse to ease understanding.

Rózsa Péter, *Playing with Infinity* (1957; Dover, 1976), English translation from Hungarian; an excellent collection of clearly written mathematical explorations and excursions.

Leo Zippen, *Uses of Infinity,* New Mathematical Library (L. W. Singer Co., 1962); monograph for high school students and lay readers.

Historical references

Eric T. Bell, *Men of Mathematics* (Simon & Schuster, 1937; Fireside paperback), chapters on Dedekind and Cantor.

Edward Kasner and James R. Newman, *Mathematics and the Imagination* (Simon & Schuster, 1940, 1967; Fireside paperback), Ch. 2, "Beyond the Googol," pp. 24–67; a collection of fascinating insights into higher mathematics that has captured many a reader with its wit and clarity.

Morris Kline, *Mathematics: The Loss of Certainty* (Oxford University Press, 1980), Ch. VI, "The Morass of Analysis;" discussion of the controversial infinitesimals that even the greatest mathematicians could not explain precisely; pp. 273–275 on the twentieth-century theory legitimizing infinitesimals. This book is written for adult readers, but calculus is not presupposed.

See also transfinite ARITHMETIC.

INTEREST

INTEREST: a fee paid for the use of money.

If you lend a friend $20 for a month, for that month you cannot use that money. If during that month a jacket that you want is on sale for $20, you will not be able to buy it unless you have another twenty dollars. You have been inconvenienced by not having your money available for your own use.

To compensate the lender for the inconvenience of not having ready cash, the borrower pays the lender a fee. The borrower pays back the original amount plus an extra amount called *interest*.

Similarly, when a person invests money in some kind of savings plan, the investor is paid some amount of interest by the bank for the use of his or her money. The bank in this case is the borrower.

FACTORS IN COMPUTING INTEREST

The amount of interest paid will depend on three things:

Principal: the amount of money borrowed or invested
Rate of interest: a PERCENT telling how many dollars per hundred will be paid as interest
Time: the number of years or months during which the money is borrowed or invested

There are two types of interest commonly used by banks and other institutions—simple interest and compound interest. The older form of interest and the one that is easier to compute is simple interest.

SIMPLE INTEREST: interest computed only on the original principal.

Fractal Dragon's Tail

Growth under compound interest is illustrated by the growth in size of the "segments" of this fractal spiral, as one moves away from its center. This is a detail of a fractal dragon analogous to that shown on page 566.
Copyright © 1982 Benoit B. Mandelbrot

276

> *Simple Interest =* Principal × Rate × Time (in years)
>
> $\quad$ $I = PRT$, where $\quad I =$ Interest
>
> $\qquad\qquad\qquad\qquad P =$ Principal
>
> $\qquad\qquad\qquad\qquad R =$ Rate per year (expressed
>
> $\qquad\qquad\qquad\qquad\qquad$ as a DECIMAL)
>
> $\qquad\qquad\qquad\qquad T =$ Time (in years)

Examples. What would be the simple interest on a $1000 loan borrowed at 18% for 2 years?

$\qquad P =$ \$1000 $\qquad R =$ 18% $= 0.18$ $\qquad T = 2$

$\qquad I =$ \$1000 × 0.18 × 2

$\qquad I =$ \$360

How much simple interest would be earned on $200 invested at $7\frac{1}{2}\%$ for 6 months?

$\qquad P =$ \$200 $\quad R = 7\frac{1}{2}\% = 0.075$ $\quad T = \frac{6}{12} = \frac{1}{2}$ (year)

$\qquad I =$ \$200 × 0.075 × $\frac{1}{2}$

$\qquad I =$ \$7.50

COMPOUND INTEREST: interest computed on the original principal and on any accumulated interest.

Compound interest is computed at regular intervals, or time periods. At the end of the first period, interest is computed on the original principal by multiplying principal times rate times time in years. The interest is then added to the principal (or converted to principal), creating a new principal. At the end of the second time period, interest is figured on the new principal. This interest is then converted to principal, and the process continues.

Compound interest may be computed, or *compounded*, at different time intervals. The interest may be compounded once a year (annually), twice a year (semiannually), four times a year (quarterly), or even more frequently. Banks and other institutions usually advertise how often the interest on savings accounts is compounded. The more frequently it is compounded, the faster the total amount (principal plus interest) grows.

Because the principal changes every time interest is compounded, there is no easy formula for computing, in a single step, the compound interest earned over several time periods. Thus, in banks and other institutions, compound interest is either read from a chart or figured on a computer. However, the formula for computing compound interest for a single time period is the same as the formula for computing simple interest: $I = P \times R \times T$.

Example.   How much interest would $1000 earn in a year invested at 18% compounded quarterly?

$$\text{Original } P = \$1000 \quad R = 18\% = 0.18 \quad T = \tfrac{3}{12} = \tfrac{1}{4} \text{ year}$$

At the end of the *first* quarter:

$$I = \$1000 \times 0.18 \times \tfrac{1}{4}$$
$$I = \$45$$

Interest is converted to principal:

$$\$1000 + \$45 = \$1045 = \text{new principal}$$

At the end of the *second* quarter:

$$I = \$1045 \times 0.18 \times \tfrac{1}{4}$$
$$I = \$47.03$$

Interest is converted to principal:

$$\$1045 + \$47.03 = \$1092.03 = \text{new principal}$$

At the end of the *third* quarter:

$$I = \$1092.03 \times 0.18 \times \tfrac{1}{4}$$
$$I = \$49.14$$

Interest is converted to principal:

$$\$1092.03 + \$49.14 = \$1141.17 = \text{new principal}$$

At the end of the *fourth* quarter:

$$I = \$1141.17 \times 0.18 \times \tfrac{1}{4}$$
$$I = \$51.35$$

The total interest on $1000 invested at 18% for one year compounded quarterly will be the sum of the interest earned in each of the four periods:

$$I = \$45.00 + \$47.03 + \$49.14 + \$51.35$$
$$I = \$192.52 \quad \textit{Compound interest}$$

Simple interest on the same amount of money ($1000) invested at the same rate (18%) for the same period of time would be $180.

$$I = \$1000 \times 0.18 \times 1 = \$180 \quad \textit{Simple interest}$$

Thus $1000 invested for a year at 18% interest compounded quarterly will earn $12.52 more than the same amount invested at the same rate of simple interest. Because compound interest is paid on accumulated interest and not just on the original principal, any investment will grow faster if it is earning compound interest than it will earning the same rate of simple interest.

FORMULAS FOR TOTAL AMOUNT OF MONEY ACCUMULATED

If you have money invested in a savings account, you will usually receive a quarterly statement indicating the total amount that has accumulated in your account. The total amount includes the principal invested plus the interest earned. There are formulas for computing the amount of money accumulated at the end of a specified period of time.

Simple interest: $A = P + (P \times R \times T)$, where

A = Amount of money accumulated
P = Principal
R = Rate per year (expressed as a decimal)
T = Time (in years)

Example. If $5000 is invested at 9%, what will be the amount of the investment after 12 years?

$$A = \$5000 + (\$5000 \times 0.09 \times 12)$$
$$A = \$5000 + \$5400$$
$$A = \$10,400$$

Compound interest: $A = P(1 + \frac{R}{n})^{nT}$, where

A = Amount of money accumulated
P = Principal
R = Rate per year (expressed as a decimal)
T = Time (in years)
n = number of times compounded per year

The EXPONENT in this formula indicates how many times the number in parentheses must be used as a factor. If the exponent is large, solving the formula becomes a long, repetitious problem involving very large numbers. For this reason, the formula for compound interest is usually solved by LOGARITHMS or by using a calculator.

Example. If $5000 is invested at 9%, compounded semiannually, what will be the amount of the investment after 12 years?

$$A = \$5000\left(1 + \frac{0.09}{2}\right)^{2 \times 12}$$
$$A = \$5000\,(1 + 0.045)^{24}$$

$$A = \$5000(1.045)^{24}$$
$$A = \$5000(2.876)$$
$$A = \$14,380.07$$

APPLICATIONS

At some time in your life, you will almost certainly either receive interest or pay interest, and you may do both.

If you invest in any type of savings plan, you will receive interest. For example, if you put $100 in a passbook savings account that pays 7% compounded quarterly, at the end of six months if you withdraw your money you will receive $3.53 in interest. If you buy a government bond (lend money to the government), after a period of time you will get back your original purchase price plus some amount of interest.

On the other hand, if you do not pay your credit card bill on time, you may have to pay interest. A common rate of interest on charge accounts is $1\frac{1}{2}\%$ per month (equivalent to $12 \times 1\frac{1}{2}\%$, or 18% per year). This means that if you receive a credit card bill for $49.95 and do not pay it within the specified time period, you will have to pay $0.75 interest for that month.

You must pay interest on money that you borrow from a bank or finance company. If you borrow $2000 from a bank to buy a car, the amount of interest you pay will depend upon the rate that the bank charges and the length of time you keep the money. If you borrow $2000 for two years and the bank charges 12% simple interest, at the end of the two years you will owe the bank $480 interest in addition to the original $2000 you borrowed.

Some banks withhold, or subtract, from the original loan the amount of interest that will be due when the loan is repaid. This practice of paying the interest at the beginning is called a *bank discount*. In the example above, if the bank discounted your $2000 loan, you would receive only $1520 from the bank. But at the end of the two years, you would owe the bank $2000. The $480 that you did not receive paid the interest in advance.

HISTORY

The practice of charging a fee for the use of money is an ancient one. Clay tablets from the Babylonian era record interest payments made as early as 2000 B.C. And these Babylonian interest rates were not to be taken lightly, as they sometimes reached a hefty 33%. Charging a fee for the use of money was common in a number of ancient civilizations, including those of the Hebrews, the Greeks, and the Romans. The interest rates varied with time and place, at one point rising to a staggering 60% in twelfth-century India.

Although the practice of charging for the use of money was common throughout the ancient world, it was strongly disapproved of or forbidden by three major religions—Judaism, Christianity, and Islam. In addition, many people, such as Plato, Aristotle, Cicero, Seneca, and Thomas Aquinas, spoke out against the practice of charging for the use of money, which was in those days called *usury*.

The argument that Church fathers and others brought against usury was that one should only charge for the use of something that can be worn out, damaged, or destroyed. For example, they thought it fair to charge for the use of a house, since when the house is returned to the owner it may not be in as good condition as it was before it was rented. However, they felt that when the lender of money had been repaid the full sum, he should not charge an additional fee since the money he now had was as valuable, or as usable, as the money he had lent.

Despite this disapproving attitude toward usury, the practice continued on a modest scale throughout the Middle Ages. With the vastly increased trade and industry that marked the end of the Middle Ages, there was a tremendous demand for cash loans, and the practice of charging for the use of money became more and more commonplace. Borrowers were willing to pay a fee for the use of funds because they expected to invest the money in ventures that would earn far more than the fee they were paying for their loans. Lenders felt they should be compensated for missing opportunities to invest the money themselves.

Gradually, the Church began to relax its attitude toward charging for the use of money, conceding that it was all right to compensate the lender for the difference between an exact repayment of the loan and what he might have earned with the money had he not lent it. Our word "interest" comes from the Latin phrase "id quod interest," meaning "that which is between." The word "interest" soon displaced the word "usury" for a fee charged for the use of money. Today *usury* means the charging of illegally high interest rates.

Since the Renaissance, charging interest for the use of money has become an accepted economic practice. Theories about interest have been developed to predict how much interest the borrower will be willing to pay, based on the supply of and demand for money. Laws have been passed to regulate the interest rates that may be charged under various conditions. This practice of charging for the use of money— once so ill thought of—has become a way of life for governments, businesses, individuals, and even churches.

REFERENCES

Thomas F. Divine, *Interest: An Historical and Analytical Study in Economics and Modern Ethics* (Marquette University Press, 1959); a full and more advanced treatment of the topic.

Historical Topics for the Mathematics Classroom, 31st Yearbook of the National Council of Teachers of Mathematics (1969), pp. 325–326; more on the history of usury and interest.

LINES

LINE: in mathematics a *straight* line, unless otherwise specified; one of three *undefined* terms in GEOMETRY, the other two being POINT and PLANE.

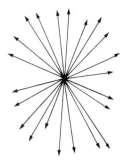

"Line" is a word familiar to everyone. There are telephone lines and clotheslines and airlines. You stand in checkout lines and ticket lines. Football players line up and try to get the ball across the other team's goal line.

In mathematics the word "line" stands for a basic concept that is like our everyday idea of the word line in some ways, but is quite different in others. Because *line* is one of the basic geometric concepts that are used to define all the other terms, it is itself undefined. (See DEFINITION.) Thus, no one can tell you exactly what a line is. However, there are some properties of a mathematical line that may help you understand the idea.

PROPERTIES OF A LINE

Imagine a point moving forever through space. The path made by such a moving point is the mathematician's concept of a line. Although this path may be straight or curved, the word "line" in mathematics usually means a straight line.

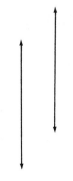

A line has the property of *length*. But the length of an entire line can never be measured, because a line is conceived of as extending on and on without end.

Moreover, a line is thought of as having no width and no thickness. That is, a line is conceived of as being *one-dimensional*. You may find it difficult to conceive of anything as having only one dimension; nothing in the physical world, no matter how thin, has only one dimension. A mathematical line, however, is not a thing; it is an idea.

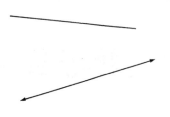

MODELS OF LINES

There are times when it is helpful to have a picture, or model, of a line. The most common one is a pencil or ink line of some measurable length drawn along a straightedge such as a ruler. Sometimes arrows are added to the model of a line to indicate that the line being represented extends on and on in opposite directions.

However, it is important to remember that all models of lines differ from the mathematical concept of a line in two respects: (1) all models of lines have some width and some thickness; and (2) all models of lines have endpoints.

Symbols:

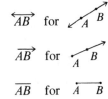

$\overleftrightarrow{AB}$ for

$\overrightarrow{AB}$ for

$\overline{AB}$ for $A \quad B$

PORTIONS OF A LINE

Ray: a portion of a line starting at one point and going on forever in one direction.

Half-line: a ray, including its endpoint (closed half-line) *or* excluding its endpoint (open half-line).

Segment: a portion of a line between and including two specific points.

A line segment has measurable length. The length of a line segment connecting two points is the shortest distance between the two points (in Euclidean geometry).

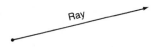

WAYS OF CLASSIFYING LINES

One way of classifying lines is by their *relationships to other lines:*

Intersecting lines (or concurrent lines): lines that meet or cross.

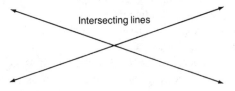

Symbol: ‖

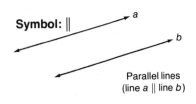

Parallel lines
(line a ‖ line b)

The intersection of two distinct lines is exactly one point.

Parallel lines: lines on a flat surface (in a plane) that do not intersect; lines in the same plane that have no point in common and will never meet, no matter how far they are extended.

Symbol: ⊥

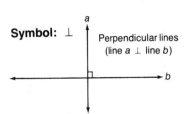

Perpendicular lines
(line a ⊥ line b)

Perpendicular lines: lines that meet and form right ANGLES; lines whose intersection forms congruent adjacent angles.

Skew lines: lines that are neither intersecting *nor* parallel.

Skew lines fail to intersect not because they are parallel (they are not), but because they are in different planes; for example, a line along a highway passing on a bridge over a line along a railroad track.

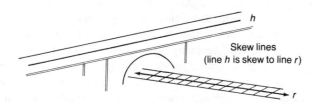

Skew lines
(line *h* is skew to line *r*)

Transversal: a line that intersects two or more lines.

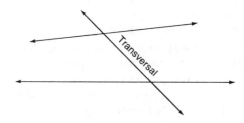

Another way of classifying lines is by their *orientation* or position *relative to the earth's surface:*

Vertical line: a line that is straight up and down, or upright; the direction of a plumb line. (A plumb line is a string supporting a weight.)

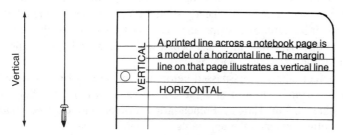

Horizontal line: a line that is perpendicular to a vertical line.

The word "horizontal" comes from the word "horizon," because a horizontal line appears to be parallel to the horizon formed by the sky and a calm sea. However, because of the curvature of the earth, the horizon and a horizontal line are not truly parallel.

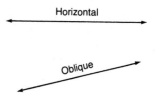

Oblique line: a line that is neither horizontal nor vertical.

DRAWING A STRAIGHT LINE

How would you go about drawing a straight line segment? Probably you would do it by running your pencil along the edge of something straight, such as a ruler. But how would you know whether the edge you drew along was really straight? Could you determine whether or not something was a straightedge without holding it next to another straightedge? And, in any case, where did the first straightedge come from?

Although Euclidean geometry was based on the existence of two drawing tools—the straightedge and the compass—there was for centuries no satisfactory instrument or procedure for making a straightedge. During that time, straightedges were made by grinding down an edge until it stood flat on a plane surface. However, this was a somewhat circular procedure, since one way to tell whether a surface was completely flat was by seeing whether a straightedge would stand completely along the surface. Clearly what was needed was a way to generate a straight line without using an already existing line segment.

In the eighteenth century there was still no way to make a perfectly straight line, but a very practical need brought an approximate solution to the problem. James Watt, the inventor of the steam engine, needed a device that would connect a piston to a flywheel and move the piston along a straight line. In 1784 he developed a revolutionary apparatus, which he called Parallel Motion, which approximates a straight line long enough for the piston stroke.

Watt's Parallel Motion linkage is made of three rods, two of which are long (length a) and hinged to the ends of a shorter one (length b). The free ends of the long rods are then set to pivot at fixed points, with the long rods parallel to each other and perpendicular to the short rod. As the long rods rotate about their fixed pivots, the center of the short rod, C, traces a line that is nearly straight. You can make a model of the device from cardboard strips and paper fasteners. If you then insert a pencil through a hole at C, the pencil will trace a straight-line approximation for a fair distance.

Another eighty years passed before the invention of the first device that *accurately* drew a straight line segment without the help of a straightedge. In 1864 a French army officer and engineer named Peaucellier invented the apparatus named in his honor.

Peaucellier's Cell is made up of four rods of the same length (x), hinged to form a rhombus $ABCD$, and two other rods (length y, with y greater than x) hinged to two opposite vertices of the rhombus. These two rods are joined at E. Another rod is hinged at B with its other end at F so that $FB = EF$, thus causing B to trace a circle when the linkage is in motion. As B moves and forms the circle, D moves and produces a straight line.

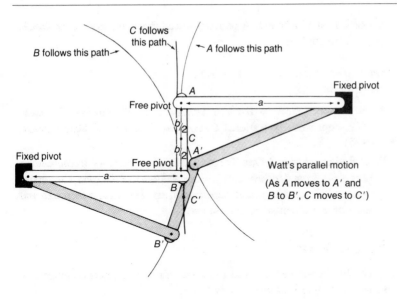

B follows this path →

C follows this path

← A follows this path

Fixed pivot

A

Free pivot

a

b/2 C

b/2 A'

B

Free pivot

Fixed pivot

a

Watt's parallel motion

(As A moves to A' and
B to B', C moves to C')

B'

C'

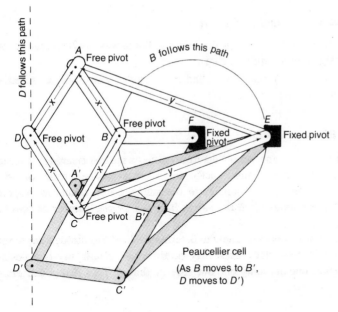

D follows this path

A

Free pivot

B follows this path

x

x

y

Free pivot

F

E

D

Free pivot

B

Fixed
pivot

Fixed pivot

A'

x

x

y

C

Free pivot

B'

D'

C'

Peaucellier cell

(As B moves to B',
D moves to D')

You can make a Peaucellier Cell with strips of cardboard and paper fasteners. The distances y and x are measured between pivot points—in other words, between holes for the paper fasteners. The last rod is cut to half the distance from B to E when the rest of the apparatus is laid out as illustrated. Then pivots F and E can be fastened to a large piece of cardboard, or to a board. A pencil inserted through a hole at D should trace a straight line.

References on linkages for drawing a
straight line

A. B. Kempe, *How to Draw a Straight Line* (Macmillan: London, 1877, reprinted by National Council of Teachers of Mathematics, 1977).

Hans Rademacher and Otto Toeplitz, *The Enjoyment of Mathematics: Selections from Mathematics for the Amateur* (Princeton University Press, 1957, hardcover and paperback), pp. 119–129; a thorough and accessible mathematical discussion.

THE LINE IN ART

The line alone can be used to create intricate geometric designs. A sequence of lines can create a curve.

References for making line art

Lois Kreischer, *Symmography* (Crown Publishers, 1971); creative line designs with yarn or string.

Dale Seymour, Linda Silvey, and Joyce Snider, *Line Designs* (Creative Publications, 1974).

Sculpture by George Richardson, photo by Adrian Ketchum.

DETERMINING A LINE

In geometry, the word "determine" has a special meaning. It means to describe or pinpoint exactly one thing as distinct from all other similar things. For example, to determine a line means to pinpoint exactly one unique line as distinct from the infinite number of possible lines.

One point is not sufficient to determine a line. For through any single point infinitely many lines may be drawn. Through any two points, however, one and only one line may be drawn. Thus *two points determine a line.*

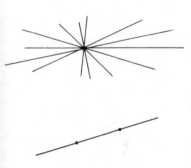

THE SHORTEST PATH BETWEEN TWO POINTS

In plane, or Euclidean, geometry a straight line segment is the shortest path between two points. But that is not true in every geometry. On a curved surface, the shortest path between two points follows the curve of the surface. For example, on the surface of the earth the shortest path between two points follows a great circle (a circle on the surface of the sphere with its center at the center of the sphere). For short distances a straight line segment is a fine approximation, but as distances get larger and larger, so does the difference between the straight-line distance and the curved one.

In the early twentieth century Albert Einstein, a German-born physicist, proposed that space and time formed a *curved* rather than a plane surface and that light rays followed the shortest path on such a surface. He suggested that gravitational fields cause the curvature of the space-time surface; tests confirm that light rays passing near a distant star are indeed bent by the effects of its gravitational field. Einstein's idea, called the *theory of general relativity,* is necessary when dealing with the enormous distances in space.

References on the curvature of space

J. J. Callahan, "The Curvature of Space in a Finite Universe," *Scientific American,* August 1976, pp. 90–100.

P. Le Corbeiller, "The Curvature of Space," *Scientific American,* November 1954; reprinted in *Mathematics in the Modern World: Readings from Scientific American* (W. H. Freeman & Co., 1968), pp. 128–133.

Morris Kline, "The Straight Line," *Scientific American*, March, 1956.

References on Einstein's theory of relativity
(for the beginner)

Martin Gardner, *The Relativity Explosion: A Lucid Account of Why Quasars, Pulsars, Black Holes and the New Atomic Clocks Are Vindicating Einstein's Revolutionary Theory* (Random House, Vintage paperback, 1976).

Martin Gardner, *Relativity for the Million* (Macmillan, 1962).

Lillian Lieber, *The Einstein Theory of Relativity* (Rinehart, 1945).

For a discussion of the non-Euclidean geometry of curved surfaces, see GEOMETRY. You will notice that because "line" is undefined for geometry in general, different geometries can assign concepts to the word "line" that are not the same as the Euclidean straight line.

For equations of a line, see SLOPE and GRAPHS. Another article related to the idea of line is NUMBER LINES.

LOCUS

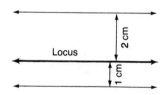

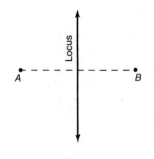

LOCUS (plural, *loci*): the SET of all POINTS that satisfy each condition in a given set of conditions.

"Locus" is the Latin word for "place"; it is the word from which our English word "location" is derived.

Finding the locus of all points that satisfy certain conditions means finding the location of those points with respect to other points, LINES, or PLANES.

Examples.

- The locus of all points in a plane one centimeter from a fixed point *A* is a circle, with center at *A* and radius one centimeter.
- The locus of all points in space one centimeter from a fixed point *A* is a sphere, with center at *A* and radius one centimeter.
- The locus of all points in a plane that are between two horizontal lines but are twice as far from the upper line as from the lower line is a line parallel to both the given lines but closer to the lower line as stated.
- The locus of all points in a plane that are equally distant from two fixed points *A* and *B* is the perpendicular bisector of the line segment joining the two points.

In these examples, each locus satisfies a single condition. However, sometimes a problem asks for the point or points that satisfy more than one condition. If so, the final locus is only those points that satisfy *all* conditions. The final locus is the intersection of the separate loci, each satisfying one condition.

Example. Find the locus of all points in a plane that are one centimeter from a point *A and* equally distant from two other points, *B* and *C,* in the same plane.

The first locus described in this problem is a circle with center at *A* and radius of one centimeter. The second locus is the perpendicular bisector of the line segment joining *B* and *C*.

The *intersection* of these two loci is the *final* locus. The final locus may be two points, one point, or no points at all, depending on the positions of *A, B,* and *C*.

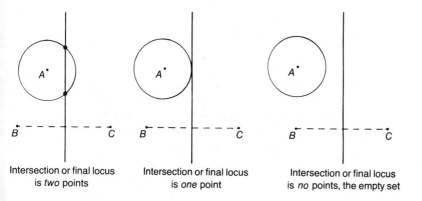

| Intersection or final locus is *two* points | Intersection or final locus is *one* point | Intersection or final locus is *no* points, the empty set |

The most famous examples of loci are the CONIC SECTIONS; see that article for interesting results and applications of considering loci.

LOGARITHMS

LOGARITHM: the *exponent,* or power, to which a *fixed base* must be raised in order to obtain a given number.

The word "logarithm," which can be abbreviated as "log," is a fancy name for EXPONENT. But "logarithm" is used only in the sense of the exponent, to a fixed base, *of a given number.*

Notation: $\log_b N = x$ means x is the exponent to which b must be raised to obtain N.

That is,

$$\log_b N = x \quad \text{means} \quad b^x = N.$$

Examples. $\log_2 32 = x$ means $2^x = 32$.

This equation asks the question "What power of 2 will give 32?" The answer is "$x = 5$."

$$\log_2 32 = 5 \quad \text{because} \quad 2^5 = 32.$$

This expression is read "The log to the base 2 of 32 is 5."

In like manner,

$$\log_{10} 1 = 0, \qquad \text{because } 10^0 = 1;$$
$$\log_{10} 1000 = 3, \qquad \text{because } 10^3 = 1000;$$
$$\log_{100} 1000 = 1.5, \quad \text{because } 100^{1.5} = 1000.$$

LOGARITHMIC SCALES

Some quantities are most conveniently measured on a logarithmic scale. The quantity to be measured is expressed as powers of a fixed base, and only the logarithms, or exponents, are marked on the scale.

For example, the intensity of sound is measured in *decibels*. A decibel (dB) is one-tenth of a *bel,* a unit named after Alexander Graham Bell, the American inventor of the telephone.

The bel scale is logarithmic to base 10. This means that

0 bels is set at a level representing the softest audible sound;

1 bel represents a sound 10^1 or 10 times as great as the softest sound;

2 bels represents a sound 10^2 or 100 times as great as the softest sound;

10 bels represents a sound 10^{10} times as great as the softest sound, and so on.

−1 bels represents a sound 10^{-1} or $\frac{1}{10}$ as great as the softest sound. (The reduction can be accomplished by moving the softest sound farther away, for example.)

Scales of sound intensity, however, are always marked in *deci*bels:

$$
\begin{aligned}
0 \text{ bels} &= 0 \text{ decibels} \\
1 \text{ bel} &= 10 \text{ decibels} \\
2 \text{ bels} &= 20 \text{ decibels} \\
10 \text{ bels} &= 100 \text{ decibels}
\end{aligned}
$$

Take a look at the resulting scale, with some common sounds, as shown on the next page.

The use of a logarithmic scale for sound intensity means that delicate measurements can be made at the low end of the scale. This delicacy is necessary because far less *difference* in sound intensity is required to distinguish between the volumes of two soft sounds than is required to distinguish between the volumes of two very loud sounds. A whisper is significant if added to a whisper, because it doubles the total sound intensity. However, a whisper does not add a distinguishable increase to the total sound intensity in heavy traffic or to the peak sound of a thunderclap. The logarithmic approach stretches the bottom of the scale and compresses the top.

Doubling a sound intensity means multiplying by 2, which equals approximately $10^{0.3}$. Hence, doubling a sound intensity means an increase of 0.3 bel or 3 decibels. Therefore, doubling the intensity of a sound of ten decibels gives a result of 10 + 3, or 13, decibels. Doubling

the intensity of a sound of 100 decibels gives a result of 100 + 3, o
103, decibels.

Decibel Scale for Sound Intensity

Times as great as softest sound	Decibels	
10^{14}	140	a jet airplane 100 feet, or 30 meters, away
10^{13}	130	a boiler factory
10^{12}	120	nearby thunder; the English pop music group "Th
10^{11}	110	Who" in 1976, at 50 meters from the sound system
10^{10}	100	a riveting machine 30 feet, or 9 meters, away
10^{9}	90	the threshold of pain for the human ear
10^{8}	80	
		busy traffic
10^{7}	70	an office typing room
10^{6}	60	normal speech from 3 feet or 1 meter
10^{5}	50	
		the overall noise level in the average home
10^{4}	40	
10^{3}	30	
10^{2}	20	the rustle of leaves; a whisper
10^{1}	10	
10^{0}	0	the softest audible sound; threshold of hearing

(A sound registering 210 decibels has been produced in a laboratory by a horn
Holes can be bored in solid material by the energy of a sound of such high
intensity.)

References on sound intensity

Sir James Jeans, *Science & Music* (Cambridge University Press, 1937
Dover, 1968), pp. 217–231.

S. S. Stevens and Fred Warshofsky, *Sound and Hearing*, Life Scienc
Library (Time, 1965).

Another phenomenon that is most conveniently measured by
logarithmic scale is the magnitude of an earthquake. The study of earth
quakes is called seismology, and tremors and quakes are recorded by a
instrument called a seismograph. American seismologist Charles F
Richter in 1935 set up the *Richter scale* which is used in reportin
earthquakes throughout the world. Newspaper, radio, and televisio

accounts give the Richter readings of an earthquake to indicate its severity.

The base for the Richter scale is also ten, and the zero point is fixed at the level of some of the smallest true earthquakes that could be recorded by good seismographs. However, it is possible to have Richter readings of less than zero, representing smaller detectable tremors. For example, a Richter reading of -1 represents 10^{-1} or $\frac{1}{10}$ the magnitude of a small quake of the level set at zero on the scale. Remember that on a logarithmic scale, zero is an exponent rather than a magnitude.

A Richter reading of 7 (meaning 10^7 or 10,000,000 times as great as the small quakes set at zero) represents a major earthquake. The largest earthquakes recorded so far occurred in Japan in 1933, with Richter readings estimated between 8.5 and 8.9, and in Alaska in 1964, with readings reported between 8.4 and 8.9.

Richter Scale for Earthquakes

Magnitude of quake	Richter reading	
10^9	9	largest quakes: San Francisco 1906; Japan 1933; USSR
10^8	8	1952; Chile 1960; Alaska 1964
10^7	7	major earthquake
10^6	6	large earthquake—potentially quite destructive
10^5	5	small earthquake—causes minor damage
10^4	4	
10^3	3	
10^2	2	more than 1000 earthquakes per day are recorded at
10^1	1	a reading of 2 or greater
10^0	0	fixed at the level of smallest true earthquake recordable
10^{-1}	-1	by good seismographs

Another logarithmic scale is that of music. Each musical sound has a *frequency,* which is the number of vibrations per second. For instance, on a piano keyboard the note C above middle C has a classical standard frequency of 512 vibrations per second; this means that the piano string for this note vibrates 512 times per second.

To sound a note an octave higher, it is necessary to double the number of vibrations per second. That is, the next higher C has a frequency of 1024. On the other hand, to sound a note an octave lower, it is necessary to halve the frequency. Thus, middle C has only 256 vibrations per second, and the C below that, 128 vibrations per second.

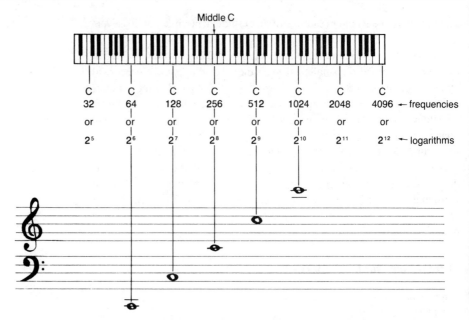

The frequency of each C note can be expressed as some power of 2. Thus, the musical scale is logarithmic, with base two. On a piano keyboard, the lower frequencies are spread out at the left and the higher frequencies are compressed at the right.

The entire musical scale, not only the C's, is logarithmic in the same way. The table shows the frequencies of all tones in this system. Notice that for every note, raising an octave doubles the frequency. (Sometimes the doubled frequency appears as one less than you would expect, due to rounding; the logarithms for notes other than C's are not integers.)

Frequencies of Tones, Classical Scale (C = 512)

C	16	32	64	128	256	512	1024	2048	4096
C♯	17	34	68	136	271	542	1085	2170	4340
D	18	36	72	144	287	575	1149	2299	4598
D♯	19	38	76	152	304	609	1218	2436	4871
E	20	40	81	161	323	645	1290	2580	5161
F	21	43	85	171	342	683	1367	2734	5468
F♯	23	45	91	181	362	724	1448	2896	5793
G	24	48	96	192	384	767	1534	3069	6137
G♯	25	51	102	203	406	813	1625	3251	6502
A	27	54	108	215	431	861	1722	3444	6889
A♯	29	57	114	228	456	912	1825	3649	7298
B	30	60	121	242	483	967	1933	3866	7732
C	32	64	128	256	512	1024	2048	4096	8192

Actually, the well-tempered scale used today differs slightly from these classical frequencies. In 1939 an international standard of pitch was set at A = 440 vibrations per second, giving slightly higher frequencies for the middle octave of the piano. But this scale is also logarithmic with base 2, because the octaves for each note are found by doubling or halving the frequency.

References on musical frequencies

Sir James Jeans, *Science & Music* (Cambridge University Press, 1937; Dover, 1968), especially pp. 21–27 and 160–177.

Evans G. Valens, *The Number of Things: Pythagoras, Geometry, and Humming Strings* (E. P. Dutton & Co., 1964), Chs. 14–16, especially pp. 162–171 on harmony and harmonics.

Frequencies of Tones, International Scale (A = 440)

C	261.6
C♯	277.2
D	293.6
D♯	311.1
E	329.6
F	349.2
F♯	370.0
G	392.0
G♯	415.3
A	440.0
A♯	466.2
B	493.9
C	523.2

LOGARITHMS AS AN AID TO COMPUTATION

> Because *logarithms are exponents,* they obey all the laws of EXPONENTS.

For example, *multiplication* of two numbers can be done by *adding* their logarithms:

Given: $\log_{10} a = s$ means $a = 10^s$ and
$\log_{10} c = t$ means $c = 10^t$.

Therefore:

$$\log_{10} a \times c = \log_{10} 10^s \times 10^t \qquad \text{substitution for } a \text{ and } c \text{ as given}$$
$$= \log_{10} 10^{s+t} \qquad \text{law of exponents}$$
$$= s + t \qquad \text{definition of logarithm}$$
$$= \log_{10} a + \log_{10} c \qquad \text{substitution for } s \text{ and } t \text{ as given}$$

Hence, if logarithms are known, the operation of multiplication can be reduced to the simpler operation of addition. And, in fact, many logarithms are known. They are listed in tables in mathematical reference books (and at the end of this one), and they are available on many calculators. This use of logarithms is especially helpful for performing operations on very large and very small numbers.

However, in order to use logarithms in this way, the logarithm of every number must be to the *same fixed base*.

$$\boxed{\log_{10} ac = \log_{10} a + \log_{10} c}$$

Choosing a Base for Logarithms

Any positive number other than one can serve as the fixed base. Fc example, it would be possible to work out the logarithm of 64 to a variet of different bases.

$$\log_2 64 = 8 \quad \text{because} \quad 2^8 = 64$$
$$\log_4 64 = 3 \quad \text{because} \quad 4^3 = 64$$
$$\log_8 64 = 2 \quad \text{because} \quad 8^2 = 64$$
$$\log_{\frac{1}{8}} 64 = -2 \quad \text{because} \quad (\tfrac{1}{8})^{-2} = 64$$

However, it is impossible to find the logarithm of 64 to base 0, 1, or $-$ because no power of 0, 1, or -4 is equal to 64.

Powers of 0	Powers of 1	Powers of -4
$0^1 = 0$	$1^1 = 1$	$-4^1 = -4$
$0^2 = 0$	$1^2 = 1$	$-4^2 = +16$
$0^3 = 0$	$1^3 = 1$	$-4^3 = -64$
$0^4 = 0$	$1^4 = 1$	$-4^4 = +256$

Because of the constant value of all powers of zero and one, an because of the alternating signs of powers of negative numbers, th negative numbers, zero, and one are excluded as logarithmic bases Furthermore, only positive numbers have logarithms to a positive base For example, there is no logarithm of -64 to any positive base. O course, the logarithm of a number may be negative, just as an exponer may be negative. Moreover, the log of a number may be 0 or 1, just a an exponent may be 0 or 1. In general then, for $\log_b N$,

b must be positive and unequal to one;
N must be positive;
$\log_b N$ may be any real number, positive, zero, or negative.

COMMON LOGARITHMS

Since our number system is based on 10, logarithms using 10 as th fixed base are the most convenient in most computations. Logarithms t base 10 are so widely used, they are called *common logs*. (They are als. known as *Briggsian logs* in honor of Henry Briggs, who first worked o deriving a table of logs to base 10.)

Consider for a moment how you might go about finding the log of number to the base 10. Suppose that you wanted to find the logarithm o 200. You are looking for the power of 10 that equals 200.

Powers of 10	Logarithmic notation
$10^0 = 1$	$\log_{10} 1 = 0$
$10^1 = 10$	$\log_{10} 10 = 1$
$10^2 = 100$	$\log_{10} 100 = 2$
$10^3 = 1000$	$\log_{10} 1000 = 3$

From the chart, you can see that the log of 200 to the base 10 must be some number between 2 and 3, because 10^2 is less than 200 and 10^3 is greater than 200. Thus, the log of 200 must be 2 plus a fraction.

Finding the fraction is a tedious procedure. However, as it happens, it is no longer necessary to calculate the fractional portions of common logarithms. Tables of common logs are accurate to as many as twenty decimal places. Thus, you can find the log of any positive number by looking it up in a table of logarithms (as given—with instructions—in APPENDIX I). However, for this article a short table is sufficient. Here in the margin you can find the log of 200.

Every common logarithm consists of a whole number portion (which may be zero), and a fractional, or decimal, portion. The whole number part of a log is called the *characteristic*. The decimal part is called the *mantissa*. For example.

Number	Log to Base 10
1	0.0000
2	0.3010
5	0.6990
10	1.0000
20	1.3010
50	1.6990
100	2.0000
200	2.3010
500	2.6990
1000	3.0000

$$\log_{10} 200 = \underset{\text{characteristic} \quad \text{mantissa}}{2.3010}$$

Thus, $\log_{10} 200 = 2.3010$.

If you compare the logarithms of 2, 20, and 200 in the table above, you will find that the mantissa is the same for all three numbers. One advantage of common logs is that numbers that differ only by a power of ten have logarithms that differ only in their characteristics. For this reason, log tables usually give only the mantissas of logarithms for numbers from 1 to 10.

Since the logarithms of the numbers

$$2.147 \quad 2{,}147 \quad 2{,}147{,}000 \quad 0.02147$$

all have the same mantissa, the mantissa of any of these numbers can be found by looking up the mantissa of 2.147. The characteristic can then be found either by finding the power of 10 bounding the number (as was done above when 200 was found to lie between 10^2 and 10^3), or by writing the number in SCIENTIFIC NOTATION. In scientific notation, a number is written as the product of 2 factors—a number between 1 and 10, and a power of 10. For example, 2147 in scientific notation is 2.147×10^3. The exponent of 10 when a number is written in scientific notation (in this case 3) will be the characteristic of the common log of that number.

Antilogarithms

Number	Log to Base 10
1	0.0000
2	0.3010
5	0.6990
10	1.0000
20	1.3010
50	1.6990
100	2.0000
200	2.3010
500	2.6990
1000	3.0000

Computation with logarithms usually leads to a result that is itself a logarithm. To get the answer you are seeking, you must find the number for which your result is the logarithm. Instead of having a number and finding its logarithm in the table, you have a logarithm and must use the table to find the number associated with it. This process is called finding the *antilogarithm,* or finding the *antilog.* For example, suppose you have the logarithm 3.6990 and want to find its antilog. Using the short log table given, you can find the mantissa .6990. Thus, you can see that the antilog will be 5 times some power of 10. Since the characteristic of the log is 3, the antilog is 5×10^3, or 5000.

LAWS OF LOGARITHMS

Remember that *logarithms are exponents.* The laws of logarithms are derived from the laws of EXPONENTS, as shown on p. 297 for multiplication.

Multiplication

$$\log_b (ac) = \log_b a + \log_b c$$

To multiply two numbers, find the log of each number, add the logs, and then find the antilog of the sum.

Example. 2×500

$$\log_{10} 2 \qquad = 0.3010$$
$$\log_{10} 500 \qquad = 2.6990$$
$$\qquad\qquad\qquad\quad 3.0000$$

antilog of $3.0000 = 1000$

therefore 2×500 $= 1000$

Although this example can be done easily without logarithms, it illustrates the procedure to be followed when using more complicated numbers.

Division

$$\log_b \frac{a}{c} = \log_b a - \log_b c$$

To divide one number by another, find the logarithm of each number, subtract the log of the divisor from the log of the dividend, and then find the antilog of the difference.

Example. $1000 \div 200$

$$\log_{10} 1000 \qquad = \quad 3.0000$$
$$\log_{10} 200 \qquad = -2.3010$$
$$\qquad\qquad\qquad\qquad 0.6990$$

antilog of $0.6990 = 5$

therefore $1000 \div 200$ $= 5$

Raising to a Power

To raise a number to the nth power, find the log of the number, multiply the log by n, and then find the antilog of the product.

$$\log_b a^n = n \log_b a$$

Example. 10^3 $\log_{10} 10 = 1.0000$

$$\underline{\times 3}$$
$$3.0000$$

antilog of $3.0000 = 1000$
therefore $10^3 = 1000$

Extracting a Root

To find the nth root of a number, find the log of the number, divide the log by n, and then find the antilog of the quotient.

$$\log_b \sqrt[n]{a} = \log_b a^{\frac{1}{n}}$$
$$= \frac{1}{n} \log_b a$$

Example. $\sqrt[2]{100}$ $\log_{10} 100 = 2$

$2 \div 2 = 1$
antilog of $1 = 10$
therefore $\sqrt[2]{100} = 10$

Logarithms provide the *only* practical way of raising numbers to high or fractional powers and of extracting difficult roots.

NATURAL LOGARITHMS

Natural logarithms are logarithms to the base e. The number e is an *irrational number* that can only be approximated:

$$e = 2.7182818284. \ldots$$

Notation

Natural logarithm of x
$= \log_e x$, or, $\ln x$

The value of e can be approximated by substituting large numbers for n in the formula

$$\left(1 + \frac{1}{n}\right)^n.$$

This formula shows up in problems dealing with natural growth or decay, such as the population growth of bacteria or the decay of uranium. It is in this sense that logs to the base e are called natural logs and not in the sense that they are any simpler or more natural than other logarithms. Natural logs are also the logarithms that occur most often in CALCULUS.

Natural logs obey all the laws of logarithms. You can confirm from the short table that $\log_e 6 = \log_e (2 \times 3) = \log_e 2 + \log_e 3$. Natural logarithms, like common logs, can be used to great advantage in working with

x	$\log_e x$
1	0.000
2	0.693
3	1.099
4	1.386
5	1.609
6	1.792
7	1.946
8	2.079
9	2.197
10	2.303

complicated expressions involving exponents and radicals. Tables for natural logs are given in reference books for higher mathematics. Tables are calculated by using formulas like

$$\log_e (1 + x) = (x - \frac{x^2}{2} + \frac{x^3}{3} - \frac{x^4}{4} + \ldots) \quad \text{and}$$

$$\log_e \frac{1 + x}{1 - x} = 2(1 + \frac{x^3}{3} + \frac{x^5}{5} + \ldots),$$

where x is between -1 and 1 (that is, $-1 < x < 1$). It is through the use of these same formulas that many high-speed computers and calculators are programmed to handle logarithms.

GRAPHS OF LOGARITHMIC FUNCTIONS

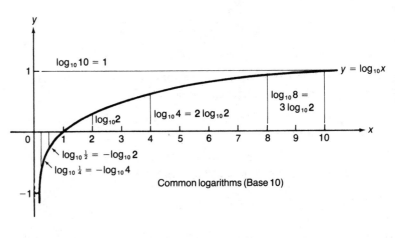

Common logarithms (Base 10)

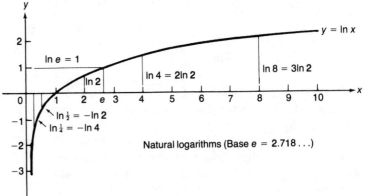

Natural logarithms (Base e = 2.718...)

HISTORY

Before the seventeenth century, solving problems that had many numbers or very large numbers was both difficult and time-consuming. Yet the pressure to solve such problems was constantly increasing, as physical scientists, particularly astronomers, collected vast quantities of data involving large numbers. Perhaps this is what inspired John Napier, a Scot, to search for an easier method of computation, leading to his invention of logarithms. After working for nearly 20 years on the idea, Napier published in 1614 his tables of logarithms and his explanation of them.

Although logarithms are now understood to be exponents, Napier did not think of them in this way. Napier derived his logarithms by setting up RATIOS in which one term came from a geometric SERIES and the other term came from an arithmetic series. In fact, the name "logarithms," which Napier gave to his invention, means "ratio numbers."

In setting up his system of logarithms, Napier used the number 10,000,000 as his starting point, giving it a log of 0. However, shortly after Napier published his work on logs, the English mathematician Henry Briggs suggested to Napier that the logarithms should be based on 10 like the decimal numeral system. Briggs pointed out the advantages of a system in which the log of 1 would be 0 and the log of 10 would be 1. Napier agreed, and in 1624, Briggs published a table of common (or base 10) logarithms for the numbers from 1 to 20,000 and from 90,000 to 100,000. The tables were completed after Briggs's death by Adriaen Vlacq, a Dutch mathematician, who is credited with first using the term "characteristic." The term "mantissa" was introduced by Briggs.

One other mathematician associated with the invention of logarithms is Jobst Bürgi, a Swiss. Bürgi is believed to have invented logarithms independently of Napier. However, since Napier published his first, the credit is given to him.

Still, exponential notation and the laws of exponents as we know them today were not invented until after the deaths of Napier, Briggs, and Bürgi. Not until the end of the seventeenth century, after both logarithms and exponents had been widely accepted, did mathematicians recognize that logarithms were exponents.

SLIDE RULE AND CALCULATOR

Less than a decade after the invention of logarithms, men began to use logarithmic scales in making computing devices. In 1620, Edmund Gunter, an English mathematician, invented a device on which he could

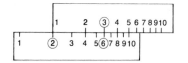

Slide rule multiplication, showing

$2 \times 3 = 6$

$\log_{10} 2 + \log_{10} 3 = \log_{10} 6$

multiply and divide. Gunter's device consisted of a logarithmic scale and a pair of dividers, or pointers. Two years later, William Oughtred, another Englishman, improved upon Gunter's invention by using two scales, with one of them sliding along the other. Oughtred's apparatus was the forerunner of the modern slide rule.

A slide rule consists of two rules marked off in logarithmic scales. The units on these scales get closer and closer together just as the common logs of successive numbers get closer and closer together. These logarithmic scales are labeled with the corresponding antilogs. To multiply two numbers on the slide rule, such as 2×3, you place the end of the top scale over the 2 on the bottom scale. Then you find 3 on the top scale, and looking directly below it, you read the product from the bottom scale. Actual slide rules are illustrated in the article on COMPUTERS, under the history of computing machines.

In the twentieth century, both common and natural logarithms have been used in the design of electronic computers and calculators. Since pocket calculators are now widely available, you might wonder how useful or necessary logarithms are today. In working with very large or very small numbers, you will find that the pocket calculator has its limitations. For example, a number such as 500^{39} is too large for most pocket calculators, yet the answer can be quickly and easily approximated using logarithms. Logarithms are also useful in extracting roots. For example, you would probably use logarithms to find the fifth root of 407.2. And even if you had a calculator capable of taking the fifth root, it would also use logs to perform the calculation.

REFERENCES

Isaac Asimov, *The Realm of Numbers* (Houghton Mifflin Co., 1959; Fawcett paperback); a good elementary exposition of exponents and logarithms.

Historical Topics for the Mathematics Classroom, 31st Yearbook of the National Council of Teachers of Mathematics (1969), pp. 142–145 and 271–273; more on the development of logarithms and the slide rule.

See GRAPHS for the use of logarithmic (semi-log and log-log) graph paper.

Tables of logarithms, both common and natural, are listed in APPENDIX I.

LOGIC

LOGIC: the science of proper reasoning.

People use logic every day to figure out answers to problems or to see if their reasoning is correct. However, reasoning can be difficult to develop, to follow, or to criticize unless the *structure* of the reasoning is clear.

This set of statements may seem rather tangled at first glance:

> No dragons are unintelligent.
> No intelligent beast expects impossibilities.
> Conclusion: ?

Can you draw a conclusion from these statements? The proper conclusion becomes clearer if the statements are replaced by a set of equivalent statements:

> Dragons are intelligent beasts.
> Intelligent beasts do not expect impossibilities.
> Conclusion: Dragons do not expect impossibilities.

The structure of this logical reasoning can be clarified by the use of letters to represent the following statements:

> p = "A beast is a dragon."
> q = "A beast is intelligent."
> r = "It will not expect impossibilities."

Then the argument can be written in the following form, which reduces to a very clear argument in symbols:

If a beast is a dragon, then the beast is intelligent.   If p, then q.

If a beast is intelligent, then it will not expect impossibilities.	If q, then r.
Conclusion: if a beast is a dragon, then it will not expect impossibilities.	Therefore, if p, then r.

The above argument can be further condensed to a single line by using the symbol $\rightarrow$ to replace the expression "if . . . , then . . . ." In mathematics, $\rightarrow$ can be read "implies."

$$[(p \rightarrow q) \text{ and } (q \rightarrow r)] \rightarrow (p \rightarrow r).$$

In logic, this type of argument is called a *syllogism*. A syllogism involves two premises, or assumptions, and a conclusion reached by DEDUCTION from these two premises. Another example of a syllogism is

$$[(p \rightarrow q) \text{ and } (\text{given } p)] \rightarrow (q),$$

which may be illustrated:

All dragons are covered with scales.
Puff is a dragon.
Conclusion: Puff is covered with scales.

LOGICAL TERMS AND SYMBOLS

Proposition: an idea that can be pronounced either true or false.

Premise: a proposition accepted as true and used to prove a conclusion.

Conclusion: a statement that can be proved from premises by logical reasoning.

The study of the logical relationships among statements may be called the *algebra of propositions,* or the *calculus of propositions.*

Symbolic logic is the use of symbols to expose the basic structure of reasoning, as has been illustrated by syllogisms. The following table lists other symbols employed by logicians and the names of the various combinations of propositions:

For two statements, p and q,

$$\sim p = \text{not } p \qquad\qquad \textit{negation}$$
$$p \wedge q = p \text{ and } q \qquad\qquad \textit{conjunction}$$

$$p \lor q = p \text{ or } q \qquad \textit{disjunction}$$
$$p \to q = \text{if } p, \text{ then } q \qquad \textit{conditional}$$
$$p \leftrightarrow q = p \text{ if and only if } q \qquad \textit{biconditional}$$

Examples.   Let p = "It is sunny."
and q = "We shall have a picnic."

Then,

$$\sim p = \text{"It is \textit{not} sunny."}$$
$$p \land q = \text{"It is sunny \textit{and} we shall have a picnic."}$$
$$p \lor q = \text{"It is sunny \textit{or} we shall have a picnic."}$$

(The possibility of sunshine *and* picnic is not excluded in logic by a disjunction.)

$$p \to q = \text{"\textit{If} it is sunny, \textit{then} we shall have a picnic."}$$
$$\sim p \to \sim q = \text{"\textit{If} it is \textit{not} sunny, \textit{then} we shall \textit{not} have a picnic."}$$
$$p \leftrightarrow q = \text{"We shall have a picnic \textit{if, and only if,} it is sunny."}$$

TRUTH VALUE

Every proposition has a *truth value;* that is, it is either true or false. Two propositions with the same truth value are *equivalent;* that is, both are true or both are false.

When two propositions p and q are combined by any of the logical connectives $\sim$, $\land$, $\lor$, $\to$, or $\leftrightarrow$, the resulting combination has a truth value that depends on the individual truth values of p and q. For example,

- if p is true, then $\sim p$ is false.
- if p is false, then $\sim p$ is true.
- $p \land q$ is true only in the case that p is true *and* q is true.
- $p \leftrightarrow q$ is true only in the case that $(p \to q)$ is true *and* $(q \to p)$ is true.

A *truth table* is a chart that shows for a set of propositions such as p and q, and their negations, the truth value of any combinations of these propositions. The following truth table displays the truth values for many possible combinations of two propositions.

Truth Table, for two statements p and q (T = true, F = false)

p q	$\sim p$ negation	$\sim q$ negation	$p \rightarrow q$ conditional	$q \rightarrow p$ converse	$\sim p \rightarrow \sim q$ inverse	$\sim q \rightarrow \sim p$ contrapositive	$p \wedge q$ conjunction	$p \vee q$ disjunction	$p \leftrightarrow q$ biconditional
T T	F	F	T	T	T	T	T	T	T
T F	F	T	F	T	T	F	F	T	F
F T	T	F	T	F	F	T	F	T	F
F F	T	T	T	T	T	T	F	F	T

Consider the conditional (fifth) column of the truth table. For a conditional statement, "if p, then q," the first two entries in the truth table seem natural:

If p is true and q is true, then $(p \rightarrow q)$ is true.
If p is true and q is false, then $(p \rightarrow q)$ is false.

However, if in a conditional statement, "if p, then q," p is false, then the truth table says that, regardless of whether q is true or false, $(p \rightarrow q)$ is true! That is,

If p is false and q is true, then $(p \rightarrow q)$ is true.
If p is false and q is false, then $(p \rightarrow q)$ is true.

It might seem strange at first glance, but this reasoning makes the whole system of logic fall into a pattern. And it is possible to illustrate these conditional truth values so that they seem less strange:

Example.   A woman running for political office promises to vote against all tax increases if elected. In other words, she says

"If I am elected, then I shall vote against all tax increases."

p q

Obviously, if she is elected and then votes against all tax increases, then her campaign statement is true.

(p is true, q is true, $(p \rightarrow q)$ is true.)

However, if she is elected and votes *for* a tax increase, then she has made her campaign statement false.

(p is true, q is false, $(p \rightarrow q)$ is false.)

On the other hand, consider the possibilities when the premise p is false:

If she is not elected but still votes against all tax increases whenever she can, then her campaign statement remains true.

$$(p \text{ is false, } q \text{ is true, } (p \rightarrow q) \text{ is true.})$$

And if she is not elected and later votes *for* a tax increase, then her campaign statement still remains true because it made promises for her actions only *if* she were elected.

$$(p \text{ is false, } q \text{ is false, } (p \rightarrow q) \text{ is true.})$$

So, according to logic, a conditional statement is true in all cases except when the premise p is true and the conclusion q is false.

The entire truth table represents the classical system of logic, constructed to give a consistent valid system of reasoning for any pair of statements p and q, regardless of their content (or sense, or meaning).

THE CONDITIONAL AND ITS VARIATIONS

Conditional: a statement of the form "if p, then q."

Example.   If it is sunny, then we shall have a picnic

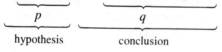

| p | q |
| hypothesis | conclusion |

Alternative phrasings: **Examples.**

$p \rightarrow q$

> *If* it is sunny, *then* we shall have a picnic.

p implies q

> A sunny day *implies* we shall have a picnic.

$p \subset q$ (p is a SUBSET of q)

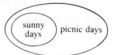

p is sufficient for q

> A sunny day is *sufficient* for a picnic.

q is necessary for p

> A picnic is *necessary* on a sunny day.

The "if" clause of a conditional is called the *hypothesis* or *antecedent*. The "then" clause is called the *conclusion* or *consequent*.

From a conditional statement $p \rightarrow q$ it is possible to form three related statements:

$(q \rightarrow p)$ **Converse:** "If q, then p." To form the converse of $p \rightarrow q$, the hypothesis and the conclusion of the original conditional are interchanged.

$(\sim p \rightarrow \sim q)$ **Inverse:** "If not p, then not q." To form the inverse of $p \rightarrow q$, the hypothesis and the conclusion of the original conditional are both negated.

$(\sim q \rightarrow \sim p)$ **Contrapositive:** "If not q, then not p." To form the contrapositive of $p \rightarrow q$, the hypothesis and the conclusion of the original conditional are interchanged and negated.

Examples.   Given that the conditional statement as a whole is true:

Conditional:	If it is sunny, then we shall have a picnic.	True.
Converse:	If we shall have a picnic, then it is sunny.	Not necessarily true— we might have our picnic on a cloudy day or under some shelter.
Inverse:	If it is not sunny, then we shall not have a picnic.	
Contrapositive:	If we shall not have a picnic, then it is not sunny.	Same truth as conditional— if it *were* sunny, the conditional says we'd have the picnic.

It may be noted that the contrapositive is *equivalent* to the conditional, because if one is true, so is the other. The inverse is also equivalent to the converse. But the conditional is *not* necessarily equivalent to its converse. These equivalences are summarized in the truth table and in the following display:

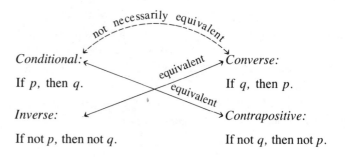

Conditional:
If p, then q.

Converse:
If q, then p.

Inverse:
If not p, then not q.

Contrapositive:
If not q, then not p.

The truth value of the converse and the inverse is *independent* of the truth value of the conditional and the contrapositive, and must be considered separately.

A case in which the conditional *is* equivalent to its converse is called a *biconditional $p \longleftrightarrow q$*. The biconditional is a statement for which the conditional, converse, inverse, and contrapositive all have the same truth value. That happens when p and q have the same truth value.

HISTORY

No one knows when people first began to use principles of sound reasoning to arrive at conclusions. But the methods of classical logic—the use of syllogisms and deductive reasoning—were formally presented by the Greek philosopher Aristotle in the fourth century B.C. The classical logic of Aristotle was based on the following three laws:

The Law of Identity:	A thing is itself.
The Law of the Excluded Middle:	A statement is either true or false.
The Law of Noncontradiction:	No statement is both true and false.

Aristotle's methods were used implicitly by another Greek scholar, Euclid, about 300 B.C. in his *Elements* (of GEOMETRY). Euclid's work was regarded as the model, by example, of classical logic for more than two thousand years. Aristotle's laws are still the foundation of most mathematical logic today.

The first ambitious effort at symbolic logic was presented in the seventeenth century by Gottfried Wilhelm von Leibniz, the German mathematician who helped create CALCULUS. Leibniz' idea was an international language for logic—a symbolic language within which the symbols, vocabulary, and rules would be a guide to logical reasoning. However, Leibniz only outlined his idea, and it was not until the nineteenth century that there were any further significant developments.

Giuseppe Peano, an Italian logician, worked from Leibniz' proposal and produced an international symbolic scientific language. Peano spent ten years, 1895–1905, on his *Formulario Mathematico,* a five-volume treatise in which all of mathematics was rewritten in his new symbolic language. Peano's symbolic logic is not simple, however, and has never been widely used.

Meanwhile, a much simpler symbolic logic had been developed by a self-taught British mathematician, George Boole, who had been working independently. In 1847 Boole published a short *Mathematical Analysis of Logic,* and seven years later he published a more thorough study, *Investigation of the Laws of Thought.* In these two works, Boole developed the fundamental ideas of using mathematical symbols and operations to represent statements and to solve problems in logic. He applied these techniques to an ALGEBRA of SETS, which has come to be called *Boolean algebra*. Boole's symbols and system of reasoning provided the model for the symbolic logic used today.

In the early twentieth century, Bertrand Russell and Alfred North Whitehead extended the symbolic logic of Leibniz, Boole, Peano, and others in their great work, *Principia Mathematica* (1910–1913). Russell and Whitehead tried to set mathematics on a solid logical foundation. In the attempt, they made important contributions both to the idea of a universal scientific language and to the field of logic in general.

The twentieth century has also seen challenges to Aristotle's laws of classical logic. For example, in 1912 a Dutch logician, L. E. J. Brouwer, while working with infinite sets, objected to the Law of the Excluded Middle, which says that any statement is either true or false. This law is the foundation of indirect DEDUCTION, or proof by contradiction, which says that if a statement can be proved to be not false, then it must be true. Brouwer, however, allowed the possibility that a statement might be neither true nor false. And for some modern mathematics, Brouwer's logic is indeed necessary.

Thus, while classical logic is by no means dead, modern logic is a lively subject with many new possibilities. For more on the history of logic, particularly on the matter of undecidability, see MATHEMATICAL SYSTEMS.

The history of logic includes many important mathematicians not mentioned in this short article. For a more complete picture, see references, Kline and Kramer.

REFERENCES

Irving Adler, *Thinking Machines: A Layman's Guide to Logic, Boolean Algebra, and Computers* (The John Day Co., 1961); logic applied to practical problems.

Lewis Carroll, *Pillow Problems and A Tangled Tale* (Dover, 1958). Lewis Carroll was the pseudonym of the mathematician Charles Dodgson, who lectured at Cambridge University in England and who wrote *Alice in Wonderland* and *Through the Looking-Glass*. The pillow problems were Carroll's method of escaping unpleasant aspects of life; the tangled tale is a collection of ten knots (chapters) of delightful Carroll prose, each of which poses logical problems. Answers and solutions are provided to all the problems in the collections.

Peter D. Cook, *The Ages of Mathematics, Volume IV: The Modern Age* (Doubleday, 1977), Ch. 6, "Logic and Mathematics." This chapter is primarily history, and it includes excerpts from *Alice in Wonderland* and from Lewis Carroll's other writings.

Oswald Jacoby, *Mathematics for Pleasure* (McGraw-Hill, 1962; Fawcett, 1970), Ch. 4, "Where Inference and Reasoning Reign." This chapter includes 55 intriguing problems requiring different kinds of reasoning; solutions and commentary are given as well.

Donovan A. Johnson, *Logic and Reasoning in Mathematics,* from the series Exploring Mathematics on Your Own (Webster Publishing Co., 1963). This booklet includes logic puzzles.

Morris Kline, *Mathematical Thought from Ancient to Modern Times* (Oxford University Press, 1972), "The Rise of Mathematical Logic," pp. 1187–1192.

Edna E. Kramer, *The Nature and Growth of Modern Mathematics* (Hawthorn Books, 1970; Princeton University Press, 1982), Ch. 3, "Mathematical Reasoning" and Ch. 6, "A Universal Language;" a thorough and pleasant discussion if you have some mathematical background.

Frederick C. Kreiling, "Leibniz," *Scientific American,* May 1968; reprinted in *Mathematics: An Introduction to Its Spirit and Use: Readings from Scientific American* (W. H. Freeman & Co., 1978).

Raymond Smullyan, *What Is the Name of this Book? The Riddle of Dracula and Other Logical Puzzles* (Prentice-Hall, 1978). Smullyan presents over 200 puzzles and paradoxes, proceeding from simple diversions all the way to complex problems of undecidability; an excellent and most entertaining presentation.

For an elaboration of two types of logical reasoning, see DEDUCTION and INDUCTION.

See also MATHEMATICAL SYSTEMS, PROOFS.

MATHEMATICAL SYSTEMS

MATHEMATICAL SYSTEM: the combination of a set of assumptions and the set of conclusions that can be proved from them by DEDUCTION.

ASSUMPTIONS OF A MATHEMATICAL SYSTEM

A mathematical system is based on some *undefined terms* that are used to *define* other terms (see DEFINITIONS), and on some *unproven statements* that are used to *prove* other statements.

The reason it is necessary to start with a few basic statements that are assumed true rather than proved true is illustrated in the following argument by Edna E. Kramer*:

> "Why must I go to sleep?" Johnny asks. "Because you need rest," says Dad. "*Why* do I need rest?" Johnny continues. "Because it will give you the strength to play games with your friends tomorrow." "*Why* should I play games with my friends tomorrow?" "Because a little boy needs exercise." "Why do I need exercise?" At this point, Dad says, "*Because!* And that's that! Go straight to bed and *no more questions!*"
>
> Dad is declaring as *axiomatic* the proposition that a child requires exercise; that is, he is stating that Johnny must accept this proposition *without proof*. It is a necessity to stop at some point in a regressive argument and "lay down the law." Even if one does not attempt to answer an endless chain of "whys," there is a certain logical danger in permitting a *finite* sequence to become too lengthy. Let us imagine that Dad decides to argue a little longer. When Johnny asks "*Why* do I need exercise?", Dad may answer, "Because it provides healthy fatigue." "*Why* do I need healthy fatigue?" "Because it will make you *sleepy and ready to go to bed* right now." Dad is right back where he started. He has just involved himself in a "vicious circle" or he is "begging the question," since if we fuse all Dad's answers into one long chain, we find that Johnny must go to sleep because he must go to sleep.

*From *The Nature and Growth of Modern Mathematics* (Hawthorn Books, 1970; Princeton University Press, 1982), p. 43; by permission of the author.

To prevent an endless argument, or circular reasoning, some statement must be chosen as an *axiom*—a statement not requiring proof. And for the same reason it is necessary to choose some of the terms to be undefined.

Primitive: one of the undefined terms on which a mathematical system is based.

Axiom (or *postulate*): a statement that is assumed to be true without proof.

Although Euclid distinguished between axioms and postulates, stating that axioms were more general and that postulates applied only to a particular branch of mathematics, most mathematicians no longer make this distinction. Assumptions, in general, are called axioms.

CONCLUSIONS OF A MATHEMATICAL SYSTEM

The conclusions that are proved from the axioms of a mathematical system are called *theorems*.

Theorem: a statement that has been proved.

Lemma: a theorem proved only for use in the proof of a more important theorem.

Corollary to a theorem: a theorem that is added to another theorem and follows so obviously from the first theorem that little or no additional proof is necessary.

Conjecture: a proposed theorem; a statement that has not yet been proved (or disproved).

The assumptions and conclusions of a mathematical system are joined together by deductive reasoning. This method shows how certain results follow logically from certain premises or assumptions. For detail see DEDUCTION and LOGIC.

DIFFERENT MATHEMATICAL SYSTEMS

There are many mathematical systems, including

ARITHMETICS: real number arithmetic
clock, or modular, arithmetic
transfinite arithmetic
arithmetics without numbers

GEOMETRIES: Euclidean geometry
spherical geometry
other non-Euclidean geometries

ALGEBRAS: algebra with REAL NUMBERS or COMPLEX NUMBERS
MATRIX algebra
VECTOR algebra
algebra of SETS

Each of these systems has its own set of axioms. The mathematical system for Euclidean geometry is based on the set of axioms and postulates given by Euclid in the third century B.C. They are listed in the GEOMETRY article. A mathematical system for the real numbers is built up in many standard algebra and analysis texts.

It is impossible to tell just by reading a statement whether it is an axiom or a theorem. Remember that different mathematical systems are built on different sets of axioms, and a statement may be an axiom in one branch of mathematics and a theorem in another. To work with a mathematical system, you must know what its axioms are.

EXPLORING THE FOUNDATIONS OF MATHEMATICAL SYSTEMS

Mathematicians have long been intrigued with the questions that arise in choosing a set of axioms. When do you have enough axioms? When do you have too many? These questions are not easily answered. Somehow, exploring them seems to give rise to more and more questions. For example, efforts to show that Euclid's fifth postulate was an unnecessary axiom for GEOMETRY eventually led to the discovery of non-Euclidean geometries with different fifth postulates.

Two goals for mathematical systems in general are *completeness* and *consistency*. That is, mathematicians naturally desire that a set of axioms be complete and that it not lead to contradictions. Consider any statement (A) and its negation (not A):

- In a *complete* system it is possible to prove either A *or* its negation;
- In a *consistent* system it is *not* possible to prove *both A and* its negation.

Early in the twentieth century, David Hilbert, an outstanding German mathematician, worked hard on a consistent foundation for all of mathematics. He tried to describe an effective list of axioms for arithmetic of the whole numbers and then to show that two contradictory statements could not both be derived from his set of axioms. If he had been able to do so, then the axioms would have been proven consistent. But neither Hilbert nor anyone else could prove this.

Then in 1931 a young Austrian mathematician, Kurt Gödel, shook the mathematical world to its foundations by showing that consistency for an effective axiomatic system (such as Hilbert's) can *never* be proved using only resources of the system. Hilbert wanted his system to be complete as well as consistent, and therein lies the difficulty—the assumption that such a system can be found produces a *paradox*. (A paradox is a case of apparently valid deductive reasoning that leads to a contradiction of a fact or premise.) A precise discussion of this paradox is highly technical; roughly speaking, it arises when you consider a sentence in the language of arithmetic that says essentially

"This statement is not provable."

If this statement is false, then you can prove it using the axioms, but that means the system is inconsistent. If the statement is true, then you cannot prove it and the system is incomplete.

Gödel showed that Hilbert's system cannot be both consistent and complete. Such a system is then called *incomplete,* and the question of consistency is called *undecidable.* Gödel's work with incompleteness and undecidability opened up new questions and new methods. And in many branches of modern mathematics, other propositions have since been proved undecidable.

The questions of consistency, completeness, and undecidability are extremely difficult advanced topics. The paradox is one key to understanding; the idea of self-reference is another. *Self-reference* is the ability of a statement to talk about itself. "This statement is not provable" is a self-referential statement, and that is what leads to the paradox. A third key to understanding is the fact that Hilbert and Gödel were working with a very special set of axioms. For any mathematical system that includes the integers, a finite set of axioms is not sufficient. So the goal is to get an *effective* list of axioms, such as a set of axioms that a computer could be programmed to list if it were given an infinite amount of time. This gives a finite way to describe an infinite list.

For further contemplation of these puzzling ideas, see the references. Hofstadter and Smullyan have both written for the nonmathematician in a most entertaining and thought-provoking manner.

Sierpinski Gasket

This figure decomposes into three parts, each of which is a reduced-scale replica of the whole. This geometric property, called *self-similarity,* illustrates a form of self-reference. Self-similarity is important in the study of shapes called *fractals,* of which this is an example. (See page iv.)

REFERENCES

Douglas R. Hofstadter, *Gödel, Escher, Bach: An Eternal Golden Braid* (Basic Books, 1979); a hefty book, but if you like Escher's drawings and Bach's music and if you are intrigued by paradoxes, you may enjoy this immensely. The key to this book is the idea of self-reference. Hofstadter has written further on this topic in *Scientific American,* January 1981 and January 1982.

Raymond M. Smullyan, *What Is the Name of this Book? The Riddle of Dracula and Other Logical Puzzles* (Prentice-Hall, 1978); leads in clear, elementary, and entertaining fashion from problems and riddles of simple deduction right to the very heart of Gödel's work on undecidability and the paradoxes involved.

References on mathematical foundations

The following references are popular rather than highly technical discussions of the ongoing search for a firm foundation for mathematics, but some mathematical background is nevertheless required.

Howard Eves and Carroll V. Newsom, *An Introduction to the Foundations and Fundamental Concepts of Mathematics* (Holt, Rinehart, and Winston, 1965), pp. 334–338; a particularly succinct and clearly organized exposition of Gödel's revelation of the limitations of the axiomatic method.

Edna E. Kramer, *The Nature and Growth of Modern Mathematics* (Hawthorn Books, 1970; Princeton University Press, 1982), pp. 41–49 on mathematical reasoning; Ch. 24, "Infinite Hierarchy," and Ch. 29, "Twentieth-Century Vistas—Logic and Foundations."

Ernest Nagel and James R. Newman, *Gödel's Proof;* an entry in Newman's *World of Mathematics* (Simon & Schuster, 1956; available in paperback), pp. 1668–1695.

Constance Reid, *Hilbert* (Springer-Verlag, 1970).

Reference on computability

Closely related to the question of decidability is the question of *computability*—which classes of problems can be adapted for solution by computer? In many cases, it can be proved that there is no single algorithm, or sequence of instructions, that will solve a particular class of problem, even though an algorithm may be found for *some* problems within that class.

B. A. Trakhtenbrot, *Algorithms and Automatic Computing Machines,* translated from Russian (D. C. Heath & Co., 1963); designed as enrichment for high school students.

Reference on applied mathematical systems

Mathematical systems can be devised to solve practical problems. For example, a system can be created for electrical circuits and then analyzed; the resulting algebra suggests implications for future circuit design. The following source provides details and also sets up a mathematical system in botany to study transmission of plant disease.

Enrichment Mathematics for the Grades, 27th Yearbook of the National Council of Teachers of Mathematics (1963), Ch. 21, "The Anatomy of a Mathematical System," by Bruce R. Vogeli; an unusual and thorough exposition in applied mathematics, well-written for junior high, with additional references.

Reference on a mathematical system for the real numbers

Grace E. Bates and Fred Kiokemeister, *The Real Number System* (Allyn & Bacon, 1960); an excellent source.

See also DEFINITIONS, DEDUCTION (with more references on para-doxes), LOGIC, PROOFS, GEOMETRY, HISTORY.

MATRICES

MATRIX (plural, Matrices): a rectangular array of numbers.

Examples.

$$\begin{bmatrix} 1 & 2 & 3 & 4 & 5 \\ 6 & 7 & 8 & 9 & 10 \end{bmatrix} \qquad \left\| \begin{matrix} 1 & 0 \\ 0 & 1 \end{matrix} \right\| \qquad \begin{pmatrix} 1 & 0 & 6 \\ -2 & 4 & 7 \\ 3 & -1 & 5 \end{pmatrix}$$

Notation: A matrix is enclosed on the left and right by brackets, double lines, or large parentheses. An entire matrix may be represented by a single capital letter, such as

$$A = \begin{bmatrix} 1 & 3 \\ 5 & 8 \end{bmatrix}$$

Matrices are used to record and summarize information. For instance, after an election, the newspapers are filled with tables like the following:

	Votes for A	*Votes for B*	*Votes for C*
First precinct	125	87	13
Second precinct	96	97	53
Third precinct	113	79	23
Fourth precinct	59	147	40
Totals	393	410	129

The array of numbers is a shorthand statement of the whole story, provided the reader knows what is represented by each *row* (horizontal

line) and *column* (vertical line). Each of the numbers in a matrix is
called an *entry*, or *element*.

$$V = \begin{bmatrix} 125 & 87 & 13 \\ 96 & 97 & 53 \\ 113 & 79 & 23 \\ 59 & 147 & 40 \\ 393 & 410 & 129 \end{bmatrix}$$

For example, the number 79 in the third row, second column, is the
entry that represents the third precinct votes for *B*. The number 410 in
the fifth row, second column, is the entry (or element) representing the
total number of votes for *B*.

The size of a matrix is called its *dimension*. Dimension is expressed
as $m \times n$ (which is read "m by n"), where m = the number of rows
and n = the number of columns. The matrix V above is a 5×3 matrix.

SPECIAL KINDS OF MATRICES

Row Matrix: a matrix with only one row.

Example. [1 2 3]

Column Matrix: a matrix with only one column.

Example. $\begin{bmatrix} 1 \\ 2 \\ 3 \end{bmatrix}$

Square Matrix: a matrix in which the number of rows equals the
number of columns.

Examples. $\begin{bmatrix} 1 & 2 \\ 3 & 4 \end{bmatrix}$ $\begin{bmatrix} 0 & 0 & 2 \\ 4 & 11 & 11 \\ -1 & 3 & 9 \end{bmatrix}$

Zero Matrix: a matrix in which all the entries are 0.

Example. $\begin{bmatrix} 0 & 0 & 0 \\ 0 & 0 & 0 \end{bmatrix} = 0$

Identity Matrix: a square matrix in which the entries on the main diagonal (from upper left to lower right) are one, and all other entries are zero.

Notation: I represents an identity matrix.

Example.
$$I = \begin{bmatrix} 1 & 0 & 0 & 0 \\ 0 & 1 & 0 & 0 \\ 0 & 0 & 1 & 0 \\ 0 & 0 & 0 & 1 \end{bmatrix}$$

Transpose of a Matrix: the matrix resulting from interchanging the rows and the columns.

Notation: A^T = transpose of A.

Example. If $A = \begin{bmatrix} 1 & 2 \\ 3 & 4 \\ 5 & 6 \end{bmatrix}$, then $A^T = \begin{bmatrix} 1 & 3 & 5 \\ 2 & 4 & 6 \end{bmatrix}$

ARITHMETIC OPERATIONS ON MATRICES

Under certain conditions, it is possible to perform ARITHMETIC OPERATIONS on entire matrices.

Addition of Matrices

Matrices can be added only if they have the same dimension, that is, the same number of rows and the same number of columns. The sum will also be a matrix of the same dimension. To add two matrices, add corresponding elements and enter each sum in the corresponding place in the sum matrix.

Example.

$$\begin{bmatrix} 1 & 3 \\ 0 & -2 \end{bmatrix} + \begin{bmatrix} 7 & -1 \\ 1 & 6 \end{bmatrix} = \begin{bmatrix} 1+7 & 3+(-1) \\ 0+1 & -2+6 \end{bmatrix} = \begin{bmatrix} 8 & 2 \\ 1 & 4 \end{bmatrix}$$

Multiplication of a Matrix by a Scalar

A *scalar* is simply a real number, and not an array of numbers. To multiply a matrix by a scalar, multiply each element in the matrix by the scalar.

Example.

$$3\begin{bmatrix} 4 & -2 \\ 0 & 6 \end{bmatrix} = \begin{bmatrix} 3 \times 4 & 3 \times (-2) \\ 3 \times 0 & 3 \times 6 \end{bmatrix} = \begin{bmatrix} 12 & -6 \\ 0 & 18 \end{bmatrix}$$

Multiplication of a Matrix by a Matrix

An $m \times n$ matrix can be multiplied only by an $n \times p$ matrix, where the number of columns of the first matrix must equal the number of rows of the second matrix. The order in which the matrices are multiplied is important. The result will be an $m \times p$ matrix.

To find the product of two such matrices, take a row from the first matrix and a column from the second, then multiply corresponding elements (starting at the left of the row and at the top of the column), and sum the results.

Examples.

$$\begin{bmatrix} 3 & 1 & 2 \end{bmatrix}\begin{bmatrix} -1 \\ 4 \\ 5 \end{bmatrix} = \begin{bmatrix} 3 \times (-1) + 1 \times 4 + 2 \times 5 \end{bmatrix} = \begin{bmatrix} 11 \end{bmatrix}$$

$$\begin{array}{cc} (1 \times 3) \times (3 \times 1) \\ m \times n \qquad n \times p \end{array} \qquad\qquad\qquad \begin{array}{c} = (1 \times 1) \\ m \times p \end{array}$$

$$\begin{bmatrix} 3 & 1 & 2 \\ 0 & 7 & 6 \end{bmatrix}\begin{bmatrix} -1 \\ 4 \\ 5 \end{bmatrix} = \begin{bmatrix} 3 \times (-1) + 1 \times 4 + 2 \times 5 \\ 0 \times (-1) + 7 \times 4 + 6 \times 5 \end{bmatrix} = \begin{bmatrix} 11 \\ 58 \end{bmatrix}$$

$$\begin{array}{cc} (2 \times 3) \times (3 \times 1) \\ m \times n \qquad n \times p \end{array} \qquad\qquad\qquad \begin{array}{c} = (2 \times 1) \\ m \times p \end{array}$$

$$\begin{bmatrix} 3 & 1 & 2 \\ 0 & 7 & 6 \end{bmatrix}\begin{bmatrix} -1 & 9 \\ 4 & 0 \\ 5 & 8 \end{bmatrix} = \begin{bmatrix} 3 \times (-1) + 1 \times 4 + 2 \times 5 & 3 \times 9 + 1 \times 0 + 2 \times 8 \\ 0 \times (-1) + 7 \times 4 + 6 \times 5 & 0 \times 9 + 7 \times 0 + 6 \times 8 \end{bmatrix} = \begin{bmatrix} 11 & 43 \\ 58 & 48 \end{bmatrix}$$

$$\begin{array}{cc} (2 \times 3) \times (3 \times 2) \\ m \times n \qquad n \times p \end{array} \qquad\qquad\qquad \begin{array}{c} = (2 \times 2) \\ m \times p \end{array}$$

APPLICATIONS OF MATRICES

The definitions of different kinds of matrices and the operations that can be performed on them form an ALGEBRA of matrices. But the question arises: "Where would you use such an algebra?" One answer:

"Wherever you need a systematic approach to dealing with an array of numbers."

Consider, for example, the voting returns mentioned at the beginning of this article. Suppose that every voter had indicated on his or her ballot a party affiliation. Then, if every voter were either a Republican or a Democrat, the results might have appeared in the newspaper like this:

	Votes for A		Votes for B		Votes for C	
	Rep.	Dem.	Rep.	Dem.	Rep.	Dem.
First precinct	120	5	13	74	7	6
Second precinct	91	5	17	80	8	45
Third precinct	101	12	30	49	13	10
Fourth precinct	57	2	13	134	39	1
Totals	369	24	73	337	67	62

And it would make sense to write the total voting matrix V as the *sum* of the Republican voting matrix R and a Democratic voting matrix D:

$$
\begin{bmatrix} 120 & 13 & 7 \\ 91 & 17 & 8 \\ 101 & 30 & 13 \\ 57 & 13 & 39 \\ 369 & 73 & 67 \end{bmatrix} + \begin{bmatrix} 5 & 74 & 6 \\ 5 & 80 & 45 \\ 12 & 49 & 10 \\ 2 & 134 & 1 \\ 24 & 337 & 62 \end{bmatrix} = \begin{bmatrix} 125 & 87 & 13 \\ 96 & 97 & 53 \\ 113 & 79 & 23 \\ 59 & 147 & 40 \\ 393 & 410 & 129 \end{bmatrix}
$$

$$
R \qquad + \qquad D \qquad = \qquad V
$$

When would you use *multiplication of a matrix by a scalar*? This matrix shows the costs of photographic film:

	20-exposure roll	36-exposure roll
black and white film	$1.98	$2.98
color print film	$2.76	$3.76
color slide film	$3.38	$5.58

A half-price sale would yield a new matrix, found by multiplying the original price matrix by the scalar $\frac{1}{2}$:

$$
\text{Sale matrix} = \frac{1}{2} \begin{bmatrix} 1.98 & 2.98 \\ 2.76 & 3.76 \\ 3.38 & 5.58 \end{bmatrix} = \begin{bmatrix} .99 & 1.49 \\ 1.38 & 1.88 \\ 1.69 & 2.79 \end{bmatrix}
$$

The labels for the rows and columns in the sale matrix are the same as those in the original price matrix. So a 36-exposure roll of color slide film costs $2.79 on sale. Some salespeople find it easier to consult a new matrix than to do mental arithmetic for each sale.

A good illustration of *multiplication of a matrix by a matrix* is provided by the following manufacturing situation.* An electronics company uses raw materials: copper, zinc, glass, and plastic. From these materials it produces electronic components: transistors, resistors, buttons, cases, and computer chips. Using these components, it produces three different models of hand calculators, called *T-1*, *T-2*, and *T-3*. The manufacturing details are summarized in two matrices *A* and *B*.

Units of	*Transistor*	*Resistor*	*Button*	*Case*	*Computer chip*	
Copper	2	2	0	0	3	
Zinc	1	1	0	0	2	
Glass	1	2	0	1	1	= Matrix *A*
Plastic	0	0	1	3	0	

	T-1	*T-2*	*T-3*	
Transistors	5	6	10	
Resistors	7	8	16	
Buttons	20	25	45	= Matrix *B*
Cases	1	1	1	
Computer Chips	4	6	10	

For example, the first row in *A* indicates that there are 2 units of copper in each transistor, 2 units in each resistor, no copper in either the buttons or the cases, and 3 units in each computer chip; the first column in *B* indicates that there are 5 transistors, 7 resistors, 20 buttons, 1 case, and 4 computer chips in each *T-1* calculator.

An overall matrix *C* relating raw materials to finished products could be constructed as follows:

The amount of copper in a *T-1* =

$$2 \text{ units copper per transistor} \times 5 \text{ transistors}$$
$$+ \ 2 \text{ units copper per resistor} \times 7 \text{ resistors}$$
$$+ \ 0 \text{ units copper per button} \times 20 \text{ buttons}$$
$$+ \ 0 \text{ units copper per case} \times 1 \text{ case}$$
$$+ \ 3 \text{ units copper per computer chip} \times 4 \text{ chips}$$
$$= \quad 36 \text{ units copper total in a } T\text{-}1$$

*From R. M. Thrall and E. L. Perry, "An Everyday Approach to Matrix Operations," produced in 1976 at a Mathematical Association of America Summer Workshop, Writing Modules in Applied Mathematics, under W. F. Lucas, 334 Upson Hall, Cornell University, Ithaca, N.Y., 14853.

Notice that this is exactly the first element that would be obtained in multiplying together the two given matrices. The amount of copper in a *T-1* is obtained from the copper row of matrix *A* and the *T-1* column of matrix *B*. This same procedure may be used to complete the matrix of raw materials for each finished product

$$
\begin{bmatrix} 2 & 2 & 0 & 0 & 3 \\ 1 & 1 & 0 & 0 & 2 \\ 1 & 2 & 0 & 1 & 1 \\ 0 & 0 & 1 & 3 & 0 \end{bmatrix}
\begin{bmatrix} 5 & 6 & 10 \\ 7 & 8 & 16 \\ 20 & 25 & 45 \\ 1 & 1 & 1 \\ 4 & 6 & 10 \end{bmatrix}
=
\begin{bmatrix} 36 & 46 & 82 \\ 20 & 26 & 46 \\ 24 & 29 & 53 \\ 23 & 28 & 48 \end{bmatrix}
$$

$$A \qquad\qquad B \quad = \quad C$$

This product matrix is represented by the table,

Raw material	Calculators		
	T-1	T-2	T-3
Copper	36	46	82
Zinc	20	26	46
Glass	24	29	53
Plastic	23	28	48

The mechanics of matrix multiplication are easily programmed into a computer. So in a situation where matrix multiplication makes sense, the computation can all be done by computer.

An exciting application of matrices has been to the field of *computer graphics*. A three-dimensional object is described for the computer by stating the geometric COORDINATES of each point of the object. Then the computer, using matrix operations, displays a two-dimensional image in *perspective* (see PROJECTION). By further matrix operations, it can show the object from the different perspectives of an observer who has changed position.

Reference on computer graphics

Kellogg S. Booth, *Tutorial: Computer Graphics* (IEEE Computer Society (The Institute of Electrical and Electronics Engineers, Inc.), 1979); a self-contained collection of papers on computer graphics, giving a good snapshot of the field in the late 1970's. A good introduction, showing a breadth of applications as well as explanation of the use of matrices (pp. 172–185), this provides an excellent overview at whatever level of mathematical background the reader brings to it.

DETERMINANTS

For *square* matrices, the following additional term may be defined for more advanced work:

Determinant: a number obtained from a square matrix by multiplying and summing the elements in a particular way.

Notation: det A or $|A|$

For a 2×2 matrix, the determinant is defined as the product of the elements on the main diagonal ($\searrow$, from upper left to lower right) minus the product of the elements on the other diagonal ($\nearrow$).

Example. $\begin{vmatrix} 2 & 3 \\ 1 & 5 \end{vmatrix} = \begin{vmatrix} 2 & 3 \\ 1 & 5 \end{vmatrix} = 2 \times 5 - 3 \times 1 = 7$

For a 3×3 matrix, the determinant may also be found by products of elements on the diagonals, but there are more diagonals. Each element in the top row heads one diagonal going down to the right and another diagonal going down to the left. The determinant equals the sum of the three products on diagonals going down to the right ($\searrow$), minus the sum of the three products on diagonals going down to the left ($\nearrow$). In order to include all the elements of the matrix on the diagonals, the second and third rows are extended in a cyclic manner, as illustrated below.

Example. $\begin{vmatrix} 1 & 2 & 3 \\ 4 & 5 & 6 \\ 7 & 8 & 9 \end{vmatrix}$

$$= \begin{matrix} 1 & 2 & 3 \\ 4 & 5 & 6 \\ 7 & 8 & 9 \end{matrix} \begin{matrix} 1 & 2 & 3 \\ 4 & 5 & 6 \\ 7 & 8 & 9 \end{matrix} \begin{matrix} 1 & 2 & 3 \\ 4 & 5 & 6 \\ 7 & 8 & 9 \end{matrix}$$

$$= 1 \times 5 \times 9 + 2 \times 6 \times 7 + 3 \times 4 \times 8$$
$$- 1 \times 6 \times 8 - 2 \times 4 \times 9 - 3 \times 5 \times 7$$

$$= 45 + 84 + 96 - 48 - 72 - 105$$

$$= 225 - 225$$

$$= 0$$

Determinants can be used to solve systems of algebraic equations in two or more unknowns. And since computers can be programmed to calculate determinants, the number of unknowns can be very large indeed. This is another important application of matrix algebra.

SOLUTIONS TO SYSTEMS OF SIMULTANEOUS LINEAR EQUATIONS

A system of simultaneous linear EQUATIONS can be written as a matrix equation.

Example. $\begin{aligned} x + 2y &= 3 \\ 4x + 5y &= 6 \end{aligned}$ can be written as

$$\begin{bmatrix} 1 & 2 \\ 4 & 5 \end{bmatrix} \begin{bmatrix} x \\ y \end{bmatrix} = \begin{bmatrix} 3 \\ 6 \end{bmatrix},$$

because of the definition of matrix multiplication. (Multiply out the matrices, and your results will give the equations above.)

If a system of simultaneous linear equations has a unique solution, that solution can be found using determinants. Swiss mathematician Gabriel Cramer developed the method, based on the matrix form for a system, in the eighteenth century.

Cramer's Rule

The general form for a system of two equations in two variables is

$$\begin{aligned} a_{11}x + a_{12}y &= b_1 \\ a_{21}x + a_{22}y &= b_2 \end{aligned} \quad \text{or} \quad \underbrace{\begin{bmatrix} a_{11} & a_{12} \\ a_{21} & a_{22} \end{bmatrix}}_{\substack{\text{matrix } A \\ \text{of coefficients}}} \begin{bmatrix} x \\ y \end{bmatrix} = \begin{bmatrix} b_1 \\ b_2 \end{bmatrix}$$

Then the solutions are

$$x = \frac{\begin{vmatrix} b_1 & a_{12} \\ b_2 & a_{22} \end{vmatrix}}{\begin{vmatrix} a_{11} & a_{12} \\ a_{21} & a_{22} \end{vmatrix}} \quad \text{and} \quad y = \frac{\begin{vmatrix} a_{11} & b_1 \\ a_{21} & b_2 \end{vmatrix}}{\begin{vmatrix} a_{11} & a_{12} \\ a_{21} & a_{22} \end{vmatrix}}$$

In other words, x and y are each the ratio of two determinants; in both cases the denominator is simply $|A|$. The numerators also start with A, but the appropriate column is replaced with the column of constants (the b's).

Example. The system of equations

$$\begin{aligned} x + 2y &= 3 \\ 4x + 5y &= 6 \end{aligned}$$

which can be represented as

$$\begin{bmatrix} 1 & 2 \\ 4 & 5 \end{bmatrix} \begin{bmatrix} x \\ y \end{bmatrix} = \begin{bmatrix} 3 \\ 6 \end{bmatrix}$$

has the solution

$$x = \frac{\begin{vmatrix} 3 & 2 \\ 6 & 5 \end{vmatrix}}{\begin{vmatrix} 1 & 2 \\ 4 & 5 \end{vmatrix}} = \frac{3 \times 5 - 2 \times 6}{1 \times 5 - 2 \times 4} = \frac{15 - 12}{5 - 8} = -1$$

$$y = \frac{\begin{vmatrix} 1 & 3 \\ 4 & 6 \end{vmatrix}}{\begin{vmatrix} 1 & 2 \\ 4 & 5 \end{vmatrix}} = \frac{1 \times 6 - 3 \times 4}{1 \times 5 - 2 \times 4} = \frac{6 - 12}{5 - 8} = 2$$

Cramer's Rule may be extended to larger systems of n equations in n variables and can be programmed for a computer or programmable calculator. Hence, Cramer's Rule provides an easy way to solve systems with 2, 3, or more variables.

Note, however, that if $|A| = 0$, you will find no solutions by Cramer's Rule. This means there is indeed no *unique* solution. But it does not necessarily mean there is no solution at all. There may be an infinite number of solutions (see EQUATIONS, simultaneous equations section). To distinguish between these two possibilities when $|A| = 0$, you will need different matrix methods.

Reference for theory of matrices

John G. Kemeny, J. Laurie Snell, Gerald L. Thompson, *Introduction to Finite Mathematics* (Prentice-Hall, 1957, 1966), Ch. V, "Vectors and Matrices," pp. 217–307 in the second edition; a classic reference.

See also VECTORS.

MEASURE

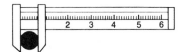

MEASURE: determination of the size, capacity, or extent of somethin
by comparing it to some standard unit.

    Examples. The diameter of a ball bearing can be measured by
caliper rule; this one measures 7.5 millimeters.

    Truck-weighing stations are used to assess road-use taxes; this truc
with its load weighs 38,000 pounds.

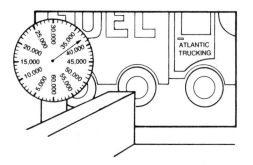

    A body temperature above normal (98.6°F) is a sign of illness; thi
thermometer shows 102°F.

    People have long had a desire or a need to measure. Very early the
probably became concerned with the size and number of things they ha
in relation to what someone else had, for example, who had more horse
or larger horses. Two persons could have compared the number o
horses they had by pairing one of the first person's horses with one o
the other's until one of them ran out of horses. (This comparison b

pairing is called making a one-to-one correspondence.) They might have compared the height of two horses by standing one beside the other. Or they might have wanted to compare the weight of two horses. The early Egyptians were able to make weight comparisons on a balance.

There was a need, however, for a movable third object, a standard unit, with which to compare measurements of two objects that could not be compared directly.

LENGTH

The early units for measurement of length were parts of the body, because one's arm or foot is always available. The *cubit* was the length of the forearm from the elbow to the tip of the middle finger (about 18 inches). The *ell* was a unit for measuring cloth equal to the distance from the tip of the nose to the end of the outstretched arm (varying from 27 inches to 45 inches in different parts of old Europe). The width of a man's *hand* (about 4 inches) was used for measuring the height of horses and is still used today. Distance was paced by the *foot*. A foot was equivalent to 12 thumb-widths, called "uncia," (the Roman word for "one-twelfth"), which has today become the *inch*. A thousand paces were to the Romans "milia passuum," which we now call the *mile*.

Eventually these units had to be standardized, because hands and feet were subject to variation. A standard must be something that does not change and that can be duplicated.

Standards for Length

The English system began to be standardized in the early thirteenth century when King Henry I set the *yard* as the measurement from the tip of his nose to the tip of his thumb when his royal arm was outstretched. In the fourteenth century, King Edward I made a standard yard from an iron bar about two cubits in length. In the early nineteenth century, Great Britain and then the United States legally adopted their own systems of measure based on similar standards for length—the yard. Since 1965, Great Britain has been converting to the METRIC SYSTEM, called *Système Internationale* or SI. The United States is making a slower conversion to the metric system.

The metric system of measurement was developed by the French in the late eighteenth century, with a carefully specified standard for length, the *meter*. The international standard meter was made of a nonrusting mixture of platinum and iridium and has been kept with the utmost care under constant conditions of temperature and atmospheric pressure. (Differences in temperature and pressure would make metal expand or contract.) The original standard meter is at Sèvres, France, home of the International Bureau of Weights and Measures, which was set up in 1875 to provide international agreement about standards of measurement. A precise copy of the standard meter is in Washington, D.C., at the National Bureau of Standards, established in 1901 to direct the standardization of measurement in the United States.

The United States officially retains the English system of measure, with the standard U.S. Customary *yard* defined in terms of the *metric* standard:

$$\text{the standard U.S. yard} = \frac{3600}{3937} \text{ of the standard meter}$$

This U.S. Customary yard serves as a standard for all the English units of linear measure (foot, mile, nautical mile, etc.) used in the United States today. Furthermore, the units of AREA measure (square foot, square yard, square mile) and the units of VOLUME measure (cubic foot, cubic yard) are also based on the standard yard. Tables for all these units and their metric equivalents appear in APPENDIX I.

WEIGHT AND MASS

A *grain*, probably of wheat, was the original unit used for comparison of weight. Eventually the grain became standardized as the smallest basic unit for all English systems of weight.

Three separate systems arose. The system for commercial use is called *avoirdupois,* from old French words meaning "goods having weight." The *apothecary* system is used for weighing drugs, which are sold in apothecary shops; from old Greek and Latin, "apotheke" or "apotheka" is a "place where things are stored up." And for weighing precious metals and gems, there is the *troy* system, named for Troyes, France, where it was first used.

All of these systems use units called *pound,* from the Roman "pondus" meaning "weight hanging down," and *ounce*, also from the Roman "uncia," meaning for weight "one-twelfth" of a pound, which is indeed the value of an ounce in the apothecary and troy systems.

Standards for Weight

In the early nineteenth century, Great Britain, followed by the United States, legally adopted a system of measure for weight based on the *pound*. There are some differences between the subsequent British and

U.S. systems; they are explained with all the tables of units of measure in APPENDIX I.

Today nearly all the countries of the world have officially adopted the international standards of the METRIC SYSTEM or Système Internationale (SI). The metric system measures *mass* by *kilogram* instead of *weight* by *pound* (the difference is explained in the next section), but an equivalence is used to convert between systems. The original standard kilogram, made of a special nonrusting mixture of platinum and iridium, is kept under constant temperature and pressure at the International Bureau of Weights and Measures in Sèvres, France. A precise copy of the standard kilogram is kept at the U.S. National Bureau of Standards in Washington, D.C.

The United States is moving slowly toward conversion to SI. The U.S. standard is still the *pound,* but the pound is now defined in terms of the *metric* standard.

the standard U.S. avoirdupois pound	= 0.4535924277	of the weight of the standard kilogram at sea level

Weight Versus Mass

There is an important technical difference between the concepts of weight, commonly used in the English system, and mass, commonly used in the metric system. Confusion results because in ordinary speech the terms "weight" and "mass" are frequently used interchangeably, though incorrectly. For technical work the difference must be understood. The definitions are:

Mass: the *amount* of substance, the amount of material. Mass can be measured on a balance, with standards.

Weight: the gravitational *force* exerted by the given amount of substance.

Weight = gravitational force
= mass × acceleration due to gravity.

Weight depends on mass *and* gravity.

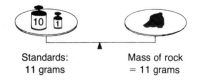

Standards: 11 grams   Mass of rock = 11 grams

The gravitational force we feel on the surface of the earth is due to the earth's immense mass and our closeness to its center. But at a great distance from the earth, or on a smaller mass like the moon, the gravitational force is far less.

Example.   An astronaut on the moon *weighs* 25 pounds because the gravitational pull of the moon is only $\frac{1}{6}$ that of earth. An astronaut in space is *weightless*—no significant gravitational force at a distance from both earth and moon. The same astronaut on earth *weighs* 150 pounds, due to the gravitational pull of earth. But in all three places, the astronaut would balance a *mass* of 68.2 kilograms.

Weight can vary, but mass remains constant. On or near the surface of the earth, however, differences in weight for a given mass are negligible. At sea level, a mass of one kilogram weighs approximately 2.2 pounds on a spring scale. So, for earthbound practical purposes, although these two measurements of weight and mass are not the same, they can be considered equivalent.

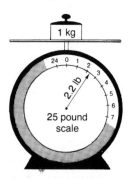

Scales in the metric system are marked according to mass; in the U.S. system they are marked in pounds. Meat and produce are sold by the kilogram (mass) under the metric system, by the pound (weight) under the U.S. system. *As long as these measurements are made on the surface of the earth,* they have the constant equivalence given.

TIME

For thousands of years, a *day* has been divided into 24 *hours,* an hour into 60 *minutes,* and a minute into 60 *seconds.* The number 24 is apparently due to the Egyptian practice of considering the day and the night as 12 hours each; 60 was the base of the Babylonian NUMERAL SYSTEM.

Standard for Time

Today the international standard for time is a cesium-beam clock that gives billions of ticks per second from the vibration of electrons within n atom of cesium, a rare metal. The vibrations are extremely stable, nd the clock will not lose or gain more than a second in 30,000 years. ynchronized cesium-beam clocks have been flown from Washington, .C., to various time-keeping stations around the world; synchroniza- ions are also made by satellites.

> the standard *second* = 9,192,631,770 vibrations
> of a cesium beam clock

1 minute (min) = 60 seconds (sec)
1 hour (hr) = 60 minutes
1 day (da) = 24 hours
1 week (wk) = 7 days
1 common year (yr) = 365 days
1 leap year = 366 days
1 decade = 10 years
1 century = 100 years
1 millennium = 1000 years

TEMPERATURE

Temperature is commonly measured on three different scales:

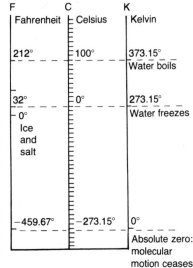

- *Fahrenheit (F):* The first temperature scale was devised in 1724 by a German physicist, Gabriel Daniel Fahrenheit. He used as a fixed cold point (which he called 0°, or zero degrees) a mixture of ice and salt, and as a fixed hot point (which he called 96°) normal body temperature. He divided the distance between these points into 96 equal degrees. (Later it was determined that normal body tempera- ture is actually 98.6° on Fahrenheit's scale.)
- *Celsius (C)* (formerly called centigrade): In 1742 a Swedish as- tronomer, Anders Celsius, invented an easier temperature scale. He used as cold point (0°) the freezing point of pure water, and as hot point (100°) the boiling temperature of water, with 100 evenly spaced degrees between.
- *Kelvin (K) or absolute:* In 1848 a British physicist, Lord Kelvin, proposed using a Celsius scale with the numbers moved downward so that 0° would be the temperature at which all molecular motion was believed to cease (*absolute zero*). This makes 0° K occur at −273.15°C.

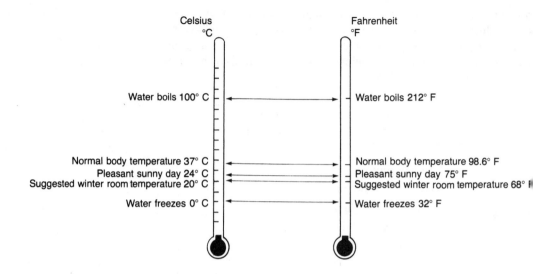

Standards for Temperature

Since 1948 the Kelvin scale has been the international standard for temperature, with measurements expressed in degrees Celsius for convenience. In 1960 six standard reference points along the scale were chosen; a thermometer may be calibrated using whichever are convenient:

The standard reference points for temperature

boiling or condensation point of oxygen	$-182.97°C$
triple point of water	$0.01°C$
(where ice, water, and water vapor coexist)	
boiling point of water	$100.00°C$
boiling point of sulfur	$444.60°C$
melting point of silver	$960.8°C$
melting point of gold	$1063.0°C$

The United States has always used the Fahrenheit scale; the metric system has always used the Celsius scale. The United States is gradually converting to Celsius. Conversions and comparisons follow:

- To change from Celsius to Fahrenheit: $F = \frac{9}{5}C + 32$

Example. Start with $100°C$.   Then $F = \frac{9}{5} \times 100 + 32$
$= \frac{900}{5} + 32$

$$= 180 + 32$$
$$= 212$$

So $100°C = 212°F$.

• To change from Fahrenheit to Celsius: $C = \frac{5}{9}(F - 32)$

Example.   Start with $212°F$.   Then
$$C = \frac{5}{9}(212 - 32)$$
$$= \frac{5}{9}(180)$$
$$= \frac{900}{9}$$
$$= 100$$

So $212°F = 100°C$.

ACCURACY AND PRECISION OF MEASUREMENT

Accuracy tells how *correctly* a measurement is made. An accurate supermarket scale will give the same reading each time you set your bag of tomatoes on it and will be properly adjusted to match standard weights.

Precision tells how *finely* a measurement is made. Precision tells you what are the smallest units on a measuring device. For example, precision may refer to whether your scales are marked in kilograms, grams, or milligrams.

Bathroom scales are marked in pounds or kilograms. Kitchen scales are used for weighing smaller quantities and are marked in ounces or grams, which are smaller units. The kitchen scales will therefore give a more precise measurement. A pumpkin might appear to weigh 4 lb on a bathroom scale and 3 lb 14 oz on a kitchen scale. Both measurements are accurate, but the latter is more precise.

Accuracy and precision are further discussed under SIGNIFICANT DIGITS.

METHODS OF MEASUREMENT

It is important to remember that every measurement is an approximation that is only as accurate as the method and the devices used. Measuring is usually done in one of two ways. The most common method is to use an instrument of *direct* comparison, such as a meter stick or a scale.

The second method is *indirect* measurement, for something that cannot be directly or accurately compared. A length such as the thickness of a sheet of paper is too small to measure accurately with an ordinary ruler. Nevertheless, you can often measure indirectly with an instrument that is too large: you can count and stack enough sheets (perhaps 100) to get an accurate measurement of the thickness of the stack and then

Thickness of stack of 100 sheets of paper = 11 mm

Thickness of single sheet of paper = 0.11 mm

divide the total thickness by the number of sheets. The more sheets you stack, the more accurate will be this method of indirect measurement.

As another example, it would be difficult to use an instrument to directly measure the height of a tall flagpole or the width of a fast-flowing river. These measurements can be made indirectly by calculations using, for instance, SIMILARITY of geometric figures, the PYTHAGOREAN THEOREM for right triangles, or TRIGONOMETRY.

For extremely large or extremely small lengths, other methods of indirect measurement may be necessary. For example, astronomers may use either the phenomenon of parallax or the spectrum of light emitted by a star or galaxy to indirectly measure distance and velocity in outer space. On the other end of the size scale—with individual atoms and their components—measurement becomes even more difficult. In 1927 German physicist and subsequent Nobel Prize-winner Werner Heisenberg stated the *Heisenberg Uncertainty Principle:* the measurement of the distance and velocity of atomic particles cannot be accomplished without the very act of measuring disturbing the measurement. Hence, there are definite limits on precision of measurement at the atomic level.

REFERENCES

Isaac Asimov, *Realm of Measure* (Houghton Mifflin Co., 1960).

Jeanne Bendick, *How Much and How Many* (McGraw-Hill, 1947).

Melvin Berger, *For Good Measure: The Story of Modern Measurement,* (McGraw-Hill, 1969).

R. Houwink, *Sizing Up Science* (John Murray, London, 1975); a delightful book that gives a feeling for measurements of different scales and units, with hundreds of examples like these:

Animals
In terms of weight, the mightiest animal that has ever lived is the blue whale; a specimen weighing 125 tonnes and measuring 29 metres (96 feet) in length was caught in 1931. This is equal to the weight of 4 brontosauri, 23 elephants, 230 cows or 1800 men—whichever you prefer. But the whale occupied only one-tenth of the volume of the 'General Sherman' Sequoia.

Sunspots
During a typical eruption on the surface of the Sun, amounts of energy up to 10^{22} kilocalories (4×10^{25} joules) are observed to be stored in distortions of the magnetic field. This is enough to bring one-third of the water in the Atlantic Ocean to the boil.

See also ANGLES, PERIMETER, AREA, VOLUME, and METRIC SYSTEM.

Tables of units of measure (English and metric) for length, area, volume, and weight or mass are gathered in APPENDIX I.

METRIC SYSTEM

METRIC SYSTEM: a DECIMAL system of MEASURE, based on ten. This means that any unit is ten times larger than the next smaller unit, or one tenth the next larger unit. The word "metric" is from the Greek "metron," meaning "to measure."

The metric system was originally set up in 1790 by the French Academy of Science for the measurement of length, volume, mass, time, and temperature. This system has been expanded to include various other scientific units and is now officially called *Système Internationale d'Unites,* or SI for short. SI is governed by the International Bureau of Weights and Measures at Sèvres, France.

BASIC METRIC UNITS

Symbols are given in parentheses.

Meter (m): basic unit for length

Gram (g): basic unit for mass (See MEASURE for a discussion of "mass" versus "weight.")

Liter (l): basic unit for VOLUME or capacity

Are (a): basic unit for AREA or surface

The basic unit in SI is the *meter,* the unit of *length.* The meter was originally defined as one ten-millionth of the distance from the North Pole to the Equator along the line of longitude near Dunkirk, France, and Barcelona, Spain. A nonrusting bar of platinum (90 percent) and iridium (10 percent) was marked to this length and has been carefully kept at Sèvres at a constant temperature and pressure, to be used as the official standard for actual comparison. Today the standard meter length remains the same, but it is now measured by 1,650,763.73 wavelengths of the orange-red light of the element krypton (obtained by heating krypton gas and using a spectroscope on the light emitted). This new official standard was adopted because it can be reproduced anywhere in the world and eliminates the need for direct comparison with the standard meter in France.

Other basic units are derived from the meter. The *liter* is the VOLUME of 1000 cubic centimeters, which is contained in a cube 10 centimeters ($\frac{10}{100}$ meters) on each edge. The *kilogram* (1000 grams) is the *mass* of one liter of water at a temperature of 4° Celsius (the temperature at which water has maximum density). The *are* is the AREA of a square ten meters on each side.

The basic unit for *time* is the *second*, as in the U.S. and British systems of measure. Time measure is not based on ten except for units smaller than the second, such as the microsecond. The standard for *temperature* is the Kelvin scale, with measurements made in *degrees Celsius*. See MEASURE for details on scales and units for time and temperature.

PREFIXES

Prefixes are used to indicate the relationship between a unit and the basic unit. (Symbols are in parentheses.) For example,

$$1 \text{ centimeter (cm)} = \tfrac{1}{100} \text{ meter (m)}$$

$$1 \text{ hectare (ha)} \quad = 100 \text{ ares (a)}$$

Prefix		Number of times	Equivalent powers of ten	Multiple	Root
tera-		1,000,000,000,000 times	10^{12}	trillion	Greek: "monster"
giga-		1,000,000,000 times	10^9	billion	Greek: "giant"
mega-	(M)	1,000,000 times	10^6	million	Greek: "great"
kilo-	(k)	1,000 times	10^3	thousand	Greek: "thousand"
hecto-	(h)	100 times	10^2	hundred	Greek: "hundred"
deka- or deca-	(da)	10 times	10^1	ten	Greek: "ten"
		1 time	10^0	one	
deci-	(d)	0.1 times	10^{-1}	tenth	Latin: "ten"
centi-	(c)	0.01 times	10^{-2}	hundredth	Latin: "hundred"
milli-	(m)	0.001 times	10^{-3}	thousandth	Latin: "thousand"
micro-	(μ)	0.000 001 times	10^{-6}	millionth	Latin: "small"
nano-		0.000 000 001 times	10^{-9}	billionth	Greek: "dwarf"
pico-		0.000 000 000 001 times	10^{-12}	trillionth	Spanish: "small"
femto-		0.000 000 000 000 001 times	10^{-15}	quadrillionth	Danish: "fifteen"
atto-		0.000 000 000 000 000 001 times	10^{-18}	quintillionth	Danish: "eighteen"

Originally, the metric system used Greek prefixes to show units larger than the basic unit and Latin prefixes for smaller units. But when extension was necessary, the original convention was dropped for lack of additional Latin roots. The International Committee on Weights and Measures at Paris in 1958 added tera-, giga-, nano-, and pico-, and in 1962, femto- and atto-.

The resulting system gives convenient units of measure for global distances (megameters), solar distances (gigameters), and galactic distances (terameters); for ordinary microscopic distances (micrometers) and atomic distances (picometers). Molecular masses are measured in attograms, time for computer operations in nanoseconds.

Reference on prefixes

Isaac Asimov, *Asimov on Numbers* (Doubleday and Co., 1977), Ch. 10, "Pre-fixing it up," pp. 123–135; an excellent source (and delightful reading) that gives a sense of these units, the orders of magnitude, and the extent of measurability of length, mass, and time.

COMPARISONS OF METRIC SYSTEM UNITS WITH U.S. SYSTEM UNITS

- Dimensional measure (actual size)

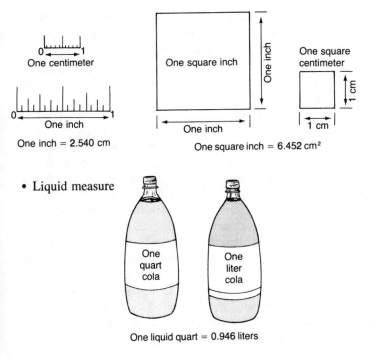

One centimeter

One inch

One inch = 2.540 cm

One square inch

One square centimeter

One inch

1 cm

One square inch = 6.452 cm²

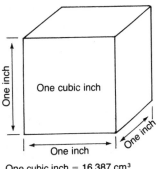

One cubic inch

One inch

One inch

One cubic inch = 16.387 cm³

- Liquid measure

One quart cola

One liter cola

One liquid quart = 0.946 liters

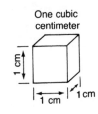

One cubic centimeter

1 cm

1 cm

1 cm

- Statistics for average thirteen-year-olds (according to the 1973 National Health Survey)

	girls		*boys*
average height:	62.5 in	average height:	62.9 in
	158.8 cm		159.8 cm
average weight:	110.7 lbs	average weight:	109.7 lbs
average mass:	50.3 kg	average mass:	49.8 kg

- Highway signs

```
┌──────┐   ┌──────┐   ┌────────────────────┐
│  50  │   │  80  │   │ BOSTON 69 MI       │
│ M.P.H.│  │ KM/HR│   │        111 KM      │
└──────┘   └──────┘   └────────────────────┘
```

Units for the U.S. Customary System of measure and conversions to the metric system are given in the tables of Units of Measure in APPENDIX I.

HISTORY

The metric system, with its new standards, was set up in 1790 by a Committee of Weights and Measures of the French Academy of Sciences. At the time, there was much discussion about what number should be used as a base. A duodecimal base (12) and a prime base (11) were both earnestly considered by the committee before the decimal base (10) won out and was adopted.

The metric system has been extended to make a more complete scientific system of measure, adding basic units for electric current, amount of substance, light intensity, and temperature to those for length, mass, volume, and time. The expanded system, adopted in 1960 by the 11th International General Conference on Weights and Measures, is called in English the International System of Units. Following its French antecedents, it is abbreviated SI, (short for *Système Internationale d'Unites*).

Now almost every country of the world is officially using or changing to SI, the metric system. Although the metric system was already established, the British and United States governments in the early nineteenth century persisted in standardizing their own systems of measure, which have endured into more modern times. Changing to the metric system involves a lot more than making new rulers and changing road signs. People will have to become accustomed to new numbers for speed limits, temperatures, and weights and volumes at the supermarket.

Tools, machinery, and screws are only some of the items that must be adapted to standard metric measurements. All this takes time. In the first ten years of conversion, the British had still not completed the switch, but they also had to change their money to a decimal system. That conversion is one hurdle the United States does not have to face.

A Brief Chronology

1790   The French Academy of Sciences developed the metric system. The United States Congress turned down Thomas Jefferson's suggestion to use a decimal system of measure.

1795   France adopted the metric system.

1812   Napoleon decreed that in France both the metric system and the old French units of weight and measure were legal. Much confusion resulted for the next quarter of a century.

1821   The United States Congress again turned down the suggestion to convert to the metric system.

1840   France made it compulsory to use only the metric system in all public commerce.

1866   The United States made it legal to use the metric system—but voluntarily.

1875   The International Bureau of Weights and Measures was established. The United States joined with seventeen other nations.

1893   The United States made the international meter and kilogram the official standards for its own units, the yard and avoirdupois pound (see MEASURE).

1902   Once again, the United States Congress defeated a bill requiring the use of the metric system in all federal departments and contracts.

1957   The United States Army and Marine Corps started using the metric system.

1960   Countries using the metric system agreed on rules for its use. SI (*Système Internationale d'Unites*) was adopted at the 11th General Conference of the International Committee on Weights and Measures.

1965   Great Britain adopted the metric system, with a planned ten-year conversion.

1970   Canada and Australia converted to the metric system.

1975   The Metric Conversion Act was passed by the United States Congress and signed by the president. The Metric Conversion Act of 1975 states, "The policy of the United States shall be to coordinate and plan the increasing use of the metric system in the United States and to establish a United States Metric Board to coordinate the voluntary conversion to the metric system.''

REFERENCES

Isaac Asimov, *Realm of Measure* (Houghton Mifflin Co., 1960).

Frank Ross, *The Metric System: Measures for All Mankind* (S. G. Phillips, 1974).

See also MEASURE and tables of units of measure in APPENDIX I.

NUMBER LINES

NUMBER LINE: a mathematical model that pictures NUMBERS as points on a line.

Examples.

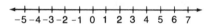

STANDARD CONVENTIONS AND SYMBOLS

Certain conventions and symbols have traditionally been used in picturing a number line. Although it would not be mathematically incorrect to use other conventions or other symbols, such departures from tradition would need to be fully explained. Here are some of the standard conventions and symbols:

Order: on a horizontal number line, the numbers are displayed in order, increasing from left to right. When two numbers are pictured on a horizontal line, the smaller will lie to the left of the larger. On a vertical number line, the numbers are ordered from bottom to top. When two numbers are pictured on a vertical line, the smaller will lie below the larger.

Arrowhead at the end of a number line: an indicator that the numbers continue indefinitely in that direction.

Origin: the point on the number line representing zero.

Unit distance: the length of the line segment between zero and one. For a given number line, the unit distance must be the same between any two consecutive integers. However, the unit distance is arbitrarily chosen and may be different for different number lines.

The length of the unit distance and the position of the origin will usually be determined by the numbers required on the line. If you wish to show more negative numbers than positive, your number line might look like. this:

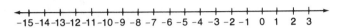

If you want to show more large numbers than small ones, you might use a number line like this:

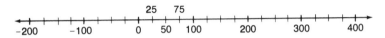

GEOMETRIC CONSTRUCTION OF A NUMBER LINE

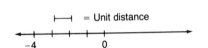

- *Integers:* Any integer can be constructed on the number line by straightedge and compass once the unit distance has been chosen. To construct a positive integer, you start at the origin and mark off to the right the number of units indicated by the integer. To construct a negative integer, you mark off the number of units to the left of the origin. For example, to construct −4, you would mark off 4 units to the left of the origin.
- *Rational numbers:* Any RATIONAL NUMBER (a number that can be expressed as the RATIO of two integers) can also be constructed with straightedge and compass alone. This can be done because there is a GEOMETRIC CONSTRUCTION to subdivide a line segment into any number of equal parts. Since the unit distance is a line segment, it can be divided into 8 equal parts, 17 equal parts, or (theoretically) a million equal parts.

Example.   To construct a rational number such as $2\frac{5}{7}$ (or $\frac{19}{7}$), you first mark off two unit distances to the right of the origin for the integer 2 (point A). Then mark off one more unit distance to the right (point B) and divide AB into 7 equal parts:

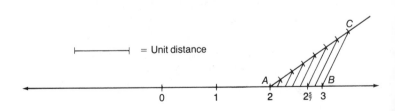

Draw a line segment through point A. On this segment, mark off some distance 7 times. Connect the last mark (C) with point B. Then construct six lines parallel to CB. These parallel lines will divide the unit distance between 2 and 3 into 7 equal parts. To locate the number $2\frac{5}{7}$ on the number line, you start at the number $+2$ and count over five sevenths to the right.

- *Irrational numbers:* Some, but not all, of the irrational numbers (see RATIONAL AND IRRATIONAL NUMBERS) can be constructed with only straightedge and compass. For example, $\sqrt{2}$, $\sqrt{3}$, and the square root of any positive number can be so constructed. The geometric construction of such irrational numbers is based on a property of right triangles described by the PYTHAGOREAN THEOREM; that is, the square of the hypotenuse (the longest side of a right triangle) is equal to the sum of the squares of the other two sides.

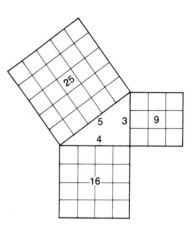

Examples.

$5^2 = 3^2 + 4^2$

$25 = 9 + 16$

$c^2 = a^2 + b^2$

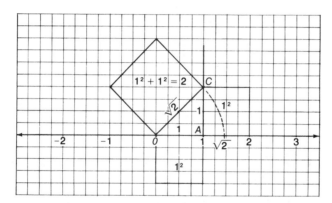

To construct the irrational number $\sqrt{2}$, you mark off one unit from the origin and erect a perpendicular at that point. Then you mark off one unit on the perpendicular. These two unit distances form the legs of a right triangle OAC. The hypotenuse of the triangle is OC, and the square of the hypotenuse must equal the sum of the squares of the other two sides—$1^2 + 1^2$, or 2. Therefore, the length of the hypotenuse must be $\sqrt{2}$. To locate $\sqrt{2}$ on the number line, you simply set your compass on O and C and make an arc that cuts the line.

To construct $\sqrt{3}$, you construct a right triangle using $\sqrt{2}$ as one leg and the unit distance, or 1, as the other leg. This will give a triangle with a square of the hypotenuse equal to $1^2 + (\sqrt{2})^2$, or 3. Thus the length of the hypotenuse will be $\sqrt{3}$. To construct $\sqrt{5}$, you construct a triangle using $\sqrt{4}$, or 2, as one leg and the unit distance as the other, and so on.

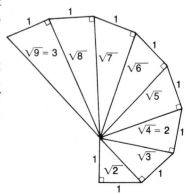

REAL NUMBER LINE: A CONTINUUM

All REAL NUMBERS—both the ones that can be constructed and the ones that cannot—are represented on the real number line. The real number line is a model of a continuum. It represents an endless line along which lie infinitely many points, between any two of which—no matter how close together—there are infinitely many other points. Similarly, the set of real numbers constitutes a continuum. It is an endless ordered set of numbers, between any two of which there are infinitely many other numbers. Therefore, every point on the real line corresponds to exactly one real number, and every real number corresponds to exactly one point on the real line.

APPLICATIONS OF THE NUMBER LINE

Because a number line is a visible model of abstract numbers, it is a useful tool for illustrating certain relationships and arithmetic operations.

Examples.   Given $A = -2$ and $B = 3$,

$B > A$ (B is greater than A because B is to the right of A.)

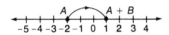

$A + B = 1$ (To add a positive number to A, start at A and move B units to the right.)

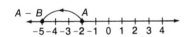

$A - B = -5$ (To subtract a positive number from A, start at A and move B units to the left.)

Another important application of number lines is to COORDINATE systems.

For more information on the different numbers pictured on a number line and for their historical background, see NUMBERS, RATIONAL AND IRRATIONAL NUMBERS, REAL NUMBERS, and SIGNED NUMBERS.

There are other numbers that cannot be represented on the real number line. Such numbers must be shown in a plane. For more on this kind of number, see COMPLEX NUMBERS.

NUMBERS

NUMBER: an undefined but basic concept in arithmetic.

Although there is no formal mathematical DEFINITION of the term "number," a number is understood to be a concept that answers the question of "how many." For example, how many members are there in each of the sets illustrated? There are five. And the idea of "fiveness" —which can be abstracted from sets of 5 triangles, 5 squares, 5 circles, 5 fingers, and so on—is a number.

A number is an abstract notion of quantity. The word "abstract" means "drawn from," and almost certainly our abstract numbers were drawn from particular physical objects. For example, before people had the general idea of "twoness," they probably first had the idea of "as many as my eyes." And, in fact, the word for "two" in some languages is the same as the word for "eyes." In our own language, the words "five" and "fist" come from a common source, reminding us that at least some of our early ancestors' idea of numbers probably developed from counting on their fingers.

But an abstract notion exists only in someone's mind. In order to talk or write about a number, we must use either a "number word" such as "five" or a number symbol such as "5." A symbol that is used for a number is called a *numeral*. Because there are different number words in different languages, because there are different NUMERAL SYSTEMS, and because one number can be represented by various combinations of numerals, it is possible to represent a single number in many different ways. For example, the number of fingers on one hand could be represented by any of the words and numerals in the table on p. 350.

Occasionally, people use the term "number" when they are really talking about a numeral. For example, someone might tell a first-grader, "You have made the number 5 backwards." However, to be precise, what should be said is "the numeral 5." We figure with numbers, and

{△ △ △ △ △}

{○ ○ ○ ○ ○}

{□ □ □ □ □}

we write numerals. A numeral or a number word can be erased, but a number is an idea and cannot be erased.

In number words		In numerals	
five	(English)	5	(Hindu-Arabic)
cinq	(French)	V	(Roman)
cinco	(Spanish)	五	(Chinese)
pente	(Greek)	|⁀|	(Egyptian hieroglyphics)
fünf	(German)		
pięć	(Polish)	3 + 2	(arithmetic expression)
viisi	(Finnish)	$\left(\dfrac{7+3}{2}\right)$	(arithmetic expression)
лать	(Russian)		

CLASSIFYING NUMBERS BY USE

Cardinal Numbers: numbers used to indicate *how many* members a SET has.

Examples.

Set	Cardinal number associated with set
{□ □ □}	3
(triangular arrangement of 10 dots)	10

The numbers {0, 1, 2, 3, ...} make up the set of cardinal numbers.

Ordinal Numbers: numbers used to indicate the *order* of members in a set.

Example.   Set of people in line

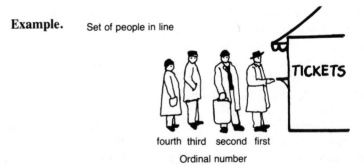

fourth third second first

Ordinal number

Nominal Numbers: numbers used to *identify* someone or something.

Examples.

Numbers on license plates

Numbers on athletes' uniforms

OTHER WAYS OF CLASSIFYING NUMBERS

Natural Numbers: the *counting numbers* $\{1, 2, 3, 4, \ldots\}$. The natural numbers include all the cardinal numbers *except zero*. The natural numbers, excluding the number 1, are either *prime* or *composite*.

Prime Number: a natural number greater than 1 that has only *two* FACTORS—itself and 1.

Examples. *Prime numbers*   *Single set of factors*

7	$= 1 \times 7$
11	$= 1 \times 11$
2	$= 1 \times 2$

Composite Number: a natural number that has *more than two factors*.

Examples. *Composite numbers*   *Sets of factors*

$$9 \quad \begin{cases} = 1 \times 9 \\ = 3 \times 3 \end{cases}$$

$$12 \quad \begin{cases} = 1 \times 12 \\ = 2 \times 6 \\ = 3 \times 4 \end{cases}$$

The number 1 is neither prime nor composite because it has only *one factor,* namely itself.

Whole Numbers: the set of natural numbers plus the number zero: $\{0, 1, 2, 3, 4, \ldots\}$.

Integers: a set of numbers including the *positive* integers, the *negative* integers, and *zero*.

Positive Integers: the set of natural numbers: $\{1, 2, 3, 4, \ldots\}$. A positive integer may be written with a plus sign ($+$) before the numeral to indicate that the number represents a quantity greater than zero: $\{+1, +2, +3, \ldots\}$.

Negative Integers: the set of numbers $\{-1, -2, -3, -4, \ldots\}$ representing quantities less than zero. Negative integers are always written with a minus sign before the numeral to indicate their direction from zero.

Zero: the integer indicating no change in magnitude (or size) and no change in direction.

When the integers are displayed on a NUMBER LINE, zero is the dividing point between the positive and the negative integers. Zero is said to be the point of *origin* (or starting point) for both sets of integers.

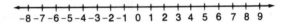

$$-8\ -7\ -6\ -5\ -4\ -3\ -2\ -1\ \ 0\ \ 1\ \ 2\ \ 3\ \ 4\ \ 5\ \ 6\ \ 7\ \ 8\ \ 9$$

The integers are sometimes called *signed numbers* because of the plus and minus signs that are affixed to the numerals. These numbers can be used in various ARITHMETIC OPERATIONS. Numerous practical applications are described in the article SIGNED NUMBERS.

An integer is either *even* or *odd*.

Even Number: an integer that has the number 2 as one of its factors.

Examples.

Even numbers	because
6	$6 = 2 \times 3$
18	$18 = 2 \times 9$
0	$0 = 2 \times 0$
-10	$-10 = 2 \times -5$

Odd Number: an integer that does not have the number 2 as one of its factors; a number that if divided by 2 gives a remainder of 1.

Examples.

Odd numbers	because
7	$\begin{array}{r} 3 \\ 2\overline{)7} \\ \underline{6} \\ 1 \text{ Remainder} \end{array}$
11	$\begin{array}{r} 5 \\ 2\overline{)11} \\ \underline{10} \\ 1 \text{ Remainder} \end{array}$

The first numbers used were the natural or counting numbers. But as people became more civilized—as commerce, industry, and the sciences grew more complex—the natural numbers were no longer adequate. As a consequence, other kinds of numbers were developed. Some are discussed in the articles on SIGNED NUMBERS, FRACTIONS, DECIMALS, RATIONAL AND IRRATIONAL NUMBERS, REAL NUMBERS, COMPLEX NUMBERS, and HISTORY.

NUMBER THEORY

Since at least the sixth century B.C., when the Pythagoreans flourished in the Greek city of Crotona, mathematicians have been fascinated by the properties of numbers. They have been interested in the factors of numbers and in those numbers that, when represented as sets, can be arranged in various shapes or configurations. Such numbers are called *figurate numbers*.

Examples. The numbers 3, 6, and 10 are said to be *triangular numbers,* because sets of 3, 6, or 10 members can be arranged in triangles.

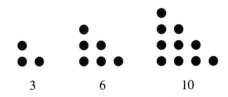

Triangular numbers

The numbers 4, 9, and 16 are said to be *square numbers,* because sets of 4, 9, or 16 members can be arranged in squares.

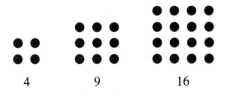

Square numbers

Mathematicians have investigated the properties of *odd* and *even* numbers and those of *primes* and *composites*. Over the years, this interest in studying the properties of numbers has developed into a branch of mathematics called *number theory*.

Prime Numbers

Of all the questions raised in number theory, probably none have intrigued more mathematicians than those about prime numbers: Is there a largest prime number? Is there a formula for the primes? Is there a formula for calculating the number of primes between two given numbers? Is there a largest pair of *twin primes*—two prime numbers differing only by 2, such as 11 and 13, or 17 and 19? Can every even number greater than 4 be expressed as the sum of 2 odd primes? And so on.

Some of these questions were answered long ago. For example, in the third century B.C., the Greek geometer Euclid was able to prove that there is no largest prime and thus that the set of primes is infinite.

Other questions about the primes were answered later. It has since been shown that even though an infinite set of primes is scattered among the integers, it is still possible to find a string of consecutive composite numbers as long as you like. The integers 8, 9, 10 form a sequence of three consecutive composites, and you can probably find a longer sequence of consecutive composites by trial and error. But there is a formula that for any number n gives a sequence of n consecutive composites:

$$(n + 1)! + 2, (n + 1)! + 3, (n + 1)! + 4, \ldots, (n + 1)! + (n + 1)$$

where "!" is a mathematical symbol called "*factorial.*" The expression $(n + 1)!$ means the product of $(n + 1)$ multiplied by every positive integer less than $(n + 1)$.

Example.   If $n = 5$, then

$$(n + 1)! = (5 + 1)! = 6! = 6 \times 5 \times 4 \times 3 \times 2 \times 1 = 720.$$

And five consecutive composites, by the above formula, are

$$6! + 2 = 720 + 2 = 722$$
$$6! + 3 = 720 + 3 = 723$$
$$6! + 4 = 720 + 4 = 724$$
$$6! + 5 = 720 + 5 = 725$$
$$6! + 6 = 720 + 6 = 726.$$

Using this same formula, you could find a string of a million consecutive composites. However, as you can imagine, these numbers would be very large indeed. Note: the formula does not find the *first* five composite numbers. For instance, 24, 25, 26, 27, 28 also form a string of five composites.

Still other questions about the primes remain to be answered. For example, there is still no formula that will generate all the prime numbers. There is a formula that will generate all of the *even numbers: e =* $2n$, where n is any integer.

Examples.   If $n = 0$, then $e = 0$

$\qquad\qquad n = 1, \quad e = 2$

$\qquad\qquad n = 2, \quad e = 4$

Similarly, there is a formula that will generate all of the *odd numbers:* $o = 2n + 1$, where n is any integer.

Examples.   If $n = 0$, then $o = 1$

$\qquad\qquad n = 1, \quad o = 3$

$\qquad\qquad n = 2, \quad o = 5$

Many mathematicians have searched for a formula that would generate all the primes. And some have even thought for a time they had found it, but so far no formula has been discovered.

Although there is no formula for generating the primes, as early as the third century B.C., Eratosthenes—a Greek contemporary of Euclid—invented a method for sifting out the primes from a finite set of integers. The method is known as *the sieve of Eratosthenes.*

To work Eratosthenes' sieve, you write down the integers in order until you have as large a set as you want.

$$1\ 2\ 3\ 4\ 5\ 6\ 7\ 8\ 9\ 10\ldots$$

Then you proceed as follows:

(1) Cross out 1, since it is neither a prime nor a composite.

$$\cancel{1}\ 2\ 3\ 4\ 5\ 6\ 7\ 8\ 9\ 10\ldots$$

(2) The next number, 2, is a prime number. Cross out every second number after 2, to eliminate multiples of 2.

$$\cancel{1}\ ②\ 3\ \cancel{4}\ 5\ \cancel{6}\ 7\ \cancel{8}\ 9\ \cancel{10}\ldots$$

(3) The next number, 3, is a prime number. Cross out every third number after 3, to eliminate multiples of 3.

~~1~~ ② ③ ~~4~~ 5 ~~6~~ 7 ~~8~~ ~~9~~ ~~10~~ . . .

(4) Continue by going to the next number which has not been crossed out. This number will be prime. Eliminate all multiples of the number greater than itself. Then go to the next uncrossed number and do the same.

~~1~~	②	③	~~4~~	⑤	~~6~~	⑦	~~8~~	~~9~~	~~10~~
⑪	~~12~~	⑬	~~14~~	~~15~~	~~16~~	⑰	~~18~~	⑲	~~20~~
~~21~~	~~22~~	㉓	~~24~~	~~25~~	~~26~~	~~27~~	~~28~~	㉙	~~30~~
㉛	~~32~~	~~33~~	~~34~~	~~35~~	~~36~~	㊲	~~38~~	~~39~~	~~40~~
㊶	~~42~~	㊸	~~44~~	~~45~~	~~46~~	㊼	~~48~~	~~49~~	~~50~~
~~51~~	~~52~~	(53)	~~54~~	~~55~~	~~56~~	~~57~~	~~58~~	(59)	~~60~~
(61)	~~62~~	~~63~~	~~64~~	~~65~~	~~66~~	(67)	~~68~~	~~69~~	~~70~~
(71)	~~72~~	(73)	~~74~~	~~75~~	~~76~~	~~77~~	~~78~~	(79)	~~80~~
~~81~~	~~82~~	(83)	~~84~~	~~85~~	~~86~~	~~87~~	~~88~~	(89)	~~90~~
~~91~~	~~92~~	~~93~~	~~94~~	~~95~~	~~96~~	(97)	~~98~~	~~99~~	~~100~~ . . .

The sieve of Eratosthenes can be used to sift out the primes from as large a set of integers as you like. And in fact an enterprising Austrian astronomer of the nineteenth century named Kulik used this method to find all the prime numbers between 1 and 100,000,000. Unfortunately, this Herculean labor (which took the better part of twenty years to complete) was not properly appreciated. The library to which Kulik gave his manuscripts lost the sections that contained primes between 12,642,000 and 22,852,800.

NUMEROLOGY

While mathematicians have long been interested in the mathematical properties of numbers, both mathematicians and nonmathematicians alike have long been interested in the magical powers said to be associated with certain numbers. Even among those who claim to be unsuperstitious, there may be a reluctance to seat 13 people at a table or a belief that sorrows come in threes or a conviction that a good lecture ought to have three main points. The strength of these number superstitions is reflected in the fact that most motels have no room numbered 13 and most hotels have no thirteenth floor. Explaining events in terms of magical powers attributed to certain numbers is called *numerology*.

The Pythagoreans were nearly as interested in numerology as they were in number theory. They believed that the first natural number—1—was the divine source of all other numbers. And for centuries thereafter, the number 1 was believed to be somehow so different from the rest of the numbers that it was not called an odd number, nor a number at all.

The Pythagoreans believed that the even numbers (2, 4, 6, . . .) were feminine and the odd numbers (3, 5, 7, . . .) were masculine. They believed that the odd numbers were superior to the even, and that the odd numbers were associated with good luck (except 13) and the even numbers with bad luck. This belief was apparently held by other people as late as the sixteenth century, for in *The Merry Wives of Windsor*, Shakespeare wrote:

> This is the third time; I hope good luck lies
> in odd numbers . . . . They say there is divinity
> in odd numbers, either in nativity, chance or death.
> (Act V, Scene 1)

The Pythagoreans believed that the number 4 stood for justice because it was a perfect square (2^2). They believed that 5 stood for marriage because it was the sum of the first feminine number and the first masculine number. They believed that the number 6 was a *perfect number* because it was equal to the sum of all its FACTORS other than itself.

Not only the Pythagoreans but many others since have believed that 7 is a lucky number. The number 7 appears many times in the Bible; in Jesus' exhortation to forgive a brother seventy times seven, in Elisha's advice to the leper to wash seven times in the Jordan, and in the seven sneezes of the child brought back to life by the prophet. Seven is such a popular number that people tend to group things in sevens—the seven wonders of the world, the seven ages of man, the seven liberal arts, the seven deadly sins, and so on.

REFERENCES

References on number lore

Irving Adler, *Magic House of Numbers* (The John Day Co., New American Library, 1974).

Henry Bowers and Joan E. Bowers, *Arithmetical Excursions: An Enrichment of Elementary Mathematics* (Dover, 1961).

Philip J. Davis, *The Lore of Large Numbers* (L. W. Singer Co., New Mathematical Library, 1961).

J. Newton Friend, *Numbers: Fun and Facts* (Charles Scribner's Sons, 1972).

William H. Glenn and Donovan A. Johnson, *Number Patterns*, Exploring Mathematics on Your Own Series (Webster Publishing Co., 1960); examples are

$$(1 \times 9) + 2 = 11$$
$$(12 \times 9) + 3 = 111$$
$$(123 \times 9) + 4 = 1111$$
$$(1234 \times 9) + 5 = 11111$$
$$\vdots$$

$$6 \times 7 = 42$$
$$66 \times 67 = 4422$$
$$666 \times 667 = 444222$$
$$6666 \times 6667 = 44442222$$
$$\vdots$$

$$333\ 667 \times 222\ 3 = 741\ 741\ 741$$
$$3333\ 6667 \times 222\ 33 = 7411\ 7411\ 7411$$
$$33333\ 66667 \times 222\ 333 = 74111\ 74111\ 74111$$
$$\vdots$$

Karl Menninger, *Number Words and Number Symbols: A Cultural History of Numbers* (M.I.T. Press, 1969); this tome is a major source, with much illustration and extreme detail.

Constance Reid, *From Zero to Infinity: What Makes Numbers Interesting* (Thomas Y. Crowell Co., 1955); the story, historical and mathematical, of each of the digits 0, 1, 2, . . . , 9 in well-done presentations that include much general mathematics.

Frederick H. Young, *Random Numbers, Mathematical Induction, Geometric Numbers* (Ginn, 1962); a pamphlet in the series, Topics in Modern Mathematics. Some algebra background is required, but the section on random numbers is especially good.

References on number theory

I. A. Barnett, *Some Ideas About Number Theory* (National Council of Teachers of Mathematics, 1961); a great variety of elementary results.

Martin Gardner, "The remarkable lore of the prime numbers," *Scientific American*, March 1964, pp. 120–128.

C. Stanley Ogilvy and John T. Anderson, *Excursions in Number Theory* (Oxford University Press, 1966); a very entertaining collection of curious facts and significant theorems, with simple proofs and no opportunity for boredom.

More on number theory appears under FACTORS and PYTHAGOREAN THEOREM.

References on numbers

Isaac Asimov, *Asimov on Numbers* (Doubleday & Co., 1977); entertaining and memorable essays, drawing on history and natural science; particularly good for a feeling of the *size* of numbers. Asimov's system, based on trillions, for coping with very large numbers is intriguing.

Mathematics: An Introduction to Its Spirit and Use: Readings from Scientific American (W. H. Freeman & Co., 1978), pp. 46–89, including the following articles which may also be found in individual issues of *Scientific American:*

> Philip J. Davis, "Number," September 1964; overview of the evolution of all numbers from the natural numbers to the complex and transfinite numbers. Also in *Mathematics and the Modern World,* (W. H. Freeman & Co., 1968).
>
> Martin Gardner, "The Remarkable Lore of the Prime Numbers," March 1964;
>
> David Hawkins, "Mathematical Sieves," December 1958 (from Eratosthenes to random sieves).

See also RATIONAL AND IRRATIONAL NUMBERS, REAL NUMBERS, COMPLEX NUMBERS, and ZERO.

For *imaginary* numbers, see COMPLEX NUMBERS.

For *perfect, abundant, deficient,* and *amicable* numbers, see FACTORS.

For *Pythagorean* numbers, see PYTHAGOREAN THEOREM.

For *transfinite* numbers, see ARITHMETIC and INFINITY.

Related articles: NUMBER LINES; NUMERAL SYSTEMS.

NUMERAL SYSTEMS

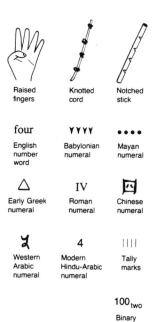

Raised fingers	Knotted cord	Notched stick
four	٧٧٧٧	• • • •
English number word	Babylonian numeral	Mayan numeral
△	IV	🀆
Early Greek numeral	Roman numeral	Chinese numeral
۴	4	۱۱۱۱
Western Arabic numeral	Modern Hindu-Arabic numeral	Tally marks
	100_{two}	
	Binary numeral	

NUMERAL: a symbol that stands for a NUMBER; a *primary numeral* is a basic numeral that contains no other numerals or digits within it.

NUMERAL SYSTEM: a set of primary numerals and rules for combining them to represent numbers.

A number is an abstraction; it is an idea. And that idea can be expressed in different kinds of symbols. For example, the number associated with this set {□ □ □ □} could be expressed in many ways. Each of these symbols stands for the idea of "fourness."

The earliest numeral systems were developed as people felt a need for keeping records. Yet long before the development of numeral systems, people had been enumerating things. *Enumeration* is the process of making a one-to-one correspondence between the members of one set of objects and the members of another. For example, suppose a shepherd wanted to keep track of the size of his flock. As the flock went out in the morning, he might place a pebble in a pile for each sheep. Then when the flock returned in the evening, he could find out whether any sheep had been lost by seeing whether there was still one sheep in the flock for every pebble in the pile. A knotted cord and a notched stick are enumeration devices that were used in the same way as the pile of pebbles.

However, by far the most convenient enumeration device is one's own body. A shepherd could enumerate a flock by putting the sheep in one-to-one correspondence with his fingers. If he had more sheep than fingers, he could continue enumerating with his toes. According to one source, the members of one tribe used 100 different parts of the body in enumeration. A one-to-one correspondence was made by naming the body parts in order, one for each object. Thus, the names of body parts came to be used as number words. For example, one Eskimo tribe counted this way:

1 — *atauseq*	(first finger)
2 — *machdlug*	(second finger)
3 — *pinasut*	(third finger)
4 — *sisamat*	(fourth finger)
5 — *tadlimat*	(fifth finger)
6 — *achfineq-atauseq*	(other hand, first finger)
7 — *achfineq-machdlug*	(other hand, second finger)

and so on through other hand, first foot, and other foot.

The process of making a one-to-one correspondence between objects and number words is called *numeration*. And the fact that our own number words may have originated long ago in finger enumeration can be seen in the common origin of the words "five" and "fist."

The first *written* numerals that could be combined systematically with other symbols in a numeral system were probably tally marks—|||. . . . For example, the first three numerals in the Roman numeral system are |, ||, and |||. For convenience in reading and writing larger numbers, the tally marks came to be arranged in groups. For example, when tally marks are grouped in fives, it is easy to read ||||| ||||| ||||| || as 17. Still later, shorthand symbols were developed for groups of tally marks. The size of such groupings in a numeral system determines the *base* of the system.

Base: in a numeral system, the number of units grouped together and represented by a single symbol.

Some common bases		Their uses
binary	base *two*	computers
quinary	base *five*	some Latin American systems
octal	base *eight*	computers
decimal	base *ten*	the Hindu-Arabic system
hexadecimal	base *sixteen*	computers
vigesimal	base *twenty*	the Mayan system
sexagesimal	base *sixty*	the Babylonian system

A further shortcut in the writing of numerals was achieved in some systems by the introduction of *place value,* or *positional notation.* In a place-value numeral system, the position of a symbol or digit in a numeral determines its value. For example, in our DECIMAL system, the numeral "11" stands for 1 ten plus 1 one. The first "1" is in the tens place and represents a value ten times that of the second "1." This is in contrast to the Roman numeral system, which is not a place-value system. In the Roman numeral "II," both of the "I's" stand for one. The place in which the symbol occurs makes no difference in its value.

In a place-value numeral system, a few symbols are sufficient to express very large numbers. For example, in the Hindu-Arabic system, the ten digits 0–9 are sufficient to represent numbers of any size.

The mathematical development of Western civilization has been linked with and influenced by the ancient Egyptian numeral system, the Babylonian numeral system, the Roman numeral system, and the Hindu-Arabic numeral system. A description of each of these follows.

EGYPTIAN NUMERAL SYSTEM

About 3000 years B.C., the ancient Egyptians began keeping records by carving into stone a picture-writing called *hieroglyphics*. Their hieroglyphics included a well-organized numeral system with base *ten*. In this system, a vertical stroke I represented one unit, and a heel mark ∩ was the shorthand symbol for ten units. These Egyptian numerals were usually written as shown. For example,

I	II	III	IIII
1	2	3	4
III II	III III	IIII III	IIII IIII
5	6	7	8
III III III	∩	∩I	∩II
9	10	11	12
∩IIII	∩IIIII	∩ III II	∩ III III
13	14	15	16

$$\cap\cap = 20 \qquad \cap\cap\cap$$
$$\cap\cap\,{}^{IIII}_{III} = 27 \qquad {}^{\cap\cap\cap}_{\cap\cap\cap}III = 93$$

Further symbols were used for additional groupings of powers of ten:

stroke	I	= one = 1
heelmark	∩	= ten = 10 or 10^1
coil of rope	୨	= one hundred = 100 or 10×10 or 10^2
lotus flower	𝓛	= one thousand = 1000 or $10\times10\times10$ or 10^3
bent finger	∕	= ten thousand = 10,000 or 10^4
bourbot fish	⌐	= one hundred thousand = 100,000 or 10^5
astonished man	𝓨	= one million = 1,000,000 or 10^6

For example, in Egyptian hieroglyphics, 32,754 would be written:

𝕚𝕚𝕚	𝓛 𝓛	୨୨୨୨ ୨୨୨	∩∩∩ ∩∩	IIII
three ten thousands	two thousands	seven hundreds	five tens	four ones

From hieroglyphic writing evolved a cursive *hieratic script,* used on papyrus. The most famous such manuscript is the *Rhind Papyrus,* discovered in 1858 by A. Henry Rhind, a Scottish antiquarian. This practical handbook of Egyptian mathematics was copied about 1700 B.C. by a scribe named A'h-mosè (Ahmes, in modern translation) from an even older manuscript. It is over 18 feet long and 13 inches high, with 60 problems written on the first side and an additional 27 problems on the reverse. A small portion is shown in the photograph, with a corresponding hieroglyphic translation. (For more information, see references, Newman.)

Rhind Papyrus, Problem 52

Scribe's mistake, written as 20, not 10

1	2,000	1	1,000
2	4,000	½	500
4	8,000		

Total: 10,000 making the area 100 *setat* (10 ten-*setat*)

Example of making a cut-off (truncated) triangle of land. Suppose it is said to thee: A cut-off triangle of land of 20 *khet* on its side, 6 *khet* on its base, 4 *khet* on its cut-off line; what is its area? Add thou its base to its cut-off line; it makes 10. Take thou ½ of 10, namely, 5, in order to get its rectangle. Make thou the multiplication: 20 times 5; it makes 10 (10 ten-*setat*). This is its area. Do it thus:

Notes:

(a) Both hieratic and hieroglyphic notation read from right to left, so in the phonetic translation, 10 appears as 01. Fractions are written with a dot (see p. 194), so ½ appears as $\dot{2}$.

(b) 1 *khet* = 100 cubits; 1 *stetat* = 1 (*khet*)². Some of the calculation is done in *cubits*, with 20 *khet* = 2,000 *cubits*.

(c) The multiplication follows a duplication method, which yields:

$$\begin{array}{r} 1 \times 2000 \\ + \ 4 \times 2000 \\ \hline = 5 \times 2000 \end{array}$$

BABYLONIAN NUMERAL SYSTEM

Also about three thousand years B.C., in Mesopotamia, the Babylonians developed a numeral system. They wrote on tablets of wet clay with a pointed stick, or stylus, so their strokes looked like this: ᛉ . This writing is called *cuneiform,* meaning "wedge-shaped." Like the Egyp-

Y	YY	YYY	YYYY	YYY YY
1	2	3	4	5

YYY	YYYY	YYY YYY YYY	YYY YYY YY	
YYY	YYY	YY	YYY	◄
6	7	8	9	10

◄Y	◄YY	◄YYY
11	12	13

tians, the Babylonians also used a shorthand symbol for ten strokes, ◄.
So the cuneiform numerals appeared as shown.

The base of the Babylonian system was *sixty*. And numbers up through sixty were written by combinations of the symbols for one and for ten. However, unlike the Egyptians, the Babylonians did *not* invent new symbols for larger numbers. They realized that the symbols for one and ten could be used to express much larger numbers by means of *place value*. For numbers greater than 60, a new grouping of symbols was made, to the left and separate from the group of symbols representing a number less than 60.

Examples.

$$\underset{}{\text{◄ ◄ ◄}}\ \underset{}{\text{YYY YYY YYY}} = 59$$

$$\underbrace{Y}_{60}\ +\ \underbrace{Y}_{1}\ = 61 \qquad \underbrace{Y}_{60}\ +\ \underbrace{\text{◄YYY YYY}}_{16}\ = 76$$

$$\underbrace{\text{YYY YY}}_{5 \times 60}\ +\ \underbrace{\text{◄◄◄ YY}}_{32}\ = 332$$
$$= 300$$

Sixty sixties, or 60^2, was indicated by still another grouping to the left.

Example.

$$\underbrace{Y\ \ Y}_{\substack{2 \times 60^2 \\ = 2 \times 3600 \\ = 7200}}\ \ \underbrace{Y}_{+\ 60}\ +\ \underbrace{\text{◄◄◄ YYY}}_{23}\ = 7283$$

Zero did not exist in early Babylonian numerals. For instance, the cuneiform numeral YY YY might represent $2 \times 60 + 2 = 122$ or $2 \times 60^2 + 2 \times 60 = 7320$ or $2 \times 60^2 + 2 = 7202$. The context in which the numeral appeared usually determined which possibility was intended. The Babylonians eventually responded to the need to cut down on confusion, and after 300 B.C. a zero symbol, ⟡, was used, at least in the middle of numerals. For example, YY ⟡ YY would have been used for 7202.

Two systems of MEASURE used today are derived from the Babylonian sexagesimal system. From this base-sixty system we get our system of measuring ANGLES by dividing a circle into 360 parts called degrees and then dividing a degree into 60 minutes and a minute into 60 seconds.

Cuneiform tablet from Nippur, about 2400 B.C., showing the divisors of 60^4 The top row shows 2, 5, and 12, with the 10 symbol crossing the 1's.

It is also from the Babylonian system that we inherited our system of measuring time, with the hour divided into 60 minutes and a minute into 60 seconds.

ROMAN NUMERAL SYSTEM

Beginning about 500 B.C., the Romans developed a numeral system that was basically a tally system, similar to that of the ancient Egyptians. Like the Egyptians, the Romans had symbols for 1, 10, 100, and 1000. But the Romans also had symbols for 5, 50, and 500, a fact which meant that each symbol would be repeated no more than four times within a single numeral.

The seven basic symbols of the Roman system were capital letters from the Roman, or Latin, alphabet. Thus the early Roman numerals were written like this:

I	II	III	IIII
1	2	3	4

I = 1
V = 5
X = 10
L = 50
C = 100
D = 500   (= I⊃ in earliest notation)
M = 1000   (= CI⊃ in earliest notation)

V	VI	VII	VIII
5	6	7	8

VIIII	X	XI	XII
9	10	11	12

and so on. In the beginning, they were written from left to right, starting with the symbol representing the largest number; and the value of a numeral was equal to the values of all the symbols added together.

XIII	XIIII	XV	XVI
13	14	15	16

Example.   LXIII = 50 + 10 + 1 + 1 + 1 = 63

and   MDCCLXXVI   = 1776
1000 + 700 + 70 + 6

500   50   5
+ 100 + 10 + 1
+ 100 + 10

Eventually (but not until the sixteenth or seventeenth century, some time after the invention of the printing press), a subtractive principle was introduced for Roman numerals. In a numeral in which a letter is immediately followed by a letter of greater value, the smaller value is subtracted from the larger value.

Examples.   IV = 5 − 1 = 4
IX = 10 − 1 = 9
XL = 50 − 10 = 40

Thus

$$\underbrace{MDCCCC}_{} \underbrace{LXXX}_{} \underbrace{IIII}_{} = 1984$$

$$
\begin{array}{ccc}
1000 + 900 + & 80 + & 4 \\
| & | & | \\
500 & 50 & 1 \\
+100 & +10 & +1 \\
+100 & +10 & +1 \\
+100 & +10 & +1 \\
+100 & &
\end{array}
$$

could be written as

$$\underbrace{M}_{} \underbrace{CM}_{} \underbrace{LXXX}_{} \underbrace{IV}_{} = 1984.$$

$$
\begin{array}{cccc}
1000 + & 900 + & 80 + & 4 \\
| & | & | & | \\
1000 & 50 & 5 & \\
-100 & +10 & -1 & \\
& +10 & & \\
& +10 & &
\end{array}
$$

Numbers greater than 10,000 have been represented by Roman numerals with additional strokes. For instance, a horizontal bar was used to indicate multiplication by 1000, so $\overline{V} = 5000$, and MM = 2000 could be written as $\overline{\overline{II}}$. (Older notations gave CCIƆƆ for 10,000 and CCCIƆƆƆ for 100,000.)

There is no zero in the Roman numeral system and no idea of place value. A Roman numeral always stands for the same value regardless of where it occurs. For example, in the numeral XX, the first X stands for ten and so does the second one. (This is in contrast to the decimal numeral system, where in the numeral 33 the two threes have different values. That is, $33 = 3 \times 10 + 3 \times 1$ rather than $3 + 3$ or 6.)

The Roman numeral system was in general use throughout Europe for centuries. In fact, Roman numerals continued to be used for hundreds of years after the Hindu-Arabic numerals were first introduced in Europe in the twelfth century. People were used to the Roman numeral system and could compute with it fairly rapidly. However, with the invention of the printing press the Hindu-Arabic system became more widely known. People discovered that it was easier to make computations such as long division with Hindu-Arabic numerals than with Roman numerals. By about 1700, even the standard use of Roman numerals for bookkeeping had disappeared.

Roman numerals are sometimes used today for formal noncomputational purposes. They may be used on clock faces and to number sections within an outline, chapters of a book, volumes in a series of books, and so on. Dates are sometimes given in Roman numerals on buildings, on monuments, and in copyright data for films and some books.

HINDU-ARABIC NUMERAL SYSTEM

Our modern numeral system originated in India around A.D. 600. The Indian Brahmi numerals were the forerunners of today's digits, with individual symbols for the numbers one through nine. These nine digits were used in a *place-value* system, and a ZERO symbol was soon added.

The Brahmi, or Hindu, numerals migrated with surprisingly little change through many cultures. The numerals were transmitted to the Arabs about A.D. 800 when works on astronomy were translated from Sanskrit into Arabic. The Hindu-Arabic numerals were used by the Persian mathematician Al-Khowarizmi in his famous algebra. And in the twelfth century, when Al-Khowarizmi's works were translated into Latin, the numerals found their way to Western Europe. The shape of some of the digits was gradually modified over the years, but by the sixteenth century the digits were close to the modern form. And by the end of the seventeenth century, Hindu-Arabic numerals had entirely replaced Roman numerals in European calculation.

Indian Brahmi numerals	—	=	≡	⼿	⼻	6	7	5	?	
Hindu-Sanskrit numerals	৭	২	੩	४	૪	६	૭	८	౭	०
East Arabic numerals (still in use today)	/	⼼	⼼	⼼	o	५	V	∧	٩	•
West Arabic numerals (transmitted to Europe)		2	⅔	⼼	५	6	7	8	9	
Hindu-Arabic numerals: fifteenth century	/	২	3	২	4	6	∧	8	9	•
twentieth century	1	2	3	4	5	6	7	8	9	0

The Hindu-Arabic numeral system is a base ten, or DECIMAL, system. The word "decimal," comes from the Latin word "decimus," meaning "tenth." There are exactly ten symbols, or *digits,* in the system: 1, 2, 3, 4, 5, 6, 7, 8, 9, 0. "Digit" also comes from Latin, from "digitus," meaning "finger," which clearly refers to the ancient use of ten fingers for counting.

The Hindu-Arabic system uses *place value* to express numbers greater than nine. That is, the value that a digit represents depends upon its position in the numeral. The value of each place is ten times the value of the place on its right. Each place has a name, as shown on p. 368 for the number 753,426,189.

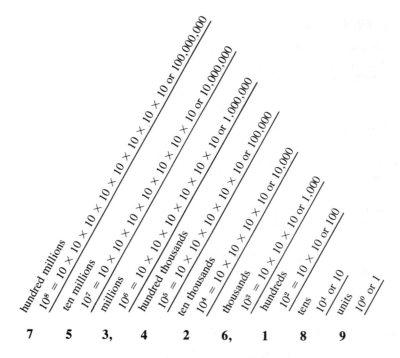

The names for places beyond the hundred-thousands place are grouped by thousands in the United States, but by millions in Great Britain:

	United States (and France)	United Kingdom (and Germany)
million	1,000,000	1,000,000
billion	1,000,000,000—a thousand millions	1,000,000,000,000—a million millions
trillion	1,000......000 12 zeros	1,000...........000 18 zeros
quadrillion	1,000.......000 15 zeros	1,000...........000 24 zeros
quintillion	1,000........000 18 zeros	1,000...........000 30 zeros
sextillion	1,000........000 21 zeros	1,000............000 36 zeros
septillion	1,000.........000 24 zeros	1,000.............000 42 zeros
octillion	1,000..........000 27 zeros	1,000...............000 48 zeros
googol	1,000,000...................000 100 zeros	
googolplex	1,000,000...........................000 a googol of zeros	

The Hindu-Arabic system can also be used to express FRACTIONS— numbers that are not whole numbers—by means of place value. A *decimal point* separates the whole number part of a numeral from the fractional part. Digits to the right of the decimal point represent the fractional part in DECIMALS, and digits to the left represent a whole number. The places to the right of the decimal point are called decimal places, and each place has a value $\frac{1}{10}$ the value of the place immediately to the left. Names of the decimal places are given in the following chart:

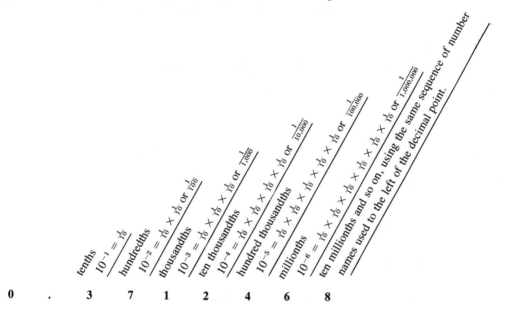

Combining whole numbers and fractions gives a numeral like

$$
\begin{array}{lll}
3 \times 10^2 = 300 & (3 \text{ hundreds}) \\
2 \times 10^1 = 20 & (2 \text{ tens}) \\
9 \times 10^0 = 9 & (9 \text{ units}) \\
7 \times 10^{-1} = 0.7 & (7 \text{ tenths}) \\
5 \times 10^{-2} = 0.05 & (5 \text{ hundredths})
\end{array}
$$

329.75

In fact, a decimal point *may* be used in the writing of every number. In whole numbers it is usually omitted, but it would be located to the right of the rightmost digit.

Examples. $470 = 470. = 470.0$
$6432. = 6432.0 = 6432$

The Hindu-Arabic numeral system has proved convenient and is now used internationally in most numerical work.

OTHER NUMERAL SYSTEMS

The systems discussed above are the ones that have been most closely connected with the history of Western civilization. However, many other numeral systems have been developed. Some are similar to the systems already described. Others exhibit quite different features. Some examples follow.

Ancient (Attic) Greek Numeral System

The early Greeks, at least from about 600 B.C., used a system of numerals very much like the Roman numerals. They are called *Attic*, or *Herodianic* numerals. The early Greek Attic numeral

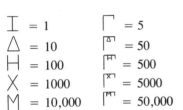

I = 1   Γ = 5
△ = 10   ᴦᴬᴵ = 50
H = 100   ᴦᴴᴵ = 500
X = 1000   ᴦˣᴵ = 5000
M = 10,000   ᴦᴹᴵ = 50,000

$$\underbrace{\text{HHH}}\underbrace{\text{ᴦ△△}}\underbrace{\text{ᴦI}} = 376.$$

300	+	70	+	6
100		50		5
+ 100		+ 10		+ 1
+ 100		+ 10		

Alphabetic Numeral Systems

In some cultures numeral systems were created by assigning number values to the letters of the alphabet. Two examples of alphabetic numeral systems are the Ionic Greek and the Hebrew systems.

Ionic Numeral System

1 A α alpha	10 I ι iota	100 P ρ rho
2 B β beta	20 K κ kappa	200 Σ σ sigma
3 Γ γ gamma	30 Λ λ lambda	300 T τ tau
4 Δ δ delta	40 M μ mu	400 Y υ upsilon
5 E ε epsilon	50 N ν nu	500 Φ φ phi
6 F digamma	60 Ξ ξ xi	600 X χ chi
(obsolete)	70 O o omicron	700 Ψ ψ psi
7 Z ζ zeta	80 Π π pi	800 Ω ω omega
8 H η eta	90 ꝗ koppa	900 ⅄ sampi
9 Θ ϑ theta	(obsolete)	(obsolete)

The Ionic, or alphabetic, Greek numeral system dates back to the fifth century B.C. However, it did not entirely replace the earlier Attic system until about 100 B.C. The letters were assigned the values as shown. Thus ΣΝΔ or σνδ = 254. Thousands were indicated by little accent marks; for example, ,α = 1000, and ,β = 2000. The Ionic Greek numerals were distinguished from words by such devices as an accent at the end or a stroke over the numeral.

Hebrew Numeral System

The Hebrew and Greek alphabets were both developed centuries before the birth of Christ, from the Phoenician alphabet, which had in turn been developed from Egyptian hieroglyphics. The Hebrews assigned numerical values to their letters as follows:

1 א alef	10 י yood	100 ק koof
2 ב baet	20 כ kaf	200 ר resh
3 ג gimel	30 ל lamed	300 ש shin
4 ד daled	40 מ mem	400 ת taf
5 ה hey	50 נ nun	(500) ך (kaf)*
6 ו vav	60 ס samek	(600) ם (mem)*
7 ז zayin	70 ע ayin	(700) ן (nun)*
8 ח haet	80 פ pey	(800) ף (fey)*
9 ט tet	90 צ tsadi	(900) ץ (tsadi)*

*The form of this letter when it appears at the end of a word.

Chinese-Japanese Numeral System

The traditional Chinese numeral system dates back to the third century B.C. The same system was later adopted by the Japanese. The Chinese system is base *ten*, with primary numerals as shown. Special symbols represent 10 十 , 100 百 , and 1000 千 .

Chinese numerals are written vertically, from top to bottom, with the special symbols telling exactly what value each numeral represents.

1 一   4 四   7 七
2 二   5 五   8 八
3 三   6 六   9 九

Examples.   2736 =   二 two
十 thousands +
七 seven
百 hundreds +
三 three
十 tens +
六 six

$$309 = \text{三 three} \\ \text{百 hundreds } + \\ \text{九 nine}$$

Because of this very explicit way of writing numerals, the Chinese had no need for a zero place holder.

Mayan Numeral System

The Central American Mayan civilization was strong in astronomy, calendar reckoning, and commerce. The Mayas developed a unique numeral system, probably by the fourth century A.D. They had twenty primary numerals, including a zero symbol.

0	5	10	15
1	6	11	16
2	7	12	17
3	8	13	18
4	9	14	19

Higher numbers were represented by a *place-value* system, with base *twenty*. The Mayan numerals were written vertically, as are the Chinese.

Example.

$$20 = \quad \begin{array}{l}\text{one twenty} \\ + \\ \text{zero units}\end{array} \quad = 1\,(20) + 0$$

$$36 = \quad \begin{array}{l}\text{one twenty} \\ + \\ \text{sixteen units}\end{array} \quad = 1\,(20) + 16$$

$$73 = \quad \begin{array}{l}\text{three twenties} \\ + \\ \text{thirteen units}\end{array} \quad = 3\,(20) + 13$$

$$340 = \quad \begin{array}{l}\text{seventeen twenties} \\ + \\ \text{zero units}\end{array} \quad = 17\,(20) + 0$$

However, there is a strange exception in the Mayas' use of base 20. The vertical positions, from bottom to top, represent *not*

$$1, \quad 20, \quad (20)^2, \quad (20)^3, \quad (20)^4, \ldots,$$

as would be expected, but

$$1, \quad 20, \quad 18\,(20), \quad 18\,(20)^2, \quad 18\,(20)^3, \ldots.$$

In other words, the ''second twenty'' is an eighteen instead! It is thought that this was because the Mayan calendar was divided into eighteen months of twenty days each, so 18×20 was a very important number in their civilization.

Therefore, translating a large number in Mayan numerals into Hindu-Arabic decimal numerals requires quite a bit of calculation on our part.

Example.

$$
=\begin{cases}
5 \times 18 \times 20^2 = 5 \times 7200 = 36{,}000 \\
3 \times 18 \times 20 = 3 \times 360 = 1{,}080 \\
12 \times 20 = 240 \\
7 \times 1 = 7 \\
\hline
37{,}327
\end{cases}
$$

Yoruba Numeral System

The oral numeral system used by the Yoruba people of Western Africa is interesting and unusual. In this spoken system, the numerals are *words*. Indeed, until Western influence brought Hindu-Arabic numerals, there were no written numerals at all. Calculation was accomplished entirely with oral numerals, and the oral numerals survive to the present.

Anthropologists suspect that the Yoruba numeration system grew out of the counting of cowrie shells, which were used as currency and were counted in fives to make piles of twenty; ten piles of twenty would have been grouped in piles of 200; 20,000 placed in a bag.

Other numerals are constructed from the primary numerals:

Primary numerals

1 = *ookan*
2 = *eeji*
3 = *eeta*
4 = *eerin*
5 = *aarun*
6 = *eefa*
7 = *eeje*
8 = *eejo*
9 = *eesan*
10 = *eewaa*
20 = *ogun*
200 = *igba*
2,000 = *egbewa*
20,000 = *egbaawaa*

11 = 10 + 1 = *ookan laa*
   (1)   (''in addition to 10,'' from *le ewa*)

12 = 10 + 2 = *eeji laa*

13 = 10 + 3 = *eeta laa*

14 = 10 + 4 = *eerin laa*

21 = 20 + 1 = *ookan le logun*
   (1)   (''in addition to 20,'' from *le ogun*)

44 = 2(20) + 4 = *eerin le logoji*
   (4)   (''in addition to 20 2s,'' from *ogun eji*)

800 = 4(200) = *egberin*
   (from *igba* and *eerin*)

Each numeral is a contraction of the pattern of primary numerals that compose it. These examples give the idea; different dialects show some variation. However, what is interesting and unusual about Yoruba numerals is the mathematical pattern by which they are constructed. The

$15 = 20 - 5$

$16 = 20 - 4$

$17 = 20 - 3$

$18 = 20 - 2$

$19 = 20 - 1$

.

.

$46 = 3 (20) - 10 - 4$
$47 = 3 (20) - 10 - 3$
$48 = 3 (20) - 10 - 2$
$49 = 3 (20) - 10 - 1$
$50 = 3 (20) - 10$
$51 = 3 (20) - 10 + 1$
$52 = 3 (20) - 10 + 2$
$53 = 3 (20) - 10 + 3$
$54 = 3 (20) - 10 + 4$
$55 = 3 (20) - 5$
$56 = 3 (20) - 4$
$57 = 3 (20) - 3$
$58 = 3 (20) - 2$
$59 = 3 (20) - 1$
$60 = 3 (20)$
$61 = 3 (20) + 1$
$62 = 3 (20) + 2$
$63 = 3 (20) + 3$
$64 = 3 (20) + 4$
$65 = 4 (20) - 10 - 5$
$66 = 4 (20) - 10 - 4$
$67 = 4 (20) - 10 - 3$
$68 = 4 (20) - 10 - 2$
$69 = 4 (20) - 10 - 1$
$70 = 4 (20) - 10$
$71 = 4 (20) - 10 + 1$
$72 = 4 (20) - 10 + 2$
$73 = 4 (20) - 10 + 3$
$74 = 4 (20) - 10 + 4$
$75 = 4 (20) - 5$
$76 = 4 (20) - 4$
$77 = 4 (20) - 3$
$78 = 4 (20) - 2$
$79 = 4 (20) - 1$
$80 = 4 (20)$

.

.

.

above examples are what you might expect from primary numerals, but other Yoruba numerals are constructed by subtraction rather than addition. This is like the Roman numeral system. The Yorubas, however, use subtraction to a far greater extent:

$$\text{although } 44 = 2 (20) + 4,$$
$$45 = 3 (20) - 10 - 5.$$

The list of numerals in the margin shows how subtraction is involved, sometimes twice, in three-fourths of the numerals. This complicated structure continues:

$$104 = 5 (20) + 4$$
$$\text{but } 105 = 6 (20) - 10 - 5$$
$$500 = 3 (200) - 5 (20)$$
$$525 = 3 (200) - 4 (20) + 5$$

The higher numerals get even more complicated:

$$3,500 = (20 - 2) (200) - 5 (20)$$

and so on.

The resulting abstract system is among the most intricate of numeral systems, and the fact that the Yoruba use it with ease is impressive. Robert G. Armstrong, who has studied Yoruba numerals, states, "It is testimony to the Yoruba capacity for abstract reasoning that they could have developed and learned such a system." (See references, Zaslavsky, p. 206.)

Binary Numeral System

There is evidence that primitive tribes of New Guinea used a binary system based on two number words: *urapun* = 1, and *okosa* = 2. In their *additive* binary system,

$$3 = \textit{okosa urapun}$$
$$4 = \textit{okosa okosa}$$
$$5 = \textit{okosa okosa urapun}$$
$$6 = \textit{okosa okosa okosa}.$$

However, a binary system is not just a curiosity or museum piece. Today we have a real need for it. A binary system based on *place value* was first developed for the Western world by the German mathematician Gottfried Wilhelm von Leibniz. In 1703, Leibniz published a description of how two digits, 0 and 1, could be used to represent any number. In a binary numeral, each place value represents a power of 2, proceeding from right to left as follows:

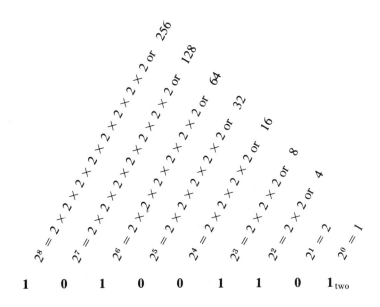

$$1 \quad 0 \quad 1 \quad 0 \quad 0 \quad 1 \quad 1 \quad 0 \quad 1_{\text{two}}$$

Examples.

Binary counting

$$
\begin{array}{rcl}
1 \times 2^2 &=& 4 \\
1 \times 2^1 &=& 2 \\
0 \times 2^0 &=& 0 \\
\hline
\mathbf{110}_{\text{two}} &=& 6 \quad \text{in decimal numerals,}
\end{array}
$$

and

$$
\begin{array}{rcl}
1 \times 2^4 &=& 16 \\
1 \times 2^3 &=& 8 \\
0 \times 2^2 &=& 0 \\
1 \times 2^1 &=& 2 \\
1 \times 2^0 &=& 1 \\
\hline
\mathbf{11011}_{\text{two}} &=& 27 \quad \text{in decimal numerals.}
\end{array}
$$

0 =	0
1 =	1
2 =	10
3 =	11
4 =	100
5 =	101
6 =	110
7 =	111
8 =	1000
9 =	1001
10 =	1010
11 =	1011
12 =	1100
13 =	1101
14 =	1110
15 =	1111
16 =	10000

The subscript$_{\text{two}}$ may follow a numeral written in the binary system so that there will be no confusion with decimal numerals. Thus, $100_{\text{two}} =$ four, not one hundred.

The binary system was not used much until electronic computers were developed in the 1940s. A COMPUTER processes information in base two because the two digits can represent a switch's two electrical states—off and on. Thus, the binary system has made computation by computers possible.

REFERENCES

Isaac Asimov, *Asimov on Numbers* (Doubleday & Co., 1977), especially Chs. 1, 2, and 4.

Arthur Buffum Chace, *The Rhind Mathematical Papyrus* (Mathematical Association of America, 1927; reprinted in lovely smaller edition by National Council of Teachers of Mathematics, 1979).

Historical Topics for the Mathematics Classroom, 31st Yearbook of the National Council of Teachers of Mathematics (1969), pp. 6–8 and 18–50.

Lancelot Hogben, *Mathematics in the Making* (Doubleday & Co. 1960), especially Ch. 2.

Harold Jacobs, *Mathematics: A Human Endeavor* (W. H. Freeman & Co., 1970), pp. 54–61 for more on the binary system.

Edward Kasner and James Newman, *Mathematics and the Imagination,* (Simon and Schuster, 1940; Fireside paperback), Ch. 1, "New Names for Old," and Ch. 2, "Beyond the Googol." The name "googol" was invented by a nine-year-old boy whose uncle, Edward Kasner, was a mathematician.

Karl Menninger, *Number Words and Number Symbols* (M.I.T. Press, 1969); a treatment so exhaustive that a reader can easily feel overwhelmed, but an excellent source; includes a chapter on Far Eastern numeral systems—China, Japan, and Korea.

Bruce E. Meserve and Max A. Sobel, *Introduction to Mathematics,* (Prentice-Hall, 1973); Chapter 4, "Systems of Numeration," gives special attention to bases other than ten and has a good discussion of the binary system and its uses.

Henrietta O. Midonick, *The Treasury of Mathematics* (Philosophical Library, 1965), "The Maya Civilization," pp. 465–495; this source holds far more than any other reference on the Mayas and includes detailed descriptions of the head numerals—glyphs of faces whose characteristics represented numbers.

James R. Newman, "The Rhind Papyrus," *Scientific American,* August 1952; reprinted in *Mathematics: An Introduction to Its Spirit and Use: Readings from Scientific American* (W. H. Freeman & Co., 1978).

David Eugene Smith, *History of Mathematics, Vol. 2: Special Topics of Elementary Mathematics* (Ginn, 1925; Dover, 1958), pp. 36–88; detailed but concise, well-illustrated; an excellent source.

4   9   17

David Eugene Smith, *Number Stories of Long Ago* (1919; National Council of Teachers of Mathematics (NCTM), 1955); a little book with old-fashioned color illustrations that tells in story form how children worked in different numeral systems.

Robert Swain, *Understanding Arithmetic* (Holt, Rinehart, 1963); an excellent discussion; also mentions the Eskimo number words.

Claudia Zaslavsky, *Africa Counts* (Prindle, Weber, and Schmidt, 1973); this is a splendid preliminary survey of African culture from the mathematical point of view. It discusses the Yoruba numeral system and many others, as well as mathematical games, numbers in everyday life, geometric form, and the effects of history and geography on pure mathematics in Africa.

PERCENT

PERCENT: hundredths; the numerator of a FRACTION that has a denominator of 100. The word "percent" comes from the Latin phrase "per centum," meaning "by the hundred."

Examples. $23\% = \frac{23}{100}$ $105\% = \frac{105}{100}$

Because percent expresses a fraction in terms of hundredths, any percent can also be written in the form of a DECIMAL fraction.

Examples. $23\% = 0.23$ $105\% = 1.05$

WHO'S FOR WHOM

The voters are not the only ones having trouble making up their minds. Many newspapers took longer than usual to issue endorsements. A survey by *Editor & Publisher* magazine shows that 26% of America's daily newspapers (168 out of 661 responding) endorsed neither candidate; in 1972 that figure was 23%.

Among the prominent onlookers are the Los Angeles *Times* and the Washington *Post*, which leans clearly to Carter but is sticking to a 24-year tradition of not officially endorsing anybody. According to *E & P*, whose questionnaire was answered by 38% of U.S. dailies, 411 dailies with 30 million circulation

TIME, NOVEMBER 8, 1976

If a poll shows that 23% of the people watching television at a certain time were watching *Popeye*, it means that 23 viewers out of every hundred (that is, 23 out of 100, or 46 out of 200, and so on) were watching *Popeye*.

Because percent expresses a fraction, it would be possible to do all calculating and all reporting of figures with fractions instead of percent. However, a glance at any newspaper will reveal that percent is extensively used. It somehow seems easier to get an idea of how big a fraction is if it is expressed as a percent. For example, how big is the fraction $\frac{168}{661}$? Apparently, the staff of *Time* magazine thought their readers would get a clearer idea of that fraction if it were expressed as a percent, and it would be easier to compare with a different figure from an earlier study.

CONVERTING OTHER FRACTIONAL FORMS TO PERCENT AND VICE VERSA

Since percent is a way of expressing a fraction in terms of hundredths, it is possible to convert (or change) any percent to a common fraction or decimal and vice versa. For example, 28% means 28 parts out of a hundred, $\frac{28}{100}$ or 0.28. The conversions between decimal fractions and percent are quite simple:

- *To convert a decimal fraction to a percent,* move the decimal point two places to the right and add the percent sign.

Examples.   0.57 = 57.% or 57%
0.385 = 38.5% or $38\frac{1}{2}$%
0.06 = 6%

- *To convert a percent to a decimal fraction,* move the decimal point two places to the left and remove the percent sign.

Examples.   28% = 0.28
12.5% = 0.125
2% = 0.02

- *To convert a common fraction to a percent,* the common fraction can first be converted to a decimal fraction by dividing the denominator into the numerator. The decimal fraction can then be converted to a percent as shown above.

Examples. $\dfrac{4}{25} = \dfrac{0.16}{25\overline{)4.00}} = 0.16$
$\phantom{\dfrac{4}{25} = }\underline{2\ 5}$
$\phantom{\dfrac{4}{25} = \ }1\ 50$
$\phantom{\dfrac{4}{25} = \ }\underline{1\ 50}$

0.16 = 16%

- *To convert a percent to a common fraction,* write the percent as numerator over the denominator 100 and omit the percent sign.

Examples.   39% $= \dfrac{39}{100}$
68.2% $= \dfrac{68.2}{100} = \dfrac{682}{1000}$
75% $= \dfrac{75}{100} = \dfrac{3}{4}$

A common fraction may also be thought of as a RATIO. That is, a fraction such as $\frac{2}{3}$ may be expressed as the ratio 2 : 3 (read "2 to 3," or "2 out of 3"). Since a common fraction may be expressed as a percent, a ratio may also be expressed as a percent and vice versa.

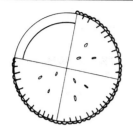

1 out of 4 pieces has been eaten, a ratio of 1 : 4

¼ of the pie has been eaten

0.25 of the pie has been eaten

25% of the pie has been eaten

Thus, there are at least four ways of expressing any fraction: (1) as a ratio, (2) as a common fraction, (3) as a decimal fraction, and (4) as a percent. In the illustration, the fraction of the pie that has been eaten is expressed in four different but equivalent forms.

ONE HUNDRED PERCENT AND BEYOND

One hundred percent of something is $\frac{100}{100}$ of it, or all of it. This is true even though the whole may not have 100 separate parts. For example, if there are 25 students enrolled in a certain math class and if all 25 are present on a particular day, then 100% of the class is present.

A percent smaller than one hundred percent denotes a fraction less than the whole. But sometimes a percent is needed to denote something larger than the original whole—a percent greater than 100%. For example, suppose that a Girl Scout troop sold 800 boxes of cookies in 1975 and 848 boxes in 1976. The number of boxes sold in 1976 compared to the number sold in 1975 is $\frac{848}{800}$. This fraction can be converted to a percent:

$$\frac{848}{800} = 800\overline{)848.00}$$

$$\begin{array}{r} 1.06 \\ 800\overline{)848.00} \\ \underline{800} \\ 48\ 00 \\ \underline{48\ 00} \end{array}$$

$$1.06 = 106\%$$

Thus, the 1976 cookie sales total was 106% of the 1975 total. Another way to report this event would be to say that the 1976 cookie sale represented a six percent increase over the 1975 sale.

Newspaper reporting is full of this sort of thing. Notice that a statement of percentage increase gives you an idea of how much the figures have changed, but unless you have more information, you cannot tell what those figures are. The first paragraph of this newspaper article does not tell how much energy the university used, only that it was 4.1 percent less than last year. On the other hand, it does tell that $580,000 is the amount of the 19.3 percent cost increase. That is,

Let x = last year's cost.

Then $580,000 = 19.3\%$ of $x = 0.193\ x$.

So,

$$x = \frac{\$580,000}{0.193} = \$3,000,000 \text{ approximately,}$$

and this year's costs will be $3,000,000 + 580,000 = $3,580,000.

The University paid $580,000 more for energy during the first half of the current fiscal year than it did for the same period the previous year despite an overall 4.1 percent decrease in energy used. It was a 19.3 percent increase in energy costs.

Although the average daily temperature was 10.7 percent warmer than the previous year, heating costs for the July-December period were up 39.6 percent over last year. And in the face of record warm during November and December,

Cornell Chronicle, February 14, 1980.

APPLICATIONS

One of the oldest applications of percent is in levying and computing taxes. The Roman Emperor Augustus is said to have levied a tax of 1% on the proceeds of all goods sold at auction. And since then import duty, property tax, sales tax, income tax, and many other taxes have been assessed and computed in terms of percent.

A familiar example is the sales tax levied by many states on all purchases made within the state. The sales tax is usually some percentage of the purchase price. Suppose the sales tax in a particular state were 5%. How much tax would you pay on a $7.00 purchase?

In order to compute some percentage of an amount, the percent is usually converted to a decimal fraction. The decimal fraction is called the *rate,* and the amount you wish to find a percentage of is called the *base.* To compute the value (in this case the value of the tax), you multiply the rate times the base.

Amount of tax = rate × base

5% tax, therefore rate = 0.05

$7.00 purchase, therefore base = $7.00

$$\begin{array}{r} \$7.00 \\ \times\ 0.05 \\ \hline \$0.3500 \end{array}$$

Thus the amount of the tax on a seven-dollar purchase in that state would be thirty-five cents.

Another important application of percentages is in computing interest. The computation of interest involves three factors—the base and rate used to compute regular percentages plus a third factor, *time.* For more on the computation of various kinds of interest, see the article on INTEREST.

HISTORY OF THE SYMBOL %

Although the use of percent in computing taxes, interest, and the like probably dates back at least to the Roman Empire, the symbol for percent is not that ancient. The percent symbol is the product of a time-saving shortcut used by scribes and clerks in the fifteenth century. At that time, there was a tremendous increase in the volume of trade all over Europe, especially in the Italian city-states. An increase in trade meant an increase in record keeping. And to lighten their work load,

Italian scribes began to abbreviate the often-used phrase "per cento." Some abbreviated it as "P 100," some as "p cento," and some as "p c⁰." Our symbol probably comes from "p c⁰," which became P ⚘ , then later became ⚘ , still later ⁰⁄₀, and finally became %.

Reference on the history of percent

Historical Topics for the Mathematics Classroom, 31st Yearbook of the National Council of Teachers of Mathematics (1969), pp. 146–147.

PERIMETER

PERIMETER: the distance around a two-dimensional or PLANE figure.

The word ''perimeter'' is from the Greek ''peri-,'' meaning around, and ''metron,'' meaning measure.

For any POLYGON, the perimeter is equal to the sum of the lengths of the sides.

For any CIRCLE, the perimeter is the circumference, πd or $2\pi r$.

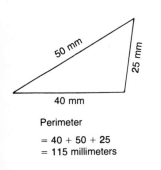

The perimeter of a lake is its shoreline.

Examples.

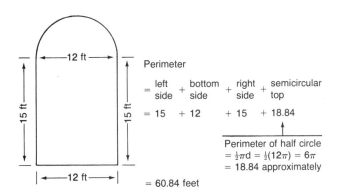

Perimeter

= 40 + 50 + 25
= 115 millimeters

Perimeter

$$= \begin{array}{c} \text{left} \\ \text{side} \end{array} + \begin{array}{c} \text{bottom} \\ \text{side} \end{array} + \begin{array}{c} \text{right} \\ \text{side} \end{array} + \begin{array}{c} \text{semicircular} \\ \text{top} \end{array}$$

= 15   + 12   + 15   + 18.84

Perimeter of half circle
$= \frac{1}{2}\pi d = \frac{1}{2}(12\pi) = 6\pi$
= 18.84 approximately

= 60.84 feet

QUEEN DIDO'S PROBLEM

A legend from about 800 B.C. concerns Queen Dido of Carthage and the matter of a perimeter. In order to escape the tyranny of her brother King Pygmalion, she fled from the Mediterranean kingdom of Phoenicia to the coast of North Africa. There she was offered as much land as she could surround with the hide of a bull. She cut the hide into narrow strips and joined them to form one long strand. Then she had only to decide how to lay out a boundary with that one long strand (a *fixed perimeter*) in order to enclose the *largest* AREA. She cleverly decided that a circular shape would give the most area and laid out her strip accordingly, establishing the city of Carthage.

It was not until the nineteenth century that mathematicians proved that the maximum area that can be enclosed by a fixed perimeter is indeed achieved by laying out the boundary in the shape of a circle. Today this is known as Queen Dido's problem.

Reference on Queen Dido's problem

Hans Rademacher and Otto Toeplitz, *The Enjoyment of Mathematics: Selections from Mathematics for the Amateur* (Princeton University Press, 1957; both hardcover and paperback), pp. 139–146; a good discussion of the circle as the only possible figure to maximize the area for a fixed perimeter.

PERMUTATIONS AND COMBINATIONS

PERMUTATION: any possible arrangement, or *ordering,* of the distinct items in a set.

Example. The three colors on a traffic light could be arranged in a number of different ways. Each arrangement, or ordering, is one permutation. How many possible permutations are there?

One way to find the number of possible permutations is by counting. For example, how many permutations of the colors red and green are possible on a two-color traffic signal? Obviously, only two. Either red is at the top and green is on the bottom or vice versa. For a three-color traffic signal there are six possible permutations, as illustrated above.

However, when there are more than two or three items to be ordered, counting permutations becomes laborious. Suppose, for example, that you have a string of holiday lights with five sockets, and that you have five bulbs, each of a different color: red, green, yellow, blue, and orange. How many different permutations are there?

Instead of screwing the bulbs in over and over again and counting all the different permutations, you might reason the problem out this way: When you begin to put the bulbs on the string, there are 5 choices for the first socket. And once you have put in the first bulb, there are still 4 choices left for the second socket. So with just the first two sockets, you already have 5 × 4, or 20, possible permutations. But you still have 3 choices left for the third socket, and 2 choices left for the fourth socket. No matter how you start, there will be only 1 choice when you get to the

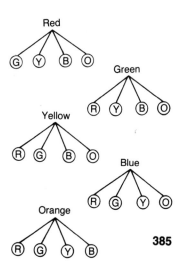

385

last socket. The total number of permutations will be $5 \times 4 \times 3 \times 2 \times 1$, or 120.

This approach to figuring the number of possible permutations is called the *fundamental principle of counting*. The principle states that if n_1 choices can be made for the first place, and if n_2 choices can be made for the second place, then the total number of permutations is $n_1 \times n_2$. Thus, if there were six sockets on the string and six different colored bulbs, the total number of permutations would be $6 \times 5 \times 4 \times 3 \times 2 \times 1$, or 720. And if there were *n* sockets (where *n* stands for any number), and *n* different colored bulbs, the number of permutations would be $n \times (n - 1) \times (n - 2) \times \ldots \times 3 \times 2 \times 1$.

The process of multiplying a whole number *n* by every positive whole number less than itself is abbreviated in mathematics as *n*!, where ! is a symbol called "factorial."

n factorial: $n! = n \times (n - 1) \times (n - 2) \times \ldots \times 3 \times 2 \times 1$

Examples. $4! = 4 \times 3 \times 2 \times 1 = 24$ four factorial
$5! = 5 \times 4 \times 3 \times 2 \times 1 = 120$ five factorial

The number of permutations of *n* distinct items can be written in factorial notation as follows:

> $_nP_n = $ the number of permutations of *n* items, using all *n* in each arrangement.
>
> $_nP_n = $ *n*!, where P = number of permutations
> n = number of distinct items
> to be arranged

Example.   The number of permutations of six different colored light bulbs in a string of six sockets is

$$_6P_6 = 6! = 6 \times 5 \times 4 \times 3 \times 2 \times 1 = 720.$$

PERMUTATIONS IN WHICH NOT ALL ITEMS ARE USED

It is possible to make permutations without using the total number of items in each permutation. For example, suppose that you had eight different-colored light bulbs to place in a string with only five sockets. How many permutations of five could you make choosing from among these eight different colors? With eight different-colored bulbs, you would have 8 choices for the first socket, 7 choices for the second, 6 choices for the third, 5 choices for the fourth, and 4 choices for the fifth. According to the fundamental principle of counting, the total number of permutations you could make would be 8 × 7 × 6 × 5 × 4, or 6,720. And this result can be expressed in general by the formula:

$_nP_r$ = the number of permutations of n items, using r of them at a time.

$_nP_r = \dfrac{n!}{(n - r)!}$, where P = number of permutations

n = number of distinct items

r = number of items to be arranged at a time

Example. The number of permutations of eight different-colored light bulbs in a string of five sockets is

$$_8P_5 = \frac{8!}{(8 - 5)!} = \frac{8!}{3!}$$

$$= \frac{8 \times 7 \times 6 \times 5 \times 4 \times 3 \times 2 \times 1}{3 \times 2 \times 1} = 6,720.$$

PERMUTATIONS WITH REPETITION

Many more permutations are possible whenever you can repeat any of the n items to be arranged. For example, suppose that to fill a five-socket string of holiday lights, you had enough bulbs of five different colors so that you could repeat any color as many times as you wished. Then for the first socket you would have 5 choices of color, for the second socket you would still have 5 choices, for the third you would have 5 choices, and so on. Thus, the total number of permutations would be 5 × 5 × 5 × 5 × 5, or 3,125.

If in addition to the red, green, yellow, blue, and orange bulbs listed above you also had pink bulbs, white bulbs, and purple bulbs, you would have eight colors possible for each socket. Assume again that you had a five-socket string of lights, with at least five bulbs of each color so that you could repeat as many times as you wished. Then the number of permutations would be 8 × 8 × 8 × 8 × 8, or 32,768.

$_n\overline{P}_r$ = the number of permutations, *with repetition*, of n distinct items, using r of them at a time.

$_n\overline{P}_r = n^r$, where $\overline{P}$ = number of permutations with repetition

n = number of distinct items

r = number of items to be arranged at a time

Example.   The number of permutations, with repetition, of eight different-colored light bulbs in a string of five sockets is

$$_8\overline{P}_5 = 8^5 = 8 \times 8 \times 8 \times 8 \times 8 = 32{,}768.$$

CIRCULAR PERMUTATIONS

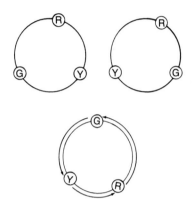

Far fewer permutations are possible when the items are arranged in a circle rather than in a line. Consider again the three colors on a traffic signal. When the colors red, green, and yellow are arranged in a straight line, there are 3!, or 6, possible permutations. But if the same three colors each represented a gem on a circular bracelet, how many permutations would there be?

There are only two possible permutations. If you try exchanging red and green in the second permutation, you will get a third permutation. But by imagining this bracelet being rotated through 120°, you can see that this third permutation is the same as the first permutation.

> $_n\mathcal{P}_n$ =   the number of *circular permutations*
> of *n* distinct items.
>
> $_n\mathcal{P}_n = (n - 1)!$

Example.   The number of circular permutations of three items taken three at a time is

$$_3\mathcal{P}_3 = (3 - 1)! = 2! = 2 \times 1 = 2.$$

PERMUTATIONS IN WHICH SOME ITEMS ARE NOT DISTINCT

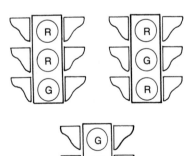

If the set of items to be arranged contains two or more items that are indistinguishable from one another, there are also fewer possible permutations. For example, suppose that the yellow glass on a traffic signal was broken and it was replaced by a red one. How many permutations would be possible with two red lights and one green one?

Although you could exchange the two red bulbs in any of the permutations, you would not get a different permutation of colors. Thus, with two red lights and one green one, there are only three possible permutations.

$_nP_n$ = the number of permutations of n items, using all n in each arrangement.

If the n items are not all distinct, there will be k distinct sets of items, where $k < n$.

a_1 = number of items in first set

a_2 = number of items in second set

.

.

.

a_k = number of items in k^{th} set

$a_1 + a_2 + \ldots + a_k = n$.

$$_nP_n = \frac{n!}{a_1! \times a_2! \times \ldots \times a_k!}$$

Example. The number of permutations of two red lights and one green light, for a total of three, is

$$_3P_3, \quad \text{with} \quad a_1 = 2 \quad \text{and} \quad a_2 = 1,$$

$$= \frac{3!}{2!1!} = \frac{3 \times 2 \times 1}{(2 \times 1)(1)} = 3.$$

COMBINATION: a set of items selected from a given set of items *without regard to order.*

In some instances it is useful to know how many possible combinations of a certain size can be drawn from a given set of items. For example, suppose that four people are running for the board of education. If the board of education is to consist of four members, then there is only one possible board that can be elected. From a given set of four items, only one combination of four can be drawn.

But if the board is to consist of three members, how many different combinations could be chosen from the following group of four candidates: Smith, Moore, Roberts, Wynn?

In this situation, order is unimportant. The combination Moore, Smith, Roberts is the same as the combination Smith, Moore, Roberts. Thus, the four combinations listed are the only possible combinations of three that can be chosen from the set of candidates.

SMITH	SMITH
MOORE	MOORE
ROBERTS	WYNN
SMITH	MOORE
ROBERTS	ROBERTS
WYNN	WYNN

$$_nC_r = \text{the number of } \textit{combinations} \text{ of } n \text{ items,}$$
$$\text{using } r \text{ of them at a time.}$$

$$_nC_r = \frac{n!}{(n - r)!(r)!}$$

Alternate notations for $_nC_r$ are $C(n,r)$ and $\binom{n}{r}$.

Example. The number of combinations of three candidates from a field of four is

$$_4C_3 = \frac{4!}{(4 - 3)!3!} = \frac{4!}{1!3!} = \frac{4 \times 3 \times 2 \times 1}{(1)(3 \times 2 \times 1)} = 4.$$

APPLICATIONS

The branch of mathematics devoted to the study of permutations and combinations is called *combinatory analysis,* or *combinatorial analysis.* The formulas derived in combinatorial analysis for computing the numbers of permutations and combinations have a wide range of practical applications.

The formulas for permutations with repetition can be used to figure out how many different telephone numbers are possible with seven digits each, how many different license plates can be made using four numerals and one letter, or how many numerals are necessary to give a different identification number to every checking account at a bank.

For example, in some states it is possible to purchase a license plate with up to three letters on it. If no numerals are used, how many different license plates can be made using permutations of three or fewer letters?

Using 1 letter, there would be 26 different plates $\quad = \quad$ 26
Using 2 letters, there would be 26×26 different plates $\quad = \quad$ 676
Using 3 letters, there would be $26 \times 26 \times 26$ different plates $= $ 17,576
    Total number of plates using 1, 2, or 3 letters: $\quad\overline{\quad18,278}$

The formula for computing permutations without repetition can be used to compute the number of different ballots needed in an election. Research has shown that *where* a candidate's name appears on the ballot can affect the number of votes he or she receives. Therefore, to be completely fair, equal numbers of different ballots should be printed, with each different ballot presenting a different permutation of the candidates' names. If, for example, a Democrat, a Republican, and a

Conservative were all running for a Senate seat, how many different permutations of the ballot should be printed to insure impartiality? The answer would be 3!, or 6 different permutations.

Formulas for permutations have recently been used to formally investigate the language of very young children. Linguists were interested in whether children who were just beginning to combine words into two- and three-word sentences were combining words according to some rule, or grammar. If these two- and three-word sentences were not the result of a rule, the linguists reasoned, then they must be either memorized permutations or random permutations. And if they were random permutations, then if enough samples of a child's speech were collected, all or nearly all of the possible permutations should appear.

When samples of children's speech were collected, it was found that of all the possible permutations, only a small percentage actually occurred. And in each child's speech, the permutations that did occur could be described or generated by one or more linguistic rules. Thus, the linguists' evidence refuted the hypothesis that the two- and three-word utterances of children were random permutations.

How many rhyming schemes can be found for five-line stanzas of verse? Here are some examples (the lines joined horizontally are those that rhyme). A complete set of diagrams like these was drawn by Lady Murasaki of Japan about A.D. 1000; there are fifty-two possibilities. See the reference for further reading on this subject.

Reference on combinations

Martin Gardner, ''Mathematical Games: The Bells: versatile numbers that can count partitions of a set, primes, and even rhymes,'' *Scientific American,* May 1978, pp. 24–30; shows complete set of Murasaki diagrams for rhyming schemes and explains that the number of possibilities can be called a Bell number; other entertaining applications of combinations.

For more on the use of permutations and combinations, see PROBABILITY and STATISTICS.

Combinations also appear in the coefficients of the *binomial theorem*. See ALGEBRAIC EXPRESSIONS.

PI

PI: the constant RATIO of the circumference of a CIRCLE to the diameter.

$$\pi = \frac{\text{circumference of a circle}}{\text{diameter of a circle}} = \text{approximately } 3.14 \text{ or } \tfrac{22}{7}$$

The *exact* ratio is denoted by the Greek letter π, called pi.

Pi is an irrational number, the value of which cannot be calculated exactly, but which can be approximated as accurately as is desired. (See RATIONAL AND IRRATIONAL NUMBERS.) Today the value is being calculated to millions of decimal places by means of computers. The decimal expansion goes on and on, without repetition. The first 527 decimal places are

3.141,592,653,589,793,238,462,643,383,279,502,884,197,169
399,375,105,820,974,944,592,307,816,406,286,208,998,628,
034,825,342,117,067,982,148,086,513,282,306,647,093,844,
609,550,582,231,725,359,408,128,481,117,450,284,102,701,
938,521,105,559,644,622,948,954,930,381,964,428,810,975,
665,933,446,128,475,648,233,786,783,165,271,201,909,145,
648,566,923,460,348,610,454,326,648,213,393,607,260,249,
141,273,724,587,006,606,315,588,174,881,520,920,962,829,
254,091,715,364,367,892,590,360,011,330,530,548,820,466,
521,384,146,951,941,511,609,433,057,270,365,759,591,953,
092,186,117,381,932,611,793,105,118,548,074,462,379,962,
749,567,351,885,752,724,891,227,938,183,011,949,129,833,
673,362,440,656,643,086,021,39.

In order to remember the value of pi to a given number of decimal places, people have written rhymes or catchy sentences in which the number of letters in each word gives each digit of the approximation.

For example, this sentence was offered by the *Scientific American* in 1914:

See, I have a rhyme assisting my feeble brain, its tasks ofttimes resisting.

3.	1	4	1	5	9	2	6	5	3	5	8	9

HISTORY OF PI

From the most ancient times, mathematicians recognized that the ratio of the circumference of a circle to the diameter was a little more than three. The same number π occurs in the formula for the area of a circle, $A = \pi r^2$; this was proved by the ancient Greeks. For centuries people sought an exact value for π by *quadrature* or *squaring of the circle*. They tried, by GEOMETRIC CONSTRUCTION, to construct a square whose area was exactly equal to the area of a given circle, in order to calculate the area of the circle and thereby find π.

As methods became more refined, greater accuracy was obtained—more decimal places were achieved in the approximations. But there was never an end to the approximation process. Finally in the late eighteenth century, it was proved that there never would be an end—that there is *no* terminating or repeating decimal number that exactly represents π.

On the following pages, a table chronicles the search for an exact value for π. The history of π has many additional chapters, some of which are very funny. There have been famous arguments among mathematicians and amateurs who truly believed they had squared the circle. In 1897 the Indiana State Legislature attempted to pass a law setting a simpler value for π. Further reading is recommended. See references, p. 396.

about	2000 B.C.	Babylonians used $\pi = 3\frac{1}{8} = 3.1250$.
		Egyptians used $\pi = (\frac{16}{9})^2 = 3.1605$.
about	1100 B.C.	Chinese used $\pi = 3$.
about	550 B.C.	Bible (I Kings 7:23) implied $\pi = 3$.
about	**240** B.C.	Archimedes determined that π is between $3\frac{10}{71}$ and $3\frac{10}{70}$, that $3.1408 < \pi < 3.1428$.

During the first millenium A.D., some improved fractional estimates of π were made by mathematicians scattered throughout the world. For example, Ptolemy of Alexandria had computed tables of chords of circles. Using the summed chords of 1° arcs as an approximation to the circumference of the circle, he effectively used a 360-sided polygon to estimate π at $\frac{377}{120}$.

about	150 A.D.	Ptolemy of Alexandria established $\pi = \frac{377}{120} = 3.14166\ldots$
about	480	Tsu Chung-Chi, a Chinese, gave $\pi = \frac{355}{113} = 3.1415929$, correct to six decimal places.
about	530	Āryabhata, a Hindu, used $\pi = \frac{62832}{20000} = 3.1416$
about	1150	Bhaskara, also Hindu, used $\pi = \frac{3927}{1250} = 3.1416$ as an "accurate" value, but noted that $\frac{22}{7} = 3.1429$ served as a less accurate value, and that $\sqrt{10} = 3.1623$ sufficed for "ordinary" work

4 to 6 decimal places

	1220	Fibonacci (Leonardo of Pisa) stated $\pi = 3.141818$
before	1436	Al-Kashî of Samarkand calculated π to 14 decimal places.

In the late sixteenth and early seventeenth centuries, Europeans used the *classical polygon method* of Archimedes, greatly increasing the number of sides of the polygon in order to extend the accuracy of the estimates of π. These were extremely laborious hand calculations.

	1579	François Viète, a Frenchman, found π correct to 9 decimal places, using polygons of 393,216 —or 6 (2^{16})—sides.
	1610	Ludolph van Ceulen, a German, computed π to 35 decimal places, using polygons of 2^{62} sides and spending much of his life on this task.
	1621	Willebrord Snell, a Dutchman, introduced trigonometric improvement to the classical polygon method, providing greater accuracy than earlier efforts.

39 decimal places

	1630	The last attempt to calculate π classically, using Snell's improvement, yielded 39 decimal places.

In the seventeenth century, several *series representations* of π were discovered. James Gregory's opened a whole new world of easily extendable calculations. For $x = 1$, Gregory's series becomes

$$\frac{\pi}{4} = 1 - \frac{1}{3} + \frac{1}{5} - \frac{1}{7} + \frac{1}{9} - \frac{1}{11} + \cdots$$

about 1650   John Wallis, an Englishman, showed

$$\frac{\pi}{2} = \frac{2 \times 2 \times 4 \times 4 \times 6 \times 6 \times 8 \times 8}{1 \times 3 \times 3 \times 5 \times 5 \times 7 \times 7 \times 9} \cdots$$

and Lord Brouncker, also English, converted this to the continued fraction

$$\frac{4}{\pi} = 1 + \cfrac{1^2}{2 + \cfrac{3^2}{2 + \cfrac{5^2}{2 + \cfrac{7^2}{2 + \cfrac{9^2}{2 + \ldots}}}}}$$

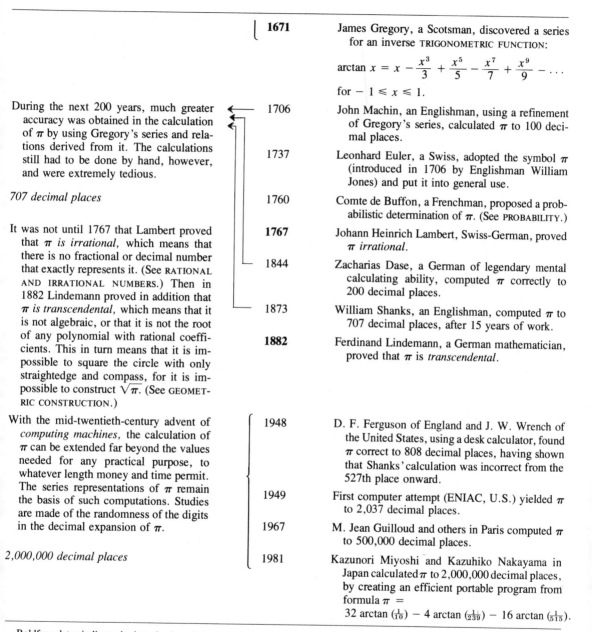

	1671	James Gregory, a Scotsman, discovered a series for an inverse TRIGONOMETRIC FUNCTION: $$\arctan x = x - \frac{x^3}{3} + \frac{x^5}{5} - \frac{x^7}{7} + \frac{x^9}{9} - \ldots$$ for $-1 \leq x \leq 1$.
During the next 200 years, much greater accuracy was obtained in the calculation of π by using Gregory's series and relations derived from it. The calculations still had to be done by hand, however, and were extremely tedious.	1706	John Machin, an Englishman, using a refinement of Gregory's series, calculated π to 100 decimal places.
	1737	Leonhard Euler, a Swiss, adopted the symbol π (introduced in 1706 by Englishman William Jones) and put it into general use.
707 decimal places	1760	Comte de Buffon, a Frenchman, proposed a probabilistic determination of π. (See PROBABILITY.)
It was not until 1767 that Lambert proved that π *is irrational,* which means that there is no fractional or decimal number that exactly represents it. (See RATIONAL AND IRRATIONAL NUMBERS.) Then in 1882 Lindemann proved in addition that π *is transcendental,* which means that it is not algebraic, or that it is not the root of any polynomial with rational coefficients. This in turn means that it is impossible to square the circle with only straightedge and compass, for it is impossible to construct $\sqrt{\pi}$. (See GEOMETRIC CONSTRUCTION.)	**1767**	Johann Heinrich Lambert, Swiss-German, proved π irrational.
	1844	Zacharias Dase, a German of legendary mental calculating ability, computed π correctly to 200 decimal places.
	1873	William Shanks, an Englishman, computed π to 707 decimal places, after 15 years of work.
	1882	Ferdinand Lindemann, a German mathematician, proved that π is *transcendental.*
With the mid-twentieth-century advent of *computing machines,* the calculation of π can be extended far beyond the values needed for any practical purpose, to whatever length money and time permit. The series representations of π remain the basis of such computations. Studies are made of the randomness of the digits in the decimal expansion of π.	1948	D. F. Ferguson of England and J. W. Wrench of the United States, using a desk calculator, found π correct to 808 decimal places, having shown that Shanks' calculation was incorrect from the 527th place onward.
	1949	First computer attempt (ENIAC, U.S.) yielded π to 2,037 decimal places.
	1967	M. Jean Guilloud and others in Paris computed π to 500,000 decimal places.
2,000,000 decimal places	1981	Kazunori Miyoshi and Kazuhiko Nakayama in Japan calculated π to 2,000,000 decimal places, by creating an efficient portable program from formula $\pi = 32 \arctan \left(\frac{1}{10}\right) - 4 \arctan \left(\frac{1}{239}\right) - 16 \arctan \left(\frac{1}{515}\right)$.

Boldface dates indicate the introduction of the most important ideas in the search.

REFERENCES

Petr Beckmann, *A History of Pi* (Golem Press, 1970, 1971).

Martin Gardner, *New Mathematical Diversions from Scientific American* (Simon & Schuster, 1966), Ch. 8, ''The Transcendental Number Pi.''

See also PROBABILITY for some surprising occurrences of π.

PLANES

PLANE: one of three *undefined* terms in GEOMETRY, the other two being POINT and LINE.

PROPERTIES OF A PLANE

Because in mathematics a plane is undefined, no one can tell you exactly what it is. (See DEFINITIONS.) However, here are some properties of a plane that may help you understand the mathematical idea:

Imagine a straight line (not a line segment, but an entire line) moving straight forever through space in a direction perpendicular to its length. The path traced by that moving line would be a plane. A plane is thought of as a completely flat surface having no edges but extending on and on, without end, into space. A straight line connecting any two points on the surface of a plane will lie entirely within the plane.

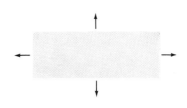

A plane has the properties of *length, width,* and *area.* However, the length, width, and area of an entire plane can never be measured, because a plane is conceived of as infinite.

A plane is thought of as having *no thickness.* In other words, a plane is *two-dimensional.* Moreover, all *plane figures*—figures that lie completely in one plane, such as a triangle, a square, a circle, and the like—are also two-dimensional. They too have no thickness.

MODELS OF A PLANE

You are already familiar with a variety of things that could serve as models for a portion of a plane; the most common models of planes used in math books are rectangles and parallelograms. These are useful because they can be seen and they fit on the page of a book. However, it is important to remember that all of these models are unlike an ideal mathematical plane in two important respects: (1) they all have thickness, even if it is imperceptible; and (2) they all have sides or edges.

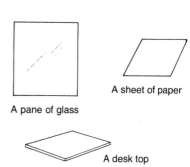

A sheet of paper

A pane of glass

A desk top

Intersecting planes

WAYS OF CLASSIFYING PLANES

One way of classifying planes is by their position, or *orientation* *relative to other planes or lines:*

Intersecting Planes: When two planes intersect, they have points i common. The intersection of two distinct planes, or the set of points i common, is a straight line.

Parallel Planes: When two planes are parallel, they do not intersec they have no points in common.

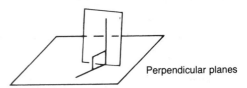

Parallel planes

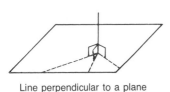

Line perpendicular to a plane

A Line Perpendicular to a Plane: When a line is perpendicular to plane, it is perpendicular to any line in the plane through its foot (th point where the line meets the plane).

Perpendicular Planes: When two planes are perpendicular, ever line in one plane that is perpendicular to the line of intersection is als perpendicular to the other plane.

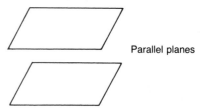

Perpendicular planes

Half-plane: A half-plane is the part of a plane extending in only o direction from a line in the plane.

Another way of classifying planes is by their *orientation,* or positio *relative to the earth's surface:*

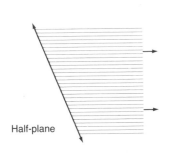

Half-plane

Vertical Plane: a plane in which a plumb line at any point in th plane lies entirely within the plane. (A plumb line is a string supporti a weight.)

Horizontal Plane: a plane that is perpendicular to a vertical line. horizontal plane is parallel to the earth's surface or to the surface water at rest *if* these surfaces are considered planes. The word "ho zontal" comes from "horizon," the line where the earth's surface a pears to meet the sky.

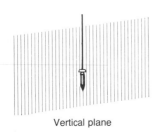

Vertical plane

Horizontal plane

Oblique Plane: a plane that is neither horizontal nor vertical.

DETERMINING A PLANE

In mathematics, the word *determine,* as in "two points determine a line," has a special meaning. It means to describe or to pinpoint exactly one thing as distinct from all other similar things. For example, to determine a line means to pinpoint exactly one unique line from the infinite number of possible lines.

Although two points are enough to determine a line, two points do not determine a plane. For through two points infinitely many planes may be drawn.

Three points determine a plane. They must be *noncollinear,* that is, not all on the same straight line. Through any three noncollinear points one and only one plane may be drawn. (Points that lie in the same plane are called *coplanar.*)

A plane is also determined by each of the following:

- one straight line and a point not on that line

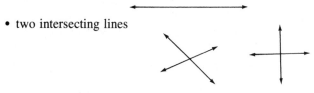

- two intersecting lines

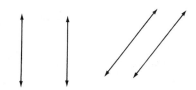

- two parallel lines

You can demonstrate that three points not in a straight line determine a plane with some thumbtacks and a flat card. If you place the card on the points of two upside-down thumbtacks, it will rock back and forth. When resting on only two points it can be in any one of a number of planes. However, if you place under the card a third upside-down tack not in a straight line with the other two, the card will not rock. When

Oblique plane

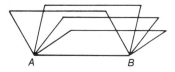

Two points:
infinitely many planes

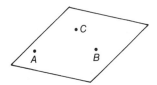

Three points: one plane

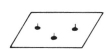

resting on three points, the card is fixed in a single plane.

A three-legged milking stool is based on the principle that three points determine a plane; it will be steady even on a rough barn floor. A four-legged chair, on the other hand, will rock if it is placed on an uneven floor or if one leg is short. A wobbly chair with one short leg goes from resting on three legs with its seat in one plane to resting on three different legs with its seat in another plane.

LIMITATIONS OF PLANE GEOMETRY

Plane, or Euclidean, geometry deals with the properties of points, lines, and figures in a plane. For centuries many people believed that the earth was flat. Thus, the mathematician's plane was viewed as an idealized model of the surface of the earth. What was true of one was believed to be true of the other. For example, if on a plane the shortest distance between two points is a straight line, then that should be true for the surface of the earth as well. And since people were dealing with relatively small portions of the earth's surface, where the curvature is so slight as to be negligible, the plane was a fairly good model. Indeed, we still measure small tracts of ground and build houses as if the earth were flat.

However, after Columbus and others demonstrated beyond a doubt that the earth was spherical, a need arose for a new geometry to describe the properties of lines and figures on a sphere or in space. For example, knowing that the shortest distance between the Old World and the New World is a straight line was not much help, since that straight line runs several hundred miles under the surface of the earth. What navigators needed to know was what is the shortest distance between two points on the surface of a sphere. (See spherical GEOMETRY.)

Once geometry was freed from the plane, it developed in different directions. In the nineteenth century three men—Nicolai Lobachevsky, a Russian; Janos Bolyai, a Hungarian; and G. F. B. Riemann, a German—developed non-Euclidean geometries in which it was no longer true that parallel lines never meet. Some of their work has helped explain some previously mysterious phenomena of astronomical space.

For more on non-Euclidean geometries, see LINE, GEOMETRY, PROJECTION, and TOPOLOGY.

REFERENCES

Anthony Ravielli, *An Adventure in Geometry* (Viking Press, 1957), pp. 44–49, 113–117; a good pictorial presentation of the plane.

References for fun

Edwin A. Abbott, *Flatland* (Seeley, 1884; Dover, 1952); a nineteenth-century science fiction classic of life in a two-dimensional world; provides clear insight into the mathematics of the plane and of higher dimensions (particularly as seen from the plane).

Alexander Keewatin Dewdney, "Exploring the Planiverse," *Journal of Recreational Mathematics*, September 1979, pp. 16–20 or "Two-dimensional Science and Technology" (97 pages, privately published, 1979; available postpaid for $5 to the United States or Canada from A. K. Dewdney, Department of Computer Science, University of Western Ontario, London, Ontario, Canada N6A 5B9); a remarkable sequel to *Flatland*.

Martin Gardner, "Mathematical Games: The pleasures of doing science and technology in the planiverse," *Scientific American*, July 1980, pp. 18–31; a report on Dewdney's ideas of chemistry, locks, engines, and chess games in two dimensions.

An ordinary key in a lock needs a third dimension in which to turn.

For the planiverse, Dewdney has invented a similar locking mechanism for which the key need not turn.

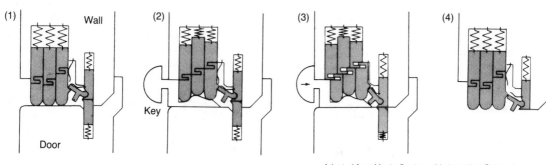

(1)   Wall

Door

(2)   Key

(3)

(4)

POINTS

POINT: one of the three *undefined* terms in GEOMETRY, the other two being LINE and PLANE.

Because point is undefined, no one can tell you exactly what a point is. (See DEFINITIONS.) However, knowing some properties of a point may help you form some idea of it. A point is thought of as having *position*. The position of a point is some location on a plane or in space. For example, the exact place where two intersecting lines meet is a point. However, a point is such an exact location that it is thought of as taking up no space at all. That is, a point has *no size of any kind*—no width, no length, no thickness. Because a point has no size, it cannot be divided into smaller parts—it is said to be *indivisible*.

To represent a point, mathematicians often use a dot. For example, point *A* on line segment *BC* would be represented as shown. However, that dot is only a model of a point; it is not itself a point. The dot, even though very small, has size; it is actually composed of an infinite set of points, just as line segments and larger geometric figures are composed of infinite sets of points. Still, the dot is a useful model because we can see it.

You certainly have an intuitive idea of what a point is. And that's all mathematicians have. But by beginning with ideas about a few basic concepts such as point, line and plane, they are then able to give more exact definitions of more complex concepts in geometry.

SPECIAL NAMES FOR POINTS

Sometimes points are labeled according to their *relationship* to one another:

Collinear Points: points on the same straight line.

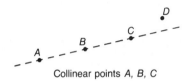

Collinear points *A, B, C*

Coplanar Points: points lying in the same plane.

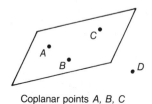

Coplanar points *A, B, C*

REFERENCES

Norman Juster, *The Dot and the Line* (Random House, 1963; available in paperback); a delightful illustrated fable of the adventures of a point meeting a line.

Anthony Ravielli, *An Adventure in Geometry,* (Viking Press, 1957), pp. 39–48; a good simple presentation of the three undefined terms in geometry.

For more on how to give the exact location of a point, see COORDI-NATES.

For a discussion of point at infinity, see INFINITY.

For *vanishing point,* see PROJECTION.

See also SYMMETRY about a point.

POLYGONS

POLYGON: A closed PLANE (two-dimensional) figure formed by the LINE segments that join (without crossing) three or more POINTS not in a straight line.

The National Defense Building in Washington, D.C. is the Pentagon
Courtesy of the Department of Defense.

Different polygonal shapes of traffic sign offer quick recognition to drivers

Bees build hexagonal honeycombs
Courtesy of Dyce Laboratory, Cornell University.

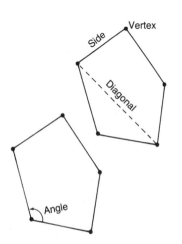

PARTS OF A POLYGON

Side: one of the line segments.

Vertex (plural, *vertices*): a point where the sides meet.

Diagonal: a line segment joining any two vertices not already joined by a side.

ANGLES OF A POLYGON

Interior Angle: an ANGLE inside a polygon and between two adjacent sides (two sides with the same vertex).

Concave Polygon: a polygon in which at least one interior angle is more than 180°. At least one straight line through a concave polygon intersects more than two sides.

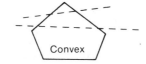

Convex Polygon: a polygon in which each interior angle is less than 180°. Any straight line through a convex polygon intersects at most two sides.

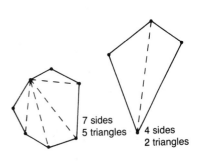

7 sides
5 triangles

4 sides
2 triangles

> The sum of the interior angles of a polygon of n sides is always $(n - 2)$ 180°.

This is true because a polygon can be divided into $(n - 2)$ triangles. Triangulation is easily done in a convex polygon by drawing all the diagonals from any one vertex. The sum of interior angles of the polygon will equal the sum of all the interior angles of the triangles. The sum of the interior angles of each TRIANGLE is 180°. Since there are $(n - 2)$ triangles, the sum of the interior angles of the polygon is $(n - 2)$ 180°.

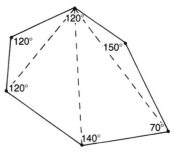

6 sides, so sum of angles is
$(6 - 2)$ 180° = 720°

CLASSIFICATION OF POLYGONS BY NUMBER OF SIDES

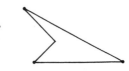

3 sides: *Triangle*   4 sides: *Quadrilateral*   5 sides: *Pentagon*

6 sides: *Hexagon*   7 sides: *Heptagon*   8 sides: *Octagon*   9 sides: *Nonagon*   10 sides: *Decagon*

These names reflect the ancient Greek origin of the study of polygons. The Greek word "poly" means many, and "gonia" means angle. Most of the other prefixes are the Greek names for the number of angles (or sides). Two exceptions are from Latin: "quadrilateral," meaning four sides, and "nona-," meaning nine.

12 sides: *Dodecagon*

n sides: *n-gon*

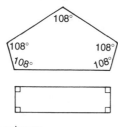

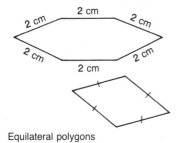

Equiangular polygons

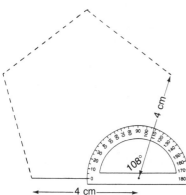

Equilateral polygons

For regular pentagon, $\dfrac{(5-2)180°}{5}$

$= 108°$ in each angle.

OTHER CLASSIFICATIONS OF POLYGONS

Equiangular Polygon: a polygon in which all angles have equal measure.

Equilateral Polygon: a polygon in which all sides have equal length.

Regular Polygon: a polygon in which all sides have equal length *and* all angles have equal measure; a polygon that is both equilateral and equiangular.

Regular polygons

MAKING REGULAR POLYGONS

There are many possible methods of creating regular polygons. For instance:

- You can use a ruler and a protractor. Use the ruler to make sides of equal length, and the protractor to make angles of equal measure. For a regular n-gon, each angle will have

$$\frac{(n-2)\,180}{n} \text{ degrees.}$$

Example. For a regular pentagon,

$$\frac{5-2}{5}\,180° = 108° \text{ in each angle.}$$

Start with one side. Measure one angle. Measure the next side. Measure the next angle at the end of that side, and so on. If you do this carefully, you should reach your starting point at the end of the fifth side.

- Some polygons can be created by paper folding. For instructions, see references for this section.
- Certain regular polygons can be obtained by a GEOMETRIC CONSTRUCTION using only straightedge and compass. These are the ones with 3, 4, 5, 15, 17, 257, and 65,537 sides, or with even multiples of these numbers (for instance, 3, 6, 12, 24, ... or 4, 8, 16, 32, ...) for the number of sides.

The construction of the seventeen-sided regular polygon was not discovered until the end of the eighteenth century, although mathematicians had been working on the problem since the time of Euclid (300 B.C.). This construction was discovered in 1796 by an eighteen-year-old German student, Carl Friedrich Gauss. It was because of this discovery that Gauss decided to spend his life working with mathematics—a wise decision, as he became one of the greatest mathematicians of all time.

Gauss also proved that a regular n-gon could be geometrically constructed if the number of sides were a *prime number* of the form

$$F_n = 2^{(2^n)} + 1, \text{ where } n \text{ is an integer.}$$

Example. $F_3 = 2^{(2^3)} + 1 = 2^8 + 1 = 256 + 1 = 257.$

Numbers of this form are called Fermat numbers, and they are not necessarily prime; for example, F_5 is not a prime number. But the first five Fermat numbers are prime:

$$F_0 = 3, F_1 = 5, F_2 = 17, F_3 = 257, \text{ and } F_4 = 65,537.$$

So Gauss' theorem showed that regular polygons could be geometrically constructed with these numbers of sides. A 257-gon was constructed in 1832. And a manuscript, ten years in the making, for the construction of a 65,537-gon occupies a large box at the University of Göttingen.

Detailed here are some methods of creating common polygons. See GEOMETRIC CONSTRUCTION for basic constructions such as perpendiculars and bisectors.

Regular Hexagon

Construct a circle. Without changing the compass (so it is still set to the radius of the circle), mark off—with the point of the compass anywhere on the circle—an arc that cuts the circle. Next, place the metal point of the compass on the intersection of the first arc and the circle and mark off a second arc. Continue around the circle in this manner until you reach your starting point. You should have six arcs that do not overlap. Then, using the straightedge, connect the consecutive points where the arcs intersect the circle.

Equilateral Triangle (Two Methods)

- Use the method for the hexagon, but connect only every other point marked on the circle.

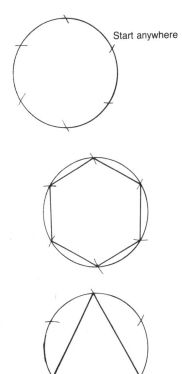

Start anywhere

- Draw a line. With the compass, mark off on the line the length yo[u] want for one side of the triangle. Without changing the compass[,] put its metal point on one end of the segment and draw an arc above the segment. Next, place the metal point on the other end of th[e] segment and draw an arc that intersects the first arc. The point a[t] which these two arcs intersect will be the third vertex. Use th[e] straightedge to draw the remaining two sides.

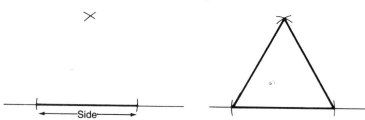

Square (Two Methods)

- Draw a line. With the compass, mark off on the line the length yo[u] want for one side of the square. Construct a perpendicular at eac[h] end of the line segment. Again, set the compass to the length of th[e] side and mark off this distance on the perpendicular sides. Use th[e] straightedge to connect these two marks for the fourth side.

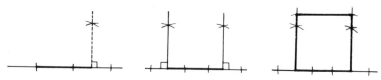

- Construct a circle. Draw a diameter of the circle. Construct a per-pendicular to this diameter at its midpoint. Make a second diamete[r] along this perpendicular. Use the straightedge to connect the fou[r] points where the diameters intersect the circle.

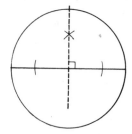 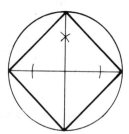

Regular Octagon

Construct a circle. Construct two perpendicular diameters, as described in the construction of the square. These meet at the center of the
circle in central angles. To double the number of sides of the square,
thereby creating a figure with eight sides, you must bisect each of these
central angles. Where the bisectors meet the circle, and where the
original perpendicular diameters meet the circle, you now have eight
points marked. Use the straightedge to join these eight equally spaced
points.

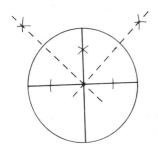
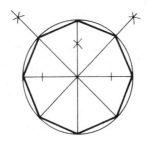

Regular Pentagon (Two Methods)

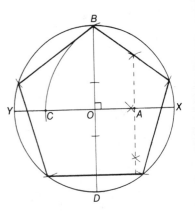

- Draw a circle. (The construction must be done very accurately, and
  points should be labeled to make the instructions clear.) Label the
  center O. Draw any diameter BD. Construct diameter YX perpendicular to BD. Bisect radius OX and label that midpoint A. Measure the length of AB with a compass. Make $AC = AB$ (with C on
  YX as shown). The length of BC will be the side of the pentagon.
  Set your compass to that length and mark off arcs on the circle. If
  you start at B and have been very accurate, five arcs should bring
  you back to B. Use the straightedge to connect the five equally
  spaced marks.
- Take a long strip of paper, of uniform width; tie it into a knot as
  shown; carefully pull it tight and press flat.

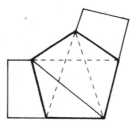

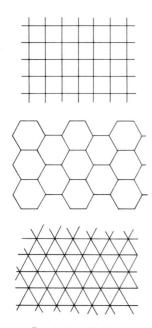

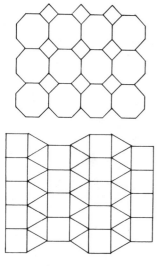

Regular tessellations

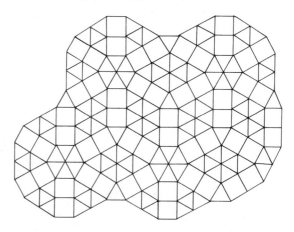

References on making regular polygons

T. Sundara Row, *Geometric Exercises in Paper Folding* (Dover, 1966)

Ian Stewart, "Gauss," *Scientific American,* July 1977, pp. 122–131; a
fascinating article on Carl Friedrich Gauss; shows the construction of
the seventeen-sided polygon.

TESSELLATIONS

A *tessellation* is a mosaic pattern formed by fitting together (without
overlapping or leaving spaces) an infinite number of repeating polygons
so that they cover the entire plane. The process of doing this is called
tiling the plane.

Tessellations are used in designs for such things as floor coverings,
quilts, and bathroom tiles. In nature the honeycomb illustrates a tessellation.

The Greeks knew and proved that there are only three regular polygons that tile the plane using only one shape per tessellation. *Regular
tessellations* are produced by the equilateral triangle, the square, and the
regular hexagon.

Combinations of regular polygons may be used to tile the plane.

When the same combination of regular polygons meets at every vertex,
the pattern is called a *semi-regular* or *homogeneous* tessellation. Certain nonregular polygons may also be used to tile the plane. They are
called *nonhomogeneous tessellations*.

Semi-regular tessellations

References on tessellations

M. C. Escher, *The Graphic Work of M. C. Escher* (Hawthorn Books,
1960); *The World of M. C. Escher* (Harry N. Abrams, Inc., 1971).

"Reptiles," by M. C. Escher

Martin Gardner, "Extraordinary nonperiodic tiling," *Scientific American,* January 1977, pp. 110–121.

E. R. Ranucci and J. L. Teeters, *Creating Escher-type Drawings* (Creative Publications, 1974); how to do it yourself.

POLYGONAL PUZZLES

Geometric Dissections

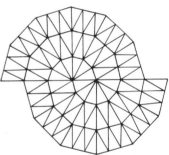

Adapted from Martin Gardner, "Mathematical Games." Copyright © 1977 by Scientific American, Inc. All rights reserved.

A geometric dissection puzzle is a plane figure that must be divided into pieces and reassembled in another specified shape. The object of the puzzle is to do the dissection in as few pieces as possible. The cuts are to be straight lines or composed of straight line segments.

For example, given a 16 by 9 rectangle, can you dissect it into two pieces that can be recombined to make a square? This problem can be solved with a single cut, as shown.

A similar geometric dissection puzzle creates a *paradox:* the area of the figure seems to increase when the pieces are reassembled.

If a square 8 units on a side is cut as shown on p. 412, the pieces can be rearranged to form a rectangle 5 units by 13 units. The area of the square is $8 \times 8 = 64$ square units, but the area of the rectangle is $5 \times 13 = 65$ square units. Where did the other square unit come from?

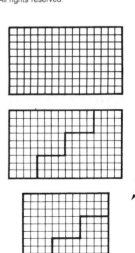

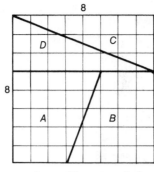

Area = 64 square units

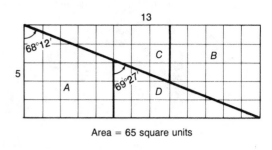

Area = 65 square units

The explanation of this paradox is that the edges of the parts do not fit exactly along the diagonal of the rectangle. They *appear* to fit because the angle is so small (less than $1\frac{1}{2}°$) between the sloping sides of the pieces.

Reference on geometric dissections

Harry Lindgren, *Geometric Dissections* (Van Nostrand, 1964); a whole book full of these puzzles.

Polyominoes

A *polyomino* is a polygonal plane figure made of congruent (identical) squares joined so as to share sides. Each polyomino has a name whose prefix tells how many squares are joined together:

monomino:	one square	□
domino:	two squares	⊏⊐
tromino:	three squares	⊏⊏⊐ *or* ⊏⊐
tetromino:	four squares	⊏⊏⊏⊐ *or* ⊏⊏⊐ *or* ⊏⊏⊐ *or* ⊏⊐ *or* ⊞
pentomino:	five squares	
hexomino:	six squares	
heptomino:	seven squares	

There is only one configuration for a monomino or domino, but two different shapes are possible for a tromino. There are five different tetrominoes, twelve pentominoes, and thirty-five hexominoes.

Many puzzles can be made with polyominoes. A highly versatile collection uses the set of twelve pentominoes. All twelve can be arranged to form a 3 × 20 rectangle *or* a 10 × 6 rectangle *or* a 5 × 12 rectangle *or* a 15 × 4 rectangle. (You may find it necessary to flip over a piece,

such as   to   ,

from one rectangular puzzle to another.)

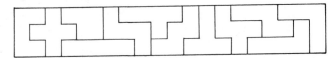

The twelve pentominoes are illustrated in the solution to the 3 × 20 rectangle. You can cut out a set following this illustration and try to form the other rectangles—4 × 15, 5 × 12, 6 × 10. There are many other pentomino puzzles as well. For instance, they can be made to cover an 8 × 8 checkerboard leaving a 2 × 2 hole at any desired location.

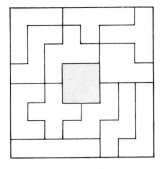

Another puzzle that can be solved by many polyominoes is the problem of tiling the plane. For example, try tiling the plane with

this pentomino   or with this heptomino

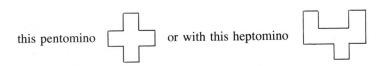

A heptomino solution is given:

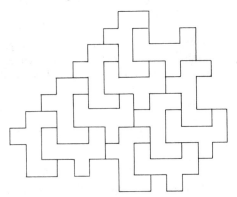

References for additional polyomino puzzles

Martin Gardner, *New Mathematical Diversions from Scientific American* (Simon & Schuster, 1966), pp. 150–161.

Solomon W. Golomb, *Polyominoes* (Charles Scribner's Sons, 1965).

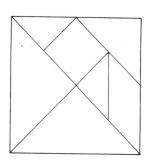

Tangrams

The tangram is an ancient Chinese puzzle, consisting of a square divided into seven parts as shown. The object is to assemble these seven parts to form different designs. All seven pieces must be used in each design.

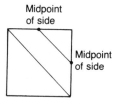

Midpoint of side

Perpendicular to diagonal

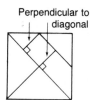

Midpoint of side

Parallel to side, perpendicular to top & bottom

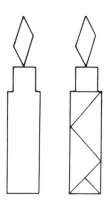

You can make your own tangram puzzle by copying the square diagram onto a cardboard square (of any size) according to these instructions. Now cut the pieces apart and reassemble them. You might try these examples.

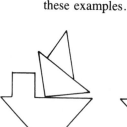

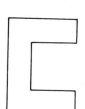

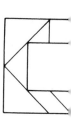

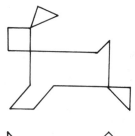

By the early nineteenth century, many books of tangrams had been printed in China. Many additional puzzles have been provided by the Western world, and there are now hundreds and hundreds of tangram designs.

Reference on tangrams

Ronald C. Read, *Tangrams: 330 Puzzles* (Dover, 1965); includes much background.

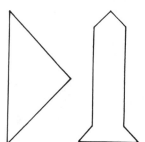

For specialized detail on three- and four-sided polygons, see TRIANGLES and QUADRILATERALS. Suggested further reading: POLYHEDRA.

POLYHEDRA

POLYHEDRON (plural, Polyhedrons or Polyhedra): a three-dimensional figure (a solid, or space figure) bounded by plane POLYGONS.

A quartz crystal   A cereal box   A star ornament   An Egyptian pyramid

PARTS OF A POLYHEDRON

Face: one of the plane polygons bounding the figure.

Edge: a line segment formed by the intersection of two faces.

Vertex (plural, *vertices*): a point where three or more edges meet.

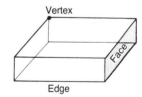

CLASSIFICATION OF POLYHEDRA BY NUMBER OF FACES

It was the ancient Greeks who studied polygons and polyhedra in detail and gave them their names. "Poly" means "many," and "hedra" means "seat." Thus, a polyhedron was considered capable of being seated on any of its faces. Greek prefixes for numbers specify the exact number of seats or faces in a particular polyhedron. The simplest three-dimensional figure possible is one with *four* faces, the tetrahedron.

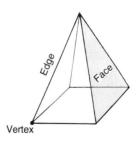

415

The commonly named polyhedra are as follows:

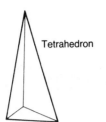

Tetrahedron

Hexahedron

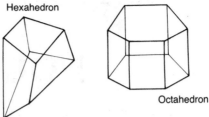

Octahedron

4 faces: *tetrahedron*
6 faces: *hexahedron*
8 faces: *octahedron*
12 faces: *dodecahedron*
20 faces: *icosahedron*

CLASSIFICATION OF POLYHEDRA BY PROPERTIES OF FACES

Prism: a polyhedron with bases that are CONGRUENT parallel polygons and with lateral faces that are parallelograms. (The word *lateral* means "side" and is used to describe side faces and side edges of a polyhedron.) A prism is named according to the shape of its bases, such as a triangular prism or a hexagonal prism.

Right Prism: a prism with lateral edges and lateral faces *perpendicular* to the bases.

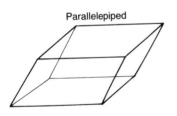

Hexagonal prism

Lateral edge

Base

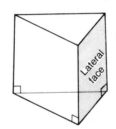

Right triangular prism

Lateral face

Parallelepiped: a prism with parallelogram bases; hence, a hexahedron with all six faces parallelograms.

Pyramid: a polyhedron in which the base may be any polygon and in which the remaining faces are all triangles that meet in a common vertex, or *apex*. A pyramid is named according to the shape of its base, such as a rectangular pyramid.

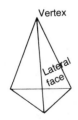

Parallelepiped

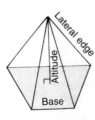

Vertex

Lateral face

Triangular pyramid

Lateral edge

Altitude

Base

Quadrilateral pyramid

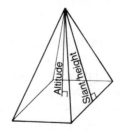

Altitude

Slant height

Regular rectangular pyramid

Frustum of a pyramid

Regular Pyramid: a pyramid whose base is a regular polygon and whose lateral edges are of equal length.

Altitude of a pyramid: the line segment from the vertex *perpendicular* to the plane of the base.

Slant Height of a pyramid: the altitude of the triangular *face* of a regular pyramid.

Frustum of a pyramid: any part of a pyramid between the base and a plane parallel to the base.

Regular Polyhedron: a polyhedron in which all faces are CONGRUENT *regular polygons,* and in which the ANGLES between the sides are also congruent.

Regular Tetrahedron: a tetrahedron in which each of the four faces is an equilateral triangle. There are three triangles at each vertex of a regular tetrahedron.

Regular Hexahedron or Cube: a hexahedron in which each of the six faces is a square. Three squares meet at each vertex of a cube.

Regular Octahedron: an octahedron in which each of the eight faces is an equilateral triangle. There are four triangles at each vertex of a regular octahedron.

Regular Dodecahedron: a dodecahedron in which each of the twelve faces is a regular pentagon. Three pentagons meet at each vertex of a regular dodecahedron.

Regular Icosahedron: an icosahedron in which each of the twenty faces is an equilateral triangle. There are five triangles at each vertex of a regular icosahedron.

Many other polyhedra have special names. Most of them are based on regular polygons.

A *semi-regular polyhedron* is one in which the faces consist of at least two different types of regular polygons combined in the same way at each vertex. A familiar example of a semi-regular polyhedron is a soccer ball, whose faces are pentagons and hexagons. This figure can be made by cutting off the point of each of the twelve vertices of a regular icosahedron, in such a way that the new faces are regular pentagons and the old faces become regular hexagons. This figure is called a "*truncated* icosahedron." At each new vertex there are two hexagons and one pentagon. The basic semi-regular polyhedra are the *Archimedean solids*, a collection of thirteen of these figures studied by Archimedes about 200 B.C. and illustrated on p. 418.

Star-shaped polyhedra may be *stellated* (formed with pyramids built up on the faces of a regular polyhedron) or *faceted* (formed with pyramids turned inward). These are also shown on p. 418.

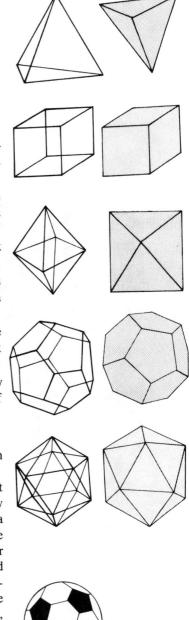

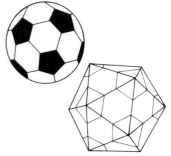

Semi-regular polyhedra

Truncated tetrahedron
Cuboctahedron
Snub cube

Snub dodecahedron
Icosidodecahedron
Rhombicuboctahedron
Truncated cube

Stellated and faceted polyhedra

From left to right: great icosahedron, great stellated dodecahedron, small stellated dodecahedron, great dodecahedr⟨⟩
From Alan Holden, *Shapes, Space, and Symmetry*.

The *geodesic domes* of R. Buckminster Fuller are polyhedra t⟨⟩
maximize structural efficiency—the triangular faces give strength a⟨⟩
rigidity; the volume is enclosed within a minimum of material.

References on geodesic domes

Ruth R. Howell, *The Dome People*, illustrated by Arline Stro⟨⟩
(Atheneum, 1974); a photographic chronicle of the actual buildi⟨⟩
of a large geodesic-domed clubhouse by teenagers (with help fr⟨⟩
children and adults).

Robert W. Marks, *The Dymaxion World of R. Buckminster Full*⟨⟩
(Southern Illinois University Press, 1966); a more technical source ⟨⟩
geodesic domes.

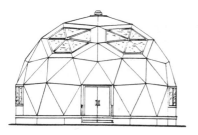

Geodesic dome

Truncated dodecahedron
Truncated octahedron
Truncated icosahedron
Rhombiicosidodecahedron

Cubocatahedron (or great rhombicuboctahedron)

Truncated icosidodecahedron (or great rhombiicosidodecahedron)

From *Convex Figures and Polyhedra*, by L. A. Lyusternick, translated by T. J. Smith (© Dover Publications, Inc., N.Y., 1963).

MAKING MODELS OF POLYHEDRA

The first step in making a regular polyhedron is to make a pattern for the regular polygon that forms its sides. Directions for constructing the equilateral triangle, the square, and the regular pentagon are given in the POLYGONS article. If you make a cardboard pattern for a polygon, you can trace around it again and again, following one of the configurations below. The polyhedron is created by cutting out the entire configuration of faces and folding along the lines. You must be sure to leave a small tab where necessary to glue or tape the sides together. One possible set of tabs is given on each configuration.

Great dodecahedron

Mountain folds ------
Valley folds _____

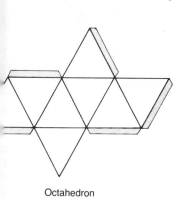
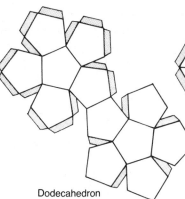
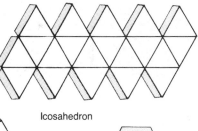

Icosahedron

Octahedron

Dodecahedron

Hexahedron (cube)

Kaleidocycles are a fascinating extension of polyhedra, first developed in 1958 by graphic designer Wallace Walker. A kaleidocycle is a chain of tetrahedra formed into a ring such that it can be rotated in a continuous cycle of different shapes. Brief instructions for building a kaleidocycle are as follows:

(1) Make a cardboard pattern of an isosceles triangle with base equal to height. ($b = h = 3$ inches works well.) Then, using your pat-

Tetrahedron

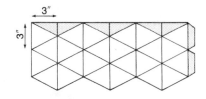

Kaleidocycle

tern, lay out a configuration as shown. Cut out along the outside of this configuration.

(2) Fold face-to-face on the vertical lines, back-to-back on the diagonal lines.

(3) A chain of tetrahedra forms—glue the chain into a ring. (The shaded areas will be where you should put the glue. But do *not* glue two shaded areas together—they should slide under non-shaded areas.)

(4) When glue dries thoroughly, rotate your kaleidocycle by pushing the points of the tetrahedra through the center hole.

For other patterns and more detailed instructions, see Schattschneider and Walker in reference list.

References for making models of polyhedra

H. Martyn Cundy and A. P. Rollett, *Mathematical Models* (Oxford University Press, 1961); a technical and exhaustive treatment with detailed measurements; includes stellated and faceted polyhedra.

Alan Holden, *Shapes, Space, and Symmetry* (Columbia University Press, 1971); also includes stellated and faceted polyhedra.

Harold R. Jacobs, *Mathematics: A Human Endeavor* (W. H. Freeman & Co., 1970), pp. 209–239; varied discussion with directions for many models.

Doris Schattschneider and Wallace Walker, *M. C. Escher Kaleidocycles* (Ballantine Books, 1977); includes complete explanation plus a kit of printed cardboard patterns all ready to cut and assemble.

Magnus J. Wenninger, *Polyhedron Models* (Cambridge University Press, 1974; available in paperback); also includes stellated and faceted polyhedra.

MORE ABOUT REGULAR POLYHEDRA

How Many Regular Polyhedra Are There?

There are exactly five regular polyhedra. The reason for this can be seen by examining the number of degrees in each angle of a regular polygon and then considering how many could be fit about a common vertex. In order to form a three-dimensional figure, at least three polygons are needed at each vertex.

If a regular polyhedron is formed from equilateral triangles, three, four, or five of them can be fitted together at the same vertex, giving tetrahedron, an *octahedron,* and an *icosahedron,* respectively. Since each equilateral triangle has an angle of 60°, six of them grouped about common vertex would give a sum of 360°, and the six triangles would lie flat when they fit together. More than six equilateral triangles will not fit around a single point, because the sum of the angles would be more than 360°. Hence, there are only three regular polyhedra that can be formed with triangular faces.

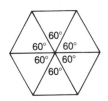

If a regular polyhedron is formed with square faces, three of them will fit together at a common vertex, giving the *cube* or *hexahedron*. Four squares meeting at a common point would lie flat, for four angles of 90° make a total of 360°, and more than four could not be used, because they would give an angle sum greater than 360°. So the cube is the only possible square-faced regular polyhedron.

A regular polygon may also be formed from regular pentagons, giving a *dodecahedron*. Each regular pentagon has 108° in each angle, so three of them will fit around a common vertex. However, four or more pentagons cannot meet at a single vertex, because their angles would sum to more than 360°.

These five figures exhaust the list of possible regular polyhedra. If you were to try to construct a regular polyhedron with hexagonal sides, you would discover that three would lie flat, for each angle of a hexagon is 120° and three of them total 360°. More than three hexagons would total more than 360° at each vertex, as would three of any polygon of more than six sides. There are simply no other possibilities.

Historical Notes

The five regular polyhedra were studied as far back as the time of Pythagoras (around 500 B.C.) and maybe even earlier. These regular figures are often called the *Platonic solids* because they were described in detail by Plato (around 400 B.C.).

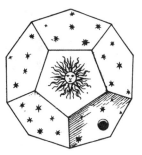

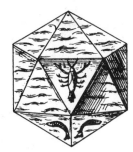

From Johannes Kepler, *Harmonices Mundi.*

The ancient Greeks thought that the world was composed of fou elements—fire, water, earth, and air—and they gave mystical signifi cance to the Platonic solids. The tetrahedron, with its minimum volum per surface area, represented fire, and the icosahedron, with it maximum volume per surface area, represented water. The stable cub represented the solid earth, while the more mobile octahedron repre sented the air. The twelve faces of the dodecahedron corresponded t the twelve signs of the zodiac, and thus this figure represented the entir universe.

In the late sixteenth century a German astronomer, Johannes Keple became intensely interested in the work that the Greeks had done wit the Platonic solids. As a scientist trying to unravel the secrets of th universe, Kepler wondered whether there was a connection between th mathematical fact that there were exactly five regular polyhedra and th astronomical fact (according to the knowledge at that time) that ther were exactly six planets (Mercury, Venus, Earth, Mars, Jupiter, an Saturn) orbiting the sun. He thought long and hard and developed thi ingenious explanation: the planets moved on imaginary spheres neste within a set of the five polyhedra. The figures were snugly nestled a follows:

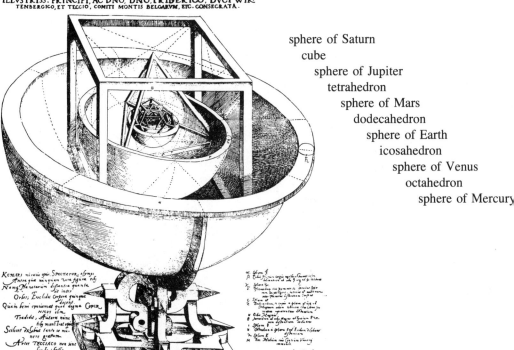

sphere of Saturn
cube
sphere of Jupiter
tetrahedron
sphere of Mars
dodecahedron
sphere of Earth
icosahedron
sphere of Venus
octahedron
sphere of Mercury

From Johannes Kepler, *Mysterium Cosmigraphicum.*

Kepler was so excited by this "discovery" that he tried to persuade his patron, the Duke of Württemberg, to finance the construction, in gold, of a model of the nested spheres and polyhedra. His plea was in vain, and in the end Kepler's beautiful theory also failed. Although his calculated interplanetary distances were very close to reality, they did not match exactly the spaces between the spheres separating the nested polyhedra (although the discrepancy had been minimized somewhat by making the spherical shells of different thicknesses). Furthermore, additional planets have been discovered (there are also at least Uranus, Neptune, and Pluto). And as Kepler himself later discovered, the planets move not in circular paths on the surface of a sphere but in *elliptical* paths about the sun. (See CONIC SECTIONS.)

POLYHEDRA IN NATURE

Naturally occurring polyhedra abound. For example, many different *mineral crystals* have been formed in the earth's crust. Cooling of the crust from very high temperatures has resulted in unique crystalline structures that are both beautiful and useful in classifying and identifying the minerals.

Reading clockwise, starting at far left:

Pyrite (fool's gold), pyritohedron form;

Pyrite, cube form;

Galena, cube form;

Orthoclase, prism and pinacoid forms;

Garnet, dodecahedron form;

Quartz, hexagonal prism with two rhombohedrons.

Center: Glauberite, prism and pinacoid forms.

Courtesy of William A. Bassett, Department of Geological Sciences, Cornell University.

Mineral crystals

Common table salt crystals have the shape of a cube. Chromite, iron, gold, and diamond occur in octahedral crystals. Quartz occurs in a variety of crystal forms, many of which are hexagonal prisms or pyramids. Many crystals are semi-regular polyhedra, such as galena

Radiolaria

From Ernst Haeckel, *Kunstformen der Natur.* Courtesy of the Fine Arts Library, Cornell University.

(lead), which occurs as truncated octahedra and cubes, or garnet, which appears as a rhombic dodecahedron.

Radiolaria are tiny sea animals whose skeletons occur in a variety of shapes resembling polyhedra.

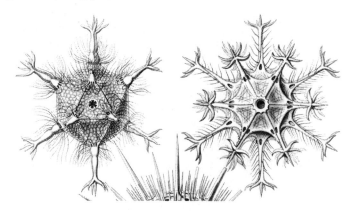

Polyhedra occur naturally in large-scale *geological formations*. The Devil's Post Pile in California is composed of tall columns of rock in the shapes of hexagonal and pentagonal prisms.

EXTENDING POLYHEDRA TO HIGHER DIMENSIONS

A three-dimensional cube (all edges equal) seems a natural extension of a two-dimensional square. From a cube, a natural extension to four-dimensional space is called a *tesseract* or *hypercube*. Mathematicians and others often want to consider a four-dimensional space. What does it look like? You can get a little idea by realizing that we often represent three-dimensional objects by two-dimensional drawings. In like fashion, perhaps you can get a three-dimensional ''picture'' of a four-dimensional object. In the case of the cube, notice that you can consider the three-dimensional cube as two two-dimensional squares, connected at the vertices by edges of the same length. Likewise, one way to consider the four-dimensional hypercube is as two three-dimensional cubes, connected at all corresponding vertices by edges of equal length. This only gives a very limited three-dimensional idea of a four-dimensional object, but it's a beginning.

References on four dimensions

George Gamow, *One Two Three . . . Infinity* (Viking Press, 1947; Mentor paperback), Ch. IV, ''The World of Four Dimensions.''

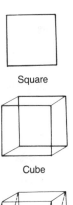

Square

Cube

Hypercube

Martin Gardner, ''Mathematical Games: Is it possible to visualize a four-dimensional figure?'' *Scientific American,* November 1966, pp. 138–143.

FOOD FOR FURTHER THOUGHT

The surface of a single three-dimensional polyhedron usually forms a *rigid* (not flexible) figure if every face is rigid. In fact, it was conjectured for millennia that all polyhedral surfaces with rigid faces were rigid. But in 1977 American topologist Robert Connelly constructed a counterexample. He found a polyhedral surface for which the faces are rigid but the surface is not! For details, including instructions for building a flexible polyhedron, see PROOFS.

Finally, an interesting characteristic of all polyhedra (providing they have no holes) is that the number V of vertices plus the number F of faces is always two more than the number E of edges: $V + F = E + 2$. For details, see TOPOLOGY.

Devil's Post Pile
Courtesy of National Park Service.

PROBABILITY

Probability of tossing heads = $\frac{1}{2}$

PROBABILITY: a RATIO expressing the chance or likelihood that a certain event will occur, given the number of possible outcomes of an experiment.

Example. When a coin is tossed, there are 2 possible outcomes—"heads" or "tails." With a fair coin, these two outcomes are equally likely. Only 1 of these outcomes is heads. Therefore, the probability of a fair coin's coming up heads in a single toss is 1 out of 2, or $\frac{1}{2}$.

Probability can be expressed as a common FRACTION, a DECIMAL fraction, or a PERCENT. For the probability of heads in a single toss of a fair coin,

$$P = \tfrac{1}{2} = 0.50 = 50\%.$$

The word "probable" is used in everyday language to mean "likely to happen." For example, suppose that someone asked you, "Which is more probable—that you will get heads in one toss of a coin or that you will get the queen of hearts in one draw from a deck of cards?" You would probably say that getting heads in a single toss is more probable. It is more likely to happen. And you would be right. But without mathematics, you would have difficulty showing exactly *how much* more probable the one event is than the other.

Probability of drawing queen of hearts = $\frac{1}{52}$

In mathematics a probability is expressed as a number that estimates how often an event will occur. For example, the probability of getting heads in a single toss of a fair coin is $\frac{1}{2}$. And the probability of getting the queen of hearts in a single draw from a full deck of 52 different cards is $\frac{1}{52}$. Once these probabilities have been expressed as numbers, it is easy to compare them:

$$\tfrac{1}{2} = 26 \times \tfrac{1}{52}.$$

Thus, the probability of getting heads in a single toss is 26 times as great as the probability of getting the queen of hearts in a single draw.

The probability of an event is always between 0 and 1. If an event is *certain* to happen, the probability of that event is *one*. For example, consider the probability that on a single toss of a die, you will get a number smaller than 10. There are six numbers on a die—1, 2, 3, 4, 5, and 6. All of these numbers are equally likely to occur, and all of them are smaller than 10. Thus, the probability of getting a number smaller than 10 is $\frac{6}{6} = 1$.

On the other hand, if an event is *impossible*, the probability of that event is *zero*. For example, the probability that on a single toss of a die you will get a number larger than 10 is $\frac{0}{6} = 0$.

For events that are neither certain nor impossible, the probability is somewhere between 0 and 1. The more likely an event is to happen, the closer the probability is to 1, and the less likely an event, the closer the probability is to 0.

However, an event may sometimes occur for which the stated probability is zero. In any experiment that has infinitely many possible outcomes, the probability of any single outcome is zero. For example, consider a spinner that will come to rest at some point on the rim of a circle. The probability that the spinner will stop at any given point P is zero, because there are infinitely many possible stopping points; nevertheless, each time the spinner is spun, it does in fact stop at some point. Thus, an event occurs for which the probability is zero.

Similarly, an event with a stated probability of 1 is not necessarily certain to happen in every repetition of an experiment. In the example of the spinner, the probability that the spinner will *not* come to rest on a given point P is 1. However, the spinner could come to rest on point P, in which case an outcome with a stated probability of 1 will not have occurred.

The probability of an event is not much good as a predictor of what will happen in a small number of cases. For example, although the probability of getting heads in one toss of a coin is $\frac{1}{2}$, this does not mean that if you toss a coin twice, you will get one heads and one tails. Nor does it mean that if you toss the coin 10 times, it will come up heads $\frac{1}{2}$ of 10, or 5, times. But it does mean that if you toss the coin a great number of times, it is more likely to come up heads half the time. The laws of probability predict only what will happen when a very large number of events is surveyed.

Probability of number smaller than 10 = 1

Probability of number greater than 10 = 0

The chances of you getting a 6 total from spinning the dice is 1 in 6, where as

Probability of spinning exactly 2.15000 = 0

the chances of not getting a 6 is 5/6.

TERMS USED IN PROBABILITY

Experiment: a procedure which has the same possible outcomes every time it is repeated but for which no single outcome is predictable.

Example.   Tossing a die is an experiment, because the only possible outcomes are for the die to show a 1, 2, 3, 4, 5, or 6 on its top face, but it is impossible to predict which face will be on top.

Sample Space: the set of all possible outcomes of an experiment.

Example.   The sample space for a single toss of two dice can be listed as ordered pairs. If you toss a black die and a white die, you can consider these pairs as listing first the number on top of the black die and second the number on top of the white die.

Event: a subset of a sample space.

Example.   In the sample space for tossing two dice, one event would be the subset in which the *sum* of the dice is 5:

$$(1, 4)   (2, 3)   (3, 2)   (4, 1).$$

These outcomes that make up this event are underlined in the sample space. You can see that the probability of this event is 4 out of 36 equally likely possible outcomes, which reduces to $\frac{1}{9}$.

Independent Events: two events such that the outcome of one does not affect the outcome of the other.

Examples.   A die is rolled twice. Consider the event of getting a 2 on the first roll and the event of getting a 3 on the second roll. The outcome of the first roll does not affect the outcome of the second roll. Therefore, these two events are independent.

On the other hand, if two dice are rolled, consider the event of rolling doubles—like (2, 2)—and the event of rolling an even sum—like (2, 4). Every double guarantees an even sum (although not all even sums are doubles). Therefore, these two events are *not* independent.

Mutually Exclusive Events: two events that cannot both occur at the same time.

Examples.   Two dice are tossed. What is the probability that the sum of the dice is less than five and greater than nine? These two events are mutually exclusive, because it is impossible for the sum to be both less than five *and* greater than nine. The probability of two mutually exclusive events occurring at the same time is 0.

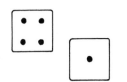

Probability of tossing a sum of
$5 = \frac{4}{36} = \frac{1}{9}$

On the other hand, it would be possible for the sum of the dice to be less than five *and* an even number:

$$(1, 1) \quad (1, 3) \quad (3, 1) \quad (2, 2)$$

These two events are *not* mutually exclusive.

Conditional Probability: the probability that an event B will occur, *given* the condition that an event A has already occurred. The fact that event A has already occurred usually *reduces* the sample space for calculating the conditional probability of B.

Example.   From a bag containing five green balls and four yellow balls, two balls are drawn, one at a time. If the first ball is green, what is the probability that the second ball is also green?

In the beginning, there are 9 balls, and 5 of them are green. But the fact that 1 green ball has already been drawn reduces the sample space to 8 balls, of which only 4 are green.

Therefore, the probability that the second draw is also green is

$$\frac{4}{8} = \frac{1}{2} .$$

LAWS OF PROBABILITY

Probability of A

$$P(A) = \frac{\text{number of outcomes of event } A}{\text{number of possible outcomes}},$$

as long as all possible outcomes are *equally likely*.

Example.   When a die is rolled, what is the probability of rolling a 5 or a 6?

$$P(A) = \frac{2}{6} = \frac{1}{3} .$$

Probability that A Does Not Occur

$$P(\text{not } A) = 1 - P(A)$$

Example.   When a die is rolled, what is the probability of rolling a number less than or equal to 4? That is, what is the probability of *not* rolling a 5 or a 6, for which $P(A) = \frac{1}{3}$?

$$P(not\ A) = 1 - \frac{1}{3} = \frac{2}{3}$$

Probability of A or B

$$\boxed{P(A\ or\ B) = P(A) + P(B) - P(A\ and\ B)}$$

$$= P(A) + P(B) \text{ if } A \text{ and } B \text{ are}$$
mutually exclusive events.

Example. When one die is rolled, what is the probability of rolling a 2 *or* a 3?

$$P(A) = \frac{1}{6}\ ;\ P(B) = \frac{1}{6}\ ;$$

$P(A\ and\ B) = 0$, because events A and B are mutually exclusive;

$$P(A\ or\ B) = \frac{1}{6} + \frac{1}{6} = \frac{1}{3}.$$

The probability of one event *or* another generally *increases* the probability of a favorable outcome. A square divided into six equal rectangles illustrates why. The probability of rolling a 2 is represented by the area of rectangle number 2. The probability of rolling a 3 is represented by the area of rectangle number 3. And the probability of rolling a 2 or a 3 is represented by the combined area of rectangles 2 and 3.

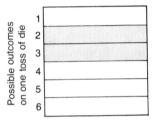

Possible outcomes on one toss of die

Probability of tossing
2 or 3 = $\frac{2}{6} = \frac{1}{3}$

Probability of A and B

$$\boxed{P(A\ and\ B) = P(A,\ given\ B)\ P(B)}$$

$$= P(A)\ P(B) \text{ if } A \text{ and } B$$
are *independent events*.

Example. When a die is rolled twice, what is the probability of getting a 2 on the first roll *and* a 3 on the second roll?
A and B are independent events, so $P\ (A\ and\ B) = P(A)\ P(B)$.

$$P(A) = \frac{1}{6}\ ;\ P(B) = \frac{1}{6}\ ;$$

$$P(A\ and\ B) = \frac{1}{6} \times \frac{1}{6} = \frac{1}{36}.$$

The probability of one event *and* another generally *decreases* the probability of a favorable outcome. To see why this is so, consider another square. The area of each horizontal rectangle represents the

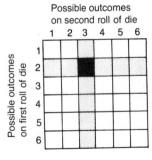

Possible outcomes
on second roll of die

Possible outcomes on first roll of die

Probability of tossing
first 2 then 3 = $\frac{1}{36}$

probability of a possible outcome on the first roll, and the area of each vertical rectangle represents the probability of a possible outcome on the second roll. The area where horizontal rectangle number 2 and vertical rectangle number 3 intersect represents the probability of getting a 2 on the first roll and a 3 on the second.

Conditional Probability of *A*, Given *B*

$$P(A, \textbf{given } B) = \frac{P(A \text{ and } B)}{P(B)}$$

where all these probabilities are calculated on the entire *original* sample space.

Example. From a bag containing five green balls and four yellow balls, two balls are drawn, one at a time. If the first ball is green, what is the probability that the second ball is also green?

$$P(A \text{ and } B) = \frac{5 \times 4}{9 \times 8} = \frac{20}{72}$$ (See PERMUTATIONS AND COMBINATIONS, or construct the sample space of the two draws: there are 72 outcomes possible.)

$$P(B) = \frac{5}{9}$$

$$P(A, \textbf{given } B) = \frac{\frac{20}{72}}{\frac{5}{9}} = \frac{1}{2}.$$

The reduced sample space explained earlier is an alternate method for conditional probability which is often easier to calculate.

ODDS, EXPECTATION, AND GAMES

Odds: the ratio of the probability of an event's happening to the probability of its not happening.

Example. When a die is tossed, the odds of its coming up 4 are one to five. There are six possible outcomes, and one of them is a 4. Therefore, the probability of getting 4 is $\frac{1}{6}$. Since there are five outcomes that will not be 4, the probability of not getting a 4 is $\frac{5}{6}$.

$$\text{The odds of getting a 4 are } \frac{\frac{1}{6}}{\frac{5}{6}} = \frac{1}{5}.$$

Note: The popular use of odds at a *race track* is exactly the *opposite* of mathematical odds. If the odds on a particular horse are 5 to 1, those are the odds that the horse *loses*.

$$\text{Its probability of losing is } \frac{5}{5 + 1} = \frac{5}{6}, \text{ and}$$

$$\text{its probability of winning is } \frac{1}{5 + 1} = \frac{1}{6}.$$

Mathematical Expectation or Expected Value: the product of the probability of an event and the value of that event. The value of an even might be in terms of money or in terms of points, as in a game.

Mathematical expectation applies only to experiments in which an outcome has a value. The mathematical expectation of the entire exper iment is the sum of the expected values for each possible outcome.

Example.   A mail-order company sends out a mailing with a gold seal. Each customer is told that if an order is placed, then the gold sea may be peeled off to see if the customer has won a prize. The space unde the seal may be blank, or it may read $2, $10, or $25. Suppose that the mailing is produced according to the following percentages:

> 80% are blank;
> 15% read $2;
> 4% read $10;
> 1% read $25.

Then the mathematical expectation of reward is

$$0.80 \times \$0 + 0.15 \times \$2 + 0.04 \times \$10 + 0.01 \times \$25 = \$0.95.$$

That is, the company could expect to pay an equivalent of 95¢ in prize money to every customer, although 80% of the customers would actu ally receive nothing at all, 15% would receive $2, 4% would receive $10, and 1% would receive $25. Nevertheless, this averages out to ar expected value of 95¢ per customer. If the mailing brings in orders tha net more than 95¢ per customer, the company gains.

Mathematical expectation is an important concept in *game theory—* the study of games of strategy. A *fair game* is defined as a game for which the *mathematical expectation is zero*.

Example.   Someone offers to pay 10¢ if a coin comes up heads and to take 10¢ if it comes up tails. If the coin is fair, the expected value for this player is

$$(0.10)(\tfrac{1}{2}) + (-0.10)(\tfrac{1}{2}) = 0$$

value probability value probability
of   of   of   of
heads   heads   tails   tails

Thus, the game is fair.

Game theory deals with far more than recreational games. Any situation involving strategy can be investigated with game theory, from social and economic problems to political power and military strategy. As the situations become more complex, the mathematics becomes more complex. The following references, listed roughly in order of increasing difficulty, are for the general but serious reader; each begins in an interesting and elementary way and proceeds to build up the complexity of games that can be analyzed.

References on game theory

Morton D. Davis, *Game Theory: A Nontechnical Introduction* (Basic Books, 1970).

J. D. Williams, *The Compleat Strategyst (being a primer on the theory of games of strategy)* (McGraw-Hill, 1966).

Anatol Rapoport, *Fights, Games, and Debates* (University of Michigan Press, 1960).

John McDonald, *The Game of Business* (Doubleday & Co.; Anchor paperback, 1977).

HISTORY AND APPLICATIONS OF PROBABILITY THEORY

Many of the examples in this article involve cards and dice. These tools of the professional gambler are perfect to illustrate the laws of probability, because if the cards or dice haven't been tampered with, the draw of a card or the cast of the die will depend solely upon chance.

But there is another reason why cards, dice, and coins have long been used as examples in probability. The mathematical study of probability originated with a mathematician's desire to improve his luck at dice. The great Italian mathematician Girolamo Cardano was also a great gambler. In the sixteenth century, he published a gambler's manual dealing with the various possible outcomes of casting two or three dice.

However, the men usually given credit for starting work on a systematic theory of probability are two seventeenth-century Frenchmen—Pierre Fermat and Blaise Pascal. They too began working on problems connected with games of chance. But Pascal, an intensely religious man, was eager to show that the theory of probability could be used for more moral purposes. To this end he used the idea of mathematical expectation to argue in favor of the godly life—an argument that has been known ever since as *"Pascal's Wager."*

The argument goes: If there is a heavenly reward for leading a religious life, surely its value is infinite. And if the value of the reward or prize is infinite, then your mathematical expectation is infinite no matter how small the probability that you will receive such a reward (because any fraction times infinity gives infinity as the product). Therefore, since your expectation is infinite, you should take a chance on the godly life.

Pascal need not have looked to eternity for applications of probability theory. Predictions based on probability can be made in any situation for which there is sufficient data to estimate the likelihood that an event will occur. Often this data is collected by observation of statistics. For example, consider the probability that an elderly person living in the United States can receive a flu shot this year. This probability could be expressed as the ratio:

$$\frac{\text{the number of doses of vaccine that can be supplied by laboratories}}{\text{the number of elderly people living in the U.S. this year}}$$

These fragile systems are under constant threat. And the situation could further deteriorate as searchers probe the ocean for oil. The fields that may soon be opened in the fertile fishing grounds of Georges Bank, writes Mrs. Simon, will have a 20-year life, during which there is a 91% chance of at least one major spill and near certainty that there will be more than 1,700 "nickel-and-dime" disasters.

Time, January 30, 1978, p. 84.

Today probability is widely used in making predictions and decisions in fields ranging from business to the physical sciences. Probability is used in forecasting the weather. It is used in assessing and reporting the dangers of various undertakings such as the construction of a nuclear energy plant. The insurance business depends heavily on probability—this and other applications of probability are illustrated under STATISTICS.

An advanced but important topic of probability theory is called *Markov chains,* developed at the turn of the twentieth century by Russian probabilist Andrey Andreyevich Markov. Markov chains describe a system in which future states are completely determined by the present state, regardless of how that present state arose. These chains have many applications in physical, biological, and social sciences. Calculations of the probabilities involved usually involve MATRICES, and are beyond the scope of this book. If you wish further information on an elementary level, see references.

PROBABILISTIC DETERMINATION OF π

Finally, an application of probability that is of special interest to mathematicians is its use in approximating the value of π—PI, the ratio of the circumference of a circle to its diameter.

In 1760, the French mathematician Comte de Buffon worked out his famous *Needle Problem:* parallel lines, a distance d apart, are drawn on a plane surface. A needle is dropped at random onto the ruled plane surface. The needle is of length n, with $n \leqslant d$. Buffon discovered that the probability P that the needle will fall across one of the ruled lines is given by the formula

$$P = \frac{2n}{\pi d}.$$

If Buffon's needle experiment is repeated a great number of times and the results recorded, the probability

$$P = \frac{\text{number of times needle touches a line}}{\text{number of times needle is dropped}}.$$

This gives an experimental value of P, which can be substituted into Buffon's formula along with the values of n and d, to compute an approximate value of π.

If $P = \dfrac{2n}{\pi d}$, then $\pi = \dfrac{2n}{Pd}$.

If $n = d$, the calculations are simplified, and $\pi = \dfrac{2}{P}$.

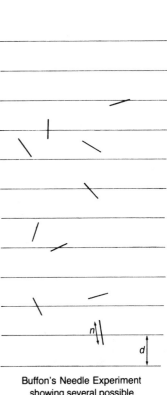

Buffon's Needle Experiment showing several possible positions of the needle

If you try this experiment, use only one needle so that there will be no interference from other needles. To obtain a good approximation of π, you must expect to drop the needle a great many times.

For more information on Buffon's formula and other occurrences of π in probability, see references.

REFERENCES

Howard F. Fehr, Lucas N. H. Bunt, and George Grossman, *An Introduction to Sets, Probability, and Hypothesis Testing* (D. C. Heath & Co., 1964); a good concise classroom text with examples from science, psychology, and opinion polls written for the senior year of high school or first year of college.

Warren Weaver, *Lady Luck* (Doubleday & Co., 1963; Anchor pa
perback); an engaging rather than technical discussion—a good blend
of problems and theory written for students.

Warren Weaver, "Probability," *Scientific American,* October 1950
reprinted with other articles on probability in *Mathematics in the
Modern World: Readings from Scientific American* (W. H. Freeman
& Co., 1968) and in *Mathematics: An Introduction to Its Spirit and
Use: Readings from Scientific American* (W. H. Freeman & Co.
1978).

References on Markov chains

Philip Davis and William G. Chinn, *3.1416 and All That* (Simon &
Schuster, 1969). Chapter 23 concerns the children's game of "Chute
and Ladders," a delightful elementary introduction to Markov
chains. The other chapters are different imaginative explorations into
the world of mathematics.

James Emile Mosimann, *Elementary Probability Theory for the Biolog
ical Sciences* (Appleton-Century-Crofts, 1968); serious information
on Markov chains, with applications.

*References on the occurrence of π in
probability*

George Gamow, *One Two Three . . . Infinity* (Viking Press, 1947; Men
tor paperback), pp. 210–213; a full explanation of how Buffon's
formula is derived for $n = d$.

Ross Honsberger, *Ingenuity in Mathematics* (Random House, 1970)
Essay One: "Probability and π," pp. 3–6; other surprising occur
rences of π in probability, with further references and exercises
discussed for the serious reader.

PROJECTION

PROJECTION: the mapping of a geometric figure onto a PLANE, producing a two-dimensional figure called the *image*.

The verb "project" means "throw forward." Mathematical projection is a systematic throwing forward of every point in a figure onto a plane called the *plane of projection*. This is accomplished by a bundle of straight lines called *projection rays,* each of which takes one point of the original figure into the corresponding point of the projected figure, or image. The word "projection" is used to refer to both the process and the image.

The illustration shows the projection of a figure *AB* in one plane onto another plane, where the projected image is *A'B'*.

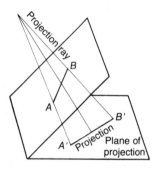

DIFFERENT TYPES OF PROJECTION

Different types of projection are possible, depending upon the source of the projection rays and upon the relationship of the rays to the plane of projection, as defined on the next page.

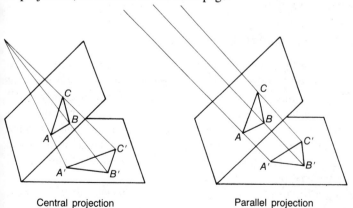

Central projection

Parallel projection

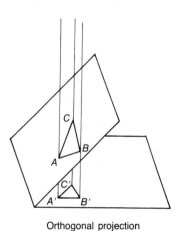

Orthogonal projection

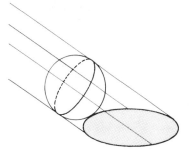

Central Projection: a projection with all rays coming from a fixed point called the *center of projection*.

Parallel Projection: a projection in which all projecting rays are parallel; that is, a central projection with the center of projection at infinity.

Orthogonal Projection: a parallel projection with all rays *perpendicular* to the plane of projection.

EXAMPLES OF PROJECTION

The outline of a *shadow* is the projection or image of an object formed by the light rays projected by the sun or some other light source. Every point in the object corresponds to exactly one point in the image. The projection rays throwing forward the outline of a shadow are the light rays that pass from the light source tangent to the object.

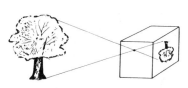

A pinhole *camera* projects an image of a scene onto light-sensitive film in the back of the camera. The projection rays are again light rays, which have been reflected by the objects in the scene. The pinhole is the center of projection, and each ray from the scene that passes through the opening locates the corresponding point of the image. Because the light rays travel in straight lines, the projected image is upside down, or inverted, as shown.

In most cameras there is a lens rather than a pinhole, but the lens serves the same purpose of focusing rays from points of the scene onto corresponding image points on the film.

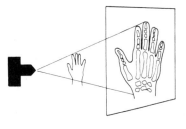

An example of projection that is related both to the shadow and to photography is the *X-ray*. In this case, however, the projection rays are not light rays, but much more powerful X-rays. X-rays are able to penetrate soft materials, such as clothing and flesh, and to project the outline of harder objects, such as bones, teeth, and pieces of metal, onto a sensitive X-ray film.

PROJECTION IN MAP MAKING

Since the world is round, a spherical globe provides the most accurate map of the earth. However, a globe is certainly not the most convenient map. A globe must be of tremendous size to represent clearly small areas on the surface of the earth. A globe can show an observer only one half of the earth at a time. And a globe cannot be folded and put in the glove compartment. So, ever since people discovered that the earth was round, they have tried to project this three-dimensional figure onto a two-dimensional piece of paper.

Making a flat map of the world is not easy, because distance, area, shape, and direction cannot all be preserved in a single projection. Any flattening of a curved surface requires that at least some of these qualities change. But map makers, or *cartographers*, can emphasize the preservation of different qualities, depending on the uses that will be made of different maps. Two of the most common map projections are conic and cylindrical.

Conic Projection

A map of half of the globe may be projected onto a cone sitting on top of the globe. The center of projection is the center of the sphere. The projection rays start from this center, pass through a point on the surface of the sphere, and project it onto a corresponding point on the cone. To make a flat map, the cone can be cut from base to apex (point) and flattened out into a plane.

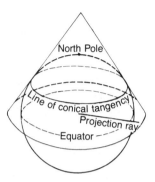

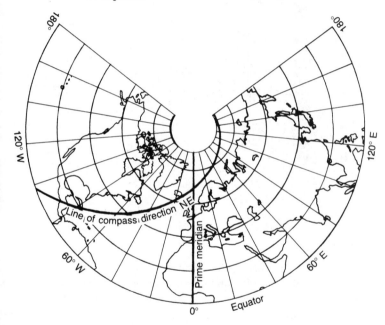

A simple conic projection like this is a good compromise on the qualities of *distance, area,* and *shape.* Although none of these qualities is preserved perfectly, none is excessively distorted. The conic projection is most accurate near the points where the cone is tangent to the globe, and it is most distorted at points farthest from the circle of tangency.

Direction, however, is *not* preserved in the usual sense by a conic projection. For example, an oblique compass direction such as "northeast" appears as a spiraling line on this projection.

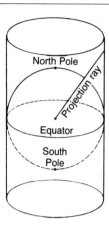

Cylindrical Projection

The global map may also be projected onto a cylinder wrapped around the globe at the Equator. In this case also, the center of projection is the center of the globe, and the projection rays pass from this center through the surface of the sphere to the corresponding points on the cylinder.

The cylindrical projection gives a good representation of the global map at the Equator. But distance, area, and shape become exceedingly distorted nearer the poles, because the meridians (vertical lines of longitude) do not converge as on a globe. In fact, the poles themselves are not even captured on a cylindrical projection.

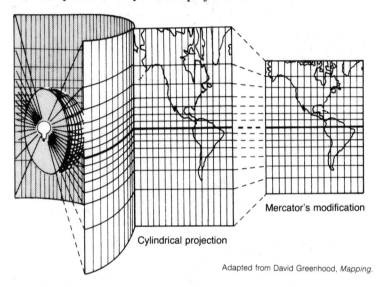

Cylindrical projection

Mercator's modification

Adapted from David Greenhood, *Mapping*.

In the sixteenth century, the Flemish cartographer Gerhard Kremer, known as Mercator, dealt with the distortion of *shape* by readjusting the vertical spacing of the parallels (horizontal lines of latitude) that resulted from the cylindrical projection of a global map. He adjusted the parallels precisely so that each region stretched horizontally in the cylindrical projection was stretched vertically in the *same ratio*. For instance, at 60° latitude the horizontal spacing on the cylindrical projection is double that on the globe, so Mercator made the vertical spacing between that latitude and the next just double the vertical spacing on the globe.

The effect of Mercator's readjustment of vertical spacing on the flattened cylindrical map is to make shapes look much more nearly as they appear on the globe, although distance and area remain ever more distorted at greater distances from the Equator. Although Canada appears twice as big as the first forty-eight United States (in contrast to its relative size on the conic projection or on the globe), shape is fairly well preserved in small regions. The distortions of distance and area are handled by different scales for different latitude. For example:

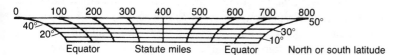

| 0 | 100 | 200 | 300 | 400 | 500 | 600 | 700 | 800 |

40° 20°   50°   30° 10°

Equator   Statute miles   Equator   North or south latitude

Something else is achieved by Mercator's modification—every *angle* on the globe is preserved, so it is sometimes called a *conformal projection*. Most important, this conformity means that *compass direction* is preserved. A northeast compass direction will cross every meridian at 45°, and on a Mercator map, a compass direction appears as a straight line. The adjusted vertical scale is such that a ship sailing directly northeast (or in any other straight course) will be following a straight line course on the map. The *Mercator Projection* provided exactly the sort of map mariners needed for navigation, and it became widely used.

Other Projections

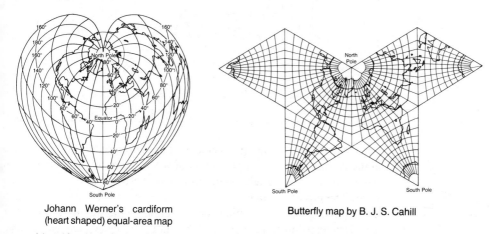

Johann Werner's cardiform (heart shaped) equal-area map

Butterfly map by B. J. S. Cahill

References on map projections

Martin Gardner, "Mathematical games: On map projections (with special reference to some inspired ones)," *Scientific American*, November 1975, pp. 120–125.

David Greenhood, *Mapping* (University of Chicago Press, 1964; available in paperback); a detailed, informative, superbly illustrated, and clearly written manual.

PROJECTION IN PAINTING AND VIEWING

Another need for projection of a three-dimensional scene onto a two-dimensional surface is in painting. The fifteenth-century Renaissance artists were the first to introduce *perspective* into their paintings, which accurately represented a scene as it would be seen by a viewer. For instance, objects in the foreground were larger than those of the same size in the background, and the paintings appeared to have depth. These techniques implied the importance of the individual who viewed the scene, and, in fact, emphasis on the individual was an important characteristic of the Renaissance.

One of the most famous examples of perspective in Renaissance art is Leonardo da Vinci's *The Last Supper*. Perspective is used to concentrate the viewer's gaze on the central figure, Christ, because the lines of the painting all follow the dotted rays toward a vanishing point behind his head. (A photograph of this painting appears on p. 589.)

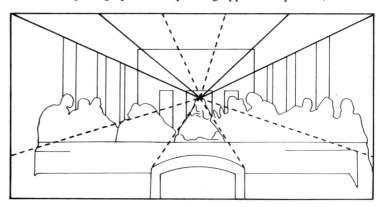

Perspective in a painting is achieved through projection. The image on the canvas represents a projection of the scene at which the artist is looking onto an imagined plane positioned between the eye and the scene. The projection rays in this case are light rays reflected from the scene, passing through the plane of projection on the way to the artist's eye. German painter and engraver Albrecht Dürer made many woodcuts showing the literal use of this process.

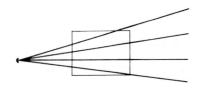

The size of any line in the image plane depends on the size of the line in the scene *and* on the distance of that portion of the scene from the eye. If two identical objects are placed so that one is twice as far from the eye as the other, the more distant object will appear half as big to the observer as the nearer. Hence, parallel railroad tracks, viewed head-on, appear to meet in the distance, as the ties appear to become smaller and smaller. To duplicate this perceptual phenomenon, a painter making use

Albrecht Durer, "Artist Drawing a Vase," about 1525

of perspective will represent more distant objects with smaller images than nearer objects of equal size.

In the theater, set designers often employ tricks of perspective to give the illusion of more space. For example, a narrowing wing appears to be a long street, and a narrowing floor pattern makes the stage seem much deeper, as shown below on the left.

Perspective can also be used to create illusions by applying the rules improperly. Impossible situations will result, as shown above by Hogarth.

On the left, Sebastiano Serlio, woodcut illustration of stage set from *De Architectura Libra Quinque*, Venice, 1569; on the right, William Hogarth, "Satire on False Perspective," engraving, 1754.

Reference on perspective

Morris Kline, *Mathematics in Western Culture* (Oxford University

Courtesy of The New York Public Library—Astor, Lenox and Tilden Foundations. Serlio from Print Collection: Art, Prints and Photographs Division; Hogarth from Rare Books and Manuscripts Division.

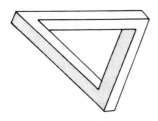

The Penrose Triangle, another impossible situation

Press, 1953; Galaxy paperback), "Painting and Perspective," pp. 127–143; "Science Born of Art: Projective Geometry," pp. 144–158; detail on perspective and projection, well illustrated with plates and drawings.

PROJECTION IN GEOMETRY

The first formal study of projection was undertaken in the fifteenth century by a number of artists interested in perspective. Many of the Renaissance painters like Leonardo da Vinci and Albrecht Dürer were highly versatile. Schooled in the sciences as well as the arts, they used their knowledge of geometry in depicting realistically the three-dimensional world on their two-dimensional canvases.

A whole new branch of geometry, *projective geometry,* grew out of these studies of perspective. Two Frenchmen, Gerard Desargues and Blaise Pascal, are credited with laying the mathematical foundations of projective geometry early in the seventeenth century.

Late in the eighteenth century, at the French École Polytechnique, Gaspard Monge led geometers in techniques of two-dimensional projections of three-dimensional objects. The "elevation" and "plan" drawings, which are used in all building trades today, were a new idea at that time. These studies were supported for a highly practical reason—they were extremely useful in the design of military fortifications.

In the early nineteenth century, an outstanding student at the École Polytechnique, Jean Victor Poncelet, made significant contributions in the field of projective geometry. Upon graduation from the École, Poncelet became a lieutenant in the Napoleonic army. He followed the Emperor on his disastrous Russian campaign and was taken prisoner during the retreat. In captivity, Poncelet recreated from memory all of the projective geometry that he had learned at the École Polytechnique and developed new theorems of his own. Poncelet's results were spectacular, which is particularly remarkable since they were done in isolation. When he returned to France and published his work, projective geometry was reborn.

Finally, in the late nineteenth century, projective geometry contributed to another branch of mathematics, TOPOLOGY, which was developed to deal with the properties of figures that remain unchanged when the figures are *distorted.*

Projective Geometry: the study of the properties of geometric figures that are unchanged by a *central projection.*

Projective geometry is very different from Euclidean GEOMETRY, where properties like length, angle, and area are measured and compared. In projective geometry, length, shape, ANGLES, AREA, SIMILARITY, and CONGRUENCE are *not preserved* under projection. However, many other properties *are* preserved.

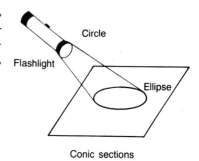

Examples of Properties Preserved under Projection

- Straight lines are projected into straight lines.
- CONIC SECTIONS are projected into conic sections, although not necessarily the same ones. For example, here a circle is projected into an ellipse.
- Length is not preserved, but a complicated *cross ratio* made by any four points on a line *is* preserved under projection.

Conic sections

For *any* points A, B, C, D on a line, with projected images A', B', C', D', then

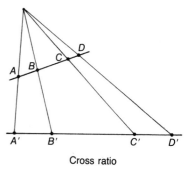

$$\text{Cross ratio} = \dfrac{\dfrac{AC}{BC}}{\dfrac{AD}{BD}} = \dfrac{\dfrac{A'C'}{B'C'}}{\dfrac{A'D'}{B'D'}}$$

Cross ratio

Cross ratio was one of Poncelet's ideas. Another was *duality* concerning POINTS and LINES. Duality means that in any statement about projection, the word "point" can be replaced by "line," and "line" by "point," throughout the statement, and the resulting statement will also be true.

Examples of Duality

- Two points determine a line.
  and
  Two lines determine a point.

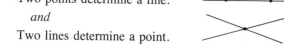

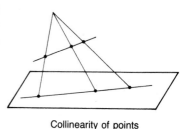

Collinearity of points

(In modern projective geometry, each pair of lines in a plane intersects in a unique point. See GEOMETRY.)

- The collinearity (lying on the same line) of points is preserved under projection.
  and
  The concurrence ("lying on" the same point) of lines is preserved under projection.

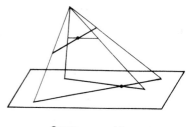

Concurrence of lines

The duality of projective geometry is one of the most beautiful principles of mathematics. Surprisingly, it relates many phenomena. And it saves an enormous amount of work, because any theorem that is proved about points and lines will have a dual theorem, complete with a dual proof, that is obtained simply by interchanging the words "line" and "point" throughout.

REFERENCES

Reference on projective geometry

Morris Kline, "Projective Geometry," *Scientific American,* January 1955; reprinted in *Mathematics in the Modern World: Readings from Scientific American* (W. H. Freeman & Co., 1968) and in *Mathematics: An Introduction to Its Spirit and Use: Readings from Scientific American* (W. H. Freeman & Co., 1978); a superb treatment, well illustrated, from Renaissance artists' study of perspective through the historical development of many interesting mathematical results.

Biographical references

Eric T. Bell, *Men of Mathematics* (Simon & Schuster, 1937; Fireside paperback); Pascal, Desargues, Monge, and Poncelet.

Julian Lowell Coolidge, *The Mathematics of Great Amateurs* (Oxford University Press, 1949; Dover, 1963); da Vinci and Dürer.

PROOFS

PROOF: a demonstration that one statement follows from another by a sequence of purely logical steps.

Different disciplines have different methods of proving that a statement is true. Mystics, for example, use divine revelation or sudden insight as a proof of some truth. Physicists, on the other hand, use the results of physical experiments. If the results of an experiment uphold a certain theory each time the experiment is repeated, then these results are accepted as proof of the theory. Mathematics, however, is an exact science of *ideas* rather than happenings or experiments. And in mathematics, proof is the means by which mathematical ideas are shown to be true or false.

A mathematical proof is a sequence of valid DEDUCTIONS. Proving something mathematically involves finding a proper sequence of deductions that will lead from a given statement, called a *premise* or *hypothesis,* to a final statement, called a *conclusion.*

Example. If you are *given,* in GEOMETRY, the line postulate,

> "For every two points there is exactly
> one line that contains both points,"

then you can *prove* the statement,

> "If two different lines intersect, their
> intersection contains only one point."

Proof: If two different lines intersected at two different points, *P* and *Q,* then there would be two lines containing *P* and *Q.* The line postulate tells us this would never happen.*

*From Edwin E. Moise and Floyd L. Downs, Jr., *Geometry* (Addison-Wesley, 1971), pp. 62–63.

The raw materials permitted in a mathematical proof include *assumptions* and *previously proven statements*. The assumptions (DEFINITIONS, axioms, postulates) are the essential foundation of any MATHEMATICAL SYSTEM.

A proof might also be defined as "an argument that convinces." A valid proof will have to convince even the most critical reader. Can you find the error in the following, which is *not* a valid proof?

Example.   Prove that $1 = 0$.

Proof: Assume that $x = 0$. Then

$x = 0$	assumption
$x (x - 1) = 0$	multiplication of both sides by $(x - 1)$
$(x - 1) = 0$	division of both sides by x
$x = 1$	addition of 1 to both sides
$0 = 1$	substitution, from original assumption, $x = 0$.

This argument fails in only one spot—all the other steps are valid. The error is in the step where both sides of the equation are divided by x; the division operation is valid only if x is *not zero*. But here, since $x = 0$, the division operation is not valid. (See ZERO.)

This example illustrates that construction of a valid proof requires care and precision. It is all too easy to neglect some crucial detail. A mathematician must consider all the consequences of every step.

THE ROLE OF PICTURES OR EXAMPLES
IN PROOFS

A particular picture or example alone never *proves* that a general statement is *true*. For instance, consider

$$\sqrt{a^2 + b^2} \overset{?}{=} a + b.$$

The question is whether this statement is true of all values of a and b. You might try substituting $a = 1$ and $b = 0$, which gives

$$\sqrt{1^2 + 0^2} \overset{?}{=} 1 + 0,$$

a statement that is indeed true: $\sqrt{1} = 1$. But this example proves only that the original question is true *if $a = 1$ and $b = 0$*. It also suggests that the statement might be true in general. But it does not *prove* anything about the statement with other values of a and b. If, for instance, you try substituting $a = 1$ and $b = 1$, you will get

$$\sqrt{1^2 + 1^2} \stackrel{?}{=} 1 + 1$$

which is false: $\sqrt{2} \neq 2$. This is a *counterexample* to the original hypothesis; it is an example that proves that the original statement is not always true.

Thus, although an example alone never proves that a general statement is true, a counterexample *does* prove that a general statement is *false*. In mathematical LOGIC a statement is either true or false—there is no middle ground.

In summary, drawing pictures and looking at examples may be helpful in deciding whether a statement is true or false. If you can find a counterexample, you have definitely proven the statement false. If your examples seem to confirm the statement in question, you may well be on the right track, but you will have to look to other means to *prove* that the statement is true. For another illustration, see INDUCTION.

Is this a true statement?

"A quadrilateral with all sides equal is a square."

☐ An example that supports statement.

▱ A counterexample that shows statement is false.

METHODS OF PROOF

Valid methods of proof include direct reasoning, indirect reasoning (also called proof by contradiction, or *reductio ad absurdum*), and mathematical induction. For details and examples, see DEDUCTION and INDUCTION.

MATHEMATICAL USES OF PROOF

The power of mathematical proofs can be seen when they demonstrate the truth of statements that are not obviously true. The following are examples of such statements:

- For any three-dimensional polyhedron without holes, the sum of the number of vertices plus the number of faces equals the number of edges plus two. (See TOPOLOGY.)
- For any ratio of two integers, the decimal expansion either terminates or repeats. (See DECIMALS.)
- The square root of two is irrational. (See RATIONAL AND IRRATIONAL NUMBERS.)
- The set of real numbers is so numerous that it cannot be counted. (See REAL NUMBERS.)

On the other hand, mathematicians also prove statements that seem obvious, just to be sure. In fact, occasionally a statement that seems obviously true turns out to be false. Here is a case in point:

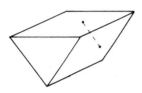

Convex polyhedron—
every line between points on
the surface lies entirely inside

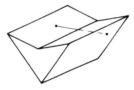

Nonconvex polyhedron—
some lines between points on
the surface pass outside

Rigidity of Polyhedra

For two thousand years, from the time of Euclid, it had been thought that the surface of a POLYHEDRON with rigid faces must be *rigid*, or not flexible.

A good way to consider rigidity is to first look at something that is *not* rigid. A polyhedral *framework* of edges alone may be *flexible*, or not rigid. For example, consider a framework of rigid edges for a rectangular solid. If the corners are hinged, this framework can be flexed, or skewed, into a different shape without changing the length of any of the edges in the process. But when a framework is flexed, some of the *faces* may change shape, as the ends of the rectangular solid illustrated. So, what happens if the framework is given *rigid faces* that do not change in shape or size? A rectangular box cannot flex at all if the faces are rigid. A natural *conjecture*, or guess, is that any polyhedral surface with rigid faces will be entirely rigid.

However, a proof for this conjecture was very hard to find. In 1813, French mathematician A.-L. Cauchy proved that any *convex* polyhedron is rigid. ("Convex" means having no dents or dimples. On a convex polyhedron, every line from one point of the polyhedron to another point of the polyhedron will lie entirely inside the polyhedron.)

But the more general question of rigidity for *any* polyhedron with rigid faces remained unproved until 1977, when an American topologist, Robert Connelly, constructed a *counterexample*. Connelly has found a polyhedron, not convex, with rigid faces, that is *flexible*. Always, even while flexing, the faces remain rigid.

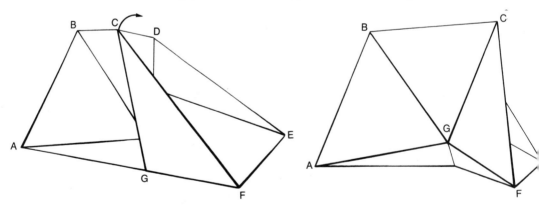

Flexible polyhedron in two different flexed positions
Illustration by Inez Wolins.

Connelly's flexible polyhedron is a "triangulated sphere" with a "crinkle." All the faces are TRIANGLES, which are always rigid, and they enclose a single volume, like a sphere. The crinkle is constructed in such a way that it can be wiggled in or out without changing the shape o the faces, but the shape of the crinkle, and hence the shape of the polyhedron, *is* changed by this flexing.

Connelly's counterexample has finally *proved* that the "obvious," partly proven, experimentally verified, centuries-old conjecture was false.

You might like to construct your own model of a flexible polyhedron. A later version by Klaus Steffen is easy to build, following this pattern. The pattern should be considerably enlarged on rather stiff lightweight cardboard—a piece of posterboard 21 inches × 14 inches will do if you make all the indicated measurements in inches. Deeply score the fold lines with a sharp instrument—on the face for lines marked as mountain folds and on the reverse for lines marked as valley folds. Make the folds and then join the seams edge to edge with masking tape so they can flex. The result will be a strange object somewhat nested in itself.

If you grab your model at the ★'s, you will be able to flex it quite a bit, with all the edges and faces remaining rigid. The amount of possible flexing is not great, but you will see that it is definite. The model indeed is a polyhedron that is not rigid, a polyhedron that shows the rigidity conjecture is false. See references, Klarner, for further details of Connelly's achievement and construction of models as explained for the amateur.

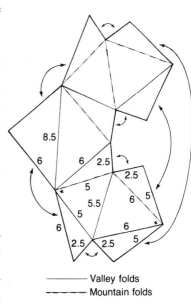

——————— Valley folds
— — — — — Mountain folds

Pattern for making a flexible polyhedron.

REFERENCES

Martin Gardner, "Mathematical Games: Geometric fallacies: hidden errors pave the road to absurd conclusions," *Scientific American,* April 1971; reprinted in *Mathematics: An Introduction to Its Spirit and Use* (W. H. Freeman & Co., 1978).

David A. Klarner, editor, *The Mathematical Gardner* (Prindle, Weber, & Schmidt, 1981), "Flexing Surfaces," pp. 79–89; details of Robert Connelly's flexible polyhedron counterexample to the rigidity conjecture. This book is a collection of thirty fascinating articles in tribute to Martin Gardner, who has delighted and inspired so many readers.

"Proof" was the theme of the 1978 Christmas Lectures by British mathematician Christopher Zeeman for the Royal Institution in London. This series of six popular lectures was created for public television; they will also be printed in book form by the BBC.

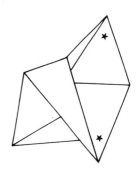

Examples of mathematical proofs in this book, in addition to those already listed, are given under DEDUCTION, mathematical INDUCTION, PYTHAGOREAN THEOREM, exact value of the GOLDEN SECTION, VOLUME of a pyramid, and TOPOLOGY (the seven bridges of Konigsberg and the four-color problem).

See also LOGIC, MATHEMATICAL SYSTEMS.

PROPERTIES
OF EQUALITY

PROPERTIES OF EQUALITY: the properties of *reflexivity, symmetry,* and *transitivity*. Each of these properties occurs (or does not occur) in a *binary relation*.

Binary relation: an ordered pairing of the elements of a single set. A RELATION is an ordered pairing of the elements from one set with the elements of another. A binary relation is a particular relation in which the first and second sets are the same set.

Examples.

Set	Binary relation	Possible pairings
$\{3, 4, 5\}$	$>$ ("is greater than")	$5 > 4$ $5 > 3$ $4 > 3$
mother father Carol Sue Tom	"is a sister of"	Carol is a sister of Sue Sue is a sister of Carol Carol is a sister of Tom Sue is a sister of Tom

A *mathematical sentence* states a binary relation between two quantities. Some of the relations given in mathematical sentences are the following:

$=$ is equal to

$\neq$ is not equal to

$>$ is greater than

$\geq$ is greater than or equal to

$<$ is less than

$\leq$ is less than or equal to

Notation: There is a general notation, *R,* for a relation which can include any of these relations. The general notation is useful in statements about more than one relation.

If *a* and *b* are two elements of a set, and *R* is a specified relation, then

> *a R b* means "*a* is related to *b* in the specified way";
>
> *a R̸ b* means "*a* is *not* related to *b* in the specified way."

Example.   *R* = "is taller than"

$$h = \text{Hank} \qquad d = \text{Dave}$$

> *h R d* says in symbols, "Hank is taller than Dave."
>
> *d R̸ h* says in symbols, "Dave is *not* taller than Hank."

PROPERTIES A BINARY RELATION MAY HAVE

Reflexive Property

A relation, *R,* is *reflexive* if *a R a* is true for any *a.*

Examples.

	Reflexivity
	a R a or *a* = *a.*

Set	Relation	Reflexive because
{1, 2, 3, 4, ...}	=	any number in the set is equal to itself.
{all living people}	"is as tall as"	anyone is as tall as herself.

Set	Relation	Not reflexive because
{1, 2, 3, 4, ...}	>	no number is greater than itself.
all possible straight lines	⊥ ("is perpendicular to")	no line is perpendicular to itself.

Symmetric Property

A relation, *R,* is *symmetric* if whenever *a R b* is true, *b R a* is also true.

Symmetry
If *a R b,* then *b R a.*
or
If *a* = *b,* then *b* = *a.*

Examples.

Set	Relation	Symmetric because
$\{x, y, z\}$	$\neq$	if $x \neq y$, then $y \neq x$.
{Kent, Nell, Ted}	"is a cousin of"	if Nell is a cousin of Ted, then Ted is cousin of Nell.

Set	Relation	Not symmetric because
$\{a, b, c\}$	$<$	if $a < b$, then $b \not< a$.
{Tim, Bob}	"is the uncle of"	if Bob is the uncle of Tim, then Tim is not the uncle of Bob.

Transitive Property

A relation, R, is *transitive* if when $a\,R\,b$ is true and $b\,R\,c$ is true then $a\,R\,c$ is also true.

<table>
<tr><td>

Transitivity

If $a\,R\,b$ and $b\,R\,c$,
then $a\,R\,c$.
If $a = b$ and $b = c$,
then $a = c$.

</td></tr>
</table>

Examples.

Set	Relation	Transitive because
	$\parallel$ ("is parallel to")	if $AB \parallel CD$ and $CD \parallel RS$, then $AB \parallel RS$.
{Todd, Josh, Nate}	"is older than"	if Todd is older than Josh and Josh is older than Nate, then Todd is older than Nate.

Set	Relation	Not transitive because
	$\perp$ ("is perpendicular to")	$AB \perp CD$ and $CD \perp LM$, but $AB \not\perp LM$.
{Mary, John, Jane}	"is in love with"	If Mary is in love with John and John is in love with Jane, then Mary might not be in love with Jane.

A binary relation may possess all three of the properties. It may possess only one or two or it may possess none of them.

Examples.

Relation	Properties		
	Reflexive	Symmetric	Transitive
= ("is equal to")	x	x	x
≠ ("is not equal to")		x	
> ("is greater than")			x
"is divisible by"	x		x
"is the mother of"			

EQUIVALENCE RELATION

A relation R is an equivalence relation if it possesses all three of the properties, *reflexivity*, *symmetry*, and *transitivity*.

Example.

Set	Relation	Equivalence relation because
{ ⃝ ○ ○ } A B C	~ ("is similar to")	$A \sim A$ (reflexive); if $A \sim B$, then $B \sim A$ (symmetric); if $A \sim B$ and $B \sim C$, then $A \sim C$ (transitive).

EQUIVALENCE CLASSES

Any two elements of a set that are related to each other by an equivalence relation are said to be *equivalent*. And, in a set, all the elements equivalent to a given element are said to form an *equivalence class*.

An equivalence relation divides a set into equivalence classes. Every element in a set will be in *exactly one* equivalence class with respect to a given relation. For example, every integer when divided by three must have some remainder, though that remainder may be zero. The possible remainders are zero, one, and two. And no integer when divided by three can have more than one remainder.

Examples.

Set	Equivalence relation	Equivalence classes
Flakies @ 79¢ a lb Popsies @ 79¢ a lb Crumbies @ 89¢ a lb Chewies @ 89¢ a lb Soggies @ 95¢ a lb	"costs the same as"	{Flakies, Popsies} all cost the same as Flakies {Crumbies, Chewies} all cost the same as Crumbies {Soggies} all cost the same as Soggies.

Set	Equivalence relation	Equivalence classes
the integers from 1 to 10	"when divided by 3 has the same remainder as"	{1, 4, 7, 10} all have a remainder of one. {2, 5, 8} all have a remainder of two. {3, 6, 9} all have a remainder of zero.

For a discussion of equivalent fractions, see FRACTIONS. For equivalent ratios, see RATIOS.

The properties of equality are important assumptions in a MATHEMATICAL SYSTEM.

PROPORTIONS

PROPORTION: a mathematical sentence that states that two RATIOS are equal.

Examples. $\dfrac{3}{6} = \dfrac{5}{10}$

$\dfrac{2}{5} = \dfrac{6}{15}$

$\dfrac{3}{21} = \dfrac{1}{7}$

The components in a proportion are referred to as:

$$\frac{\text{first term}}{\text{second term}} = \frac{\text{third term}}{\text{fourth term}}$$

Terms: the four numbers related in a proportion.

Means: the second and third terms in a proportion.

Extremes: the first and fourth terms in a proportion.

Mean Proportional: if the means are equal, this expression is used to refer to their relationship to the extremes. In the proportion

$$\frac{4}{6} = \frac{6}{9}$$

6 is the mean proportional to 4 and 9.

WAYS OF WRITING PROPORTIONS

The above examples of proportions are all written in FRACTION form. Another way of writing

$$\frac{3}{6} = \frac{5}{10} \quad \text{is} \quad 3 : 6 :: 5 : 10.$$

This is read "Three is to six as five is to ten." The fractional form of writing proportions is generally preferred because it is more suitable for

457

$$3 : 6 :: 5 : 10$$

means

extremes

solving equations. However, it is from the other way of writing proportions that we get the terms *means* and *extremes*. In the older linear form, the *means* were in the middle of the proportion and the *extremes* were on the outside.

MEANS-EXTREMES PRODUCT PROPERTY

In any true proportion, the product of the means equals the product of the extremes. In the proportion

$$\frac{3}{6} = \frac{5}{10}$$

the means are 6 and 5, and the extremes are 3 and 10.

$$\frac{3}{6} \times \frac{5}{10}$$

$$6 \times 5 = 3 \times 10$$

$$30 = 30$$

Since a proportion is a mathematical sentence, it may be true, it may be false, or it may be neither true nor false. (See EQUATIONS.) You can use the means-extremes product property to determine if a proportion is true or false.

True	*False*
$\frac{4}{8} \overset{?}{=} \frac{6}{12}$	$\frac{1}{2} \overset{?}{=} \frac{5}{14}$
$8 \times 6 = 4 \times 12$	$2 \times 5 \neq 1 \times 14$
$48 = 48$	$10 \neq 14$

You can also use the means-extremes product property to find the missing term that makes a proportion true.

$$\frac{2}{a} \times \frac{6}{12}$$

$$a \times 6 = 2 \times 12$$

$$6a = 24$$

$$a = 4$$

APPLICATIONS

Solving a proportion for a missing term is a common procedure. For example, a druggist making up a 5% solution of boric acid knows that the ratio of boric acid to water must be 5 parts acid to 95 parts water, or $\frac{5}{95}$, which equals $\frac{1}{19}$. If the druggist wishes to make up a solution from 3 ounces of acid, he solves the following proportion to find how many ounces of water to use:

Let w = number of ounces of water.

$$\frac{1}{19} = \frac{3}{w}$$

$$19 \times 3 = 1 \times w$$

$$57 = w$$

Solving for the missing term tells you that if 3 ounces of acid are used, 57 ounces of water must be used.

Another common use of proportion is in determining how many representatives a certain group or district may have in the government. If the number of representatives a group may have depends on the size of the group, then the representation is said to be *proportional representation*. An example is the representation in the U.S. House of Representatives.

The number of U.S. Representatives allotted to a given state, such as Arkansas, is determined by setting up a proportion:

$$\frac{\text{population of Arkansas}}{\text{population of U.S.}} = \frac{\text{number of Representatives from Arkansas}}{\text{number of members of U.S. House of Representatives}}$$

The number of members of the House of Representatives is fixed at 435. If the population of the United States is 200,000,000 and the population of Arkansas is 2,000,000, then we can set up the following proportion and solve for the missing term:

Let A = the number of representatives from Arkansas.

$$\frac{2,000,000}{200,000,000} = \frac{A}{435}$$

$$200,000,000 \times A = 2,000,000 \times 435$$

$$A = \frac{2,000,000 \times 435}{200,000,000}$$

$$A = 4.35$$

Thus, Arkansas would be entitled to at least 4 representatives.

Another important application of proportion occurs in indirect measurement. See SIMILARITY.

For direct and inverse proportion and for proportional variation, see VARIATION.

For Divine Proportion, see GOLDEN SECTION.

PYTHAGOREAN THEOREM

PYTHAGOREAN THEOREM: the statement that in any *right* TRIANGLE, the square of the length of the hypotenuse is equal to the sum of the squares of the lengths of the legs. This is sometimes called the *Right Triangle Principle*.

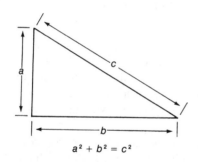

$$a^2 + b^2 = c^2$$

The most famous example of the Pythagorean Theorem is the 3-4-5 right triangle. In this diagram you can count the unit squares making up the squares on each of the sides of the triangle and confirm that

$$3^2 + 4^2 = 5^2$$
$$9 + 16 = 25.$$

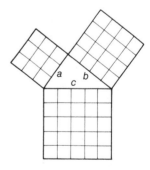

However, a *theorem* is a statement that has been proved. The example shows only that $a^2 + b^2 = c^2$ in a 3-4-5 right triangle.

The general theorem for any right triangle is named after the great Greek mathematician Pythagoras, who lived roughly 580–500 B.C. Certainly many examples of this theorem were known and used by the Babylonians a good thousand years earlier. At least by 600 B.C., before Pythagoras was born, the theorem was stated with details of construction in an ancient Hindu handbook for temple builders, the *Sulbasutram*, by Baudhayana. In the ancient Chinese *Chou Pei Suan Ching*,

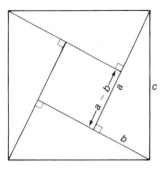

dating from approximately the same era as Pythagoras, there is a diagram indicating that perhaps the theorem was known there as well. But Pythagoras was popularly credited with first demonstrating the truth of this theorem.

Many people have written different PROOFS for the Pythagorean Theorem. One of the simplest comes from this diagram, attributed to Bhaskara, a Hindu mathematician of the twelfth century, who accompanied it with the single word "Behold!"

$$\begin{array}{ccccc} \text{area of} & = & \text{area of} & + & \text{area of} \\ \text{large square} & & \text{small square} & & \text{four triangles} \end{array}$$

$$c^2 = (a - b)^2 + 4\left(\tfrac{1}{2}ab\right)$$
$$= a^2 - 2ab + b^2 + 2ab$$
$$= a^2 + b^2.$$

CONVERSE OF THE PYTHAGOREAN THEOREM

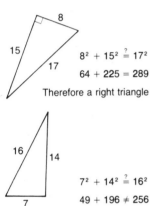

$8^2 + 15^2 \overset{?}{=} 17^2$

$64 + 225 = 289$

Therefore a right triangle

$7^2 + 14^2 \overset{?}{=} 16^2$

$49 + 196 \neq 256$

Therefore not a right triangle

The *converse* of a theorem reverses what is known and what is to be proved. For example, if a theorem states, "If A is true, then B is true," the converse of that theorem states, "If B is true, then A is true." The converse of a theorem may or may not be true.

The converse of the Pythagorean Theorem may be stated,

"If the sum of the squares of the lengths of two sides of a triangle is equal to the square of the length of the third side, then the triangle is a right triangle."

This converse theorem is also true, and can be used to find out whether a given triangle is a right triangle.

SOME APPLICATIONS OF THE PYTHAGOREAN THEOREM

• Find the altitude of the equilateral triangle with side equal to 2.

$$1^2 + x^2 = 2^2$$
$$1 + x^2 = 4$$
$$x^2 = 3$$
$$x = \sqrt{3}$$
$$x \doteq 1.732, \text{ approximately}$$

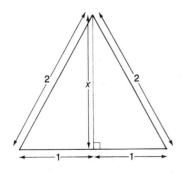

(For an explanation of $\sqrt{}$, or square root, see ARITHMETIC OPER-ATIONS.)

- A man drives 9 miles due north, 5 miles due east, and 3 miles due north. How far is he from his starting point? In the diagram, the unknown distance is A to D. The man drives from A to B to C to D. Line DC has been extended, and line AE drawn perpendicular to it.

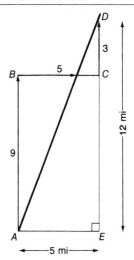

$$AD^2 = AE^2 + ED^2$$
$$= 5^2 + 12^2$$
$$= 25 + 144 = 169$$
$$AD = 13 \text{ miles}$$

- The Pythagorean theorem is the basis of the formula for *distance* between any two points in a COORDINATE SYSTEM:

$$|AB| = \text{distance between point } A \text{ and point } B$$
$$= \sqrt{(x_b - x_a)^2 + (y_b - y_a)^2}$$

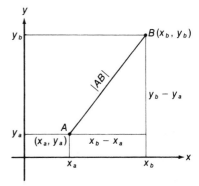

Examples. If $A = (1, 2)$
$$B = (3, 5)$$
$$C = (-2, 3)$$

then

$$|AB| = \sqrt{(3 - 1)^2 + (5 - 2)^2}$$
$$= \sqrt{2^2 + 3^2}$$
$$= \sqrt{13}, \text{ and}$$

$$|AC| = \sqrt{(-2 - 1)^2 + (3 - 2)^2}$$
$$= \sqrt{(-3)^2 + 1^2}$$
$$= \sqrt{10}.$$

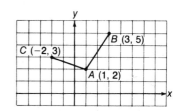

THE PYTHAGOREAN THEOREM AND NUMBER THEORY

Pythagorean Triples

Pythagorean triples are any set of three integers a, b, c that satisfy the equation $a^2 + b^2 = c^2$. To find some of the different combinations of numbers, you can do *either* of the following:

- Choose any two positive integers. Represent them by m and n, with m greater than n. Then a Pythagorean triple will be given by

$$a = m^2 - n^2 \qquad b = 2mn \qquad c = m^2 + n^2$$

Example. $m = 6;\ n = 3$
$$a = m^2 - n^2 = 6^2 - 3^2 = \enclose{circle}{27}$$
$$b = 2mn = 2 \times 6 \times 3 = \enclose{circle}{36}$$
$$c = m^2 + n^2 = 6^2 + 3^2 = \enclose{circle}{45}$$
$$Check:\ 27^2 + 36^2 \overset{?}{=} 45^2$$
$$729 + 1296 \overset{?}{=} 2025$$
$$2025 = 2025$$

- Choose any odd positive integer and represent it by r. Then a Pythagorean triple will be given by

$$a = r \qquad b = \tfrac{1}{2}(r^2 - 1) \qquad c = \tfrac{1}{2}(r^2 + 1)$$

Example.   Choose $r = 9$
$$a = r = \enclose{circle}{9}$$
$$b = \tfrac{1}{2}(r^2 - 1) = \tfrac{1}{2}(9^2 - 1) = \enclose{circle}{40}$$
$$c = \tfrac{1}{2}(r^2 + 1) = \tfrac{1}{2}(9^2 + 1) = \enclose{circle}{41}$$
$$Check:\ 9^2 + 40^2 \overset{?}{=} 40^2$$
$$81 + 1600 \overset{?}{=} 1681$$
$$1681 = 1681.$$

Fermat's Last Theorem

The relationship expressed by $a^2 + b^2 = c^2$ and its solutions (the sets of three integers a, b, c) led to the question of whether the equation could be solved if the EXPONENT were higher than 2. For example, could you find sets of integers a, b, c such that $a^3 + b^3 = c^3$, or $a^4 + b^4 = c^4$? In general terms, this equation would be $a^n + b^n = c^n$.

Pierre de Fermat was a famous French mathematician of the early seventeenth century. He left a tantalizing statement scribbled on the page of a book that this general equation, $a^n + b^n = c^n$, has *no* solution in positive integers for n greater than 2, but that "this margin is too narrow to contain [the proof]." His proof has never been found. Although later mathematicians have been able to show that Fermat's statement is correct for all numbers n less than 600, it has never been proved correct for *all* values of n.

Fermat's Last Theorem is an extension of the Pythagorean Theorem, but it is generally considered part of *number theory*—see NUMBERS and its references for other theorems and curiosities.

REFERENCES

References for other proofs of the Pythagorean Theorem

Historical Topics for the Mathematics Classroom, 31st Yearbook of the National Council of Teachers of Mathematics (1969), pp. 215–218; includes a version of Euclid's classic proof.

Harold R. Jacobs, *Geometry* (W. H. Freeman & Co., 1974), pp. 350–355 and 421–424; includes proofs by Leonardo da Vinci and U.S. President James A. Garfield.

References on Fermat's Last Theorem

Philip J. Davis and William G. Chinn, *3.1416 And All That* (Simon & Schuster, 1969); an entertaining collection of 24 explorations, with bibliographies, of many areas of mathematics; Fermat's Last Theorem is the first.

Harold M. Edwards, "Fermat's Last Theorem," *Scientific American*, October 1978, pp. 104–122; a well-illustrated and detailed chronicle of 300 years of efforts to solve the problem, including interesting biographical information on Fermat.

References on Pythagoras and Fermat

Eric T. Bell, *Men of Mathematics* (Simon & Schuster, 1937; Fireside paperback).

Carl B. Boyer, *A History of Mathematics* (John Wiley & Sons, 1968).

Howard Eves, *An Introduction to the History of Mathematics*, 3rd ed. (Holt, Rinehart & Winston, 1969); discusses formulas for Pythagorean triples and the evidence that the Babylonians knew many of these triples.

Evans G. Valens, *The Number of Things: Pythagoras, Geometry, and Humming Strings* (E. P. Dutton & Co., 1964); more about Pythagoras and his work, both in geometry and music, told in clear and delightful detail.

More uses of the Pythagorean Theorem are given in the articles on GEOMETRIC CONSTRUCTION and TRIGONOMETRY. And a little more about Pythagoras and his followers is told in the GOLDEN SECTION article.

QUADRILATERALS

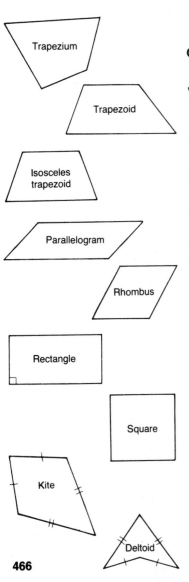

QUADRILATERAL: a POLYGON with exactly four sides.

VARIOUS TYPES OF QUADRILATERALS

Trapezium: a quadrilateral in which no pair of sides is parallel. (*Trapezium* in British usage means trapezoid.)

Trapezoid: a quadrilateral in which one and only one pair of sides is parallel.

Isosceles Trapezoid: a trapezoid in which the nonparallel sides are equal in length.

Parallelogram: a quadrilateral in which both pairs of opposite sides are parallel. The opposite sides of a parallelogram are equal, and the opposite angles are equal.

Rhombus: a parallelogram in which two adjacent sides are equal. Since a rhombus is a parallelogram, opposite sides are equal. Therefore, all four sides of a rhombus are equal.

Rectangle: a parallelogram in which one angle equals 90°. Since a rectangle is a parallelogram, opposite angles are equal, and adjacent angles are supplementary (total 180°). Therefore, every angle of a rectangle equals 90°.

Square: a rectangle in which two adjacent sides are equal. Since a square is a rectangle, which is a parallelogram, opposite sides are equal. Therefore, all four sides of a square are equal.

Kite-shaped Quadrilateral: a convex quadrilateral in which two pairs of adjacent sides are equal, but opposite sides are not parallel. (In a *convex* POLYGON, every interior angle is less than 180°.)

Deltoid: a concave quadrilateral in which two pairs of adjacent sides are equal, but opposite sides are not parallel. (In a *concave* polygon, at least one interior angle is greater than 180°.)

SUM OF THE INTERIOR ANGLES

The sum of the interior angles of any quadrilateral is 360°. You can prove this to yourself if you know that the sum of the interior angles of any TRIANGLE is 180°. Any quadrilateral can be divided into two triangles by connecting opposite vertices.

A HIERARCHY OF QUADRILATERALS

In addition to the definition of *trapezoid* given above, there is an alternative definition which some mathematicians prefer. The alternative definition is: A trapezoid is a quadrilateral in which *at least* one pair of opposite sides is parallel. One reason that some mathematicians prefer this definition is that it enables them to arrange the quadrilaterals in a hierarchy:

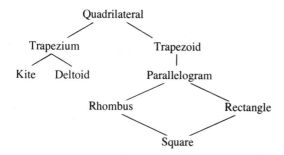

The diagram shows that every square is both a rhombus and a rectangle, that every rectangle is a parallelogram, that every parallelogram is a trapezoid, and that every trapezoid is a quadrilateral.

REFERENCE

Bruno Munari, *Discovery of the Square* (George Wittenborn, Inc., 1965); full of fascinating geometric and arithmetic facts about the square, with dozens of striking photographs of its use in art and architecture.

One of the most interesting quadrilaterals is a special rectangle called the Golden Rectangle. For a description and discussion of the Golden Rectangle, see GOLDEN SECTION.

For formulas for finding the area of quadrilaterals, see AREA.

RATIONAL AND IRRATIONAL NUMBERS

RATIONAL NUMBER: any real number that can be expressed as the *ratio* of two *integers*, with the second integer not equal to zero.

The word "rational" when applied to numbers comes from the word "ratio," and does not mean "reasonable" or "logical," as it does in more general English usage. A rational number is a RATIO. Therefore, a rational number may be represented symbolically as

$$\frac{a}{b} \quad \text{where } a \text{ may be any integer and } b \text{ may be any integer except zero.}$$

Examples.

$$\frac{1}{3} = 0.333333333333\ldots$$

$$-\frac{3}{4} = -0.750000000000\ldots$$

$$\frac{18}{11} = 1.636363636363\ldots$$

$$-3\tfrac{1}{8} = -3.125000000000\ldots$$

$$\frac{1}{7} = 0.142857142857\ldots$$

Every rational number can be expressed as a *repeating decimal fraction*. And every repeating decimal fraction is a rational number. For the conversion from a ratio to a repeating decimal and from a repeating decimal to a ratio of two integers, see DECIMALS.

The rational numbers also include all the integers—positive, negative, and zero—and all the rational FRACTIONS, both positive and negative. Any of these numbers can be expressed as the ratio of two integers.

Every rational number is a REAL NUMBER, but *not* every real number is rational.

IRRATIONAL NUMBER: any real number that is *not rational*.

An irrational number *cannot* be expressed as the ratio of two integers, so it cannot be expressed as a repeating decimal. Every irrational number can be represented by a *nonrepeating decimal expansion*.

Examples.   0.12122122212222122222...

0.1234567891011121314...

−0.12123123412345123456...

$\sqrt{2} = 1.414214...$

$\sqrt[3]{2} = 1.259921...$

$\pi = 3.141592653589...$ (PI, the ratio of the circumference to the diameter of a circle)

$e = 2.7182818284...$ (the base of natural LOGARITHMS)

Irrational Numbers that are Roots of Rational Numbers

It is possible to obtain some irrational numbers by taking the root of a rational number. A *root* of some number, N, is a number that can be multiplied by itself a given number of times to produce N. For example, 4 is the square (or second) root of 16 because $4 \times 4 = 16$. Similarly, 2 is the cube (or third) root of 8 because $2 \times 2 \times 2 = 8$.

But suppose you wanted to find the square root of 7; that is, the number that can be multiplied times itself to equal 7. The square root of 7 (written $\sqrt{7}$) can be estimated to be between 2 and 3, because $2 \times 2 = 4$ and $3 \times 3 = 9$, and 7 is between 4 and 9. If you try 2.5 as the estimate, you will find it too small because $2.5 \times 2.5 = 6.25$. The number 2.6 is still too small because $2.6 \times 2.6 = 6.76$. But 2.7 is too large because $2.7 \times 2.7 = 7.29$.

If you keep on trying numbers, you will find that $2.63 \times 2.63 = 6.9169$. By using a calculator or computer, you could get even closer. For example, $2.6457513 \times 2.6457513 = 6.9999994145169$. But no matter what number you try, you will never get exactly 7 because $\sqrt{7}$ cannot be represented by any terminating decimal or by any repeating decimal. The square root of 7 is an irrational number.

If you are not familiar with the idea of roots, you may wonder whether irrational numbers have anything to do with the real world. The answer is yes. Irrational numbers do represent the measure of distances

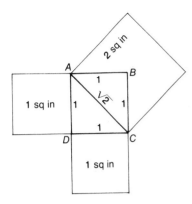

1 sq in

2 sq in

1 sq in

in the real world. In fact, it is easy to *construct* a line segment the measure of which is an irrational number.

Consider, for example, the square *ABCD*, which is one inch on a side. The diagonal of that square, *AC*, forms the hypotenuse (longest side) of two right triangles. From the PYTHAGOREAN THEOREM, it is known that the sum of the squares of the two shorter sides of a right triangle is equal to the square of the hypotenuse. Thus, a square on the diagonal *AC* has an area of 2 square inches. And the length of *AC* is $\sqrt{2}$ inches. But $\sqrt{2}$ is irrational. (A formal *proof* of the fact that $\sqrt{2}$ is irrational is provided at the end of this article; construction of line segments for other irrational numbers is shown under NUMBER LINES.)

There are infinitely many other numbers which, like $\sqrt{7}$ and $\sqrt{2}$, have decimal expansions that neither terminate nor repeat. In fact, irrational numbers are *more numerous* than rational numbers. Consider, for example, the rational number 2. From this one number, you can derive the following irrational numbers: $\sqrt{2}$, $\sqrt[3]{2}$, $\sqrt[4]{2}$, $\sqrt[5]{2}$, $2^{\sqrt{2}}$, and so on.

An irrational number that is a root of a rational number is sometimes called a *surd;* arithmetic expressions involving terms with surds may also be called surds.

Examples. $\sqrt{3}$
$\sqrt[3]{2}$
$5\sqrt{2} + \sqrt{3}$
$\sqrt{6} + \sqrt{3}$

Irrational Numbers that are not Roots

There are infinitely many irrational numbers that are *not* roots. Perhaps the most famous of these is PI (π), the ratio of the circumference of a circle to its diameter. For hundreds of years, mathematicians struggled to figure out this ratio. In the Bible, pi is given as 3. The ancient Babylonians, knowing π to be a little greater than 3, used $3\frac{1}{8}$. In the third century B.C., the great Greek mathematician Archimedes calculated π correct to two decimal places. And in the seventeenth century, a German mathematician, Ludolph van Ceulen, devoted years to calculating π to thirty-five decimal places. In the eighteenth century, however, a Swiss-German mathematician, Johann Lambert, proved that no matter how many decimal places of pi were computed, they would *never* give the *exact* ratio of circumference to diameter; Lambert proved that the ratio π is *irrational*.

Other irrational numbers that are not roots include certain ratios in TRIGONOMETRY and certain LOGARITHMS. The irrational number *e* is the base of *natural logarithms,* which are important in higher mathematics.

And there are infinitely more irrational numbers that have no special mathematical name. For example, the number 0.1211211121111211112 ... is irrational. Although the decimal expansion of this number has a pattern, it is not a pattern with a repeating sequence of digits, and therefore the number is not rational.

OPERATIONS ON RATIONAL AND IRRATIONAL NUMBERS

The REAL NUMBERS are composed of all the rational numbers and all the irrational numbers. Any two real numbers can be added, subtracted, multiplied, or divided (excluding division by zero). These four basic arithmetic operations can be performed on pairs of rational numbers, on pairs of irrational numbers, or on pairs in which one number is rational and one is irrational.

It is common for operations involving irrational numbers to be performed without using their decimal representations. For example, the result of adding π and π can be expressed as 2π; and the result of subtracting $\sqrt{2}$ from 3 can be expressed as $3 - \sqrt{2}$. A number such as $3 - \sqrt{2}$ is considered a unique and exact number.

But often it is necessary to use a decimal representation of an irrational number in working a problem. Although the true decimal representation of an irrational number goes on forever, in order to work a problem with such a number you have to terminate it at some point. When the decimal expansion of an irrational number is terminated after a given number of places, the result is referred to as the *rational approximation* of the original number.

Examples. *Irrational number*   *Rational approximation*

$$\sqrt{2} \quad \doteq \quad 1.414$$

$$\pi \quad \doteq \quad 3.1416$$

$$2 + \sqrt{3} \quad \doteq \quad 3.732$$

The "dotted" equality sign means "approximately equal."

A rational approximation can never be exact. But it can be calculated to any desired level of accuracy before being terminated.

A Ladder for Approximating $\sqrt{2}$

An intriguing ladder grew out of work done by the early Greek Pythagoreans (roughly 500–300 B.C.). This ladder provides an algorithm for approximating $\sqrt{2}$ as accurately as one wishes.

Ladder for Rational
Approximation of $\sqrt{2}$

x	y	$\frac{y}{x}$
1	1	1.000000 ...
2	3	1.500000 ...
5	7	1.400000 ...
12	17	1.416666 ...
29	41	1.413793 ...
70	99	1.414285 ...
169	239	1.414201 ...
408	577	1.414216 ...
.	.	.
.	.	.
.	.	.

Each rung of the ladder consists of a pair of numbers. On the first rung there is a 1 on the left and a 1 on the right. On each successive rung, the left-hand number equals the sum of the numbers on the previous rung, and the right-hand number equals the sum of its left-hand mate and the left-hand element from the preceding rung. The process of calculating rungs can be repeated any number of times.

To get a rational approximation of $\sqrt{2}$, you form a ratio of the right-hand element on one rung over the left-hand element of the same rung. The approximations on successive rungs alternate above and below the true value of $\sqrt{2}$. The farther down the ladder you choose the rung, the more accurate the approximation will be. For example, the first rung approximation is $\frac{1}{1}$, or 1, which is not too accurate. However, the fifth rung approximation, $\frac{41}{29}$, is accurate to three decimal places: 1.414. (The $\sqrt{2} = 1.414214 \ldots$)

Reference on ladders for rational
approximation

James R. Newman, ed., *The World of Mathematics*, four volumes (Simon & Schuster, 1956; available in paperback), Vol. I, pp. 97–98.

PROOF OF THE IRRATIONALITY OF $\sqrt{2}$

The fact that $\sqrt{2}$ is irrational can be *proved* by a combination of direct DEDUCTION and indirect reasoning:

Either $\sqrt{2}$ is rational *or* $\sqrt{2}$ is irrational (*not* rational).

To show that the first statement is false is to prove that the second is true. This is done as follows:

(1) If $\sqrt{2}$ is rational, it can be written as a FRACTION. That is,

$$\sqrt{2} = \frac{a}{b} \quad,$$

a fraction in lowest terms.

(2) If a/b is in lowest terms, a and b cannot both be even numbers. If a and b were both even numbers, then numerator and denominator could be reduced by a FACTOR of 2, which would mean that the fraction was not in lowest terms.)

(3) Squaring both sides of

$$\sqrt{2} = \frac{a}{b} \text{ gives } 2 = \frac{a^2}{b^2}.$$

(4) Multiplying by b^2 both sides of the equation

$$2 = \frac{a^2}{b^2} \quad \text{gives } 2b^2 = a^2.$$

(5) The left side of $2b^2 = a^2$ is an even number, because it has a factor of 2.

(6) Because the left side of $2b^2 = a^2$ must equal the right side, the right side, a^2, is also an even number.

(7) If a^2 is an even number, then a is an even number (a^2 must be either an odd number times an odd number, which gives an odd a^2, or an even number times an even number, which gives an even a^2 as in step 6).

(8) If a is even, a can be written as 2 times some other quantity c. That is, $a = 2c$.

(9) From step 4, $a^2 = 2b^2$. From step 8, $a^2 = (2c)^2 = 4c^2$. These two expressions for a^2 must be equal. Therefore, $2b^2 = 4c^2$.

(10) Dividing by 2 both sides of $2b^2 = 4c^2$ gives $b^2 = 2c^2$.

(11) If $b^2 = 2c^2$, then b is an even number, by the same reasoning used to show a is an even number in steps 5, 6, and 7.

(12) Now a and b have *both* been shown to be even numbers, which is a contradiction of step 2.

(13) Therefore, the original assumption in step 1 cannot be true, since step 2 and all that followed came from step 1.

(14) If step 1 is not true, $\sqrt{2}$ is *not* rational and is therefore *irrational*.

Reference on proving $\sqrt{n}$ irrational

Mary P. Dolciani, Simon L. Berman, and Julius Freilich, *Modern Algebra, Book 1* (Houghton Mifflin, 1965), p. 407; proof that $\sqrt{n}$ is irrational for any n that is not a perfect square.

For a continuation of the discussion of rational and irrational numbers, with references, see REAL NUMBERS.

See also FRACTIONS and DECIMALS. And for more on the history of π, see PI.

RATIOS

RATIO: a comparison of two similar measures by means of division. A ratio is usually written in one of two ways: as two numbers separated by a colon, or as a FRACTION. Hence the ratio "24 to 8" could be written as

$$24 : 8 \text{ or as } \frac{24}{8}.$$

Familiar examples of ratios are the pupil-teacher ratio in the schools, the ratio of wins to losses for a baseball team, the different ratios of bleach to water recommended for different cleaning jobs.

A ratio is a comparison by *division*. The ratio of a boy's height to his father's height tells what fraction of his father's height the boy has reached. Other comparisons could be made, such as the difference between the boy's height and his father's height, but such a comparison by subtraction would not be a ratio.

The *order* of two numbers in a ratio is extremely important. The quantity mentioned first in the comparison is written first in the ratio. A pupil-teacher ratio of $18 : 1$ would mean there were 18 pupils to every teacher. The ratio $1 : 18$ would represent the number of teachers to pupils.

A ratio is usually a comparison of *similar measures*. For example, in a pupil-teacher ratio, both numbers represent the number of people. In the ratio of wins to losses for a ball team, both numbers represent games. If a bleach bottle recommends a ratio of 1 to 8 for a certain purpose, the numbers refer to units of liquid measurement. In each of these cases the numbers in the ratio have the same units, and the ratio is a pure number. It is possible, however, to find the quotients of numbers representing different measures, such as miles per gallon or dollars per hour. In cases like these, the ratio must be labeled with the units.

If both numbers in a ratio represent similar measures, they must be expressed in the *same units*. If a boy's height is given as 54 inches and his father's as six feet, a ratio cannot be formed until the measurements are both expressed in the same units. Both can be expressed in inches or both in feet.

54 inches, or $4\frac{1}{2}$ feet   6 feet, or 72 inches

Ratio of $\dfrac{\text{boy's height}}{\text{father's height}}$ is $\dfrac{54 \text{ inches}}{72 \text{ inches}} = \dfrac{3}{4}$ or $\dfrac{4\frac{1}{2} \text{ feet}}{6 \text{ feet}} = \dfrac{3}{4}$

When the two numbers in a ratio represent similar measures, expressed in the same units, the ratio itself is not in any specific units. As a result, the ratio of the boy's height to his father's is the same whether the measurements are both expressed in feet or both expressed in inches. The ratio would still be the same if both measurements were expressed in centimeters:

$$\frac{\text{boy's height}}{\text{father's height}} = \frac{54 \text{ inches}}{72 \text{ inches}} = \frac{137.16 \text{ centimeters}}{182.88 \text{ centimeters}} = \frac{3}{4}$$

EQUIVALENT RATIOS: ratios that may be set equal to one another.

The different ratios for comparing a boy's height with his father's given in the previous example are all equal to $\frac{3}{4}$. Therefore, they are all *equivalent ratios.*

$$\frac{54}{72} = \frac{4\frac{1}{2}}{6} = \frac{137.16}{182.88} = \frac{3}{4} .$$

Equivalent ratios can be illustrated by *grouping*. Suppose you have 24 black marbles and your friend Bill has 8 white marbles. It would be possible to group those two sets of marbles in a number of ways. For example, each of you might divide your marbles into two equal groups. You would then have two groups of 12 marbles, and Bill would have two groups of 4 marbles. Thus, for every 12 marbles you have, Bill has 4.

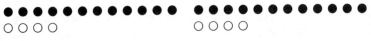

$$12 : 4 \text{ or } \frac{12}{4} = 3$$

Or you could divide your marbles into eight equal groups, in which case you would have eight groups of 3, and Bill would have eight groups of

1. For every 3 marbles you have, he has 1.

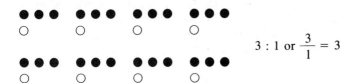

$$3 : 1 \text{ or } \frac{3}{1} = 3$$

A third possibility is that you could each put your marbles into one group—a group of 24 for you and a group of 8 for him. For every 24 marbles you have, Bill has 8. Each of these comparisons forms a ratio, and all of these ratios are equivalent.

$$24 : 8 \text{ or } \frac{24}{8} = 3$$

The grouping of marbles shows that a ratio does not necessarily tell how many black or white marbles there are. The ratio just says that there are three times as many black marbles as white.

Two equivalent, or equal, ratios form a PROPORTION. For example, the following equality is a proportion:

$$\frac{24}{8} = \frac{12}{4}$$

Many arithmetic and algebra problems are solved by finding a ratio that is equal to some other ratio by completing a proportion.

For instance, in cooking if you want to change the quantity of a recipe, it is necessary to maintain equivalent ratios between ingredients to get the proper consistency and taste in the finished product. If your cookie recipe calls for two cups of flour and one cup of sugar, you will want to keep the flour-to-sugar ratio at 2 : 1. If the recipe is doubled, you will need four cups of flour to two cups of sugar.

$$\frac{\text{flour}}{\text{sugar}} = \frac{2}{1} = \frac{4 \text{ cups}}{2 \text{ cups}}$$

If, on the other hand, you were to make one third the quantity, your proportion would now be:

$$\frac{\text{flour}}{\text{sugar}} = \frac{2}{1} = \frac{\frac{2}{3} \text{ cup}}{\frac{1}{3} \text{ cup}}$$

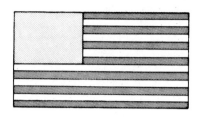

APPLICATIONS OF RATIO

The shape of the flag of the United States is determined by federal regulations set by President William Howard Taft in 1912. The width-to-length ratio of any official United States flag must be

$$1 : 1.9 \quad (\text{or } \frac{1}{1.9} = \frac{10}{19}).$$

Therefore, someone wanting to make a flag three feet wide could determine how long the flag should be from the following proportion:

$$\frac{\text{width of flag}}{\text{length of flag}} = \frac{1}{1.9} = \frac{3 \text{ ft}}{x \text{ ft}} = \frac{3}{5.7}$$

$$x = 3 \times 1.9 = 5.7 \text{ ft.}$$

An architect drawing the plans for a building cannot make the drawing the same size as the building. She can give a good idea of what the finished product will look like, however, by keeping the ratio of the dimensions of the drawing to the dimensions of the building constant. Such a drawing is called a *scale drawing*. The usual ratio between the dimensions of an architect's scale drawing and the dimensions of the building is $\frac{1}{48}$. This means that $\frac{1}{4}''$ on the scale drawing would represent twelve inches, or one foot, on the building.

$$\frac{1}{48} = \frac{\frac{1}{4} \text{ inch}}{12 \text{ inches}}$$

Thus, a room 8 feet by 15 feet would appear on the architect's plan as 2 inches by $3\frac{3}{4}$ inches, because

$$\frac{8'}{15'} = \frac{\frac{1}{48}(8')}{\frac{1}{48}(15')} = \frac{\frac{1}{48}(96'')}{\frac{1}{48}(180'')} = \frac{2''}{3\frac{3}{4}''}$$

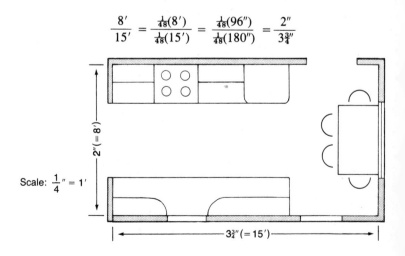

Scale: $\frac{1}{4}'' = 1'$

Another important application of ratio is in the design of gears. A gear is a wheel with teeth on it. The gear is fastened to a shaft, and either the gear is used to apply a twisting force called *torque* to this shaft or the shaft is turned by some other means and turns the gear. To increase the torque a machine can produce, a small gear can be put on the motor shaft to drive a bigger gear on another shaft. The amount the torque is increased will depend upon the relative size, or ratio, of the gears. If the second gear has twice as many teeth as the first gear, a *gear ratio* of 2 : 1, the torque will be doubled. A gear with 28 teeth being driven by a gear with 22 teeth has a gear ratio of

$$\frac{28}{22} = 1.27 : 1.$$

The gear ratio of a combination of gears is equivalent to the product of the individual gear ratios.

For example, in the transmission of a car, a typical gear ratio might be 2.78 : 1 for low gear, 1.70 : 1 for second gear, and 1 : 1 for high gear.

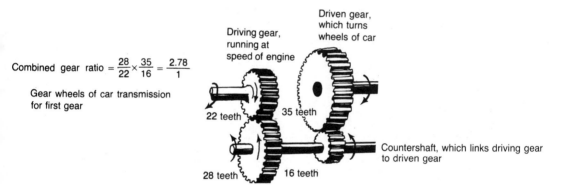

Combined gear ratio $= \dfrac{28}{22} \times \dfrac{35}{16} = \dfrac{2.78}{1}$

Gear wheels of car transmission for first gear

Driving gear, running at speed of engine

Driven gear, which turns wheels of car

22 teeth   35 teeth

Countershaft, which links driving gear to driven gear

28 teeth   16 teeth

SPECIAL RATIOS IN MATHEMATICS

Certain ratios in mathematics have been studied so extensively and used so often that they have been given special names. One such ratio is PI (π), the ratio of the circumference of a circle to its diameter. Finding the exact value of the ratio π occupied mathematicians for hundreds of years and led to several important mathematical discoveries.

Another familiar ratio is the GOLDEN SECTION, also known as the Divine Proportion. *Section* here means "cutting." And the Golden Section is formed when a line segment or rectangle is cut into two parts so that the ratio of the larger part to the smaller part is equal to the ratio of the whole to the larger part. This ratio is thought to be particularly pleasing to the eye, and it has been used repeatedly in art and architecture.

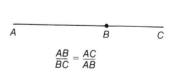

A B C

$$\frac{AB}{BC} = \frac{AC}{AB}$$

The ratio of SIMILARITY relates the dimensions of similar figures. When two geometric figures are similar, the lengths of their corresponding parts are always in the same ratio. This information often makes possible an indirect calculation of some inaccessible measure.

Still other ratios are important in TRIGONOMETRY. The trigonometric ratios are formed by comparing various pairs of sides of a right triangle. The values of these ratios have been computed for angles of various sizes, and these values can be used in making various indirect measurements.

For other articles related to ratio, see PROPORTIONS, FRACTIONS, PERCENT, and RATIONAL NUMBERS.

REAL NUMBERS

REAL NUMBER: any number that can be located on a *number line*. A NUMBER LINE is a mathematical model that pictures NUMBERS as points on a line. The real numbers are in one-to-one correspondence with the points on such a line.

Examples.

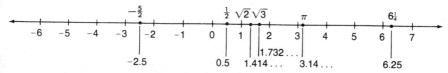

Any number can be located on a number line if it has an expansion as a DECIMAL fraction. A real number is any number that can be represented by a decimal expansion.

Any number that can be represented by an *infinite repeating decimal expansion* is a *rational* number. (Rational numbers include those that have finite decimal expansions, such as 1.7, because the finite decimal can be followed by a repeating sequence of zeros, such as 1.700000. . . .) Any number that can be represented by an *infinite non-repeating decimal expansion* is an *irrational* number. The set of rational numbers and the set of irrational numbers are mutually exclusive sets. The union of these two sets, the RATIONAL AND IRRATIONAL NUMBERS, is exactly the set of real numbers. Every real number is either rational or irrational.

Examples.

$$
\left.
\begin{array}{rl}
1.000 = & 1.00000000000\ldots \\
13.712 = & 13.71200000000\ldots \\
-2 = & -2.00000000000\ldots \\
\tfrac{2}{3} = & .66666666666\ldots
\end{array}
\right\}
\begin{array}{l}
\text{Rational} \\
\text{numbers}
\end{array}
\left.
\right\}
\begin{array}{l}
\text{Real} \\
\text{numbers}
\end{array}
$$

$$-\tfrac{1}{2} = -.50000000000\ldots$$
$$\tfrac{1}{7} = .142857142857\ldots$$

Rational numbers

$$.12122122212222\ldots$$
$$\pi = 3.14159\ldots$$
$$\sqrt{2} = 1.4142\ldots$$
$$\sqrt[5]{3} = 1.245\ldots$$
$$-10^{0.6} = -3.98\ldots$$
$$5^{\sqrt{2}} = 9.738\ldots$$
$$5^{-\sqrt{2}} = .10269\ldots$$

Irrational numbers

Real numbers

THE SYSTEM OF REAL NUMBERS

The set of real numbers is a vast system. It includes as subsets not only the rational numbers and the irrational numbers but several other sets of numbers, including the integers, the positive numbers, and the negative numbers. The relationships between these subsets are illustrated by a diagram.

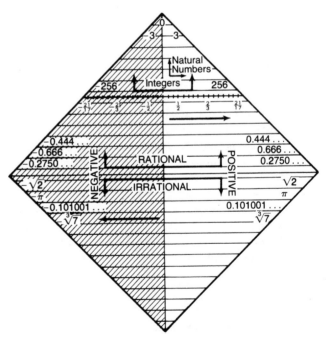

Real number system

THE REAL NUMBERS AS A FIELD

The real numbers constitute what is known in mathematics as a *field*. That is, the real numbers satisfy all of the FIELD PROPERTIES: closure, commutativity, associativity, distributivity, identity elements, and inverses.

The field property of *closure* means that when any two elements of the field are added, subtracted, multiplied, or divided (excluding division by zero), the result will always belong to the field. This property of closure is satisfied by the real numbers. It is also satisfied by the rational numbers. When any two rational numbers are added, subtracted, multiplied, or divided (excluding division by zero), the results will always be a rational number. In fact, the rational numbers alone also constitute a field, because they satisfy all of the other field properties as well.

The irrational numbers, on the other hand, though a more numerous set than the rationals, do *not* alone constitute a field. This is so because the set of irrational numbers does not have closure. When two irrational numbers are added, subtracted, multiplied, or divided, the result will not always be irrational.

Example. $\quad 3 - \sqrt{2}$ (irrational)

$\qquad \underline{ + \sqrt{2}}$ (irrational)

$\qquad 3 \qquad\quad$ (rational)

In order to obtain a field that includes the irrational numbers, the rational numbers must also be included. In fact, adding, subtracting, multiplying, or dividing (excluding division by zero) any combination of rational and irrational numbers will always produce either a rational or an irrational result. The real numbers are the smallest closed set that includes the irrational numbers. And, as stated above, the real numbers satisfy all the other field properties as well. So the real numbers are the smallest field that includes the irrational numbers.

The COMPLEX NUMBERS constitute a yet larger field that includes all of the real numbers.

ORDER IN THE REAL NUMBERS

The real numbers form an *ordered* set. That is, it is always possible to decide whether two real numbers are equal or to decide which of the two is the larger and which the smaller. The real numbers are ordered by looking at their decimal expansions.

Example.

$$\sqrt{2} \quad < \quad \sqrt{3} \quad < 3 < \quad \pi \quad < 3.15 < 3.51,$$

because $1.414\ldots < 1.732\ldots < 3 < 3.14159\ldots < 3.15 < 3.51.$

This property of the real numbers is noteworthy because the COMPLEX NUMBERS are *not* ordered. The real numbers are ordered on a one dimensional number line, but the complex numbers require representation in two dimensions.

DENSITY OF THE REAL NUMBERS

The real numbers are said to be everywhere *dense*. The property of *density* means that between any two real numbers, no matter how close together, there exist infinitely many other real numbers.

Example.   Consider the real numbers $\frac{1}{100}$ and $\frac{1}{101}$. These numbers can be written as follows:

$$\frac{1}{100} = \frac{1010}{101,000} \quad \text{and} \quad \frac{1}{101} = \frac{1000}{101,000}.$$

Therefore, the numbers

$$\frac{1001}{101,000}, \frac{1002}{101,000}, \ldots, \frac{1009}{101,000} \text{ all lie between } \frac{1}{100} \text{ and } \frac{1}{101}$$

In a similar way, it is possible to find infinitely many other numbers between $\frac{1}{100}$ and $\frac{1}{101}$, or between *any* two real numbers.

As this example illustrates, the rational numbers alone also satisfy the property of density.

THE REAL NUMBERS AS A CONTINUUM

The set of real numbers constitutes a *continuum*. To illustrate the nature of a continuum, consider again the number line.

Then consider the rational numbers alone. On a number line such as the one above, it would be possible to locate infinitely many rational numbers. Each unit could be subdivided into hundredths, thousandths, ten-thousandths, hundred-thousandths, and so on, until it would seem that every point on the line would be represented by some rational number. But this would not in fact be true. For example, there would be some point on that line exactly equal to $\sqrt{2}$, and there would be no rational number to represent that point no matter how finely you subdivided each unit. Thus, the *rational numbers* are not sufficient to describe every point on the line. They *do not form a continuum*.

Nor do the irrational numbers constitute a continuum. A number line marked off only in irrational numbers would not contain a number for any points equal to integers or rational fractions. Thus, the set of irrational numbers is insufficient to describe all the points on the line.

But the set of real numbers does form a continuum. This means that every real number corresponds to exactly one point on the line, and for every one of the infinite number of points on the line, there exists exactly one real number.

NUMBERS THAT ARE NOT REAL NUMBERS

Since the real numbers describe every possible point on a number line, you might wonder whether the real numbers include all the numbers there are. The answer is no. There are yet other numbers, such as *imaginary numbers*. See COMPLEX NUMBERS.

HISTORY OF THE REAL NUMBERS

The historical development of the real number system traces a path almost exactly parallel to the overall history of mathematics. Nearly every time people have learned to manipulate numbers in more sophisticated ways to solve more complicated problems, they have had to expand their idea of the real number system. See HISTORY for further information.

THE UNCOUNTABILITY OF THE REAL NUMBERS

A set of numbers may be infinite yet *countable*. For example, the natural numbers $1, 2, 3, 4, \ldots$ can be counted. And any set of numbers that can be put in a one-to-one correspondence with the natural numbers is countable, for example, the set of unit fractions:

1	$\frac{1}{2}$	$\frac{1}{3}$	$\frac{1}{4}$	$\frac{1}{5}$	$\frac{1}{6}$	$\frac{1}{7}$	$\frac{1}{8}$	$\frac{1}{9}$	$\frac{1}{10}$	$\frac{1}{11}$	$\cdots$
$\updownarrow$	$\updownarrow$	$\updownarrow$	$\updownarrow$	$\updownarrow$	$\updownarrow$	$\updownarrow$	$\updownarrow$	$\updownarrow$	$\updownarrow$	$\updownarrow$	
1	2	3	4	5	6	7	8	9	10	11	$\cdots$

The set of real numbers is *uncountable*. That is, the real numbers are so numerous that they cannot be counted. There are more real numbers than can be put in one-to-one correspondence with the natural, or counting, numbers.

The uncountability of the real numbers can be proved by DEDUCTION, in a famous diagonal argument that is based on *contradiction*. The idea is to assume that the set of real numbers is countable, and then to show that this assumption leads to a contradiction. The conclusion then is that the assumption must be false, and the set of real numbers is therefore *not* countable. The entire proof follows:

Proof that the set of real numbers is uncountable

(1) Assume that the infinite set of real numbers from

$$0.000000\ldots \text{ to } 0.9999999\ldots$$

is *countable*.

(2) "Countable" means that all the numbers of the set can be listed in a one-to-one correspondence with the natural counting numbers. That is, if this set of real numbers is countable, *all* these real numbers can be listed in some numerical order. This can be done by using the *decimal expansion* of each real number.

(3) Imagine this infinite *list* of decimals that will include *all* the real numbers from $0.00000\ldots$ to $0.99999\ldots$:

first	$0. a_1 a_2 a_3 a_4 a_5 a_6 a_7 a_8 a_9 a_{10} a_{11} a_{12} \cdots$
second	$0. b_1 b_2 b_3 b_4 b_5 b_6 b_7 b_8 b_9 b_{10} b_{11} b_{12} \cdots$
third	$0. c_1 c_2 c_3 c_4 c_5 c_6 c_7 c_8 c_9 c_{10} c_{11} c_{12} \cdots$
fourth	$0. d_1 d_2 d_3 d_4 d_5 d_6 d_7 d_8 d_9 d_{10} d_{11} d_{12} \cdots$
fifth	$0. e_1 e_2 e_3 e_4 e_5 e_6 e_7 e_8 e_9 e_{10} e_{11} e_{12} \cdots$
sixth	$0. f_1 f_2 f_3 f_4 f_5 f_6 f_7 f_8 f_9 f_{10} f_{11} f_{12} \cdots$

(4) Look at the main *diagonal* formed by this display—the first digit from the first number on the list, the second digit from the second number on the list, the third digit from the third number on the list, and so on, as shown by the circles.

first	$0.\bigcirc a_2 a_3 a_4 a_5 a_6 a_7 a_8 a_9 a_{10} a_{11} a_{12} \ldots$
second	$0.b_1 \bigcirc b_3 b_4 b_5 b_6 b_7 b_8 b_9 b_{10} b_{11} b_{12} \ldots$
third	$0.c_1 c_2 \bigcirc c_4 c_5 c_6 c_7 c_8 c_9 c_{10} c_{11} c_{12} \ldots$
fourth	$0.d_1 d_2 d_3 \bigcirc d_5 d_6 d_7 d_8 d_9 d_{10} d_{11} d_{12} \ldots$
fifth	$0.e_1 e_2 e_3 e_4 \bigcirc e_6 e_7 e_8 e_9 e_{10} e_{11} e_{12} \ldots$
sixth	$0.f_1 f_2 f_3 f_4 f_5 \bigcirc f_7 f_8 f_9 f_{10} f_{11} f_{12} \ldots$
seventh	$0.g_1 g_2 g_3 g_4 g_5 g_6 \bigcirc g_8 g_9 g_{10} g_{11} g_{12} \ldots$
eighth	$0.h_1 h_2 h_3 h_4 h_5 h_6 h_7 \bigcirc h_9 h_{10} h_{11} h_{12} \ldots$
ninth	$0.i_1 i_2 i_3 i_4 i_5 i_6 i_7 i_8 \bigcirc i_{10} i_{11} i_{12} \ldots$
tenth	$0.j_1 j_2 j_3 j_4 j_5 j_6 j_7 j_8 j_9 \bigcirc j_{11} j_{12} \ldots$

(5) Now form a new number, another infinite decimal: make every digit of the new number *different,* without using 0 or 9, from the corresponding digit circled on the main diagonal of the list of all real numbers.

(6) This new number so formed is a *real* number, because it is an infinite decimal.

(7) But this new real number is *not* already on the list of all real numbers, because the new number differs in at least the diagonal digit from every number on the list of all real numbers.

(8) This is a contradiction to step 2, because the list was assumed to include all real numbers.

(9) Hence assumption 1—that the set of real numbers is countable—is *false*. This means that the set of real numbers from 0.00000 ... to 0.99999 ... is *uncountable*.

(10) And if the set of real numbers from 0.00000 ... to 0.99999 ... is uncountable, the set of *all* real numbers, which includes this subset, must also be uncountable.

The fact that some infinite sets, such as the real numbers, are uncountable is the basis of *transfinite arithmetic*. See articles on INFINITY and ARITHMETIC, and references, Yarnelle.

REFERENCES

Grace E. Bates and Fred Kiokemeister, *The Real Number System* (Allyn & Bacon, 1960); an elementary systematic exposition (82 pages) of the mathematical system, starting from definitions, postulates, and field properties.

Robert Hackworth and Joseph Howland, *Real Number System,* a module from Introductory College Mathematics: The Saunders Series in Modular Mathematics (W. B. Saunders, 1976); a good elementary source.

Ivan Niven, *Numbers: Rational and Irrational* (Random House, 1961); a more advanced treatment of the real numbers.

Reference on uncountability

John E. Yarnelle, *An Introduction to Transfinite Mathematics* (D. C. Heath & Co., 1964); clearly written on an elementary level to explain arithmetic with uncountable sets; includes an expanded proof of the uncountability of the real numbers.

For more on the real numbers, see HISTORY, FIELD PROPERTIES, NUMBERS, and NUMBER LINES.

The real numbers include FRACTIONS, DECIMALS, SIGNED NUMBERS, RATIONAL AND IRRATIONAL NUMBERS.

RELATIONS

RELATION: an *ordered pairing* of the elements from one SET with elements from another set.

The word "relation" is used in many ways. Within a family there are many relations, such as the relation between an uncle and his nieces and nephews. On a test there is a relation between your numerical score and your letter grade. When you boil an egg, there is a relation between the hardness of your egg and the number of minutes it was boiled.

In each of these examples there is a *pairing* between the things that are related. This pairing is called a *relation*.

Mathematicians *order* the pairs in a relation so that information can be given most efficiently. Consider Uncle Guram: "Guram is an uncle of Rebecca" can be reduced to (Guram, Rebecca) if it is understood that the first person is an uncle of the second.

The result of such a pairing is a whole *set of ordered pairs*. The first element of each pair is from a set called the *domain* of the relation. The second element of each pair is from another set called the *range*.

Example.

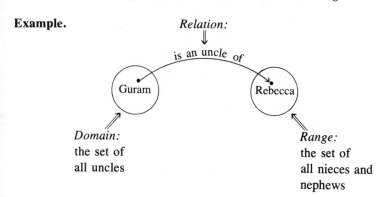

Relation:
⇓
is an uncle of

Guram   Rebecca

Domain:
the set of
all uncles

Range:
the set of
all nieces and
nephews

(Guram, Rebecca) is one of the ordered pairs shown by this relation;
(Uncle Ted, Joe) might be another pair in this relation, and so on.

489

WAYS OF EXPRESSING A RELATION

A relation can be expressed in a number of different ways:

Example.   *Relation:*
Each number in the domain
is paired with its double
in the range

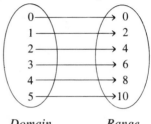

Domain   Range

This first way is called a *mapping diagram*. Another way of expressing this relation is to *list* the ordered pairs.

$$\{(0, 0), (1, 2), (2, 4), (3, 6), (4, 8), (5, 10)\}$$

And still another way of expressing the same relation is by using a *table*.

Domain	0	1	2	3	4	5
Range	0	2	4	6	8	10

Any ordered pairing of the members from one set with the members from another is a relation.

Example.   The number of points scored by the home team in a season of basketball games could be paired with the number of points scored by their opponents:

Home town	51	West City	32
Home town	69	East Overshoe	28
Home town	86	North Boondocks	87
Home town	79	South Podunk	110
Home town	45	Centerville	41

or $\{(51, 32), (69, 28), (86, 87), (79, 110), (45, 41)\}$

Each integer could be paired with its square, resulting in an infinite number of pairs.

1	2	3	4	5	6	7	8	. . .
1	4	9	16	25	36	49	64	. . .

Usually, however, the pairing of two sets is given by some rule or pattern. In particular, a mathematical relation of pairs (x, y) is most commonly expressed by an EQUATION or an INEQUALITY in x and y. The domain in this case is the set of all values of x for which the equation is true, and the range is the set of resulting values for y.

Examples. $y = x^2$ domain: all real numbers

range: all nonnegative real numbers

$y > x$ domain: all real numbers

range: all real numbers

Since an equation or inequality expressing a relation involves two variables, the relation can be shown on a GRAPH.

Examples. $\{(x, y) \text{ such that } x + y = 7\}$

The graph of this relation is a straight line. The domain (possible values of x) and the range (possible values of y) both include all the real numbers, as shown below on the left.

$\{(x, y) \text{ such that } y = x^2 + 4\}$

The graph of this relation is a parabola. The domain is the set of all the real numbers. The resulting range is limited to positive numbers $\geqslant 4$.

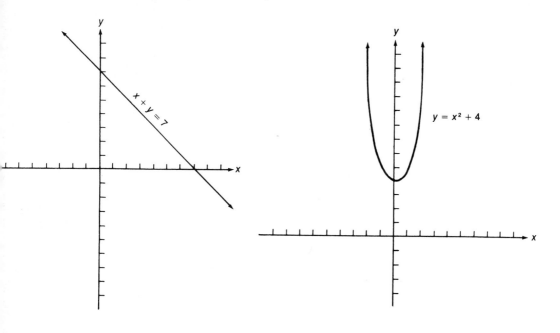

$$\{(x, y) \text{ such that } x^2 + y^2 = 25\}$$

The graph of this relation is a circle. The domain and range are both limited as follows: $-5 \leqslant x \leqslant 5$, $-5 \leqslant y \leqslant 5$, as shown below on the left.

$$\{(x, y) \text{ such that } x \geqslant 5\}$$

The graph of this relation is a half plane. The domain is restricted to $x \geqslant 5$, but the range includes all the real numbers.

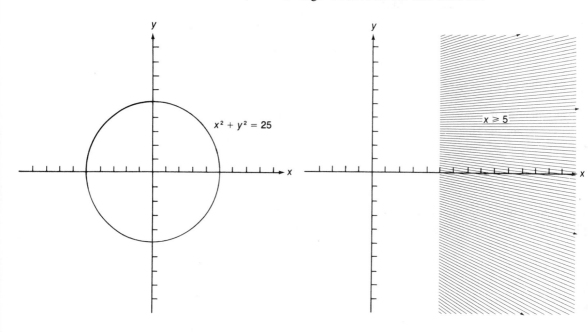

FUNCTION: a *relation* in which each element in the domain is paired with *exactly one* element in the range.

Examples. $\{(1, 2), (2, 3), (3, 4)\}$ is a function.

$\{(1, 2), (1, 3), (3, 4)\}$ is *not* a function, because the element 1 of the domain is paired with two *different* values in the range.

{(x, y) such that x + y = 7}   is a function, because
any given first
element x is paired
with exactly one
second element y,
equal to 7 − x.

Although all functions are relations, *not all relations are functions*. A relation is a function only if, in a set of ordered pairs in which no pair is repeated, every first element is different.

A graph gives a good way to tell if a relation is or is not a function. If a relation is a function, no two points of the graph will be on the same vertical line.

Examples.

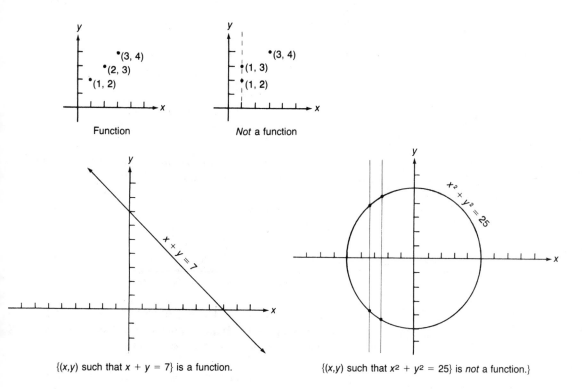

{(x,y) such that x + y = 7} is a function.

{(x,y) such that x² + y² = 25} is *not* a function.}

See also FUNCTIONS.

For *binary relation* and *equivalence relation*, see PROPERTIES OF EQUALITY.

SCIENTIFIC NOTATION

SCIENTIFIC NOTATION: a way of writing a number as a product of two factors: the first factor has exactly one nonzero digit to the left of the decimal point; the second factor is the necessary power of ten.

Examples.

Decimal notation		Scientific notation
347.1	=	3.471×10^2
0.00098	=	9.8×10^{-4}
7000	=	7×10^3
0.00000005	=	5×10^{-8}

The EXPONENT of 10 in scientific notation is the key to changing from decimal notation to scientific notation, or vice versa.

A *positive integer exponent* indicates how many times 10 is to be used as a factor. Therefore,

$$3.471 \times 10^5 = 3.471 \times \underbrace{10 \times 10 \times 10 \times 10 \times 10}_{5 \text{ factors of } 10} = 347,100.$$

When a number greater than ten is written in scientific notation, the power of 10 has a positive integer exponent. The procedures for changing from one notation to another are as follows:

- To change from scientific notation to decimal notation, move the decimal point to the right the number of places indicated by the exponent of 10.

$$3.471 \times 10^5 = 347,100$$

5 places

- To change from decimal notation to scientific notation, move the decimal point to the left until only one digit remains to the left of the decimal point; the resulting number is the first factor. The second factor is a power of 10 with an exponent equal to the number of places the decimal point was moved.

$$347{,}100 = 3.471 \times 10^5$$

5 places

A *negative integer exponent* for a number in scientific notation indicates how many times $\frac{1}{10}$ is to be used as a factor. Therefore,

$$1.9 \times 10^{-6} = 1.9 \times \tfrac{1}{10} \times \tfrac{1}{10} \times \tfrac{1}{10} \times \tfrac{1}{10} \times \tfrac{1}{10} \times \tfrac{1}{10} = 0.0000019.$$

$$\longrightarrow 6 \text{ factors of } \tfrac{1}{10}$$

When a number with absolute value less than one is written in scientific notation, the power of 10 will have a negative integer exponent. The procedures for changing from one notation to another are as follows:

- To change from scientific notation to decimal notation, move the decimal point to the left the number of places indicated by the negative exponent of 10.

$$1.9 \times 10^{-6} = 0.0000019$$

6 places

- To change from decimal notation to scientific notation, move the decimal point to the right until there is only one nonzero digit to the left of it; this number is the first factor. The second factor is a negative power of 10. The exponent is equal to the number of places the decimal point was moved.

$$0.0000019 = 1.9 \times 10^{-6}$$

6 places

ADVANTAGES OF SCIENTIFIC NOTATION

Scientific notation is a particular way of writing numbers so that the *size* and *precision* of numbers can be easily compared. When a number is written in scientific notation, the first factor shows the precision and the second factor shows the size.

Size

Extremely large and extremely small numbers are difficult to read and difficult to compare when they are written in decimal form. Consider the following examples. Sir Henry Cavendish in 1798 computed the earth's mass at 6,000,000,000,000,000,000,000,000,000 grams, or weight of 6,600,000,000,000,000,000,000 tons. Under certain conditions of temperature and pressure, there are 27,000,000,000,000,000,000 molecules in a cubic centimeter of any gas. In an electronic computer, an electrical impulse travels through 9 inches of wire in 0.000000001 of a second. The diameter of a hydrogen atom is 0.00000001016 centimeters.

In these examples it is difficult to tell, without stopping to count the zeros, just how big or how small each number is. And it is equally difficult to tell just by looking how much bigger one number is than another. Therefore, in the physical sciences, where it is often necessary to work with very large and very small numbers, it is usual to express such numbers in scientific notation. The table shows how the examples would be written in scientific notation.

Decimal notation	Scientific notation	Description
6,000,000,000,000, 000,000,000,000,000	$= 6. \times 10^{27}$	Mass of earth in grams
6,600,000,000,000, 000,000,000	$= 6.6 \times 10^{21}$	Weight of earth in tons
27,000,000,000,000, 000,000	$= 2.7 \times 10^{19}$	Number of molecules per cubic centimeter of gas
0.000000001	$= 1. \times 10^{-9}$	Seconds required for an electrical impulse to travel through 9 inches of wire in a computer
0.00000001016	$= 1.016 \times 10^{-8}$	Diameter of hydrogen atom in centimeters

When a number is written in scientific notation, the power of 10 indicates roughly how big or how small the number is. It tells you whether the number is in the hundreds, thousands, ten thousands, and so on; or whether it is in the hundredths, thousandths, ten thousandths, and so on. The power of 10 indicates the *order of magnitude* of a number. Two numbers are of the same order of magnitude if they have the same power of 10 when written in scientific notation.

The power of 10 is also useful in making *rough comparisons* between two numbers. For example, you can compare the number of grams that earth weighs with the number of tons it weighs, by comparing the second factors of the two weights. The weight in grams has a second factor of 10^{27}; the weight in tons has a second factor of 10^{21}. Thus, the first number is roughly 10^6 times as large as the second, or approximately a million times as great.

Precision

When a number is written in scientific notation, the first factor indicates how many SIGNIFICANT DIGITS there are in the number. A *significant digit* is one that indicates the result of some measurement. In any number, the digits other than zero are always significant. However, zero may or may not be significant. If it indicates that a measurement was made and found to be zero, it is significant.

For example, if the weight of a girl is given as 108 pounds, all the digits in that number are significant. They indicate a measurement of 1 one hundred, 0 tens, and 8 ones. However, if the weight of an elephant is given as 12,000 pounds, the last three digits of this number may not be significant. It may not be true that the weight of the elephant has been found to be between 11,999 and 12,001 pounds. The number 12,000 may only represent a measurement correct to the nearest thousand pounds, in which case the last 3 digits would be nonsignificant. They would simply serve to place the decimal point.

All significant digits of a number are included in the first factor when that number is expressed in scientific notation. All nonsignificant zeros are dropped. Thus, if the weight of a twelve-thousand-pound elephant were measured only to the nearest thousand pounds, it would be written in scientific notation as 1.2×10^4 (two significant digits). However, if the weight were measured to the nearest hundred pounds, it would be expressed in scientific notation as 1.20×10^4 (three significant digits). And if it were correct to the nearest ten pounds, it would be expressed as 1.200×10^4 (four significant digits). In scientific notation, all zeros are significant, and final zeros indicate the precision of the measurement.

See also SIGNIFICANT DIGITS.

SEQUENCES AND SERIES

SEQUENCE: a SET of elements ordered in some specified way.

Examples.

Sequence	Way of ordering
$\{1, 3, 9, 27, 81\}$	Each term after the first $= 3 \times$ the preceding term.
$\{3, 7, 11, 15, 19, \ldots\}$	Each term after the first $=$ the preceding term $+ 4$.
$\{1, 3, 4, 7, 11\}$	Each term after the first two terms $=$ the sum of the two preceding terms.
$\{1, \frac{1}{2}, \frac{1}{4}, \frac{1}{8}, \frac{1}{16} \ldots\}$	Each term after the first $= \frac{1}{2} \times$ the preceding term.
$\{2, -2, 2, -2, 2\}$	Each term after the first $= -1 \times$ the preceding term.

TYPES OF SEQUENCES

Finite Sequence: a sequence with a finite number of terms. The number of terms in a finite sequence can be counted. In every finite sequence there is a last term.

Examples.

Sequence	Number of members
$\{2, 4, 6, 8, 10\}$	5
$\{1, 2, 3, 4, 5, 6, 7, 8\}$	8

Infinite Sequence: a sequence with infinitely many terms. The counting of the terms of an infinite sequence would never come to an end because there is no last term in an infinite sequence.

Examples.

Sequence	Number of members
$\{3, 7, 11, 15, 19, \ldots\}$	infinitely many
$\{1, \frac{1}{2}, \frac{1}{4}, \frac{1}{8}, \frac{1}{16}, \ldots\}$	infinitely many

Arithmetic Sequence (or *arithmetic progression*): a sequence in which there is a common *difference* between successive terms.

Examples.

Sequence	Common difference
$\{2, 5, 8, 11, 14, \ldots\}$	3
$\{7, 5, 3, 1, -1, -3\}$	-2

Each successive term of an arithmetic sequence is found by adding the common difference to the preceding term.

Formula for the nth Term of an Arithmetic Sequence

nth term $= a + (n - 1)d$ where $a = $ first term of the sequence

$n = $ the ordinal number of the term to be found

$d = $ common difference

Example. Find the twenty-first term of $\{3, 7, 11, 15, 19, \ldots\}$

$$a = 3 \qquad n = 21 \qquad d = 4$$

$$\begin{aligned}
\text{21st term} = a + (n - 1)d &= 3 + (21 - 1)4 \\
&= 3 + (20)4 \\
&= 3 + 80 = 83
\end{aligned}$$

Geometric Sequence (or *geometric progression*): a sequence in which there is a common RATIO between successive terms.

Examples.

Sequence	Common ratio
$\{1, 3, 9, 27, 81\}$	3
$\{1, \frac{1}{2}, \frac{1}{4}, \frac{1}{8}, \frac{1}{16}, \ldots\}$	$\frac{1}{2}$

Each successive term of a geometric sequence is found by multiplying the preceding term by the common ratio.

Formula for the nth Term of a Geometric Sequence

nth term $= ar^{(n-1)}$ where $a = $ first term of the sequence

$n = $ the ordinal number of the term to be found

$r = $ common ratio

Example. Find the tenth term of $\{3, 6, 12, 24, \ldots\}$

$$a = 3 \qquad n = 10 \qquad r = 2$$

$$
\begin{aligned}
\text{10th term} = ar^{n-1} &= 3 \times 2^{(10-1)} \\
&= 3 \times 2^9 \\
&= 3 \times 512 \\
&= 1536
\end{aligned}
$$

SERIES: the *sum* of the terms of a sequence.

Symbol:

$\sum$ indicates that a *sum* is to be found.

Examples.

Sequence	Series
$\{1, 3, 9, 27, 81\}$	$1 + 3 + 9 + 27 + 81$
$\{3, 7, 11, 15, 19, \ldots\}$	$3 + 7 + 11 + 15 + 19 + \ldots$

The summation sign $\sum$ (the Greek letter sigma) can be used to abbreviate the writing of a series.

Examples.

$\displaystyle\sum_{n=1}^{5} 3n$ This expression indicates that n is to be replaced in turn by $1, 2, 3,$ 4, and 5, and then the results added.

$$
\begin{aligned}
\sum_{n=1}^{5} 3n &= 3 \times 1 + 3 \times 2 + 3 \times 3 + 3 \times 4 + 3 \times 5 \\
&= \quad 3 \quad + \quad 6 \quad + \quad 9 \quad + \quad 12 \quad + \quad 15 \\
&= 45
\end{aligned}
$$

$\displaystyle\sum_{k=3}^{\infty} (k+1)$ This expression indicates that k is to be replaced sequentially by $3, 4, 5, 6, 7, \ldots$ and the results added.

$$
\begin{aligned}
\sum_{k=3}^{\infty} (k+1) &= (3 + 1) + (4 + 1) + (5 + 1) + (6 + 1) + \ldots \\
&= \quad 4 \quad + \quad 5 \quad + \quad 6 \quad + \quad 7 \quad + \ldots
\end{aligned}
$$

TYPES OF SERIES

Finite Series: the sum of the terms of a finite sequence.

Example. $3 + 6 + 9 + 12 + 15$

which can also be written as $\displaystyle\sum_{n=1}^{5} 3n$.

Infinite Series: the sum of the terms of an infinite sequence.

Some infinite series represent a sum that becomes infinitely greater than zero or a sum that becomes infinitely less than zero. Such infinite series cannot be evaluated.

Example. $4 + 5 + 6 + 7 + 8 + 9 + 10 + \ldots$

which can also be written as $\sum_{k=3}^{\infty} (k + 1)$.

There are other infinite series that oscillate; some of these cannot be evaluated either.

Example. $1 - 1 + 1 - 1 + 1 - 1 + 1 - 1 \ldots$

An even number of terms sums to 0, an odd number to 1. It is not possible to assign a single sum to this series.

However, some infinite series represent a sum that approaches some finite number as more and more terms are added.

Example. $\frac{1}{2} + \frac{1}{4} + \frac{1}{8} + \frac{1}{16} + \frac{1}{32} + \ldots = 1$

This sum is illustrated by the following line segment:

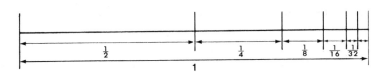

This series can also be written as

$$\sum_{n=1}^{\infty} \left(\tfrac{1}{2}\right)^n = \tfrac{1}{2} + \left(\tfrac{1}{2}\right)^2 + \left(\tfrac{1}{2}\right)^3 + \left(\tfrac{1}{2}\right)^4 + \ldots$$

This is a *geometric series* of a geometric sequence with ratio of $\frac{1}{2}$. Such an infinite series may be evaluated by means of a formula as shown on the next page.

Arithmetic Series: the sum of the terms of an arithmetic sequence.

Examples. $3 + 7 + 11 + 15 + 19 + \ldots$

$-2 + 0 + 2 + 4 + 6 + 8 + 10$

Formula for the Sum of a Finite Arithmetic Series

$$\text{sum} = \frac{n}{2}[2a + (n - 1)d] \quad \text{where} \quad n = \text{number of terms}$$
$$a = \text{first term}$$
$$d = \text{common difference}$$

Example.   Find the sum of the first 22 terms of
$$3 + 7 + 11 + 15 + 19 + \ldots$$

$$n = 22 \quad a = 3 \quad d = 4$$

$$\text{sum} = \frac{n}{2}[2a + (n - 1)d] = \frac{22}{2}[2 \times 3 + (22 - 1) \times 4]$$

$$= 11(6 + 21 \times 4) = 990.$$

Geometric Series: the sum of the terms of a geometric sequence.

Examples. $1 + 3 + 9 + 27 + 81$

$$1 + 2 + 4 + 8 + 16 + 32 + 64 + \ldots$$

Formula for the Sum of the First n Terms of a Geometric Series

$$\text{sum} = \frac{a - ar^n}{1 - r} \quad \text{where} \quad a = \text{first term}$$
$$r = \text{common ratio } (r \neq 1 \text{ required})$$
$$n = \text{number of terms}$$

Example.   Find the sum of the first eight terms of
$$1 + 2 + 4 + 8 + \ldots$$

$$n = 8 \quad a = 1 \quad r = 2$$

$$\text{sum} = \frac{a - ar^n}{1 - r} = \frac{1 - 1 \times 2^8}{1 - 2} = \frac{1 - 256}{-1} = \frac{-255}{-1} = 255.$$

Formula for the Sum of an Infinite Geometric Series When the Common Ratio is Between −1 and 1

$$\text{sum} = \frac{a}{1 - r} \quad \text{where} \quad a = \text{first term} \quad \left(\begin{array}{c} -1 < r < 1 \\ \text{required} \end{array} \right)$$
$$r = \text{common ratio}$$

Example.   Find the sum of the infinite series
$$\tfrac{1}{2} + \tfrac{1}{4} + \tfrac{1}{8} + \tfrac{1}{16} + \tfrac{1}{32} + \ldots$$

$$a = \tfrac{1}{2} \quad r = \tfrac{1}{2}$$

$$\text{sum} = \frac{a}{1 - r} = \frac{\tfrac{1}{2}}{1 - \tfrac{1}{2}} = \frac{\tfrac{1}{2}}{\tfrac{1}{2}} = 1.$$

An infinite geometric series cannot be summed unless $-1 < r < 1$.

ARITHMETIC VERSUS GEOMETRIC SEQUENCES

If two infinite sequences—one arithmetic and one geometric—are both increasing, the geometric sequence will always overtake the arithmetic sequence, no matter how great a headstart the arithmetic sequence has at the beginning.

In 1798, an English economist, Thomas Malthus, used this property of sequences to make a startling prediction. Malthus observed that the population of the world when unchecked tends to increase in a geometric progression, whereas food production increases only in an arithmetic progression. Thus, Malthus predicted that if population growth continues unchecked, we must eventually reach a point where the world's population exceeds the world's food production. In other words, in the case of unchecked population growth, there would be mass starvation. To see how Malthus came to this conclusion, consider the following:

Example.   Planet X has a population of 100,000 individuals and is able to produce food for exactly 100,000 in a given year. But every year after that, the food production capacity increases by 50,000 (an arithmetic progression) and the population increases by 7% (a geometric progression).

At first the increases in food production capacity far exceed the increases in population. But as the table illustrates, eventually the population will overtake food production:

Time	Population	Food Production Capacity	
Beginning year	100,000	100,000	
1	107,000	150,000	At first, the food production
2	114,490	200,000	capacity seems to be building
3	122,540	250,000	up a wide margin over the
4	131,079	300,000	population increases.
5	140,254	350,000	
6	150,072	400,000	
7	160,579	450,000	
8	171,819	500,000	
9	183,846	550,000	
10	196,715	600,000	
11	210,485	650,000	
12	225,219	700,000	During these years, food
13	240,984	750,000	production capacity is about

Time	Population	Food Production Capacity	
14	257,853	800,000	three times the population each year.
15	275,903	850,000	
16	295,216	900,000	
17	315,881	950,000	
18	337,993	1,000,000	
19	361,652	1,050,000	
20	386,968	1,100,000	
21	414,056	1,150,000	
22	443,040	1,200,000	But the food production capacity begins to lose ground. It is now less than three times the population each year.
23	474,053	1,250,000	
24	507,237	1,300,000	
25	542,744	1,350,000	
26	580,736	1,400,000	
27	621,388	1,450,000	
28	664,885	1,500,000	
29	711,427	1,550,000	
30	761,227	1,600,000	
31	814,513	1,650,000	←During the 31st year, population increases 53,286 over the preceding year, while food production increases only 50,000. It is now only a matter of time before the population will overtake the food production capacity.
32	871,529	1,700,000	
33	932,536	1,750,000	
34	997,814	1,800,000	
35	1,067,661	1,850,000	
36	1,142,397	1,900,000	
37	1,222,365	1,950,000	
38	1,307,930	2,000,000	
39	1,399,485	2,050,000	
40	1,497,449	2,100,000	The gap is narrowing between the population and the food production, because the population *increase* (7% annually) is now so much more than the food production increase (a constant 50,000 annually).
41	1,602,270	2,150,000	
42	1,714,429	2,200,000	
43	1,834,439	2,250,000	
44	1,962,848	2,300,000	
45	2,100,247	2,350,000	
46	2,247,264	2,400,000	
47	2,404,572	2,450,000	
48	2,572,892	2,500,000	←In the 48th year, the total population *exceeds* the total food production capacity.

Food production—Arithmetic series
Linear growth

Population—Geometric series
Exponential growth

Food production capacity
Population

2,500,000
2,000,000
1,500,000
1,000,000
500,000

0 5 10 15 20 25 30 35 40 45 50
→ Time, in years

FIBONACCI SEQUENCE

An interesting sequence that is neither arithmetic nor geometric was discovered by Leonardo of Pisa, also known as Fibonacci—an Italian mathematician of the thirteenth century—whose greatest achievement was popularizing for the Western world the Hindu-Arabic numerals in his famous arithmetic, *Liber Abaci*. The Fibonacci sequence progresses as follows:

$$\{1,\ 1,\ 2,\ 3,\ 5,\ 8,\ 13,\ 21,\ 34,\ 55,\ 89,\ 144,\ 233,\dots\}$$

The pattern for this sequence is simple but unusual. The first two terms are 1, and every term thereafter is the sum of the two preceding terms.

Fibonacci first presented the sequence as the answer to a problem posed in *Liber Abaci*. The problem asked:

> If a pair of rabbits produces another pair of rabbits at the end of two months and after that produces another pair of rabbits every month, and if each pair of rabbits produced follows this same pattern, then how many pairs of rabbits will there be at the beginning of each month if all the rabbits live?

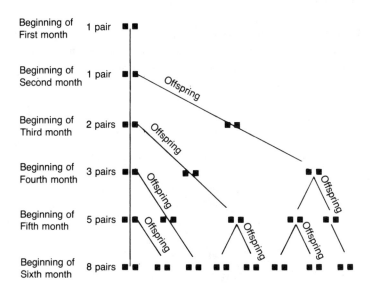

The pine cone has 13 clockwise spirals and 8 counterclockwise; the sunflower has 89 clockwise and 55 counterclockwise.

The Fibonacci sequence might appear to be a mathematical curiosity of interest only to those who dote on solving medieval arithmetic problems. But in fact, the terms of the Fibonacci sequence, 1, 1, 2, 3, 5, 8, 13, 21, 34, 55, 89, ... , turn up in so many unexpected places that the terms alone have been given the name *Fibonacci numbers*.

The Fibonacci numbers describe a surprising variety of natural phenomena. For example, the *spirals* at the center of a sunflower, or on the bottom of a pineapple or a pine cone, are arranged so that the ratio of the number of spirals in one direction to the number of spirals in the

Sunflower photograph by Andreas Feininger.

other direction is composed of two consecutive Fibonacci numbers. If you turn the diagram of rabbits upside down, you can see that the pattern of *branching* is like that of many plants, and the numbers that occur naturally in branching patterns are indeed Fibonacci numbers. Furthermore, part of the Fibonacci sequence can be found in an *octave* on the piano keyboard. In one octave there are

One octave

13 keys altogether,
8 white keys,
5 black keys,
3 black keys in one cluster,
2 black keys in another cluster.

Mathematical curiosities abound. There is a Fibonacci Association that publishes a quarterly journal of these alone.

Example. Consider *Pascal's triangle,* the pattern of coefficients for the *binomial theorem* (see ALGEBRAIC EXPRESSIONS). If you sum the numbers on diagonal lines as shown, the results are the Fibonacci numbers.

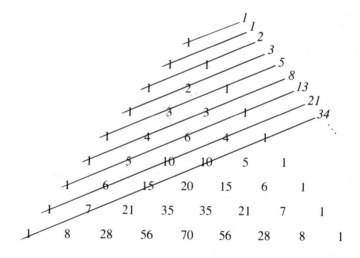

Finally, although the Fibonacci sequence is *not* a geometric sequence, the further the sequence is extended, the more closely it approaches a geometric series with an approximate ratio of 1.6 between successive terms. Actually, this ratio approaches ever more closely the *golden ratio* (or GOLDEN SECTION), of 1.618 . . . that appears so often in art and architecture.

SEQUENCES IN GEOMETRY

n = 1

The idea of a sequence is not limited to arithmetic and algebra. Consider the geometric snowflake figures in the margin. The sequence begins with an equilateral triangle. Then along each side a new equilateral triangle is built up on the middle third of that side. Each successive figure is made in exactly the same way, using the new sides of the preceding figure.

n = 2

This snowflake sequence has a most curious aspect. As the steps continue, the AREAS of the figures increase, and the PERIMETERS also increase. The areas cannot grow larger than the area of a circle containing the snowflake: ◕ ❂ . The perimeters, however, increase without any bound. If the sequence goes on forever, the perimeter becomes INFINITE in length, although the area remains finite!

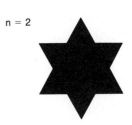

REFERENCES

n = 3

Teri Perl, *Math Equals: Biographies of Women Mathematicians + Related Activities* (Addison-Wesley, 1978), pp. 138–147; gives some exploration of sequences in general as an introduction to the work of Sonya Kovalevskaya, a nineteenth-century Russian woman who overcame many difficulties to become a leading mathematician in Germany and Sweden.

References on the Fibonacci sequence

Joseph and Frances Gies, *Leonard of Pisa and the New Mathematics of the Middle Ages* (Thomas Y. Crowell Co., 1969).

C. Stanley Ogilvy and John T. Anderson, *Excursions in Number Theory* (Oxford University Press, 1966), ch. 11; additional curiosities of the Fibonacci numbers.

N. N. Vorob'ev, *Fibonacci Numbers*, Popular Lectures in Mathematics Series, translated from Russian (Blaisdell, 1961).

References on sequences in geometry

Benoit B. Mandelbrot, *Fractals: Form, Chance, and Dimension* (W. H. Freeman and Co., 1977).

Benoit B. Mandelbrot, *The Fractal Geometry of Nature* (W. H. Freeman and Co., 1982); a reorganized version of the first book, with new developments and even better illustrations. The graphics capabilities of the computer provide a valuable tool for mathematical research.

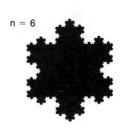

n = 6

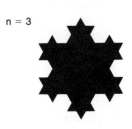

See also the final example of inverse TRIGONOMETRIC FUNCTIONS for the use of infinite series in computing approximations to PI.

SETS

Symbols:

{ ... } A set is usually enclosed in braces.

∈ symbol for "is an
element of"

∉ symbol for "is not
an element of"

SET: a group or collection of items. Each item in a set is called an *element*, or *member*, of the set.

Examples.   {2, 4, 6, 8} = the set with elements 2, 4, 6, and 8
{red, blue, yellow} = the set with elements red, blue, and yellow

$$4 \in \{2, 4, 6, 8\}$$

$$10 \notin \{2, 4, 6, 8\}$$

Set is a basic concept in mathematics. In fact, many mathematicians believe that the concept of set is even more basic than the concept of NUMBER. And in some branches of mathematics, set is a basic undefined term, just as LINE is an undefined term in GEOMETRY.

A set may be any collection of items. It may be a set of individuals, a set of cities, a set of numbers, or a set of points. Furthermore, the elements in a set do not all have to be the same kind of elements. For example, {z, 213, George Washington} constitutes a set.

A set is an *unordered* collection of elements. The set {5, 11, 20} is the same as {20, 5, 11}.

But one property that all sets have in common is that they must be *well-defined*. A set must be defined so that it is always possible to decide whether a given item is or is not a member of that set. The collection of all movies that won an Oscar in 1978 constitutes a set because the list of Oscar winners would determine exactly which movies were members of that set. However, the collection of the five best movies of 1978 does not constitute a set because not everyone would agree on which movies should be included in this group.

WAYS OF DEFINING A SET

A set may be defined by listing all the elements of the set. Such a list is called a *roster*.

Examples. {2, 4, 6, 8}

{John Kennedy, Lyndon Johnson, Richard Nixon}

Sometimes a set is so large that it is impractical or impossible to list all the members. If the members of such a set can be listed in SEQUENCE, then three dots can be used to represent other members following the same sequence.

Examples. {1, 2, 3, 4, . . . ,99, 100}

{5, 10, 15, 20, 25, . . .}

A set may be defined by a written *description*.

Examples. {even integers between 0 and 10}

{presidents of the U.S. who took office in the 1960s}

There may be more than one way to describe a set. For instance, the set in the first example could be defined as {even whole numbers less than 10}. But any description must fit all members of the set and only members of the set. Otherwise the set is not well-defined.

A set may be defined by using a *variable* to represent an arbitrary element of the set and then making a statement about the variable.

Example. {x | x is an even integer and 2 ≤ x ≤ 8} (Read ''the set of all x such that x is an even integer, equal to or greater than 2 and equal to or less than 8.'')

A set of numbers or a set of points may be shown on a NUMBER LINE or on a GRAPH.

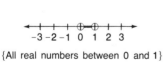

{All real numbers between 0 and 1}

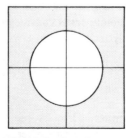

{All points interior to the square and exterior to the circle}

TYPES OF SETS

Finite Set: a set with a finite number of elements; a set whose members can be counted.

Examples. {2, 4, 6, 8}

{1, 2, 3, 4, . . . ,99, 100}

A set may be very large and still be finite. For example, the set of grains of sand needed to fill a swimming pool would be very large indeed. However, if enough people worked together, the counting of all the grains in the pool would eventually come to an end. Thus, this very large set is still finite.

Infinite Set: a set with infinitely many elements. (See INFINITY.)

Examples. {1, 2, 3, 4, 5, 6, . . .}

$\{\frac{1}{2}, \frac{1}{4}, \frac{1}{8}, \frac{1}{16}, \frac{1}{32}, \ldots\}$

The set of natural numbers is an infinite set. No matter how many people worked together on the job, the counting of its elements would never end because there is no last element.

Symbol: { } or ∅

(Either symbol represents the empty set.)

Empty Set (or *null set*): a set with no elements.

Examples. {whole numbers between 2 and 3} = { }

{crocodiles living at the North Pole} = ∅

The empty set is often the result of placing various restrictions or qualifications on the members of a set. For example, {women in the U.S. in the 1960s} is a set with millions of members. The set {women who worked for the U.S. government in the 1960s} is still a large set, but it has fewer members than the first set. And finally, {women who worked for the U.S. government as president of the U.S. in the 1960s} is a well-defined set with no members at all.

The empty set is considered to be a *finite* set since it does not have infinitely many members.

Symbol:

U universal set

Universal Set: a set containing (but not limited to) all the elements being considered in a given problem or discussion.

Examples. If a problem deals with juniors, seniors, basketball players, and band members—all students at Lincoln High, then *U* = {students at Lincoln High}.

If a problem deals with lengths or distances, then U = {positive real numbers}.

SET RELATIONS

Equal Sets: two or more sets that have exactly the same elements.

Examples.   {2, 4, 6, 8} = {even integers between 0 and 10}

{x, y, z} = {z, y, x}

{U.S. Presidents who took office in the 1960s} =
{John Kennedy, Lyndon Johnson, Richard Nixon}

Symbol:

= is equal to

Equivalent Sets: two or more sets that have the same number of elements.

Example.   {x, y, z} $\longleftrightarrow$ {1, 3, 5}   (three elements in each set)

Symbol:

$\longleftrightarrow$ is equivalent to

If two sets are equivalent, then every element in one set can be paired with exactly one element in the other set, and vice versa.

Example.   {x, y, z}
                ↓ ↓ ↓
               {1, 3, 5}

This pairing of elements is called making a *one-to-one correspondence* and can be done with infinite sets as well as finite ones.

Example.   {1, 2, 3, 4, 5, ...}   set of natural numbers
                ↓ ↓ ↓ ↓ ↓
               {2, 4, 6, 8, 10, ...} set of even natural numbers

It is possible to pair every element in the infinite set of natural numbers with exactly one element in the infinite set of even natural numbers. Thus, these two sets are equivalent.

$$\{1, 2, 3, 4, 5, \ldots\} \longleftrightarrow \{2, 4, 6, 8, 10, \ldots\}$$

Disjoint Sets: two or more sets with no elements in common.

Example.   {1, 3, 5, 7, ...}   is disjoint from   {2, 4, 6, 8, ...}

Symbols:

$\subset$ is a subset of

$\not\subset$ is not a subset of

Subset: set A is a *subset* of set B if every element in A is also contained in B.

Examples. $\{1, 2\} \subset \{1, 2, 3\}$

$\{6, 19, 100\} \subset \{1, 2, 3, 4, 5, \ldots\}$

$\{1, 2, 3\} \not\subset \{1, 2\}$

Proper Subset: set A is a *proper* subset of B if A is a subset of B containing at least one element *and* if A is not equal to B.

Examples. $\{a, b\}$ is a proper subset of $\{a, b, c\}$

$\{a, b, c\}$ is a subset of $\{a, b, c\}$ but *not* a proper subset.

The subset relation can be restated in a slightly different way. Set A is a subset of B if A contains no elements that are not also contained in B. Note that the empty set contains no members that are not contained in other sets. Thus, the empty set is a subset of every set.

Example. $\{\ \} \subset \{a, b, c\}$

Power Set: the power set of a given set is the collection of all the possible subsets of the given set.

Example.   The power set of $\{1, 2, 3\}$ is

$$\{1, 2, 3\}, \{1, 2\}, \{1, 3\}, \{2, 3\}, \{1\}, \{2\}, \{3\}, \{\ \}.$$

The *number of subsets* in the power set of a given finite set is equal to 2^n, where n is the number of elements in the given set.

Example. $\{1, 2, 3\}$ has three elements. Thus, $\{1, 2, 3\}$ has 2^3 or 8 subsets in its power set.

VENN DIAGRAMS

Venn diagrams are geometric figures used to picture sets and set relations as shown.

Although such figures were used as early as the eighteenth century by the Swiss mathematician Leonhard Euler, they are called Venn diagrams in honor of John Venn. Venn was an English mathematician in the late nineteenth century who used these diagrams extensively to illustrate set relations and who introduced the idea of using a rectangle to represent the universal set.

The size and shape of Venn diagrams are unimportant. But generally a rectangle is used to represent the universal set, and circles are used to represent subsets of the universal set.

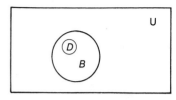

$D \subset B \subset U$

Example. U = {students at Lincoln High}
B = {band members at Lincoln High}
D = {band members at Lincoln High who play the drums}

Venn diagrams are useful for illustrating set operations.

SET OPERATIONS

Symbol:

$\cap$ intersection

Set Intersection: the *intersection* of two sets A and B is the set of elements common to *both A and B*.

Example.   Set A = {1, 2, 4, 8}
Set B = {0, 4, 8, 12, 16}

$A \cap B$ = {4, 8}

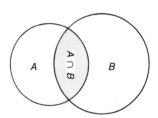

Shaded area = $A \cap B$

When the intersection of two sets is the empty set, the two sets are *disjoint*.

Example. R = {1, 3, 5}
S = {2, 4, 6}

$R \cap S$ = { }; R and S are disjoint.

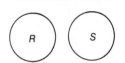

R and S are disjoint

Set Union: the *union* of two sets A and B is the set of all elements contained *either* in A or in B or in both.

Symbol:

$\cup$ union

Example. A = {1, 2, 4, 8}
B = {0, 4, 8, 12, 16}

$A \cup B$ = {0, 1, 2, 4, 8, 12, 16}

The *number of elements* in the union of two finite sets A and B is equal to the number of elements in A, plus the number of elements in B, minus the number of elements in $A \cap B$.

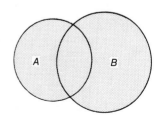

Shaded area = $A \cup B$

In the previous examples, each set is involved in only one operation. However, the results of one set operation may be used in another operation.

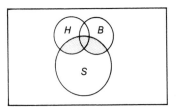

Shaded area = $S \cap \{H \cup B\}$

Example. $H = \{$members of the Honor Society at Lincoln High$\}$
$B = \{$members of the band at Lincoln High$\}$
$S = \{$members of the senior class at Lincoln High$\}$

$S \cap \{H \cup B\} = \{$seniors at Lincoln who are either in the Honor Society or in the band or in both$\}$

Set Complementation: if set A is a subset of B, then the *complement of A in B* is the set of elements contained in B but not in A.

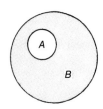

Shaded area = $B - A$ =
complement of A in B

Example. $A = \{1, 3, 5\}$
$B = \{1, 2, 3, 4, 5\}$

Thus $A \subset B$, and the complement of A in $B = B - A = \{2, 4\}$.

The phrase "complement of A" alone, without a specific "in B," refers to the complement of A in the universal set U. That is, the complement of A is the set of all elements in U but not in A. The complement of A may be symbolized by A'.

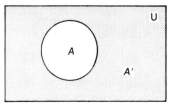

Shaded area = A' =
complement of A

Example. $U = \{$students at Lincoln High$\}$
$A = \{$members of athletic teams at Lincoln High$\}$
$A' = $ the complement of A
$= \{$all students at Lincoln High who are not members of athletic teams$\}$

Set operations can also be performed on more complicated sets:

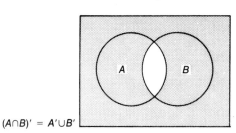

$(A \cap B)' = A' \cup B'$

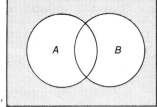

$(A \cup B)' = A' \cap B'$

These two statements are often referred to as *DeMorgan's rules*, after the nineteenth-century British logician Augustus DeMorgan.

CARTESIAN PRODUCT (or Cross Product): the Cartesian product of two sets A and B is the set of *ordered pairs* that can be formed by pairing every element from A with every element from B, always listing the A element first and the B element second.

Symbol:

$A \times B$ A cross B

Example.   Set A = toppings for ice cream
Set B = flavors of ice cream

Cartesian product $A \times B$ lists all combinations of toppings and ice cream flavors.

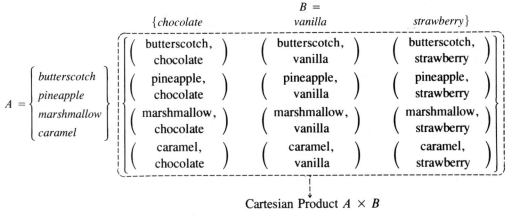

Cartesian Product $A \times B$

Although for sets in general the elements are not ordered, the individual pairs in a Cartesian product are ordered. The first element in each pair is always taken from the first set named in the cross product. Thus, from the two sets C and P two different cross products may be formed. The set $C \times P$ will be entirely different from the set $P \times C$.

Example. $C = \{1, 2, 3\}$
$P = \{4, 5\}$

$$P = \{4, 5\}$$

$$C = \left\{ \begin{array}{c} 1 \\ 2 \\ 3 \end{array} \right\} \quad \left\{ \begin{array}{cc} (1, 4) & (1, 5) \\ (2, 4) & (2, 5) \\ (3, 4) & (3, 5) \end{array} \right\}$$

Cartesian product $C \times P$

$$C = \{1, 2, 3\}$$

$$P = \left\{ \begin{array}{c} 4 \\ 5 \end{array} \right\} \quad \left\{ \begin{array}{ccc} (4,\ 1) & (4,\ 2) & (4,\ 3) \\ (5,\ 1) & (5,\ 2) & (5,\ 3) \end{array} \right\} \dashrightarrow \begin{array}{c} \text{Cartesian product} \\ P \times C \end{array}$$

The *number of pairs* in a Cartesian product is equal to the number of elements in the first set multiplied by the number of elements in the second set.

If $\mathcal{R}$ = the set of REAL NUMBERS, then $\mathcal{R} \times \mathcal{R}$ represents the set of all possible ordered pairs of real numbers. Members of this set can be represented on a GRAPH.

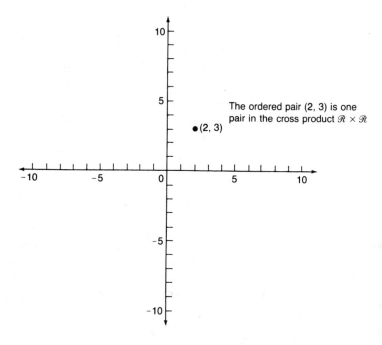

The ordered pair (2, 3) is one pair in the cross product $\mathcal{R} \times \mathcal{R}$

The idea of representing ordered pairs of real numbers as POINTS in a PLANE was first proposed by the French mathematician René Descartes in the early seventeenth century. And it is in his honor that the cross product of two sets is called a *Cartesian product;* the cross product of two real number lines is called a *Cartesian* COORDINATE *plane.*

DEVELOPMENT OF SET THEORY

The notion of set as a collection of elements is doubtless nearly as ancient as the human race. Evidence from primitive tribes and from ancient artifacts suggests that long before people could count they were able to keep track of how many sheep they had by carving one notch on a stick for every animal. These people were really making a one-to-one correspondence between the elements in a set of animals and the elements in a set of notches. Thus, even before people used numbers, they used equivalent sets.

Although mathematicians had long used an intuitive notion of set, the idea of set as a formal mathematical concept was not proposed until the nineteenth century. At that time, two men—George Boole of England and Georg Cantor of Germany—working independently on quite different problems came to the conclusion that set was an important basic concept.

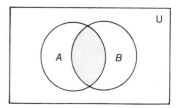

Shaded area = A *and* B are true

Boole began working with sets in an attempt to construct a LOGIC that used symbols instead of words. He saw that the logical condition "*A and B* are both true" is equivalent to set intersection, and that the logical condition "Either *A or B or* both are true" is equivalent to set union.

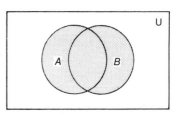

Shaded area = A *or* B or both are true

Example. U = {applicants to Center College}
A = {applicants who have graduated from high school}
B = {applicants who scored more than 500 on entrance exam}

Then $A \cap B$ = {applicants who graduated from high school *and* scored more than 500 on entrance exam}
and $A \cup B$ = {applicants who graduated from high school *or* scored more than 500 on entrance exam or both}

Using the concept of set, Boole worked out operations for a symbolic logic called the ALGEBRA of sets, or Boolean algebra.

Georg Cantor discovered the importance of sets while investigating the properties of NUMBERS, and he became convinced that set was an even more basic concept than number. He developed a MATHEMATICAL SYSTEM for operating with sets called *set theory*. Cantor was the first to define formally many of the terms appearing in this article, such as "equivalent sets." He showed how the concept of equivalent sets made it possible to compare the magnitudes of INFINITE sets. And he developed an ARITHMETIC called transfinite arithmetic that operated on cardinal numbers assigned to infinite sets.

Cantor's theory of sets was so revolutionary that many of his fellow mathematicians rejected it and ridiculed him. During his lifetime, Cantor received little acclaim for his discoveries and he was unable to get a teaching post at a first-rate university. Possibly as a result of harsh criticism from some fellow mathematicians, Cantor suffered a nervous breakdown and spent the final years of his life in a mental hospital.

But Cantor's theory ultimately prevailed. In the twentieth century, various eminent mathematicians, including David Hilbert of Germany, concluded that Cantor had been right. As a consequence many mathematical concepts, such as ARITHMETIC OPERATION, RELATION, and FUNCTION, were redefined in terms of set.

Biographical references

Eric T. Bell, *Men of Mathematics* (Simon and Schuster, 1937; Fireside paperback), Ch. 23, "Complete Independence" (Boole) and Ch. 29, "Paradise Lost?" (Cantor).

SET THEORY AND ELECTRIC CIRCUITRY

The algebra of sets has a number of applications, including the design of electric circuitry for electronic computers. Given adequate data, a COMPUTER is able to carry out either of the following commands:

"If *A and B* are true, do *C*."
"If *A or B* is true, do *D*."

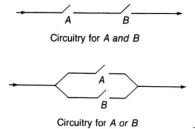

Circuitry for *A and B*

Circuitry for *A or B*

To carry out these commands, a computer has what are called "and-gates" and "or-gates." In an and-gate, two switches are wired in series, and the current only flows when both switches are closed. The switches are closed when both logical conditions are true—the equivalent of set intersection. In an or-gate the two switches are wired in parallel. Thus, current can flow if either switch or both switches are closed; that is, if either logical condition is true—the equivalent of set union.

References on logical circuit design

Irving Adler, *Thinking Machines: A Layman's Introduction to Logic, Boolean Algebra, and Computers* (The John Day Co., 1961); a complete treatise, clearly written.

Historical Topics for the Mathematics Classroom, 31st Yearbook of the National Council of Teachers of Mathematics (1969), pp. 284–287; simple circuits.

Nicholas Pippinger, "Complexity Theory," *Scientific American,* June 1978, pp. 114–124; how to establish efficient switching networks for a computer or telephone exchange.

James Poirot and David Groves, *Computer Science for the Teacher* (Sterling Swift Publishing Co., 1976), pp. 86–96; simple circuits.

For more on infinite sets, see INFINITY and ARITHMETIC.
Boolean algebra is mentioned under ALGEBRA and LOGIC.

SIGNED NUMBERS

SIGNED NUMBER (or Directed Number): a number that is either positive or negative. A *positive* number is greater than zero. A *negative* number is less than zero. The number *zero* is neither positive nor negative.

Symbols:

+ positive, or plus
− negative, or minus

Examples. +15
−8
3 (An unsigned number is assumed to be positive.)

Signed numbers indicate both *magnitude* (size) and *direction* with respect to some starting point or zero point. There are many everyday situations in which such numbers are commonly used.

Examples. When the temperature is 15 degrees above zero, it is reported as +15° (or 15°); but when it falls 15 degrees below 0, it is reported as −15°.

In football, a five-yard gain is +5 yards, while a five-yard loss is −5 yards.

On a bank statement, a deposit of $12 is listed as +$12, but a check or withdrawal for the same amount is listed as −$12.

The signed numbers and zero form a continuous sequence of numbers that can be represented on a NUMBER LINE. Starting at zero, the positive numbers go on to infinity in one direction and the negatives go on to infinity in the other. Thus, every signed number on the line can be paired with another number which is the same distance from zero but in

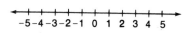

Opposites

$-5\frac{1}{2}$ -3 Opposites   3 $5\frac{1}{2}$

−6 −5 −4 −3 −2 −1 0 +1 +2 +3 +4 +5 +6

519

the opposite direction. For example, -3 can be paired with $+3$ (or 3); $5\frac{1}{2}$ can be paired with $-5\frac{1}{2}$. Each member in such a pair is said to be the *opposite*, or *additive inverse*, of the other.

A signed number and its opposite are the same *distance from zero*, which is called the *absolute value* of the number. For example, $+3$ and -3 have the same absolute value, written $|3|$ or $|-3|$, which equals 3.

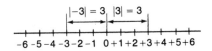

Thus, both members of a pair of opposites have the same absolute value since they are the same distance from zero, although in opposite directions. The positive member of a pair of opposites gives the absolute value of each member of the pair. (For more on absolute values, see a later section of this article.)

ARITHMETIC OPERATIONS ON SIGNED NUMBERS

Signed numbers can be added, subtracted, multiplied, or divided. However, there are special rules for performing these operations. And the result is correct only if it bears the correct sign. The rules for performing operations with signed numbers are called the *rules (or laws) of signs*.

Addition

> To add two numbers with the *same sign*, add the absolute values and affix the common sign to the sum.

Examples.

$$\begin{array}{r} (+3) \\ + \ (+6) \\ \hline +9 \end{array} \qquad \begin{array}{r} (-3) \\ + \ (-2) \\ \hline -5 \end{array}$$

> To add two numbers with *different signs*, find the difference in their absolute values and affix the sign of the larger absolute value to the difference.

Examples.

$$\begin{array}{r} (+12) \\ + \ (-17) \\ \hline -\ 5 \end{array} \qquad \begin{array}{r} (+19) \\ + \ \ (-4) \\ \hline +15 \end{array}$$

Addition of signed numbers is like moving forward and backward on football field. If a football team loses 5 yards on one play and gains 2 ards on the next play, the net result of the two plays will be a 3-yard)ss.

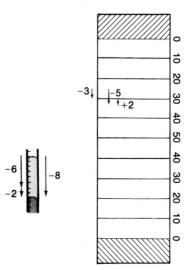

$$-5 + 2 = -3 \text{ yards}$$

If the temperature falls 6 degrees in one hour and then falls 2 more egrees during the next hour, the net change in temperature at the end of ıe two hours would be −8 degrees.

$$-6 + (-2) = -8°$$

The addition of signed numbers can be illustrated on a number line:

- to *add* a *positive* number, you move that many units forward (*in a positive direction*);
- to *add* a *negative* number, you move that many units backward (*in a negative direction*).

Examples.

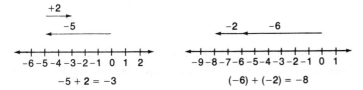

$$-5 + 2 = -3 \qquad (-6) + (-2) = -8$$

Subtraction

Subtraction is the *inverse* or *opposite* of addition. Thus, if you are ubtracting on a number line, you move in the opposite direction:

- to *subtract* a *positive* number, you move backwards (*in a negative direction*);
- to *subtract* a *negative* number, you move forward (*in a positive direction*).

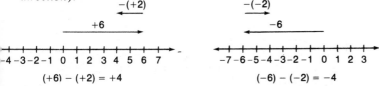

$$(+6) - (+2) = +4 \qquad (-6) - (-2) = -4$$

Examples. Notice that subtracting a +2 leads to the same result as adding -2. And subtracting -2 is the same as adding $+2$. Thus, the rule of signs for subtraction is as follows.

> To subtract one signed number from another, replace the number to be subtracted with its opposite and then add.

Examples.

$$\frac{(+12)}{- (-17)} = \frac{\begin{array}{r}(+12)\\ + (+17)\end{array}}{+29} \qquad \frac{(+105)}{- (+17)} = \frac{\begin{array}{r}(+105)\\ + (-17)\end{array}}{+88}$$

$$\frac{(-33)}{- (-14)} = \frac{\begin{array}{r}(-33)\\ + (+14)\end{array}}{-19}$$

An everyday example of subtracting a negative number is the taking away of a debt. For example, if you owe $25 to a store, then the balance of your account with that store is $-$25. However, if you return a shirt that you just bought from the store for $16 and they subtract that sixteen-dollar debt from your account, you will then owe the store only $9.

$$\frac{\begin{array}{r}-\$25\\ - \quad -16\end{array}}{-9}$$

That is, subtracting a debt of $16 is the same as making a payment of $16. Subtracting a negative number is the same as adding a positive one.

Multiplication

> To multiply two numbers with the *same sign*, multiply the absolute values of the numbers and affix a positive sign to the product.

Examples.

$$\frac{\begin{array}{r}(+3)\\ \times (+2)\end{array}}{+6} \qquad \frac{\begin{array}{r}(-7)\\ \times (-4)\end{array}}{+28}$$

> To multiply two numbers with *different signs*, multiply the absolute values of the numbers and affix a negative sign to the product.

Examples. $(+8)$ (-5)
$$\underline{\times\ (-4)}\qquad\underline{\times\ (+2)}$$
$$-32\qquad\quad -10$$

The rule of signs for multiplication is set to be consistent with conventional arithmetic:

- Multiplying *two positive* numbers gives a *positive product,* as everyone knows from elementary arithmetic.
- Multiplying a *positive* number by a *negative* number gives a *negative product,* as can be shown by repeated addition:

Examples. $3 \times 2 = 2$ $3 \times (-2) = -2$
$$\qquad\qquad 2\qquad\qquad\qquad\qquad -2$$
$$\qquad\quad\underline{+2}\qquad\qquad\qquad\underline{+\ -2}$$
$$\qquad\qquad 6\qquad\qquad\qquad\qquad -6$$

- Multiplying a *negative* number by a *positive* number also gives a *negative product,* because the order of multiplication does not affect the product.
- Multiplying *two negative* numbers gives a *positive* product, which works mathematically but is not so easy to explain. One approach is to consider an enormous oil tank at a refinery:

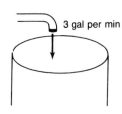

Refined oil is produced to fill the tank at the rate of 3 gallons a minute. During filling, you can observe that

> 10 minutes hence $(+10)$,
> at a fill rate of 3 gallons/minute $(+3)$,
> the tank will hold 30 gallons more $(+30)$.

$(+10) \times (+3) = +30$

> 10 minutes ago (-10),
> at a fill rate of 3 gallons/minute $(+3)$,
> the tank held 30 gallons less (-30).

$(-10) \times (+3) = -30$

After the tank is full, production moves on to other tanks. When it is time to ship the oil from this tank, it will be pumped out at the rate of 45 gallons per minute. In each minute the level of oil *drops* by 45 gallons. During pumping, you can observe that

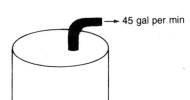

> 10 minutes hence $(+10)$,
> at a pump rate of 45 gallons/minute (-45),
> the tank will hold 450 gallons less (-450).

$(+10) \times (-45) = -450$

$$(-10) \times (-45) = +450$$

$$\begin{cases} \text{10 minutes ago } (-10), \\ \text{at a pump rate of 45 gallons/minute } (-45), \\ \text{the tank held 450 gallons more } (+450). \end{cases}$$

Division

> To divide one signed number by another with the *same sign*, divide the absolute values and affix a positive sign to the quotient.

Examples.
$$\frac{+12}{+3} = +4 \qquad \begin{array}{r} +5 \\ -3\overline{)-15} \end{array}$$

> To divide one signed number by a number with a *different sign*, divide the absolute values and affix a negative sign to the quotient.

Examples.
$$\frac{+7}{-2} = -3\tfrac{1}{2} \qquad \begin{array}{r} -5 \\ +6\overline{)-30} \end{array}$$

Division is the *inverse* operation of multiplication. Therefore the rule of signs for division is determined by the rule of signs for multiplication.

Examples. Since $(+3) \times (+2) = +6$, then $(+6) \div (+2) = +3$
Since $(+3) \times (-2) = -6$, then $(-6) \div (-2) = +3$
Since $(-3) \times (-2) = +6$, then $(+6) \div (-2) = -3$
Since $(-3) \times (+2) = -6$, then $(-6) \div (+2) = -3$

Symbol: $|-3|$

the absolute value of negative three

ABSOLUTE VALUE: The absolute value of a signed number is its *distance from zero*, without regard to direction.

Examples.

$$|0| = 0$$

$$|-3| = 3 \qquad |3| = 3$$
$$|-5\tfrac{1}{2}| = 5\tfrac{1}{2} \qquad |5\tfrac{1}{2}| = 5\tfrac{1}{2}$$

The absolute value can be found for any number or ALGEBRAIC EXPRESSION:

|positive number| = the positive number

|negative number| = − the negative number (that is,

the *opposite* of the negative number;

this opposite is positive.)

Given any two numbers A and B on a number line, the distance between them is always equal to $|A - B|$, which is in turn always equal to $|B - A|$.

Examples.   Distance from A to B is 4 units.

$$|A - B| = |B - A|$$
$$|7 - 3| = |3 - 7|$$
$$|4| = |-4|$$
$$4 = 4$$

Distance from A to B is 6 units.

$$|A - B| = |B - A|$$
$$|-1 - 5| = |5 - (-1)|$$
$$|-6| = |6|$$
$$6 = 6$$

Care must be taken in *combining* absolute values: $|A| + |B|$ sometimes, but not always, equals $|A + B|$.

Examples. $$|A| + |B| = |A + B|$$
$$|3| + |7| = |3 + 7|$$
$$3 + 7 = 10$$
$$10 = 10$$

$$|A| + |B| > |A + B|$$
$$|-1| + |5| > |-1 + 5|$$
$$1 + 5 > 4$$
$$6 > 4$$

The only certain general statement you can make is that

$$|A| + |B| \geq |A + B|.$$

When solving EQUATIONS or INEQUALITIES involving the absolute value of a *variable*, it is usually necessary to consider separately the cases of positive and negative quantities between the vertical bars.

Example. Find all real numbers x such that $|x + 3| = 5$. (The absolute value of the sum is equal to 5.)

Since 5 is the absolute value of both $+5$ and -5, the value of the sum $x + 3$ could be either $+5$ or -5. Therefore, there are two possible EQUATIONS and two possible solutions:

$$x + 3 = 5, \text{ which gives } x = 2$$
$$or$$
$$x + 3 = -5, \text{ which gives } x = -8$$

two solutions

Example. Find all real numbers x such that $|x| < 2$. (The absolute value of x is less than 2.)

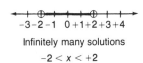

Infinitely many solutions

$-2 < x < +2$

This INEQUALITY has many possible solutions. For example, $+1$, -1, $+\frac{1}{2}$, $-\frac{1}{2}$, $+\frac{1}{4}$, $-\frac{1}{4}$, and 0 all have an absolute value less than 2. However, all possible solutions to this inequality must be less than $+2$ and greater than -2, as shown on the number line. Any number outside this range would have an absolute value equal to or greater than 2.

Thus, $|x| < +2$ is true if and only if $x < +2$ *and* $x > -2$. A short way to write this is $-2 < x < +2$ (read "x is greater than -2 and less than $+2$").

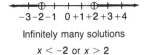

Infinitely many solutions

$x < -2$ or $x > 2$

Example. Find all real numbers x such that $|x| > 2$. (The absolute value of x is greater than 2.)

This is true if and only if $x > 2$ *or* $x < -2$. There is no shorter way to write this combination.

WHY NEGATIVE NUMBERS ARE CALLED NEGATIVE

Negative numbers were introduced by the Hindus about A.D. 700 to represent debits. Both Hindus and Arabs used them rather freely, but for many centuries Europeans were very reluctant to do so. One of the earliest examples of Western use of signed numbers is found in a German business arithmetic of the fifteenth century, where the signs $+$ and $-$ are used to indicate surplus and deficiency.

But business people were not the only ones who needed to use numbers less than zero. Mathematicians also needed such numbers to solve problems in ALGEBRA. In 1545, the Italian mathematician Girolamo Cardano showed negative solutions to problems in his famous algebra *Ars Magna*.

Although other mathematicians soon began to work with negative numbers and used them as solutions to problems, many were still very uncomfortable with the idea of numbers smaller than zero. One six-teenth century German mathematician, Michael Stifel, called such numbers "absurd." René Descartes, the French mathematician who in the seventeenth century first stated the rules of signs, called them "false" numbers. And as late as the eighteenth century, the authors of some textbooks declared that multiplication of a negative by a negative was impossible.

The word "negative" comes from a Latin word meaning "to deny or say no to." And the fact that numbers smaller than zero were called "negative" reflects the skeptical attitude of early mathematicians toward them.

REFERENCE

Martin Gardner, "Mathematical Games: The concept of negative numbers and the difficulty of grasping it," *Scientific American,* June 1977, pp. 131–134; an engaging account of history, rules, and persistent uneasiness—with many nice tidbits.

See also NUMBER LINES and REAL NUMBERS.

SIGNIFICANT DIGITS

SIGNIFICANT DIGIT: any digit that is obtained by actual measurement and thus is not simply a placeholder used to position the decimal point.

Examples.   (significant digits are underlined)

108 pounds	the weight of a person
3.2 kilograms	the mass of a newborn baby
12,000 pounds	the weight of an elephant
56,290 square miles	the area of the state of Iowa
0.00000001016 centimeters	the diameter of a hydrogen atom

EXACT NUMBERS AND APPROXIMATE NUMBERS

Numbers that represent discrete, or countable, quantities are said to be *exact numbers*. For example, in the statement "There are 100 counties in North Carolina," the number 100 is an exact number. There are not $100\frac{1}{2}$ counties or $99\frac{3}{4}$ counties. The counties can be counted, and there are exactly 100.

However, numbers that are arrived at by measurement of a continuous quantity, by estimation, or by rounding off are said to be *approximate numbers*. For example, in the statement "It is 100 kilometers from here to Chicago," the number 100 is an approximate number. It represents a measurement of distance, and depending upon the precision of the measurement, 100 kilometers may mean that the distance is between $99\frac{1}{2}$ and $100\frac{1}{2}$ kilometers, or it may mean that the distance is between 95 and 105 kilometers.

SIGNIFICANT DIGITS IN APPROXIMATE NUMBERS

In approximate numbers, some digits are significant and some digits may be nonsignificant. The *significant digits* are those that represent the result of some measurement. *Nonsignificant digits* are zeros that serve only to place the decimal point correctly.

Example.   Suppose you read that a spacecraft headed for Saturn was 64,000,000 miles from Earth. If you thought about it, you would probably conclude that the final zero in that measurement was nonsignificant. That is, you would hardly suppose that the distance had been measured to the mile and found to be exactly 64 million, with no thousands of miles, no hundreds of miles, not even one mile left over. In fact, the approximate number in this example would probably represent a measurement to the nearest million miles, in which case all six of the final zeros would be nonsignificant. They would serve only to place the decimal point.

In our NUMERAL SYSTEM there are 10 digits—0, 1, 2, 3, 4, 5, 6, 7, 8, 9; and the digits 1 through 9 are always significant. The digit zero, however, may or may not be significant depending upon where it occurs in a number; there are a few special rules:

- Zeros that occur between significant digits are *significant*.

Examples.   108 (3 significant digits)
          2003 (4 significant digits)

- In a number between 0 and 1, zeros that occur to the left of the first nonzero digit are *nonsignificant*. They serve only to place the decimal point.

Examples.   0.00000001016 (4 significant digits)
          0.00032   (2 significant digits)

- After a decimal point, zeros that occur to the right of the last nonzero digit are *significant*. They indicate the precision of the measurement.

Examples.   0.3800   (4 significant digits)
          0.00320   (3 significant digits)

• In a whole number ending in one or more zeros, the final zeros are assumed to be *nonsignificant* unless they are marked in some way as being significant.

Examples.   123,000   (3 significant digits)

470,500   (4 significant digits)

The significant digits in an approximate number convey two kinds of information: they indicate the smallest unit of measure used in obtaining the approximate number and they indicate how many of those units there are in the number.

Approximate number	Smallest unit of measure	Number of units	Number of significant digits
108 pounds	pound	108	3
3.2 kilograms	tenth of a kilogram	32	2
12,000 pounds	thousand pounds	12	2
56,290 square miles	10 square miles	5,629	4
0.00000001016 centimeters	hundred billionth of a centimeter	1,016	4

MARKING SIGNIFICANT ZEROS

Consider the number 5600. As it is written, you would assume that it is correct to the nearest hundred. There are 56 hundreds; hence, there are 2 significant digits. However, it would be entirely possible for something to measure 5600 when measured to the nearest ten or even when measured to the nearest unit. That is, under certain circumstances, the number 5600 might have 3 or even 4 significant digits. For example, the area of a house might measure 5600 square feet to the nearest 10 square feet, or a bank account might contain exactly 5600 dollars.

If the final zeros of a whole number are significant, they are usually marked in some way to distinguish them from nonsignificant zeros. There are a number of ways of calling attention to significant zeros:

• The precision of the measurement can be stated *in words*.

Examples.   5600 correct to the nearest ten (3 significant digits)

5600 correct to the nearest unit (4 significant digits)

• A *dot* can be placed over the last significant digit.

Examples.   5600   (3 significant digits)
5600   (4 significant digits)

• *Nonsignificant* zeros can be written *smaller* than the significant digits.

Examples.   240,000   (3 significant digits)
240,000   (4 significant digits)

• The number can be written in SCIENTIFIC NOTATION. All zeros that appear in a number written in scientific notation are significant.

Examples. 5.6×10^3 (2 significant digits)
5.60×10^3 (3 significant digits)
5.600×10^3 (4 significant digits)

Scientific notation is the most common way of indicating significant zeros.

PRECISION AND ACCURACY

The *precision* of an approximate number refers to the absolute size of possible errors. For example, if a measurement is made to the nearest centimeter, the maximum possible error would be $\frac{1}{2}$ centimeter, or 0.5 centimeter. If two distances were measured to the nearest centimeter, and one was found to be 105 centimeters and the other was found to be 5 centimeters, both measurements would be to the same level of precision. The maximum possible error in each case would be 0.5 centimeter.

The *accuracy* of an approximate number, however, refers to the RATIO of the size of the maximum possible error to the size of the number. This ratio is called the *relative error*. For example, the relative error of a measurement of 105 centimeters to the nearest centimeter would be

$$\frac{0.5}{105}, \quad \text{or} \quad 0.0048.$$

However, the relative error of a measurement of 5 centimeters to the nearest centimeter would be

$$\frac{0.5}{5}, \quad \text{or} \quad 0.1.$$

Thus, although the measurements 105 centimeters and 5 centimeters are equally precise, they are not equally accurate. The measurement of 105 centimeters is more accurate because it has the smaller relative error.

The precision of an approximate number depends upon the size of the smallest measuring unit, for example, whether the measurement is to the nearest 10 feet, to the nearest foot, to the nearest tenth of a foot. The accuracy of a measurement depends on the number of significant digits in the measurement. Two measurements with the same number of significant digits have been measured to the same level of accuracy though they may not be measured to the same level of precision.

ROUNDING OFF

Exact numbers and approximate numbers are often rounded off to some desired level of precision. For example, if the distance between 2 towns is found to be 57 miles, this measurement may be rounded off to 60 miles if precision is desired only to the nearest 10 miles.

To round off a number to a certain level of precision, you consider only the digit immediately to the right of the place to which the number is to be rounded. For example, if a number is to be rounded to the nearest hundred, you consider only the digit in the tens place.

- If the digit immediately to the right is less than 5, this digit and all digits to the right of it are dropped;
- If the digit immediately to the right is greater than or equal to 5, this digit and all digits to the right of it are dropped and the last digit to be retained is increased by one.
- If, and only if, the number being rounded is a whole number, the dropped digits are replaced by zeros.

Examples.   349 rounded to the nearest hundred = 300
                    351 rounded to the nearest hundred = 400
                    60.075 rounded to the nearest tenth = 60.1

Some authorities recommend one exception to the rule. They point out that since the digit 5 is exactly halfway between 1 and 9, rounding every 5 upward tends to inflate the size of the results. To correct this problem, it has been suggested that when rounding a 5 that is the last digit or is followed only by zeros, you should round so that the result is always an even number.

Examples.   7.625 rounded to the nearest hundredth = 7.62

$$4.750 \text{ rounded to the nearest tenth} = 4.8$$
$$4.650 \text{ rounded to the nearest tenth} = 4.6$$

Since there are likely to be the same number of odds and evens in the data, this procedure rounds upward only about half the numbers ending in five, therefore preventing an inflation of the results.

COMPUTING WITH APPROXIMATE NUMBERS

When doing computations with approximate numbers, it is possible to get a result that appears to be more precise than the original data in the problem. For example, if the dimensions of a room are 12.5 feet by 10.5 feet, multiplying length times width gives an area of 131.25 square feet. However, it makes no sense to suppose that this answer is correct to the nearest hundredth, when the original measurements used to get the answer were correct only to the nearest tenth. As this example illustrates, computation with approximate numbers can lead to results in which final digits other than zero are really nonsignificant. Such results are usually rounded off to the nearest significant digit:

- When *adding* or *subtracting* approximate numbers, round the result to the same level of precision as the least precise number in the problem. For example, if the least precise number is correct only to the nearest tenth, then the result should be rounded off to the nearest tenth.

Examples.

```
  4.375                              65.05   (least precise)
  1.2    (least precise)           − 11.252
+ 5.07                              ─────────
─────────                            53.798 = 53.80 approximately
 10.645 = 10.6 approximately
```

- When *multiplying* or *dividing* with approximate numbers, round off the result so that it has the same number of significant digits as the number with the fewest significant digits in the problem. For example, if the number with the fewest significant digits has 2, the result should be rounded to 2 significant digits.

Examples.

```
         12.5
  ×       11  (fewest significant digits)
  ─────────────
         12 5
       125
  ─────────────
        137.5 = 140 approximately
```

$$\frac{58.2}{1.2 \text{ (fewest significant digits)}} = \quad \frac{4\ 8.5}{1.2)\overline{58.2\,0}} = 49 \text{ approximately}$$

$$\begin{array}{r} 48 \\ \hline 10\ 2 \\ 9\ 6 \\ \hline 6\ 0 \\ 6\ 0 \\ \hline \hline \end{array}$$

It is important to note that these rules apply only to computation with approximate numbers. In computations with exact numbers such as the exact amount of money in a bank account and an exact rate of interest, these rules for rounding do not apply.

See also SCIENTIFIC NOTATION.

SIMILARITY

SIMILARITY: in geometry, the property of having exactly the same shape, though not necessarily the same size.

The phrase "similar to" in everyday usage means "a little bit like." Its definition in mathematics is more precise because it involves being alike in only one sense: *identical in shape, not* necessarily identical in *size.*

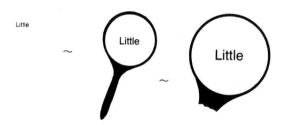

You are already familiar with numerous examples of similar figures. When you look at something through a magnifying glass, what you see is similar to the original object, only larger. In the enlargement of a photograph, the images are similar to the images in the original smaller photograph. In the directions accompanying a sewing pattern, the illus-

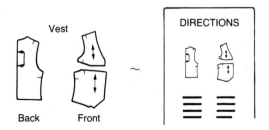

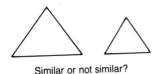

Similar or not similar?

tration of each pattern piece is similar to the pattern piece itself. The members of each pair of similar figures have exactly the same shape though not necessarily the same size.

Just by looking at two figures, it is often difficult to decide whether or not they are similar. Two triangles appear to have the same shape, but is it exactly the same? What conditions are sufficient to insure that two figures are geometrically similar?

CONDITIONS FOR SIMILARITY

Figures that are geometrically similar have two important properties:

- their corresponding angles are congruent, *and*
- their corresponding linear dimensions are in proportion.

Corresponding parts of two figures are those parts that occur in the same relative position when the two figures have the same orientation. *Congruent* ANGLES are angles of equal measure. *Linear dimensions* are lengths, such as length of a side or diameter of a circle. To be in PROPORTION means to have the same RATIO. These two properties are sufficient conditions to insure similarity. That is, they insure that figures have the same shape, whether or not they have the same size.

Congruent angles are commonly indicated by marking their arcs with the same number of little slashes—⌧⌧ and ⩘⩘—as shown in the examples to follow.

The second property of similarity—that corresponding lengths are in constant ratio—is of crucial importance in applications involving measurement. The constant ratio is called the *scale factor*. A "half-scale" drawing or model has every length half the original length.

Examples. Polygons $ABCD$ and $A'B'C'D'$ are similar. Angle A of the first figure corresponds to angle A' of the second, and so on, so

$$\angle A = \angle A', \ \angle B = \angle B', \ \angle C = \angle C', \ \angle D = \angle D'.$$

Side AB of the first figure corresponds to side $A'B'$ of the second, and so on, so

$$\frac{AB}{A'B'} = \frac{BC}{B'C'} = \frac{CD}{C'D'} = \frac{DA}{D'A'}$$

$$\frac{6}{3} = \frac{5}{2.5} = \frac{3}{1.5} = \frac{4}{2} = 2 \leftarrow \text{Scale factor: } ABCD \text{ has a scale 2 times that of } A'B'C'D'$$

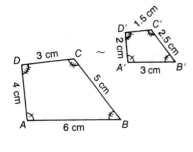

Similar polygons

These two polygons are also similar to $A''B''C''D''$, which can be rotated into the same orientation as $ABCD$ and $A'B'C'D'$.

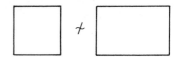

For two polygons to be similar, *both* properties must be true. If only one holds true, the polygons may not be similar.

Examples.   If angles are congruent but sides are not in proportion, figures are *not* similar.

If sides are in proportion (in this case they are even congruent), but angles are *not* congruent, figures are *not* similar.

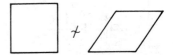

Sides in proportion (in fact, congruent), but angles not congruent

Therefore figures are *not* similar

Similarity of Geometric Figures

The following pairs of similar figures each demonstrate exactly the same shape, though not necessarily the same size. Each pair satisfies the two conditions for similarity. (For a circle, the diameter is considered a linear dimension.)

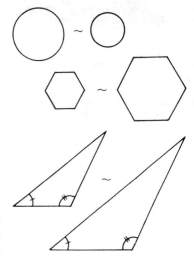

- Any two straight *line segments* are similar.
- Any two *circles* are similar.
- Any two *congruent figures* (having identical shape *and* size) are similar.
- Any two *polygons* are similar if their corresponding angles are congruent *and* their corresponding sides are in proportion. (See the preceding section.)
- Any two *regular polygons* with the same number of sides are similar. Regular polygons have all sides congruent and all angles congruent.
- Any two *triangles* are similar if two pairs of corresponding angles are congruent. (Since the sum of the angles of a triangle must equal 180°, if two triangles contain two pairs of congruent corresponding angles, the third angles must also be congruent. In triangles with corresponding angles congruent, the corresponding sides are automatically in proportion.)
- Any two *solids* or *space figures* are similar if they are bounded by similar surfaces. (A familiar example of similar solids is a set of nested blocks for small children. The blocks are all the same shape but vary in size. If one of the smaller blocks were uniformly enlarged, it would coincide exactly with one of the larger blocks.)

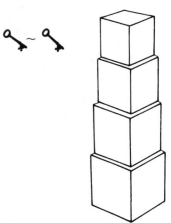

SCALE DRAWING AND MODEL BUILDING

A common application of the principles of similarity is in making scale drawings—drawings of similar figures much reduced or enlarged in size. Almost all plans for proposed constructions are scale drawings.

Indeed, it would be rather unwieldy for a contractor to have to work from plans equal in size to the construction itself. Although the scale drawing is reduced in size, the reduction of all parts is proportional.

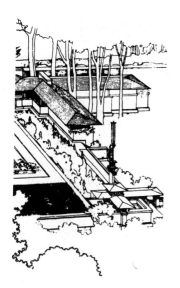

McCormick House by Frank Lloyd Wright, with half-scale playhouse.

From Lionel March and Philip Steadman, *The Geometry of Environment.* Courtesy of RIBA Publications, Limited, London.

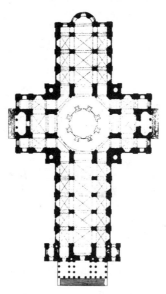

Early plan for St. Paul's Cathedral, London, by Christopher Wren

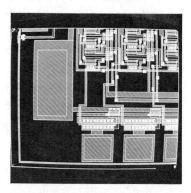

From this layout of circuitry is built a tiny part of a quarter-inch computer chip, such as is shown on p. 58 or p. 100. This diagram represents a portion of the chip that is only 1 mm wide, so it is here enlarged about 50 times. The actual design work is done by comput- er graphics on a CRT terminal—this means that the electrical engineers are working on a screen at a scale of more like 400 to 1.

Courtesy of *Engineering: Cornell Quarterly,* Vol. 16. No. 3. photo by Jon Reis.

Thus, the drawing gives a good representation of what the finished construction will look like. Design of miniature electronic circuits in COMPUTER chips requires greatly enlarged scale drawing.

Three-dimensional scale models are important in architectural plan- ning. The design of automobiles, ships, and airplanes requires scale models for testing properties like wind resistance. River turbulence can be studied by making an environmental model. In ways like these, similarity in model-building is indispensable.

DRAWING SIMILAR FIGURES

Suppose you wanted to draw a rectangle similar to rectangle *ABCD* below, but larger. How would you go about it? You could measure the base of *ABCD,* and then draw a line segment twice as long for the base of your new rectangle. Then you could erect two sides at right angles to this base and make them twice as long as the sides of the first rectangle. And finally, you could join the endpoints of the two sides to make the fourth side of the rectangle, which is larger by a scale factor of 2. For a different scale factor you would replace "twice as long" by the scale you choose. By knowing some of the GEOMETRIC CONSTRUCTION techniques, you could construct polygons similar to any other polygons.

But suppose you wanted to draw a figure similar to some irregular curvilinear shape such as the silhouette shown. Could you draw a figure exactly similar to this sketch, only larger? You could if you had a pantograph.

A *pantograph* is an instrument used to draw a plane figure similar to a given plane figure. It consists of four bars linked together to form a parallelogram with two long arms. In the illustration, *ABCD* is a parallelogram, and *P* and *E* are at the ends of the arms. Triangle *PAD* is similar to triangle *PBE*.

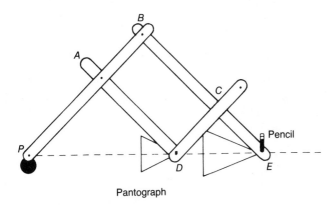

Pantograph

When the pantograph is used, *P* remains fixed, but at points *A*, *B*, *C*, and *D* the bars can move. Yet no matter how the bars are moved, *P*, *D*, and *E* will always lie in a straight line.

A pencil is placed at *D* and another pencil is placed at *E*. As the pencil at *D* traces any figure, the pencil at *E* traces an enlarged figure similar to it. To make a reduced figure, the pencil at *E* traces the given figure while the pencil at *D* traces a smaller but similar figure.

INDIRECT MEASUREMENT

Certain things, such as the height of a tree or the distance across a pond, are difficult to measure directly. The properties of similarity can be used to measure such inaccessible heights and distances *indirectly*.

Example.   Suppose that you wanted to know the height of a flagpole. You could calculate it by using similar triangles. First you could place a straight stick in the ground at right angles. The stick and its

Similar triangles

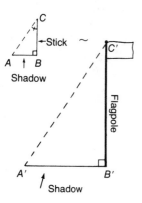

shadow form two sides of a right triangle, and the imaginary line joining the tip of the shadow to the top of the stick forms the third side. Similarly, the flagpole, its shadow, and the imaginary line connecting the top of the pole to the tip of its shadow form another triangle.

The two triangles are similar triangles because they have two congruent angles. Angles B and B' are congruent because both are right angles (90°). Angles C and C' are congruent because they are formed by the rays of the sun striking the pole and the stick, and at the same time of day the sun will strike both at the same angle.

Since triangles ABC and $A'B'C'$ are similar, corresponding sides are proportional. Thus, the height of the flagpole can be calculated by measuring the height of the stick and the lengths of the two shadows and setting up the following proportion:

$$\frac{\text{length of stick shadow}}{\text{length of pole shadow}} = \frac{\text{height of stick}}{\text{height of pole}}$$

If the height of the stick is 3 feet, the shadow of the stick is 2 feet long, and the shadow of the pole is 18 feet long, the following proportion can be solved to find the height of the pole, P:

$$\frac{2}{18} = \frac{3}{P}$$
$$2 \times P = 3 \times 18$$
$$2P = 54$$
$$P = 27$$

Thus the height of the flagpole is 27 feet.

Indirect measurement using similar triangles was particularly useful to surveyors of the eighteenth and nineteenth centuries. Lacking instrumentation and technology like the aerial photography available to surveyors today, earlier surveyors measured all accessible distances and angles. Then on a plotting board they made scale drawings, and by using similar triangles (or by TRIGONOMETRY) they set up proportions to calculate inaccessible distances.

For another method of indirect measurement by similar triangles, see ANGLE—the section on angle of incidence and angle of reflection.

Reference on indirect measurement

Elizabeth A. Wood, *Science from Your Airplane Window* (Houghton Mifflin, 1968; Dover, 1975), especially Ch. 8 on quantitative measurement, pp. 108–129. This book is a superb air-travel companion.

SLOPE

SLOPE: a number representing the RATIO of the vertical change (or *rise*) to the horizontal change (or *run*) between two points on an incline or line.

$$\text{slope} = \frac{\text{rise}}{\text{run}} = \frac{\text{vertical change}}{\text{horizontal change}}$$

A train goes up a "grade"; a roof has a "pitch" so water will drain off. The grade of a railroad and the pitch of a roof are examples of the concept in mathematics known as slope. Slope shows the relationship between how much the road or the roof, for example, goes up (vertical change, or rise) and how much it goes straight across (horizontal change, or run).

Slope is calculated by measuring the rise and run and finding their ratio.

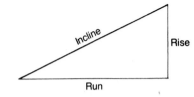

9% GRADE
7 MILES

Examples.

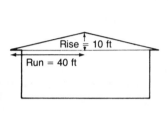

Rise = 10 ft
Run = 40 ft

$$\text{Slope} = \frac{10}{40} = \frac{1}{4} \text{ or 1 to 4}$$

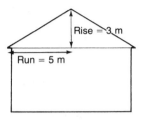

Rise = 3 m
Run = 5 m

$$\text{Slope} = \frac{3}{5}$$

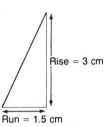

Rise = 3 cm
Run = 1.5 cm

$$\text{Slope} = \frac{3}{1.5} = 2$$

These facts about slope may be noted:

- The *steeper* the incline, the *larger the number* representing the slope.

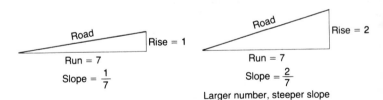

- For a *straight line*, the slope may be calculated from *any portion of*

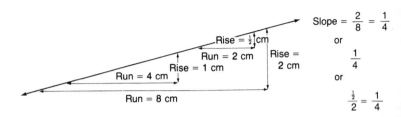

A horizontal line and a vertical line are special cases:

- A *horizontal* line has *zero* slope.

$$\text{slope} = \frac{\text{rise}}{\text{run}} = \frac{0}{\text{run}} = 0.$$

- A *vertical* line has *no* slope (which is not the same as zero slope).

$$\text{slope} = \frac{\text{rise}}{\text{run}} = \frac{\text{rise}}{0} \text{, which is } \textit{undefined. (See ZERO.)}$$

SLOPE FROM GRAPHS AND COORDINATES

A more formal mathematical approach to slope uses GRAPHS and COORDINATES.

For an oblique line drawn on graph paper, the slope may be calculated simply by counting squares for rise and run.

The slope of a line may also be calculated just from the Cartesian coordinates (x, y) of *any two points* on the line. Then

$$\text{slope} = \frac{\text{difference between } y\text{-coordinates}}{\text{difference between } x\text{-coordinates}}$$

Example.

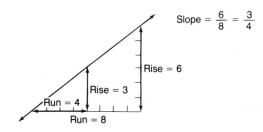

Slope $= \dfrac{6}{8} = \dfrac{3}{4}$

Rise = 6

Rise = 3

Run = 4

Run = 8

Example.

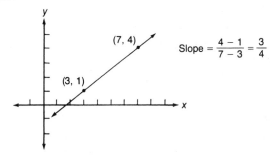

(7, 4)

(3, 1)

Slope $= \dfrac{4 - 1}{7 - 3} = \dfrac{3}{4}$

Finding the slope in this manner from the coordinates of two points is just a shortcut for counting squares. It is usually written as the following formula:

$$\text{slope} = m = \frac{y_2 - y_1}{x_2 - x_1}$$

where

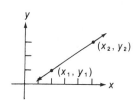

(x₂, y₂)

(x₁, y₁)

$m =$ the standard notation for slope,

(x_1, y_1) are the coordinates of the first point, and

(x_2, y_2) are the coordinates of the second point.

If this formula is used carefully, it can be quite handy, especially if some of the coordinates are negative.

Example.   If $(x_1, y_1) = (3, -3)$ and $(x_2, y_2) = (-2, 2)$, then

$$x_1 = 3, \; y_1 = -3$$
$$x_2 = -2, \; y_2 = 2.$$

$$\text{slope} = m = \frac{y_2 - y_1}{x_2 - x_1} = \frac{2 - (-3)}{-2 - 3} = \frac{2 + 3}{-5} = \frac{5}{-5} = -1$$

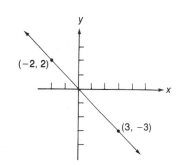

(-2, 2)

(3, -3)

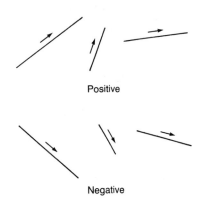

Positive

Negative

If you switch the order of the points, by letting $(x_1, y_1) = (-2, 2)$ and $(x_2, y_2) = (3, -3)$, you will get the same slope. The order of the points does not matter.

The fact that this last slope is a negative number is significant:

- A line of *positive slope* goes *upward* as you move from left to right.
- A line of *negative slope* goes *downward* as you move from left to right.

The mathematical formulation of slope for graphs leads to these statements about parallel and perpendicular lines—provided neither are vertical, for vertical lines have no slope:

- *Parallel* lines have the *same* slope.

Example.

slope $\overleftrightarrow{AB}$ = slope $\overleftrightarrow{CD}$

$\overleftrightarrow{AB} \parallel \overleftrightarrow{CD}$

($\overleftrightarrow{AB}$ is parallel to $\overleftrightarrow{CD}$)

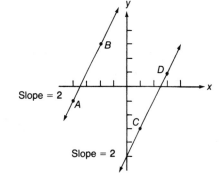

Slope = 2

Slope = 2

- *Perpendicular* lines (providing neither is vertical) have slopes that are *negative reciprocals*. The product of the slopes of two perpendicular lines will be -1.

Example.

Slope = $\dfrac{-3}{2}$

Slope = $\dfrac{2}{3}$

$$(\text{slope } \overleftrightarrow{AB}) \times (\text{slope } \overleftrightarrow{CD}) = \frac{2}{3} \times (\frac{-3}{2}) = \frac{-6}{6} = -1$$

$$\overleftrightarrow{AB} \perp \overleftrightarrow{CD}$$

$$(\overleftrightarrow{AB} \text{ is perpendicular to } \overleftrightarrow{CD})$$

SLOPES FOR STRAIGHT LINES

Slope is the defining characteristic of a straight line. If the slope of a curve is *constant,* the curve is a straight line.

Example. Consider the line that connects the points A, B, C, D, and E.

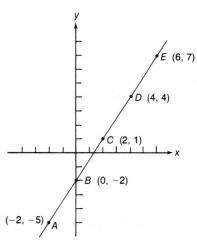

$$\text{slope } AB = \frac{\text{rise}}{\text{run}} = \frac{3}{2}$$

$$\text{slope } CE = \frac{6}{4} = \frac{3}{2}$$

You can pick any other pair of points on the line and confirm that the slope is constant. The graph that goes through all these points is a straight line.

A straight line on a graph represents *all* the points (x, y) that lie on it.

Example. The line of this graph passes through not only A, B, C, D, and E, but also through all other points between and beyond, such as

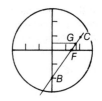

A portion of the same graph

$$(1\tfrac{1}{3}, 0) \quad \text{point } F$$
$$(1\tfrac{2}{3}, \tfrac{1}{2}) \quad \text{point } G$$

For any point on the line, you can find its Cartesian coordinates approximately by reading off the graph.

There is an exact mathematical relationship between the x and y coordinates of each point on a straight line. This relationship can be expressed as an equation, called a *linear equation* because the graph is a straight line. The equation of a line can be used to calculate the y-coordinate of any point on the line if the x-coordinate is known, or to calculate the x-coordinate if the y-coordinate is known.

Example. The line AE has slope $\tfrac{3}{2}$, and when $x = 0$, $y = -2$. The equation of this line can be written

$$y = \tfrac{3}{2}x - 2.$$

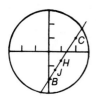

The same portion of the graph

You can confirm for yourself that points A, B, C, D, and E satisfy this equation. For example,

for point B where $x = 0$,
$$y = \tfrac{3}{2}(0) - 2 = -2.$$

for point C where $x = 2$,
$$y = \tfrac{3}{2}(2) - 2 = 1.$$

And you can also use the equation to compute a y-coordinate given any x-coordinate at all. For example,

$$\text{for } x = 1,\ y = \tfrac{3}{2}(1) - 2 = -\tfrac{1}{2} \quad \text{point } H;$$

$$\text{for } x = \tfrac{1}{2},\ y = \tfrac{3}{2}(\tfrac{1}{2}) - 2 = -1\tfrac{1}{4} \text{ point } J.$$

The equation of a line may be written in several different forms, including the *slope-intercept form,* the *point-slope form,* and the *general linear form.* For any given line, these forms are all equivalent.

Slope-intercept form	*Point-slope form*	*General linear form*
$y = mx + b$	$y - y_1 = m(x - x_1)$	$Ax + By + C = 0$
where m is the slope, and b is the *y-intercept,* the ordinate of the point where the line crosses the y axis.	where m is the slope, $(x_1\ y_1)$ is one point on the line, and (x, y) is *any* point on the line.	where A, B, and C are all real numbers and where A and B cannot both be zero.
For line $ABCDE$, $m = \tfrac{3}{2}$ and $b = -2$.	For line $ABCDE$, $m = \tfrac{3}{2}$, and point A $(-2, -5)$ may be taken as one point.	For line $ABCDE$, the general linear form equivalent to the other forms is
$\boxed{y = \tfrac{3}{2}x - 2}$	$y - (-5) = \tfrac{3}{2}[x - (-2)]$, or $\boxed{y + 5 = \tfrac{3}{2}(x + 2)}$	$\boxed{3x - 2y - 4 = 0,}$ so $A = 3$, $B = -2$, $C = -4$.
	You could also use any other point on the line, such as C $(2, 1)$. This gives $\boxed{y - 1 = \tfrac{3}{2}(x - 2),}$ which looks very different from $$y + 5 = \tfrac{3}{2}(x + 2).$$ But if you multiply out both of these equations, you get the same general linear form.	

Any linear equation may be transformed from one form to another by the rules of ALGEBRA.

Example.

$y = \dfrac{3}{2}x - 2$ ⟵——— slope-intercept equation

⟩ multiplying both sides by 2 in order to clear fractions

$2y = 3x - 4$ ⟵

adding $-2y$ to both sides in order to get zero on one side

$0 = 3x - 2y - 4$ ⟵

general linear form, with $A = 3$, $B = -2$, and $C = -4$

Horizontal and vertical lines illustrate special cases of the general linear equation:

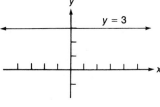

- For a *horizontal* line, $A = 0$.

Example. $y = 3$ (which can be written as $y - 3 = 0$, with $A = 0$, $B = 1$, and $C = -3$).

- For a *vertical* line, $B = 0$.

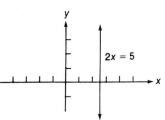

Example. $2x = 5$ (which can be written as $2x - 5 = 0$, with $A = 2$, $B = 0$, and $C = -5$).

For further discussion of linear equations and nonlinear equations, see GRAPHS and EQUATIONS.

SLOPES FOR CURVES

Does it make sense to talk about slope for anything other than straight lines? Yes, if the slope of a *curve* at a point means the slope of an appropriate *line* through that point.

$$\begin{array}{c} \text{slope of a curve} \\ \text{at a point} \end{array} = \begin{array}{c} \text{slope of a line } \textit{tangent} \text{ to the curve} \\ \text{at that point.} \end{array}$$

Example. Consider the smooth curve through points P, Q, and R.

As you can see, the slope may be different at each point on a curve. The shape of a curve is determined by these slopes. Finding its slope at each point can enable one to reproduce such a curve.

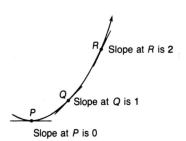

Slope at R is 2

Slope at Q is 1

Slope at P is 0

For example, the aiming of cannon required knowledge of the path the cannonball would take. The slopes of the cannonball's path could be calculated from physics, so the curve the ball would follow could be visualized.

Another application is the making of lenses for eyeglasses and optical instruments. Lenses are designed to bend light rays, but the amount of bending is determined by the angle between each ray and the tangent to the surface of the lens. Hence the designing and making of lenses require very careful attention to the slope of the lens surface at every point.

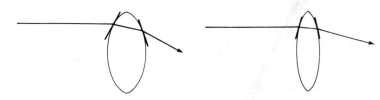

Calculating slopes of a curve is the topic of *differential calculus*, an important branch of higher mathematics. Calculus gives an easy calculation of slope at *every* point on a curve, once one has a thorough working knowledge of algebra. For further discussion of slope of a curve, see CALCULUS.

STATISTICS

STATISTICS: the branch of mathematics consisting of methods for collecting, organizing, and summarizing numerical facts and for making predictions based on these facts. The numerical facts that are collected are called *data*. An individual numerical fact, or piece of data, is sometimes called a *statistic*.

Nearly everyone is familiar with statistics in some form. For example, newspapers print statistics for baseball teams, including the number of hits each player had, the number of times each player struck out, and the number of innings each pitcher pitched. Safety organizations publish statistics on the number of traffic accidents occurring in a given region, the number of deaths resulting from these accidents, and the number of accident victims wearing seat belts. On the night of a national election, television networks give statistics on the number of people who have voted, the percent of the vote that has been counted, and the number of votes for each candidate; and on the basis of what is known about the voters whose votes have been counted, statisticians attempt to predict the winner in a given race.

Basic to an understanding of mathematical statistics are the concepts of *population* and *sample*.

Population: the group of all the individuals (or objects or events) that fit a particular description.

Example. All eighth-grade boys in the United States in the fall of 1980 form a statistical population.

Sample: a number of individuals (or objects or events) chosen from a given population as *representative* of the entire group.

Example. 300 eighth-grade boys in the United States in the fall of 1980 form a sample of the above population.

Mets 4, Giants 3

NEW YORK	ab	r	h	bi	SAN FRAN	ab	r	h	bi
Mazzilli cf	3	1	0	0	Morgan 2b	4	1	1	0
Bckmn 2b	3	1	1	0	Bergmn 1b	5	0	2	1
Yongbld rf	5	1	2	1	Clark rf	5	0	0	0
Kingmn lf	4	1	3	2	DEvans 3b	0	0	0	0
Wilson lf	0	0	0	0	Cabell 3b	5	0	1	0
Jorgnsn 1b	3	0	1	0	Herndon lf	4	1	2	1
Staub ph	1	0	0	0	Martin cf	5	0	0	0
Trevino c	0	0	0	1	May c	3	0	1	0
Stearns c	4	0	0	0	Sadek c	1	1	0	0
Brooks 3b	4	0	2	0	LeMstr ss	2	0	1	0
Flynn ss	4	0	0	0	Griffin p	2	0	0	0
Reardon p	0	0	0	0	Stennet ph	1	0	1	1
Harris p	2	0	0	0	Lavelle p	0	0	0	0
Cubbag ph	1	0	0	0	Whlfrd ph	1	0	0	0
Allen p	0	0	0	0	Minton p	0	0	0	0
Bailor ss	1	0	0	0					
Total	35	4	9	4	Total	38	3	9	3

New York   200 001 000 1— 4
San Francisco   001 100 100 0— 3

E—Brooks, Harris. DP—New York 1, San Francisco 2. LOB—New York 7, San Francisco 9. 2B—Youngblood, Jorgensen, Bergman, Brooks. HR—Herndon (1), Kingman (6). SB—Backman, Brooks, Stennett, Herndon. S—LeMaster. Backman. SF—Trevino.

	IP	H	R	ER	BB	SO
New York						
Harris	6	4	2	2	2	5
Allen	2	2	1	1	1	1
Reardon W,1-0	2	3	0	0	0	3
San Francisco						
Griffin	7	6	3	3	1	5
Lavelle	2	1	0	0	2	1
Minton L,1-2	1	2	1	1	1	1

WP—Griffin. PB—Trevino. T—3:22. A—5,189.

May 20, 1981.

BASEBALL

American League
Eastern Division

	W	L	Pct.	GB
Detroit	32	18	.640	—
Boston	33	19	.635	—
Cleveland	27	24	.529	5½
Milwaukee	27	24	.529	5½
New York	25	25	.500	7
Baltimore	25	26	.490	7½
Toronto	24	29	.453	9½

Western Division

	W	L	Pct.	GB
Kansas City	29	21	.580	—
California	31	23	.574	—
Chicago	29	22	.569	½
Seattle	26	29	.473	5½
Oakland	25	30	.455	6½
Texas	17	30	.362	10½
Minnesota	13	43	.232	19

BASKETBALL

NBA Playoffs
CHAMPIONSHIP FINALS
Best of Seven
Sunday's Game

Philadelphia 135, Los Angeles 102. Los Angeles leads series 3-2

76ers 135, Lakers 102
LOS ANGELES (102)

	fg	fga	ft	fta	r	a	pf	pts
Rambis	3	10	0	1	6	0	4	6
Wilkes	6	17	1	2	7	4	3	13
Abdul-Jabbar	3	6	0	2	4	4	5	6
Nixon	9	19	2	3	5	13	1	20
E.Johnson	4	9	2	4	10	4	4	10
McAdoo	11	14	1	2	4	1	5	23
Cooper	8	11	2	2	3	4	5	18
C.Johnson	0	2	0	0	1	0	1	0
Landsberger	0	2	0	6	0	1	0	0
Jordan	0	1	0	0	0	1	0	0
McGee	2	8	0	0	2	0	0	4
Brewer	1	1	0	0	1	0	0	2
Team Rebonds					8			
Totals	47	100	8	16	49	1	29	102

PHILADELHIA (135)

	fg	fga	ft	fta	r	a	pf	pts
Erving	10	19	3	3	12	4	1	23
B.Jones	7	9	7	8	3	2	4	21
C.Jones	2	7	0	1	4	1	3	4
Cheeks	5	9	3	6	3	8	0	13
Toney	13	18	5	6	2	8	2	31
Bantom	1	3	0	2	4	2	2	2
Dawkins	9	15	2	6	7	1	4	20
Richardson	4	8	3	4	5	4	2	11
Mix	2	2	0	0	0	1	0	4
Hollins	0	1	0	0	1	4	0	0
Edwards	3	3	0	0	0	0	0	6
Team Rebonds					14			
Totals	56	94	23	34	39	37	18	135
Los Angeles			20	34	27	21	—	102
Philadelphia			20	34	37	44	—	135

Fouled Out—None. Total Fouls—Los Angeles 29, Philadelphia 18. Technical Fouls—Philadelphia, illegal defense. Los Angeles, illegal defense. A—18,364.

June 7, 1982.

Random Sample: a sample in which every individual in the population has equal chance of being chosen for the sample.

Biased Sample: a sample in which some portion of the population is represented more heavily than it actually occurs; often a nonrandom sample.

A famous example of a biased sample was the one used in 1936 by the *Literary Digest* to predict the American voters' choice for president. The statistical population in this case was all the Americans eligible to vote in 1936. The sample used in the poll was selected from telephone directories for various American towns and cities. It was not random because voters who did not have a telephone had no chance to be included in the sample, and a significant percentage of the population at that time had no telephone. The *Digest* predicted victory for Alfred Landon, but his opponent, Franklin Roosevelt, won the election by a landslide.

TYPES OF STATISTICS

Descriptive Statistics: the science of *collecting, organizing, and summarizing* the numerical data that characterize a particular group.

Example. You might collect data on the heights of 300 eighth-grade boys, organize this data in a chart or graph, and then summarize by giving the average height of the group studied.

Inferential Statistics: the science of *making inferences or predictions* about a population, based on characteristics of a sample of that population.

Example. A medical research group tests a new drug on a sample group of volunteer patients. The researchers gather data on responses to the drug and possible side effects. They will then make inferences and predictions about its effectiveness and safety.

Descriptive statistics is a necessary first step to inferential statistics. Every ten years, since 1790, the United States Census Bureau has counted the total number of people in the nation. The census was established to allot to each state the proper number of seats in the U.S. House of Representatives. It also helps to insure proper representation in state legislatures and local governments. Distribution of government funds to communities and school districts depends on an accurate population count as well.

Every household fills out a short questionnaire listing each member's age, sex, marital status, and national origin. Once this information is collected, organized, and summarized, the proper apportionment of representation and funds can be decided. Trends in the growth of various populations will be evident in comparison to earlier census counts; predictions will be made.

A certain percentage of households receive longer questionnaires that collect data about occupations, income, expenses, housing, and so forth. Having organized and summarized this more detailed data, the Census Bureau can make inferences—region by region—about the entire population. Inferences can also be made about standards of living, use of energy, and sociological factors; trends can be predicted.

How likely are these figures to be accurate? Inferential statistics includes methods of calculating the PROBABILITY that a statistic based on a sample is representative of the entire population.

WAYS OF ORGANIZING DATA

One way to organize facts once they have been collected is simply to list them in a *table*. A more visual presentation can be provided by a statistical GRAPH. This might be a bar graph, a pictograph, a broken-line graph, or a circle graph. Consider the following U.S. census data:

Bar Graph

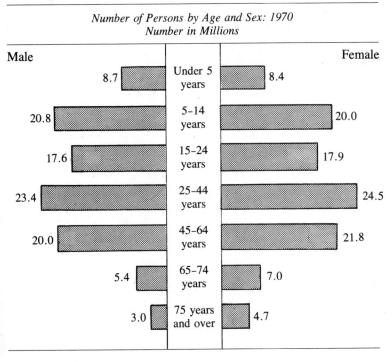

Number of Persons by Age and Sex: 1970
Number in Millions

Table

Number of Persons by Age and Sex: 1970

Age	Male	Female
Total persons in U.S.	98,912,192	104,299,734
Under 5 years	8,745,499	8,408,838
5 to 14 years	20,759,233	19,986,482
15 to 24 years	17,551,116	17,890,253
25 to 44 years	23,448,593	24,546,641
45 to 64 years	19,992,043	21,817,726
65 to 74 years	5,437,084	6,998,372
75 years and over	2,978,624	4,651,422

The bar graph and the table organize the same data, illustrating how different presentations emphasize different aspects.

The data used in statistics can be either *discrete* or *continuous*. The number of hits by a baseball player and the number of students in a class are examples of *discrete* data, because the measurements can have only certain values. In these examples measurement must be in whole numbers. On the other hand, measurements of height or temperature are examples of *continuous* data, because these measurements can have any value, including fractional values. A girl might be $59\frac{3}{4}$ inches tall; a fever thermometer may register 99.8 degrees Fahrenheit. For the purposes of organizing data, however, continuous data is often broken into discrete sets. For example, heights might be measured to the nearest inch.

Example.   *Distribution of heights in a class of 51 eighth-grade boys*

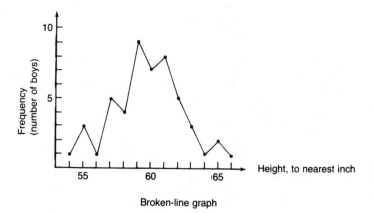

Broken-line graph

The *number* of individuals having a measurement within each interval is called the *frequency* of individuals appearing in that interval of measurement. In statistics, a display of measurements and related frequencies is called a *distribution*.

Frequency Distribution: a method of presenting data that shows the frequency (number) of individuals in each possible interval of measurement.

Examples. *Scores on a seventh-grade math test*

**Four Different Presentations
of the Frequency Distribution**

Scores	Frequency (tally marks)	Frequency (numerical)	Frequency (bar graph)
90–100	IIII	4	
80–89	III	3	
70–79	⊬⊬ III	8	
60–69	II	2	
50–59	II	2	
40–49		0	
30–39	I	1	
20–29		0	
10–19		0	
0–9		0	

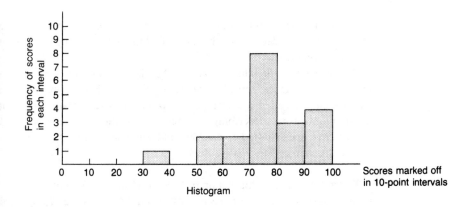

Histogram

A frequency distribution can be pictured in a number of ways, such as by tally marks, a broken-line graph, a bar graph, or a histogram. A *histogram* looks like a bar graph in which there are no spaces between the bars; it is a convenient form for further study of frequency distributions.

Example. In the previous example, only 20 students' scores are represented. But suppose that the same test were given to 100 students and that their scores were distributed in 5-point intervals:

Scores	Frequency
95–100	5
90–94	7
85–89	9
80–84	10
75–79	13
70–74	15
65–69	8
60–64	10
55–59	9
50–54	6
45–49	5
40–44	1
35–39	1
30–34	1
Below 30	0

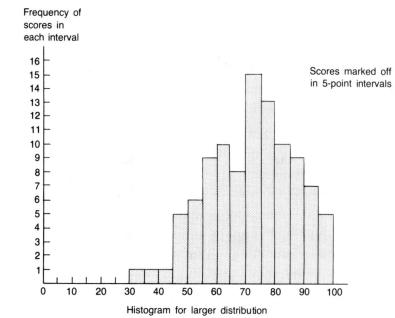

Histogram for larger distribution

As the number of scores in a distribution is increased and as the size of the interval is decreased, the shape of the corresponding histogram becomes smoother.

As the number of intervals approaches infinity and the size of the intervals approaches zero, the shape of the histogram approaches a smooth curve, called a *distribution curve*. There are many different distribution curves describing different distributions. Many of these curves have been studied extensively and some have been given names, as listed under *special distributions*, pp. 555–557.

Example. The histogram on p. 555 shows the distribution of scores of 1021 seventh graders on a math test when the scores are arranged in 2-point intervals.

Frequency of
scores in
each interval

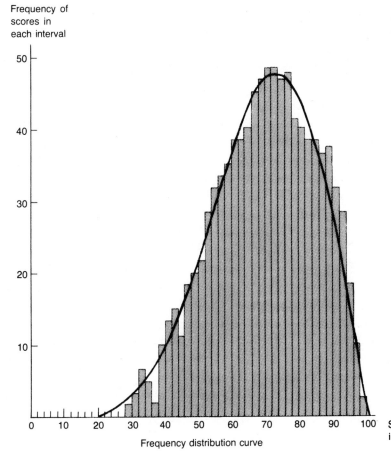

Frequency distribution curve

Scores marked off
in 2-point intervals

Special Distributions

Uniform Distribution: a frequency distribution in which there are an equal number of scores (or measures) in each interval.

Example. Suppose that you toss one die 96 times and keep a record of the results. If the die is "honest"—that is, if no factor other than chance determines the outcome—you should get approximately the same number of ones, twos, threes, fours, fives, and sixes. And if the die were tossed enough times, the distribution should be equal. Such a distribution approaches a uniform distribution, as shown on p. 556.

Number	Frequency
1	16
2	14
3	17
4	15
5	15
6	19

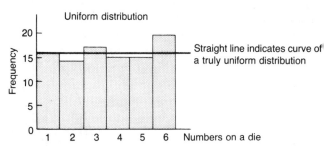

Tossing one die 96 times

The distribution curve of a true uniform distribution is a straight line.

Normal Distribution: a symmetrical frequency distribution in which most scores (or measures) occur in the intervals closest to the center of the distribution and fewer scores are found in the intervals farther from the center.

Example. Suppose that you toss ten pennies at a time until you have made one hundred tosses and that you keep a tally of the number of heads appearing on each toss. If the pennies are all "honest," you should get five heads more often than any other result. And you should get zero heads or ten heads least often. Such a distribution approaches a normal distribution.

Tossing 10 pennies at a time

Number of heads per toss	Frequency
0	0
1	2
2	4
3	11
4	20
5	25
6	19
7	12
8	5
9	1
10	1

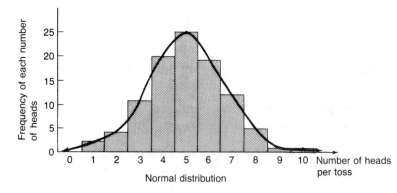

In a true normal distribution, the data is continuous—the highest frequency occurs in the center of the distribution, and the lowest frequencies are found at the extremes. When such a distribution is graphed, the result is a *bell-shaped curve* called the *normal curve*.

The normal distribution is a very common distribution. If you were to measure the heights of all the men in your town or the heights of all the pine trees or of all the cats or of just about anything that grows, in each case you would get a distribution of measurements that would be nearly normal. Since many distributions of data are normal or nearly normal, the normal curve serves as a mathematical model in the study of statistics.

Skew Distribution: a frequency distribution in which the measurements cluster about a certain value, but this value is not in the center of the distribution.

Example. The following distribution of ninety test scores is a skew distribution:

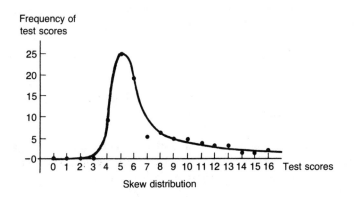

Distribution of test scores

Skew distribution

Score	Frequency
16	2
15	1
14	1
13	3
12	3
11	4
10	5
9	5
8	7
7	6
6	19
5	25
4	9

WAYS OF SUMMARIZING DATA

Organizing data into a frequency distribution brings order to a set of measurements. However, it does not summarize the data. Suppose, for example, that you wish to know the approximate height of an eighth-grade boy. A frequency distribution of the heights of a group of eighth-grade boys will give you more data and less information than you are seeking. What you are looking for is a single measurement that is typical of the whole group. This typical height will not be that of the tallest boy or of the shortest but will be found somewhere in the middle of the distribution. A measure that summarizes a whole set of measurements by representing the approximate center of a distribution is called a *measure of central tendency*. And there are other *measures of location* as well which summarize in some sense where a given measurement is located in a distribution. The various measures of location can be defined and illustrated as follows:

Statistical Measures of Location

Mean or Average: the measure found by adding together all the scores (or measurements) of a distribution and dividing by the total number of scores.

The mean is the only measure of central tendency that is dependent upon the exact value of every measurement. The mean is like the pivot point of a balanced seesaw. A change in any measurement will produce a change in the mean.

Median: the middle score (or measurement) in a distribution when all scores are arranged in order from largest to smallest.

If the total number of scores is even, the median is the mean, or average, of the middle two scores.

Mode: the score (or measurement) that occurs most often in a distribution.

A distribution may have more than one mode, for two or more scores may occur an equal number of times.

Percentile: the point in a distribution of scores (or measurements), arranged in order from largest to smallest, below which a given PERCENT of the scores lie. Percentile is sometimes abbreviated as *%-ile*.

The median of a distribution represents the 50th percentile because half, or 50%, of the scores fall below the median and half are above the median. If on a weight chart for ten-year-old boys a weight of 102 pounds represents the 96th percentile, then 96% of the ten-year-old boys on whom that chart is based weighed less than 102 pounds.

The mean, median, and mode are three different ways of locating a "center" of a distribution. But, as shown by the example of test scores, these measures may represent three different centers. In a *normal distribution,* however, the mean, median, and mode are all equal. In the penny-tossing example, which approximates a normal distribution, the mean = 5.05, the median = 5, and the mode = 5.

Examples. For a particular distribution of test scores, the following measures have been calculated:

Test
scores

100
100
95
80th *percentile* → 95
95
90
85 $\swarrow$ *mean*   = 82.3 $\left(\dfrac{\text{total sum of scores}}{\text{number of scores}} = \dfrac{1235}{15} \right)$
50th *percentile* → 80 ← *median* = 80 (middle score in list)
75
75
75 ← *mode* = 75 (most frequent score)
75
75
65
55

Measures of central tendency

Statistical Measures of Scatter

Measures of central tendency and other statistical measures of location such as percentile do not always give a proper or complete picture of a distribution. A single measure may not be representative of all the scores.

Example. Suppose that five men who ride a commuter train together earn the following annual salaries:

Smith: $20,000
Jones: $12,000
Taylor: $16,500
Brown: $14,000
Wilson: $145,000
    5)$207,500 = $41,500 = mean salary

The mean salary of these five men would be $41,500, but actually this figure is more than double any of the salaries except Wilson's.

In order to interpret how well the mean is likely to represent an entire group, statisticians calculate what is called a *measure of scatter*. A measure of scatter indicates whether the measurements in a distribution are bunched together or scattered apart. The usual statistical measures of scatter are:

Range: the difference between the lowest score (or measurement) and the highest in a distribution.

Example.   For the five salaries of the men listed above, $12,000, $14,000, $16,500, $20,000, and $145,000,

highest   lowest

range = $145,000 − $12,000 = $133,000.

The range does not reveal very much about how the scores are distributed. The scores could be clustered at either end of the scale or in the middle, without affecting the range.

The range is useful, though, in a distribution like temperature measurement. If you were packing for a trip to another climate, it would not be enough to know that the average daily temperature is 60° Fahrenheit. You would want to know the range as well, because a range of 60° will require packing a great deal more clothing than a range of 20°.

Deviation: the difference between a single score and the mean of the set of scores in a distribution.

Example.   For the salaries of the five men listed above, with a mean of $41,500, the deviation of Wilson's salary of $145,000 is

salary   mean salary

$145,000 − $41,500 = $103,500 = *deviation from mean*

For *standard* deviation, see below.

Variance: the mean of the squared deviations in a distribution.

Squaring the deviations allows a negative deviation to have the same effect as a positive deviation of the same size. And because the deviation is squared, the further it is from the mean, the more pronounced its effect on the size of the variance.

Example.   Consider this set of ten scores:

	Scores	Deviation from mean	Square of deviation	
	13	5	25	
	13	5	25	
	12	4	16	
	10	2	4	
	8	0	0	
	7	−1	1	
	5	−3	9	
	5	−3	9	
	5	−3	9	
	2	−6	36	
sum of scores:	80		134	= total of squares of deviations
mean = 8.00 =	$\frac{80}{10}$		$\frac{134}{10}$	= *mean* of squares of deviations
				= 13.4 = *variance*

Variance gives a better measure of scatter than does the range, because variance takes into account how much each score deviates from the mean. If most scores cluster near the mean, the variance will be small. But if many scores deviate widely from the mean, the variance will be large.

Standard Deviation: the square root of the *variance;* that is, the square root of the mean of the sum of the squared deviations in a distribution.

Comparison of two normal distributions with same mean but different standard deviations

Example. The variance of the scores in the previous example is 13.4. Therefore,

$$s = standard\ deviation = \sqrt{variance} = \sqrt{13.4} = 3.66$$

Standard deviation is much more commonly used than variance as a measure of scatter because it is expressed in the same unit as the scores, instead of in square units as the variance is. Being expressed in the same units allows easy comparison with the mean, and a statement of just the mean and the standard deviation is enough to give a rough picture of a whole distribution, even if no other data is available.

In a *normal* distribution, approximately 68% (or roughly two thirds) of all the measurements lie within one standard deviation on either side of the mean, approximately 95% of all the measurements lie within two

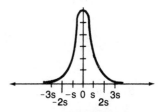

Number of standard deviations from mean for small s

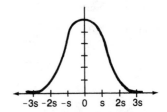

Number of standard deviations from mean for large s

standard deviations on either side of the mean, and approximately 99% of all the measurements lie within three standard deviations of the mean. Thus, standard deviation gives a good indication of how widely the scores in a distribution are scattered. An illustration shows that a small standard deviation indicates a much narrower distribution than a large standard deviation.

APPLICATIONS

The concepts of statistics are sometimes useful in quite unexpected ways. Suppose you were asked to find the sum of all the numbers from 1 to 100. The answer is fairly large, and most people would take a long time to compute it. In 1787 in Germany, a teacher gave this problem to his class, and a ten-year-old boy solved the problem within seconds. This boy, Carl Friedrich Gauss, later became the foremost mathematician of his time. Nevertheless, no one, not even a Gauss, can add a hundred numbers in a few seconds. He had to have a method for finding the sum, and Gauss's method was to use the mean.

Since the numbers between 1 and 100 are evenly distributed, the mean of the set of numbers is the same as the mean of 1 and 100—the first and last terms of the set. Since the mean equals 50.5 and there are 100 numbers, the sum must be 100×50.5, or 5050. To test this method quickly, you can try it on the sum of the first five numbers: 1, 2, 3, 4, 5.

In the twentieth century, statistics has become indispensable in scientific research, in industry, in commerce, in education, in government, and in hundreds of other areas of life. Statistical techniques are used to predict the weather, to determine the location of subatomic particles, and to determine the effectiveness of a new drug. Statistical procedures are used by opinion polls to determine which political candidate people favor, which television programs people watch, and which cereal they prefer. Statistical tests are used to decide how significant is the amount of pollution found in a sample of air or a sample of water. Statistical tests are used to analyze the findings of scientific experiments so that decisions can be made on whether a food product is likely to harm consumers' health.

One business that depends heavily on statistics and PROBABILITY is the insurance business. Insurance companies continually collect statistics from which they determine the probabilities of such events as death, fire, and accidents. These statistics and probabilities vary, of course, for different segments of the population. For example, a mortality table might show that for every 1000 persons 26 years of age there is 1 death per year, but that for every 1000 persons 66 years of age there are 41 deaths per year. To the life insurance company, this means that unless a person has known health problems, the probability of a twenty-six-

Two Ways to Add Consecutive Numbers

By addition

$$
\begin{array}{r}
1 \\
2 \\
3 \\
4 \\
+\ 5 \\
\hline
15
\end{array}
$$

By Gauss's method

$$\text{Mean} = \frac{1 + 5}{2} = 3$$

There are 5 numbers in the set.

$$\text{Sum} = 5 \times 3 = 15$$

year-old's dying within the year is 0.001, whereas the probability of a sixty-six-year-old's dying within the year is 0.04. Using such information, insurance companies can calculate the starting premiums they must charge a twenty–six-year-old, a twenty–seven-year-old, and so on, in order to cover the cost of payments to the beneficiaries of customers expected to die and to make a profit for the company.

Until the 1960s, statistics was taught only as an advanced math course in colleges and universities. But today it pervades so many areas of life that elements of statistics are now routinely taught in high school and often even in elementary school.

REFERENCES

Lee Arthur, Elizabeth James, and Judith B. Taylor, *Sportsmath: How It Works* (Lothrop, Lee and Shepard Co., 1975); the use of statistics in football, baseball, basketball, hockey, and tennis.

Bradley Efron and Carl Morris, "Stein's Paradox in Statistics," *Scientific American,* May 1977, pp. 119–127. In some circumstances the future can be predicted by better methods than an average of the past; detailed examples are given from baseball (batting averages of major league players) and from the spread of a blood disease.

David Freedman, Robert Pisani, and Roger Purves, *Statistics* (W. W. Norton & Co., 1978); for the serious reader who wants more than a taste. This is often called "Statistics Without Numbers"; it is an excellent introductory college text, giving a thorough background in the subject but allowing the student to avoid the distractions of manipulating the immense lists and tables of numbers found in most texts.

Darrell Huff, *How to Lie with Statistics* (W. W. Norton and Co., 1954); a delightful, easy to read discussion on the pitfalls of being too easily swayed by statistics; it sharpens awareness of what lies behind them—definitely recommended to anyone who reads newspapers or watches TV.

Morris Kline, ed., *Mathematics in the Modern World: Readings from Scientific American* (W. H. Freeman & Co., 1968); reprints of articles such as "Statistics" by Warren Weaver, January 1952; "Mathematics in the Social Sciences" by Richard Stone, September 1964; and "The Practice of Quality Control" by A. G. Dalton, March 1953.

Manfred Reidel, *Winning with Numbers: A Kids' Guide to Statistics* (Prentice-Hall, 1978).

Judith M. Tanur, ed., *Statistics: A Guide to the Unknown* (Holden-Day, 1972). Forty-four essays effectively explore important applications of statistics to a great variety of problems in government, science, and business. Examples include the safety, effectiveness, and dosage levels of drugs, pesticides, and anesthetics; police manpower versus crime; election night on television and the control of error; deciding authorship; when walks and bunts are good strategies; cloudseeding and rainmaking; antiaircraft fire. An excellent supplement for courses in statistics, written nontechnically and clearly to explain the design of experiments and to answer the question, "What does statistics have to do with me?"

See also PROBABILITY.

SYMMETRY

SYMMETRY: the property of exact balance in a geometric figure or in a relation.

Symmetry gives a harmony of design and can be formed in different ways: by reflection, by rotation, and by translation.

A symmetrical figure or design involves *repetition* and *balance*. Usually there is a *center;* this center may be a point, a line, or a plane. If the figure is symmetric, or symmetrical, every part of the figure on one side of the center is balanced by a *corresponding part* on the opposite side. These corresponding parts must be equally distant from the center. (The word "symmetry" comes from two Greek words meaning "measured together.") Moreover, the corresponding parts must have the *same size and shape*.

From Ernst Haeckel, *Kunstformen der Natur*.
Courtesy of the Fine Arts Library, Cornell University.

Examples. The first house is a symmetrical figure. The center in this case is along the dotted line. However, the other houses are *not* symmetrical, for various reasons: Some parts are not balanced by a corresponding part. Some parts are not the same distance from the center as their corresponding parts. Some corresponding parts are not the same size or shape.

 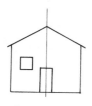 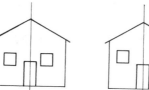

Symmetrical   *Not* symmetrical →

This discussion of symmetry has not been mathematically exact, because it generalizes all types of symmetry. But whenever the type of symmetry is specified and the center is defined as a point, a line, or a plane, it is possible to give more precise definitions.

565

Symmetry

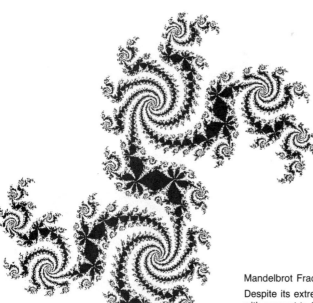

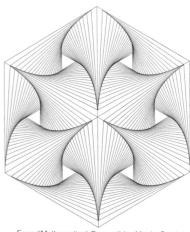

Mandelbrot Fractal Dragon

Despite its extreme complexity, this shape is symmetric with respect to its central point. This "dragon" was found in the study of a certain highly simplified dynamical system. (See page iv.)

Cloth Hall, 14th century, Market Square, Cracow

Polish Easter eggs

This stunning rosette is not the inspired design for a window in a great cathedral, but the supporting structure of the wildflower Queen Anne's lace.

Photograph by Andreas Feininger.

SYMMETRY BY REFLECTION: the property of being divisible into halves that are *reflections* of each other.

Lace trim from Lillian Baker and Doris Schattschneider,
The Perceptive Eye: Art and Math (Allentown Art Museum).

Polish papercutting

Shir-Dor Medresseh, 17th century
Registan, Samarkand

Symmetry with Respect to a Line

Two points are symmetric with respect to a line if, and only if, that line perpendicularly bisects the line segment joining the two points.

Example. Points A and B are symmetric with respect to line L, which is called the *axis of symmetry*, or a *line of symmetry*.

A geometric figure is symmetric with respect to a line if, and only if, every point of the figure on one side of the line is balanced by a symmetrical point on the opposite side of the line or axis of symmetry.

Example. The ellipse is symmetric with respect to a line L. For every point P of the ellipse on one side of the line L, there is a symmetrical point P' on the opposite side. The ellipse is also symmetric with respect to another line, L'.

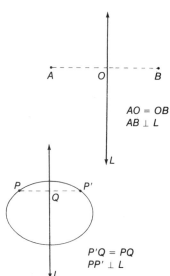

$AO = OB$
$AB \perp L$

$P'Q = PQ$
$PP' \perp L$

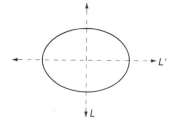

Any geometric figure may have more than one line of symmetry, exactly one line of symmetry, or no lines of symmetry. The axis of symmetry divides a figure into two symmetrical halves. If a symmetrical figure is folded along its line of symmetry, the halves exactly match. How many axes of symmetry can you find in each of these figures?

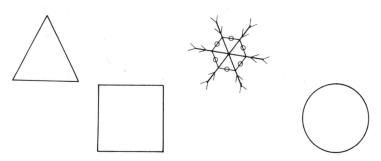

Plane figures symmetric with respect to a *line*

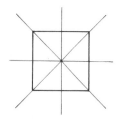

Four axes of symmetry

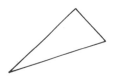

No axis of symmetry

The equilateral triangle has three, the square has four, the snowflake has six, the circle has infinitely many. On the other hand, a scalene triangle (with no sides of equal length) has no axis of symmetry at all.

All of these examples are plane or two-dimensional figures. It is also possible for a solid, or three-dimensional, figure to be symmetric with respect to a line. A cylinder such as a tin can is symmetric with respect to the line perpendicular to the base of the cylinder that passes through the center of the base. A salt shaker or a chair leg turned on a woodworking lathe is symmetric about the line of rotation. Again, it is possible to have more than one axis of symmetry in three-dimensional figures. A sphere has infinitely many axes of symmetry, as it is symmetric with respect to any line passing through its center.

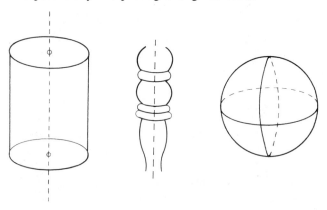

Solid figures symmetrical with respect to a *line*

Symmetry with Respect to a Plane

Two points are symmetric with respect to a PLANE if, and only if, the plane perpendicularly bisects the line segment joining the two points.

Example.   Points A and B are symmetric with respect to plane P, which is called the *plane of symmetry*.

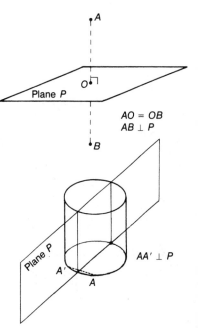

A geometric figure is symmetric with respect to a plane if, and only if, every point of the figure on one side of the plane is balanced by a symmetrical point on the opposite side of the plane.

Example.   The cylinder is symmetric with respect to a plane P. For every point A of the cylinder on one side of the plane P, there is a symmetrical point A' on the opposite side.

A geometric figure may have more than one, exactly one, or no planes of symmetry. The cylinder has infinitely many planes of symmetry. Each plane of symmetry divides the figure into two symmetrical halves.

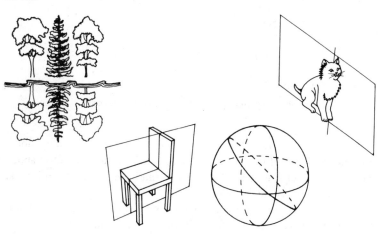

Solid figures symmetrical with respect to a *plane*

A calm lake appears as a plane of symmetry for the scene of trees and sky and its reflection. Nearly every manufactured object you buy is symmetric with respect to a plane: a chair, a table, a teacup, a spoon, a book, a light bulb, and so on. You have to look hard not to see symmetry. Many flowers and most animals are symmetric with respect to some plane. Even you yourself are roughly symmetric with respect to the plane that perpendicularly bisects the line segment joining your two eyes.

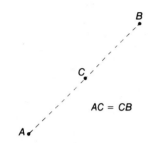

$AC = CB$

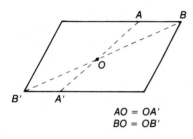

$AO = OA'$
$BO = OB'$

Symmetry with Respect to a Point

Two points are symmetric with respect to a third point if, and only if, the third point bisects the line segment joining the other two.

Example. Points A and B are symmetric with respect to point C, which is called the *point of symmetry*.

A geometric figure is symmetrical with respect to a point if, and only if, for every point on the figure there is another point on the figure symmetric to it with respect to the point of symmetry.

Example. A parallelogram is an example of a figure symmetric with respect to a point O in the middle.

In a figure symmetrical with respect to a point, any line segment drawn from a point on the figure to the corresponding symmetrical point on the other side of the figure passes through and is bisected by the point of symmetry.

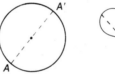

Plane figures symmetric with respect to a *point.*

Notice that figures symmetric about a point may or may not be symmetric about a line. The circle and snowflake are symmetric about a point and about lines, but the letter **S** (and the letters **N** and **Z**) are symmetric only about a point.

Solid figures may also be symmetric with respect to a point. Examples are a sphere, a cube, and a Christmas tree ornament.

Solid figures symmetric with respect to a *point.*

SYMMETRY BY ROTATION: the property that a figure coincides with its original position when rotated (about a point of symmetry) through an angle of less than 360°.

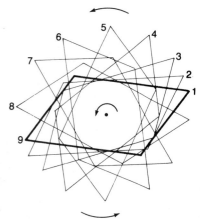

For example, consider a parallelogram, which is symmetric with respect to a point at its center. Rotate the parallelogram about that point and it will coincide with its original position when it has turned through an angle of 180°.

A snowflake will coincide with its original position if rotated about its point of symmetry through only 60°.

Ship's Propeller

Snowflakes from W. A. Bentley and
W. J. Humphreys, *Snow Crystals*.

In fact, any figure that is symmetric about a point also exhibits rotational symmetry. However, some figures such as propellers that have rotational symmetry have *no* symmetry of reflection. Notice that rotational symmetry is often a necessity for rotating engine parts.

SYMMETRY BY TRANSLATION: the property that a figure coincides with its original position when translated or shifted a fixed distance. A *translation* is a rigid motion that preserves exactly the size, shape, and orientation of a figure.

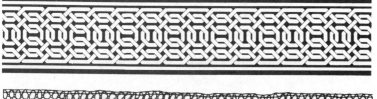

Lace trim from Lillian Baker and Doris Schattschneider,
The Perceptive Eye: Art and Math (Allentown Art Museum).

Some other symmetries are combinations of the above, such as the *glide reflection,* a combination of translation and reflection.

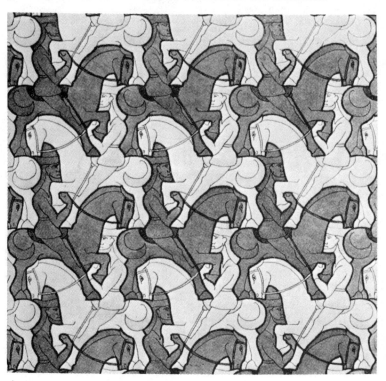

"Horseman," by M. C. Escher

© BEELDRECHT, Amsterdam/VAGA, New York. Collection Haags Gemeentemuseum—The Hague, 1981. Courtesy of The Vorpal Galleries; New York, San Francisco, Laguna Beach.

Bilateral symmetry

SYMMETRY IN NATURE

Examples of symmetry in nature abound. Leaves, flowers, seashells, animals, and mineral crystals often have a symmetry that is pleasing to the eye and may be functional as well.

The symmetry in nature is more than a pretty ornament. Recently, the presence of different kinds of symmetry in animals has been used by biologists to classify species. A number of species of simpler animals exhibit *radial symmetry*—a rotational symmetry about a central axis. Examples are hydras, jellyfish, sea anemones, and coral.

More complex species exhibit external *bilateral symmetry*. Members of these species have a front and a back and are symmetrical with respect to one central vertical plane running from front to back. For example, a horse exhibits bilateral symmetry. A vertical plane running from a horse's nose to its tail divides the horse into two symmetrical halves. Bilaterally symmetric species include all mammals, birds, fish, reptiles, amphibians, and insects.

Symmetry in Nature

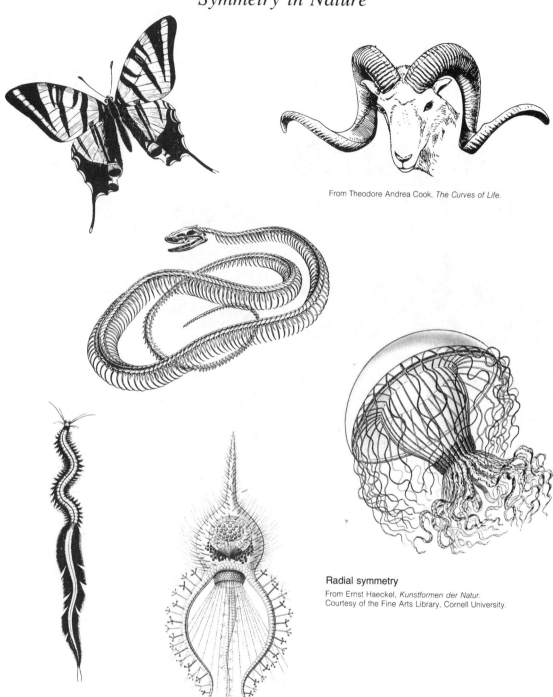

From Theodore Andrea Cook, *The Curves of Life.*

Radial symmetry
From Ernst Haeckel, *Kunstformen der Natur.*
Courtesy of the Fine Arts Library, Cornell University.

Still another example of symmetry in nature is found in the structure of crystals. Here again there are different kinds of symmetry, and the different kinds have been used by scientists to classify crystals. Some are symmetrical with respect to a point, some with respect to a line or lines, some with respect to a plane or planes, and some with respect to all three. By knowing the type of symmetry a crystal exhibits, scientists are able to predict how it will react when changed, or transformed.

Mineral crystals

Courtesy of William A. Bassett, Department of Geological Sciences, Cornell University.

  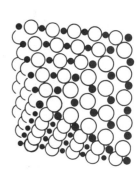

Left: Sand calcite, hexagonal symmetry results from the calcite cement holding the sand grains together.

Center: Phlogopite mica. Although it is monoclinic, it is very nearly a hexagonal prism.

Right: Fluorite and atomic model of fluorite showing octahedral cleavage faces. The atoms are enlarged approximately 50 million times.

The more closely one studies the natural world—from salamanders to salt crystals—the more apparent it becomes that symmetry in nature is not the exception but the rule.

SYMMETRY OF RELATIONS

Perhaps because the balance of symmetry is so familiar in the realm of physical objects, the word "symmetric" is used to describe a certain kind of balanced relation in algebra and logic.

A *symmetric relation* is a relation that is *always reversible*. For example, the relation "is married to" is symmetric. That is, if it is true that Edgar is married to Polly, then it must also be true that Polly is married to Edgar. Equality is a symmetric (or reversible) relation. (See PROPERTIES OF EQUALITY.) If $a + b = c$, then $c = a + b$. Other examples of symmetrical relations are the following:

- is parallel to
- is perpendicular to
- is next to
- is as tall as
- is a cousin of

An *asymmetric relation* is a relation that is *never reversible*. For example, the relation "is the wife of" is asymmetric. That is, if it is true that Polly is the wife of Edgar, then it can never be true that Edgar is the wife of Polly. Another asymmetric (or nonreversible) relation is "is greater than." If a is greater than b, then b cannot be greater than a. Some other examples of asymmetric relations are the following:

- is less than
- is ahead of
- is surrounded by
- is taller than
- is the mother of

A *nonsymmetric relation* is a relation that *may or may not be reversible*. For example, the relation "likes" is nonsymmetric. That is, if it is true that John likes Marsha, it may or may not be true that Marsha likes John. Another nonsymmetric relation is "is a brother of." Sometimes it is reversible and sometimes not. If Clarence is a brother of Fred, then Fred must be a brother of Clarence. However, if Clarence is a brother of Sue, it does not follow that Sue is a brother of Clarence. Some other examples of nonsymmetric relations are the following:

- is afraid of
- is looking at
- is moving toward

The examples above illustrate how the idea of symmetry (or lack of it)—a concept originally associated with geometric shapes—can be extended to describe abstract relations in algebra and logic.

REFERENCES

W. A. Bentley and W. J. Humphreys, *Snow Crystals* (McGraw-Hill, 1931; Dover, 1962); lovely photographs of over 2000 snowflakes, with related forms of dew, ice, and frost.

Howard W. Bergerson, *Palindromes and Anagrams* (Dover, 1973). Palindromes are symmetries in language that read the same forward and backward. A famous example, created by Leigh Mercer of London, is "A man, a plan, a canal, Panama."

H. A. Elliott, James MacLean, and Janet Jorden, *Geometry in the Classroom* (Holt, Rinehart & Winston of Canada, 1968), pp. 103–106.

Martin Gardner, *The Ambidextrous Universe: Left, Right, and the Fall of Parity* (Basic Books, 1964); from atoms, molecules, and crystals through plants, animals, and human intellect to the cosmos beyond; entertaining and enlightening exploration.

S. Haak, "Transformation Geometry and the Artwork of M. C. Escher," *Mathematics Teacher,* December 1976, pp. 647–652.

Alan Holden, *Shapes, Space, and Symmetry* (Columbia University Press, 1971); lattices and POLYHEDRA.

Teri Perl, *Math Equals: Biographies of Women Mathematicians + Related Activities* (Addison-Wesley, 1978), pp. 72 and 98–99 on the symmetric patterns caused by vibration of a surface. They were discovered by Ernest Chladni, a German physicist, and later explained in 1816 by Sophie Germain, a French mathematician who won for this effort an important prize from the French Academy of Science.

J. Troccolo, "A Strip of Wallpaper," *Mathematics Teacher,* January 1977, pp. 55–58.

Hermann Weyl, *Symmetry* (Princeton University Press, 1952); a well-illustrated classic—a mathematician's exploration of symmetry and beauty in biology, art, mathematics, chemistry, and physics.

TOPOLOGY

TOPOLOGY: the study of those properties of geometric figures that are unchanged when the shape of the figure is twisted, stretched, shrunk, or otherwise distorted without breaking.

Points that were close to each other before a topological distortion must remain close afterwards. Topology is sometimes called "rubber-sheet GEOMETRY."

Example. Consider a triangular patch drawn on a thin sheet of rubber. Stretching the sheet without tearing it produces a topological distortion of the triangular patch.

TOPOLOGICAL PROPERTIES

When the rubber sheet is stretched, a number of properties of the triangular patch may change: straight lines may become curved, short lines may become longer, and angles between lines may become greater. These properties—straightness, distance, and angle—are *not* topological properties.

There are other properties of the figure that will *not* change when the figure is stretched and distorted. For instance, the patch *ABC* has no holes in it either before or after stretching. Furthermore, the figure has bounds, or edges, both before and after distortion. Finally, the points *A*, *B*, and *C*—and all the points between—remain in the same circular order both before and after distortion. These are all examples of *topological properties:* those properties of a figure that do not change when the figure is distorted.

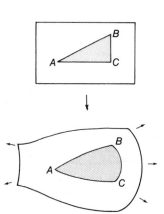

TOPOLOGICAL EQUIVALENCE

If one figure can be distorted into another figure without breaking, then the two figures are *topologically equivalent*. For instance, the boundary of the rubber-sheet triangle is topologically equivalent to a

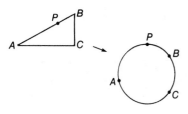

circle. And any point P between A and B on the triangle lies between the points A and B on the circle.

The letters of the alphabet provide a number of examples of topologically equivalent figures. For example, the letters **C, I, L, M, N, S, U, V, W,** and **Z** are all topologically equivalent. If you imagine the letters being made out of pipe cleaners, you can see that the **C** could be straightened out to make an **I**, the **I** could be bent to make an **L**, and so on.

The letters **O** and **D** are topologically equivalent to each other, but not to the previous set of letters. To make an **O** or a **D** from pipe cleaners, the two ends of a pipe cleaner must be joined together. Thus an **O** cannot be distorted into a **C** without breaking.

What other sets of topologically equivalent letters do you find? It may depend upon your style of letters. The letters **E, F, G, T,** and **Y** are topologically equivalent because each requires two pipe cleaners, one attached to the "middle" of the other:

E F G T Y

But the letter **J** might belong to either this set or to the first set of letters, depending on whether you write it **J** or **J**.

An interesting pair of solid figures that are topologically equivalent are the coffee cup and the doughnut. The mathematical term for an object shaped like a doughnut is a *torus*. A torus is topologically equivalent to a coffee cup because a flexible torus can be molded into the shape of a cup without tearing or breaking. You can try this with soft clay:

THE MOEBIUS STRIP

Distortions that break a figure so that points next to each other do not remain so are not topological. Making such a nontopological distortion can lead to completely new and surprising figures. A marvelous example is a surface with only one side, which was discovered in 1858 by August Moebius, a German mathematician and astronomer.

Moebius took a closed belt-shaped loop. He cut the belt, gave one end a half twist, and fastened the ends back together. The new loop is called a *Moebius strip,* or a *Moebius band.* You can make one yourself from a long strip of paper, giving one end a half twist, and gluing or taping the ends together.

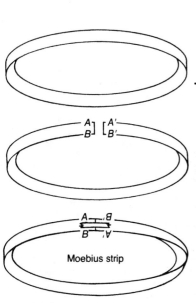

Moebius strip

Because one end is only half twisted, the points such as A and A' that were originally close to each other on the closed loop are now separated on the band. Even though an untwisted loop clearly has two sides and two edges, the Moebius band has only *one* side and *one* edge.

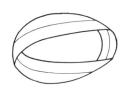

To discover some of the surprising properties of the Moebius strip, try the following:

(1) Draw a lengthwise line down the center of your strip until you reach your starting point. Now see if you can find a side of the strip that has no line.

(2) Next cut the strip along the line you have just drawn. You will then have a new closed band twice as long as the original with two twists in it. It is now a two-sided strip. Cutting it apart has changed the topological property of one-sidedness.

(3) Now cut your new loop down the middle again. The result will be even more surprising—you will have two intersecting loops.

(4) What would happen to the original Moebius strip if you cut around it one third of the way in from the edge? Make another Moebius strip and try it. You'll probably be surprised yet again.

The Moebius strip may appear to be an intriguing novelty of little practical value. But such is not the case. One practical application has been in the design of driving belts such as fan belts and conveyor belts. Ordinarily, friction wears the belts out more quickly on the inside than on the outside. Belts made with a half twist like a Moebius strip have only one side or surface. Thus, they wear uniformly and more slowly.

THE SEVEN BRIDGES OF KOENIGSBERG

Another important discovery resulting from the distortion of a figure was Leonhard Euler's solution to the problem of the seven bridges of Koenigsberg. The old German city of Koenigsberg (now the Russian city of Kaliningrad) was built on two islands in the Pregel River and on the banks on either side of the Pregel. The different parts of the city were connected by seven bridges.

A favorite question in the early eighteenth century was whether it was possible to take a walk through the city crossing each bridge exactly once, that is, without skipping any bridge or crossing any bridge twice. Most people felt that it was impossible, but they couldn't prove that it was. Then in 1736, Euler, a Swiss mathematician, came up with a proof of the impossibility of taking such a walk.

Euler solved the problem by distorting the map, or diagram, into a *topologically equivalent network*. In Euler's network, the *arcs* (which may be curved or straight line segments) represent the bridges and the *vertices* represent land. In such a network, a vertex is where two or

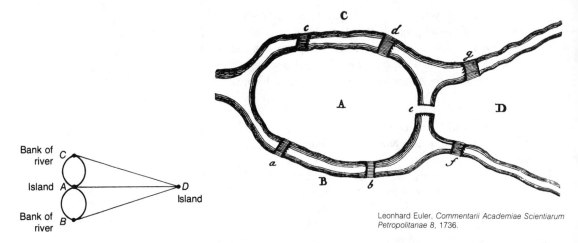

Bank of
river C

Island A •————————• D
Island

Bank of
river B

Leonhard Euler, *Commentarii Academiae Scientiarum Petropolitanae 8*, 1736.

more arcs meet or intersect. A vertex where an even number of arcs meet is said to be an *even* vertex; a vertex where an odd number of arcs meet is said to be *odd*.

Look at vertex *D*, which is odd. You can pass through *D* once, arriving on one arc (bridge) and leaving on a second. But there is a third arc left over, which must be either the beginning or the end of the walk. In fact, any odd vertex must, by this type of argument, be either the beginning or the end of the required walk. In the Koenigsberg network, vertices *D*, *B*, and *C* each have three arcs, while vertex *A* has five. All four vertices are odd. It is impossible for all four vertices to be either the beginning or the end of a walk, so this network can*not* be traced without repetition in a single walk.

Euler showed in general that a network can be traveled crossing each arc exactly once *only if the number of odd vertices is zero or two.*

Today there is a whole field of study called *network theory* with a host of practical applications. Network theory is used in planning where to run electric power lines, in designing more efficient city bus and garbage routes, and in channeling information flow in large organizations. However, the most important application of network theory has been in designing electric circuits for everything from small appliances to computers.

THE EULER-DESCARTES FORMULA FOR POLYHEDRA

Euler again considered networks when he proved the following famous formula for POLYHEDRA:

Consider any polyhedron without holes.

Let V = number of vertices,

E = number of edges,

F = number of faces.

Then $\boxed{V - E + F = 2,}$ always!

Examples. A tetrahedron has 4 vertices, 6 edges, and 4 faces.

$$V - E + F = 4 - 6 + 4 = 2$$

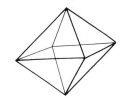

An octahedron has 6 vertices, 12 edges, and 8 faces.

$$V - E + F = 6 - 12 + 8 = 2$$

You can confirm that this formula works for a hexahedron as well, and for any other polyhedron.

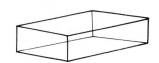

This interesting fact was first stated by René Descartes about 1635. Without any knowledge of Descartes' work, Leonhard Euler in 1752 also stated the formula. For this reason it is known as the Euler-Descartes formula.

But there is more to this idea. If a polyhedron has a hole, $V - E + F$ will be a different number. Consider a solid figure with a hole, as shown. Here $V - E + F = 16 - 32 + 16 = 0$. It turns out that any polyhedron with one hole will have $V - E + F = 0$.

The quantity $V - E + F$ is *topologically invariant,* which means it is unchanged even if a figure is topologically distorted. For any polyhedron topologically equivalent to a solid ball (in other words, without holes), $V - E + F = 2$. For any polyhedron topologically equivalent to a solid torus (with one hole), $V - E + F = 0$. The discovery that a *numerical* quantity is unchanged by a topological distortion was one of the origins of the branch of topology called *algebraic topology.*

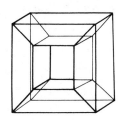

References on The Euler-Descartes Formula

Richard Courant and Herbert Robbins, *What Is Mathematics?* (Oxford University Press, 1941), pp. 236–240; a *proof* that this formula works for *any* polyhedron.

Imre Lakatos, *Proofs and Refutations: The Logic of Mathematical Discovery,* (Cambridge University Press, 1976); discusses Euler's Formula, $V - E + F = 2$, and its extensions in great detail while illustrating methods and difficulties in mathematical proofs. The subject matter is not at all trivial, but it is presented as an entertaining dialogue between a teacher and his students.

MAP COLORING

How many colors do you think are necessary to color this map, including the border? You will obviously want each region to be a different color from those that border it. If two regions meet only at a corner, they need not be of different colors. But if two regions share any length of boundary, they must have different colors. With that as the only requirement, the question is, "How *few* colors can you use?" (Since you will probably wish to make several tries, a good way to do it is to copy the map once and then make your coloring patterns on tracing paper placed over the map.)

In this particular map, it is possible to get by with just four colors. One solution is shown, with R = red, Y = yellow, B = blue, G = green.

But what about the more general question of how many colors are necessary to color any map? Wouldn't that depend on the number of regions in the map, the shapes of the regions, and their arrangement? If you try a few experiments, you will find that although the arrangement of the regions does matter, their shape does not. The map-coloring question will not be changed by rubber-sheet distortion of the map. For instance, these maps are topologically equivalent:

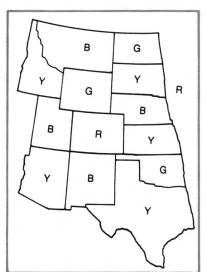

These two maps can be colored in exactly the same way. But it is easier to consider the general question of map-coloring in terms of the second, topologically equivalent, map (just as networks are a good way of considering the Koenigsberg bridge problem). For instance, a simpler map shows exactly how many regions border each region. Triangular and pentagonal regions each indicate that at least four colors will be necessary. (Try it: you cannot get by with fewer.)

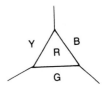

But what about the polygons that form other regions? And what does the overall *configuration,* or arrangement of regions, require?

It had been thought for more than a century that four colors would suffice to color any planar map (flat map in a PLANE), but nobody was able to prove it. Mathematicians could prove that five colors would be enough, but they could not find a map that *required* five colors. So they kept looking for a proof that four colors would do. Just as in the three famous GEOMETRIC CONSTRUCTION problems of the ancient Greeks (squaring the circle, trisecting the angle, and duplicating the cube), the tantalizing four-color problem has attracted mathematicians and amateurs by the score. Some have labored for years seeking a solution.

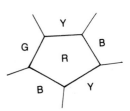

However, unlike the ancient Greek construction problems which were eventually proved to be impossible, it seems that the four-color problem has finally been solved. In 1976, Kenneth Appel and Wolfgang Haken, mathematicians at the University of Illinois, announced that they had obtained a proof that four colors are enough for any planar map.

Not only do Appel and Haken believe they have answered this long-standing question, but they worked at it in truly revolutionary fashion, using over 1000 hours of COMPUTER time. The proof is so complicated that after five years it had not been confirmed by others.

However, Appel and Haken's basic approach is a common one in mathematics—*proof by contradiction.* In this case that means showing that if five colors are necessary, an argument can be made leading to an impossible situation, or contradiction.

If five colors were required by some maps, some map would have the smallest number of regions that would require five. Appel and Haken found a collection of configurations, at least one of which must occur in any "smallest map" requiring five colors. This was an enormous set of 1,936 configurations. They then showed that each five-color map containing one of these configurations could be reduced to a smaller five-color map. Therefore, every "smallest" map requiring five colors could be reduced to a smaller map requiring five colors. This would prove that there simply is no smallest five-color map and hence no map at all requiring five colors.

The computer was necessary to check and determine this set of configurations. So many computations were required that the scope of the project was beyond human calculation. This was the first time that such a problem was solved by a machine, and the idea opens the door to other exciting possibilities.

Meanwhile, immediately after Appel and Haken's announcement, others who had been trying to prove the four-color theorem set to work with renewed vigor. Within the year some mathematicians claimed to have found other proofs, by entirely different methods and without use of a computer. This often happens in mathematics—knowing that a question has been answered allows someone to work harder and to think more clearly.

The question of the sufficient number of colors for coloring a map was asked and answered long ago for surfaces other than the plane. For example, six colors suffice for a map on a Moebius strip, but a map on a torus may require seven different colors.

References on map coloring

Kenneth Appel, ''The Proof of the Four Colour Theorem,'' *New Scientist,* October 21, 1976, pp. 154–155; short and not too technical, but outlining the whole idea.

Kenneth Appel and Wolfgang Haken, ''The Solution of the Four-Color-Map Problem,'' *Scientific American,* October 1977, pp. 108–121; contains more elaborate detail.

Martin Gardner, ''Mathematical Games: The coloring of unusual maps leads into uncharted territory,'' *Scientific American,* February 1980, pp. 14–21.

HISTORY OF TOPOLOGY

Topology as a branch of mathematics did not spring full-blown into the mind of some mathematician. It developed as a number of mathematicians experimented with the distortion of geometric figures. In the eighteenth and nineteenth centuries, Euler distorted a map into a network and Moebius discovered a one-sided surface. Carl Friedrich Gauss, an eminent German mathematician, explored the distortion in knots, and others worked with distortion in projective geometry (see PROJECTION).

The fruit of all these individual efforts was the eventual development of a branch of mathematics devoted exclusively to studying the constant properties of figures under distortion. The first attempt to systematize topology was made by Henri Poincaré, a French mathematician. In 1895, he published five papers developing topology as a purely qualitative, not quantitative, subject in its own right. Since their publication, the field of topology has grown at such an explosive rate that today it is one of the major branches of mathematics.

FURTHER THOUGHTS

There are many other interesting topological problems concerning knots, mazes, and puzzles. Many of the topics discussed here can also be developed further. For instance, as well as the one-sided Moebius strip, there is the single-surfaced Klein bottle.

Martin Gardner asks whether a torus can swallow a torus: There is a hole or "mouth" in torus *B*. Can torus *A*, which is linked with torus *B*, be "swallowed" through this hole so it ends up inside *B?* Either torus may be stretched and deformed as much as you like, as long as there is no tearing. But in the end *B* should have its original shape and *A* must be entirely inside *B*.

For more on topics like these, see the references.

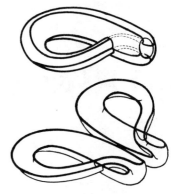

Klein bottle

REFERENCES

Stephen Barr, *Experiments in Topology* (Thomas Y. Crowell Co., 1964); clearly written and illustrated.

David Bergamini, *Mathematics,* Life Science Library (Time, 1963), p. 176 ff.; a beautifully illustrated picture essay on "Topology, The Mathematics of Distortion."

Leonhard Euler, "The Koenigsberg Bridges," (1736, reprinted by *Scientific American,* July 1953 and in the Kline books below)

Martin Gardner, "Mathematical Games," *Scientific American,* April 1977 (for the question "Can a torus swallow a torus?") and May 1977 (for the solution).

William H. Glenn and Donovan A. Johnson, *Topology,* Webster Publishing Company's series, Exploring Mathematics on Your Own (Transatlantic, 1960).

Morris Kline, ed., *Mathematics: An Introduction to Its Spirit and Use: Readings from Scientific American* (W. H. Freeman & Co., 1978), pp. 123–134; a collection of interesting articles on topology.

Morris Kline, ed., *Mathematics in the Modern World: Readings from Scientific American* (W. H. Freeman & Co., 1968), pp. 134–150; a different collection of interesting articles on topology.

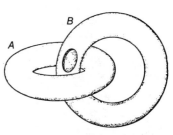

Can torus *B* swallow torus *A*?

Reference for a more rigorous approach

B. H. Arnold, *Intuitive Concepts in Elementary Topology* (Prentice-Hall, Inc., 1962).

TRIANGLES

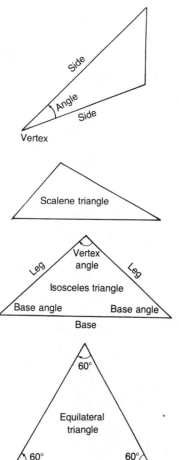

Side

Angle

Side

Vertex

Scalene triangle

Vertex angle

Leg

Leg

Isosceles triangle

Base angle

Base angle

Base

60°

Equilateral triangle

60°

60°

TRIANGLE: a closed plane figure formed by the line segments joining three points not in a straight line; a POLYGON of three sides.

Side: the line segment joining two of the points.

Vertex (plural, *vertices*): the point where two sides meet.

Angle: the ANGLE formed inside the triangle by two sides meeting at a vertex.

CLASSIFICATION OF TRIANGLES BY SIDES

Scalene Triangle: a triangle in which each side is of a different length.

Isosceles Triangle: a triangle in which at least two sides are congruent. In an isosceles triangle, the angles opposite the sides of equal length have equal measure.

The *legs* of an isosceles triangle are the two sides of equal length; the *base* is the third side. The two angles opposite the two sides of equal length are the *base angles*; the third angle, formed by the legs, is the *vertex angle*.

Equilateral Triangle: a triangle in which all three sides are congruent.

An equilateral triangle is also isosceles. All the angles of an equilateral triangle are equal; each has a measure of 60°. Therefore, this triangle can also be called *equiangular*.

CLASSIFICATION OF TRIANGLES
BY ANGLES

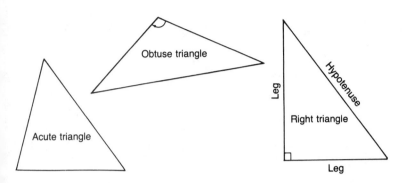

Acute Triangle: a triangle in which the measure of every angle is less than 90°.

Obtuse Triangle: a triangle in which the measure of one angle is greater than 90°. The other two angles of an obtuse triangle are each of measure less than 90°.

Right Triangle: a triangle in which the measure of one angle is equal to 90° (a right angle). The other two angles of a right triangle are complementary; the sum of their measures is 90°.

The *legs* of a right triangle are the two sides forming the 90° angle. The *hypotenuse* of a right triangle is the side opposite the 90° angle.

SPECIAL LINES IN A TRIANGLE

Base: *one* side of a triangle. Except in an isosceles triangle, *any* side could be considered the base of the triangle. Usually the side on which the triangle is resting is labeled the base.

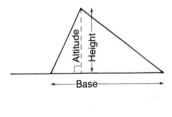

Altitude: a line segment from a vertex perpendicular to the opposite side (or the extension of that side). An altitude may also lie outside a triangle (as in an obtuse triangle) or along a side (as in a right triangle).

Every triangle has three altitudes and they meet at a point. The point may be either inside or outside the triangle. If it is outside the triangle, it is necessary to extend the altitudes beyond the sides of the triangle until they intersect, as shown at the top of p. 588.

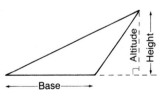

Height: the length of an altitude. The height of a triangle from any given base is the length of the altitude to that base.

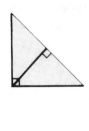

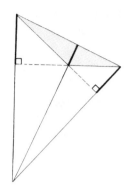

The altitudes of a triangle meet at a point

Median: a line segment from a vertex to the midpoint of the opposite side.

Every triangle has three medians and they meet at a point.

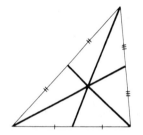

The medians of a triangle meet at a point

FACTS ABOUT TRIANGLES

- *The triangle inequality:* The sum of any two sides of a triangle is always greater than the third side. This is also discussed under INEQUALITIES.
- *The sum of the three angles* of a triangle is always 180°.

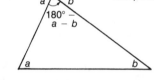

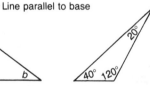

$$90° + 45° + 45° = 180°$$

$$40° + 20° + 120° = 180°$$

- *The area of a triangle* = $\frac{1}{2}$ base × height.

$$A = \tfrac{1}{2}bh$$

The *base* is the length of any side. The *height* is the length of the altitude to the side used as base. See AREA for further discussion of the area of a triangle, including Hero's formula for calculating the area using only the lengths of the three sides.

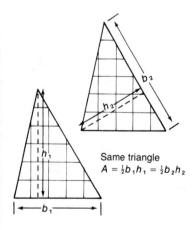

Same triangle
$A = \tfrac{1}{2}b_1h_1 = \tfrac{1}{2}b_2h_2$

- *The theorem of Pythagoras:* The sides of a *right* triangle always satisfy the following condition (see PYTHAGOREAN THEOREM):

$$(\text{one leg})^2 + (\text{other leg})^2 = (\text{hypotenuse})^2.$$

TRIANGLES, TRIANGLES, EVERYWHERE

You will find triangles in many situations. Nearly every schoolchild is familiar with the *musical triangle*. In literature you will often find a *lovers' triangle*. People are baffled by the unusual disappearance of ships and planes in an area of the Atlantic called the *Bermuda Triangle* or the *Devil's Triangle*.

The Bermuda Triangle

The Triangle in Art

In the arts of painting and sculpture, triangular forms have long been popular. Not only have abstract geometric triangles been explicitly painted or sculpted, but an underlying triangular configuration has often been used to give order and balance to paintings and other works of art. In the Middle Ages, the triangle in art had a symbolic meaning as well: it represented the Christian trinity of Father, Son, and Holy Spirit. During the Renaissance, there was a revival of interest in the works of Greek scholars. Many artists such as da Vinci, Raphael, and Dürer were students of classical geometry and made extensive use of triangular forms in their work. Da Vinci's *Mona Lisa,* for example, has the underlying form of an equilateral triangle. His *Last Supper* portrays Christ as an equilateral triangle (symbolizing perfection) and Judas, his betrayer, as a scalene triangle (totally lacking in perfection).

"The Last Supper," by Leonardo da Vinci, about 1495–1498

Courtesy of Stehli Brothers Ltd., Zurich.

Triangles in Construction

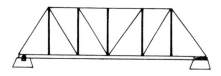

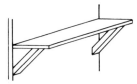

Unitarian Church, Madison, Wisconsin, by Frank Lloyd Wright

Triangles in Construction

Because of its *rigidity,* the triangular form is basic to the construction of any number of practical objects, from simple shelf supports to bridges and steel towers.

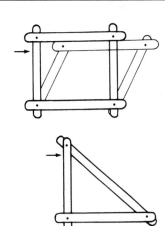

You can test this rigidity for yourself. With some cardboard strips and paper fasteners, try making a figure of four sides and a figure of three sides. You can easily distort the four-sided figure by holding one side and pushing against one of the adjacent sides. But the three-sided triangular figure holds its shape and cannot be pushed into a different form.

Triangles can produce striking architectural forms, as in this church designed by renowned twentieth-century architect Frank Lloyd Wright.

Triangulation

Surveying and *navigation* rely heavily on *triangulation* to measure unknown distances, both earthbound and astronomical. Some distances can be measured directly, and those that are inaccessible can often be

A the top of the hill, B the foote, C my station or the place of mine eye, A B 60 pace, C B 200 pace, the Square of 60 is 3600, the Square of 200 is 40000, these two ioyned together make 43600, whose Quadrate roote being about 208 pace 3 foote is the Hypothenusall line A C. Likewise A B the breadth of the Ditche being 30 foote, and B C the altitude of the Curtaine 20 foote, there two squares added together bring foorth 1300, whose Quadrate roote being 36 foote very nigh, is the length of the scaling ladder A C. But if the base of your mountaine be not visible, then ereare vp your Geometricall Square, the index placed (as was before declared) toward the top of the Hill A, and remoouing the Index:(your Square standing immoueable)espie your second station Orthogonally at D where ye must place the Centre of your Instrument, and so situate your square againe, that you may behold bothe your station and the mountaine toppe without stirring of the Square, onely remoouing the Index : in all the rest do as is before already sufficiently declared, behold the Figure, there needeth no other Example . The last Chapter well vnderstood, openeth this most plainely.

Two examples of triangulation for military purposes, from Leonard Digges, *A geometrical practical treatize named Pantometria* (A. Jeffes, London, 1591).

calculated from the SIMILARITY of triangles or by the PYTHAGOREAN THEOREM for right triangles. Even more inaccessible distances can be calculated by TRIGONOMETRY, which is the branch of mathematics dealing with triangles, angles, and their relationships. See the indicated articles for examples of triangulation.

REFERENCE

Martin Gardner, "Mathematical Games: Elegant triangle theorems not to be found in Euclid," *Scientific American,* June 1970; reprinted in *Mathematics: An Introduction to Its Spirit and Use: Readings from Scientific American* (W. H. Freeman & Co., 1978); interesting mathematical facts about triangles are still being discovered.

For more on triangles, see TRIGONOMETRY. Applications appear under ANGLES of incidence and reflection, and SIMILARITY: indirect measurement.

TRIGONOMETRIC FUNCTIONS

TRIGONOMETRIC FUNCTION: a FUNCTION that pairs the measure of an angle with a real number that is a *trigonometric ratio*.

The more basic article on TRIGONOMETRY (the study of triangles, angles, and their relationships) defines the six basic *trigonometric ratios* for an angle. Each of these ratios is a *function* of the given angle, because the value of each trigonometric ratio depends on the measure of the angle. In that article the six ratios are explained and defined in terms of a right triangle; they can also be defined in terms of a circle.

It is most convenient to use a circle with radius $r = 1$, called a *unit circle*, centered at the origin of a Cartesian COORDINATE system. The ANGLE, represented by the Greek letter θ (theta), has vertex at the origin and is measured from the positive x-axis. The point P is where the terminal side of the angle meets the circle; P has coordinates (x,y). Then, for any angle θ, the basic trigonometric functions can be defined as follows:

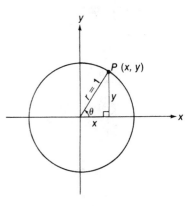

$$\textit{sine function} = \text{Sin } \theta = y$$

$$\textit{cosine function} = \text{Cos } \theta = x$$

The other trigonometric functions are

$$\textit{tangent function} = \text{Tan } \theta = \frac{y}{x} = \frac{\text{Sin } \theta}{\text{Cos } \theta}$$

$$\textit{cotangent function} = \text{Cot } \theta = \frac{x}{y} = \frac{\text{Cos } \theta}{\text{Sin } \theta}$$

$$\textit{secant function} = \text{Sec } \theta = \frac{1}{x} = \frac{1}{\text{Cos } \theta}$$

$$\textit{cosecant function} = \text{Csc } \theta = \frac{1}{y} = \frac{1}{\text{Sin } \theta}$$

593

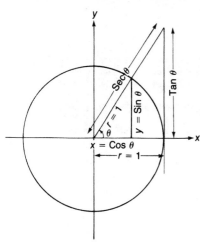

The tangent and secant functions are named for their positions as lines in the CIRCLE. By similar right triangles, large and small, you can see in the diagram that

$$\frac{\text{vertical leg}}{\text{horizontal leg}} = \frac{\text{Tan }\theta}{1} = \frac{\text{Sin }\theta}{\text{Cos }\theta}$$

$$\frac{\text{hypotenuse}}{\text{horizontal leg}} = \frac{\text{Sec }\theta}{1} = \frac{1}{\text{Cos }\theta}$$

For any angle θ between 0° and 90°, *the six trigonometric ratios in terms of the circle can be seen to be the same as those in terms of the triangle*, if you note that

$$x = \text{adjacent side} \qquad y = \text{opposite side} \qquad 1 = \text{hypotenuse.}$$

The circle definitions, however, allow angles with measure greater than 90°, or greater than 360°, or less than 0°.

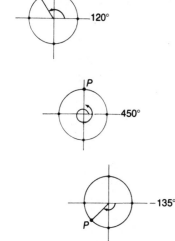

The measure of the angle θ is always determined by starting at the positive x-axis. If the measurement is made in a *counterclockwise* direction, the measure is assigned a *positive* value. If the measurement is made in a *clockwise* direction, the measure is assigned a *negative* value.

Whenever the measure of an angle θ is less than 0° or greater than 90°, some of the trigonometric ratios may be negative. By convention the quadrants are numbered counterclockwise, and in some quadrants the sine or the cosine is negative.

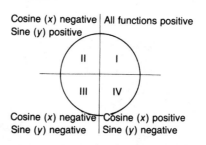

Cosine (x) negative | All functions positive
Sine (y) positive

II   I

III   IV

Cosine (x) negative   Cosine (x) positive
Sine (y) negative   Sine (y) negative

Trigonometric ratios for angles from 0° to 90° are listed in *tables,* such as the one provided in APPENDIX I, or they may be found on CALCULATORS. Ratios can be hand-calculated easily for angles of 0°, 30°, 45°, 60°, and 90°, as shown in the TRIGONOMETRY article. The results are summarized in the following very brief table:

θ	Measure of angle θ in degrees	$y = sine\ \theta$	$x = cosine\ \theta$	$\dfrac{y}{x} = tangent\ \theta$
	0°	$0 = 0.000$	$1 = 1.000$	$\dfrac{0}{1} = 0.000$
	30°	$\dfrac{1}{2} = 0.500$	$\dfrac{\sqrt{3}}{2} \doteq 0.866$	$\dfrac{1}{\sqrt{3}} \doteq 0.577$
	45°	$\dfrac{1}{\sqrt{2}} \doteq 0.707$	$\dfrac{1}{\sqrt{2}} \doteq 0.707$	$\dfrac{1}{1} = 1.000$
	60°	$\dfrac{\sqrt{3}}{2} \doteq 0.866$	$\dfrac{1}{2} = 0.500$	$\dfrac{\sqrt{3}}{1} \doteq 1.732$
	90°	$1 = 1.000$	$0 = 0.000$	$\dfrac{1}{0}$: does not exist

Trigonometric ratios for any angle at all can be calculated from those for angles between 0° and 90° by using the SYMMETRY visible in the circle diagram.

Examples. $\text{Sin } 240° = -\text{Sin } 60° = -\dfrac{\sqrt{3}}{2}$

$\quad\quad\quad\quad \text{Cos } 240° = -\text{Cos } 60° = -\dfrac{1}{2}$

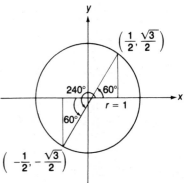

Therefore, the trigonometric tables for angles from 0° to 90° actually give all the information necessary for the trigonometric ratios of any angle at all.

Frequently in trigonometry, angles are measured in *radians* rather than degrees. Radians are the measure of distance along the circumference of the unit circle. This measure is further discussed under ANGLES.

RELATIONSHIPS BETWEEN TRIGONOMETRIC FUNCTIONS

The trigonometric functions are sine, cosine, tangent, cotangent, secant, and cosecant. Special relationships exist between certain pairs of these functions, and these relationships may be expressed as identities. An *identity* in θ is a relationship that is true regardless of the value of θ. For example, every trigonometric function may be expressed in terms of the sine and cosine ratios, as in the definitions. The following are additional trigonometric identities:

Reciprocal Functions

sine and cosecant:

$$\text{Sin } \theta = \frac{1}{\text{Csc } \theta} \qquad \text{Csc } \theta = \frac{1}{\text{Sin } \theta}$$

cosine and secant:

$$\text{Cos } \theta = \frac{1}{\text{Sec } \theta} \qquad \text{Sec } \theta = \frac{1}{\text{Cos } \theta}$$

tangent and cotangent:

$$\text{Tan } \theta = \frac{1}{\text{Cot } \theta} \qquad \text{Cot } \theta = \frac{1}{\text{Tan } \theta}$$

Example.   Sin 30° = ½, while Csc 30° = 2.

These identities follow from the definitions of the trigonometric ratios.

Cofunctions (Complementary Functions)

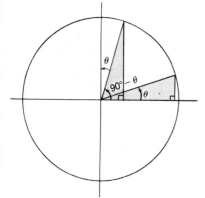

sine and cosine:

$$\text{Sin } \theta = \text{Cos } (90° - \theta)$$
$$\text{Cos } \theta = \text{Sin } (90° - \theta)$$

tangent and cotangent:

$$\text{Tan } \theta = \text{Cot } (90° - \theta)$$
$$\text{Cot } \theta = \text{Tan } (90° - \theta)$$

secant and cosecant:

$$\text{Sec } \theta = \text{Csc } (90° - \theta)$$
$$\text{Csc } \theta = \text{Sec } (90° - \theta)$$

Example.   Sin 30° = Cos (90° − 30°) = Cos 60° = ½.

The truth of these identities may be illustrated by the circle diagram.
The right triangles formed by the complementary angles are CONGRUENT.

Other Identities

There are many other trigonometric identities. The most important is
the fact that $(\text{Sin } \theta)^2 + (\text{Cos } \theta)^2 = 1$.

Example. $(\text{Sin } 30°)^2 + (\text{Cos } 30°)^2 =$

$$\left(\frac{1}{2}\right)^2 + \left(\frac{\sqrt{3}}{2}\right)^2 =$$

$$\frac{1}{4} + \frac{3}{4} = 1.$$

This identity is also illustrated by applying the PYTHAGOREAN THEOREM
to the unit circle diagram.

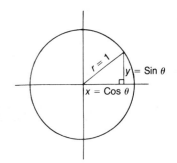

$$y^2 \quad + \quad x^2 \quad = 1$$

$$(\text{Sin } \theta)^2 + (\text{Cos } \theta)^2 = 1$$

It is often written $\boxed{\text{Sin}^2 \ \theta + \text{Cos}^2 \ \theta = 1}$

And from this identity, two others are derived:

dividing by Cos$^2 \ \theta$: $\boxed{\text{Tan}^2 \ \theta + 1 = \text{Sec}^2 \ \theta,}$

or,

dividing by Sin$^2 \ \theta$: $\boxed{1 + \text{Cot}^2 \ \theta = \text{Csc}^2 \ \theta.}$

Other trigonometric identities that you may encounter are listed here
for reference without their proofs. You can consult a trigonometry text
for elaboration.

$$\boxed{\text{Sin } (A + B) = \text{Sin } A \ \text{Cos } B + \text{Cos } A \ \text{Sin } B}$$

$$\boxed{\text{Cos } (A + B) = \text{Cos } A \ \text{Cos } B - \text{Sin } A \ \text{Sin } B}$$

$$\boxed{\text{Tan } (A + B) = \frac{\text{Tan } A + \text{Tan } B}{1 - \text{Tan } A \ \text{Tan } B}}$$

From these can be derived double angle formulas, such as

$$\text{Sin } 2A = \text{Sin } (A + A) = 2 \ \text{Sin } A \ \text{Cos } A$$

and others, such as

$$\text{Sin } (A - B) = \text{Sin } (A + -B)$$
$$= \text{Sin } A \ \text{Cos } -B + \text{Cos } A \ \text{Sin } -B$$
$$= \text{Sin } A \ \text{Cos } B - \text{Cos } A \ \text{Sin } B,$$

which can help to solve trigonometric equations.

Finally, there are some trigonometric identities that help to solve
triangle problems when the triangle is not a right triangle. In any

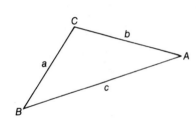

triangle, if you label the three sides a, b, c and then label the opposite angles respectively A, B, C, you can use the following laws:

> Law of Sines: $\dfrac{\text{Sin } A}{a} = \dfrac{\text{Sin } B}{b} = \dfrac{\text{Sin } C}{c}$

> Law of Cosines: $c^2 = a^2 + b^2 - 2ab \text{ Cos } C$

Example.   A soccer goal is 24 feet wide. A player shoots the ball when he is 54 feet from one goal post and 60 feet from the other. Calculate the angle within which the player must execute a ground shot to score. All three sides are known and we want an angle, so the law of cosines applies.

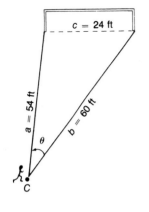

$$(24)^2 = (54)^2 + (60)^2 - 2\,(54)\,(60) \text{ Cos } \theta$$
$$576 = 2916 + 3600 - 6480 \text{ Cos } \theta$$
$$6480 \text{ Cos } \theta = 5940$$
$$\text{Cos } \theta = \frac{5940}{6480} \doteq 0.9167 \quad \text{From a table of cosines, } \theta \doteq 24°.$$

GRAPHS OF TRIGONOMETRIC FUNCTIONS

Each trigonometric function has a GRAPH. The horizontal axis represents the values of the angle θ, while the vertical axis represents the values of the trigonometric function, as shown on the opposite page.

From the graphs of the trigonometric functions, you can see that each curve has one pattern, or *cycle*, which repeats itself. Repeating functions like these are called *periodic*. The *period* of such a function is the horizontal length of the cycle, from any point to the closest point where the cycle begins to repeat.

For both the sine function and the cosine function, the period is 360°. For the tangent function, the period is 180°.

THE SINE WAVE

The graph of the sine function looks like a wave. In fact, it does represent many types of waves.

Various concepts are associated with this graph. The *amplitude* is the maximum height of the wave. The *period* can be measured from any point to the next point horizontally where the cycle begins anew. The *frequency* tells how many cycles occur in a given interval. It depends on the reciprocal of the period. If the horizontal axis is a function of time

Sin θ

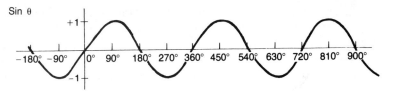

Cos θ

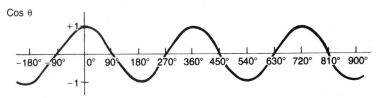

Tan θ

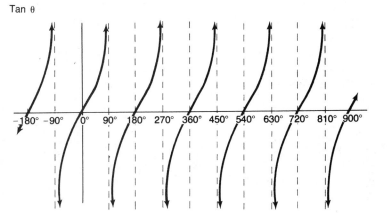

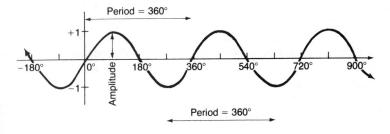

(that is, if the angle θ depends on time), then the frequency might be expressed in *cycles per second*, as in the broadcasting of radio waves.

This sine wave and other similar graphs, such as Sin 2θ, 2 Sin θ, and Cos θ, occur in the study of the behavior of alternating electric current,

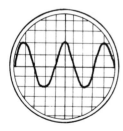

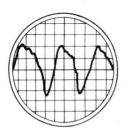

a swinging pendulum, or almost any sort of *vibration*. Although neither a pendulum nor a vibrating spring has motion that looks like a sine wave, a physicist working with these phenomena uses equations that result in these graphs.

Sound travels in waves of air compression; mathematical analysis of these waves also yields a sine function. The loudness of a sound depends upon the amplitude of the wave. Pitch depends upon the frequency of the sound wave—the number of cycles per second. The higher the pitch, the higher the frequency. A musical note one octave higher than another has exactly twice the frequency. Musical sounds are discussed in more detail in the articles on LOGARITHMS and VARIATION.

The *oscilloscope* is an electronic instrument used to test television sets and other electronic devices, to find distortions in high fidelity equipment, and to study electrical impulses from the heart and brain. The oscilloscope shows the mathematical analysis of these phenomena by means of changing electrical signals, which appear on a screen as wavy lines in patterns ranging from a simple sine curve to more complex periodic waves.

In fact, the complex pattern shown second is nothing but the *sum* of simple sine waves of different frequencies and amplitudes. For example, the dark wave in the following graph is the sum of the two lighter sine waves:

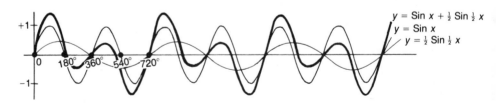

$$y = \text{Sin } x + \tfrac{1}{2} \text{Sin } \tfrac{1}{2} x$$
$$y = \text{Sin } x$$
$$y = \tfrac{1}{2} \text{Sin } \tfrac{1}{2} x$$

This amazing fact was first discovered in the early nineteenth century by the French mathematical physicist Joseph Fourier during his studies of heat flow. Furthermore, Fourier showed that *any* mathematical curve could be considered as a sum of simple sine functions (though it might take hundreds for a good approximation). This demonstrates that trigonometry underlies a good deal more of mathematics and science than just the study of triangles.

References on the sum of sine waves

Edward E. David, Jr., "The Reproduction of Sound," *Scientific American,* August 1961.

The Physics of Music: Readings from Scientific American (W. H. Freeman & Co., 1978). Some of this material is also reprinted in

Mathematics: An Introduction to Its Spirit and Use: Readings from Scientific American (W. H. Freeman & Co., 1978), pp. 198–213, with additional references.

INVERSE TRIGONOMETRIC FUNCTIONS

Each trigonometric function has an *inverse,* defined as follows:

inverse sine function = arcsin x
        = the angle with *sine* equal to x.

> y = arcsin x is *equivalent* to x = sin y.

inverse cosine function = arccos x
        = the angle with *cosine* equal to x.

> y = arccos x is *equivalent* to x = cos y.

inverse tangent function = arctan x
        = the angle with *tangent* equal to x.

> y = arctan x is *equivalent* to x = tan y.

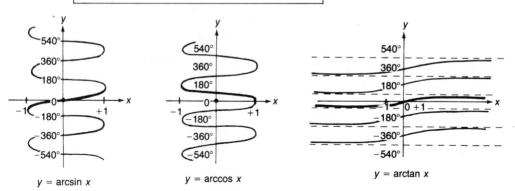

   y = arcsin x y = arccos x y = arctan x

The thickened portion of each graph indicates the conventional *principal values* of y for each x, which define an inverse trigonometric FUNCTION. (Note: In CALCULUS these principal values must be given in radians rather than in degrees. See ANGLES for conversion of degrees to radians.)

Although you may never need to know about inverse trigonometric functions, they are useful in higher mathematics. An interesting example is the *inverse tangent* function, which can be expressed as an infinite series (the sum of an infinite SEQUENCE).

$$\arctan x = x - \frac{x^3}{3} + \frac{x^5}{5} - \frac{x^7}{7} + \frac{x^9}{9} - \frac{x^{11}}{11} + \ldots$$

For any value of x such that $-1 \leqslant x \leqslant 1$, this sum converges to the angle, *measured in radians*, with tangent equal to x.

In particular, arctan 1 is the angle with tangent equal to 1. That angle is 45°, or $\frac{\pi}{4}$ radians. Thus,

$$\frac{\pi}{4} = \arctan 1 = 1 - \frac{1}{3} + \frac{1}{5} - \frac{1}{7} + \frac{1}{9} - \frac{1}{11} + \ldots$$

This series, and faster-converging variations, are the basis of earlier hand approximations and modern computer calculations of PI.

REFERENCE

Deborah Hughes-Hallett, *The Math Workshop: Elementary Functions* (W. W. Norton & Co., 1980), pp. 293–466; a thorough text that is exceptionally readable.

TRIGONOMETRY

TRIGONOMETRY: the study of TRIANGLES, ANGLES, and their relationships.

The word "trigonometry" comes from the ancient Greeks, who studied the subject extensively. Trigonometry literally means triangle measurement. *Plane trigonometry* is the study of triangles in the PLANE.

Basic to the study of trigonometry is the *measurement of angles*. ANGLES can be measured in degrees: place a *protractor* with its center on the vertex of the angle and its base line on one side of the angle. Where the other side of the angle meets the protractor, you can read the number of degrees in the angle.

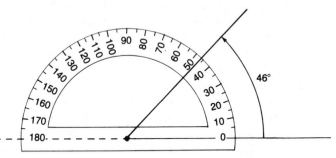

You can also make from your protractor a simple instrument to measure less accessible angles. You need to add a pivoting sighting device—a piece of straight clear plastic tubing will do nicely. Drill a hole near one end of the tubing and another hole in the center of the base of the protractor. Fasten the two objects together with a nut and bolt or a paper fastener through the holes so the sighting tube can rotate snugly. Fix the pivot point at the vertex of the angle you wish to measure and fix the protractor so that one side of the angle is along the base line (this can be determined by sighting if necessary). Look through the tube and rotate it until the object comes into view. The angle can be read from the protractor right under the middle of the sighting tube.

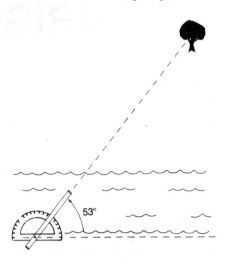

THE TRIGONOMETRIC RATIOS OF PLANE TRIGONOMETRY

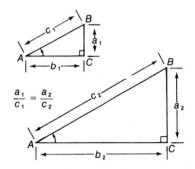

The "triangle measurement" of trigonometry refers to the use of similar triangles to measure inaccessible distances. The RATIOS of corresponding sides of similar triangles are equal (see SIMILARITY). Therefore, the length of one side of a triangle can be found if the length of one other side is known, by setting up a PROPORTION using the lengths of corresponding sides of a similar known triangle. Right triangles are frequently used to make such measurements because any two right triangles with a common acute angle are similar. Thus, for all right triangles containing a given angle A, the ratio of side a to side c will be constant, as will be the ratio of side b to side c, and so on.

$$\frac{a_1}{c_1} = \frac{a_2}{c_2}.$$

With any angle are associated six *trigonometric ratios:* sine, cosine, tangent, cotangent, secant, and cosecant. One way to define trigonometric ratios is in terms of a *right triangle*. The angles of the triangle are usually labeled by capital letters A, B, and C, with C denoting the right angle. For a given acute angle A, the legs of the triangle can be labeled "opposite" and "adjacent." For angle A:

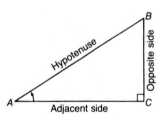

$$sine \text{ ratio} = \text{Sin } A = \frac{\text{opposite side}}{\text{hypotenuse}}$$

$$cosine \text{ ratio} = \text{Cos } A = \frac{\text{adjacent side}}{\text{hypotenuse}}$$

The sine and cosine are the basic trigonometric ratios. The others are:

$$tangent \text{ ratio} = \text{Tan } A = \frac{\text{opposite side}}{\text{adjacent side}} = \frac{\text{Sin } A}{\text{Cos } A}$$

$$cotangent \text{ ratio} = \text{Cot } A = \frac{\text{adjacent side}}{\text{opposite side}} = \frac{\text{Cos } A}{\text{Sin } A}$$

$$secant \text{ ratio} = \text{Sec } A = \frac{\text{hypotenuse}}{\text{adjacent side}} = \frac{1}{\text{Cos } A}$$

$$cosecant \text{ ratio} = \text{Csc } A = \frac{\text{hypotenuse}}{\text{opposite side}} = \frac{1}{\text{Sin } A}$$

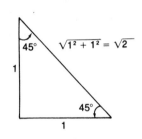

For several angles, you can calculate the trigonometric ratios your-self:

- A 45° angle occurs in an isosceles right triangle—a triangle in which the ratio of the legs is $1:1$. Since all right triangles contain-ing a 45° angle are similar, make each of the legs 1 unit long. The hypotenuse of this triangle can then be found, by the PYTHAGOREAN THEOREM, to be $\sqrt{1^2 + 1^2} = \sqrt{2}$.
- The ratios associated with angles of 30° and 60° can be found by using an equilateral triangle. A right triangle can be formed by an altitude and half of the equilateral triangle as shown in the diagram. The hypotenuse of this right triangle is twice as long as the short leg. Since all equilateral triangles are similar, make each side 2 units long. Then you can use the Pythagorean Theorem to show that the longer leg of the right triangle $= \sqrt{2^2 - 1^2} = \sqrt{3}$.
- An angle A of 0° can be thought of as the result of shrinking the opposite side, a, to 0, which would make the adjacent side, b, equal to the hypotenuse, c.
- An angle A of 90° can be thought of as the result of shrinking the adjacent side, b, to 0, which would make the opposite side, a, equal to the hypotenuse, c.

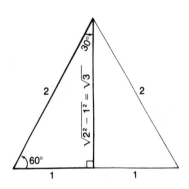

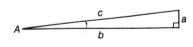

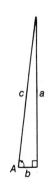

From these triangles, you can calculate all six trigonometric ratios of 0°, 30°, 45°, 60°, and 90° simply by forming the ratios of the appropriate sides. Decimal equivalents may be calculated from the approximation of $\sqrt{2} \doteq 1.414$ and $\sqrt{3} \doteq 1.732$. Results for the three most common ratios of the five angles are listed on the next page.

Measure of angle in degrees	Sine	Cosine	Tangent
0°	$\dfrac{0}{c} = 0.000$	$\dfrac{b}{c} = 1.000$	$\dfrac{0}{b} = 0.000$
30°	$\dfrac{1}{2} = 0.500$	$\dfrac{\sqrt{3}}{2} \doteq 0.866$	$\dfrac{1}{\sqrt{3}} \doteq 0.577$
45°	$\dfrac{1}{\sqrt{2}} \doteq 0.707$	$\dfrac{1}{\sqrt{2}} \doteq 0.707$	$\dfrac{1}{1} = 1.000$
60°	$\dfrac{\sqrt{3}}{2} \doteq 0.866$	$\dfrac{1}{2} = 0.500$	$\dfrac{\sqrt{3}}{1} \doteq 1.732$
90°	$\dfrac{a}{c} = 1.000$	$\dfrac{0}{c} = 0.000$	$\dfrac{a}{0}$: does not exist

For angles other than these five, calculating the trigonometric ratios is a laborious process requiring very precise measurement and calculation. Fortunately this work has been done, and the results are listed in *trigonometric tables,* one of which appears in APPENDIX I. These values can also be found on hand CALCULATORS.

Examples of Problems that can be Solved by Trigonometry

Estimating Distance from an Airplane

The navigator of an airplane flying over the ocean sights a small boat off his wing, at an angle of depression of 30°. From his altimeter, he reads that the plane is 3700 feet above the water. Will the plane receive a radio message if the boat's transmitter has a range of only one mile?

The situation can be sketched as a right triangle, with the airplane at *A* and the boat at *B*. Angle *B* measures 30°, for it also is an angle between the line of sight and a horizontal line. The distance of the boat from the plane is *c*.

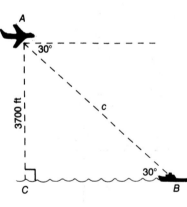

$$\text{Sin } 30° = \frac{3700}{c}, \text{ so } c = \frac{3700}{\sin 30°} = \frac{3700}{0.500} = 7400 \text{ feet.}$$

Since a mile equals 5280 feet, the airplane will not hear the radio signal unless it turns toward the boat.

Measuring the Width of a River

A stake is driven into the ground at point *C*, which is directly across the river from some landmark *A*. Then another stake is driven some distance down the bank at a point B, determined by sighting to be along a line at an angle of 90° to CA. The distance, a, from C to B can be measured directly, and the angle B determined by sighting first from B to C and then to A. The width of the river is b.

If a measures 30 yards, and angle B measures 52°, then

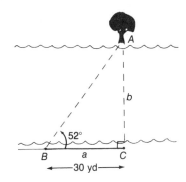

$$\tan 52° = \frac{b}{30}, \text{ and}$$

$$b = 30 \, (\tan 52°) \doteq 30 \, (1.280) \doteq 38.40 \text{ yards.}$$

SPHERICAL TRIGONOMETRY

Trigonometry on a sphere concerns *spherical triangles*. The sides of a spherical triangle are the arcs of great circles. On the surface of a sphere, such as our earth, the arc of a great circle is the shortest distance between two points.

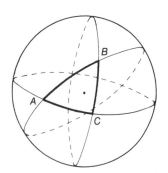

Spherical triangles have different properties from triangles in the plane. Some details are discussed under spherical GEOMETRY. Spherical trigonometry involves finding unknown sides and angles of spherical triangles using trigonometric functions.

The solution of spherical triangles was necessary even in very early astronomy, for the stars appeared to move on circular paths. Each star seemed fixed on a great imaginary *celestial sphere*. The rotation of the earth on its axis makes the stars appear to rotate in the heavens.

Reference on Spherical Trigonometry

Lancelot Hogben, *Mathematics for the Million* (published in Great Britain and by W. W. Norton & Co. in the United States in many editions, from 1936 to 1967), the chapter titled "The World Encompassed, or Spherical Triangles" in the first edition and "Mathematics for the Mariner" in the fourth; a brief but full discussion of the spherical triangle and its applications.

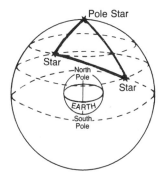

HISTORY OF TRIGONOMETRY

From very early times, surveyors, navigators, and astronomers have employed triangles to measure distances that could not be measured directly. Babylonian clay tablets and ancient Egyptian papyri, dating from at least 1600 B.C., show considerable evidence of practical problems solved by triangle measurement.

Trigonometry as the science of trigonometric ratios grew out of early astronomical observations, such as those of Hipparchus of Alexandria, about 140 B.C. By the second century A.D. there existed Claudius

Ptolemy's "Table of Chords" and Menelaus of Alexandria's treatise on spherical geometry and trigonometry.

And it was astronomy again which led to vast improvements in trigonometry. In the early sixteenth century, the Polish astronomer Nicolas Copernicus challenged the prevailing view of the universe by proposing the theory of a sun-centered solar system rather than the traditional earth-centered universe. To prove or disprove the Copernican theory, more accurate astronomical observations and calculations were needed, leading to the extension of trigonometric tables to ten and fifteen places, for every angle from 0° to 90°, in ten-second increments. By 1700 this enormous task had been accomplished, entirely by hand calculation.

REFERENCES

William R. Ransom, *Trigonometric Novelties* (J. Weston Walch, 1959); recreations in new topics for someone with trigonometric background.

David Eugene Smith, *History of Mathematics, Vol. II: Special Topics of Elementary Mathematics* (Ginn, 1925; Dover, 1958), pp. 600–633; thorough detail on the history of trigonometry; includes the history of work in Persia, India, China, and Japan.

Elizabeth A. Wood, *Science from Your Airplane Window* (Houghton Mifflin, 1968; Dover, 1975), especially ch. 8 on quantitative measurement using trigonometry and similarity and pp. 72–79 on angles; includes a goniometer to measure angles.

Related articles: ANGLES, TRIANGLES, TRIGONOMETRIC FUNCTIONS.

Another way to define the trigonometric ratios is in terms of a *circle*; for these definitions, see TRIGONOMETRIC FUNCTIONS.

VARIATION

VARIATION: a statement of how one quantity changes relative to the way another quantity changes. A variation may be expressed as an equation that states a constant relationship between the values of two or more variables.

Everything in the world is constantly changing. For some of these changes there seems to be little or no pattern. Or to be more accurate, the pattern of change is so complicated that it cannot be easily stated in a mathematical equation. For example, the changes in your mood could depend on your health, how tired you are, the events that have happened to you, your personality, the number of friends you have, and a host of other factors. Thus, it would be almost impossible to write an equation stating how your mood changes relative to the way other factors change.

Other kinds of change are more predictable. For example, it has been discovered that when pressure is held constant, the length of a column of mercury of a given diameter will increase as the temperature increases and will decrease as the temperature decreases. Because this pattern of change, or variation, is constant, thermometers can be made to measure changes in temperature in terms of changes in the length of a column of mercury. One of the goals of physical science is to discover these patterns of change and state them in mathematical formulas.

A formula, or equation, stating *how* one quantity changes relative to the way other quantities change is called a *variation*. And a *variable* is a symbol for one of the quantities that may change.

Example. If the pay for a job is $4 per hour, the total wages will depend on the number of hours worked. You can let w = wages and h = number of hours worked. Then

$$w \text{ and } h \text{ are variables};$$
$$w = 4h \text{ is a variation.}$$

Different patterns of change between variables can be observed. For example, if one quantity increases as another increases, this is one pattern of change. However, if one quantity increases as another decreases, this is another pattern of variation. Four different types of variation commonly observed are discussed below.

DIRECT VARIATION (or Direct Proportion): a variation in which the RATIO between the values of two variables remains constant.

Direct variation

$$\frac{y}{x} = k \quad \text{or} \quad y = kx$$

where k is constant

In a direct variation, as the value of one variable *increases,* the value of the other variable *increases* proportionally. Or, if the value of one of the variables decreases, the value of the other decreases proportionally.

A familiar example of direct variation is the relationship between the amount you pay for gasoline at a particular pump and the number of gallons you buy. In this example, two values can change—the number of gallons and the total cost. These are the variables. On the other hand, the price per gallon at a given pump (at a given time) does not change. This constant, or unchanging, value is called the *constant of variation.* When you buy gasoline at a pump, the total amount you pay will equal the constant price per gallon times the number of gallons you buy. The more you buy, the more you'll have to pay.

Total cost

Number of gallons

Direct variation

T = total cost in dollars   (variable)
k = price per gallon in dollars   (constant)
n = number of gallons   (variable)

Then $T = kn$ or $\dfrac{T}{n} = k$, where $\dfrac{T}{n}$ is a constant ratio.

If the price per gallon is \$1.50 and you buy 5 gallons, your total cost will be 5 × \$1.50, or \$7.50. If you buy 10 gallons at the same price, your total cost will be \$15.00. The graph illustrates how the total cost varies directly with the number of gallons purchased.

Proportion form for direct variation

$$\frac{x_1}{x_2} = \frac{y_1}{y_2}$$

Problems Involving Direct Variation

A problem involving direct variation can be solved by setting up the problem either in EQUATION form or in PROPORTION form.

• *In equation form:*

$$\frac{y}{x} = k \text{ or } y = kx,$$

where x and y are two variables and where k is the constant of variation. In solving a variation in equation form, it may be necessary to compute the value of k if it is not given in the problem.

- *In proportion form:*

$$\frac{x_1}{y_1} = \frac{x_2}{y_2} \text{ or } \frac{x_1}{x_2} = \frac{y_1}{y_2}$$

where x_1 and x_2 are two values of one variable and y_1 and y_2 are corresponding values of another variable. The two ratios

$$\frac{x_1}{y_1} \text{ and } \frac{x_2}{y_2} \text{ are each equal to } k,$$

the constant of variation. So, in solving a variation in proportion form, it is not necessary to compute the value of k.

Example. If an automatic doughnut machine can produce 500 doughnuts in 3 hours, how long would it take to produce 300 doughnuts?

- *Solution using equation form:*

$$d = \text{total number of doughnuts} = 300$$
$$k = \text{number of doughnuts produced per hour}$$
$$h = \text{number of hours}$$
$$d = kh$$

Since the machine produces 500 doughnuts in 3 hours, the number produced per hour, or the value of k, is $500 \div 3$.

Therefore, $300 = \dfrac{500}{3}h$ and $h = \dfrac{300 \times 3}{500} = 1\dfrac{4}{5}$ hours.

- *Solution using proportion form:*

$$x_1 = 500 \text{ doughnuts}$$
$$y_1 = \text{number of hours to produce 500 doughnuts} = 3 \text{ hours}$$
$$x_2 = 300 \text{ doughnuts}$$
$$y_2 = \text{number of hours to produce 300 doughnuts}$$

$$\frac{x_1}{x_2} = \frac{y_1}{y_2}$$

$$\frac{500}{300} \diagdown \frac{3}{y_2}$$

$$y_2 = \frac{300 \times 3}{500} = 1\frac{4}{5} \text{ hours.}$$

> *Inverse variation*
>
> $$yx = k \text{ or } y = \frac{k}{x}$$
>
> where k is constant

INVERSE VARIATION (or Inverse Proportion): a variation in which the *product* of two variables remains constant.

In an inverse variation, as the value of one variable *increases,* the value of the other variable *decreases.* Or, if the value of the first variable decreases, the value of the second increases.

A familiar example of inverse variation is the relationship between rate of speed and the time required to travel a *fixed distance.* The distance in this example does not change; it is the constant of variation. The two variables in this example are the rate of speed and the time required to travel the distance. As one of these variables increases, the other decreases. The greater the speed, the less time is needed to travel the distance. The lower the speed, the more time is needed.

Hours needed to travel
100 miles

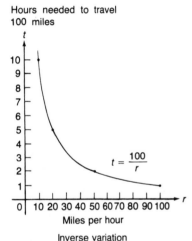

Miles per hour

Inverse variation

$$d = \text{distance in miles} \qquad \text{(constant)}$$
$$r = \text{rate of speed in miles per hour} \quad \text{(variable)}$$
$$t = \text{time in hours} \qquad \text{(variable)}$$

Then $d = rt$ or $t = \dfrac{d}{r}$, where d is constant.

If the fixed distance is 100 miles and the rate of speed is 40 miles per hour, the time needed to travel the distance will be $100 \div 40$, or $2\frac{1}{2}$ hours. However, if the speed is increased to 50 miles per hour, the time will be reduced to 2 hours. A graph illustrates the inverse variation between rate of speed and the time needed to travel 100 miles.

> *Proportion form for inverse variation*
>
> $$\frac{x_1}{x_2} = \frac{y_2}{y_1}$$

Problems Involving Inverse Variation

A problem involving inverse variation can be solved by setting up the problem either in equation form or in proportion form.

• *In equation form:*

$$xy = k \text{ or } y = \frac{k}{x} ,$$

where x and y are variables and k is the constant of variation.

• *In proportion form:*

$$\frac{x_1}{x_2} = \frac{y_2}{y_1},$$

where x_1 and x_2 are two values of one variable and y_1 and y_2 are corresponding values of the other variable.

Example. The force needed to pry up a rock varies inversely with the length of the crowbar used. If a certain rock can be pried up using a 6-foot crowbar and a force of 160 pounds, how long a crowbar is needed if the force is only 120 pounds?

• *Solution using equation form:*

> F = force needed in pounds
> L = length of crowbar in feet
> K = total number of foot-pounds needed to lift the rock
> $FL = K$

Since a force of 160 pounds is needed using a 6-foot crowbar, the total number of foot-pounds needed, or the value of K, is 160×6, or 960 foot-pounds.

$$\text{Therefore, } 960 = 120L, \text{ so } L = \frac{960}{120} = 8 \text{ feet.}$$

• *Solution using proportion form:*

> x_1 = force of 160 pounds
> y_1 = length of crowbar in feet using 160 pounds of force
> x_2 = force of 120 pounds
> y_2 = length of crowbar in feet using 120 pounds of force

$$\frac{x_1}{x_2} = \frac{y_2}{y_1}$$

$$\frac{160}{120} \diagdown\!\!\!\!\diagup \frac{y_2}{6}$$

$$120\, y_2 = 960$$

$$\text{so } y_2 = \frac{960}{120} = 8 \text{ feet.}$$

> *Joint variation*
>
> $y = kxz$
>
> where k is constant

JOINT VARIATION: a direct variation involving more than two variables.

A familiar example of joint variation can be seen in the amount of interest earned on money invested at a *constant rate*. If the rate of interest is constant, the amount of interest earned will vary directly both with the amount of money invested (the *principal*) and with the length of time the money is invested. The more money you invest, the more interest you will earn. And similarly, the longer you leave the money invested, the more money you will earn. Thus, interest varies jointly with both principal and time.

$$I = \text{amount of interest earned} \quad \text{(variable)}$$
$$p = \text{principal} \quad \text{(variable)}$$
$$r = \text{rate of interest} \quad \text{(constant)}$$
$$t = \text{time in years} \quad \text{(variable)}$$
$$I = prt$$

> *Combined variation*
>
> $y = \dfrac{kx}{z}$
>
> where k is constant

COMBINED VARIATION: a variation involving both direct and inverse variation.

One example of combined variation is in the relationship between the pressure needed to force water through a pipe, the speed of the water, and the diameter of the pipe. The pressure needed varies directly with the square of the speed of the water and varies inversely with the diameter of the pipe. That is, the greater the speed of the water, the greater the pressure must be. However, the smaller the pipe, the greater the pressure must be. This combined variation can be expressed in the following formula:

$$p = \frac{ks^2}{d} \text{ , where } p = \text{pressure} \quad \text{(variable)}$$
$$s = \text{speed of water} \quad \text{(variable)}$$
$$d = \text{diameter of pipe} \quad \text{(variable)}$$
$$k = \text{constant of variation} \quad \text{(constant)}$$

APPLICATION

An interesting example of combined variation can be seen in the design of stringed instruments. Pythagoras, a famous Greek mathematician, and his band of fellow scholars discovered in the sixth century B.C. that the pitch of a note produced by plucking a string is inversely proportional to the length of the string. That is, the longer the string, the lower the pitch. Moreover, they discovered that doubling the length of the string lowered the pitch by one octave. That is, the RATIO of the lengths of two strings with pitches an octave apart is 2:1.

If the only variable affecting the pitch produced by a string were the length of the string, no one could design an instrument like the modern piano, which has a range of over 7 octaves. For if the shortest string were only 5 inches long, the longest string would need to be over 50 feet long—a rather cumbersome instrument to say the least.

However, the length of the string is not the only variable that affects pitch. Thicker or heavier strings produce lower pitches, and tighter strings produce higher pitches. Although these general truths were probably known by the Pythagoreans, it was not until the middle of the seventeenth century that the exact combined variation was discovered by Marin Mersenne, a French mathematician. Mersenne's Laws include the following:

- Pitch is inversely proportional to the length (L) of the string. (Pythagoras' Law)
- Pitch is directly proportional to the square root of the tension (T) applied to the string.
- Pitch is inversely proportional to the square root of the weight (W) of the string.

$$\text{In summary, pitch} = \frac{k}{L}\sqrt{\frac{T}{W}}.$$

So, increased tension for high-sounding strings and thicker, heavier strings for the low notes are what bring the piano down to size. You can see and hear the same effects on any stringed instrument, such as a violin, guitar, or harp.

References on variation in the design of musical instruments

Sir James Jeans, *Science & Music* (Cambridge University Press, 1937; Dover, 1968), especially pp. 61–65; a marvelous compendium of detail on all mathematical aspects of music.

Charles F. Linn, *The Golden Mean: Mathematics and the Fine Arts* (Doubleday & Co., 1974), pp. 9–13 and 79–87; a clear and simple presentation.

The Physics of Music: Readings from Scientific American (W. H. Freeman, 1978); includes E. Donnell Blackham, "The Physics of the Piano," December 1965, and Carleen Maley Hutchins, "The Physics of Violins," November 1962.

For other articles related to variation, see RATIOS and PROPORTIONS.

VECTORS

Symbols: $\vec{v}$ *or* **v**

A half-arrow above a letter or a boldface letter is used to indicate a vector.

$\overrightarrow{AB}$ or **AB** represents a vector from point A to point B.

$\|\overrightarrow{AB}\|$ represents only the magnitude of $\overrightarrow{AB}$ and is called the *norm* or *absolute value* of $\overrightarrow{AB}$.

VECTOR: a quantity that has both *magnitude* (size) and *direction*. In contrast, a quantity that has only magnitude is called a *scalar*.

Examples. The following quantities are vectors:

- a river current flowing *two miles per hour* in a *northwest direction;*
- a force of *fifty pounds* pulling *downward;*
- a wind blowing at *30 miles per hour from the south.*

GRAPHIC REPRESENTATION OF A VECTOR

A vector can be represented by a line segment drawn to scale to show the magnitude of the vector and oriented and capped with an arrowhead to indicate the direction of the vector.

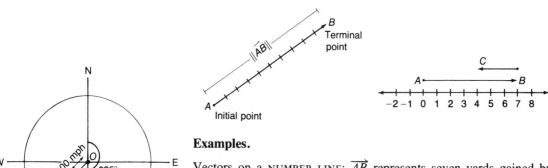

Examples.

Vectors on a NUMBER LINE: $\overrightarrow{AB}$ represents seven yards gained by a football player rushing toward the defensive team's goal. $\overrightarrow{BC}$ represents three yards lost on the next play, moving the ball back toward the offensive team's goal.

Vector in a PLANE: $\overrightarrow{OB}$ represents a velocity of 600 miles per hour at a compass heading of 225°.

Unit Vector: a vector with a magnitude of 1 unit.

Equivalent Vectors: vectors that have the same size and the same direction.

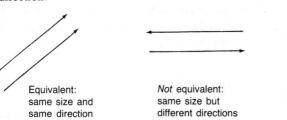

Equivalent:
same size and
same direction

Not equivalent:
same size but
different directions

Not equivalent:
same direction but
different sizes

ADDITION OF VECTORS

To find the sum of two vectors, you find a single vector called the *resultant,* which has the same effect as the two vectors being added.

Examples.

- If a football team gains seven yards on one play, $\overrightarrow{AB}$, and loses three yards on the next play, $\overrightarrow{BC}$, the resultant of the two plays is a four-yard gain, $\overrightarrow{AC}$.

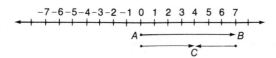

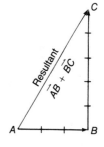

- If a man walks three blocks due east, $\overrightarrow{AB}$, then walks five blocks due north, $\overrightarrow{BC}$, the resultant of his walk is shown by $\overrightarrow{AC}$.
- If two forces, $\overrightarrow{AB}$ and $\overrightarrow{AC}$, are pulling on an object at A, the resultant vector can be found in the following way: Construct $\overrightarrow{BD}$ equivalent to $\overrightarrow{AC}$ or construct $\overrightarrow{CD}$ equivalent to $\overrightarrow{AB}$. (Remember that equivalent vectors have the same magnitude and the same direction.) Then the diagonal $\overrightarrow{AD}$ is the resultant force vector. The object at A would be pulled in the direction of D, with a force equal to the magnitude of $\overrightarrow{AD}$.

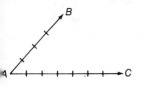

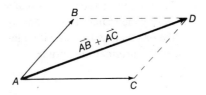

A parallelogram such as *ABDC* is called a parallelogram of forces. And this method of adding vectors geometrically is known as the *Parallelogram Law* (or Triangle Law).

The Parallelogram Law can be used to find the sum of three or more vectors. Three vectors can be added by first finding the resultant of two of the vectors and then adding that resultant to the third vector.

Example.

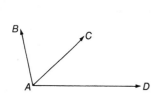
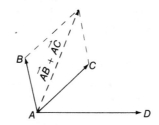
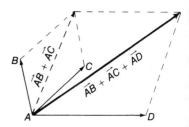

Components *of a vector:* vectors the sum of which is the given vector.

Examples.

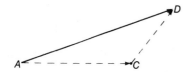

$\vec{AC} + \vec{CD} = \vec{AD}$

Components of $\vec{AD}$

$\vec{AE} + \vec{ED} = \vec{AD}$

Perpendicular components of AD

A single vector $\vec{AD}$ can have an infinite number of components. These are but two examples.

MULTIPLICATION OF A VECTOR BY A SCALAR

Scalar: a REAL NUMBER, a quantity with magnitude but no direction.

To multiply a vector by a scalar, you multiply the magnitude of the vector by the scalar. The product is a new vector with the same direction as the original vector but with a length equal to the product of the scalar times the original magnitude.

Examples.

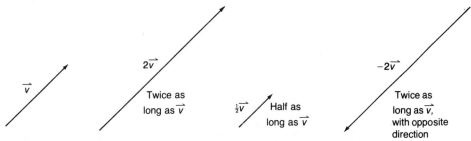

Multiplication of a vector by a scalar results in a stretching or shrinking of the original vector. Multiplication of a vector by a negative scalar also reverses the direction.

ORDERED PAIR NOTATION

Any vector can be viewed as the sum of its perpendicular components. For example, in the diagram, $\overrightarrow{AB}$ is the sum of $\overrightarrow{AC}$ and $\overrightarrow{CB}$.

Furthermore, any vector lying in the plane of a Cartesian COORDINATE system may be considered the sum of a horizontal component, parallel to the x-axis, and a vertical component, parallel to the y-axis. In such a system, the vector can be expressed algebraically by an *ordered pair* of numbers. The first element of the pair represents the horizontal component of the vector; the second element represents the vertical component.

Example.

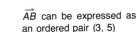

$\overrightarrow{AB}$ can be expressed as an ordered pair (3, 5)

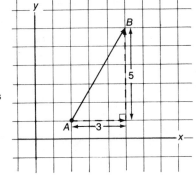

When a vector is represented as an ordered pair, its magnitude can be calculated from the PYTHAGOREAN THEOREM because the vector and its components form a right triangle. Thus, the magnitude of the vector equals the square root of the sum of the squares of the components.

Example.

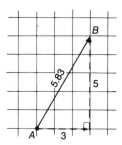

If $\overrightarrow{AB}$ = (3, 5), then

$$\|\overrightarrow{AB}\| = \sqrt{3^2 + 5^2}$$
$$= \sqrt{34}, \text{ or approximately 5.83}$$

Expressing vectors as ordered pairs has a number of advantages. One advantage of ordered-pair notation is that it simplifies the performing of ARITHMETIC OPERATIONS with vectors. When vectors are expressed as ordered pairs, addition of vectors becomes addition of components.

Example.

(1, 4) + (5, 3) = (1 + 5, 4 + 3) = (6, 7)

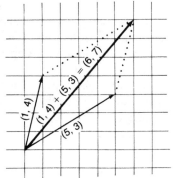

Multiplication of a vector by a scalar becomes multiplication of the components by the scalar.

Example.

$3\overrightarrow{AB}$ = 3 (5, 2) = (3 × 5, 3 × 2) = (15, 6)

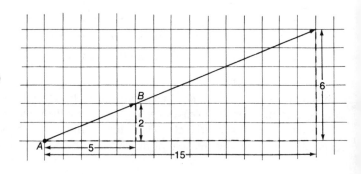

Moreover, when vectors are expressed as ordered pairs of numbers, these numbers can be entered into a computer, or calculator, thereby making arithmetic operations with vectors even easier.

EXTENSION OF VECTOR ALGEBRA BEYOND GEOMETRY

Just as it is possible to have a two-dimensional vector in a plane, so it is possible to conceive of a three-dimensional vector in space. Such a vector would have three components with respect to a three-dimensional coordinate system—one component parallel to the x-axis, one parallel to the y-axis, and one parallel to the z-axis, which represents the direction perpendicular to the xy-plane. Such a three-dimensional vector would be represented algebraically as an *ordered triple* of numbers. The first element of the ordered triple would represent the component parallel to the x-axis; the second would represent the component parallel to the y-axis; and the third, the component parallel to the z-axis.

Example.

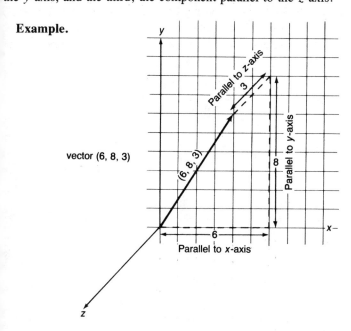

Another advantage of expressing vectors algebraically as ordered sets of numbers is that it allows the idea of vectors to be extended even beyond three dimensions. In the same way that ordered pairs represent two-dimensional vectors and ordered triples represent three-dimensional vectors, ordered quadruples represent four-dimensional vectors and ordered *n*-tuples represent *n*-dimensional vectors. It is possible for mathematicians to use an ordered hundred-tuple to represent a vector, even though such a hundred-dimensional vector could not possibly be drawn geometrically. Still, hundred-tuples are used by mathematicians whenever a hundred different variables must be accounted for.

When $n = 2$ or 3, *direction* of the vector can be thought of in terms of the *components*; finding the direction means specifying the components. For *n* greater than 2 or 3, the "direction" of the vector is no longer something you can *see* in the plane or in space. But the notion is extended abstractly by still focusing on the components. The components give all the necessary information, whether or not you can actually draw the vector.

The point is that listing dozens of variables in vector form provides *organization* to guide calculation of sums and products. For example, a vector could be formed for a week's production at a factory that manufactures 53 different types of chain. That means a standard listing is specified for the 53 types, so the vector simply lists production in that standard order; the weekly production vector has 53 components, each of which is just a number representing the quantity of that type of chain produced that week. Then the factory's quarterly production can be stated simply as "the vector sum of the thirteen weekly production vectors" for that calendar quarter; this single statement covers all 53 component sums of thirteen terms each.

MORE ON MULTIPLICATION

There are actually three different kinds of vector multiplication. The simplest—multiplication by a scalar—has been explained. But a vector may also be multiplied by a vector in several ways. One possibility is called the *dot product*. The dot product $\vec{U} \cdot \vec{V}$ of two vectors, $\vec{U}$ and $\vec{V}$ (having the same dimension), is a *scalar,* equal to the *sum of the products of the respective components*.

Example. $(3, 2) \cdot (5, 4) = (3 \times 5) + (2 \times 4) = 23$

The dot product has many applications. For a nongeometric example, consider an order blank for a home-delivery milkman. This order could be considered as a six-dimensional vector $(3, 2, 0, 1, 0, 0)$, because the delivery order is always printed in this sequence. Another six-dimensional vector could be formed with the prices for the items listed in the same sequence $(0.99, 0.89, 1.87, 0.65, 1.15, 0.79)$. Then the total bill for the customer is the dot product of these two vectors, the order vector and the price vector.

HOME DELIVERY		
how many?		cost
3	MILK @ .99/half gallon	
2	EGGS @ .89/dozen	
	BUTTER @ 1.87/pound	
1	CREAM @ .65/half pint	
	EGGNOG @ 1.15/quart	
	ORANGE JUICE @ .79/quart	
	total bill	

$$3 \times 0.99 + 2 \times 0.89 + 0 \times 1.87 + 1 \times 0.65 + 0 \times 1.15 + 0 \times 0.79$$
$$= \$5.40$$

Although the milkman probably does not know it, when he calculates this bill, he is computing a dot product.

The concept of dot product has organized the separate multiplications and subsequent addition into a single vector operation. A computer can easily be programmed to carry out this operation; then all you need to do is feed in the two vectors.

Economists often compute dot products to find the net result of changes in several variables. For example, the cost of living in a given city is regularly found on a computer by calculating the dot product of a typical shopping-list vector and the corresponding price vector. Each month as prices change, a new price vector is entered into the machine and a new dot product, representing the cost of living, is computed using the same typical shopping-list vector.

HISTORY OF VECTORS

The roots of vector analysis go back at least to the sixteenth century. In 1586, a Flemish mathematician and physicist, Simon Stevin, gave the Parallelogram Law for finding the resultant of two physical forces expressed as vectors. In the eighteenth century the Swiss mathematician Leonhard Euler used a vector approach to solving at least one problem.

Yet though the roots of vector analysis are to be found earlier, the full flowering of the study came in the nineteenth century. An Irish mathematician, William Rowan Hamilton, was searching for a three-dimensional number to represent the rotation of a vector in space. In 1843 he suddenly realized that he needed a four-dimensional number, *and* he made the revolutionary discovery that it is possible to construct an algebra in which one of the basic ground rules, or FIELD PROPERTIES, of conventional algebra does not hold. Specifically, Hamilton developed an algebra of vectors (which he called *quaternions*) in which multiplication is *not commutative*. In other words, in Hamilton's quaternion algebra, $a \times b \neq b \times a$. Hamilton was stunned. The insight came to him while he was out walking, and he is said to have stopped and carved the equation representing his discovery into a bridge.

Hamilton's ideas were soon generalized and applied by other mathematicians. In 1844, Hermann Grassmann, a German geometer, independently published a much more general algebra of n-dimensional quantities. And in the late nineteenth century an American, Josiah Willard Gibbs, applied the work of Hamilton and Grassmann to physics. From their theories, Gibbs developed a complete vector analysis for three-dimensional geometric vectors. Finally, in 1887, an

Multiplication Table for Hamilton's Quaternions

	1	i	j	k
1	1	i	j	k
i	i	-1	k	$-j$
j	j	$-k$	-1	i
k	k	j	$-i$	-1

NOTE:
$i \times j = k$, but $j \times i = -k$

Italian mathematician, Gregorio Ricci, developed an even more general theory of vector quantities called *tensor analysis*.

The fruits of vector analysis have been numerous. One of the most significant applications was made in the twentieth century by Albert Einstein. In developing his general theory of relativity, Einstein found that he needed a way of representing gravitational force that was not tied to any particular coordinate system. Tensor analysis provides a way. Luckily, a friend of Einstein's, Marcel Grossman, was a mathematician who specialized in tensor analysis. "Without Grossman's powerful mathematical aid, Einstein would have been long delayed in bringing the general theory of relativity to fruition."*

REFERENCES

Kurt O. Friedrichs, *From Pythagoras to Einstein,* New Mathematical Library #16 (Random House, 1966).

Abraham M. Glicksman, *Vectors in Three Dimensional Geometry* (National Council of Teachers of Mathematics, 1961).

Banesh Hoffman, *About Vectors* (Prentice-Hall, 1966); excellent and entertaining attention to disturbing questions, as well as instruction for beginners that goes all the way to tensors.

M. Scott Norton, *Basic Concepts of Vectors,* Exploring Math on Your Own series (Webster Publishing Co., 1963).

Biographical references

E. T. Bell, *Men of Mathematics* (Simon & Schuster, 1937; Fireside paperback), Ch. 19, "An Irish Tragedy."

Sir Edmund Whittaker, "William Rowan Hamilton," *Scientific American,* May 1954, reprinted in *Mathematics in the Modern World: Readings from Scientific American* (W. H. Freeman & Co., 1968).

Vectors have been further generalized to MATRICES. Consider a vector as an n-tuple; then a *matrix* can be considered as a set of vectors—an $m \times n$, or "m by n," rectangular array of m n-tuples. A $1 \times n$ matrix is a single vector, and any vector can be considered a special case of a matrix.

*Banesh Hoffman and Helen Dukes, *Albert Einstein: Creator and Rebel* (Viking Press, 1972), pp. 116–117.

VOLUME

VOLUME: an amount of three-dimensional space; a MEASURE of capacity.

The word "volume" comes from the Latin *volumen,* meaning "scroll." As printing became common, "volume" came to mean "book." Eventually, the word came to refer to the size or bulk of a book, and finally in the seventeenth century, to the size or bulk of other objects or materials.

Examples.

• Milk for a recipe might be measured in any of these containers:

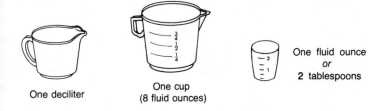

One deciliter

One cup
(8 fluid ounces)

One fluid ounce
or
2 tablespoons

• Firewood is sold by the cord (128 cubic feet) or the stere (1 cubic meter).

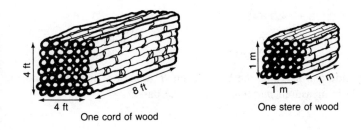

One cord of wood

One stere of wood

• A wagon might have the capacity to carry 400 bushels of corn.

CALCULATION OF VOLUME

Volume is calculated by counting or approximating the number of cubic units contained in the object in question. In many cases this counting can be done quickly by a formula.

Volumes of Polyhedra and other Figures

See POLYHEDRA for definitions of prism, pyramid, and frustum. See AREA for formulas for area for bases.

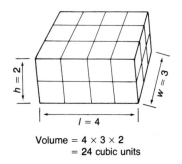

Volume = 3 × 3 × 3
       = 27 cubic units

Volume = 4 × 3 × 2
       = 24 cubic units

Cube: volume = edge × edge × edge

$$V = e^3$$

Rectangular Solid: volume = length × width × height

$$V = lwh$$

or

volume = area of base × height

$$V = Bh$$

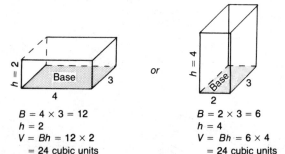

$B = 4 \times 3 = 12$
$h = 2$
$V = Bh = 12 \times 2$
   = 24 cubic units

or

$B = 2 \times 3 = 6$
$h = 4$
$V = Bh = 6 \times 4$
   = 24 cubic units

Any side can serve as the base. Then B = area of the base, and the height is measured *perpendicular* to the base.

Prism: volume = area of base × height

$$V = Bh$$

The base is one of the parallel ends of the prism. Then B = area of the base, and the height is measured *perpendicular* to the base.

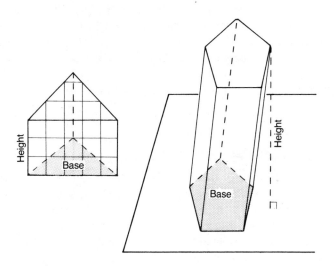

Cylinder: volume = area of base × height

$$V = Bh = \pi r^2 h$$

The base is a circle of area πr^2. The height is measured *perpendicular* to the base.

Pyramid: volume = $\frac{1}{3}$ (area of base × height)

$$V = \frac{1}{3} Bh$$

B is the area of the base, and the height is measured *perpendicular* to the base.

Cone: volume = $\frac{1}{3}$ (area of base × height)

$$V = \frac{1}{3} Bh = \frac{1}{3} \pi r^2 h$$

The base is a circle of area πr^2. The height is measured *perpendicular* to the base.

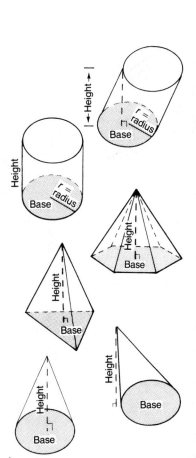

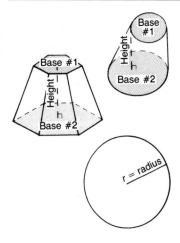

Frustum of a Pyramid or Cone:

$$\text{volume} = \tfrac{1}{3} \text{ height} \times (\text{area } B_1 + \text{area } B_2 + \sqrt{(\text{area } B_1)(\text{area } B_2)})$$

$$V = \tfrac{1}{3} h (B_1 + B_2 + \sqrt{B_1 B_2})$$

A frustum of a pyramid or cone is the part of the solid between two parallel planes that form two bases, of areas B_1 and B_2. The height is the *perpendicular* distance between the bases. To find the volume of a frustum, it is necessary to calculate the *square root* of the product $B_1 B_2$. For calculation of square root, see ARITHMETIC OPERATIONS.

Sphere: volume $= \tfrac{4}{3} \times$ pi $\times$ cube of radius

$$V = \tfrac{4}{3} \pi r^3$$

A Closer Look at Base x Height

Consider a deck of 52 cards neatly stacked into a rectangular pile. If the pile is then skewed, the shape of the pile changes, but the volume does not. In terms of the formula $V = Bh$ (which is a good approximation to the volume of a deck of cards), the area of the base (one card) has not changed, and the height of the pile (52 × thickness of each card) has not changed when the deck is skewed.

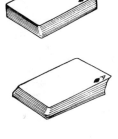

This idea lies behind all the volume formulas that include area of base × height. For instance, the position of the vertex of a pyramid is not important as long as the area of the base and the height perpendicular to that base are known. Consider the following sketch:

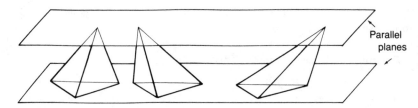

Parallel planes

Because the planes are parallel, the height of each pyramid is the same. The base of each pyramid is the same triangle. Therefore, the volumes of each pyramid are the same.

A Closer Look at $\frac{1}{3} Bh$

Why does $\tfrac{1}{3}$ appear in formulas for the volume of a pyramid or cone? For the case of a triangular pyramid, it can be shown this way:

(1) Consider a pyramid with triangle *ABC* as its base.

(2) On the base of this *pyramid*, a *prism* can be constructed with the same base and the same height as the pyramid, using *BD* as one of the parallel edges.

(3) This prism is the union of the three pyramids, I, II, and III.

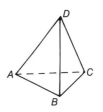

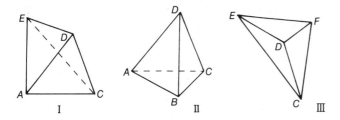

I   II   III

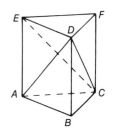

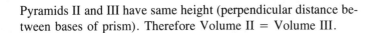

Base *ABC* of II = Base *EDF* of III.

Pyramids II and III have same height (perpendicular distance between bases of prism). Therefore Volume II = Volume III.

Base *EDA* of I = Base *ADB* of II,

because *EDA* and *ADB* are two halves of a parallelogram *AEDB* forming a side of the prism. I and II have the same height (perpendicular distance from *C* to base of each pyramid, since the bases are in the same plane). Therefore, Volume I = Volume II.

(4) Therefore Volume I = Volume II = Volume III. Hence, the volume of the pyramid is contained three times in the volume of the prism (*Bh*), showing that the volume of the pyramid is indeed $\frac{1}{3}Bh$.

Origin of Other Volume Formulas

For nonrectangular figures, such as the sphere, the volumes may be calculated as the *limit of a sum* of the volumes of thin *cylindrical slices*. That is, if the figure is sliced by a number of equally spaced parallel planes, each slice approximates a cylinder whose volume can be calculated. The sum of these volumes approximates the total volume of the figure. If the spacing between slices were made smaller, a better approximation would result. The actual volume of the whole figure is the *limit* of a sequence of approximations to the volume, with each approximation having a shorter distance between the parallel planes. The branch of mathematics known as integral CALCULUS is concerned with finding this

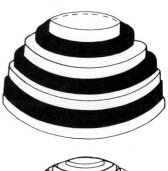

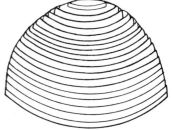

limit. Similar calculations of limits are used to find the AREA of irregular figures.

Calculation of Volume Without a Formula

One way to find the volume of an irregular solid, such as a rock, is by water displacement. If the object is dropped into a measured amount of water (enough to cover the object), then the water level rises by an amount equal to the volume of the object.

Example.

Start with 6 ounces of water

Add the rock: water level rises to 8 ounces

Difference = 2 fluid ounces

Volume of rock = 2 ounces × 1.805 cubic inches per ounce

= 3.610 cubic inches

The equivalence of 1.805 cubic inches per ounce comes from the *Table of Liquid Measure* in APPENDIX 1.

CONSIDERING VOLUME IN NATURE

Surprisingly many qualities of animal existence and behavior depend upon the *volume* of the animal. The weight of an animal depends upon its volume, because weight is distributed throughout the body. The animal also produces heat throughout its body when it consumes food. Furthermore, the energy the animal uses during activity depends on the quantity of muscle, which is also distributed throughout the body. So heat production and energy for activity also depend on volume.

Other quantities, such as heat loss or the friction against a swimming animal, depend upon the *surface area* of the animal. For instance, the amount of heat that is lost by evaporation of perspiration in hot weather or by chilling in cold weather depends on the amount of surface in contact with the air. On the other hand, an aquatic animal, such as a whale, is slowed in its swimming activity by the friction between the skin and the water at a rate that depends upon the amount of skin.

Mathematically, this leads to some interesting implications, because the larger an animal, the smaller is its RATIO of surface area to volume. This idea can most easily be shown with a cube.

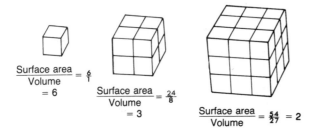

$$\frac{\text{Surface area}}{\text{Volume}} = \frac{6}{1} = 6$$

$$\frac{\text{Surface area}}{\text{Volume}} = \frac{24}{8} = 3$$

$$\frac{\text{Surface area}}{\text{Volume}} = \frac{54}{27} = 2$$

This means, for instance, that a larger animal suffers less heat loss (in proportion to its weight or volume) in cold weather, because it has less surface area per volume. Polar bears are far better suited to an arctic climate than chipmunks, for they have less trouble keeping warm. A larger animal also needs to eat much less food (in proportion to its body weight or volume) to maintain enough heat production to match its natural losses.

For aquatic animals there is another advantage to large size, for the larger animal has greater speed. That is because its energy for activity depends upon its volume, while the friction opposing its swimming depends upon its surface area. Since a larger animal has a smaller surface area to volume ratio, it has a smaller friction to energy ratio. This smaller ratio can mean greater speed.

Reference on volume in nature

D'Arcy Thompson, *On Growth and Form* (Cambridge University Press, 1917; revised edition, 1961), Ch. 2, "On Magnitude"; details of these examples and many other considerations of the comparative measurements of living things; the classic reference.

Related articles: MEASURE, METRIC SYSTEM, POLYHEDRA. Tables of *Units of Measure* for measuring volume are given in APPENDIX I.

ZERO

ZERO: the NUMBER symbolized by the numeral 0 and having all the properties listed below.

Zero is the *cardinal number* that denotes none, or not any. For example, the number of tigers living at the North Pole is zero, for there are no tigers living at the North Pole. Thus, the set of all tigers living at the North Pole is an empty set. Zero is the numeral that denotes the number of elements in the *empty set*.

Zero is a *place holder*. In our numeral system there is a difference between 57, 507, and 570. In the numeral 570, the 5 denotes five hundreds, the 7 denotes seven tens, and the zero is a place holder denoting no units, or ones. In the numeral 507, the zero denotes no tens. The number 57 could be written 057 or 000057 because 57 contains no hundreds, no thousands, and so on. However, for convenience, fifty-seven is usually written 57.

Zero is a starting place, or point of *origin*. In a game, the score at the beginning before any points have been scored is 0 to 0. On a graph, the place from which you start counting to locate 5 years or 10,000 bushels is zero.

Zero is a REAL NUMBER that is *neither positive nor negative*. Rather, it is the point between the positive and the negative numbers. Positive numbers are those greater than zero; negative numbers are those less than zero. Thus, zero occupies the point between the positives and the negatives on the NUMBER LINE.

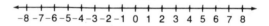

$$-8\ -7\ -6\ -5\ -4\ -3\ -2\ -1\ \ 0\ \ 1\ \ 2\ \ 3\ \ 4\ \ 5\ \ 6\ \ 7\ \ 8$$

Zero belongs to some subsets of the set of real numbers—the whole numbers and the integers. In the set of integers it is considered an even integer.

Zero is the *additive identity element*. That is, when zero is added to any given number, the sum is always identical to the given number. For example,

$$3 + 0 = 3 \qquad -5 + 0 = -5 \qquad \tfrac{1}{2} + 0 = \tfrac{1}{2}.$$

Zero is a *factor* that always gives *zero as the product*. That is, when zero is multiplied by any number, the product is always zero. For example,

$$0 \times 3 = 0 \qquad 0 \times -5 = 0 \qquad 0 \times \tfrac{1}{2} = 0.$$

Zero is the only factor that yields a product of zero. Thus, if a product is zero, at least one of the factors must be zero. For example,

$$\text{if } (3n = 0), \text{ then } n = 0.$$

Zero is the only number that *cannot be used as a divisor*. To understand why division by zero is impossible, consider the quantity $6 \div 0$. When 6 is divided by 2, the answer is 3, because $3 \times 2 = 6$. When 6 is divided by 1, the answer is 6, because $6 \times 1 = 6$. But when 6 is divided by 0, what can the answer be? What number times 0 equals 6? The answer is that there is no number, because when zero is a factor the product is always zero. Thus, division by zero is said to be undefined.

However, zero can be divided by any number other than zero, and the quotient is always zero. For example,

$$\frac{0}{6} = 0 \qquad \frac{0}{-7} = 0 \qquad \frac{0}{\frac{1}{2}} = 0.$$

HISTORY

The concept of zero is full of complexities that we take for granted. Its discovery took a long long time. Despite its importance to progress in arithmetic, the amazing fact is that the sophisticated early Greeks never discovered this concept. Western mathematics had to wait for the Hindu-Arabic zero.

Zero was the last Hindu-Arabic numeral to come into use, and its origin is not certain. It was formerly believed that the Hindus invented zero. Newer evidence indicates, though, that a symbol like zero was used intermittently in other numeration systems even before the time of Christ, and that it was gradually incorporated into the Hindu system. The symbol for zero does appear in a Hindu manuscript of the seventh century. The concept and symbol for zero were probably transmitted from the Hindus to the Arabs and thus eventually became a part of our Hindu-Arabic numeral system.

Zero was first used as a place holder rather than as a separate numeral. According to some sources, the word "zero" comes from a form of the Arabic *sifr,* which in turn comes from the Hindu *sunya,* meaning "void," or "empty."

See NUMERAL SYSTEMS for other cultures that used zero. About 300 B.C. the Babylonians had a symbol for zero as a place holder. The Mayan civilization in Central America developed a system including a zero symbol, probably by the fourth century A.D. (It is also interesting to examine other systems, such as Roman, early Greek, Hebrew, Chinese, and Yoruba to see how they avoided the need for a zero.)

REFERENCES

Robert K. Logan, "The Mystery of the Discovery of Zero," *Et Cetera,* March 1979, pp. 16–27; a fascinating essay on why the ideas of zero and algebra were developed in India and not in ancient Greece.

Marnie Luce, *Zero is Something* (Lerner Publications, 1969); brief and elementary, but interesting.

Constance Reid, *From Zero to Infinity: What Makes Numbers Interesting* (Thomas Y. Crowell Co., 1955); contains a chapter on the history and meaning of zero: why 0 as a digit was invented before 0 as a number was discovered.

Appendix I **TABLES**

MATHEMATICAL SYMBOLS

$=$	is equal to
$\doteq$	is approximately equal to
$\overset{?}{=}$	is equal to? (question)
$\neq$	is not equal to
$>$	is greater than
$\geq$	is greater than or equal to
$<$	is less than
$\leq$	is less than or equal to

} INEQUALITIES

$\cong$	is congruent to
$\not\cong$	is not congruent to

} CONGRUENCE

$\sim$	is similar to
$\nsim$	is not similar to

} SIMILARITY

$+$	plus (addition)
$-$	minus (subtraction)
$\pm$	plus or minus
$\times$	times (multiplication)
$a \cdot b$	a times b
ab	a times b
$\div$	divided by
$\dfrac{a}{b}$	a divided by b; FRACTION
$\sqrt{a}$	the positive square root of a
$\sqrt[n]{a}$	the nth root of a
a^n	a to the nth power

} ARITHMETIC OPERATIONS

(x, y)	rectangular coordinates of a point in a plane
(r, θ)	polar coordinates of a point in a plane

} COORDINATES

m	slope
b	y-intercept of a line

} SLOPE

h	height of geometric figure
b	base of geometric figure

GREEK ALPHABET

A	α	alpha
B	β	beta
Γ	γ	gamma
Δ	δ	delta
E	ϵ	epsilon
Z	ζ	zeta
H	η	eta
Θ	θ	theta
I	ι	iota
K	κ	kappa
Λ	λ	lambda
M	μ	mu
N	ν	nu
Ξ	ξ	xi
O	o	omicron
Π	π	pi
P	ρ	rho
Σ	σ	sigma
T	τ	tau
Y	υ	upsilon
Φ	ϕ	phi
X	χ	chi
Ψ	ψ	psi
Ω	ω	omega

635

l	length of geometric figure	
w	width of geometric figure	
c	circumference	
r	radius	CIRCLE
d	diameter	
s	semiperimeter of triangle	
$\times 10^n$	SCIENTIFIC NOTATION	
$\log a$	logarithm of a	
$\log_e a$ or $\ln a$	natural logarithm of a	
antilog	antilogarithm	LOGARITHMS
e	$2.71828\ldots$, the base of natural logarithms	
π	$3.14159\ldots$, PI	
$0.7\overline{3}$	$0.73333\ldots$, repeating DECIMAL	
∞	INFINITY	
$\aleph_0$	cardinal number of a countable infinite set	INFINITY
$\mathcal{R}$	the set of REAL NUMBERS	
i	$\sqrt{-1}$, an imaginary number	
$a + bi$	COMPLEX NUMBER	COMPLEX NUMBERS
$\lvert x \rvert$	the absolute value of x	SIGNED NUMBERS
$\%$	PERCENT	
$a{:}b$	the RATIO of a to b	
$::$	is in PROPORTION to	
LCD	least common denominator	FRACTIONS
LCM	least common multiple	
GCF	greatest common factor	FACTORS AND
GCD	greatest common divisor	MULTIPLES
$\sum$	summation	SEQUENCES AND SERIES
$P(A)$	probability of A	
$P(A\lvert B)$	probability of A given B (conditional probability)	PROBABILITY
$\%$-ile	percentile	
$\bar{x}$	mean of a sample	
s^2	variance of a sample	STATISTICS
s	standard deviation of a sample	
$f(x)$	f is a FUNCTION of x	
$\therefore$	therefore	
$\exists$	there exists	
$\forall$	for all	
$\ni$	such that	
$\angle A, \measuredangle A$	ANGLE A	
$^\circ$	degrees	
$'$	minutes	ANGLES
$''$	seconds	
$\llcorner$	right angle	

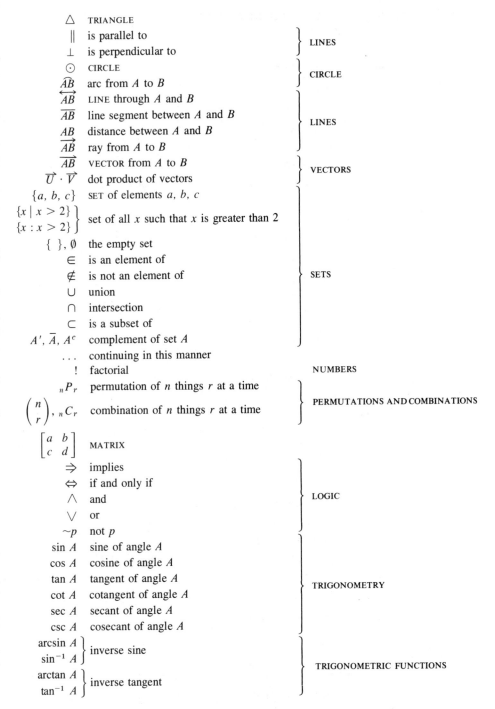

$\triangle$	TRIANGLE	
$\parallel$	is parallel to	} LINES
$\perp$	is perpendicular to	
$\odot$	CIRCLE	} CIRCLE
$\overset{\frown}{AB}$	arc from A to B	
$\overleftrightarrow{AB}$	LINE through A and B	
$\overline{AB}$	line segment between A and B	
AB	distance between A and B	} LINES
$\overrightarrow{AB}$	ray from A to B	
$\overrightarrow{AB}$	VECTOR from A to B	} VECTORS
$\vec{U} \cdot \vec{V}$	dot product of vectors	
$\{a, b, c\}$	SET of elements a, b, c	
$\{x \mid x > 2\}$ $\{x : x > 2\}$	set of all x such that x is greater than 2	
$\{\ \}, \emptyset$	the empty set	
$\in$	is an element of	
$\notin$	is not an element of	} SETS
$\cup$	union	
$\cap$	intersection	
$\subset$	is a subset of	
$A', \overline{A}, A^c$	complement of set A	
$\ldots$	continuing in this manner	
$!$	factorial	NUMBERS
$_nP_r$	permutation of n things r at a time	
$\binom{n}{r}, \ _nC_r$	combination of n things r at a time	} PERMUTATIONS AND COMBINATIONS
$\begin{bmatrix} a & b \\ c & d \end{bmatrix}$	MATRIX	
$\Rightarrow$	implies	
$\Leftrightarrow$	if and only if	
$\wedge$	and	} LOGIC
$\vee$	or	
$\sim p$	not p	
$\sin A$	sine of angle A	
$\cos A$	cosine of angle A	
$\tan A$	tangent of angle A	
$\cot A$	cotangent of angle A	} TRIGONOMETRY
$\sec A$	secant of angle A	
$\csc A$	cosecant of angle A	
$\arcsin A$ $\sin^{-1} A$	inverse sine	
$\arctan A$ $\tan^{-1} A$	inverse tangent	} TRIGONOMETRIC FUNCTIONS

See APPENDIX I, *Table of Units of Measure* for additional symbols and abbreviations.

TABLE OF U.S. CUSTOMARY SYSTEM OF MEASURE

Length, or Distance (basic unit: one *inch* = 0.02540 meter)

1 foot (1 ft, or 1′) = 12 inches (12 in, or 12″)
1 yard (yd) = 3 feet = 36 inches
1 rod (rd) = $5\frac{1}{2}$ yards
1 furlong (fur) = 40 rods = $\frac{1}{8}$ mile
1 statute mile (mi) = 1760 yards = 5280 feet
1 nautical mile = 1.1516 statute miles = 6080.20 feet
1 fathom = 6 feet
1 (land) league = 3 statute miles
1 (marine) league = 3 nautical miles

Area (basic unit: one *square inch*)

1 square foot (sq ft, or ft²) = 144 square inches (sq in, or in²)
1 square yard (sq yd, or yd²) = 9 square feet
1 square rod (sq rd, or rd²) = $30\frac{1}{4}$ square yards
1 acre = 160 square rods = 4840 square yards = 43,560 square feet
1 square mile (sq mi, or mi²) = 640 acres

Volume

Different units are used for different materials. The basic distinction is between dry and liquid measure.

Dry and cubic measure (basic unit: one *cubic inch*)

1 cubic foot (cu ft, or ft³) = 1728 cubic inches (cu in, or in³)
1 cubic yard (cu yd, or yd³) = 27 cubic feet
1 dry pint (pt) = 33.60 cubic inches
1 dry quart (qt) = 2 pints = 67.2006 cubic inches
1 peck (pk) = 8 quarts = 537.605 cubic inches
1 bushel (bu) = 4 pecks = 32 quarts = 2150.42 cubic inches
1 cord (for firewood, a pile 8 ft long, 4 ft wide, 4 ft high) = 128 cubic feet

Liquid measure (basic unit: one *fluid ounce* = 1.8047 cubic inches)

1 tablespoon (tbsp, or T) = 3 teaspoons (tsp or t)
1 fluid ounce (fl oz) = 2 tablespoons

1 cup (c) = 8 fluid ounces

1 pint (pt) = 16 fluid ounces = 28.875 cubic inches

1 quart (qt) = 2 pints = 57.75 cubic inches

1 gallon (gal) = 4 quarts = 128 fluid ounces = 231 cubic inches

1 barrel (bbl) = 31½ gallons, usually. There are many other "barrels."
A barrel of petroleum products = 42 gallons; a barrel of fermented
liquors = 31 gallons. Most U.S. state laws set the "barrel for
liquids" at 31½ gallons, but others use different equivalents, such as
36 gallons or 42 gallons.

Weight (basic unit for all systems below: one *grain*, which is the weight
equivalent, on the surface of the earth, of 0.000064799 kilograms mass.
See MEASURE for discussion of weight versus mass.)

Avoirdupois (Avdp) (used for commerce)

1 dram (dr) = 27.343475 grains (gr)

1 ounce (oz*) = 16 drams = 437½ grains

1 pound (lb*) = 16 ounces = 7000 grains

1 hundredweight (cwt*) = 100 pounds

1 ton (T) = 20 hundredweight = 2000 pounds

Apothecary (used for drugs)

1 scruple = 20 grains

1 dram = 3 scruples = 60 grains

1 ounce = 8 drams = 480 grains

1 pound = 12 ounces = 5760 grains

Troy (used for precious metals and gems)

1 carat (c) = 3.086 grains

1 pennyweight (pwt, or dwt*) = 24 grains

1 ounce (oz t) = 20 pennyweight = 480 grains

1 pound (lb t) = 12 ounces = 5760 grains

Notice the many differences in these systems. For example, an avoirdupois dram is less than half an apothecary dram, yet an avoirdupois pound
is considerably greater than an apothecary pound.

*These abbreviations are from Latin:
  lb   from *libra* for "pound,"
  oz   from *onzia* for "ounce,"
  cwt   from *centum* for "hundred," plus English "weight,"
  dwt   from *denarius,* a Roman silver coin, plus English "weight."

DIFFERENCES BETWEEN U.S. UNITS AND
TRADITIONAL BRITISH UNITS OF MEASURE

The U.S. and British systems of MEASURE grew out of a common heritage and use the same names for units which are similar but not exactly the same. The differences are quite significant in avoirdupois weight and liquid measure.

Although both the U.S. and British systems use the same avoirdupois pound, they define the hundredweight and the ton very differently, as shown in the table:

Avoirdupois Weight

	U.S. Customary System	Traditional British System
1 pound	16 ounces, or 7000 grains	16 ounces, or 7000 grains
1 stone	—	14 pounds
1 hundredweight	1 hundredweight = 100 pounds	1 (*gross* or *long*) hundredweight = 8 stones = 112 pounds
1 ton	1 ton = 2000 pounds	1 (*long*) ton = 20 long hundredweight = 2240 pounds

Liquid measure is even more confusing. The British Imperial gallon has 160 fluid ounces, while the U.S. gallon has 128 fluid ounces, a ratio of 5:4. However, an 18-gallon gas tank in a U.S. automobile holds only 15 Imperial gallons in Canada, a ratio of 6:5, which does not match the other ratio, as you would expect. The awful truth of the matter is that the British fluid ounce is different from the U.S. fluid ounce. The pint, quart, and gallon all hold different numbers of different fluid ounces in the two systems.

Liquid Measure

	U.S. Customary System	*Traditional British System*
1 fluid ounce	1.8047 cubic inches	1.734 cubic inches
1 pint	16 U.S. fluid ounces = 28.88 cubic inches	20 British fluid ounces = 34.68 cubic inches
1 quart	2 U.S. pints = 57.75 cubic inches	2 British pints = 69.36 cubic inches
1 gallon	1 U.S. gallon = 4 U.S. quarts = 128 U.S. fluid ounces = 231 cubic inches	1 Imperial gallon = 4 British quarts = 160 British fluid ounces = 277.42 cubic inches

Conversions: 1 U.S. gallon = 0.833 British Imperial gallons.
1 British Imperial gallon = 1.201 U.S. gallons.

Although conversion to the metric system will eventually wipe out these differences, the use of these units in many places is slow to change. Furthermore, British literature of all sorts and from all periods makes its way to the United States. So it is wise to note the differences and beware. A British recipe calling for a pint of milk needs quite a bit more milk than a U.S. pint. The British have always weighed people in stones, not in pounds. Traditions die hard; shipbuilders on both sides of the Atlantic have always worked in long tons.

**TABLE OF METRIC SYSTEM OF MEASURE
OR SYSTÈME INTERNATIONALE (SI)**

See METRIC SYSTEM for further discussion of these units.

Length, or Distance (basic unit: one *centimeter*)

1 centimeter (cm) = 10 millimeters (mm)
1 meter (m) = 100 centimeters = 1000 millimeters
1 kilometer (km) = 1000 meters

Area (basic unit: one *square centimeter*)

1 square centimeter (cm^2) = 100 square millimeters (mm^2)
1 square meter (m^2) = 10,000 square centimeters
1 are (a) = 100 square meters
1 hectare (ha) = 100 ares = 10,000 square meters
1 square kilometer (km^2) = 100 hectares
= 1,000,000 square meters

Volume

Dry and cubic measure (basic unit: one *cubic centimeter*, abbreviated
cu cm, cc, or cm^3)

1 cubic centimeter = 1000 cubic millimeters (cu mm, or mm^3)
1 cubic meter (cu m, or m^3) = 1,000,000 cubic centimeters
1 stere (for firewood) = 1 cubic meter

Liquid measure (basic unit: one *milliliter* = 1 cubic centimeter)

1 deciliter (dl) = 100 milliliters (ml)
1 liter (l) = 1000 cubic centimeters = 1000 milliliters
1 kiloliter (kl) = 1000 liters

Mass (basic unit: one *gram*, the mass of one cubic centimeter of water
at maximum density)

1 gram (g) = 1000 milligrams (mg)
1 kilogram (kg) = 1000 grams

**Conversion Factors for Changing from U.S. Customary
System to Metric System (SI)**

1 inch = 2.540 centimeters   1 yard = 0.9144 meters
1 foot = 30.48 centimeters   1 mile = 1.609 kilometers

1 square inch = 6.452 square centimeters
1 square foot = 929.030 square centimeters
1 square yard = 0.836 square meters
1 square mile = 2.5899 km² = 258.99 hectares
1 acre = 0.4047 hectares

1 cubic inch = 16.387 cubic centimeters
1 cubic foot = 28,317 cubic centimeters
1 cubic yard = 0.765 cubic meters

1 teaspoon = 5 milliliters
1 fluid ounce = 29.573 milliliters
1 dry quart = 1.101 liters
1 liquid quart = 0.9465 liters
1 gallon = 3.785 liters

1 pound avoirdupois weight is equivalent, on the earth's surface, to
0.4536 kilograms mass.

**Conversion Factors for Changing from Metric System (SI)
to U.S. Customary System**

1 millimeter = 0.03937 inches
1 centimeter = 0.3937 inches
1 meter = 3.281 feet
1 meter = 1.094 yards
1 kilometer = 0.6214 miles

1 square centimeter = 0.155 square inches
1 square meter = 1.196 square yards = 10.764 square feet
1 square kilometer = 0.386 square miles
1 hectare = 2.471 acres

1 cubic centimeter = 0.061 cubic inches
1 cubic meter = 1.308 cubic yards

1 liter = 1.057 liquid quarts = 0.908 dry quarts = 61.024 cubic inches

1 kilogram mass weighs, on the earth's surface, 2.205 pounds avoirdupois.

TABLE OF SQUARES, CUBES, AND ROOTS

n	n^2	$\sqrt{n}$	$\sqrt{10n}$	n^3	$\sqrt[3]{n}$	$\sqrt[3]{10n}$	$\sqrt[3]{100n}$
1	1	1.000 000	3.162 278	1	1.000 000	2.154 435	4.641 589
2	4	1.414 214	4.472 136	8	1.259 921	2.714 418	5.848 035
3	9	1.732 051	5.477 226	27	1.442 250	3.107 233	6.694 330
4	16	2.000 000	6.324 555	64	1.587 401	3.419 952	7.368 063
5	25	2.236 068	7.071 068	125	1.709 976	3.684 031	7.937 005
6	36	2.449 490	7.745 967	216	1.817 121	3.914 868	8.434 327
7	49	2.645 751	8.366 600	343	1.912 931	4.121 285	8.879 040
8	64	2.828 427	8.944 272	512	2.000 000	4.308 869	9.283 178
9	81	3.000 000	9.486 833	729	2.080 084	4.481 405	9.654 894
10	100	3.162 278	10.00000	1 000	2.154 435	4.641 589	10.00000
11	121	3.316 625	10.48809	1 331	2.223 980	4.791 420	10.32280
12	144	3.464 102	10.95445	1 728	2.289 428	4.932 424	10.62659
13	169	3.605 551	11.40175	2 197	2.351 335	5.065 797	10.91393
14	196	3.741 657	11.83216	2 744	2.410 142	5.192 494	11.18689
15	225	3.872 983	12.24745	3 375	2.466 212	5.313 293	11.44714
16	256	4.000 000	12.64911	4 096	2.519 842	5.428 835	11.69607
17	289	4.123 106	13.03840	4 913	2.571 282	5.539 658	11.93483
18	324	4.242 641	13.41641	5 832	2.620 741	5.646 216	12.16440
19	361	4.358 899	13.78405	6 859	2.668 402	5.748 897	12.38562
20	400	4.472 136	14.14214	8 000	2.714 418	5.848 035	12.59921
21	441	4.582 576	14.49138	9 261	2.758 924	5.943 922	12.80579
22	484	4.690 416	14.83240	10 648	2.802 039	6.036 811	13.00591
23	529	4.795 832	15.16575	12 167	2.843 867	6.126 926	13.20006
24	576	4.898 979	15.49193	13 824	2.884 499	6.214 465	13.38866
25	625	5.000 000	15.81139	15 625	2.924 018	6.299 605	13.57209
26	676	5.099 020	16.12452	17 576	2.962 496	6.382 504	13.75069
27	729	5.196 152	16.43168	19 683	3.000 000	6.463 304	13.92477
28	784	5.291 503	16.73320	21 952	3.036 589	6.542 133	14.09460
29	841	5.385 165	17.02939	24 389	3.072 317	6.619 106	14.26043
30	900	5.477 226	17.32051	27 000	3.107 233	6.694 330	14.42250
31	961	5.567 764	17.60682	29 791	3.141 381	6.767 899	14.58100
32	1 024	5.656 854	17.88854	32 768	3.174 802	6.839 904	14.73613
33	1 089	5.744 563	18.16590	35 937	3.207 534	6.910 423	14.88806
34	1 156	5.830 952	18.43909	39 304	3.239 612	6.979 532	15.03695
35	1 225	5.916 080	18.70829	42 875	3.271 066	7.047 299	15.18294
36	1 296	6.000 000	18.97367	46 656	3.301 927	7.113 787	15.32619
37	1 369	6.082 763	19.23538	50 653	3.332 222	7.179 054	15.46680
38	1 444	6.164 414	19.49359	54 872	3.361 975	7.243 156	15.60491
39	1 521	6.244 998	19.74842	59 319	3.391 211	7.306 144	15.74061
40	1 600	6.324 555	20.00000	64 000	3.419 952	7.368 063	15.87401
41	1 681	6.403 124	20.24846	68 921	3.448 217	7.428 959	16.00521
42	1 764	6.480 741	20.49390	74 088	3.476 027	7.488 872	16.13429
43	1 849	6.557 439	20.73644	79 507	3.503 398	7.547 842	16.26133
44	1 936	6.633 250	20.97618	85 184	3.530 348	7.605 905	16.38643
45	2 025	6.708 204	21.21320	91 125	3.556 893	7.663 094	16.50964
46	2 116	6.782 330	21.44761	97 336	3.583 048	7.719 443	16.63103
47	2 209	6.855 655	21.67948	103 823	3.608 826	7.774 980	16.75069
48	2 304	6.928 203	21.90890	110 592	3.634 241	7.829 735	16.86865
49	2 401	7.000 000	22.13504	117 649	3.659 306	7.883 735	16.98499

n	n^2	$\sqrt{n}$	$\sqrt{10n}$	n^3	$\sqrt[3]{n}$	$\sqrt[3]{10n}$	$\sqrt[3]{100n}$
50	2 500	7.071 068	22.36068	125 000	3.684 031	7.937 005	17.09976
51	2 601	7.141 428	22.58318	132 651	3.708 430	7.989 570	17.21301
52	2 704	7.211 103	22.80351	140 608	3.732 511	8.041 452	17.32478
53	2 809	7.280 110	23.02173	148 877	3.756 286	8.092 672	17.43513
54	2 916	7.348 469	23.23790	157 464	3.779 763	8.143 253	17.54411
55	3 025	7.416 198	23.45208	166 375	3.802 952	8.193 213	17.65174
56	3 136	7.483 315	23.66432	175 616	3.825 862	8.242 571	17.75808
57	3 249	7.549 834	23.87467	185 193	3.848 501	8.291 344	17.86316
58	3 364	7.615 773	24.08319	195 112	3.870 877	8.339 551	17.96702
59	3 481	7.681 146	24.28992	205 379	3.892 996	8.387 207	18.06969
60	3 600	7.745 967	24.49490	216 000	3.914 868	8.434 327	18.17121
61	3 721	7.810 250	24.69818	226 981	3.936 497	8.480 926	18.27160
62	3 844	7.874 008	24.89980	238 328	3.957 892	8.527 019	18.37091
63	3 969	7.937 254	25.09980	250 047	3.979 057	8.572 619	18.46915
64	4 096	8.000 000	25.29822	262 144	4.000 000	8.617 739	18.56636
65	4 225	8.062 258	25.49510	274 625	4.020 726	8.662 391	18.66256
66	4 356	8.124 038	25.69047	287 496	4.041 240	8.706 588	18.75777
67	4 489	8.185 353	25.88436	300 763	4.061 548	8.750 340	18.85204
68	4 624	8.246 211	26.07681	314 432	4.081 655	8.793 659	18.94536
69	4 761	8.306 624	26.26785	328 509	4.101 566	8.836 556	19.03778
70	4 900	8.366 600	26.45751	343 000	4.121 285	8.879 040	19.12931
71	5 041	8.426 150	26.64583	357 911	4.140 818	8.921 121	19.21997
72	5 184	8.485 281	26.83282	373 248	4.160 168	8.962 809	19.30979
73	5 329	8.544 004	27.01851	389 017	4.179 339	9.004 113	19.39877
74	5 476	8.602 325	27.20294	405 224	4.198 336	9.045 042	19.48695
75	5 625	8.660 254	27.38613	421 875	4.217 163	9.085 603	19.57434
76	5 776	8.717 798	27.56810	438 976	4.235 824	9.125 805	19.66095
77	5 929	8.774 964	27.74887	456 533	4.254 321	9.165 656	19.74681
78	6 084	8.831 761	27.92848	474 552	4.272 659	9.205 164	19.83192
79	6 241	8.888 194	28.10694	493 039	4.290 840	9.244 335	19.91632
80	6 400	8.944 272	28.28427	512 000	4.308 869	9.283 178	20.00000
81	6 561	9.000 000	28.46050	531 441	4.326 749	9.321 698	20.08299
82	6 724	9.055 385	28.63564	551 368	4.344 481	9.359 902	20.16530
83	6 889	9.110 434	28.80972	571 787	4.362 071	9.397 796	20.24694
84	7 056	9.165 151	28.98275	592 704	4.379 519	9.435 388	20.32793
85	7 225	9.219 544	29.15476	614 125	4.396 830	9.472 682	20.40828
86	7 396	9.273 618	29.32576	636 056	4.414 005	9.509 685	20.48800
87	7 569	9.327 379	29.49576	658 503	4.431 048	9.546 403	20.56710
88	7 744	9.380 832	29.66479	681 472	4.447 960	9.582 840	20.64560
89	7 921	9.433 981	29.83287	704 969	4.464 745	9.619 002	20.72351
90	8 100	9.486 833	30.00000	729 000	4.481 405	9.654 894	20.80084
91	8 281	9.539 392	30.16621	753 571	4.497 941	9.690 521	20.87759
92	8 464	9.591 663	30.33150	778 688	4.514 357	9.725 888	20.95379
93	8 649	9.643 651	30.49590	804 357	4.530 655	9.761 000	21.02944
94	8 836	9.695 360	30.65942	830 584	4.546 836	9.795 861	21.10454
95	9 025	9.746 794	30.82207	857 375	4.562 903	9.830 476	21.17912
96	9 216	9.797 959	30.98387	884 736	4.578 857	9.864 848	21.25317
97	9 409	9.848 858	31.14482	912 673	4.594 701	9.898 983	21.32671
98	9 604	9.899 495	31.30495	941 192	4.610 436	9.932 884	21.39975
99	9 801	9.949 874	31.46427	970 299	4.626 065	9.966 555	21.47229
100	10 000	10.00000	31.62278	1 000 000	4.641 589	10.00000	21.54435

TABLES OF LOGARITHMS

To find log₁₀N | $\log_{10}N = x$ means $10^x = N$

Two SIGNIFICANT DIGITS of N appear at the left of the table, and the first column of the table gives the *mantissa,* or decimal part, of $\log_{10}$ for the two-digit N. The *characteristic,* or whole number part, of $\log_{10}N$ is determined by the placement of the decimal point in N.

$$\log_{10}5.2 = 0.7160 \quad \text{because 5.2 is between } 10^0 \text{ and } 10^1;$$
$$\log_{10}52 = 1.7160 \quad \text{because 52 is between } 10^1 \text{ and } 10^2.$$

A third significant digit of N is given across the top (and bottom) of the table, labeling additional columns of mantissas.

$$\log_{10}5.24 = 0.7193 \quad \text{from the column headed 4.}$$

For a more detailed explanation, see LOGARITHMS: *common logarithms.*

Common Logarithms (base 10; $\log_{10} N$)

N	0	1	2	3	4	5	6	7	8	9
10	0000	0043	0086	0128	0170	0212	0253	0294	0334	0374
11	0414	0453	0492	0531	0569	0607	0645	0682	0719	0755
12	0792	0828	0864	0899	0934	0969	1004	1038	1072	1106
13	1139	1173	1206	1239	1271	1303	1335	1367	1399	1430
14	1461	1492	1523	1553	1584	1614	1644	1673	1703	1732
15	1761	1790	1818	1847	1875	1903	1931	1959	1987	2014
16	2041	2068	2095	2122	2148	2175	2201	2227	2253	2279
17	2304	2330	2355	2380	2405	2430	2455	2480	2504	2529
18	2553	2577	2601	2625	2648	2672	2695	2718	2742	2765
19	2788	2810	2833	2856	2878	2900	2923	2945	2967	2989
20	3010	3032	3054	3075	3096	3118	3139	3160	3181	3201
21	3222	3243	3263	3284	3304	3324	3345	3365	3385	3404
22	3424	3444	3464	3483	3502	3522	3541	3560	3579	3598
23	3617	3636	3655	3674	3692	3711	3729	3747	3766	3784
24	3802	3820	3838	3856	3874	3892	3909	3927	3945	3962
25	3979	3997	4014	4031	4048	4065	4082	4099	4116	4133
26	4150	4166	4183	4200	4216	4232	4249	4265	4281	4298
27	4314	4330	4346	4362	4378	4393	4409	4425	4440	4456
28	4472	4487	4502	4518	4533	4548	4564	4579	4594	4609

N	0	1	2	3	4	5	6	7	8	9
29	4624	4639	4654	4669	4683	4698	4713	4728	4742	4757
30	4771	4786	4800	4814	4829	4843	4857	4871	4886	4900
31	4914	4928	4942	4955	4969	4983	4997	5011	5024	5038
32	5051	5065	5079	5092	5105	5119	5132	5145	5159	5172
33	5185	5198	5211	5224	5237	5250	5263	5276	5289	5302
34	5315	5328	5340	5353	5366	5378	5391	5403	5416	5428
35	5441	5453	5465	5478	5490	5502	5514	5527	5539	5551
36	5563	5575	5587	5599	5611	5623	5635	5647	5658	5670
37	5682	5694	5705	5717	5729	5740	5752	5763	5775	5786
38	5798	5809	5821	5832	5843	5855	5866	5877	5888	5899
39	5911	5922	5933	5944	5955	5966	5977	5988	5999	6010
40	6021	6031	6042	6053	6064	6075	6085	6096	6107	6117
41	6128	6138	6149	6160	6170	6180	6191	6201	6212	6222
42	6232	6243	6253	6263	6274	6284	6294	6304	6314	6325
43	6335	6345	6355	6365	6375	6385	6395	6405	6415	6425
44	6435	6444	6454	6464	6474	6484	6493	6503	6513	6522
45	6532	6542	6551	6561	6571	6580	6590	6599	6609	6618
46	6628	6637	6646	6656	6665	6675	6684	6693	6702	6712
47	6721	6730	6739	6749	6758	6767	6776	6785	6794	6803
48	6812	6821	6830	6839	6848	6857	6866	6875	6884	6893
49	6902	6911	6920	6928	6937	6946	6955	6964	6972	6981
50	6990	6998	7007	7016	7024	7033	7042	7050	7059	7067
51	7076	7084	7093	7101	7110	7118	7126	7135	7143	7152
52	7160	7168	7177	7185	7193	7202	7210	7218	7226	7235
53	7243	7251	7259	7267	7275	7284	7292	7300	7308	7316
54	7324	7332	7340	7348	7356	7364	7372	7380	7388	7396
55	7404	7412	7419	7427	7435	7443	7451	7459	7466	7474
56	7482	7490	7497	7505	7513	7520	7528	7536	7543	7551
57	7559	7566	7574	7582	7589	7597	7604	7612	7619	7627
58	7634	7642	7649	7657	7664	7672	7679	7686	7694	7701
59	7709	7716	7723	7731	7738	7745	7752	7760	7767	7774
60	7782	7789	7796	7803	7810	7818	7825	7832	7839	7846
61	7853	7860	7868	7875	7882	7889	7896	7903	7910	7917
62	7924	7931	7938	7945	7952	7959	7966	7973	7980	7987
63	7993	8000	8007	8014	8021	8028	8035	8041	8048	8055
64	8062	8069	8075	8082	8089	8096	8102	8109	8116	8122
65	8129	8136	8142	8149	8156	8162	8169	8176	8182	8189
66	8195	8202	8209	8215	8222	8228	8235	8241	8248	8254
67	8261	8267	8274	8280	8287	8293	8299	8306	8312	8319
68	8325	8331	8338	8344	8351	8357	8363	8370	8376	8382
69	8388	8395	8401	8407	8414	8420	8426	8432	8439	8445

Common Logarithms, (base 10; $\log_{10} N$)—*continued*

N	0	1	2	3	4	5	6	7	8	9
70	8451	8457	8463	8470	8476	8482	8488	8494	8500	8506
71	8513	8519	8525	8531	8537	8543	8549	8555	8561	8567
72	8573	8579	8585	8591	8597	8603	8609	8615	8621	8627
73	8633	8639	8645	8651	8657	8663	8669	8675	8681	8686
74	8692	8698	8704	8710	8716	8722	8727	8733	8739	8745
75	8751	8756	8762	8768	8774	8779	8785	8791	8797	8802
76	8808	8814	8820	8825	8831	8837	8842	8848	8854	8859
77	8865	8871	8876	8882	8887	8893	8899	8904	8910	8915
78	8921	8927	8932	8938	8943	8949	8954	8960	8965	8971
79	8976	8982	8987	8993	8998	9004	9009	9015	9020	9025
80	9031	9036	9042	9047	9053	9058	9063	9069	9074	9079
81	9085	9090	9096	9101	9106	9112	9117	9122	9128	9133
82	9138	9143	9149	9154	9159	9165	9170	9175	9180	9186
83	9191	9196	9201	9206	9212	9217	9222	9227	9232	9238
84	9243	9248	9253	9258	9263	9269	9274	9279	9284	9289
85	9294	9299	9304	9309	9315	9320	9325	9330	9335	9340
86	9345	9350	9355	9360	9365	9370	9375	9380	9385	9390
87	9395	9400	9405	9410	9415	9420	9425	9430	9435	9440
88	9445	9450	9455	9460	9465	9469	9474	9479	9484	9489
89	9494	9499	9504	9509	9513	9518	9523	9528	9533	9538
90	9542	9547	9552	9557	9562	9566	9571	9576	9581	9586
91	9590	9595	9600	9605	9609	9614	9619	9624	9628	9633
92	9638	9643	9647	9652	9657	9661	9666	9671	9675	9680
93	9685	9689	9694	9699	9703	9708	9713	9717	9722	9727
94	9731	9736	9741	9745	9750	9754	9759	9763	9768	9773
95	9777	9782	9786	9791	9795	9800	9805	9809	9814	9818
96	9823	9827	9832	9836	9841	9845	9850	9854	9859	9863
97	9868	9872	9877	9881	9886	9890	9894	9899	9903	9908
98	9912	9917	9921	9926	9930	9934	9939	9943	9948	9952
99	9956	9961	9965	9969	9974	9978	9983	9987	9991	9996

To find $\log_e N$ | $\log_e N = x$ means $e^x = N$

Only two significant digits of N are given, one at the left and one across the top, with the decimal placement specified. The entire $\log_e$ is then given in the columns.

$$\log_e 5.2 = 1.649$$

Numbers N that are not between 1.0 and 10.9 must be expressed as a product of numbers that *are* between 1.0 and 10.9 in order to use this table. By the laws of LOGARITHMS,

$$\log_e xy = \log_e x + \log_e y$$

Example. $\log_e 52 = \log_e 5.2 + \log_e 10$
$$= 1.649 + 2.303$$
$$= 3.952$$

For either table, if you wish to use an N with more significant digits than given, you can approximate the logarithm by *linear interpolation* (see GRAPHS: *estimation*).

Example. $\log_e 5.24$ is about $\frac{4}{10}$ of the way from $\log_e 5.2$ to $\log_e 5.3$

$\log_e 5.2 = 1.649$
$\log_e 5.24 \doteq 1.657$ approximation, from $1.649 + 0.4\,(1.668 - 1.649)$
$\log_e 5.3 = 1.668$

Natural Logarithms (base e; $\log_e N$ or $\ln N$)

N	0.0	0.1	0.2	0.3	0.4	0.5	0.6	0.7	0.8	0.9
1	0.000	0.095	0.182	0.262	0.336	0.405	0.470	0.531	0.588	0.642
2	0.693	0.742	0.788	0.833	0.875	0.916	0.956	0.993	1.030	1.065
3	1.099	1.131	1.163	1.194	1.224	1.253	1.281	1.308	1.335	1.361
4	1.386	1.411	1.435	1.459	1.482	1.504	1.526	1.548	1.569	1.589
5	1.609	1.629	1.649	1.668	1.686	1.705	1.723	1.740	1.758	1.775
6	1.792	1.808	1.825	1.841	1.856	1.872	1.887	1.902	1.917	1.932
7	1.946	1.960	1.974	1.988	2.001	2.015	2.028	2.041	2.054	2.067
8	2.079	2.092	2.104	2.116	2.128	2.140	2.152	2.163	2.175	2.186
9	2.197	2.208	2.219	2.230	2.241	2.251	2.262	2.272	2.282	2.293
10	2.303	2.313	2.322	2.332	2.342	2.351	2.361	2.370	2.380	2.389

TRIGONOMETRIC TABLES (for angles from 0° to 90°)

For a detailed explanation of these tables, see TRIGONOMETRY (and ANGLES). For angles greater than 90°, see TRIGONOMETRIC FUNCTIONS. For angles between the values listed, the trigonometric ratios can be approximated by *linear interpolation* (see GRAPHS: *estimation*).

Example.   sine 18°   = 0.314
                sine 18°30′ ≐ 0.323 approximation, halfway between
                                          0.314 and 0.332
                sine 19°   = 0.332

Angle		Sine	Cosine	Tangent
degrees	*radians*			
0°	0.000	0.0000	1.0000	0.0000
1°	0.017	0.0175	0.9998	0.0175
2°	0.035	0.0349	0.9994	0.0349
3°	0.052	0.0523	0.9986	0.0524
4°	0.070	0.0698	0.9976	0.0699
5°	0.087	0.0872	0.9962	0.0875
6°	0.105	0.1045	0.9945	0.1051
7°	0.122	0.1219	0.9925	0.1228
8°	0.140	0.1392	0.9903	0.1405
9°	0.157	0.1564	0.9877	0.1584
10°	0.175	0.1736	0.9848	0.1763
11°	0.192	0.1908	0.9816	0.1944
12°	0.209	0.2079	0.9781	0.2126
13°	0.227	0.2250	0.9744	0.2309
14°	0.244	0.2419	0.9703	0.2493
15°	0.262	0.2588	0.9659	0.2679
16°	0.279	0.2756	0.9613	0.2867
17°	0.297	0.2924	0.9563	0.3057
18°	0.314	0.3090	0.9511	0.3249
19°	0.332	0.3256	0.9455	0.3443
20°	0.349	0.3420	0.9397	0.3640
21°	0.367	0.3584	0.9336	0.3839
22°	0.384	0.3746	0.9272	0.4040
23°	0.401	0.3907	0.9205	0.4245
24°	0.419	0.4067	0.9135	0.4452
25°	0.436	0.4226	0.9063	0.4663

Angle		Sine	Cosine	Tangent
degrees	radians			
26°	0.454	0.4384	0.8988	0.4877
27°	0.471	0.4540	0.8910	0.5095
28°	0.489	0.4695	0.8829	0.5317
29°	0.506	0.4848	0.8746	0.5543
30°	0.524	0.5000	0.8660	0.5774
31°	0.541	0.5150	0.8572	0.6009
32°	0.559	0.5299	0.8480	0.6249
33°	0.576	0.5446	0.8387	0.6494
34°	0.593	0.5592	0.8290	0.6745
35°	0.611	0.5736	0.8192	0.7002
36°	0.628	0.5878	0.8090	0.7265
37°	0.646	0.6018	0.7986	0.7536
38°	0.663	0.6157	0.7880	0.7813
39°	0.681	0.6293	0.7771	0.8098
40°	0.698	0.6428	0.7660	0.8391
41°	0.716	0.6561	0.7547	0.8693
42°	0.733	0.6691	0.7431	0.9004
43°	0.750	0.6820	0.7314	0.9325
44°	0.768	0.6947	0.7193	0.9657
45°	0.785	0.7071	0.7071	1.0000
46°	0.803	0.7193	0.6947	1.0355
47°	0.820	0.7314	0.6820	1.0724
48°	0.838	0.7431	0.6691	1.1106
49°	0.855	0.7547	0.6561	1.1504
50°	0.873	0.7660	0.6428	1.1918
51°	0.890	0.7771	0.6293	1.2349
52°	0.908	0.7880	0.6157	1.2799
53°	0.925	0.7986	0.6018	1.3270
54°	0.942	0.8090	0.5878	1.3764
55°	0.960	0.8192	0.5736	1.4281
56°	0.977	0.8290	0.5592	1.4826
57°	0.995	0.8387	0.5446	1.5399
58°	1.012	0.8480	0.5299	1.6003
59°	1.030	0.8572	0.5150	1.6643
60°	1.047	0.8660	0.5000	1.7321
61°	1.065	0.8746	0.4848	1.8040
62°	1.082	0.8829	0.4695	1.8807
63°	1.100	0.8910	0.4540	1.9626
64°	1.117	0.8988	0.4384	2.0503
65°	1.134	0.9063	0.4226	2.1445

Angle		Sine	Cosine	Tangent
degrees	*radians*			
66°	1.152	0.9135	0.4067	2.2460
67°	1.169	0.9205	0.3907	2.3559
68°	1.187	0.9272	0.3746	2.4751
69°	1.204	0.9336	0.3584	2.6051
70°	1.222	0.9397	0.3420	2.7475
71°	1.239	0.9455	0.3256	2.9042
72°	1.257	0.9511	0.3090	3.0777
73°	1.274	0.9563	0.2924	3.2709
74°	1.292	0.9613	0.2756	3.4874
75°	1.309	0.9659	0.2588	3.7321
76°	1.326	0.9703	0.2419	4.0108
77°	1.344	0.9744	0.2250	4.3315
78°	1.361	0.9781	0.2079	4.7046
79°	1.379	0.9816	0.1908	5.1446
80°	1.396	0.9848	0.1736	5.6713
81°	1.414	0.9877	0.1564	6.3138
82°	1.431	0.9903	0.1392	7.1154
83°	1.449	0.9925	0.1219	8.1443
84°	1.466	0.9945	0.1045	9.5144
85°	1.484	0.9962	0.0872	11.4301
86°	1.501	0.9976	0.0698	14.3007
87°	1.518	0.9986	0.0523	19.0811
88°	1.536	0.9994	0.0349	28.6363
89°	1.553	0.9998	0.0175	57.2900
90°	1.571	1.0000	0.0000	undefined

If you need greater detail or accuracy than is provided by any of the accompanying tables, consult *Mathematical Tables from Handbook of Chemistry and Physics* (Chemical Rubber Publishing Co., numerous editions since 1931).

Appendix II **History**

BIOGRAPHICAL LIST

Articles in which each person is mentioned are listed following the biographical information.

Abbott, Robert (American, contemporary) INDUCTION

Abel, Niels Henrik (Norwegian, 1802–1829) EQUATIONS

Ahmes [A'h Mosè] (Egyptian scribe, about 1650 B.C.) CIRCLE, FRACTIONS, NUMERAL SYSTEMS

Aiken, Howard (American, 1900–1973) COMPUTERS

Alembert, Jean le Rond d' (French, 1717–1783) COMPLEX NUMBERS

al-Kashî, Jamshid (Arabian, died about 1436) PI

al-Khowârizmî, Muhammed ibn Mûsâ (Arabian, about A.D. 780–850) ALGEBRA, EQUATIONS, HISTORY, NUMERAL SYSTEMS

Apollonius of Perga (Greek, 262–190 B.C.) CONIC SECTIONS

Appel, Kenneth (American, 1932–   ) TOPOLOGY

Archimedes of Syracuse (Greek, 287–212 B.C) ANGLES, CALCULUS, CIRCLE, INFINITY, LOGARITHMS, PI, POLYHEDRA

Archytas of Tarentum (Greek, about 400 B.C.) GEOMETRIC CONSTRUCTION

Argand, Jean-Robert (Swiss, 1768–1822) COMPLEX NUMBERS

Aristotle (Greek philosopher, 384–322 B.C.) GEOMETRY, INFINITY, LOGIC

Āryabhata (Hindu, A.D. 476–550) PI

Babbage, Charles (English, 1792–1871) COMPUTERS

Barbour, E. D. (American, nineteenth century) COMPUTERS

Bhaskara (Hindu, 1114–1185) PI, PYTHAGOREAN THEOREM

Bolyai, János (Hungarian, 1802–1860) GEOMETRY, HISTORY

Boole, George (English, 1815–1864) ALGEBRA, LOGIC, SETS

Brahmagupta (Hindu, born A.D. 598) HISTORY

Briggs, Henry (English, 1561–1631) LOGARITHMS

Brouncker, Lord William (English, 1620–1684) PI

Brouwer, Luitzen E. J. (Dutch, 1881–1967) LOGIC

Buffon, Comte George Louis Leclerc de (French naturalist, 1707–1788) PI, PROBABILITY

Bürgi, Joost (Swiss, 1552–1632) EXPONENTS, LOGARITHMS

Bush, Vannevar (American electrical engineer, 1890–1974) COMPUTERS

Buteo, Jean (French, 1492–about 1565) EXPONENTS

Cantor, Georg (German, 1845–1918) ARITHMETIC, FUNCTIONS, INFINITY, PI, PROBABILITY, SETS

Cardano, Girolamo [Jerome Cardan] (Italian, 1501–1576) COMPLEX NUMBERS, EQUATIONS, HISTORY, PROBABILITY, SIGNED NUMBERS

Carroll, Lewis—see Dodgson, Charles

Cataldi, Pietro (Italian, about 1548–1626) EXPONENTS

Cauchy, Augustin-Louis (French, 1789–1857) HISTORY, PROOFS

Cavendish, Henry (English chemist, 1731–1810) SCIENTIFIC NOTATION, ALGEBRA

Cayley, Arthur (English, 1821–1895) ALGEBRA

Celsius, Anders (Swedish astronomer, 1701–1744) MEASURE, METRIC SYSTEM

Ceulen, Ludolph van (German, 1540–1610) PI, RATIONAL AND IRRATIONAL NUMBERS

Châtelet, Marquise du [Emilie de Breteuil] (French, 1706–1749) CALCULUS

Chladni, Ernest (German physicist, 1756–1827) SYMMETRY

Connelly, Robert (American, 1942–   ) PROOFS

Copernicus, Nicholas (Polish astronomer, 1473–1543) TRIGONOMETRY

Cramer, Gabriel (Swiss, 1704–1752) MATRICES

Curie, Marie Sklodovska (Polish-born chemist and physicist, 1867–1934) EXPONENTS

Curie, Pierre (French physicist and chemist, 1859–1906) EXPONENTS

d'Alembert—see Alembert

Dase, Zacharias (German, 1824–1861) PI

da Vinci—see Vinci

Dedekind, Richard (German, 1831–1916) INFINITY

del Ferro—see Ferro

DeMorgan, Augustus (British, 1806–1871) INFINITY, LOGIC, SETS

Desargues, Gérard (French, 1591–1661) PROJECTION

Descartes, René (French, 1596–1650) COORDINATES, EXPONENTS, POLYHEDRA, SETS, SIGNED NUMBERS, TOPOLOGY

Dido, Queen of Carthage (Phoenician, about 800 B.C.) PERIMETER

Diophantus of Alexandria (Greek, about A.D. 250) ALGEBRA, EQUATIONS

Dodgson, Charles L. [Lewis Carroll] (English, 1832–1898) LOGIC

du Châtelet, Emilie—see Châtelet

Dürer, Albrecht (German painter and engraver, 1471–1528) GOLDEN SECTION, PROJECTION

Eckert, J. Presper (American electrical engineer, 1919–   ) COMPUTERS

Eddington, Sir Arthur (British astronomer and physicist, 1882–1944) INFINITY

Einstein, Albert (German-born American, 1879–1955) FUNCTIONS, GEOMETRY, INFINITY, LINES, VECTORS

Eratosthenes of Cyrene (Greek, about 284–192 B.C.) NUMBERS

Escher, Maurits Cornelis (Dutch graphic artist, 1898–1971) GEOMETRY, POLYGONS, SYMMETRY

Euclid of Alexandria (Greek, about 365–300 B.C.) DEFINITIONS, GEOMETRIC CONSTRUCTION, GEOMETRY, NUMBERS, PLANES

Euler, Leonhard (Swiss, 1707–1783) FUNCTIONS, PI, POLYHEDRA, SETS, TOPOLOGY, VECTORS

Fahrenheit, Gabriel Daniel (German physicist, 1686–1736) MEASURE

Ferguson, D. F. (English, contemporary) PI

Fermat, Pierre de (French, 1601–1665) COORDINATES, POLYGONS, PROBABILITY, PYTHAGOREAN THEOREM

Ferrari, Lodovico (Italian, 1522–1565) EQUATIONS

Ferro, Scipione del (Italian, 1465–1526) EQUATIONS

Fibonacci—see Leonardo of Pisa

Fior, Antonio Maria (Italian, about 1515) EQUATIONS

Fontana, Niccolò [Tartaglia] (Italian, about 1499–1557) EQUATIONS

Fourier, Jean-Baptiste Joseph (French, 1768–1830) TRIGONOMETRIC FUNCTIONS

Fuller, R. Buckminster (American, 1895–   ) POLYHEDRA

Galileo [Galilei, Galileo] (Italian astronomer and physicist, 1564–1642) ALGEBRA, FUNCTIONS, INFINITY

Galois, Evariste (French, 1811–1832) EQUATIONS

Gauss, Carl Friedrich (German, 1777–1855) COMPLEX NUMBERS, GEOMETRY, POLYGONS, STATISTICS, TOPOLOGY

Germain, Sophie (French, 1776–1831) ARITHMETIC, SYMMETRY

Gibbs, Josiah Willard (American physicist, 1839–1903) VECTORS

Gödel, Kurt (Austrian, 1906–1979) HISTORY, MATHEMATICAL SYSTEMS

Goldbach, Christian (Russian, 1690–1764) INDUCTION

Grassman, Hermann Günther (German, 1809–1877) VECTORS

Gregory, James (Scottish, 1638–1675) CALCULUS, PI

Grossman, Marcel (Swiss, 1878–1936) VECTORS

Guilloud, M. Jean (French, contemporary) PI

Gunter, Edmund (English, 1581–1626) COMPUTERS, LOGARITHMS

Haken, Wolfgang (German-born, 1928–   ) TOPOLOGY

Hamilton, William Rowan (Irish, 1805–1865) ALGEBRA, COMPLEX NUMBERS, VECTORS

Heisenberg, Werner (German physicist, 1901–1976) MEASURE

Hero [Heron] of Alexandria (Greek, about A.D. 70) AREA

Hilbert, David (German, 1862–1943) HISTORY, INFINITY, MATHEMATICAL SYSTEMS, SETS

Hipparchus of Alexandria (Greek, about 180–125 B.C.) TRIGONOMETRY

Hollerith, Herman (American, 1860–1929) COMPUTERS, COMPUTER PROGRAMMING

Hypatia of Alexandria (Greek, A.D. 370–415) CONIC SECTIONS

Kashî—see al-Kashî

Kelvin, Lord [William Thomson] (English, 1824–1907) MEASURE

Kepler, Johannes (German astronomer, 1571–1630) CALCULUS, CONIC SECTIONS, POLYHEDRA

Khayyám, Omar (Persian poet, about 1048–1122) GEOMETRY

Khowârizmî—see al-Khowârizmî

Kovalevsky, Sonya [Kovalevskaya] (Russian, 1850–1891) SEQUENCES AND SERIES

Kremer, Gerhard [Mercator] (Flemish cartographer, 1512–1594) PROJECTION

Kulik, J. P. (Austrian astronomer, 1773–1863) NUMBERS

Lambert, Johann Heinrich (German, 1728–1777) COMPLEX NUMBERS, HISTORY, PI, RATIONAL AND IRRATIONAL NUMBERS

Le Corbusier [Charles Edouard Jeanneret] (Swiss-French architect, 1887–1965) GOLDEN SECTION

Leibniz, Gottfried Wilhelm von (German, 1646–1716) CALCULUS, COMPUTERS, FUNCTIONS, INFINITY, LOGIC, NUMERAL SYSTEMS

Leonardo of Pisa [Fibonacci] (Italian, about 1170–1250) EQUATIONS, HISTORY, PI, SEQUENCES AND SERIES

Lindemann, Ferdinand (German, 1852–1939) HISTORY, PI

Liouville, Joseph (French, 1809–1882) HISTORY

Lobachevsky, Nikolai Ivanovich (Russian, 1793–1856) GEOMETRY, HISTORY

Lovelace, Lady Ada Byron (English, 1815–1852) COMPUTER PROGRAMMING, COMPUTERS

Machin, John (English, 1680–1751) PI

Malthus, Thomas (English political economist, 1766–1834) SEQUENCES AND SERIES

Markov, Andrey Andreyevich (Russian, 1856–1922) PROBABILITY

Mauchly, John (American, 1907–   ) COMPUTERS

Menelaus of Alexandria (Greek, about A.D. 100) TRIGONOMETRY

Mercator—see Kremer

Mersenne, Marin (French, 1588–1648) VARIATION

Miyoshi, Kazunori (Japanese, contemporary) PI

Moebius, August Ferdinand (German, 1790–1868) TOPOLOGY

Monge, Gaspard (French, 1746–1818) PROJECTION

Murasaki, Lady (Japanese novelist, 978–about 1031) PERMUTATIONS AND COMBINATIONS

Nakayama, Kazuhiko (Japanese, 1934–   ) PI

Napier, John (Scottish, 1550–1617) COMPUTERS, DECIMALS, LOGARITHMS

Neumann—see von Neumann

Newton, Sir Isaac (English, 1642–1727) ALGEBRA, CALCULUS, INFINITY, LOGIC

Noether, Emmy (German, 1882–1935) ALGEBRA, ARITHMETIC

Oresme, Nicole (French, 1323–1382) FUNCTIONS

Oughtred, William (English, 1574–1660) COMPUTERS, LOGARITHMS

Pascal, Blaise (French, 1623–1662) ALGEBRAIC EXPRESSIONS, COMPUTERS, PROBABILITY, PROJECTION

Peano, Giuseppe (Italian, 1858–1932) HISTORY, LOGIC

Peaucellier, A. (French army officer, 1832–1913) LINES

Plato (Greek philosopher, 427–347 B.C.) POLYHEDRA

Playfair, John (Scottish, 1748–1819) GEOMETRY

Poincaré, Jules Henri (French, 1854–1912) TOPOLOGY

Poncelet, Jean Victor (French, 1788–1867) PROJECTION

Ptolemy, Claudius of Alexandria (Greek astronomer and geographer, about A.D. 85–168) TRIGONOMETRY

Pythagoras of Samos (Greek, about 585–507 B.C.) PYTHAGOREAN THEOREM, TRIANGLES, TRIGONOMETRY, VARIATION

Pythagoreans (Greek, for 200 years following Pythagoras) FACTORS, GOLDEN SECTION, HISTORY, NUMBERS

Rhind, A. Henry (Scottish antiquarian, 1833–1863) CIRCLE, FRACTIONS, NUMERAL SYSTEMS

Ricci, Curbastro Gregorio (Italian, 1853–1925) VECTORS

Richter, Charles F. (American seismologist, 1900–   ) LOGARITHMS

Riemann, Georg Friedrich Bernhard (German, 1826–1866) GEOMETRY

Rudolff, Christoff (German, about 1500–1545) ARITHMETIC OPERATIONS

Ruffini, Paolo (Italian physician, 1765–1822) EQUATIONS

Russell, Bertrand Arthur William (English, 1872–1970) DEDUCTION, HISTORY, LOGIC

Saccheri, Girolamo (Italian, 1667–1733) GEOMETRY

Shanks, William (English, 1812–1882) PI

Snell, Willebrord (Dutch physicist, 1581–1626) PI

Steffen, Klaus (German, contemporary) PROOFS

Steinmetz, Charles (German-born American electrical engineer, 1865–1923) COMPLEX NUMBERS

Stevin, Simon (Flemish, 1548–1620) DECIMALS, EXPONENTS, FRACTIONS, VECTORS

Stifel, Michael (German, about 1486–1567) SIGNED NUMBERS

Tartaglia—see Fontana

Theano (Greek, sixth century B.C.) GOLDEN SECTION

Trachtenberg, Jakow (Russian, 1888–   ) ARITHMETIC OPERATIONS

Tsu Chung-chi (Chinese, about A.D. 480) PI

Turing, Alan Mathison (British, 1912–1954) COMPUTERS

Bibliographical Index

662

General Index

668

Exponential function, 165
Exponential growth and decay, 165–66, 276, 279
Exponential notation, history, 167
Exponents, 46, 159–67
  decimal, 161
  fractional, 146, 160–61, 164
  laws of, 162–64
  as logarithms, 292, 297, 300–03
  multiplication and division with, 162
  negative, 159–60, 161, 163–64
  positive, 159, 160
  in scientific notation, 494–95
  variable, 165
  zero, 161, 164
Expressions, algebraic, see Algebraic expressions
Exterior angles, 20
Exterior, of circle, 67
Externally tangent circles, 67
Extracting a root, 42, 47–50, 163
Extrapolation, 246
Extreme and mean ratio, 227 see also Golden Section
Extremes, of a proportion, 457

Faceted polyhedra, 417–18
Factor, 44, 168–74
  greatest common factor (G.C.F.), 169
  prime, 169
  scale, 536
  zero as factor, 633
Factor tree, 168–69
Factorial, 354, 386
Factoring, 168–69
  of algebraic expressions, 171–72
Fahrenheit temperature, 335–37
  versus Celsius temperature, 238–39, 336–37
Fahrenheit, Gabriel Daniel, 335–37, 655
Fair game, 432–33
Falling bodies, law of, 204
False Perspective (Hogarth), 443
False solution for trisecting angle, 23
The Family at Work (Oude), 71
Family tree of complex numbers, 75
Feininger, Andreas, 505, 566
Femto- (prefix), 340–41
Ferguson, D. F., 395, 655
Fermat numbers, 407
Fermat, Pierre de, 256, 464–65, 655
  Cartesian coordinates, 119
  probability, 434
Fermat's last theorem 464–65
Ferrari, Lodovico, 157, 655
Ferro, Scipione del, 156–57, 655
Fibonacci, see Leonardo of Pisa
Fibonacci Association, 506
Fibonacci numbers, 504–07
Fibonacci sequence, 234, 504–07

Field properties, 175–83
  in algebra, 5
  associativity, 176–77, 180–81
  closure, 175–76, 180
  commutativity, 176, 180–81
  of complex numbers, 76, 180
  distributivity, 177–78, 180–81
  everyday applications, 181
  identity elements, 178, 180
  inverses, 178–80
  summary, 180
Field, 175
  finite, 182
  of real numbers, 483
Figurate numbers, 353
Finite decimal, 129–31, 469, 481
Finite fields, 182
Finite sequence, 498
Finite series, 500
Finite set, 270, 510
Fior, Antonio Maria, 156–57, 655
First degree equations, graphing, 238–41
Flag, U.S., 478
Flexible polyhedron or sphere, 450–51
Flow chart, 81–82
Fluid ounce, 638, 640–42
Focal radius, 115
Foci, 115
Focus, of conic sections, 115
Folding of conic sections, 113
Fontana, Niccolò, 156–57, 158, 655
Formula, Euler-Descartes, for polyhedra, 580–81
Fortran, programming language, 82, 83
Foundations of mathematics, 254, 316–18
Four-color problem, 583–84
Four-dimensional polyhedra, 424–25
Fourier, Jean-Baptiste Joseph, 256, 600, 655
Fourth dimension, 110–11, 424
Fractals, ii, iv, 80, 276, 317, 507, 566
Fractional exponents, 160–61, 164
Fractions, 184–97
  in algebraic expressions, 196
  arithmetic operations, 189–92
  classification, 186–89
  complex, 187
  with complex numbers, 196
  continued, 196–97, 394
  conversions
    decimal, 127, 129
    percent, 379
  decimal, 127–37 see also Decimals
  density, 192–93, 272–73
  equivalent, 187–89, 192
  history, 194–95, 249
  indeterminate, 187
  least common denominator, 189

Fractions (cont.)
  like, 189
  as percent, 378
  as rational number, 192, 468
  reducing or simplifying, 188
  undefined, 186–87
  zero, 186
French academy of science, 339, 342–43
Frequency
  musical, 295–97, 600
  of trigonometric functions, 598–99
Frequency distribution, 553–57
Friendly numbers, 173, 174
Frustum
  of cone, 628
  of pyramid, 417, 628
Fuller rule, 98
Fuller, R., Buckminster, 418, 655
Function machine, 199
Functions, 198–205
  on calculator, 55
  discontinuous, 202, 244
  domain and range, 199–200
  exponential, 165
  graphing, 200–01, 598–99
  as mapping, 202–03
  periodic, 598–99
  as relation, 492–93
  step, 202
  trigonometric, 593–602 see also Trigonometric functions
Fundamental principle of counting, 386
Fundamental theorem of calculus, 64
Fundamental theorem of arithmetic, 169
Fundamental theorem of algebra, 78
Furlong, 638

G.C.F. (greatest common factor), 169
Galaxy, 234
Galileo, 655
  algebra, 3
  falling objects, 204
  infinity, 273–74
Galois, Evariste, 157–58, 256–57, 655
Game theory, 432–33
Games
  with graphs, 247–48
  induction, 260–61
Gauss, Carl Friedrich, 256, 257, 655
  adding, 562
  complex numbers, 78, 79, 252
  construction of regular 17-sided polygon, 407
  non-Euclidean geometry, 222, 253–54
  topology, 584
Gear ratio, 479
General linear equation of a line, 547
General relativity, 289, 624

Pantograph, 538–39
Paper tape, punched, 85, 91
Papyrus, Rhind, or Ahmes, 363, 376
  area of circle, 69
  fractions, 194
Parabola
  applications, 117
  conic section, 112, 114–15
  folding from paper, 113
  graphing from equation, 242–43, 491
Paradox
  barber, 142
  in foundations of mathematics,
    317–18
  geometric dissection, 411–12
  Zeno's, 141–43
Parallel lines, 221, 284
  construction, 210–11
  intersection, 272
  slope, 544
Parallel motion, 286–87
Parallel planes, 398
Parallel postulate, 221, 253–54, see
    also Non-Euclidean geometry
Parallel projection, 437–38
Parallelepiped, 416
Parallelogram, 466
  area, 27
Parallelogram law, 617–18, 623
Parallels of latitude, 123, 124, 126
Parentheses, to indicate order of opera-
    tions, 50–51
Pascal, Blaise, 255–57, 446, 657
  calculating machine, 99, 103
  probability, 434
  projective geometry, 444
Pascal, programming language, 83
Pascal's triangle, 11–13, 506
Pascal's Wager, 434
Patterns
  faceted polyhedron, 419
  flexible polyhedron, 451
  kaleidocycles, 420
  regular polyhedra, 419
Peano, Giuseppe, 254, 311, 657
Peaucellier, A., 286–88, 657
Peaucellier's Cell, 286–88
Peck, 638
Pennyweight, 639
Penrose Triangle, 444
Pentagon, 404–05
  construction, 409
Pentagonal prisms, 424
Pentagram of Pythagoras, 227–28
  construction, 228
Pentomino, 412–13
Percent, 195, 276, 378–82
  applications, 381
  beyond one hundred percent, 380

Percent (cont.)
  converting to fractions or decimals,
    378–79
  history, 381–82
Percentile, 558–59
Perfect number, 172, 174
Perimeter, 383–84
Period
  of repeating decimal, 129
  in square root algorithm, 48
  of trigonometric functions, 598–99
Periodic decimal, see Decimals,
    repeating
Periodic functions, 598–99
Permutations, 385–89
  applications, 390–91
  circular, 388
  groups of, 41
Perpendicular lines, 284
  construction, 208–09
  slope, 544–45
Perpendicular planes, 398
Perpendicular, to a plane, 398
Persians
  decimal fractions, 136
  history of mathematics, 255
Perspective, 442–44
  use in computer graphics, 326
Pi, 68, 392–96
  calculation of, 394–95
  history, 393–95
  as irrational number, 470
  probabilistic determination, 435–36
  use of inverse trigonometric functions,
    602
Pico- (prefix), 340–41
Pictograph, 237–38
Pictorial unit graph, 237–38
Pie chart, 238
Pine cone, 505
Pitch, of sound, 600, 614–15
PL/1, programming language, 83
Place value
  in Babylonian system, 363
  in binary system, 375
  in Hindu-Arabic system, 367–70
  in Mayan numeral system, 372–73
  in numeral systems, 361
Placeholder, zero, 364, 632
Plan
  projection, 444
  scale drawing, 478
Plane
  complex, 77
  determination of, 399
  of projection, 437
  of symmetry, 569
  tiling, 410–11, 413
  vector representation, 616

Plane geometry, 219
  limitations, 400
Plane trigonometry, 603
Planes, 397–401
  classification, 398–99
  properties, 397
Planets, Kepler's theories
  of motion, 116
  of spacing, 422–23
Planiverse, 401
Plato, 281, 421, 657
Platonic solids, 420–23
Playfair, John, 221, 657
Playfair's parallel postulate, 221
Plotter, 92
Plus, 42
Poincaré, Jules Henri, 256, 584, 657
Point
  of contact, 66
  at infinity, 272
  of symmetry, 570
  of tangency, 66
Point-slope equation of a line, 546
Points, 402–03
Polar axis, 121
Polar coordinates, 121–23
  graph paper, 245–46
  relation to Cartesian coordinates, 123
Pole, polar coordinates, 121
Polish Easter eggs, 566
Polish, reverse notation in a calculator,
    55
Polonium and exponential decay, 165
Polygonal puzzles, 411–14
Polygons, 404–14
  classification, 405–06
  congruence of, 107–08
  construction, 406–10
  puzzles, 411–14
  quadrilaterals, 466–67
  regular, 406–10
  similar, 537
  terminology, 404–05
  tesselations, 410–11
Polyhedra, 415–25
  classification, 415–18
  Euler-Descartes formula, 580–81
  four-dimensional, 424–25
  historical discussion, 421–23
  making models, 419–20
  in nature, 423–24
  rigidity, 450–51
  volume, 626–27
Polyhedral angle, 24
Polyhedrons, see Polyhedra
Polynomial, 9
  standard form, 151
Polynomial equation, 78
  solving, 153

Polynomial inequality, 264
Polyominoes, 412–13
Poncelet, Jean Victor, 256, 444–46, 657
Population, in statistics, 549
Population growth, compared to food production, 503–04
Positional notation, 361–62
Positive angle, 15, 594
Positive exponent, 159–60
Positive number, 519
Positive slope, 544
Postulates, 220, 315, 448
  Euclid's, 221, 253
  importance of, 253–54
  Playfair's parallel, 221
Potential infinity, 273
Power, 46
  of algebraic expression, 11–14
  exponent notation, 159
  inverse of, 48
  with logarithms, 301–02
  raising to, 42, 46–47, 162
Power set, 512
Precision
  of approximate number, 531–32
  of definition, 145
  of measurement, 337
  in scientific notation, 495, 497
Prefixes, metric system, 340–41
Premise, 138–40, 306, 447
Primary numeral, 360
Prime factor, 169
Prime factorization, 169
Prime Meridian, 123, 124, 125
Prime numbers, 174, 351, 354–46
  Fermat primes, 407
  induction example, 258–59
  relatively prime numbers, 170
Primitive, 315
Primitive axiom, 148
Primitive terms, 145, 146
Principal, 276
Principal values, for inverse trig-onometric functions, 601
Principia (Newton), 65
Principia Mathematica (Russell and Whitehead), 312
Prism, 416, 423, 424
  volume, 627
Probability, 426–36
  applications, 434
  conditional, 429, 431
  determination of pi, 435–36
  as fraction, 196
  game theory, 432–33
  history, 433–34
  laws, 429–31
  terminology, 427–29
Problems of antiquity, 216

Processor, computer, 90–91
Product, 44
  Cartesian, 515–16
  cross, in set theory, 515–16
  exponent notation, 159
Program, computer, *see* Computer programming
Programmable calculators, 56
Programmer, 80
Programming, *see* Computer programming
Progression, *see* Sequences
Projection, 225, 437–46
  different types, 437–38
  in geometry, 444–46
  in map making, 438–41
  in painting and viewing, 442–44
  properties preserved under, 445
  use with matrices, 326
Projection rays, 437
Projective geometry, 225, 444–46
Proofs, 447–51
  by contradiction, 140–41, 449, 583, *see also* Contradiction
  diagonal, 486–87
  geometric example, 140
  invalid, 448
  irrationality of $\sqrt{2}$, 472–73
  methods, 449
  for rational number, decimal either terminates or repeats, 130
  role of pictures or examples, 448–49
  uncountability of real numbers, 486–87
Propagation of the Divine Proportion, 233–34
Proper fraction, 186
Proper subset, 512
Properties
  of equality, 452–56
  field, 5, 175–83, *see also* Field properties
  of line, 283
  of plane, 397
  preserved under projection, 445
  topological, 577
Property
  associative, 176–77, 180–81
  commutative, 176, 180–81
  of density of fractions, 193
  distributive, 177–178, 180–81
  reflexive, 453, 455
  symmetric, 453–55, 574
  transitive, 454–55
Proportion form
  direct variation, 610–12
  inverse variation, 612–13
Proportion, 457–60, 477
  applications, 458–60
  direct, 610–12

Proportion (*cont.*)
  Divine, 227–35, *see also* Golden Section
  inverse, 612–13
Proportional representation, 459
Proportional, mean, 457
Proportions, 457–60
Proposition, 221, 306
  equivalent, 307–08, 310
Protractor, 603
Ptolemy, Claudius of Alexandria, 394, 607–08, 657
Punch-cards, 84–85, 91–92
Punched paper tape, 84, 91
Puzzles
  logical, 142
  polygonal, 411–14
Pyramid, 415–17, 423
  volume, 627–29
  of frustum, 628
Pyramids, and the Golden Section, 229–30
Pythagoras of Samos, 257, 465, 657, *see also* Pythagoreans
  Golden Section, 227
  music, 614–15
  theorem, 461–62
Pythagoras' Law, 615
Pythagorean Theorem, 461–65, 588
  applications, 462–63
  with complex numbers, 77–78
  converse, 462
  in constructing irrational numbers, 216–17, 250, 347
  and irrational numbers, 470
  number theory, 463–65
  in trigonometry, 605
  in vector calculation, 619–20
Pythagorean triples, 463–64
Pythagoreans, 235, 356–57, 657
  factors, 172
  Golden Section, 227–28
  history of irrational numbers, 249–50
  ladder for approximating irrationals, 471–72
  number theory, 353–56
  numerology, 356–57

Quadrant, 119
Quadratic equations, 150
  graphing, 241–43
  solving, 152–53
Quadratic formula, 152–53
Quadratic inequalities, 264, 266–67
Quadratrix, 23
Quadrature of the circle, 68–70, 253, 393
Quadrilateral, 466–67
  area, 26–27
Quartic equation, 151

Quaternions, 623
Queen Dido's Problem, 72, 383–84
Quinary base, of numeral system, 361
Quotient, 45

Racing odds, 432
Radial symmetry, 572
Radians, 16–18, 650–52
Radical, 47
Radicand, 47
Radii, 66
Radioactive decay, 165–66
Radiolaria, 424
Radius, 66
Raising to a power, 42, 46–47
  algebraic expression, 11–14
  with exponents, 162
RAM memory, 93
Random sample, 550
Range
  of function, 199–200, 202
  of relation, 489
  statistical, 560
Raphael, 589
Rate, of interest, 276
Ratio
  in design of musical instruments,
    614–15
  as fraction, 196
  in geometric progression, 499
  Golden, 227–235, 506, see also
    Golden Section
  as rational number, 468
  of surface area to volume, 630–31
Rational approximation, 471–72
Rational numbers, 192, 468–74, 481–82
  between 0 and 1, 272
  early use, 249
  field properties, 180
  geometric construction on a number
    line, 346
  operations, 471
Ratios, 475–80
  trigonometric, 593, 604
Ray, 15, 284
  projection, 437
Real number system, 482
Real numbers, 73, 481–88
  Cartesian product, 516
  continuum, 484–85
  density, 484
  field, 180, 483
  history, 249–57
  order, 483–84
  uncountability, 485–88
  zero, 632
Reasoning, 305, 449, see also Logic
  circular, 314–15
  deductive, 138–43, see also
    Deduction

Reasoning (cont.)
  formal, 220
  inductive, 258, 259, see also
    Induction
Reciprocal, 46, 159–60, 179, 187
Reciprocal functions, in trigonometry,
  596
Rectangle, 466
  area, 26
  Golden, 232–34
Rectangular coordinates, 119
Rectangular solid
  surface area, 30
  volume, 626
Reduced fractions, 188
Reduced sample space, 429
Reductio ad absurdum, see
  Contradiction
Reference points, for temperature,
  336
Reflection, 106, 224–25
  angle of, 21–22
  glide, 572
  symmetry by, 567–70
Reflex angle, 19
Reflexivity (reflexive property), 452, 453,
  455
Regular polygon, 406–10
Regular polyhedra, 417, 420–23
  making models, 419
Regular tesselations, 410
Relations, 489–93
  binary, 452
  equivalence, 455
  as functions, 202, 204–05
  of sets, 511–12
  symmetry of, 574–75
Relative error, 531–32
Relatively prime numbers, 170
Relativity, theory of general, 289
Remainder, 45
Renaissance painting, 442–44, 589
Repeating decimal, 129–31, 468, 481
Repetend, 129
Repetition
  in permutation, 387
  in symmetry, 565
Representation, proportional, 459
Reptiles (Escher), 411
Resultant, of vector addition, 617–18
Reverse Polish notation, in calculator,
  55
Reversible relation, 574
Rhetorical method, of solving equations,
  156, 158
Rhind Papyrus, 363, 376
  area of circle, 69
  fractions, 194
Rhind, A. Henry, 363, 657
Rhombic dodecahedron, 423–24

Rhombicuboctahedron, 418
Rhombiicosidodecahedron, 418
Rhombus, 466
Rhymes, application of permutations,
  391
Ricci, Curbastro Gregorio, 624, 657
Richardson, George W., 288
Richter scale, 295
Richter, Charles F., 294–95, 657
Riemann, Georg Friedrich Bernhard,
  256, 657
  non-Euclidean geometry, 222, 400
Right angle, 19
Right circular cone, 112
Right prism, 416
Right triangle, 587
  in trigonometry, 604
Right triangle principle, 461
Right-handed coordinate system, 121
Rigid motions, 224
Ridigity
  of polyhedra, 425, 450–51
  of triangle, 591
Rise, 541
Rods, Napier's, 96–97
Romans
  computing, 96
  fractions, 195
  interest, 281
  numeral system, 365–66, 634
Roots
  of equation, 150–53
  extracting, 42, 47–50, 163
    by logarithms, 301–02
    square root algorithm, 48–49
  fractional exponent notation, 160–
    61
  index of, 47
  inverse of, 48
  irrational, 48, 469–70
  table, 644–45
Roster, 509
Rotation, 106, 224
  using complex numbers, 79
  of a square, arithmetic without num-
    bers, 36–37
  symmetry by, 571
Rounding off, 131–32, 532–33
Row matrix, 321
RPN (Reverse Polish notation), 55
Rubaiyat (Khayyam), 222
Rubber-sheet geometry, 225, 577
Rudolff, Christoff, 47, 657
Ruffini, Paolo, 157, 657
Rule, as function, 198
Run, 541
Russell, Bertrand Arthur William, 254,
  312, 657
  barber paradox, 142
Russian abacus, 96